Public Speaking
Strategies for Success

Fourth Edition

David Zarefsky
Northwestern University

PEARSON

Boston   New York   San Francisco
Mexico City   Montreal   Toronto   London   Madrid   Munich   Paris
Hong Kong   Singapore   Tokyo   Cape Town   Sydney

For my students

Editorial Director: *Jason Jordan*
Executive Editor: *Karon Bowers*
Series Editor: *Brian Wheel*
Developmental Editor: *Shannon Morrow*
Series Editorial Assistant: *Jennifer Trebby*
Marketing Manager: *Mandee Eckersley*
Composition and Prepress Buyer: *Linda Cox*
Manufacturing Manager: *Megan Cochran*
Cover Designer: *Kristina Mose-Libon*
Photo Research: *Helane M. Prottas/ Posh Pictures*
Editorial-Production Coordinator: *Mary Beth Finch*
Editorial-Production Service: *Modern Graphics, Inc.*
Electronic Composition: *Modern Graphics, Inc.*

For related titles and support materials, visit our online catalog at www.ablongman.com

Between the time Website information is gathered and then published, it is not unusual for
some sites to have closed. Also, the transcription of URLs can result in unintended typo-
graphical errors. The publisher would appreciate notification where these errors occur so that
they may be corrected in subsequent editions.

Library of Congress Cataloging-in-Publication Data

Zarefsky, David.
   Public speaking : strategies for success / David Zarefsky.—4th ed.
      p. cm.
   Includes bibliographical references and index.
   ISBN 0-205-41487-7
      1. Public speaking.   I. Title.

PN4129.15.Z37 2004
808.5'1—dc22
                                                                    2004040985
Printed in the United States of America.

10 9 8 7 6 5 4 3   VHP 09 08 07 06 05

Photo credits appear on page 500, which constitutes a continuation of the copyright page.

Brief Contents

Special Features

Contents

Part I — Foundations of Public Speaking 2

Chapter One — Welcome to Public Speaking 3

Part 2	Invention and Development of the Speech 92

Chapter Five

Researching the Topic 121

Chapter Six

Reasoning 157

Part 3 — Arrangement of the Speech 192

Part 4 Style and Delivery of the Speech 270

Chapter Twelve

Using Visual Aids 325

Part 5 — Uses of Public Speaking 356

Chapter Thirteen

Informing 357

Chapter Fourteen

Persuading 377

To the Instructor

I wrote *Public Speaking: Strategies for Success* because I was convinced that no other book really focused on the premise that successful public speaking is *strategic*. By that I mean that it involves understanding the circumstances in which one speaks, making deliberate choices about how to deal with these circumstances, and planning for achieving one's goals. The key elements in a strategic approach to public speaking are *critical thinking* and *strategic planning*, and I emphasize these skills throughout this book.

A consequence of a strategic perspective is the recognition that public speaking is not a science with universally applicable principles or a set of formulas that can be applied mechanically or by rote. It is more complicated than that, involving subjective judgment and human choice. We do our students a disservice if we pretend otherwise. Instead, by equipping them with necessary knowledge and skills, we should help to prepare them to make these choices skillfully and intelligently. That is a goal of this book.

To say that the subject matter is complex, though, is certainly not to say that the textbook must be dull, tedious, or unreadable. This edition especially reflects my desire to make the text readily accessible to students without compromising the integrity of the subject matter.

I am grateful for the positive reception that has been given to earlier editions. I hope that this fourth edition will refine the approach and incorporate new material while maintaining the clear perspective for which the book has become known.

New To This Edition

Greater Focus on Diversity

Far from being a "buzzword" or an emblem of "political correctness," diversity of audiences on virtually every dimension is a fact with which speakers must be prepared to deal. It is not an issue that can be separated from other concerns but one that affects every aspect of public speaking. Accordingly, throughout the book it is incorporated in examples and precepts, and every chapter includes a new feature, *Strategies for Speaking to Diverse Audiences*, with tips on how that chapter can be applied in an increasingly diverse environment.

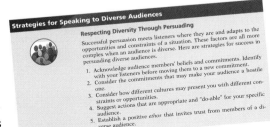

Expanded Material on Informing and Persuading

Chapters 13 and 14 have been revised to incorporate additional research findings and practical advice concerning strategies for informing and persuading. Appendix A has been more sharply focused to deal with the application of these strategies in the public forum.

Revised and Updated Examples

Throughout the book, examples of student and public speakers have been updated to reflect current issues, especially in the aftermath of the terrorist attacks of September 11, 2001. New examples also have been chosen to illustrate theoretical principles more effectively. At the same time, the book retains a depth of historical examples so that students will see how speakers over the years responded to the challenges of public speaking.

Updated Material on Technology

> **WWW. Using the Internet**
>
> **Watch or Listen to Congress**
>
> While most speeches presented on the floor of the U.S. House of Representatives or the Senate deal with specific pieces of legislation, you may also observe speeches that have a ceremonial quality. Explore **FedNet** to find out the current issues being discussed on the Hill. You can watch or listen to floor debate or observe committee hearings.
>
> Point your browser to **http://www.fednet.net**. Scroll to your right to find links for debates, hearings, press conferences, or special events to see or listen to RealVideo or RealAudio transmission. FedNet subscribers can also access the archive of past Congressional activities.

Information technology plays an increasing role in the public speaking course, both for research and in presentation. Accordingly, Chapters 5 and 12 have been carefully updated, as have the *Using the Internet* features in each chapter. Special attention has been paid to the critical notion of evaluating material available on the Internet. While its use can be beneficial, students need to understand that the information must be evaluated carefully. Those of you teaching the course without access to advanced computer technology, however, will not be left behind, because the book still focuses on the art of rhetoric, with its traditions dating back to antiquity, long before the advent of the computer. And Chapters 5 and 12 include discussion of "low tech" as well as "high tech" research sources and presentation materials.

Retained From Earlier Editions

Even with the changes described above, the principal elements that distinguished earlier editions have been maintained. These include a focus on strategies; integration of theory and practice; challenging examples and applications; stress on the skills of analysis, research, and reasoning; a holistic approach to the study of language and delivery; comprehensive treatment of visual aids and of occasions for public speaking; enriched emphasis on learning from others; and a rich presentation of audience analysis and the public forum.

Focus on Strategies

The primary focus of the book—strategic thinking and planning—clearly has been retained. Far too often, students leave a public speaking class with nothing more than a recipe for how to prepare and deliver a seven-minute speech in class. Certainly, being able to prepare and deliver that classroom speech well is a start. The goal of this book, however, is to help students also to learn how to apply the skills required for the seven-minute classroom speech to the range of public speaking situations they will encounter throughout their lives. Students should recognize how often they will find themselves participating in speaking situations, whether as a public speaker or as an audience member. They need to think through and about the public speaking process and to develop strategies to achieve their goals.

This edition includes *Choose a Strategy* boxes, which appear throughout the book and present students with a case study situation requiring that they decide how the skills and concepts discussed in the chapter (and in previous chapters) could be adapted to a concrete rhetorical situation. These case studies are geared toward students' level of experience and they focus on public speaking situations that students typically might encounter. After applying what they've learned to the initial scenario, students are asked to decide what impact a change in topic, audience, purpose, or other variable might have on the choice of strategies. These scenarios offer students a chance to explore the variables and tradeoffs that inevitably apply to any strategic decision. There are usually no "correct" solutions for these open-ended *Choose a Strategy* situations. Rather, they are exercises in what we have described as applied rhetoric: sizing up a situation, understanding its opportunities and constraints, assessing ideas, and reasoning with an audience in mind. These situations are realistic and encourage students to develop and refine their strategic thinking about the public speaking process.

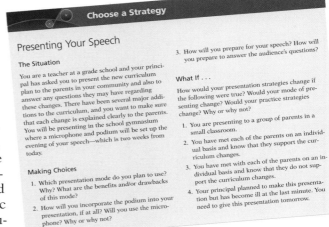

Integration of Theory and Practice

An approach that views public speaking as a set of formulas or rules to be followed is of limited value. Few actual speaking situations will match exactly those for which the "rules" were written; students need instead to be able to adapt to the particular situations in which they find themselves. In order to do that, they must understand the theory behind the rules. Recognizing this fact, some books try to "import" theory, including all the latest specialized terms and jargon. This book instead integrates theory into the underlying discussions of practice, not by highlighting obscure writers or technical terms, but by explaining clearly what students should do and why. The book is solidly grounded in rhetorical theory, but no prior knowledge of that field is either required or assumed. Theory and practice are treated as a seamless fabric.

A Variety of Challenging Examples and Applications

Because public speaking is situation-specific, this book includes a large number of cases and examples. The examples have the following characteristics. First, they encompass a wide range of topics and issues, with some examples from actual speaking situations and some hypothetical examples to illustrate points in the text. Second, some examples compare speeches in the classroom with speeches in the field. Third, there are both brief examples and some extended examples that can be followed throughout an entire chapter. The examples emphasize a need to analyze and respond to audiences as an integral part of the strategic thinking process.

Stress on the Skills of Analysis, Research, and Reasoning

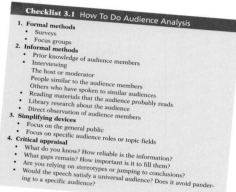

Checklist 3.1 How To Do Audience Analysis
1. **Formal methods**
   - Surveys
   - Focus groups
2. **Informal methods**
   - Prior knowledge of audience members
   - Interviewing
     The host or moderator
     People similar to the audience members
     Others who have spoken to similar audiences
   - Reading materials that the audience probably reads
   - Library research about the audience
   - Direct observation of audience members
3. **Simplifying devices**
   - Focus on the general public
   - Focus on specific audience roles or topic fields
4. **Critical appraisal**
   - What do you know? How reliable is the information?
   - What gaps remain? How important is it to fill them?
   - Are you relying on stereotypes or jumping to conclusions?
   - Would the speech satisfy a universal audience? Does it avoid pandering to a specific audience?

This book, more than others, emphasizes practical applications of critical thinking skills that are so crucial to public speaking. These skills include active listening skills for mapping ideas and critical evaluation, and topic analysis to determine underlying issues. The investigation and research process is treated in considerable detail, with specific advice and guidance for analyzing a thesis to discover new subtopics and approaches. And there is a full chapter on reasoning in the context of the entire speaking situation (not limited to persuasive speeches), a subject often ignored or slighted in other public speaking texts. These practical skills and processes are summarized regularly for students in *Checklist* sections provided in every chapter.

A Holistic Approach to the Study of Language and Delivery

Public Speaking recognizes a fundamental irony about language and delivery. They are the features of a speech that are most immediately noticeable, and the aspects on which many beginning speakers wish to concentrate. Yet to focus intensively on the details of language and delivery may be the worst way to improve them; speakers may become so self-conscious that language and delivery are distracting mannerisms. This book, while quite specific in its treatment, focuses on language as a means to achieve a personal style and on delivery as a means to improve understanding of the message.

Comprehensive Treatment of Visual Aids and of Occasions for Public Speaking

The topics of visual aids and occasions for public speaking are common to public speaking books, but the treatment here is particularly comprehensive. A wide variety of visual aids are considered, including those that make use of contemporary computer technology. Although both deliberative and ceremonial occasions for public speaking are discussed, a much wider range of speaking occasions is presented—from everyday interchange to public forums to small groups.

A careful approach to the distinction between informing and persuading is noticeable in the later chapters. One of the most venerable traditions in public speaking instruction is to distinguish between speeches that inform and speeches that persuade. There is some value to that distinction, and yet we know that matters are not so simple. Most speeches are a blend of information and persuasion, sometimes so fine a blend that the elements cannot be separated. *Public Speaking* regards informing and persuading as headings for types of strategies speakers can use, and provides more specific coverage of speech purposes that may mix information and persuasion. Nevertheless, because of the time limitations of the classroom, instructors using this text can easily assign an informative speech and a persuasive speech without confusing students if they wish to do so. The realistic discussion of the blending and overlapping of informative and persuasive strategies is developed in Chapter 13 ("Informing") and Chapter 14 ("Persuading") in order to introduce students to the notion gradually.

Enriched Emphasis on Learning from Others

In many of the chapters, there is a boxed feature called *Applying Strategies* that highlights five real-life students from Texas Tech University and describes their development throughout their public speaking course. Included are excerpts from their assignments, speeches, and journals, as well as comments and critiques from their instructor, Dr. Tonya Blivens. These boxes encourage students to learn from and be encouraged by others who are their peers.

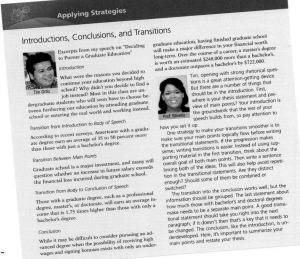

A Rich Presentation of Audience Analysis and the Public Forum

Analysis of the audience is basic to any speaking situation, yet many books offer an unrealistic presentation of what audience analysis involves. They focus primarily on quantitative demographic information that the speaker often is unable to obtain. *Public Speaking* treats three separate levels of audience analysis and draws on awareness of audience psychology and cultures—including responsiveness to cultural diversity—as well as demographics.

Public Speaking grounds public speaking in a concept of the *public forum*. All too often, the *public* dimension is missing from books on public speaking. Speakers will not always speak only about personal issues to an audience made up only of their friends. Rather than treating the classroom situation as an end in itself, this book argues that it is a simulation of the public forum. Audiences are called upon to make judgments about matters on which they cannot possibly have all the relevant information. The task of the speaker is to help in guiding listeners to make sound judgments. From this premise follow ideas about the importance of the speaker's *ethos*, about the responsibilities one incurs when speaking and the ethical standards one should meet, and about the collaborative nature of the speaker–audience relationship. These topics are all explored in this book. In addition, Appendix A focuses particularly on the public forum. It is intended to bridge the gap between the artificial speaking environment of the classroom and that of the "real world."

Organization and Pedagogy

Although unique perspectives and approaches are presented in almost every chapter, the structure of *Public Speaking* is relatively conventional, so that it might be adapted easily to public speaking classes at institutions of various types. An opening unit on the foundational skills of speaking and listening is followed by units that take up rhetorical invention, arrangement, style and delivery, and the contexts and occasions for speaking. Each chapter includes the following features:

- Learning objectives listed at chapter openings help readers anticipate key ideas they will need to keep in mind as the chapter develops.
- *Checklists* throughout every chapter provide students with a quick review and reinforcement of key guidelines as they read the chapter.
- Marginal glossaries remind students of key terms and concepts.
- End-of-chapter summaries encapsulate the highlights for easy review.
- *Using the Internet* activities within each chapter offer students suggestions for exploring information on the Internet and learning about its use in the public speaking process. Through these activities, students can see the range of resources available while also learning the limitations of that material.
- A feature, *Strategies for Speaking to Diverse Audiences,* at the end of each chapter offers specific tips about how that chapter's principles and strategies can be applied in an increasingly diverse speaking environment.
- End-of-chapter questions, projects, and case studies, as well as footnote references, show background materials that interested students can pursue.

Appendix B contains full-length speeches for classes interested in analyzing the effectiveness of speakers in more depth. In addition to the contemporary pieces—three by students—there are historical speeches that illustrate the power of applied rhetoric at key decision points in our national development. An introduction, providing context, key information, and guidelines for analysis, precedes each speech.

Supplements

Instructor Resources

Download supplements from our self-service website! Adopters of any Allyn & Bacon/Longman text can register for free and immediate access to a wide selection of instructor supplements in electronic format—including PDF,

MSWord, TestGen, CourseCompass, Blackboard, WebCT, and more. Visit www.ablongman.com/suppscentral to register for your login and password today.

Print Resources

Instructor's Resource Manual with Teaching Tool for the Companion Website, prepared by Julie R. Mactaggart of St. Cloud State University. The manual provides the instructor with an assortment of teaching materials, including chapter-at-a-glance guide to the supplements package, learning objectives, chapter outlines, discussion topics, class projects, and student exercises. A new Teaching Tool section helps integrate the text's Companion Website into an instructor's course with teaching topics, class activities, and test questions.

Test Bank, by Robert Bookwalter of Marshall University, contains multiple choice, true/false, fill-in, short answer, and essay questions. Midterm and final exam handouts also are included.

A Guide for New Public Speaking Teachers: Building Toward Success, Third Edition, by Calvin L. Troup of Duquesne University, is designed to help new instructors teach the introductory public speaking course effectively by covering such topics as preparing for the term, planning and structuring the course, evaluating speeches, utilizing the textbook, and integrating technology into the classroom. The third edition includes a brief guide on teaching students for whom English is not the first language, teaching suggestions, and student activities designed to accompany The Allyn & Bacon Classic and Contemporary Speeches DVD.

Allyn & Bacon Public Speaking Transparency Package includes 100 full-color transparencies created with PowerPoint software to provide visual support for classroom lectures and discussions.

Great Ideas for Teaching Speech (GIFTS), Thirteenth Edition, by Raymond Zeuschner of California Polytechnic State University, includes descriptions and guidelines for assignments used successfully by experienced public speaking instructors in their classrooms.

ESL Guide for Public Speaking, by Debra Gonsher Vinik of Bronx Community College of the City University of New York, provides strategies and resources for instructors teaching in a bilingual or multilingual classroom. It also includes suggestions for further reading and a listing of related Websites.

Electronic Resources

MySpeechLab Where students learn to speak with confidence! MySpeechLab is an interactive and instructive online solution for introductory public speaking. Designed to be used as a supplement to a traditional lecture course, or to completely administer an online course, MySpeechLab combines multimedia, video, speech preparation activities, research support, tests, and quizzes to make teaching and learning fun! Students benefit from a wealth of video clips that include student and professional speeches with running commentary, questions to consider, and helpful tips—all geared to help students learn to speak with confidence. For complete details and ordering information, please visit www.myspeechlab.com or consult your local Allyn & Bacon representative.

TestGen EQ: Computerized Test Bank The user-friendly interface enables instructors to view, edit, add questions, transfer questions to tests, and print tests in a variety of fonts. Search and sort features allow instructors to locate questions quickly and arrange them in preferred order.

PowerPoint Presentation for Public Speaking, by Rebecca L. Roberts of The University of Wyoming, contains over 100 slides of text-specific lecture outlines and graphic images. Available on supplements central. Log on to www.ablongman.com/suppscentral to access the presentation.

Allyn & Bacon PowerPoint Presentation Package for Public Speaking Available at www.ablongman.com/suppscentral, this package includes 125 slides that provide visual and instructional support for the classroom including material on communication theory, visual aids, and tips for organizing and outlining speeches. A brief user's guide accompanies this package.

Allyn & Bacon Digital Media Archive CD-ROM for Communication, Version 2.0 contains electronic images of charts, graphs, maps, tables, and figures, along with media elements such as video, audio clips, and related web links. These media assets are fully customizable to use with our preformatted PowerPoint outlines or to import into instructor's own lectures (Windows and Mac).

VideoWorkshop for Public Speaking, Version 2.0, by Tasha Van Horn of Citrus College and Marilyn Reineck of Concordia University- St. Paul, includes quality video footage on an easy-to-use CD-ROM plus an Instructor's Teaching Guide with textbook-specific Correlation Grids. *VideoWorkshop* brings textbook concepts to life with ease and helps students understand, analyze, and apply the objectives of the course.

CourseCompass for Public Speaking, powered by Blackboard and hosted nationally, is the most flexible online course management system on the market today. By using this powerful suite of online tools in conjunction with Allyn & Bacon's preloaded textbook and testing content, you can create an online presence for your course in under thirty minutes. The Public Speaking course features preloaded content such as quiz questions, video clips, instructor's manuals, PowerPoint presentations, still images, course preparation, and instruction materials, *VideoWorkshop for Public Speaking,* weblinks, and much more! Log on to www.coursecompass.com to access this dynamic teaching resource. The content is also compatible with Blackboard and WebCT.

CourseCompass for Public Speaking, Professional Development Edition is a collection of helpful instructional materials that feature public speaking teaching strategies, resources, and video examples that you can access on the Internet using CourseCompass. For course coordinators working with adjuncts and/or teaching assistants, our *CourseCompass Public Speaking, Professional Development Edition* helps you to provide training materials to your instructors—whether they're on campus or not. You can access our preloaded instruction materials, add your own materials, and make the resulting combination available to other instructors for their own instructional development and for the continued benefit of their students. Log on at www.coursecompass.com for more information.

The Allyn & Bacon Classic and Contemporary Speeches DVD presents a collection of over 120 minutes of video footage in an easy-to-use DVD format. Each speech is accompanied by a biographical and historical summary that helps students understand the context and motivation behind each speech. This DVD is available free to professors and students when packaged with new copies of *Public Speaking.* Contact your Allyn & Bacon sales representative for additional details and ordering information.

The Allyn & Bacon Student Speeches Video Library has a collection of student speeches videos that includes three 2-hour American Forensic Association videos of award-winning student speeches and four videos with a range of student speeches delivered in the classroom. Some restrictions apply.

The Allyn & Bacon Communication Video Library contains a collection of communication videos produced by Film for the Humanities and Sciences. Topics include: *Business Presentations, Great American Speeches,* and *Conflict Resolution.* Contact your local Allyn & Bacon sales representative for ordering information. Some restrictions apply.

The Allyn & Bacon Public Speaking Video includes excerpts of classic and contemporary speeches as well as student speeches to illustrate the public speaking process. One speech is delivered two times under different circumstances by the same person to illustrate the difference between effective and noneffective delivery based on appearance, nonverbal, and verbal style. Some restrictions apply.

The Allyn & Bacon Public Speaking Key Topics Video Library contains three videos that address core topics covered in the classroom: *Critiquing Student Speeches, Speaker Apprehension,* and *Addressing Your Audience.* Some restrictions apply.

Student Resources

Print Resources

Research Navigator Guide for Speech Communication, by Terrence Doyle of Northern Virginia Community College, is designed to teach students how to conduct high-quality online research and to document it properly. Pearson's new Research Navigator is the easiest way for students to start researching their speeches. Complete with extensive help on the research process and exclusive databases of credible and reliable source material, including EBSCO's ContentSelect Academic Journal Database and the *New York Times* Search by Subject Archive, Research Navigator helps students quickly and efficiently make the most of their research time. The guide is available on the web at www.researchnavigator.com or valuepacked with any of Allyn & Bacon's Public Speaking texts.

Preparing Visual Aids for Presentations, Third Edition, by Dan Cavanaugh, is a brief booklet that provides a host of ideas for using today's multimedia tools to improve presentations, including suggestions for how to plan a presentation, guidelines for designing visual aids and storyboarding, and a walkthrough that shows how to prepare a visual display using PowerPoint.

Speech Preparation Workbook, by Jennifer Dreyer and Gregory H. Patton of San Diego State University, takes students through the various stages of speech creation—from audience analysis to writing the speech—and provides supplementary assignments and tear-out forms.

Public Speaking in the Multicultural Environment, Second Edition, by Devorah A. Lieberman of Portland State University, includes activities in a two-chapter essay that encourages students to analyze cultural diversity within their audiences and adapt their presentations accordingly.

Outlining Workbook, by Reeze L. Hanson and Sharon Condon of Haskell Indian Nations University, touches briefly on activities, exercises, and answers that help students develop and master the critical skill of outlining.

Electronic Resources

MySpeechLab Where students learn to speak with confidence! MySpeechLab is an interactive and instructive online solution for introductory public speaking. Designed to be used as a supplement to a traditional lecture course, or completely administer an online course, MySpeechLab combines multimedia, video, speech preparation activities, research support, tests, and quizzes to make learning fun! Students benefit from a wealth of video clips that include student and professional speeches with running commentary, questions to consider, and helpful tips—all geared to help students learn to speak with confidence. For complete details and ordering information, please visit www.myspeechlab.com.

VideoWorkshop for Public Speaking, Version 2.0, by Tasha Van Horn of Citrus College and Marilyn Reineck of Concordia University- St. Paul, includes quality video footage on an easy-to-use CD-ROM plus a Student Learning Guide with textbook-specific Correlation Grids. *VideoWorkshop* brings textbook concepts to life with ease and helps students understand, analyze, and apply the objectives of the course.

Companion Website with Online Practice Tests, by Julie R. Mactaggart of St. Cloud State University, is easily accessed at www.ablongman.com/zarefsky4e. This site provides an assortment of activities to help students prepare speeches, including weblinks from the text's *Using the Internet* feature and additional examples of student work by the class featured in the text's *Applying Strategies* feature. The site also includes learning objectives, flashcards, and an online set of practice tests for each chapter.

Allyn & Bacon Public Speaking Website, by Nan Peck of Northern Virginia Community College, contains five modules students can use along with their text to learn about the process of public speaking and in preparation of their speeches. This site includes enrichment materials and interactive activities to enhance students' understanding of key concepts. Access this website at www.ablongman.com/pubspeak.

Interactive Speechwriter Software, Version 1.1, by Martin R. Cox, contains sample speeches, tutorials, self-test questions on key concepts, and templates for writing informative, persuasive, and motivated sequence speeches. This program enhances student's understanding of key concepts discussed in the text. This product is available for student purchase or FREE when valuepacked with any Allyn & Bacon public speaking text. Some restrictions apply.

The Speech Writer's Workshop CD-ROM, Version 2.0, assists students with speech preparation by including a *Speech Handbook* with tips for researching and preparing speeches; a *Speech Workshop* that guides students step-by-step through the speech writing process; a *Topics Dictionary* that gives students hundreds of ideas for speeches; and the *Documentor* citation database that helps them to format bibliographic entries in either MLA or APA style. Available FREE when packaged with any Allyn & Bacon public speaking text. Some restrictions apply.

Public Speaking Tutor, Tutor Center. (Access Code Required) www.aw.com/tutorcenter.   The Tutor Center provides students free, one-on-one interactive tutoring from qualified public speaking instructors on all material in the text. The Tutor Center offers students help with understanding major communication principles as well as methods for study. In addition, students have the option of submitting self-taped speeches for review and critique by Tutor Center instructors to help prepare for and improve their speech assignments. Tutoring assistance is offered by phone, fax, Internet, and e-mail during Tutor Center hours. For more details and ordering information, contact your Allyn & Bacon publisher's representative.

Acknowledgments

Reviewers of the Fourth Edition

Articulating this perspective on public speaking in a textbook that is accessible to students has been a stimulating challenge. All or part of the manuscript was read by:

Barbara Blackstone, Slippery Rock University; Robert Bookwalter, Marshall University; Kristina Bruss, University of Minnesota; Lisa Inzer Coleman, Southwest Tennesee Community College; Marilyn Cristiano, Paradise Valley Community College; Mark A. Gring, Texas Tech University; Douglas Kresse, Fullerton College; Craig Monroe, California State University, San Bernardino.

Reviewers of Previous Editions

Ellen Arden-Ogle, Consumnes River College; Susan Baack, Montana State University; Ernest Bartow, Bucks County Community College; John Bee, Ohio State University; Sandra Berkowitz, Wayne State University; Vincent Bloom, California State University–Fresno; Robert Bookwalter, Marshall University; Ferald J. Bryan, Northern Illinois University; Leah Ceccarelli, University of Washington; Faye Clark, DeKalb College; Marion Couvillon, Mississippi State University; Marilyn Cristiano, Paradise Valley Community College; Jim Dittus, Highland Community College; Michael Howard Eaves, Valdosta State University; Susan Redding Emel, Baker University; Patricia Faverty, Thomas More College; William Fusfeld, University of Pittsburgh; Kathleen Galvin, Northwestern University; John Giertz, Bakersfield State University; Joseph Giordana, University of Wisconsin–Eau Claire; William Goodbar, Old Dominion University; Rose Gruber, Gloucester County College; Richard Halley, Weber State University; Kelby K. Halone, Clemson University; Diane Hill, Providence College; Stephen K. Hunt, Illinois State University; Carol Jablonski, University of South Florida; Karla Kay Jensen, Texas Tech University; Richard Jensen, University of Nevada–Las Vegas; Jack Johnson, University of Wisconsin–Milwaukee; William Jordan, North Carolina State University; Elizabeth Lamoureux, Buena Vista University; Thomas A. Marshall II, Robert Morris College; Al Montanaro, SUNY Plattsburgh; John M. Murphy, University of Georgia; Stephen Neilson, University of Nevada–Las Vegas; Patrick O'Sullivan, Illinois State University; Cate Palczewski, University of Northern Iowa; Jay Pence, University of North Carolina–Chapel Hill; Lee Polk, Baylor University; Kenna J. Reeves, Emporia State University; Kurt Ritter, Texas A&M University; Kellie Roberts, University of Florida; Rebecca L. Roberts, University of Wyoming; Paul Sabelka, Iowa Wesleyan College; Noreen Schaefer-Faix, Kutztown University; Deanna Sellnow, North Dakota State University; Kenneth G. Sherwood, Los Angeles City College; Calvin Smith, Eastern Illinois University; Cynthia Duquette Smith, Indiana University, Bloomington; Jessica Stowell, Tulsa Junior College; Robert Terrill, Indiana University; Denise Vrchota, Iowa State University; Beth Waggenspack, Virginia Polytechnic Institute and State University; Rita Kirk Whillock, Southern Methodist University; Roy Wood, University of Denver.

The comments and suggestions of the reviewers listed above were quite helpful and often pointed the way for substantial improvement in the manuscript. The responsibility for what I have written, of course, remains with me.

My debt to Leah Ceccarelli, now on the faculty at the University of Washington, continues from the first edition. She helped in the development and selection of examples and end-of-chapter features and helped significantly to shape the tone of the book. I also appreciate the work of those who prepared supplementary materials for the first, second, and third editions: Victoria Gallagher, North Carolina State University; Glen Williams, University of Akron; Melissa Beall, University of Northern Iowa; Robert Brookey, Northern Illinois University; Robert Bookwalter, Marshall University; Calvin Troup, Duquesne University; Terry Doyle, Northern Virginia Community College; and Sherilyn Marrow, University of Northern Colorado.

I am grateful to those who assisted in the preparation of the fourth edition. Christine Gardner, a doctoral student at Northwestern University, worked with me on the revision and updating of examples, the *Strategies for Speaking to Diverse Audiences,* features, and the selection of speeches for Appendix B. Additionally, the following instructors prepared some of the key supplements for this fourth edition: Robert Bookwalter, Martin R. Cox, Julie R. Mactaggart, and Nan Peck.

My thanks also to Tonya Blivens and her students at Texas Tech University for their work in helping with the *Applying Strategies* feature for this edition.

At Allyn & Bacon, Steve Hull and Joe Opiela first persuaded me to undertake the task and Bill Barke placed his faith in my ability to complete the book in a reasonable period of time. I have benefited from the editing of Karon Bowers, Carol Alper, and Shannon Morrow. I also am grateful for the diligent efforts of all the production staff at Allyn and Bacon, often working against short deadlines.

The title of the book, *Public Speaking: Strategies for Success,* has a twofold meaning. The book offers a strategic perspective that should lead students to become more successful public speakers. Additionally, the art of public speaking provides many of the strategies for students to succeed in many different walks of life. My hope is that this book will help you to empower your students to achieve that goal.

David Zarefsky

To the Student

Public speaking may well be the single most important course in the entire curriculum. I make that bold statement with confidence because it has been true in my own life.

In the fall of 1961, as a sophomore in high school, I enrolled in my first course in public speaking. As the saying goes, it changed my life. I had taken the course to become more comfortable in speaking before a group and to learn how to use my voice effectively and how to control distracting mannerisms. I accomplished those goals and so much more. I learned how to think analytically, how to organize ideas, how to do research, how to assess an audience, how to inform and persuade. It was not long before I realized that these skills and habits were valuable not just in public speaking but in every other course and, indeed, in almost every aspect of life. If I were to identify one course that provided the tools I have used in my personal and professional life, without a doubt public speaking would be that course.

Thirty years later, my daughter had an almost identical experience. After taking a course in public speaking, she suddenly realized that it was easier for her to write essays and research papers and that the papers were better. She began to read more critically and to analyze what she read. She, too, had found patterns for working with ideas that have been useful well beyond the confines of the course. My son completed a public speaking course a few years later with many of the same results.

I hope that this book, and the course of which it is a part, will help you to have a similar experience. For over 2,500 years, men and women have studied the art of public speaking, both because it is valuable in its own right and because, in the best sense of the term, it is a liberal art—one that frees and empowers people. It does so by providing the knowledge, cultivating the skills, and modeling the habits of effective thought and expression that can be applied to any area of life.

The title of this book is *Public Speaking: Strategies for Success*. That title has a double meaning. First, this book is about strategies for success in public speaking. Second, the premise of the book is that public speaking will provide you with strategies for success in life. Certainly it does not promise fame or fortune, but it does offer a blend of reflective judgment

You will find *Applying Strategies* boxes throughout this text. These boxes allow you to get to know five students who attend Texas Tech University in Lubbock, Texas. Just as you are doing now, these students took a public speaking course and experienced the same questions, fears, and uncertainties that you might encounter throughout the term. The *Applying Strategies* boxes contain comments and insights from the students as well as excerpts and sample materials from their speeches that will provide you with tips and guidance. You will see how the necessary elements of a speech are implemented and how other students have used strategies discussed in this book. You will also hear from their instructor, Dr. Tonya Blivens, as she offers feedback on their outlines and speeches. From the experience of students who have "been there," you will see that speaking in public is a valuable art and skill that is not as intimidating as it might appear at first.

Tonya Blivens

Hello and welcome to the fourth edition of *Public Speaking*: *Strategies for Success* by David Zarefsky. My students have found Professor Zarefsky's textbook to be very informative and user-friendly as they navigate their way through the different strategies of effective public speaking. In this edition, you can enhance your learning of the materials by reading about the experiences of five of my students: John, Darbi, Priya, Tim, and Kyle. They have gone through some of the same things that you will go through in your class, so you will be able to relate to their experiences. You will read about their difficulties as well as their successes in public speaking. Their work,

and carefully chosen action that should enable you, whatever your experience, to enjoy a life well lived.

I have chosen the term *strategy* to emphasize that public speaking is about *choices*. It is an art and not a science. When you speak, you will be faced with situations that offer both opportunities and constraints. You will along with some of my feedback, is featured in the *Applying Strategies* boxes located within many of the text's chapters. In these boxes, they share their perspectives on the topics covered in the text and offer suggestions to make your own experience go a little smoother. We hope that this personalized approach will help you reach your goals in this course and lead you to a lifetime of successful public speaking!

John Hernandez

My name is John Hernandez, I am a 20-year-old junior at Texas Tech University. I am majoring in Food Technology. My goal is to receive my master's degree in this field and go on to work in the food industry as a quality control manager. I plan to work for Shepps Dairy when I have achieved my goals.

Darbi Howard

I'm nineteen years old and my major is psychology, more specifically child psychology. My minor is English, at least for now just because I think it will be the most beneficial for my career. I picked psychology because I love learning about the human brain and the way people learn and react. Knowing about psychology is helpful in so many careers and also just in daily life.

Right now I am classified as a sophomore. My aspirations are to finish with a Ph.D. in psychology and eventually start my own practice working with children. When I graduate I hope to work at a school or a child studies center to gain some real hands-on work. I'm very excited about my future!

Priya Mydar

I am seventeen years old and a sophomore at the wonderful Texas Tech University. I decided to major in Civil Engineering because I admire the complexity of buildings and structures, and one day I would like to help with the construction of such buildings.

Tim Ortiz

My name is Tim Ortiz and I'm a senior at Texas Tech. My major is Communication Studies and after graduation I plan to go into organizational communication. My goal is to work in the corporate setting.

Kyle Rogers

I'm an eighteen-year-old freshman and my current major is General Studies. I plan to go into business for myself full-time after college. Right now I have a small online business that I hope will continue to grow. My overall goal is to finish up college and then go into business.

want to decide how to work within this situation to achieve your goals, and your plan for doing so is a strategy. And even as you make choices in response to a situation, the pattern of your choices actually helps to define what the situation is. It affects you, but you also affect it.

Thinking strategically about public speaking means abandoning the belief that there is an all-purpose magic formula that will always produce a good speech. Although, as you will see, there are some general norms and expectations, a speech is good not because it follows some formula, but because it deals effectively with a specific situation. A speech that is good in one context may be weak in another. It is always necessary to get down to cases.

For that reason, you will find many examples and case studies in this book. Some come from student speakers and some from speakers in the "real world." Some are actual situations and some are hypothetical ones that I have designed to illustrate important principles. Some describe what speakers actually did and some ask you what you might do. Just as lawyers learn the law, in part, through the case method, so you will cultivate and sharpen the skills of public speaking by trying them out on specific cases.

Case material will be provided not only by this book, but also by your class. You will have the opportunity not only to present speeches, but to listen to many as well. Listening to speeches is also important, not just a necessary evil to be endured while you wait your turn to speak. You develop habits of analysis and memory, you see a large array of choices other students make in specific situations, and you gain skill in assessing whether strategies succeed or fail and in deciding whether or not they are strategies that you might wish to use.

At the same time, *Public Speaking* does not study cases in a vacuum. It draws on underlying theory to explain these situations. *Theory* does not refer to that which is impractical; nor does it refer to a lot of fancy terms or ideas that seem isolated from reality. Although sometimes the theory and practice of public speaking are studied in isolation, the premise of *Public Speaking* is that they need to be integrated at every step. Theory informs our understanding of practice by enabling us to explain what is happening in particular situations. And practice applies and modifies our understanding of theory. What you learn about theories of arrangement, for instance, will help you to organize a speech, but your experience in organizing speeches will also contribute to your thinking about theories of arrangement.

It is a pleasure to welcome you to this class in public speaking. This book, your own experience, and the interaction with other students and your instructor are all vital parts of the course. I hope that, like me, you will find that you not only achieve your original goals, but actually transcend them.

And I hope that a course in public speaking contributes as much to your life as it has to mine.

David Zarefsky

Public Speaking

Chapter One

Welcome to Public Speaking

In this chapter, we will:

- Identify the principal things you will learn in this course and how they will benefit you outside the classroom.

- Understand public speaking as a communication process in which the speaker and listeners jointly create meaning and understanding.

- Examine the main goals and strategies for developing a speech and learn how to prepare your first speech for this course.

- Discover how nervousness can be used to your advantage in public speaking and learn strategies to overcome anxiety.

- Recognize what makes a speech of high quality.

- Consider the ethical responsibilities of both speakers and listeners.

Welcome to Public Speaking, one of the most important courses you will ever take. If that sounds like a strong claim, consider what the following students had to say after completing a public speaking course:

> I used to be terrified of speaking in public. I've learned that solid preparation is the key to overcoming my fears. I still get nervous, but now I know how to control my nervousness and focus on communicating with my audience.

> This class has taught me to be a better listener. I'm more aware of weak arguments, fuzzy logic, and unsupported claims. I think critically about what I am being persuaded to do and why.

> Before taking this class, I used to be the most boring speaker! My speeches were well researched, but my delivery was poor. Now I make eye contact with my audience members and use my voice and pauses to set a tone and emphasize key points.

> I've learned more about the structure of speeches, especially the importance of an attention-grabber at the beginning of my speech and a preview of my main points to give the audience a "road map" of what I'm going to say.

Why Study Public Speaking?

You may have enrolled in this course because you expect to be making public presentations and you want to learn how to do that better and more easily. Maybe your goal is to speak more forcefully or to be less nervous. Perhaps you want to become better organized, to learn more about how to prepare a speech, or to think more clearly and more critically. You may even have chosen the course because it meets at a convenient time, is a requirement for graduation, or has a good instructor.

Apply What You Learn

Whatever your reasons for studying public speaking, this is one of the few courses you will take that combine theory and practice—that help you apply classroom content in your daily life. As you study creative and critical thinking, sensitivity to audiences, and effective speech presentation, the skills you learn will:

- Help you critically evaluate messages and appeals of all kinds.
- Make you more sensitive to people and situations.
- Enable you to recognize and adapt to diverse audiences and complex occasions.
- Increase your self-confidence and your willingness to engage in serious dialogue with others.[1]

Outside the classroom, these attributes will enhance your value as an employee and as a citizen. Employers and career counselors often put "good communication skills" at the top of the list of qualities they seek in people.[2] The reason is simple: Each year our economy becomes more dependent on information and the ability to communicate it.

Your study of public speaking will also help make you a more competent, more active citizen. The skills just listed will make you better able to understand public issues and social controversies, to decide what you think about them, and to participate effectively in resolving them—whether on your campus, in your neighborhood, or in the larger public forum.

When people deliberate about matters that affect themselves and others, they participate in the public forum. Decision making in a democracy is improved when the public forum is active and vibrant. Otherwise, critical decisions will be made unilaterally, either by experts or by rulers, so that those affected by the decisions really won't have any part in making them. Without a well-cultivated public forum, democracies tend to decline and are often replaced by either tyranny or anarchy. Fortunately, studying public speaking equips you to participate better in the public forum and thereby helps to strengthen democratic life. Appendix A describes the public forum in more detail.

The communication skills you learn in your public speaking class will help you throughout all aspects of your life: as a student, as an employee, and as a citizen.

Develop Specific Communication Skills

Here are some of the specific skills you will learn or improve by studying public speaking:

- How to listen carefully and critically in order to understand and evaluate what others say
- How to decide what you want to speak about and to select what to say
- How to find the material for a speech by examining your own experience, consulting with others, using the Internet, and visiting a library
- How to think critically about what you read and observe so that you will reason soundly when addressing an audience
- How to organize a speech to make it clear, coherent, sensible, and effective
- How to use language skillfully to convey both meaning and mood
- How to use your voice and your body to present yourself and your message in an effective, compelling way
- How to use visual aids to enhance your message, not distract listeners from it
- How to adapt general principles to your particular speaking situation, with emphasis on the dimensions of informing, persuading, and entertaining
- How to understand and benefit from reactions to your speeches so that the audience's response helps you improve your skills

In this chapter, we will discuss each of these skills only briefly so that you can start practicing them. Each topic introduced here will be covered more fully later in the book.

This set of skills has been studied and taught for about 2,500 years (in different ways over the years, of course), so you are taking part in a very old and valuable academic tradition.

Focus on Critical Thinking and Strategic Planning

Besides improving these specific skills as a communicator, you also will be applying and refining two invaluable general skills that are emphasized throughout this book: critical thinking and strategic planning.

Critical Thinking. Public speaking is in large measure an exercise in **critical thinking,** the ability to form and defend your own judgments rather than blindly accepting or instantly rejecting what you hear or read. Critical thinkers can analyze and understand various points of view, and they can quickly recognize the difference between fact and opinion.

Facts, as we will see in detail later, are statements that—at least in theory—can be *verified* by someone else. If a speaker says that the world's population has doubled every 25 years, that statement can be tested by checking population statistics. In contrast, **opinions** are *subjective* statements that presumably are based on experience or expertise. If a speaker asserts that the world's population is growing too fast, that opinion cannot be verified externally; it stands or falls depending on the insight and judgment of the person who offers it.

Critical thinking is the basis of those "good communication skills" that employers seek and democracies need. As a listener, critical thinking will help you to recognize a speaker's unstated assumptions. As a speaker, it will help you to form precise statements that embody your thoughts. Overall, critical thinking will place ideas into a broader context, showing how they relate to other things that you already know or believe.

The particular skills of critical thinking are the focus of Chapter 2, but they will inform all your work in this course.

Strategic Planning. A speaker operates in a world of choices: whether to speak, when to speak, what to say, how to phrase a particular point, and how to explain or defend it, how to organize the message, and what tone to give it, and exactly how to relate a message to the audience. Even all these options do not exhaust the possibilities! Some speakers make these choices unconsciously, without real thought (and relying on luck). But effective speakers make their choices *strategically;* through **strategic planning** they identify their goals and then determine how best to achieve them.

Chapter 4 will focus on strategies relating to a speaker's many choices, but throughout the book you will be reminded—and encouraged—to think strategically.

Public Speaking and Communication

When you give a speech, you and your listeners are involved in **communication,** meaning that you interact in order to build some sort of connection with them, whereby you can understand each other and recognize common interests. How does this happen? And how does public speaking differ from other forms of communication such as personal conversation and written essays?

Early theories of communication viewed public speaking as a series of one-way messages sent from speaker to audience. In fact, however, the audience participates with the speaker in creating shared meaning and understanding. The speaker's ideas and values are tested and refined through

critical thinking
The ability to form and defend your own judgments rather than blindly accepting or instantly rejecting what you hear or read.

facts
Statements that can be verified by someone other than the speaker.

opinions
Subjective judgments based on experience or expertise, not capable of being verified by someone else.

strategic planning
The process of identifying your goals and then determining how best to achieve them.

communication
Interaction that builds connections between people that helps them to understand each other and to recognize common interests.

interaction with the audience, and listeners' knowledge and understanding are modified through interaction with the speaker. Thus, public speaking is a *continuous* communication process in which messages and signals circulate back and forth between speaker and listeners.

From the audience's point of view, each listener comes to the speech with a framework of prior knowledge, beliefs, and values, and each listener "decodes," or interprets, the speaker's message within this personal framework. In a large or culturally diverse audience, the frameworks used by listeners may vary greatly.

To a particular listener, some ideas will be more important, or *salient,* than other ideas. If the speech is about vegetarian diets, for example, some listeners will approach it with special interest in health and nutrition, others will be concerned about the welfare of animals, and still others will view vegetarianism as a fad for eccentrics. The speech may support, challenge, or modify any of these frameworks, but each listener's framework will shape how he or she interprets and understands the speech. Audience members work actively to assess what the speaker says against what they already know or believe, and they constantly make judgments about the message and convey them back to the speaker through facial responses and other nonverbal clues.

From the speaker's point of view, knowing about the audience is crucial in preparing and delivering a speech. A speech about campus social life, for example, would be different for an audience of prospective students than for an audience of alumni. Even if the basic points of the speech were the same, the nature of the audience would affect how they are developed and explained and what tone or attitude the speaker projects. In preparing the speech, the speaker would analyze the audience and try to match listeners' expectations appropriately. Moreover, as listeners respond during the speech (by frowning, nodding approval, looking puzzled, etc.), the speaker would constantly modify how key points are organized and phrased and would try to acknowledge or respond to the audience's concerns.

Figure 1.1 depicts this interplay between speaker and audience. Suppose that you plan to speak about the benefits of a vegetarian diet. In preparing the speech, you'll remember that some listeners think vegetarianism is healthful; others think it is a passing fad; others come from cultures in which eating meat is prohibited, so that vegetarianism is not a matter of choice; and still others associate vegetarianism with eccentrics who don't really understand nutrition. As you speak, you'll be watching for **feedback,** responses from the audience that signal how they are reacting to what you say. Most responses will be nonverbal, such as frowns or nods of approval. Feedback might prompt you to acknowledge that some people doubt the merits of vegetarian diets; you might even admit that you had doubts yourself but now are a committed vegetarian. Throughout the speech—beginning with its preparation and lasting through its presentation—you will be sensitive to how well your ideas match your audience, and you'll use feedback to improve the fit as you speak.

WWW. Using the Internet

The Internet and Communication

In this chapter, we've explored the concept of two-way communication, particularly in Figure 1.1 (page 8), depicting the interplay between a speaker and audience. Explore how the concept of interplay works on the Internet. A good example of this is an online forum. One of the most widely respected forums is *Salon Magazine.* Point your Web browser to **http://www.salon.com/** to see the range of topics discussed in the magazine. Then, select "Table Talk" to join a forum. If this is your first time joining "Table Talk," you will need to sign on as indicated on the page.

- Click on one of the threads and observe how the interplay of users takes place.
- You can also evaluate. Which participants, in your view, demonstrate *ethos* to speak on their topic? (See page 13 for discussion of *ethos.*)

feedback
Responses from the audience to the speaker, often in the form of nonverbal cues.

Figure 1.1 Public speaking as a communication process.

You may convince some audience members to change their beliefs; others may interpret your message in ways consistent with their beliefs; and if the discrepancy between their beliefs and your message is too great, some listeners will reject your message. In any case, the audience will be actively involved as you speak, interpreting and testing what you say against their own beliefs and values and letting you know their reactions.

The Rhetorical Situation

From the preceding, we can see that one way in which public speaking differs from other forms of communication is that *the speaker and listeners simultaneously participate in creating the message.* Another unique characteristic of public speaking is that it occurs *in response to a specific situation.* Unlike great dramatic or literary works, which "speak to the ages," the principal test of a good speech is whether it responds most effectively to the needs of the situation in which it is presented.[3]

What the Rhetorical Situation Is

situation
The particular context in which a speech takes place.

The **situation** is the specific context in which a speech is given. Compared with poems and stories, which are read long after they were written, most speeches have a short life span. For example, student Warren Wilkins's first speech to his classmates concerned an important and timely issue:

Almost every week, there are new reports of ethnic violence in the Democratic Republic of the Congo. Civilians are killed every day—in their villages, in their homes, and on the market streets. It has been estimated that the civilian death toll from war and disease already is in the hundreds of thousands. This is nothing short of a human catastrophe, but we seem to be paying even less attention than we did to Bosnia or Kosovo in the 1990s. We must bring the world's conscience to bear on this crisis and do whatever we can to bring the war and disease to an end.

Although Warren's speech probably could be appreciated long after the war in the Democratic Republic of the Congo ended, it was created in response to a particular event and was designed primarily to be heard by a particular audience.

The study of how messages affect people has long been called **rhetoric.** This ancient discipline is concerned with the role that messages play in:

- Shaping, reaffirming, and modifying people's values.
- Binding people closer together or moving them farther apart.
- Celebrating significant events.
- Creating a sense of identity among people.
- Conveying information and helping people to learn.
- Nurturing, strengthening, or changing people's beliefs.
- Leading people to take (or not to take) action.

A **rhetorical situation,** then, is a situation in which people's understanding can be changed through messages.[4]

The following example shows how student Katie Jacobson responded to a rhetorical situation posed by recent armed robberies on her university campus:

It's easy to feel safe on our familiar campus, but crime is on the rise, and the university is partly to blame. Poor lighting both on and off campus provides many shadows for crimes to take place unseen. University police seem more interested in patrolling weekend parties than making weeknight walks between dorms and the library. And campus shuttle services are unreliable late at night, forcing students to walk through dangerous, unlit areas. We need to contact the university administration and let them know that they should take our safety seriously.

But it's not just up to the administration. We also need to take our personal safety seriously. Take self-defense classes. Lock your bikes. Familiarize yourself with the emergency telephone boxes on campus. Don't leave valuables in plain sight. Be careful where you publish your personal identification information. Show the university officials that you are doing what you can to be safe; then ask them to do what they can.

Katie's message addressed a particular audience and asked its members to consider a specific problem and solution. The speech was timely—Katie knew that the recent assault would be on her audience members' minds. The message also affected how students understood possible solutions, both institutional solutions that university administrators could affect and personal solutions that students could implement. An ineffective speech will leave the situation unchanged by not identifying possible causes of the problem and possible solutions that audience members can achieve.

rhetoric
The study of how messages affect people.

rhetorical situation
A situation in which people's understanding can be changed through messages.

Determinants of the Rhetorical Situation

Figure 1.2 shows the four basic factors that determine the success of any rhetorical situation: the audience, the occasion, the speaker, and the speech itself. This is a simplified presentation of the model; we will add more refinements later in the book.

The Audience.   Whereas a poem or a novel is addressed to all potential readers over time, a speech is usually presented to a specific **audience.** Most speakers, most of the time, want to present their ideas in a way that achieves **identification** with the audience; that is, they try to find common ground between what they know about the audience and what they want to say. Bear in mind, though, that a speaker sometimes might want to *avoid* common ground and even to antagonize listeners to get their attention or to motivate them to participate.

Listeners, as you know, are not passive receivers of the message. Instead, they form judgments about the speaker and message while the speech is in progress, and they communicate their judgments through feedback. Such reactions as eye contact, smiles, yawns, and frowns tell the speaker whether listeners understand the point being made, whether they are confused and need further explanation, whether they are paying close attention or seem distracted or bored, and whether the argument seems strong or needs additional support.

Ultimately, of course, the audience determines whether the speech was successful—whether a "speech to entertain" really was entertaining, whether a speech about a problem really did provide new information and insights, whether listeners actually will take the action that the speaker advocates. Because the audience is so important in determining the success of a rhetorical situation, Chapter 3 will explain in detail how to analyze the audience.

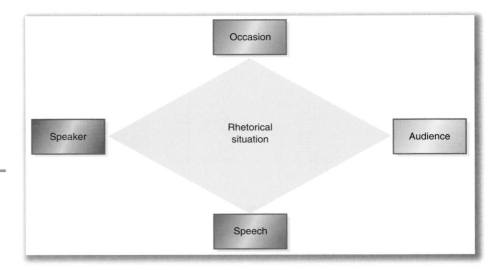

audience
The people who assemble to listen to a speech.

identification
Formation of common bonds between a speaker and the audience.

Figure 1.2 Determinants of the rhetorical situation.

The Occasion (and Purpose). The **occasion** is the specific setting for the speech, the circumstances in which it occurs. The date, time, place, and purpose help to define the occasion. Even as the speech responds to the rhetorical situation, the occasion influences what the rhetorical situation is. "A commencement speech about school reform, delivered at Western State University in June 2004" is an example of an occasion; "growing unease about the quality of public education" is the rhetorical situation to which this speech was a response. The speech responds to the rhetorical situation of growing unease among people about the quality of public education, but the expectation that a commencement speech will inspire the graduates also helps to define what the rhetorical situation is.

People speak on all kinds of occasions and for many reasons. Some speeches commemorate an important event or enact a ritual, such as presenting or accepting an award, delivering a eulogy, introducing or toasting someone, or entertaining an audience. Other speeches involve problem solving and decision making, such as giving an oral report or a sales presentation, advocating a policy, or refuting an argument. Still other occasions arise in which the speaker wants to lead the audience in deciding what is true, or in passing judgment on actions, or in applying some rule or social convention.

Whatever the occasion, the audience arrives with ideas about what is and what is not *appropriate behavior.* Such expectations have developed over time, and they limit what a speaker can do in responding to the rhetorical situation. For example, listeners expect a eulogy to offer a favorable view of the deceased, and they normally would think it inappropriate for a speaker to dwell on the person's failings. On the other hand, an after-dinner speech is usually expected to be lighthearted; a speaker who instead presents a highly technical lecture would not be responding appropriately to the occasion.

Simultaneous events further define the occasion. For example, the fact that a presidential campaign is under way helps to define the occasion for a speech about health care reform. The retirement of a popular athlete helps to set the stage for a speech about retirement trends in industry. And if listeners only last week were urged to give up tobacco, that may affect their judgments about a speech that now asks them to give up red meat.

Another way to think about the occasion is to note that it presents the speaker with an **exigence**—a problem that cannot be avoided but that can be solved, or at least managed, through the development of an appropriate message. Satisfactorily addressing the exigence, then, is the goal of the speech.

We will look closely at three basic purposes (informing, persuading, and entertaining) at the end of this chapter. Most of the speeches that you will present will be **deliberative,** meaning that your purpose is to share information and to influence listeners' beliefs and actions. Much of this book therefore will focus on the skills needed to inform and to persuade. But we also will examine other reasons for speaking, such as celebrating and entertaining, and how they affect the rhetorical situation. Finally, Chapter 15 will explore the wide range of occasions for public speaking.

The Speaker. The same speech delivered by different speakers will produce different reactions and effects in an audience. The concept of *ethos*, which we will examine in more detail later, refers to the speaker's character as the

occasion
The specific setting for the speech; the context in which it takes place.

exigence
A problem that cannot be avoided but that can be solved, or at least managed, through the development of an appropriate message.

deliberative
Intended to give listeners new information and to influence their thought and action.

audience perceives it. Developing and maintaining positive *ethos* will contribute immeasurably to the success of a speech. If you appear interested in your topic, the audience will be more likely to be interested, too. If you appear to know what you are talking about, listeners will be more likely to trust your judgment and to follow your advice. Fortunately, you can learn the skills that enable a speaker to contribute positively to a rhetorical situation, and so we will focus on ways to develop and maintain positive *ethos* throughout the book.

The Speech. Although we tend to think of the situation as something to which the speech responds, the message itself also works to *shape the situation*. Before Katie Jacobson spoke about crime on campus, her audience thought it was a problem for the campus police to solve, but during the speech, they began to see campus crime as a problem that called for individuals to take responsibility for the solution. The message had redefined the situation.

In most cases, an audience's understanding of a situation can be improved by a speech that is organized effectively, that includes interesting examples and memorable phrases, and that is presented enthusiastically. Although many factors determine whether or not a speech responds successfully to a rhetorical situation, by understanding the basic factors involved you can better shape your message as a speaker and can participate more fully as a listener.

Goals and Strategies for Your First Speech

Most instructors assign a first speech early in the course, often asking students to introduce themselves or a classmate or to briefly develop a single main idea. Whatever your specific assignment is, two goals are important for any speech:

1. Your message should be clear.
2. You should establish positive *ethos*.

Although these goals are highlighted for your first speech, they will continue to be goals for *every* speech you give. After examining what the goals entail, we will explore some strategies for achieving them.

A Clear Message

First, your speech should have a clear **purpose** and thesis. The purpose is your goal for the speech, the response you are seeking from listeners. The **thesis** is a statement of your main idea; it summarizes the basic point you want the audience to accept.

Your Purpose. Obviously, as a speaker you want listeners to pay attention to you and to think well of you. Beyond that, however, speeches can seek many different responses from the audience. Do you primarily want to impart information, to teach listeners something new? Or do you want to remind them of something they already believe so they will be more aware of it and

purpose
The goal of the speech, the response sought from listeners.

thesis
The main idea of the speech, usually stated in one or two sentences.

how it affects them? Is it your goal to make listeners see the humorous side of something they regard as serious—or perhaps to see the serious side of what they may otherwise view as a joke? Do you want them to pay more attention to something that they may tend to ignore? Do you hope to change their beliefs or attitudes about something? Do you want listeners to take some specific action as a result of your speech?

Questions like these illustrate the many possible purposes that a speaker might have, but not all of them are suitable for a brief first speech. In your first assignment, you should aim to provide new information and ask listeners to think about it. For now, this is a more realistic goal than aiming to change your listeners' beliefs or attitudes. We will look more closely at the purposes of a speech later in the chapter. At this point, it is enough that you can state your purpose clearly in a sentence or two.

Your Thesis. After you have defined your purpose for speaking, you should clearly state the thesis, or main idea, that you want the speech to establish. After your speech is over, listeners should have little doubt about what you actually said or what you meant. If you find it difficult to state your main idea in a sentence or two, you may be trying to cover too much. Even complex technical claims should be reducible to simple, basic thesis statements.

If the effort to state your thesis results in a statement like "I'm going to talk about computers," you have not focused sharply enough on your subject; you have only identified a general area. A better, more specific statement of what the speech will seek to establish might be "Using a computer has changed how I study." Similarly, if the purpose of your first speech is to introduce someone, simply saying "I am going to tell you about Jack Green" is too broad. Instead, a focused thesis statement like "Jack Green's life was greatly affected by his growing up in Europe" tells the audience exactly what your speech will claim. Stating your thesis in a single specific sentence will help ensure that you focus on the main idea rather than talk around it.

Establishing Positive Ethos

The second goal for your beginning speech is to establish positive *ethos* as a speaker. This Greek term was used by teachers of public speaking 2,500 years ago, and a rough translation is *character*.[5] But *ethos* does not refer to innate character traits, those at the core of a person's identity. Rather, **ethos** refers to the character that is *attributed to* a speaker by listeners on the basis of what the speaker says and does in the speech. *Ethos* is the character that you project when you are in a speaking situation. Some textbooks use the term *credibility* to describe this concept, but listeners make other judgments besides whether or not they should believe you. They also form impressions about what kind of person they think you are based on what you say and project as a speaker.

Try the following experiment. Select a classmate whom you don't yet know well, and listen carefully to his or her first speech. Then, based only on the speech, jot down all the adjectives you can think of with which you would describe this person. Your list might look something like this:

nervous	**deferential**	**slick**	**committed**
intelligent	**concerned**	**friendly**	**tasteful**
trustworthy	**respectful**	**unsure**	
weak	**funny**	**happy**	

ethos
The speaker's character as perceived by the audience.

When you give your first speech you can follow five steps to help turn your speech anxiety into an advantage: acknowledge your fears but recognize that you can overcome them, think about the effect your message will have on the audience, act confident, prepare a strong introduction to get you off to a good start, and prepare an effective conclusion so the speech will end on a strong note. See text discussion on pages 24–25.

Even a list this long will not capture *all* the attributes you might perceive in a speaker upon hearing a short speech. What can we conclude from this simple exercise about *ethos* and its effects?

First, *an audience's judgments about a speaker's character can be quite detailed.* From this exercise, you seem to know quite a bit about the speaker, based only on a very brief first speech. You have a sense of the person's intellect, emotions, judgment, relationships with others, power, confidence, and sense of self. Each of these is an important dimension of a person's character, and listeners make many such judgments about a speaker.

Second, *judgments about a speaker's character are made quickly.* Your classmate's speech probably lasted only a few minutes, and yet it gave you many insights into the person's apparent character. This exercise shows that assessments of *ethos* often reflect superficial first impressions. Whether the speaker walked confidently to the front of the room, looked at the audience, and then began speaking or whether the speaker seemed unsure, looked at the floor, and spoke before reaching the front of the room may give you clues about the person. As a listener you decide whether the speaker is nervous or comfortable, whether the speaker values the relationship with the audience, and how much confidence the speaker has in what she or he says. Your judgments may turn out to be wrong, of course, but you based them on the information you had. Listeners often only have first impressions to guide them in assessing a speaker, and they form judgments quickly.

Third, *assessments of* ethos *are durable.* Listeners' first impressions not only shape how they judge the speaker but also affect how they think about the speech and interpret what comes later. If the first impression you make is that you are very serious, it will seem out of character when you tell a joke later in the speech. The joke may cause listeners to revise their first impression ("Oh, that speaker's not so somber after all"), but it may also affect how they interpret the joke ("Such a serious person can't even tell a joke that's really funny").

The first speech is an icebreaker, an opportunity to learn about your classmates and to share things about yourself. Because an audience's assessments of a speaker are detailed, are formed quickly, and are durable, the goal of developing positive *ethos* in your first speech is just as important as having a clear statement of your purpose and thesis.

In addition to *ethos,* the ancient Greeks identified two other resources of a speaker: *logos* and *pathos. Logos* refers to the substance and structure of a speech's ideas, and *pathos* refers to the speaker's evoking of appropriate emotion from the audience. These resources will be considered later. However, because a listener's assessment of a speaker's character influences many other judgments about that speaker, we will emphasize establishing positive *ethos* right from the first speech you give.

Checklist 1.1 Goals for Your First Speech

1. **Develop a clear message.**
   - Choose a topic—the general subject area of the speech (unless your instructor has assigned the topic).
   - Determine the purpose of the speech.
     Informing
     Persuading
     Entertaining
   - State your thesis—the main idea of the speech.
2. **Establish positive ethos.**
   - Recognize that an audience's judgments about a speaker's character are:
     Quite detailed
     Made quickly
     Durable

Strategies for Organizing Your Speech

Once you have in mind the twin goals of presenting a clear message and establishing positive *ethos,* the next step is to think strategically about ways to organize the speech in order to achieve these goals.

Basically, every speech has three parts: a beginning, a middle, and an end. We will call these the *introduction,* the *body,* and the *conclusion,* and we will examine them fully in Chapters 7 and 8. For now, it is enough to realize that each part of a speech includes certain elements and performs certain functions.

The Introduction

Your **introduction** should be designed to (1) get the audience's attention, (2) state your thesis, and (3) preview how you will develop your ideas. Often the third function can be omitted in a short speech that has only one main point.

To get listeners' attention and put them in the right frame of mind, you might startle the audience with a significant but little-known fact. If your

introduction
The beginning of the speech, designed to get the audience's attention, to state the thesis, and to preview the development of the speech.

speech is about recycling, for example, you could begin by asking, "Do you realize that the trees of an entire forest are harvested each year to make paper for textbooks?" Or if your speech is about the benefits of technology, you might begin with a story that illustrates what it was like to practice law before the advent of computerized databases. Your opening statement is the first impression of the speech that listeners will receive; you want to get their attention and focus it appropriately on your main idea. When people want to listen to you, your *ethos* also is enhanced.

The statement of your thesis further serves to put listeners in the right frame of mind by defining the context in which you want them to interpret what you are about to say. In speaking about recycling, for example, your thesis might be, "We need to get serious about conserving and replenishing our natural resources." If you identified your thesis clearly when preparing the speech, stating it in the introduction should be easy.

To preview how you will develop your thesis, the final thing the introduction should do is make a natural transition to the body of the speech by telling listeners what to expect. For example, you might follow your thesis statement with, "After examining how our forests have been reduced over the last fifty years, I will outline some simple measures that we can take to prevent further deforestation."

The Body

The **body** is the largest portion of the speech; it develops your thesis statement and offers whatever proof you need to support your claims.

Supporting Materials. **Supporting materials** are all forms of evidence that lend weight to the truth of your thesis, whether by explaining, illustrating, or defending it. The many kinds of supporting materials can be grouped into a few broad categories:

- Experience
- Narratives (stories)
- Data
- Opinions

You can draw on your own experience with a topic or problem to make it clear that you are familiar with and have been affected by the subject of your speech. For example, if your thesis is "Health care takes too large a bite out of personal income," you could tell the audience what percentage of your own paycheck goes toward health costs. If your thesis is that travel broadens a person's mind, you could draw on your own travel experiences. To support the thesis that everyone needs to know about self-defense, student Teresa Madera described how she escaped from an assailant:

> It was late, and I was returning to the dorm after studying at the library. When I was passing an alley, a stranger jumped out at me. Luckily, I was carrying this keychain. You'll notice that it has a small canister attached to it. This is mace, and it probably saved my life. I sprayed the guy who attacked me and then didn't wait around to see what happened.

Teresa went on to explain how her experience had convinced her that all students should be prepared to defend themselves.

You can use *narratives,* or stories, for supporting material; people often explain (and understand) situations in terms of a story. For example, in a

body
The largest portion of the speech; includes the development of supporting materials to prove the thesis and any subsidiary claims.

supporting materials
All forms of evidence that lend weight to the truth of a claim.

speech about child abuse, student Stacey Gerbman illustrated the impact of the problem by telling the story of five-year-old Joey, who was abused by his father:

> Joey was afraid of his father. He hadn't meant to drop the milk jug, but it was so heavy. As he cringed in the corner of the kitchen, his father was screaming at him. Maybe he *was* a scrawny wimp, as his father said. Only a coward would whimper at the prospect of a beating. When the blows actually came, Joey couldn't stop crying. The next day, he had bruises on both body and soul.

Stacey ended the speech—and concluded the story—by telling how Joey later became a violent man himself:

> When Joey grew up and raised his own family, he too beat his children and showered them with verbal taunts. Sadly, he had learned that behavior all too well from his own father.

You can draw on *data* ("facts") for supporting material. If you claim that telephones outnumber people in the United States, you could simply use statistical tables to report the two total numbers. If the thesis is "Most American presidents have been lawyers," then naming all the lawyer-presidents would provide factual support.

You also can use *opinions* to support your thesis. As noted earlier, opinions are subjective judgments based on a person's experience; unlike facts, opinions cannot be verified. But if you use the opinions of experts to support your claims, those judgments are authoritative, because they are based on expertise in the subject. Opinions are especially useful in situations where you cannot observe things yourself or when you want to support promises or predictions. For instance, to support a prediction that inflation will not worsen over the next six months, you could cite the opinion of the chair of the Federal Reserve Board. In offering an opinion, of course, you want to be sure that the person really is an expert in the field and that he or she has no ax to grind and is not biased.

Different cultures emphasize different supporting materials. In some cultures, storytelling carries great weight, whereas in others only data really matter. Partly for this reason, speakers addressing diverse audiences usually are advised to use a variety of types of supporting material. Varying the types of support is good advice for *any* speaker, because it will help to sustain the audience's interest and may enhance the speaker's *ethos* by suggesting that he or she has deep knowledge of the topic.

Organizing the Evidence. Whenever you offer more than one piece of supporting material, you must decide in what order to arrange your evidence. Suppose, for example, that you want to use facts, narratives, and opinions to support the claim that prisons are seriously overcrowded. Which type of material should you present first?

Sometimes the decision about organization is just a matter of preference—of what seems instinctively to have the most natural "flow." You might decide on this basis to begin with a narrative, then state the facts about prison over-

WWW. Using the Internet

Using the Internet as a Library

The Internet does not replace the traditional library but should be used alongside it. You can find many valuable sources of information to use in your speeches, or you can find junk! One of the starting points for doing research on the Net is to use a site that has done some thoughtful screening of sources. An example of this is the **Librarian's Index to the Internet.** Point your browser to **http://lii.org** and select one of the topic areas.

- Explore some of the sources that the creators of the list have included.

crowding, and finally conclude with the opinions of some prisoners and corrections officers. In cases like this, you should try several organizational arrangements to see which works best. You might ask some friends whether the thesis is clearer or more effective when you organize the supporting material one way rather than another.

At other times, the supporting material may suggest an organizational arrangement. If you are speaking about three times that your town was damaged by a flood, it makes sense to arrange the occasions chronologically—either from first to last or from last to first. Disrupting this natural pattern by describing the floods in random order would make the speech harder to follow.

Time order, as in this example, is one natural organizational pattern. Another is *spatial order*—arranging items according to their location. To discuss the varied geography of Texas, for example, you might proceed clockwise, beginning with the Panhandle in the far north, then describing the hill country of central Texas and the "piney woods" of the east, then dipping southward to cover the Gulf Coast and the Rio Grande Valley, and finally heading to western Texas and the Big Bend country.

Other common organizational patterns are *cause–effect* (beginning with conditions and then describing their causes, or vice versa); *problem–solution* (first explaining a problem and then pointing to the solution); and *topical structure* (mentioning all the economic facts, for example, before mentioning all the political facts). Strategies for using different organizational patterns will be explored in later chapters.

The Conclusion

The final part of the speech is the **conclusion,** which has two basic tasks. First, it should draw together the ideas in the speech so that they are memorable. This is sometimes done by a brief summary of the argument, sometimes by a restatement of the main points or ideas, sometimes by repetition of the thesis. Second, the conclusion should give a strong note of finality to the speech. It might restate the idea in the introduction to suggest a completed circle. It might challenge the audience with an interesting question. Or it might draw on the claims in the speech to appeal for a specific belief or action on the part of the listeners.

Checklist 1.2 Decisions About Organization

1. **Develop an introduction.**
   - Get the audience's attention.
   - State your thesis.
   - Preview the development of the speech.
2. **Assemble the body of the speech.**
   - Decide which kinds of supporting materials you need.
     Experience
     Narratives
     Data
     Opinions
   - Decide how to organize the supporting materials.

---

conclusion
The ending of the speech; draws together the main ideas and provides a note of finality.

Time order
Spatial order
Cause–effect order
Problem–solution order
Topical order

3. **Prepare a conclusion.**
   - Draw together the ideas in the speech.
   - Provide a strong note of finality.

Beginning Assignments

The One-Point Speech

A common first speaking assignment is the **one-point speech,** in which the speaker's task is to establish only one main idea (the thesis). This type of speech requires a thesis that is clear and simple, and it is developed as follows:

Introduction

1. Wake up!
2. This concerns you.
3. Generally speaking

Body

4. For example

Conclusion

5. So what?

> ### WWW. Using the Internet
>
> **The Internet and Communication**
>
> Consider criteria for evaluating the quality of information you find online by examining the **10C's for Evaluating Internet Sources** that were developed at McIntyre Library at the University of Wisconsin—Eau Claire. Point your browser to
> **http://www.uwec.edu/library/Guides/tencs.html**
>
> - To what degree do you already use standards like these to judge the quality of information you find?
> - Are any of the criteria unique to evaluating sources from the Internet?

As indicated, the first three steps enact the introduction to the speech. "Wake up!" is the device to get the audience's attention, such as an interesting story, a startling statistic, or an unexpected fact. "This concerns you" shows listeners how the topic relates to them; it gives them reason to pay attention and to take the speech seriously. "Generally speaking" states the thesis of the speech.

"Generally speaking" also forms a natural transition to the body of the speech, represented by the heading "For example." The body develops the thesis by presenting whatever supporting materials are needed to support the claims in the thesis—experiences, stories, facts, and opinions, arranged in whichever order is most effective.

Finally, "So what?" signals the twofold function of the conclusion: drawing together the important ideas of the speech and making a final lasting impression on the audience. Answering "So what?" points out what the supporting material leads to and gives listeners cues about what they should believe or do.

The following short example of a one-point speech has the thesis "The Internet has changed our relationship to the world." The sections of the speech are indicated in brackets.

[WAKE UP!] When my parents went to college, they felt removed from their friends who went to schools in other parts of the country. They took time away

one-point speech
A speech in which only one main idea (the thesis) is offered and established.

Introducing Yourself to Others

The Situation

You have three minutes to introduce yourself to your classmates and your instructor in your public speaking class. Three minutes is not enough time to describe everything there is to know about you, so choices must be made.

Making Choices

1. How should you decide what you want to share about yourself?

   Should you consider: the members of your audience? your classroom setting? your goals for the class? the course subject? how much or how little you want the audience to know about you?

   What else might you consider?

2. What is the most relevant information to relay to your instructor and fellow students?

   Should you describe: your primary likes and dislikes? where you are from? what your hobbies and personal interests are? why you are fearful of speaking in public?

   What other information about yourself might you include in your speech?

What If . . .

Let's assume you are given the same assignment but with a different audience and a different purpose. How would your decisions above be affected by the following conditions?

1. Your public speaking classmates are evaluating your speech for a grade.

2. Your speech of introduction assignment will not be graded.

3. Your audience is now the entire student body, and your purpose is to announce your candidacy for student president.

4. Your audience is the active members of a fraternity/sorority that you would like to join.

---

from their books and wrote long letters, and then waited and waited for a reply. Distant as they were from their friends in this country, they couldn't imagine having strong friendships with people around the world. [THIS CONCERNS YOU.] When I told them I had friends in the Philippines and Israel, and that we had exchanged several letters over the past two weeks, they were surprised. You, too, may have found it hard to explain to your parents how you can keep up relationships with people abroad. [GENERALLY SPEAKING] The Internet has changed our relationship to the world. [FOR EXAMPLE] We can sit in our homes in Chicago, Illinois, and within seconds find out what's happening in Bielefeld, Germany. We can send e-mail to a friend in Australia. We can order music discs from stores in Japan. We can even order a movie, watch it, and return it without ever leaving our dorm rooms. [SO WHAT?] The world is now a smaller place. And we have the opportunity to take advantage of its diminishing size. We should learn more about people from far-off places and the events and rituals that mark their lives.

WWW Using the Internet

The One-Point Speech

One way to brainstorm topic ideas is to browse library and Internet resources. Review one or more of the sites below, select a topic area, and develop a one-point speech that focuses on a single significant aspect of your topic. Point your browser to **http://library.sau.edu/bestinfo/Hot/hotindex.htm** or to **http://www.libraries.psu.edu/crsweb/docs/speechtopics/topics.htm**.

Being short and simple, the one-point speech is a good way to master the basic structure of a speech. For this first speech, you may have a day or more to prepare. But the five-step structure of the one-point speech is also useful whenever you have to speak impromptu—on the spur of the moment. When you raise your hand to speak at a meeting or in class, remembering the structure of the one-point speech will help you state your point briefly, clearly, and effectively.

The Speech of Introduction

Another common first assignment is a speech to introduce yourself, a classmate, or a famous person whom you imagine inviting to class. You can easily adapt the structure of the one-point speech to a speech of introduction if you avoid reciting all the details of the person's biography. Such a recitation would have no central theme; besides lacking a sense of unity, the speech would be dull. Instead, select a key aspect of the individual's experience, and devise your thesis from that. Then follow the structure of the one-point speech.

For example, you might open with a statement such as "Unlike most of us, John Patterson has never lived outside of this town." The contrast between John and his classmates should capture the audience's attention and interest. This achieves the "Wake up!" function of the one-point speech.

Your next statement might be "John's experience can give us insight into the sense of roots that many of our ancestors had but most of us lack today." This identifies how you will make John's experience relevant to the audience, fulfilling the "This concerns you" step in the one-point speech.

Then you might state the thesis: "This town is so much a part of John's identity that he cannot imagine himself apart from it." This step matches "Generally speaking" in the one-point speech. It both states the idea that you intend to establish and provides a natural transition to the body of the speech.

The next step is to support this thesis. You might do it by referring to key events in John's life that are closely identified with the town: growing up where everyone knew everyone else, participating in parades and celebrations, living as an adult in the same house that he occupied as a child, and watching things change around him as others moved into or out of town. These experiences are the supporting material, corresponding to "For example" in the one-point speech. Decide which order to present them in and how much detail to provide.

Finally, conclude by answering the implicit question "So what?" You might say something like, "So, the next time you read statistics about how often people move, or the next time you think about how many careers you might have during your life, remember that some people choose to nurture their roots where they stand. John Patterson is a thriving example."

Practicing the Speech

Now that you have analyzed how to put a speech together, you will soon be ready to speak. First, though, you should develop an outline of the speech and practice talking through its main ideas.

Outlining Your Speech

Sometimes speakers read a speech, word for word, from a fully written manuscript. On rare occasions, they also commit the speech to memory.[6] These approaches may be helpful for highly formal speeches when every word matters and will be recorded for posterity. But for most of your speeches in this course, writing out and memorizing every word not only is a waste of time but may actually hinder your communication with the audience.

On the other hand, neither is it usually a good idea to speak impromptu—without preparation, trusting that a flash of inspiration will strike you as you speak. Most successful speakers aim for middle ground with an **extemporaneous** speech, meaning that they have a clear sense of the main ideas and how to organize them, but they have not planned the speech in advance word for word.

In speaking extemporaneously, an outline of the speech is a tremendous help. In fact, *two* outlines are even more helpful: a preparation outline and a presentation outline.

Preparation Outline. Begin developing your speech with a **preparation outline,** which is more complete than the outline you will use when presenting the speech. The preparation outline helps you to identify your main ideas and to organize them sensibly, and it lists supporting materials and how you will use them. Write complete sentences in your preparation outline, as in this example for a section of the speech discussed earlier introducing John Patterson:

Main Idea: John has a clear sense of his roots.

Support

   A. He still lives in the same house in which he grew up.
   B. He marched in the Fourth of July parade every year.
   C. He has never wanted to go anywhere else.

The rest of the speech would be outlined similarly.

Presentation Outline. Although the preparation outline is valuable in developing the speech, it is too complete to use while speaking. Your interaction with the audience will be limited if you are busy reading a fully elaborated, complete-sentence outline point by point. Instead, prepare a very brief outline of key words that will jog your memory and remind you of what comes next. You will use this **presentation outline** during the actual speech. Here is the previous example reduced to a presentation outline:

Main Idea: Sense of roots

Support

   A. Same house
   B. 4th of July
   C. No desire to leave

Because you are familiar with the ideas of the speech, seeing the phrase "Same house" will remind you of the statement you want to make about how John still lives in the room he occupied as a child and how that experience has affected his perspective on life. You may never need to refer to

---

extemporaneous
A mode of presentation in which the main ideas and structure have been worked out in advance but specific wording has not been developed.

preparation outline
An outline used in developing a speech; main ideas and supporting material are usually set forth in complete sentences.

presentation outline
An outline used while presenting a speech; typically consists only of key words written on an index card.

---

the presentation outline while you are speaking, but if you do, a quick glance at the words "Same house" will remind you of the point you want to make.

You probably can reduce the presentation outline to fit on index cards, which are easier to handle than loose sheets of paper. For the first speech, you may need only one index card; three or four cards will usually be enough even for complex speeches.

Practicing Your Delivery

Because you are going to speak extemporaneously, practicing the speech is really a way to become familiar with the ideas by talking them through. You will not say exactly the same thing each time, but you will know the content of the speech well enough that the thoughts will come to you easily and you can express them naturally. To achieve this goal, use this sequence of activities:

1. *Develop and talk through the preparation outline.* In your complete-sentence outline, fill in the explanation of your thesis and develop transitions between ideas. Don't worry about awkward pauses that occur while you figure out what to say next. These will smooth out as you practice.

After you have talked through the preparation outline once or twice to yourself, make an audio recording and listen to it. Ask yourself whether your main point is clear and easy to identify. If not, change your explanation or your transitions to present the thesis more effectively. You might also ask a friend to listen to you. Check whether your friend can identify the thesis correctly, and ask for suggestions to improve the speech.

2. *Reduce the preparation outline to a presentation outline.* Write your outline with key words on an index card, and repeat step 1. Get familiar enough with the speech so that each key word triggers the same statement that you made when following the complete-sentence outline. If a key word doesn't prompt the same statement, change the key word.

3. *Develop exact wording for the introduction and the conclusion.* Unlike the body of the speech, which will be more effective if presented extemporaneously, you may want to memorize the introduction and conclusion because of their importance in shaping the audience's first and last impressions. This is a good idea especially when precise wording is needed to make your ideas clear. Knowing exactly how you will start should give you a sense of security, and you won't have to rely on memory for strong finishing remarks. Even so, you may not wish to recite the introduction and conclusion from memory. Although you may have fairly specific wording in mind, you still are likely to speak extemporaneously.

4. *Simulate the conditions under which you will speak.* Find an empty room, and stand in front—where you will stand when you present the speech. Imagine an audience present, and think about maintaining eye contact with them. (Don't present the entire speech looking either up at the ceiling or down at your notes.) Practice walking up to speak as well as returning to your seat. Both before and after speaking, pause a second or two to "size up" the audience and to signal a sense of self-control and confidence. If you will be speaking at a lectern, practice using it (avoid the tendency to grip it and hang on for dear life). Finally, when you are familiar

> **Checklist 1.3** Practicing Your Delivery
>
> 1. **Develop and talk through the preparation outline.**
>   - Main ideas
>   - Supporting materials
> 2. **Reduce the preparation outline to a presentation outline.**
>   - Key words
>   - First and last sentences (see step 3)
> 3. **Develop exact wording for the introduction and the conclusion.**
> 4. **Simulate the conditions under which you will speak.**

with the content of your speech, practice how you will position yourself and move around and gesture. The more you can imagine yourself in the actual speaking environment, the less threatening the environment will seem.

Strategies for Overcoming Speech Anxiety

Even experienced speakers may be apprehensive when the time comes to speak.[7] In fact, researchers consistently report that most Americans fear public speaking more than anything—even more than death. As comedian Jerry Seinfeld has noted, that means that most people would rather be in the casket than delivering the eulogy! The term *communication apprehension* refers to fears and worries people have about communicating with others and can range from not wanting to speak up in a small group to worrying about talking on the telephone. Anxiety about public speaking is a widespread example. People experience communication apprehension very differently, depending on such factors as their style of thinking and their general level of self-esteem and confidence. A few generalizations may be useful.

Being nervous is normal. You believe that what you have to say is important, and you value your listeners' judgment. Wanting to please your audience and to make a good impression, you may worry about making some innocent but colossal mistake.

In response to this emotional state, our bodies undergo numerous chemical changes. More blood sugar becomes available; insulin is secreted; blood pressure, respiration, and the conductivity of nerves all increase. In turn, these chemical changes induce feelings of anxiety or fear.[8] Although most people experience this to a modest degree, in extreme situations a person may become immobilized. Such an extreme case is highly unlikely. Nevertheless, even the old term *stage fright* falls short of describing the deep-seated fear that some people have of speaking in public.[9]

Interestingly, though, the same chemical changes that cause extreme anxiety in some people bring others to a higher state of readiness and confidence. Many speakers get a boost of energy that, properly channeled, causes them to feel "psyched up" for the speech and hence in a position to do well. The following five steps can help you tap into this extra energy and turn speech anxiety into an advantage.

1. *Acknowledge your fears, but recognize that you can overcome them.* Remind yourself that your listeners are not hostile; if anything, they will be

supportive and sympathetic, especially for a beginning speaker. Also remind yourself that you have something valuable to say, that you know what you are talking about, and that it's important to share your ideas with the audience. This positive approach can convert nervous energy from a source of anxiety to a source of motivation.

2. *Think about what you are going to say and the effect you want to have on your audience.* The more you concentrate on your topic and on your relationship with the audience, the less anxiety you will feel—and the more likely you will do well. Becoming familiar with your outline through frequent practice will help boost your confidence.

3. *Act confident, even if you feel apprehensive.* Walk decisively to the front of the room, pause a moment to size up the audience, begin on a strong note, and maintain eye contact with your listeners. You may think of this as putting on a show, but remember that the audience has no idea how nervous you are. By acting confident, you will help listeners to feel positive about you, which, in turn, will help you feel more comfortable.

4. *Work carefully on the introduction so that you can start the speech on a strong note.* If you have written out the first few sentences of your speech and know exactly what you are going to say, this will propel you into the body of the speech. As you get into the speech and focus on what you are saying, your nervousness will probably subside.

5. *End the speech on a strong note and pause for a second before returning to your seat.* Even if you want to rush back to your seat, present a well-prepared conclusion in a deliberate manner; then pause to let your closing thoughts sink into the listeners' minds before you return slowly to your seat.

These simple steps will turn nervousness into an advantage for most speakers. In extreme cases of communication apprehension, however, nervousness becomes a pathological fear of relating to others in the public setting, and it may be necessary to treat the underlying anxiety through behavior modification—as is done with other phobias.[10] But such extremes are rare in a public speaking class. Even if you think that you are experiencing speech anxiety beyond the norm, remember this: You are in a relatively risk-free environment. Your classmates are likely to be friends and supporters because they are going through the same experience themselves. Your instructor's primary goal is to help you speak effectively, not to embarrass or intimidate you. Overall, there is probably no better setting in which to ac-

Checklist 1.4 Overcoming Speech Anxiety

1. **Acknowledge your fears, but recognize that you can overcome them.**
2. **Think about what you are going to say and the effect you want to have on your audience.**
3. **Act confident, even if you feel apprehensive.**
4. **Work carefully on the introduction so that you can start the speech on a strong note.**
5. **End the speech on a strong note, and pause for a second before returning to your seat.**

knowledge your fears and then go ahead anyway. With practice, you are likely to find that speech anxiety becomes manageable and actually helps you.

The Quest for Quality

With practice, you will overcome speech anxiety and will be able to get through your speech with confidence. Of course, you don't want to give just *any* speech; you want to give a *good* speech. So you need to know what makes a speech strong or weak. With practice, you will develop an instinct about this. As a starting point, you can assess the quality of a speech by focusing on its purpose and on feedback from the audience.

Purpose and Quality

Speeches are presented to achieve a purpose, and so the overriding standard of quality is that a speech succeed in attaining its goal. As you learned earlier, the three most general purposes of speeches are to inform, to persuade, and to entertain:

- **Informing** provides listeners with new information or ideas.
- **Persuading** influences listeners' attitudes and behavior (either to strengthen existing beliefs or to support new ones).
- **Entertaining** stimulates a sense of community by celebrating the common bonds among speaker and listeners.

Although these general purposes may seem to be completely separate, they often coexist in a single speech—as when a speaker aims *both* to share new information and also to use that information in influencing attitudes and behavior (or to stimulate a sense of community). For this reason, in Chapter 4 we will classify purposes in a more detailed way. For now, though, focus on the general purposes and realize that you must have (1) something about which to inform the audience or (2) some position you want to persuade them to take or (3) some subject with which to entertain them. Therefore, any speech also has one or more specific purposes. Here are some examples:

GENERAL PURPOSE: Informing

SPECIFIC PURPOSE: Explaining the main steps in the construction of the college library

GENERAL PURPOSE: Persuading

SPECIFIC PURPOSE: Urging listeners to endorse the president's education proposal and to send telegrams of support

GENERAL PURPOSE: Entertaining

SPECIFIC PURPOSE: "Roasting" the boss on the eve of her retirement

informing
Providing listeners with new information or ideas.

persuading
Influencing listeners' attitudes and behavior.

entertaining
Stimulating a sense of community through the celebration of common bonds among speaker and listeners.

How to Deal with Your Fear of Public Speaking

Priya Mydur

Though I am nervous before giving a speech, I think being in front of people and speaking about a topic that I enjoy is the most exhilarating feeling. It is very difficult to explain, because I feel like I am listening to someone else speak, as though it is not me, and I am thinking about all this while giving my speech, so I am not really paying attention to myself. All my apprehensions go away for that short period in time.

Tim Ortiz

I'm like any other "average Joe"; the thought of speaking in public isn't an experience that I find to be comfortable or pleasurable. It's comforting to know that all other college-aged people probably fall in this category as well. I do believe the key to a successful speech is the amount of time and sincere belief in the topic chosen. Comfort and knowledge in all the key areas of your speech, mixed with practice, usually always produces a smooth performance.

Prof. Blivens

Both of you identified strategies we discussed in class to cope with speech anxiety. First, the idea that everyone experiences some amount of speech anxiety is important to remember. You are not alone in your experiences of nervousness and your classmates probably are having some of the same feelings. This is a good way to keep calm and it gives you a reality check. Second, picking a topic you're comfortable with and practicing gives you much more confidence. Priya, I think that exhilarating feeling you get from speaking is a combination of being prepared and having a good attitude about public speaking.

John Hernandez

When I first stepped in front of the room, everyone stared at me. I felt as if their eyes were just pushing me against the wall. My mouth was dry, and I was getting nervous, so I took a few deep breaths and began. After my introduction, I calmed down a little and was able to give my speech. I feel more comfortable talking to a group of people when they are laughing with me, or at me, it doesn't matter as long as they're laughing.

Prof. Blivens

John, you and Tim should try using cognitive modification. Try and change your general attitude about public speaking. In class, another student mentioned that at first she didn't like public speaking because she felt like everyone was staring at her, but then she began to look at it differently. She began to think of public speaking more as her time when everyone *had* to listen to her, and it was a platform for her to speak about issues she cared about. Work on visualizing yourself doing well as you practice. This will give you an added boost of confidence. The breathing techniques we discussed in class helped, so remember to include that in your practicing. The introduction can play a major role in the flow of a speech. For you and most students, if the introduction flows smoothly it helps them calm down. John, one strategy that you use effectively is humor. Consider putting humor into your introduction since that makes you feel more comfortable. As a class, we shouldn't overlook the importance of practice in front of others before presenting it to the class. Not only does it improve your nervousness, but practice also points out structural problems you can fix before class.

In each case, the specific purpose is the standard to use in deciding whether the speech achieved its goal. Did listeners get a better understanding of the steps in constructing the college library? If so, then this specific example met the general goal of informing. Are audience members ready to send telegrams endorsing the president's education proposal? If so, then the speech succeeded at persuading. Can you and your coworkers empathize with the retiring boss and also share a laugh about the event? If so, then the entertaining speech achieved its goal.

Using purpose to assess the quality of a speech keeps things simple: Good speeches achieve the speaker's purpose; bad speeches do not. Yet few people are comfortable using only that standard. We do not want to regard as good a speech that misleads or manipulates the audience, even if it does achieve the speaker's purpose. And if the speaker's purpose itself is unworthy—such as reinforcing negative cultural or racial stereotypes, for example—we would evaluate the speech harshly even if it does achieve that purpose. Examples like these suggest that achieving one's purpose is not the only standard of quality in assessing a speech. It is a good place to begin, but the audience's reaction is another important factor.

Feedback and Quality

Take a moment to look again at Figure 1.1 (page 8). Recall that communication is mutual interplay between the speaker and the audience. As you speak, listeners provide nonverbal responses, nonverbal responses that help you sense whether you are achieving your purpose and how you might advance it better. One reason to maintain eye contact with the audience is to project that you are confident and trustworthy. But eye contact also gives you valuable feedback. If listeners frown or stare blankly when you make an important point, they may not understand you; you might want to explain that point further. If listeners appear lost, you might want to summarize your main points before moving on. If you've said something that you think is funny but no one laughs or smiles, you might either rephrase the comment or decide to let it pass. And when listeners nod supportively, you should feel more confident and reassured.

After you speak, you are likely to receive more feedback in the form of comments from your instructor and classmates. They can tell you what was most effective about your speech and what could be improved. View such feedback as being constructive. Even if you think that someone missed your point completely, reconsider the organization of your speech and whether you might revise it to avoid "losing" some future listener. It's a good idea to take notes about listeners' comments; in the flush of energy right after you speak, you are unlikely to remember everything.

You probably also will receive unsolicited comments from classmates either after class or elsewhere on campus. If the comments are positive, express your appreciation. But realize that listeners are typically generous toward speakers; the fact that classmates liked your speech does not necessarily mean that you did everything exactly right! Sometimes, too, a classmate may express disagreement with your speech or may want to argue about your conclusions. Listen carefully to the person's point of view, and clarify your point if it was misunderstood. But don't feel that your success as a speaker depends on the approval of every single audience member. A listener whose mind is dead set against your point is not likely to change, no matter what more you might say. Be grateful that the person was honest, take whatever benefit you can from the criticism, but do not feel that you have failed if some audience members disagree with you.

In addition to your audience's reactions, you can get valuable feedback by reviewing a videotape of your speech. At first you may feel uncomfortable watching yourself on tape; you may be oversensitive to details that no one else would notice. But focus on the skills that you were practicing—a clear message and positive *ethos*—to glimpse yourself as the audience saw and heard you. The tape may reveal things about your delivery that you can change before giving your next speech.

Ethics: Respect for Audience, Topic, and Occasion

Even though we sometimes say that "talk is cheap" or that "words can never hurt me," we know better. Speech has tremendous power, and the person who wields it bears great responsibility. Public speakers, in particular, set out to affect others, aiming to change what listeners believe or what they do. Furthermore, the act of addressing an audience may alter the speaker's own beliefs and values in response to listeners' reactions. Given this powerful interaction in public speaking, both speakers and listeners should seek high standards of ethical conduct.

As a listener you owe speakers your care and attention. Recognize and acknowledge the effort that went into preparing the speech, and appreciate that the speaker is disclosing something personal. Assume that the speaker is sincere, and listen intently to his or her message. Above all, listeners have the responsibility to think critically about the speech. Do not reject or refuse to consider the speaker's message simply because it differs from what you already believe. Nor, however, should you blindly accept the message. Assess the speech carefully to decide whether it merits your support. Whatever you decide, do so thoughtfully. Your agreement is especially valuable to a speaker when it reflects critical thought and you give it freely.

As a speaker you should demonstrate high ethical standards in four areas:

- Respect for your listeners
- Respect for your topic
- Responsibility for your statements
- Concern for the consequences of your speech

Respect for Your Listeners

Successful communication usually depends on evoking common bonds between the speaker and listeners. Audience members feel both that the speaker cares about them and that they are not just passive spectators. Rather, they feel that they are actively involved in the speech.

Because a speech is presented to a specific audience in a specific situation, a high-quality speech is sensitive to listeners' perspectives. A speaker who carefully analyzes the audience at hand will select materials and strategies that are appropriate and effective. In particular, the following principles demonstrate a speaker's respect for listeners.

Meet Listeners Where They Are. One sign of respect is your willingness to acknowledge the audience's current position and to make it your point of departure—whether or not you agree with it. For example, in trying to convince opponents of capital punishment to rethink their position, student Mary O'Malley chose not to attack the audience's point of view right away but instead to begin by considering it:

> I understand that you have some reservations about the death penalty because you are worried that an innocent person might mistakenly be executed. This is certainly an important consideration. Death is final, and no one wants to be responsible for such a horrible mistake. Today I want to examine the possibility that a mistake might occur in the criminal justice system and to explore the consequences of such a mistake.

Rather than ignoring her listeners' views, Mary incorporated them into the speech, showing respect by meeting listeners on their own ground.

Public speakers make claims on their listeners' attention and beliefs. Speakers therefore have a responsibility to say something worthwhile, to respect listeners' judgment, and to respect the diversity of viewpoint and cultural background that listeners represent.

Don't Insult Listeners' Intelligence or Judgment. Besides starting her speech by acknowledging listeners' views, Mary also respected their judgment and intelligence by saying that she would examine their position in her speech. Likewise, when you prepare and present a speech, avoid patronizing or "talking down to" the audience. Don't devote the entire speech to repeating what listeners already know or believe, making them wonder why they took the time to hear you. Also avoid suggesting that anyone who does not agree with you is somehow deficient in judgment. Steer clear of phrases that a listener might interpret as a put-down.

Make Sure Your Message Merits the Audience's Time. In general, although listeners could do other things with their time, they choose to attend your speech in the belief that you have something valuable and original to say. Recognize that you are receiving a gift of their time, and prepare a speech that deserves their gift.

Respect Listeners' Ability to Assess Your Message. Because you respect listeners, you want them to understand your message thoroughly and to give their approval freely. Do not mislead listeners about your purpose or conceal what you want them to believe, feel, think, or do. If you are urging them to make a choice among alternatives, do not try to manipulate them by hiding options or by casting any particular option in unduly favorable or unfavorable light. If it is your goal to advocate one option over another, you will best defend your position by explaining how it is superior to the alternatives, not by distorting or ignoring the options that you dislike.

Respect the Cultural Diversity of Your Audience. Not all listeners share your perspective. An audience often includes people with many diverse cultural backgrounds, and these affect their attitudes and experiences. As society becomes even more diverse, all public communicators must expect that some listeners will have assumptions different from their own. The tendency to imagine that one's own views are typical of everyone else's is called *ethnocentrism*. It not only demeans listeners who have different cultural backgrounds but also reduces the likelihood of successful communication.[11]

Ethnocentrism is usually unconscious. When student speaker Mary Winthrop concluded her speech on religion in American life by saying, "So in this country, it clearly doesn't matter where you go to church on Sunday," she thought she was celebrating religious freedom. She didn't realize that she alienated Muslims and Jews in her audience, whose religions focus on other days of the week and who do not call their houses of worship "churches," or that she had offended those who do not practice a religion. Likewise, when Patrick Dungan mentioned that "by eighth grade, everyone begins thinking about where to go to college," he probably didn't realize that in his audience were students who couldn't afford to go to college at all until after several years in the workforce.

Respecting cultural diversity requires being aware of one's own assumptions and resisting the temptation to assume that everyone else will share them. Although we will focus on audience culture in Chapter 3, respect for cultural diversity should influence every aspect of preparing and presenting a speech.

Respect for Your Topic

Presumably, you will be speaking about a topic that matters to you, and you will have something important to say. When you speak, you are putting yourself on the record; your words will outlast the actual speaking situation. You are also asking listeners to accept you as a credible source of ideas about the topic. To justify their confidence in you, and to meet your own high standards, you need to know what you are talking about in enough detail that you can present it clearly and fairly. You must demonstrate that you care enough about the topic to study it thoroughly. Otherwise, why should the audience take your ideas about the topic seriously?

Responsibility for Your Statements

A public speaker makes claims on the audience, and so you must take responsibility for the accuracy and integrity of your statements. This is every bit as important in speaking as it is in writing, and similar guidelines apply.

Particularly in speaking (since listeners cannot see the printed word), you need to distinguish between fact and opinion, being careful not to misrepresent one as the other. Additionally, whether you are presenting fact or opinion, a statement is made in a particular context, and you must represent that correctly; if not, you will mislead or deceive the audience. The film critic who writes, "Nothing could be better than this film if you are looking for a cure for insomnia," does not want to be quoted as saying, "Nothing could be better than this film." Likewise, stating that military spending has declined as a percentage of the gross domestic product over the past five years is not fair to the context unless you tell listeners that the source also said that actual military spending has *increased* by several billion dollars but that the economy grew at an even faster rate.

As in writing, one of the most irresponsible things you can do as a speaker is to present another person's words or ideas as though they were your own. Such **plagiarism** is nothing less than theft. To avoid plagiarism:

1. Never present someone else's unique ideas or words without acknowledging it.
2. Specify who developed the ideas or said the words that you present ("As discovered by Professor Jones," "Socrates said," and so forth).
3. Paraphrase statements in your own words rather than quoting them directly, unless the exact wording of a statement is crucial to your speech.
4. Draw on several sources rather than on a single source.

Remember that it is also a form of plagiarism to present another student's speech as your own or to use the same speech in two different classes. Every speech you present should be your own original work.

Concern for the Consequences of Your Speech

Recognizing that your speech has consequences is another important ethical responsibility. You cannot be indifferent to how your speech may affect others, even though you may not know what all the effects will be. A listener might repeat an amusing anecdote you told, might feel more closely connected to someone whose life you celebrated, might get a psychological lift from your upbeat tone, or might change health insurance based on the reasoning in your speech. You cannot be held legally responsible for such effects, of course, but high ethical standards should lead you at least to think about how your speech might affect listeners.

Moreover, in any rhetorical situation, speakers and listeners together make up a community united by experience, interests, and values. Speech is the glue that holds a community together by making us aware of our common bonds and by giving us a vision to which we might aspire. Ethical public speakers take their membership in this community seriously, and they accept their responsibility to sustain the community by adhering to high ethical standards.[12]

plagiarism
Using another person's words as if they were your own.

Respecting Diversity Through the Preparation of Your Speech

When preparing your speech it is important to consider your audience and the viewpoints held by the audience members. Here are several ideas for showing respect for your audience's perspective.

1. Research all angles of your topic. Be sure to include viewpoints that may be different from your own.
2. Think about your word choices. Do they demonstrate any bias?
3. Show respect for your audience:
   - Acknowledge audience members' current position on your topic.
   - Do not insult audience members' intelligence.
   - Be aware of your own assumptions.

Summary

By studying public speaking, you will learn essential skills of thought and expression: reading, observing, and thinking critically; selecting what to say; using language effectively; presenting yourself skillfully; and responding to others' reactions to you. These skills, which you will study by blending theory and practice, will help you to be more articulate. They will apply to a variety of business and career situations, and they will enable you to participate more effectively as a citizen.

Public speaking is communication, the joint creation of meaning and understanding by speakers and listeners. A speech is given in a specific rhetorical situation, which is determined by the audience, occasion, speaker, and speech. Listeners interpret a message within their own framework of thought and knowledge, and they provide feedback as formal or informal responses to the speaker. The speaker takes listeners into account both in developing the speech and in responding to feedback.

You have two basic goals for your first speech: clarity of purpose and thesis and establishing positive *ethos*. The purpose is your goal for the speech, the response you seek from listeners. The thesis is the main point you want to make, which you should be able to state in one sentence.

Supporting materials—experience, narratives, data, and opinions—will lend weight to your thesis and help establish your claim. After choosing which supporting materials to use, you also must decide how to arrange them to advance your thesis. The basic structure of every speech includes an introduction, a body, and a conclusion—each of which serves distinct functions and raises strategic decisions. Common first speaking assignments are the one-point speech and the speech of introduction, both of which will give you practice in organizing a speech.

Outlining is an aid both in preparing and in presenting a speech. The preparation outline, usually written in complete sentences, details the structure and supporting materials of the speech. The presentation outline reduces this to key words and is used as a guide to cue you while you speak. Working with these two outlines, you can develop a sequence of practice exercises that range from informally talking through the speech to simulating the conditions under which you will deliver the speech.

Nervousness is a natural reaction to speaking in public, but you can turn it to your advantage by acknowledging your fears, reminding yourself of the strengths of your speech, concentrating on the topic and the audience, and carefully practicing your introduction and conclusion. Both during and after your speech, you should seek feedback to improve subsequent presentations.

The overriding test of the quality of a speech is whether or not it achieves its purpose. Both formal and informal feedback will tell you whether your topic meets the requirements of the situation, whether your thesis is meaningful and important to the audience, whether your organization and presentation are effective, and whether the speech involves the audience and builds community. Beyond such practical matters, however, you also want to adhere to high ethical standards that reflect the mutual responsibilities of speaker and listeners and that recognize the significant power of public speaking as an act of communication.

In this chapter, we have introduced many concepts and skills. Each has been covered only briefly, so that you have the basic knowledge you need in order to begin giving speeches. Later chapters will cover each of these topics in more detail.

Welcome to what should be a unique, challenging, stimulating, and personally valuable class.

Discussion Questions

1. What is rhetoric? Why is it important to study rhetoric?
2. Watch a speech on television, and then identify the most important strategic choices made by the speaker. How would the speech be changed if these choices had been made differently?
3. Develop two lists of adjectives, one describing what you consider to be positive judgments about a speaker's *ethos* and the other describing negative judgments. How might a beginning speech be strategically designed to develop positive judgments and avoid negative judgments? In answering this question, consider the following elements of strategy:
   Choice of topic
   Choice of purpose
   Presentation of supporting material
   Structure of the speech
   Delivery
4. The one-point speech is arranged in five steps:

1. Wake up!
2. This concerns you.
3. Generally speaking
4. For example
5. So what?

    Why is this a good model for developing a short speech? Discuss the strategic purpose of each step and how it contributes to the goals of imparting a clear message and building positive *ethos*.

5. Someone who is having trouble hearing a speaker usually leans forward to get closer to the sound. This is a cue to the speaker to increase the volume. What are some other common feedback cues that an audience might present? Discuss how a speaker might use each cue to modify either the message or the presentation.

6. View a speech with your classmates, and then, as a group, evaluate the quality of that speech. Take into account its purpose; the degree to which the topic meets the requirements of the situation; sensitivity to cultural diversity; the meaningfulness and importance of the thesis; organization, support, and presentation; the way in which the speech builds community with the audience; and its ethical implications.

    Which of these characteristics are most helpful and most important to you in distinguishing a good speech from a bad one? Is this the same for all speeches, or do different speeches call for different evaluative emphases?

7. What are the most important ethical considerations for a speaker and for a listener in your class? Using the guidelines in this chapter, work with your classmates to establish a code of ethics that individuals will abide by when they are speakers and when they are audience members.

Activities

1. For each of the following topics, devise a thesis statement that would be appropriate for a short speech.
   Affirmative action
   Date rape
   Job training
   Computers
   Summer vacation
2. Lay out three different types of supporting material for the thesis "Parking is a serious problem at most universities."
3. Following the recommendations in this chapter, develop both a preparation outline and a presentation outline for a speech of introduction, and practice the delivery of that speech.
4. Present the speech in activity 3 to a few friends or family members. Pay close attention to their feedback, both during the speech and when you discuss it with them later. Then strategically modify your speech

to accommodate their concerns and suggestions. In one page, explain how the changes you made to your speech responded to the feedback you received.

5. Watch a speech, and then write a paper that evaluates its quality.
6. Examine your reasons for taking this public speaking course. What goals do you want to achieve? Based on your reading of this chapter, do you think this course will help you achieve your goals? Why or why not?

Notes

1. These skills will help you succeed in college. See Rebecca B. Rubin and Elizabeth E. Graham, "Communication Correlates of College Success: An Exploratory Investigation," *Communication Education* 37 (January 1988): 14–27.
2. For example, business employers have named oral communication skills as the number one priority for college graduates seeking employment and the number two priority for successful performance once they have a job. Dan B. Curtis, Jerry L. Winsor, and Ronald D. Stephens, "National Preferences in Business and Communication Education," *Communication Education* 38 (January 1989): 6–14.
3. For a discussion of this difference between literature and oratory, see Herbert A. Wichelns, "The Literary Criticism of Oratory," first published in 1925, reprinted in *Methods of Rhetorical Criticism: A Twentieth Century Perspective*, ed. Robert L. Scott and Bernard L. Brock, New York: Harper & Row, 1972.
4. See Lloyd Bitzer, "The Rhetorical Situation," *Philosophy and Rhetoric* 1 (Winter 1968): 1–14.
5. *Ethos* is discussed extensively in Aristotle, *The Rhetoric*, translated by W. Rhys Roberts, New York: The Modern Library, 1954. See especially Book II. It has been suggested that, in forming judgments about public figures, *empathy* plays a greater role than the more traditional components of *ethos*. Audiences give more weight to speakers who appear to think and feel as they do. See Brooks Aylor, "Source Credibility and Presidential Candidates in 1996: The Changing Nature of Character and Empathy Evaluators," *Communication Research Reports* 16 (Summer 1999): 296–304.
6. A taste of how oratory was different in earlier U.S. history can be had by reading Garry Wills's description of Edward Everett's address at Gettysburg in *Lincoln at Gettysburg: The Words That Remade America*, New York: Simon & Schuster, 1992, pp. 21–22, 33–34.
7. For a summary of research done in this area, see Daniel Goleman, "Social Anxiety: New Focus Leads to Insights and Therapy," *New York Times* (Dec. 18, 1984): C1.
8. For a fuller description of the physical aspect of anxiety, see the table of physiological variables associated with anxiety in Raymond B. Cattell, "Anxiety and Motivation: Theory and Critical Experiments," *Anxiety and Behavior*, ed. Charles Spielberger, New York: Academic Press, 1966, p. 33.
9. For more about the study of speaker anxiety, see Joe Ayres, "Coping with Speech Anxiety: The Power of Positive Thinking," *Communication Education* 30 (October 1988): 289–296; and Michael Beatty, "Public Speaking Apprehension, Decision-Making Errors in the Selection of Speech Introduction Strategies and Adherence to Strategy," *Communication Education* 30 (October 1988): 297–311.
10. Some colleges have programs to treat severe communication apprehension. See Jan Hoffmann and Jo Sprague, "A Survey of Reticence and Communication Apprehension Treatment Programs at U.S. Colleges and Universities," *Communication Education* 31 (July 1982): 185–194. There is extensive literature about different ways to overcome speech anxiety. For a recent example, see Joe Ayres, Tim Hopf, and Elizabeth Peterson, "A Test of Communication-Orientation Motivation (COM) Therapy," *Communication Reports* 13 (Winter 2000): 35–44.
11. One way to begin breaking down your ethnocentric views is to examine communication across cultures. See Robert Paine, ed., *Politically Speaking: Cross-Cultural Studies of Rhetoric*, Philadelphia: Institute for the Study of Human Issues, 1981.

12. For more on ethical considerations in the public speaking class, see Karl R. Wallace, "An Ethical Basis of Communication," *Communication Education* 4 (January 1955): 1–9. See also James A. Jaksa and Michael S. Pritchard, *Communication Ethics: Methods of Analysis,* Belmont, Calif.: Wadsworth, 1988; and Karen Joy Greenberg, ed., *Conversations on Communication Ethics,* Norwood, N.J.: Ablex, 1991.

Listening Critically

It's a standard scene in comic strips and television sitcoms: The husband sits at the breakfast table, face buried in the newspaper, seeming not to notice his wife seated across from him. The wife is trying to conduct a conversation about the day's events or about chores to be done around the house. Whenever she pauses, he mutters, "Mm-hmm"—never lowering the newspaper even to look at her. In desperation she finally grabs the paper and shouts, "You're not listening to me!" The husband calmly replies, "That's not true, dear. I heard every word you said."

Are You Really Listening?

The husband and wife are both right, because hearing and listening are two different things. **Hearing** is a sensory process. Nerve endings in the ear receive sound waves and transmit them to the brain; the brain receives them, and we become conscious of sound. This is a physiological process.

In contrast, **listening** is a mental operation. It involves processing the sound waves, interpreting their meaning, and storing the interpretation in memory so that we can recall it, think about it, or act on it. The husband did hear every word, but he wasn't *listening*. His attention was focused entirely on the newspaper, and so he didn't interpret and store the information he heard. Now he can't repeat it, and he can't answer questions or make decisions about it.

Hearing comes naturally to most people and requires no special training. But listening is an acquired skill that takes practice. Even though people's ability to hear may be equally strong, some people are better listeners because they have trained themselves to:

- Focus attention.
- Minimize distractions.
- Process messages accurately.
- Think **critically.**[1]

In this chapter, you will learn how to develop and improve these skills. First, though, we need to explore two questions: (1) Why should we concentrate on listening in our study of public speaking? (2) What makes listening so difficult that we need training to do it well?

Why Listening Is Important

Checking for Accuracy. To begin with, we usually want to check the *accuracy* of what we heard, because the consequences of faulty listening can be far more serious than in the scene at the breakfast table. Students who don't listen to and correctly follow the professor's instructions could do the assignment but still get a failing grade. Employees who misunderstand the supervisor's instructions could jeopardize company profits—and their own jobs. Parents who don't really listen to a child's request for help could respond inappropriately, or not at all. And diplomats who don't listen carefully to each other could overlook an opportunity for a breakthrough in negotiations.

To avoid the consequences of faulty listening, we often check that we have heard and understood correctly. Students and employees ask questions about instructions; parents try to find out what their child means; and

hearing
A sensory process in which sound waves are transmitted to the brain and someone becomes conscious of sound.

listening
A mental operation involving processing sound waves, interpreting their meaning, and storing their meaning in memory.

diplomats "feel out" each other's statements before making a formal response.

Giving (and Getting) Feedback. Beyond checking the accuracy of communication, careful listening enables hearers to provide **feedback** to speakers. We saw in Chapter 1 that even in formal situations the speaker and the audience both send and receive messages. The audience members' reactions are usually nonverbal—applause, head nodding, bored or distracted looks, and indications that they are having trouble following the speaker's argument. Such feedback enables speakers to modify their message and improve the likelihood of achieving their purpose. During the speech, careful listening makes feedback possible; after the speech, it helps listeners to remember and think about the speaker's ideas.

You will spend far more time in this course listening to speeches than delivering them. By becoming a trained listener, you will provide appropriate feedback to other speakers. In addition, listening and responding to classmates' speeches will suggest ways to improve your own speaking. Your reactions to a speaker whose voice is too quiet, or who ends too abruptly, or who seems to lack confidence will make you more determined to avoid such problems. You'll also pick up tips from classmates who perform well. As you listen attentively, you will consider more and more factors that relate to your upcoming role as a speaker. You will develop ideas about what to do—or not to do—to make your own speeches successful. In short, your reactions to classroom speeches will provide feedback to yourself.

Evaluating Messages. Ensuring that you heard a message accurately and allowing you to provide feedback to the speaker and to yourself are two reasons why listening is so important. A third benefit is that you need to listen in order to *evaluate* what you hear. Unless you listen carefully, you seldom can know how to respond to or evaluate the message.

You have a vested interest in paying close attention to a classmate's message so that you can decide how it relates to you and to others in a broader audience. You need to be able to assess how the speaker's position and technique compare with yours and whether they are models to follow when it is your turn to speak. Of course, when you listen to speeches given outside the classroom—whether by politicians, celebrities, people in business, or religious leaders—it is even more important that you be able to evaluate the message. In addition to your own assessment, you also should ask, "How will others whom I care about respond to this message?" Speeches often reach an audience beyond those who are present, and so you should consider how people who "tune in later" might react.

Finally—and unfortunately—not all speakers who seek our attention are scrupulous and ethical. Some urge listeners to do things that are unjustified or unacceptable. Be aware that their influence depends precisely on the fact that it is easy for people to hear without really listening. You need to know when a speaker is being unethical rather than just sloppy, insensitive, or misinformed. To protect yourself as a listener, you need to practice skills that will help you evaluate speakers and messages. Essentially, these are the skills of critical thinking, and you will learn to apply them to the speech situation later in this chapter.

WWW. Using the Internet

Listen to Speeches in RealAudio or RealVideo Format

Explore some of the speeches in the Archive of speeches in the **Allyn & Bacon Public Speaking Web Site.** Go to **http://www.abacon.com/pubspeak/histsit.html**.

feedback
Verbal and nonverbal audience response to a speech; usually taken seriously by a speaker and incorporated into the speech when possible.

Why Listening Is Difficult

So much, then, for the question of why speakers need to cultivate listening skills: Careful listening will help you both as an audience member and as a speaker. But what makes listening so difficult that we need training in it? Why are so many people poor listeners? At least four factors deserve close attention:

- Listener distractions
- Limited attention span
- Jumping to conclusions
- Situational distractions

Listener Distractions. We can think faster than we can listen. Because the processing of sound waves does not fully engage the brain, we can do something else at the same time we listen. Unfortunately, that "something else" may distract us from listening effectively.

Imagine a listener who is daydreaming during a speech, constructing a mental fantasy while listening. The fantasy may be more exciting and more personally relevant than the speaker's message. Gradually, without meaning to, this audience member will devote all energy to the daydream—still hearing, but not listening to, the speech. In fact, the distracting daydream may be stimulated by words in the speech. The word *video*, for example, might trigger the thought, "I wonder what video I should rent for the party tonight," which in turn might lead to "I hope my roommate remembers to pick up the pizzas," and then to a mental checklist of preparations for the party. All these thoughts might lead to "I hope Ali Rickey is going to be there." Clearly, this is not careful listening.

Worse yet, the listener might be distracted several times during the speech before snapping to attention and thinking, "Oops! I'd better listen more closely to this speech." After tuning in again for a few minutes, the listener might then be distracted by some other word or phrase. The idea of "channel surfing"—of mindlessly switching among television programs without paying much attention to any of them—aptly describes how some listeners tune a speech in and out, seemingly at random. Although a speaker can't be held responsible for listeners' habits, a well-prepared, well-delivered speech is the best defense against listener distractions.

Limited Attention Span. Another factor that makes listening difficult is that most people's **attention span**—the length of time they will attend to a message without distraction—is short. In the past, audiences were prepared for (and expected) lengthy speeches, sermons, lectures, and debates. During the eighteenth and early nineteenth centuries, political orations went on for hours, sometimes days. But today's public messages are much shorter. Until the creation of half-hour "infomercials" during the 1992 presidential campaign, the trend had been for shorter and shorter political messages. The same could be said of sermons, lectures, business presentations, and other forms of public **speaking.**[2]

The trend may have reversed somewhat in recent years. Although advertisements remain short, some speeches have become longer. The acceptance addresses at the 2000 Republican and Democratic conventions were almost an hour long, and President George W. Bush, while not matching his predecessor's record, has delivered State of the Union addresses that are nearly that long as well.

attention span
The length of time a person will attend to a message without feeling distracted.

Shorter messages are generally less complex and make fewer demands on listeners' powers of concentration. The speak-er simply doesn't have time to try out many ideas, to develop them fully, and to suggest all their implications. Messages have to fit the short time available. This trend is especially clear in political advertisements, which shrank from about five minutes in the mid-1960s to only a few seconds in the late 1980s. Such short messages can present little except slogans or sound bites. And frequent exposure to short messages—whether advertising jingles or political slogans—weakens listeners' capacity to process and evaluate longer, more intricate messages.

The trend to make messages "short and sim-

Much of today's public communication is delivered in brief "sound bites" to which people only partially pay attention while engaged in other activities. As a result, many people have not practiced the skill of listening to a sustained statement or description, even when it concerns them directly.

ple" has been accelerated by television.[3] Viewers are accustomed to changing channels frequently and may find it hard, even for entertainment, to pay attention for long. Also, the cost of advertising time (or ad space, in print media) has led to shorter, simpler messages. And, of course, television is visually stimulating. As a result, many audience members today have only limited abilities to listen carefully to a speech—which may seem long, will not be primarily visual, and may not be **entertaining.**

Jumping to Conclusions. People sometimes assume that they "know" what the speaker is going to say, but jumping to conclusions is no basis for effective listening. Early in the semester, student speaker Smita Shah gave an impromptu speech about why society should enforce capital punishment. Later in the semester, she again chose capital punishment as the topic for a different speech. But after doing her research, she changed her opinion and decided that capital punishment should be abolished. Nonetheless, when she rose to speak, some audience members were so sure that she would again favor capital punishment that they misinterpreted everything she said. Here are some of the questions they asked after she spoke:

"How can you support state-sanctioned murder?"
"What about innocent people who might be executed by mistake?"
"Doesn't it cost more to execute someone than to keep him in prison for life?"

Listening Critically

The Situation

You and a small group of classmates are working together to practice your speeches for an upcoming presentation. Won has asked you to listen to a practice run of her speech on fast food consumption in the United States and its detrimental effect on young children. You feel that Won's speech is well organized, but you don't understand why she picked this topic and you are having problems understanding its relevance. Halfway through her speech, you find yourself thinking about your plans for the evening—your dinner date, finishing your project, doing laundry, and preparing for class the next day.

Making Choices

1. What strategies could you use to help you listen more carefully to Won's speech?

2. What questions could you ask to help you better understand Won's topic and its relevance?

3. How can you use your critical thinking skills to provide useful feedback to Won? What recommendations might you have for her?

What If . . .

How would your listening strategies change if the following were true?

1. You are the manager of a fast food restaurant.

2. You are critiquing Won's speech for a graded assignment.

"Isn't it true that a disproportionately large number of those executed are black?"

These audience members thought they were asking hostile questions, but they had jumped to conclusions and showed instead that they hadn't listened carefully.

Most untrained listeners sometimes make such assumptions and misinterpretations. People who attend a speech as committed supporters of the speaker's cause already "know" that they will agree with the message and hence do not listen to it carefully. They often find themselves endorsing a position that they don't really support. Other listeners who strongly oppose a speaker's cause almost instinctively reject every part of the message.

In recent years, growing distrust of authority figures has led many listeners to reject cynically whatever a person in authority might say. In both cases—instant acceptance and instant rejection—listeners jump to conclusions through **assimilation;** they blur the distinction between two similar messages and regard them as identical. If the speaker says something that in any way seems to confirm their position, they interpret that as the thesis of the speech. They also *disregard* any parts of the message that challenge their assumptions. They simply ignore those ideas. In both cases, hasty conclusions keep them from truly **listening.**[4]

assimilation
The tendency to regard two similar messages as basically identical, blurring the distinction between them.

Situational Distractions. Distractions in the specific speaking situation can also make listening difficult. Perhaps the wind blows the door shut while you are speaking, and listeners turn to look when they hear it slam. Or an audience member may arrive late, or some lights may go out, or loud laughter may erupt in the hallway. None of these events can be controlled, yet all can interfere with effective listening. The first thing a speaker can do in such cases is to try to offset the distraction by repeating or rephrasing the part of the speech that had to compete with it.

Each of these obstacles to effective listening can lead to a bad listening habit, which careful listeners can overcome through concentration. Figure 2.1 summarizes the obstacles, bad habits, and remedies for both listeners and speakers.

- Because *thinking is faster than listening,* your mind may wander and you may not pay attention. Some remedies are to concentrate harder on the speech and to take notes. As a speaker, you can offset this tendency by keeping the speech focused; rivet the audience's attention to each main idea by showing how it relates to your thesis.
- Because *your attention span is limited,* you may not be able to follow a long, complex speech. Besides concentrating and taking notes, you can stretch your attention span gradually by listening to longer speeches. As a speaker, work to combat this obstacle by dividing the speech into small segments that you can develop quickly and memorably; again, tie each segment to your thesis.
- Because *you jump to conclusions,* you may miss the speaker's precise point. You may think that statements you like are closer to your position than they actually are; and if you disagree with statements, you may magnify the differences between your views and the speaker's. The remedy is to set aside your prejudices and concentrate on the speaker's point of view. As a speaker, you can best overcome this obstacle through careful audience analysis, which is described in Chapter 3. Basically, if

Obstacles	Listener's bad habit	Remedy	
		Listener	**Speaker**
Thinking is faster than listening.	Listener's mind may wander.	Concentrate on the speech; take notes.	Keep the speech focused; tie each point to main thesis.
Listener's attention span is short.	Not hearing speeches that are long or complex.	Practice gradually to hear longer speeches.	Divide speeches into small, compact segments.
Listener jumps to conclusions.	Missing speaker's point; judging by listener viewpoint only.	Try to set prejudices aside.	Careful audience analysis; extra effort on clarity.
Situations contain distractions.	Following the distraction rather than the speech.	Concentrate on the speech and on self-discipline.	Stay flexible; adapt to situation.

Figure 2.1 Overcoming four obstacles to good listening.

you analyze where listeners' preconceptions are likely to lead them, you can figure out exactly which points must be made especially clear.

- Because *elements in the situation distract you,* you don't listen carefully to what the speaker is saying. Again, try harder to concentrate; take notes, and exercise self-discipline. As a speaker, you can counteract distractions by remaining flexible, by adapting to the situation rather than being tied to your text. If you respond to a distraction quickly enough, you may even be able to turn it to your advantage.

As a speaker, the best defense against *all* obstacles to effective listening is precisely your awareness that listening is difficult. Knowing this, you can compensate for listeners' bad habits by finding clear and interesting supporting material, by repeating points appropriately, and by varying your delivery to fit the circumstances. Speakers must make a whole range of strategic choices about how to design and present a message, and we will examine those choices throughout this book.

As an audience member, understanding the difficulties of listening should strengthen your resolve to concentrate and to listen carefully and critically. Try to identify any bad habits in how you listen, and strive actively to correct them. In order to evaluate others' messages effectively and thus improve your own messages, become more sensitive to the obstacles of listening. By listening to others carefully and critically—discussed next— you'll gain information about audience beliefs and values that can help you make effective strategic choices as a speaker.

Strategies for Careful Listening

Some people try to overcome the difficulties of listening by going to the other extreme. They set the goal of focusing on *each and every word* the speaker utters. This approach rarely works, however, because the attempt to take in everything makes it less likely that you will think about, interpret, and assess what you are hearing. Similarly, students who try to take notes about every word in a professor's lecture often cannot explain what the lecture was about. They are so busy writing that they have little energy or time for thinking. It's a classic case of seeing the trees but missing the forest. Listening without thinking is just as flawed as hearing without listening.

Even careless listeners are quick to recognize the superficial strengths and weaknesses of a speech, such as whether the speaker tells an interesting story, mispronounces words, races through a quotation, or talks too loudly. Although these are important aspects of a speech, untrained listeners often fail to *think about* the ideas presented and whether or not those ideas support the thesis. They may be hearing the speech; they may even be listening to it; but they are not listening carefully.

Careful listeners, then, avoid both of these extremes. They do not try to remember every word, and they do not attend only to superficial aspects of a speech. They focus instead on the thesis and the main ideas that support it. Two techniques that can help you do this—and thus become a more careful listener—are *mapping* and *note taking.*

Mapping

Careful listening is encouraged by the technique of **mapping,** in which the listener draws a diagram showing the relationship between the thesis of the speech and the main ideas that support it. This involves four basic steps:

1. Extracting the thesis
2. Identifying the main ideas
3. Assessing the main ideas
4. Deciding whether the main ideas support the thesis

Extract the Thesis of the Speech. Careful listeners should be able to identify not only the general topic of a speech but also its thesis, whether stated explicitly or not. You should be able to say not only that the speech was about privacy protections on the Internet, but also that the speaker claimed that the current level of online privacy protection is inadequate. If the speaker states that thesis explicitly in the introduction, you can follow along and see how the claim is developed and supported in the body of the speech. But if the thesis is only implied by supporting material or is stated only in the conclusion of the speech, you have to listen carefully to extract the thesis and map its relationship to the main ideas.

Remember that your task in mapping a speech is not to reconstruct it word for word but to identify its main ideas and the appeals the speaker used. The thesis almost always can be expressed in one or two sentences; from this central point, the proofs and other supporting materials radiate.

Identify the Main Ideas that Develop the Thesis. Suppose, for example, that the thesis of the speech about online privacy was "The current level of online privacy protection is inadequate." To support the thesis, the speaker offered three claims as main ideas:

A. Millions of people use the Internet.
B. Online dot.com companies have little incentive to regulate Internet commerce.
C. Consumers are left without protection of their personal information.

In this case, claims A, B, and C each represent a separate idea to support the thesis, and so a map of this speech would show each main idea as being connected to the thesis. Figure 2.2 shows two examples of how you might map this **speech.**

But suppose that the relationship among the main ideas was more complex, as in the following example:

A. Internet commerce is a new industry.
B. New industries are notoriously complex and therefore difficult to regulate.
C. Absent regulation, each of the popular Web sites announces its own online privacy policies.
D. Many of these policies are contained in lengthy and tedious notices.
E. Cumbersome privacy protections will be ignored by consumers attracted to the efficiency of electronic commerce.

mapping
Diagraming the relationship between the thesis of a speech and its main ideas.

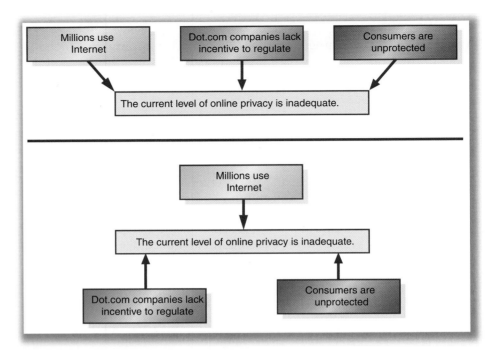

Figure 2.2 Mapping claims that separately support the thesis.

Using the Internet

Search for Audio Files and Use Mapping Skills

For this exercise, we will browse the **History and Politics Outloud** Web page, which is a digital archive of texts and audio recordings of famous speeches. Point your browser to **http://www.hpol.org/** and scroll down the page to select the option to browse the list of speakers. Choose one of the speakers on the page. Next, select a speech from the entries for that speaker. As an alternative, select a speech from the **Gifts of Speech** Web page. Point your browser to **http://gos.sbc.edu/** and browse by speaker or by year to select a speech. Map the message you've found by:

- Extracting the thesis.
- Identifying the main ideas.
- Assessing the main ideas.
- Deciding whether the main ideas support the thesis.

In this example, each claim follows from the one before it; only together—and not individually—do the main ideas support the thesis. As shown in Figure 2.3, a map of this speech would represent the relationship among the main **ideas.**

The structure of ideas in a speech map may or may not correspond to the actual structure of the speech. Again, the goal for careful listeners is not to recall exactly what was said but rather to be able to *reconstruct* the thesis and main ideas and to explain how they fit together.

Assess the Adequacy of the Main Ideas. This is an evaluation step in which you judge whether the main ideas have been advanced solidly. For example, the thesis of a speech about techniques of self-defense might be "With knowledge of simple techniques, you can defend yourself if attacked." The main ideas that you diagram on your map are the following:

A. A victim can shout for help and run.
B. A victim can use mace to stop the attacker.
C. A victim can disable the attacker.
D. A person should walk only in safe neighborhoods.

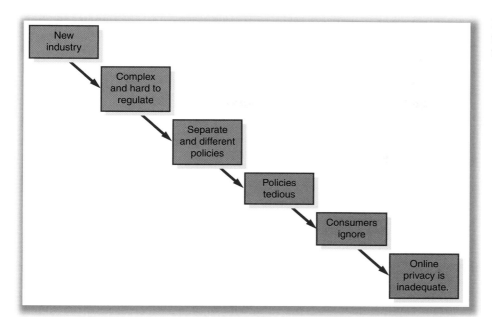

Figure 2.3 Mapping claims that only together support the thesis.

In evaluating the development of these points, you might decide that the claim about mace was not explored thoroughly. After all, you've heard that attackers sometimes grab the mace and use it against the victim. Or, in the speech about online privacy, you might conclude that the speaker failed to prove that dot.com companies lacked incentives to regulate Internet commerce.

Decide Whether the Main Ideas Truly Support the Thesis. This second evaluation step moves beyond judging the main ideas in their own right to judging whether they really link to the thesis. Even if the ideas are true, they may not support the thesis. This was not a problem in the examples about mace and regulating the Internet; the ideas were in doubt, but their links were not. *If* mace were effective or *if* commercial Web sites relied on diverse and complex notifications of privacy protections, then those ideas would provide support for their theses.

Now reconsider the speech about self-defense. The point about walking only in safe neighborhoods may be sensible, but it does not connect well to the thesis. It describes a preventive measure, not a technique for self-defense when you are attacked. So you would conclude that the link between this main idea and the thesis is weak. Or, in the speech on protecting online privacy, suppose that the speaker convinced you that millions of people use the Internet but did not prove that this makes online privacy a significant problem. After all, many people who use the Internet do not buy things online and many who do buy are not worried about their privacy. The main idea itself is not in question, but the link between that idea and the thesis is not established.

Mapping a speech enables you to listen carefully, because you have a clear purpose: to discover and evaluate the underlying structure of the speech in terms of its thesis and main supporting ideas. One handy short-cut in mapping a speech is to use plus and minus signs to record your appraisal both of the ideas and of their links. For example, a plus sign next to a claim indicates that you think the claim was established, whereas a minus sign next to a link indicates that you believe the link was not supported. Obviously, every speaker wants the audience to make positive evaluations of *both* the claims and the links.

Note Taking

You may not be able to complete the speech map while the speech is being delivered. Even if the main ideas were previewed in the introduction, you may not fully grasp them or see how they link to the thesis until the speaker has finished. And you probably will not be able to evaluate them until you have had some time to think about them. Sometimes your preliminary understanding of the thesis may turn out to be wrong, and mapping during the speech may lead you to jump to (wrong) conclusions. But if you wait until after the speech to make the map, can you confidently remember the thesis and main ideas? Most listeners cannot; they need notes to remind them.

Note taking is not a substitute for thinking about the speech during its presentation. Instead, disciplined note taking is an essential tool for careful listening. The goals are to record as much *significant* information as possible and to do so as *efficiently* as possible. The following suggestions will help you:

1. *Focus on the thesis and main ideas.* As the speech gets underway, try to identify these critical elements, and take notes that will help you recall their relationship. Avoid being sidetracked by examples and less important points.

2. *Use key words rather than sentences.* You need not record every word to remember the speech, and attempting that is inefficient and distracting. In particular, prepositions, articles *(a, an, the),* and even verbs often can be omitted without losing the sense of the idea being communicated.

3. *Organize the notes as a rough outline.* You don't need a formal outline of the speech; the crucial thing is to identify major headings and subheadings (claims and supporting ideas). If you leave plenty of space in the left-hand margin and between items in your notes, you can insert headings, subheadings, and related points wherever they belong—whenever the speaker presents them.

4. *Abbreviate and use symbols whenever possible.* By establishing some consistent, memorable abbreviations and symbols, you can take notes quickly without missing anything the speaker says. For example, some common abbreviations and symbols are w/ for *with,* w/o for *without,* = for *is,* ~ for *is not,* < for *less than,* > for *more than,* and arrows pointing either up for *increasing* or down for *decreasing.* Develop your own system of abbreviations and symbols for frequently used words and terms.

5. *Also make notes to help you evaluate the speech.* Because careful listening and evaluation are ongoing responsibilities, another level of note taking is to jot down comments that will help you prepare a critical assessment of the speech. If you think that the thesis was supported well,

write "good support"; if the structure of the speech confused you, jot down "disorganized." Put such evaluative comments in the margin, or write them in a different color, so that they don't interfere with your notes about what the speaker said. You can think of this as "making notes" to distinguish it from "taking notes."

The test of progress toward becoming a careful listener is whether, when a speech is over, you can reconstruct its basic form; not whether you have memorized the speech or can repeat it word for word, but whether you can identify the thesis and explain how it was developed.

Listening Critically

The title of this chapter is "Listening Critically," which moves far beyond listening carefully. **Critical listening** results not only in an accurate rendering of the speech, but also in a personal interpretation and assessment of it. Thus the evaluation steps of mapping and note taking are developed more thoroughly. Basically, critical listening enables you to apply critical thinking to a speech.

Critical Thinking

You know from Chapter 1 that **critical thinking** is the ability to form and defend your own judgments rather than blindly accepting or instantly rejecting what you hear or read. *Critical* does not mean "negative," "hostile," or "adversarial"; but it does mean "reflective." It is a conscious, systematic method of evaluating ideas wherever you encounter them—not only in speeches but also in conversation, in print, on television, in films and plays, and so on. By reflecting on the ideas you hear or read, you can form judgments about which are strong and which are weak.

The Characteristics of Critical Thinkers. At least six characteristics are demonstrated by critical thinkers:

1. *Critical thinkers are reluctant to accept assertions on faith.* Unsupported assertions carry little weight with critical thinkers, who are skeptical and always imagine themselves asking, "What have you got to go on?"

2. *Critical thinkers distinguish facts from opinions.* In Chapter 1, we introduced this distinction. **Facts,** at least in theory, can be independently verified by others. They are either true or false, and their truth is not subject to interpretation. The number of people who don't have health insurance is a fact, as is the historical claim that "In fourteen hundred and ninety-two, Columbus sailed the ocean blue."

Opinions are judgments that are *not* clearly true or false and so cannot be independently verified. For example, a person might hold the opinion that Paris is more beautiful than London or that the United States is the best country in which to live. Opinions may be highly individualistic, or they may be widely shared. Just because an opinion is widely shared, however, does not make it a fact—although it is not easily disregarded. Even so, remember that opinions *can* be changed. Often, the strength of an opinion depends on the *ethos* of the person who holds it (or who dismisses it).

critical listening
Listening that enables you to offer both an accurate rendering of the speech and an interpretation and assessment of it.

critical thinking
The ability to form and defend your own judgments rather than blindly accepting or instantly rejecting what you hear or read.

facts
Statements that can be independently verified by others; they are either true or false.

opinions
Judgments that cannot be independently verified and that are not clearly true or false.

Successful listeners bring their critical thinking skills to the speech-making arena. As they are listening, they also question, challenge, form opinions, and strive to put their ideas into the broader context.

Facts are not necessarily better than opinions, and both are well suited for particular kinds of statements. But you should understand the difference between them. Critical thinkers listen carefully to be sure that a speaker does not mistake an opinion for a fact or a fact for an opinion.

3. *Critical thinkers seek to uncover assumptions.* **Assumptions** are unstated, taken-for-granted beliefs in a particular situation. For example, underlying the argument that the tax cut of 2003 will threaten Social Security are the assumptions that the deficit will be financed by borrowing from the Social Security trust fund and that the fund is not large enough to withstand this loss. Often, speakers and listeners assume that they share some crucial value—an assumption that is seldom noted until it is questioned. Critical thinkers not only uncover assumptions in what other people say, but also identify and test their own assumptions.

4. *Critical thinkers are open to new ideas.* Although critical thinkers do not hold their opinions and beliefs lightly, they are willing to consider challenges to what they believe and are open to the possibility that they may have to change their minds.

5. *Critical thinkers apply reason and common sense to new ideas.* Critical thinkers ask whether a new idea makes sense, whether it seems internally consistent, and whether they can see and understand the links made by the speaker or writer in developing the idea. If reason and common sense tell them that everything is in order, they give the idea a good hearing—whether or not they expect to agree with it. But if reason and common sense tell them the idea is wrong, they are likely to reject it, even though it might support a conclusion with which they agree.

6. *Critical thinkers relate new ideas to what they already know.* They ask, "Is the new idea consistent with what I already think or know to be true?" If not, they ask how their existing attitudes and beliefs need to be modified

assumptions
Unstated, taken-for-granted beliefs in a particular situation.

and whether such modifications are justified. These steps enable them to put the idea into a broader context and to incorporate it into their constantly developing system of beliefs and attitudes.

What these six characteristics of critical thinking have in common is their emphasis on **reflective** judgment—neither blind acceptance nor automatic rejection of an idea, but a considered and thoughtful opinion about whether the idea and its support merit acceptance.

The Skills of Critical Thinking. From these six characteristics of critical thinkers we can extract four basic skills that underlie critical thinking:

1. *Questioning and challenging,* both your own ideas and the ideas of others, so that you will neither accept nor dismiss an idea without thoughtful reflection. When a speaker puts forward an assertion or a claim, you will ask yourself, "What does that speaker have to go on? Should I believe what he or she says?"

2. *Recognizing differences*—between ideas, between facts and opinions, between explicit claims and unstated assumptions, and between easily explained events and anomalies or puzzles. When hearing a speech about justifications for the 2003 Iraqi war, for example, you will be alert to the difference between reasons used to justify the war in advance and those offered as justification after the fact.

3. *Forming opinions and supporting claims* so that you can state and evaluate ideas. You can get beyond your vague uneasiness about the plan for Medicare coverage of prescription drugs and state that the plan will increase costs to the government without adequately meeting the health needs of senior citizens.

4. *Putting ideas into a broader context* by seeing how they relate to what you already know and by understanding what they imply about other things you might assert or believe.[5] After listening to a speech opposing affirmative action, you realize that the speaker has not responded to most of the justifications of affirmative action that you had encountered in your **reading.**

Checklist 2.1 Critical Thinking

1. **Characteristics of Critical Thinkers**
   - Reluctant to accept assertions on faith
   - Distinguish facts from opinions
   - Seek to uncover assumptions
   - Open to new ideas
   - Apply reason and common sense to new ideas
   - Relate new ideas to what they already know
2. **Critical Thinking Skills**
   - Questioning and challenging
   - Recognizing differences
   - Forming opinions and supporting claims
   - Putting ideas into a broader context

reflective
Considered, thoughtful (as opposed to automatic).

Applying Critical Thinking to the Speech Situation

Earlier, we noted that listeners form judgments about the strength of a speaker's ideas and about their links to the thesis. Now we will consider *how* listeners form such judgments.

Some judgments are made uncritically. A statement "sounds right," so you decide it must be true; or it is at odds with your beliefs, and you conclude immediately that it is false. If a speaker *seems* personable and sincere, you might accept the claims without investigation; but if the speaker's delivery is unappealing, you might reject the content out of hand. Each of these is an *uncritical* judgment, one made without reason or reflection.

In contrast, **critical judgments** are those that you can articulate and defend by providing reasons for them. This does not mean that you are hostile or negative toward the speech. In fact, critical listening begins with the assumption that the speaker knows what he or she is talking about; but this assumption is balanced with skepticism, which is a reluctance to be pushed prematurely into conclusions.

Critical listening begins with mapping and is aided by note taking, but it adds the step of *reflection* before judgment. Reflective listeners think consciously about the speech and ask themselves questions about it.

Another way to say this is that critical listeners *elaborate* the message. Their minds are engaged, and they think actively about the speaker's ideas and how they might be answered. They carry on a kind of internal dialogue with the speaker about the speech. This tendency makes them skeptical, but in a healthy way. They are willing to accept a speaker's ideas, but only if those ideas satisfy the appropriate tests. We will discuss the *elaboration likelihood model* more fully in Chapter 14.

Here are some examples of questions that critical listeners might pose to test a speaker's ideas.

- Are the main ideas identifiable?
- Are the links among the ideas reasonable?
- Are the ideas supported where necessary?
- How does accepting or rejecting the thesis affect my other beliefs?

Are the Main Ideas Identifiable? As emphasized earlier, it is important to know not just the general topic of the speech, but also its specific thesis and the main ideas that support it. Critical listeners are especially concerned that the thesis be clear and precise.

Suppose you were listening to a speech about multiculturalism in U.S. education. You might recognize quickly whether or not the speaker thinks multiculturalism is good. But as a critical listener, you would ask yourself additional questions, such as:

- What does the speaker mean by *multiculturalism?*
- Does she mean the same thing each time she uses the term?
- Do others whom she quotes about multiculturalism mean the same thing that she does?
- Is she saying that multiculturalism is good in principle, as it is applied, or both?
- Is she saying that multiculturalism is good regardless of other values with which it may conflict? Or is she recognizing the conflicts and saying that multiculturalism is good on balance?

critical judgments
Judgments that can be articulated and defended by providing the reasons for them.

Notice that each of these questions is raised only to develop a precise understanding of the speaker's thesis, not to object to the thesis. Obviously, you cannot assess a speech critically until you know exactly what the speaker is trying to say.

Are the Links Among the Ideas Reasonable? When we addressed this question earlier, we asked only whether the links seemed to square with common sense. But critical listeners want to know more than that; they will ask whether the speaker has proved the claims in a reasonable way.

Suppose that in a speech about the federal budget surplus of the late 1990s the speaker claims that (1) the flourishing national economy was the primary cause of the surplus and that (2) the surplus was improving our country's position in the world economy. As a critical listener, you would ask such questions as:

- *Does the speaker prove what he claims?* This speaker is claiming that one thing causes another. But if he can show only that, as the surplus increases, our international economic strength increases, he has not proved a cause–effect relationship. He has only revealed a correlation. A country's economic strength might result from some other factor or a combination of factors.
- *If the links are established, should you accept the speaker's claim?* Even though the speaker might convince you that the flourishing national economy added to the surplus and that the surplus strengthened the country's economic position, you still might not find the conclusion acceptable. For example, you may have just read in the newspaper that economists recently concluded that the U.S. economy experienced increasing competition from other countries. Something does not add up: If the surplus was so beneficial, why did the U.S. economy experience increased foreign competition? In raising this kind of question, you are recognizing that the speaker has not examined the topic completely. You want to know more about other factors that apparently are offsetting the effects of the surplus, such as high production costs.

Are the Ideas Supported Where Necessary? As we have seen, some statements are accepted at face value by most listeners, whereas other statements need to be supported by facts, narratives, data, or opinions. As a critical listener, you require a speaker to support ideas that need it, and so you would ask such questions as:

- *Does the idea need support?* Even critical listeners accept some statements at face value. Maybe the idea is clear intuitively, or perhaps the speaker's explanation makes it seem so obvious that no further support is required. For example, if the speaker clearly defines the budget surplus as "the government's taking in more than it is spending," you might see no need for additional support. But you probably will not be so quick to accept an opinion like "The budget surplus is our hard-won hope for social equality."
- *Has the speaker offered enough supporting material?* For most listeners, one or two examples of elderly people who cannot pay their medical bills will probably not be sufficient support for the thesis "The health-care system is hard on the elderly." The speaker doesn't offer enough examples to support a generalization about all elderly people. Insufficient support

may lead listeners to conclude that there *is* no other support, and so they may not take the speaker's ideas seriously.

How Does Accepting or Rejecting the Thesis Affect My Other Beliefs? Critical listeners recognize that beliefs and values do not exist in isolation. Almost always, accepting or rejecting a speaker's thesis will have consequences for your beliefs about other matters. Believing, for example, that the budget surplus justified a tax cut may not square with another belief you hold— that there are significant needs for increased spending on education and health care that the surplus made possible.

These four sets of questions are intended to help you develop a clear understanding of what a speaker is asking you to think about, to believe, or to do. They will help you to form a careful and reflective judgment about whether or not to agree with the speaker. But listening critically does not mean that you have to subject a speaker to an inquisition before accepting anything he or she says. Rather, in the language of nuclear arms agreements, it is a way to "trust, but verify"—to accept the *ethos* of the speaker but not to depend entirely on that in deciding whether the speech makes sense.

> **Checklist 2.2** Critical Thinking About a Speech
>
> 1. **Are the main ideas identifiable?**
> 2. **Are the links among the ideas reasonable?**
> 3. **Are the ideas supported where necessary?**
> 4. **How does accepting or rejecting the thesis affect my other beliefs?**

Evaluating Speeches Critically

So far, we have considered one dimension of critical listening: judging whether a speaker's ideas are sound. We saw that the basic skills of critical thinking are used as well in thinking strategically about the thesis and supporting ideas of a speech. Now we will consider a second dimension of critical listening: assessing the strength of the speech *as a speech*. This evaluation centers on three questions:

1. Did the speech demonstrate the principles and techniques of public speaking?
2. What was strong and what was weak about the speech?
3. How might the speaker improve the speech?

This dimension of critical listening is especially important in a public speaking class. Although your primary goal is to become more skilled at giving speeches, you will spend far more time listening to classmates speak than speaking yourself. Your feedback as a critical listener will help others improve, and their assessments, in turn, will strengthen your abilities as a speaker. Outside the class, too, you will spend far more time as a listener than as a speaker.

Evaluation Standards

Like judgments about the content of a speech, assessments of its quality can be made uncritically—as when an audience member says, "Wow!" or "That was a great speech!" without explaining why. But the goal is to make *critical* assessments, which depend on the four critical thinking skills described earlier: questioning and challenging, recognizing differences, forming opinions and supporting claims, and putting ideas into a broader context.

As you apply these skills to speechmaking, remember that a speech is a strategic communication. It is presented in a specific situation to achieve a specific purpose. By focusing on these two concepts—*the rhetorical situation* and *the speaker's purpose*—you will develop evaluation criteria that turn careful listening into critical listening.

Rhetorical Situation. The discussion in Chapter 1 of the **rhetorical situation** made it clear that speeches are delivered not in a vacuum but in response to a specific context. Critical listeners thus realize that it is not fair to evaluate a speech without considering the situation in which the speaker prepared and delivered it.

Abraham Lincoln, to cite a historical example, has been criticized in recent years for not coming out more strongly against slavery in the period leading to the Civil War. Indeed, in his fourth debate with Stephen A. Douglas during the 1858 senatorial campaign in Illinois, Lincoln said:

The facial expressions of critical listeners often indicate their concern about a speech. Reporters and news correspondents frequently find themselves listening critically and asking themselves: What was the speaker trying to achieve? Should I accept what he or she says?

rhetorical situation
A situation in which people's understanding can be changed through messages.

I will say then that I am not, nor ever have been in favor of bringing about in any way the social and political equality of the white and black races— that I am not nor ever have been in favor of making voters or jurors of negroes, nor of qualifying them to hold office, nor to intermarry with white people; and I will say in addition to this that there is a physical difference between the white and black races which I believe will for ever forbid the two races living together on terms of social and political equality.

This position seems far from the popular image of Lincoln as the "Great Emancipator," but some of the criticism ignores the specific situation in which he spoke—especially the fact that very few white Americans in the 1850s could imagine the races as equal. Nor did Lincoln have free rein about the content of speeches in these campaign appearances. Because his goal was to win the election, he could not antagonize listeners whose votes he was seeking. Any critique that altogether ignores the rhetorical situation in which Lincoln spoke would give a false impression of the realistic choices available to him.

The key questions, then, are:

- What was the specific rhetorical situation?
- What constraints and opportunities did it pose?
- How well did the speaker respond to the situation?

When evaluating a classmate's speech, consider *both* the constraints imposed by the immediate audience and the constraints imposed by the larger rhetorical situation. With respect to the immediate audience, ask whether or not the speaker adequately tailored the speech to the listeners' knowledge level. You also might consider whether the speaker's ideas and supporting material were interesting and effective for the specific audience. With respect to the larger rhetorical situation, ask if the speaker understands current attitudes, beliefs, and practices regarding the issue about which she spoke.

Speaker's Purpose. Besides taking into account the speaker's rhetorical situation, also consider the speaker's purpose. It's easy to say that a speaker chose the wrong purpose and should have aimed for something else. Generally, however, you should evaluate a speech *in light of* its stated or implied purpose. To condemn a speech for not accomplishing what the speaker never intended to accomplish is neither rational nor **fair.**[6]

If you understand the purpose of the speech, then the next key question is "How well did the speaker achieve the purpose?" This focuses on the means used by the speaker and whether they were the best choices available. If the purpose is to introduce a complicated subject, then a speech that assumes prior knowledge on the part of the audience and that fails to explain key concepts would not be well adapted to the purpose. The speaker may not recognize any problems, but critical listeners can point them out.

Evaluating a speech in terms of its purpose raises a third important question: "Should a speech be judged by its effects or by its artistry?" If the **effectiveness standard** is the only measure of a speech, then whatever is most likely to accomplish the purpose should be done. By this standard, to use an extreme example, Adolf Hitler would be regarded as a good speaker because he was effective in achieving his **purpose.**[7]

Most theorists, however, reject effectiveness as the sole basis for evaluating a speech. As noted in Chapter 1, the goal is not only to achieve a stated purpose but also to achieve it while following accepted principles and observing ethical norms. Public speaking is a practical art. The **artistic standard** asks whether the speaker followed the principles of the art, and hence whether he or she did the best that could be done, consistent with ethical norms, in a specific rhetorical situation. If a classmate speaks in favor of some controversial topic—say abortion or gay rights—you should not fault the speech for failing to convince those listeners whose opposition is strongly entrenched. The artistic standard does not ignore the issue of effectiveness, however, because the application of public speaking principles and the observance of ethical norms generally make a speech more effective than it otherwise would be.

Evaluating Classroom Speeches

To participate effectively in evaluating classroom speeches, you and your classmates must listen carefully and critically to each other. By exchanging valuable feedback, you will help each other become better speakers, and you will all sharpen your skills as critical listeners.

Typically, a classroom speaking assignment does not highlight all the dimensions of public speaking at once. One assignment may focus on how to organize a speech clearly; another may emphasize research skills and the selection of supporting materials. Therefore, when assessing a classmate's speech, be sensitive to the specific purpose of the assignment. If it is intended to focus on organization, for instance, that also should be the focus of your critique. To concentrate on some other factor, such as the speaker's gestures, would be unfair, since the whole point of this assignment is to deemphasize other aspects of speaking in order to put the spotlight on organization.

A constructive attitude is essential in evaluating classroom speeches, because that provides the best environment for learning from each other. If criticism is hostile or antagonistic, the speaker may become defensive and may ignore useful feedback. At the same time, listeners who are too eager to criticize a speech may not properly assess the speaker's situation and purpose. Do not overlook weaknesses in a speech, but remember that the purpose of the critique is to help your classmate improve the speech, not to undermine self-esteem. Emphasize what the speaker can improve and how to do that; and remember that the strengths of the speech need not be ignored in order to identify its weaknesses.

A classroom speech often develops only a limited number of points, and your critique, too, should focus on a few features of the speech that are most important. The value of feedback is greatly reduced when critics offer a blow-by-blow reaction to everything that was said. The speaker will not be able to benefit from the criticism, because the important points

effectiveness standard
Evaluation of a speech according to the effects it produced.

artistic standard
Evaluation of a speech according to its ethical execution of principles of public speaking without regard to its actual effects.

will be indistinguishable from superficial reactions. As a general rule, focus your critique on just a few features of the speech, and arrange them in order of importance. The critique itself is an attempt to influence others, and, like a speech, it should be composed in a way that best achieves its purpose.

Critiques of classroom speeches take a variety of forms. The most common is informal discussion. After a speech is presented, the class may spend some time talking about its strengths and about how it might be improved. Students are sometimes reluctant to participate in these discussions. Some may fear hurting their classmates' feelings, or they may believe that, if they critique others, their own speeches will be evaluated more harshly. These are short-sighted reactions. After all, a primary goal of this course is to become more skilled in speaking, and vigorous evaluation—as long as your attitude is constructive—is one of the best ways to achieve that goal.

Sometimes students fill out *rating forms* to evaluate classroom speeches. These emphasize the same features of public speaking that are stressed in the particular assignment. They are efficient—raters use check marks, circle key words, or assign numerical scores, for example—and they usually also include space to write more open-ended comments. If your class uses rating forms for evaluation, take the task seriously, and provide the most constructive feedback possible.

On some occasions, evaluation involves an *impromptu speech of criticism* in which the critic follows the speaker with a presentation that assesses the speech. This will sharpen your own critical skills and at the same time give you practice in speaking. Like any other speech, a speech of evaluation has a thesis and main ideas—in this case, whatever you think is most important to say in assessing a classmate's speech.

Evaluating Speeches in the Field

Most speeches are not delivered in a classroom for the purpose of practicing the art. Most are delivered in a variety of public settings, such as banquets, commemorative celebrations, business meetings, churches and synagogues, political campaigns, and so on.

Many of the principles of classroom evaluation also apply to speeches in the field. In particular, critics need to have a clear understanding of the rhetorical situation and the speaker's purpose. Speeches are presented in specific situations to achieve specific goals, and the critique must take these into account. It is also helpful to become familiar with the speaker and his or her particular assets and liabilities in the speaking situation. As with classroom speeches, you need to decide which standards to use for evaluation, probably including such factors as the validity of the speaker's reasoning and assertions, any value judgments made consciously or unconsciously, and the ethical implications of the speech.

An advantage of assessing speeches outside the classroom is that they have more variety, since they don't all spring from the same assignment. No doubt you'll hear speakers who ignore some of the concepts and guidelines in this book or who give them a unique twist. By assessing speakers in the field, you will encounter a great range of speaking styles and can better develop your own distinctive approach to public speaking.

Rhetorical Criticism

Evaluating the speeches of others is an elementary form of **rhetorical criticism**—the analytical assessment of messages that are intended to affect other people. Careful, critical listening and evaluation of speeches will help you develop a mindset for rhetorical criticism. It will give you experience in thinking rhetorically about speeches: asking yourself what the speaker's purpose seems to be, what opportunities and problems are presented by the speaker's situation, how the speaker has chosen to go about the task, whether other choices were available, and whether the selected means and ends were the best possible in that **situation**.[8]

Engaging in rhetorical criticism has two major by-products. First, it gives you insights into your own public speaking by providing a range of speakers to study and by drawing your attention to how they apply principles of public speaking. Second, it develops your sensitivity to public speaking and makes you more aware of how it works. Besides improving your own abilities as a speaker, this awareness should help you appreciate excellent public speaking and put you on guard against speakers who try to undermine listeners' critical abilities.

rhetorical criticism
The analytical assessment of messages that are intended to affect other people.

Strategies for Speaking to Diverse Audiences

Respecting Diversity Through Critical Listening

Listening is a cultivated skill. Listening critically requires practice and respect for the speaker. Consider these ideas when practicing critical listening.

1. Demonstrate respect for the speaker by paying attention.
2. Be open to new ideas.
3. Form a reflective—not hasty—judgment.

Summary

Although hearing is a natural physiological activity, listening is a cultivated skill that includes mental processing and assessment of what is heard. It is an important skill to develop to be sure you know what you heard, to provide feedback to the speaker, and to protect yourself from unethical or unscrupulous speakers.

Listening is difficult. People think more rapidly than they listen and therefore may be prone to daydream. They may engage in "channel surfing," tuning a speech in and out as they are stimulated by certain words to think about other things. For some people a limited attention span makes it difficult to take everything in; for others the commitment to listen to absolutely everything may get in the way of reflective judgment. People may jump to conclusions because they agree or disagree with the speaker, and they may regard what the speaker says as closer to or farther from their own beliefs than is really the case. Finally, factors in the situation such as noise or physical disruption may interfere with listening to the speech.

Overcoming these difficulties requires concerted effort to develop the skills of careful and critical listening. Careful listening includes decoding the message by identifying the thesis and mapping the links between it and the main supporting ideas. It also involves making at least some judgment about the content of the speech and the links within it. Careful listening can be aided by efficient note taking.

Critical listening begins with the skills of critical thinking and applies them to the speaking situation. Critical listeners are open to new ideas and arguments but assess them with skepticism and an insistence that they be explained and supported. The goals of critical listening are to be able to reconstruct the thesis and main ideas of a speech and to form a reflective rather than hasty judgment about them.

Critical listening makes it possible both to evaluate messages and to provide feedback to others about how they can improve their speaking performance. Clear standards of evaluation are needed, and the assessment should be guided especially by understanding of the rhetorical situation and the speaker's purpose. Although the effectiveness standard is an important criterion, by itself it usually is not the most appropriate basis for evaluating a speech. Instead, the artistic standard includes effectiveness but focuses on the question of how well the speaker applied public speaking principles and followed ethical norms in a specific situation. You will have the opportunity to practice rhetorical criticism both by critiquing classmates' speeches and by attending and evaluating speeches in the field.

Discussion Questions

1. We have all heard speeches that were interesting and speeches that were boring. What was it about the interesting speeches that grabbed your attention? What was it about the boring speeches that made them difficult to bear? Based on your answers, suggest some strategies for gaining and holding an audience's attention.

2. You are about to speak to a hostile audience. How do you get them to listen with an open mind rather than immediately discounting your position?

3. You are assigned the responsibility of grading a speech that you yourself haven't heard. You must consider the views of two critics who heard the speech and gave you their opinions about it. But their evaluations are contradictory: One says the speech was great, and the other thinks it was shoddy work. How would you reconcile these different evaluations and assign a grade to the speech?

4. You have just heard a speech that was particularly effective, but in your opinion it was ethically suspect. How would you evaluate the speech? Why?

1. Listen to a speech on television, in class, or at a lecture. Whenever your mind wanders, make a note about the last thing you heard and what you then began to think about. After the speech, write a short essay about your listening habits and how you would like to improve them.
2. Map a speech. Identify its thesis and main ideas, and evaluate its claims and links.
3. Write a three- to five-page essay to evaluate a speech. Analyze the rhetorical situation and the speaker's purpose; state and explain your evaluation standards; and apply rhetorical criticism to the speech.

1. The complexity of an individual's cognitive processes is also responsible for differences in listening comprehension. See Michael J. Beatty and Steven K. Payne, "Listening Comprehension as a Function of Cognitive Complexity: A Research Note," *Communication Monographs* 51 (March 1984): 85–89.
2. Neil Postman provides an extensive social critique of how television is responsible for this trend in *Amusing Ourselves to Death: Public Discourse in the Age of Show Business,* New York: Penguin Books, 1985.
3. For a discussion of how television tends to simplify messages, see Jeffrey Scheuer, *The Sound Bite Society,* New York: Routledge, 2001.
4. One example of this is seen in a study showing that when common citizens hear an argument about capital punishment, they judge the validity of evidence from the perspective they bring to the communication event, retaining their original beliefs regardless of the evidence presented. See Charles Lord, Ross Lee, and Mark Lepper, "Biased Assimilation and Attitude Polarization: The Effects of Prior Theories on Subsequently Considered Evidence," *Journal of Personality and Social Psychology* 37 (November 1979): 2098–2109.
5. For more about critical thinking, see Brook Noel Moore and Richard Parker, *Critical Thinking: Evaluating Claims and Arguments in Everyday Life,* 2nd ed., Mountain View, Calif.: Mayfield, 1989; and Leonard J. Rosen and Laurence Behrens, *The Allyn & Bacon Handbook,* 2nd ed., Boston: Allyn & Bacon, 1994, pp. 1–9. Although these textbooks focus on essay writing and evaluation, many of their directives apply as well to public speaking.
6. According to Mikhail Bahktin, we automatically tend to judge all utterances—from sentences to completed speeches—by what we imagine the speaker wishes to say. See "The Problem of Speech Genres," in *Speech Genres and Other Essays,* translated by Vern W. McGee, Austin: Univ. of Texas Press, 1986, p. 77.
7. Another example of why a speech should not be judged on effect alone is discussed in Edwin Black, *Rhetorical Criticism,* New York: Macmillan, 1965. For more about this debate in speech criticism, see Forbes I. Hill, "Conventional Wisdom—Traditional Form: The President's Message of November 3, 1969"; Karlyn Kohrs Campbell, "Conventional Wisdom—Traditional Form: A Rejoinder"; and Forbes I. Hill, "Reply to Professor Campbell," *Quarterly Journal of Speech* 58 (December 1972): 373–386, 451–460.
8. For more about rhetorical criticism, see James R. Andrews, Michael Leff, and Robert Terrill, *Reading Rhetorical Texts: An Introduction to Criticism,* Boston: Houghton Mifflin, 1998; Roderick P. Hart, *Modern Rhetorical Criticism,* 2d ed., Boston: Allyn and Bacon, 1997.

Chapter Three

Analyzing Your Audience

In this chapter, we will:

- Discover how the success of a speech depends on the audience.

- Explore how the audience demographics, cultures, and psychology affect listeners' receptiveness to a speech.

- Consider ways that speakers can adapt a message in particular circumstances to fit the audience.

- Identify both formal and informal methods of audience analysis.

- Examine how the speaker's *ethos* influences the audience and how speakers can improve their *ethos*.

Two students were presenting speeches to their classmates about the dangers of drunk driving. Both spent a great deal of time preparing, but they had strongly different attitudes about how to develop their speeches. The night before speaking, they met to compare their preparations. The first student said:

> There is so much statistical evidence on this topic, it was hard to pick only a few studies. I'll have lots of statistics. I had to trim my examples to stay within the time limit, but if I cite all this scholarly research, people will know that this is a serious topic and I'm well prepared to talk about it.

His classmate took a different approach:

> You're right; there is a lot of research on this topic. But our audience consists of students, and they're the age group at greatest risk of drunk driving. They don't believe anything will happen to them so they disregard all those statistical studies. I'll refer briefly to them, but I'm going to concentrate instead on the tragic drunk-driving accident just off campus last year. I want to tell a story that students can relate to, so they'll know that my speech concerns them.

The first student viewed the assignment only from his own perspective as speaker, worrying about how to include all the research and how to ensure a good grade. The second student considered the audience's perspective. She was determined to make the message interesting to classmates, and she carefully reviewed each bit of information from the viewpoint of someone hearing it in a short speech. Both speakers had the same general topic and goal, but to the audience the first speech was abstract, complicated, and dull, whereas the second was stimulating and full of common sense.

Of course, had the two students been speaking at a scientific conference, the results might have been just the opposite. The fact that the same speech could elicit such different reactions from different audiences emphasizes the importance of analyzing the audience and designing the speech with the audience in mind—the focus of this chapter.

It may seem surprising that even your attitude toward preparing a speech can create such a difference in the audience's reaction, but it's natural for listeners to give appreciation, attention, and support to a speaker who considers their comfort, interests, and beliefs. Even though an audience can thus be a constraint on a speaker's freedom, you can work with that constraint by careful audience analysis on three different levels:

- By checking *audience demographics,* you will consider how your speech should respond to certain characteristics of the audience as a whole—such as its size, age range, and educational level.
- By respecting *audience cultures,* you will become aware of how listeners approach your speech in terms of their interests, beliefs and values, prior understanding, and common knowledge.
- By understanding *audience psychology,* you will realize that listeners are selective about what they attend to and perceive.

The relationships among audience demographics, cultures, and psychology are illustrated in Figure 3.1. After studying these three levels of audience analysis, we will examine strategies for learning about your specific audience and for assessing your own resources and *ethos* in relation to audience members.

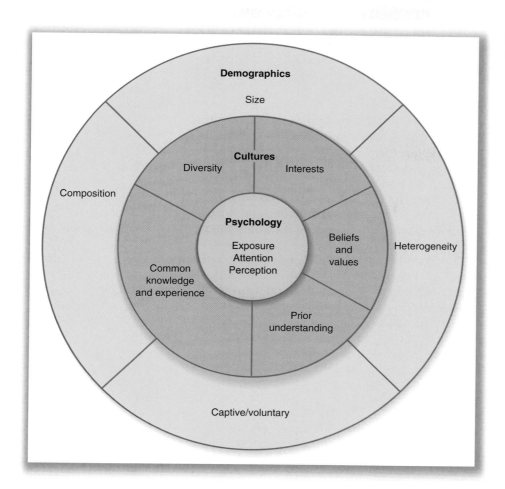

Figure 3.1 Levels of influence on audiences.

Checking Audience Demographics

Demographics refers to characteristics of the audience as a whole. The major demographic categories are the audience's size, heterogeneity, status as captive or voluntary, and composition.

Size

How large will your audience be? The more listeners there are, the greater your sense of distance from them, and consequently the more formal your presentation is likely to be. Someone speaking to a dozen people in a small room clearly faces a different situation than someone addressing a large lecture hall or a mass-media audience.

Classroom speakers probably have an audience of about 20 to 25 listeners, an audience size that is typical of many speeches to service clubs, neighborhood groups, and work-related organizations. This size lets you address a public without losing sight of individuals, and the setting is a middle ground between highly formal and extremely informal.

Heterogeneity

Heterogeneity refers to the variety or diversity of audience members—the degree of dissimilarity among them. The smaller the audience, the more likely that its members will have similar assumptions, values, and ways of thinking. Of course, even a small audience may show marked differences in these criteria, but a large audience virtually ensures that members will have different values and assumptions as well as learning styles; the audience is said to be *heterogeneous*.

The two students speaking about the dangers of drunk driving assumed that their audience of American college students would be like them, would learn about the subject in the same way, and would respond favorably to their message. But a heterogeneous audience could include experienced social drinkers and stockholders of alcohol distributors who might oppose restrictions on drinking.

The more heterogeneous your audience, the more you need to find examples and appeals that will be meaningful to all kinds of listeners; or you might combine appeals that are relevant to different segments of the audience. Avoid materials that are significant only to some listeners but beside the point to others. The goal is to appeal meaningfully to a diverse audience without resorting to vague generalizations and **platitudes** (buzzwords or phrases that are devoid of specific content).

An audience can be heterogeneous even if its members share the same cultural background, but a culturally diverse audience is particularly likely to be heterogeneous. The audience for the speeches against drunk driving might include a student or two from countries where alcohol use is unrestricted or where few people drive, and they may not share their classmates' concerns about the safety risks of drunk driving.

Voluntary Versus Captive Audience

Under what circumstances has the audience assembled? In general, people who have chosen to hear a speech are more likely to be interested and receptive than are people who have been coerced into attending. A captive audience may resent having to hear the speech, which may undercut the speaker's *ethos* and message.

Students who are required to attend an assembly, employees whose jobs depend on participation in a seminar, and churchgoers who find themselves listening to a political message when they expected a sermon are examples of captive audiences. Speakers cannot assume that captive listeners have any interest in them or their subject, and they must work particularly hard to interest and motivate their listeners.

Some of your classmates may also be captive listeners, especially if the course is required or if individuals don't recognize the value of effective listening. With luck, you can turn them into voluntary listeners as they become interested in what you have to say and as they begin to see that they can improve their own speeches by listening carefully to yours.

If you assume that your audience is there voluntarily and you make no effort to motivate them, you could be setting yourself up for disaster. If you are wrong in your assessment and your listeners see themselves as captive, their feelings of boredom or hostility are likely to overwhelm any message you present. For this reason, when you don't know the status of the audi-

heterogeneity
Variety or diversity among audience members; dissimilarity.

platitudes
Buzzwords or phrases that are devoid of specific content.

ence, it is best to assume that listeners are captive and that you need to motivate them.

Composition

Sometimes, if it will help you make choices about your speech, you can analyze the audience in terms of such demographic categories as age, gender, religion, ethnicity, educational level, or socioeconomic status. For example, it may be safe to assume that a young audience would be less interested in a speech about retirement planning than an older audience would be. Likewise, you might assume that listeners with a high level of formal education can think in figurative as well as literal terms and can deal with complex issues. And if an audience is made up mostly of members of a particular religious or ethnic group, you well may tailor your presentation to take advantage of their commonality by making brief reference to specific religious practices or perhaps by using phrases from another language with which they will be familiar.

Giving too much weight to demographic categories, however, may lead to false and unwarranted **stereotyping**—wrongly assuming that all members of a category are alike. For example, it is less true today than in the past that women and men differ in the likelihood of their being persuaded by a speaker. Nor do all people from rural areas think alike; and not everyone from a particular region has the same set of beliefs and values.[1] In short, demographic categories can provide important hints about an audience, but do not assume that the hints apply to everyone.

WWW. Using the Internet

Audience Analysis of Your Class

Use one of the three exercises included in the **Allyn & Bacon Public Speaking Web Site.** Go to **http://www.abacon.com/pubspeak/analyze/analyze.html.** Select "Draw a Demographic Profile of Your Audience," "Draw a Psychographic Profile of Your Audience," or "Credibility Self-Assessment." The exercises are about halfway down the page and are identified with an icon of a pencil. You can print out a copy of the results page after completing the exercise, send it to your own e-mail address, and/or send it to your instructor.

Respecting Audience Cultures

As applied to audiences, the term *culture* has two different meanings. First, to the degree that we can characterize particular audiences in terms of subjective factors such as interests, beliefs and values, common knowledge and experience, roles and reference groups, we can describe a distinct **audience culture.** This is likely to happen when the audience is relatively homogeneous. For example, having made a hobby of studying the stock market, Jon Koenig received several invitations to speak about investment strategies. In one week, he was asked to speak to a group of college seniors about to graduate, to a group of employed single women of various ages, and to a group of older workers interested in retirement planning. He tried to adapt his message to the culture represented by each of these different audiences, strategically planning his speech to maximize his chances of success with each audience.

The second meaning of *culture* reflects the fact that each individual listener represents one or more cultures—traditions that influence how people think, feel, believe, and act. Ethnic heritage, political orientation, and national identity are some components of culture in this second sense. From this standpoint, we can say that an audience draws from multiple cultures. A heterogeneous audience is especially likely to be culturally diverse,

stereotyping
Assuming that all members of a demographic category are alike in all respects.

audience culture
Subjective factors that characterize a particular audience and make its situation distinct.

but even an audience that is homogeneous on one factor may be quite diverse on others.

A thorough audience analysis will consider audience culture in both of these senses. We will first consider several of the factors that can give an individual audience a distinctive culture. Then we will explore how to recognize and respect the cultural diversity that characterizes many audiences today.

Self-Interest

Listeners have **self-interests;** they stand to gain or lose personally depending on what is done. For example, a proposal to raise students' tuition and fees would not be in the self-interest of those who are working their way through college, whereas a proposal to increase funds for financial aid *would* appeal to the self-interest of those same students. Self-interest goes beyond economic matters, however. A speech that advocates limits on listeners' freedom or power or that casts them in an unflattering role also will be at odds with the audience's self-interest.

Most listeners resist messages that clearly challenge their self-interest. If you feel that it is necessary to challenge the audience's self-interest, consider whether you can develop your message in a nonthreatening way while still being true to your beliefs. Perhaps you can plan the speech with a strong combination of appeals so that listeners will look beyond their self-interest to consider some broader concept of what is good.

At the time of the 2003 Iraqi war, for example, men and women whose spouses might be placed in danger nevertheless were urged to support the war. Although having their loved ones placed in harm's way was not in their self-interest, many were persuaded that more important principles were at stake and that the sacrifice of their personal interests were justified.

One common strategy for challenging listeners' self-interest is to suggest that their short-term sacrifices will bring long-term benefits (and so their self-interest will be satisfied in the long run). One student took this approach in arguing that course work should be more difficult. She began by admitting outright that her speech would challenge the audience's self-interest:

> Talk to any student at this college and you'll hear about how busy they are, how much work they have to do, how much time their classes take. I'm sure it's true, because many of us have never really been challenged to work hard before this. The last thing most students want is to hear someone say that classes should be made even harder. But if we can improve the academic reputation of this college, not only will it attract better students, but in the long run our own degrees will be more highly valued.

Personal Interests

self-interest
Personal gain or loss resulting from an action or policy.

personal interests
What an individual regards as interesting or important.

Listeners also have **personal interests,** and so you need to assess how likely it is that your topic will interest others. Even though you may be an avid student of military history, you cannot assume that others will be captivated by a speech about battle planning. And although you may be thrilled by the details of auto mechanics, realize that many listeners only want to know how to turn the ignition key to start the car.

If you think that listeners will be strongly interested in your topic, a straightforward presentation may be fine. But if interest may be low, you should deliberately plan the speech in a way that captures the audience's attention and holds their interest. Usually, you should avoid technical language, jargon, and abstractions unless you know that the audience is familiar with and interested in the topic. On the other hand, startling statements, rhetorical questions, personal anecdotes, and narratives are especially good ways to involve listeners in your topic and enhance their interest in it.

Sometimes listeners do have a casual interest in your topic but do not regard it as particularly important or of high priority. Then your task is less one of arousing initial interest and more a matter of impressing the audience with the urgency of the situation and the significance of your message. In any case, by analyzing the audience's level of interest in your topic, you are better able to determine how to frame the speech.

Beliefs and Values

Beliefs are statements that listeners regard as true; **values** are positive or negative judgments that listeners make. For example, a listener might believe that homelessness is a serious problem (belief) and might also regard government aid for the homeless as a good thing (giving it a positive value). Another listener might agree that homelessness is a serious problem (belief) yet might object to government aid (giving it a negative value). Still another listener might not believe that homelessness is a serious problem and might think that its scope has been exaggerated. For the last listener, government aid is not an issue because no problem has been acknowledged.

As these examples show, an audience's beliefs and values are starting points for crafting the strategy of your speech. You will want to uphold your own beliefs and values, of course, but you can do that and also advance your purpose if you emphasize the connections between listeners' beliefs and values and your own.

Assume that you wish to advocate increased government aid for the homeless. For the first listener, your strategy might be designed to reinforce existing beliefs and values. For the second listener, you might briefly review the extent of the problem, but most of the speech would be designed to convince the listener that government aid works better than private solutions alone; your goal would be to change the listener's value about government aid from negative to positive. For the third listener, it is pointless to consider whether public or private solutions are better unless you can demonstrate that homelessness really is a problem. In this case, much of your speech would be designed to illustrate the extent and severity of homelessness and the urgent need for action. Finally, if all three listeners are in your

WWW. Using the Internet

What Strategies of Audience Analysis Are Used for Political Advertising?

Analyze how the designers of a political advertisement use audience culture and audience psychology to formulate their strategies. Point your browser to one of the sites below.

- **CNN AllPolitics** at http://www.cnn.com/ALLPOLITICS/ 1996/candidates/ad.archive/
- **C-SPAN Campaign 2000** at http://www.c-span.org/ campaign2000/advertising.asp
- **Campaign Advertising E-Archives** at http://faculty .kutztown.edu/richards/220/ad-archive.html

Search for a message that you can view using RealVideo. Address the following:

- How are elements of the audience culture addressed? Consider examples of the listeners'
    Self-interest
    Beliefs and values
    Experiences
    Common knowledge
    Roles and reference group identification
- Relate how the designers may have developed the message with reference to the concepts of
    Selective exposure
    Selective attention
    Selective perception

beliefs
Statements that listeners regard as true.

values
Positive or negative judgments that listeners apply to a person, place, object, event, or idea.

Sometimes, listeners know a good deal about the topic and have strong feelings about it. To be successful, speakers must respond to what the audience already knows about the topic or situation.

audience, your strategy should combine appeals in the hope that one thing or another would convince each listener.

This example has focused on topic-specific beliefs and values about homelessness. But listeners also hold many general beliefs and values about a host of topics—about human nature, about their responsibilities to others, about the status of their nation in the world, about the significance of science or religion, and so on. For example, if an audience believes that things generally are better (or worse) today than in the past, speakers in a political campaign might exploit that belief by claiming that their party (or the opposing party) is responsible for the situation.

Prior Understanding

How much do your listeners already know about your topic? Have they heard about any of your points before? Do they have enough background information to follow your reasoning? Answers to questions like these can help you design a powerful speech without boring or confusing your audience.

Speakers sometimes mistake intelligence for knowledge, thus overestimating what the audience knows. Fearful of **condescending** to listeners—of talking down to them and assuming that they can't think for themselves—some speakers cover complex material too quickly, omit important steps in an explanation, or relate events out of sequence. Another danger of poor audience analysis is telling listeners nothing that they don't already know. If the listeners believe a speaker is wasting their time and saying nothing new, they are less likely to pay attention. Worse, they may become angry or resent the speaker as a person. You can avoid all these dangers by analyzing what the audience already knows.

condescending

Talking down to an audience; assuming that listeners are not capable of thinking about a subject and reaching their own conclusions.

President Reagan was dubbed "The Great Communicator" in part because he could render complex subjects in simple, understandable terms. In a 1983 speech seeking support for his Strategic Defense Initiative, he used simple terms to describe sophisticated military and strategic concepts, and he also overcame complex arguments about defense spending:

> But first, let me say what the defense debate is not about. It is not about spending arithmetic. I know that in the last few weeks you've been bombarded with numbers and percentages. . . . The trouble with all these numbers is that they tell us little about the kind of defense program America needs or the benefits and security and freedom that our defense effort buys for us.

In simple language, President Reagan then explained the importance of a defensive missile system:

> I've become more and more convinced that the human spirit must be capable of rising above dealing with other nations and human beings by threatening their existence

and

> Wouldn't it be better to save lives than avenge them?

He admitted but downplayed the difficulties of developing this new system and called on the scientific community

> those who gave us nuclear weapons, to turn their great talents now to the cause of mankind and world peace, to give us the means of rendering these nuclear weapons impotent and obsolete.

If President Reagan had focused only on technical and scientific issues in the belief that "everyone understood" the difference between offensive and defensive systems, his speech would have been far less effective.

Forty years earlier, President Franklin Roosevelt displayed the same skill. Letting the Allies use American war materials, he told his listeners, was like lending a garden hose to one's neighbor to put out a fire. The analogy enabled him, without being condescending, to make an innovative plan understandable to people who might know little about the logistics of war but who were familiar with borrowing and lending between neighbors.

Common Knowledge and Experience

What **cultural facts** in your listeners' general store of knowledge will be relevant to your speech? Surveys frequently report that embarrassing percentages of Americans cannot name their senator or representative, do not know when the Civil War was fought, or cannot locate a particular country on the globe. Such evidence does not argue that people are stupid or that a speaker must spell out everything for an audience. Rather, in recent years educators have been less concerned with teaching facts than with teaching students how to find information.[2] Thus, for a general audience, you may need to identify or explain cultural facts that are important to your argument. But if your audience is specialized—say a group of Civil War buffs—you can assume that listeners are familiar with basic information about your topic.

Speakers often make **allusions,** or brief references, to things that they assume listeners know about and understand. But if listeners don't "get" the

cultural facts
Facts that are commonly known among the members of a culture; common knowledge.

allusions
Brief references to something with which the audience is assumed to be familiar.

allusion, they also will miss the point of the comparison. So you need to have a good sense of which allusions your audience will recognize. Well into the twentieth century, speakers could assume that most listeners were familiar with the Bible and with classic literature. Late in the century, however, popular culture—especially television—became the source of many allusions, especially in the United States. For example, supporters of President John F. Kennedy fondly remembered his administration by referring to the popular musical *Camelot.* And during the fall of 1998, when President Clinton ordered the bombing of Iraq as Congress prepared to vote on his impeachment, his action was described as a "wag the dog" scenario—referring to a popular film in which a president creates a foreign crisis to divert attention from his domestic troubles.

Similarly, in a classroom speech against the feminine side of masculinity, one student alluded to an episode on the popular television series *Friends:*

> Women in the 1990s wanted men to be more emotional, more sensitive—in essence, more like women. But now men in particular are becoming threatened by this feminine side of masculinity. A recent episode of *Friends* provides a good example. Ross and Rachel's new nanny for their daughter Emma seemed perfect—he sang songs, performed puppet shows, and baked cookies. But Ross felt uncomfortable that Sandy—a man—was displaying such feminine qualities as playing a recorder and crying at a sad story in public. Ross eventually fired Sandy because of his own reluctance to acknowledge his feminine side.

By analyzing and understanding his audience's shared cultural experiences, this student was able to allude to characters on *Friends* to build a strong introduction that captured interest and prepared listeners for his main point.

Roles and Reference Groups

Each listener occupies a variety of **roles,** or socially assigned positions, and these are an important part of an audience's culture. Consider, for example, an audience made up of Girl Scouts. A listener who is a Girl Scout is also a young woman, a student, and a daughter; and she may be a member of a church, the Honor Society, and the dance club. Depending on which role is dominant for her at any given time, different topics and appeals are likely to be effective. If, while listening to a speech, she thinks of herself mainly as a Girl Scout, she may be more interested in physical adventure or social service than she would be if she thought of herself mainly as a dancer. In analyzing your audience, therefore, you need to decide which roles are most important to listeners while you speak.

Listeners also identify with many **reference groups,** whether or not they actually belong to them. Reference groups are also socially constructed categories. Because they serve as guides or models for behavior, they can influence listeners' beliefs, values, and actions. For example, a student may model his taste in clothes or hairstyle on the members of a popular band; he isn't a member of this band, but he likes people to think of him as sharing its characteristics. Another student may take cues about the importance of good study habits from older friends in her residence hall; they are a reference group for her because she likes to be thought of in reference to them. In other situations, however, each of these students will model different reference groups—family, friends, peers, public figures, and ethnic groups, for

roles
Socially assigned positions, such as "parent," "student," "employee," and "citizen."

reference groups
Groups with which listeners identify, regardless of whether they belong to them. Reference groups serve as guides or models for behavior.

instance. By knowing which reference groups and values are important to your listeners, you can strategically plan effective appeals and supporting materials.

Cultural Diversity

We have been discussing culture as though audience members all share a common culture. In some respects they probably do, but a speaker who assumes that an unfamiliar audience has a single set of beliefs, values, or experiences is inviting disaster.

The United States has increasingly become a multicultural society, and many other nations have been multicultural societies for a long time. Wherever you speak, it is important to remember that today's audience members represent a diversity of cultures and backgrounds. This is true of public speaking classes particularly, because schools, colleges, and universities have sought to attract international students and students from various racial and ethnic groups. It is also true of society at large, as racial and ethnic minority groups make up a growing proportion of the population.

There are many types of diversity, including religious, gender, age, economic, and political diversity. Everyone, whether speaker or listener, must acknowledge and relate to people who reflect a wide variety of cultural backgrounds.

Conservative commentator David Horowitz discovered this basic truth during a speech at the University of Chicago in 2001. His topic—why financial reparations for descendants of slavery is a bad idea—was controversial and generated angry protests. One student stood with her back to Horowitz throughout the entire presentation of his speech. By calling reparations "racist" and arguing that no one group was responsible for slavery, Horowitz alienated his audience, which included African Americans. Arousing hostility in order to generate publicity may have been Horowitz's purpose in this

A speaker who faces a culturally diverse audience, one likely to be made up of people with differing belief and value systems, must think about how his or her message will be received by the various members of the audience, and plan his or her speech accordingly.

specific case. Most speakers, however, prefer to obtain a hearing for their views. Controversial topics can and should be discussed in public, but they must be presented with clear acknowledgment of and sensitivity to cultural differences in order for the audience to receive the message.

Speaking to a multicultural audience challenges you to become aware of your own cultural assumptions and predispositions. It is common for people to regard as universal the values of their specific culture. This is the extension of a tendency known as *egocentrism* to a cultural scale. People tend to pay attention to what is most interesting to them. Reflection and careful self-analysis can help you avoid seeing your own values as universal and thus seeming insensitive to cultural differences.[3]

To use a simple example, U.S. culture traditionally has valued youth, whereas Japanese culture has valued age. In speaking to an audience of both American and Japanese listeners, it would not be a good idea either to discredit something by labeling it "old" or, on the other hand, to assume that our ancestors always understood things better than we do.

Another example is seen in cultural attitudes toward the role of women, which vary widely between more traditional and more modern cultures. Women's roles as professionals are not as widely recognized in some societies in the Middle East and Latin America as they are in the United States. So a speech about women in the business world might be planned and presented differently for an international audience composed mostly of men and for an audience of U.S. businesspeople.

However, even a speech on women in the business world to a group of women professionals needs to consider cultural diversity. Characterizing women professionals as engaged in "real" work as compared with homemakers would most likely alienate many audience members, considering the number of women who work both inside and outside the home. Cultural diversity is most likely present even in a seemingly homogeneous audience.

Cultures differ even with respect to who is eligible to speak in public. During the early 1800s, women in the United States often were not allowed to appear on a public platform because that would violate their "feminine" role. As recently as 1976, U.S. Representative Barbara Jordan, one of the most prominent African American politicians, began her keynote speech to the Democratic National Convention by observing:

> There is something different about tonight. There is something special about tonight. What is different? What is special? I, Barbara Jordan, am a keynote speaker.
>
> A lot of years passed since 1832, and during that time it would have been most unusual for any national political party to ask that a Barbara Jordan deliver a keynote address—but tonight here I am. And I feel that notwithstanding the past that my presence here is one additional bit of evidence that the American Dream need not forever be deferred.

Yet another example relates to people's attitudes about what is "correct" speech or language. Language is a tool for communication. You most likely do not want to use language that will alienate your audience and hinder the reception of your message. Generational differences sometimes can dictate the appropriateness of certain phrases or expressions. For example, slang such as "you guys" might be acceptable for an audience of your friends, but it is likely inappropriate for a group of older men and women. President

George W. Bush received much criticism for his use of the word *crusade* in a speech following the terrorist attacks of September 11, 2001. Although he may have meant a campaign to end global terrorism, his word choice suggested a Christian war against Muslims, which alienated American Muslims in his audience, among others.

Culturally sensitive speech can also mean awareness of different ways of speaking. The United States includes many regional, ethnic, and social dialects. In some circumstances, these are perfectly acceptable ways of speaking; in others, listeners may regard them as substandard. If you plan to quote dialect in your speech, recognize that different language patterns are legitimate, and acknowledge the validity of "standard" patterns; yet do not disparage patterns different from your own.[4]

Regional differences in culture are also important. A student who grew up in the South and attends a university in the Northeast will not understand how classmates can survive winter. Likewise, those classmates may be surprised by this student's unhurried pace and "laid back" lifestyle. But it is easy to misinterpret someone else based on the framework of your own background, without acknowledging that your cultural background creates a frame of reference through which you perceive people and events, unless you recognize and understand the validity of cultural differences.

Many beliefs about other cultures are based on negative, unflattering stereotypes, and it is particularly important to avoid these when addressing a multicultural audience. Consciously resist any such belief as that one culture is hardworking and another is lazy, or that one is educated and another is ignorant, or that one is compulsive and another is relaxed. The reality is far more complex, and such simple-minded attitudes will rightly both insult and antagonize an audience.

Speakers adapt to a culturally diverse audience in three basic ways. One approach is to derive examples from many cultures so that all listeners feel that they are being addressed within the framework of their own culture. Even if some cultures are not mentioned specifically, the speaker's acknowledgment of diversity may make everyone feel more included.[5] This approach, of course, requires the speaker to know which particular cultures are represented by audience members.

A second approach is for speakers to emphasize their own cultural heritage in a way that makes others feel that their distinctiveness is valued as well. During the 2000 presidential campaign, Joseph Lieberman made frequent references to Jewish traditions and religious practices. He did so not only to appeal to other Jews but also to make the larger point that U.S. politics welcomes diversity, a point that encouraged members of other ethnic or racial minorities.

The third approach is to resist culture-specific references altogether and to search instead for appeals that transcend cultures. An appeal based on preserving the planet for the next generation, an appeal to the common interest in peace, or an appeal based on the beauty and wonder of nature may well transcend the limits of any particular culture.[6] In a speech in 1963, President Kennedy illustrated this approach. After speaking about the need to recognize diversity among nations and cultures, he noted that all people hold certain values in common:

> For in the final analysis, our most basic common link is that we all inhabit this small planet. We all breathe the same air. We all cherish our children's future. And we are all mortal.

Understanding Audience Psychology

The final set of audience characteristics relate to psychology. These have to do with the ways people understand and respond to the messages they hear.

Selective Exposure and Selective Attention

Each day, an infinite number of potential communication stimuli are available to us. We can converse with anyone we meet and can overhear the conversations of others; we can call or write to each other; we can read newspapers, magazines, and books; we can listen to the radio or watch television; we can see films or videos; we can attend speeches, listen to lectures on tape, hear sermons, or join group discussions. And while we're busy doing all this, our computers can log on to the Internet to exchange mail and collect any information we specify.

Even if we did nothing else except engage in communication, there is clearly too much for any of us to do. How do we choose which speeches to hear, which magazines to read, which television programs to watch, and which Web sites to visit? In short, how do we select the communications to which we will expose ourselves?

Selective exposure is the concept that our communication choices are not random; rather, we are inclined to expose ourselves to messages that are important to us personally and that are consistent with what we already believe. Few of us seek out messages that we do not think will be useful or pertinent to us; nor do we listen to speeches other than entertainment speeches merely for the pleasure of hearing them. And very few of us relish an attack on what we believe. Instead, we read magazines, listen to speakers, and make friends whose views are similar to our own.

Although selective exposure governs which messages we will seek out, sometimes audience members are not given a choice. Your classmates, for instance, are captive listeners who do not have the option of not hearing you, even if you disagree with them. But both captive and voluntary audiences can exercise a second level of control over potential communications. They are selective about whether or not to focus intently on a message, to follow it, to absorb it, and to take it seriously. These choices, sometimes made unconsciously, are called **selective attention.**

As we discussed in Chapter 2, it takes effort and energy to listen carefully and critically to a speech. Listeners' minds tend to wander—to events of the day, people they want to see, things they need to do, problems they hope to solve. Making the effort to listen requires motivation, and the speaker can help to supply that for the audience.

Student speaker Scott Poggi overlooked this opportunity when he decided to develop a speech based on his own special interests. On weekends, Scott worked as a stagehand for a production company, and his speech demonstrated his expertise in the subject. He told his classmates all about the backstage area, introducing them to the light designer, the head light technician, and the light crew; mentioning the "FOH" (footlights and overheads), the electrics, and the cyclorama; telling them about the necessity of "testing and gelling the lights"; introducing them to the sound crew and their equipment; and finally describing the stage manager's many duties. By the time Scott finished, many in the audience were half asleep. Not only did

selective exposure
A tendency to expose oneself to messages that are important personally and that are consistent with what one already believes.

selective attention
Conscious or unconscious choice about whether or not to focus intently on a speech, absorb and process its contents, and take it seriously.

he provide too much technical information without explaining it (classmates still had to ask, "What is an 'FOH,' and how do you 'gel' a light?"); but he also never gave the audience any reason for wanting to know this information in the first place. Better audience analysis might have shown Scott that he would have to motivate listeners to help them pay attention.

The speaker can motivate the audience in at least three ways:

1. Make the message personally important to listeners.
2. Make the message stand out.
3. Make the message easy to follow.

Make the Message Personally Important to Listeners. Listeners are better motivated to pay attention if the speech is personally meaningful and important to them, affects them, offers new information and insights they haven't considered, solves puzzles or paradoxes, or tells a story or makes a comparison with something they already know. When you plan the strategy for your speech, focus on making it clear how your message relates to audience members personally. In effect, you are saying, "This concerns you. Sit up and take notice."

To apply these general principles, you might introduce your speech with an example that listeners will recognize or a story that describes an experience they might have had. Or you might translate statistics or abstract ideas into personal terms, as in the statement "The percentage of people wrongly sentenced to death is so large that if all of us in this room were facing capital punishment, half of us would be taken off death row upon appeal." You might even announce explicitly that listeners will benefit from your speech: "I'm going to tell you how you can get better grades in every course."

Make the Message Stand Out. The message may stand out because of a contrast between what the speaker is expected to say and what he or she actually says. Listeners will sit up and take notice if a student suggests that professors do not assign enough work, if an athlete maintains that physical fitness is unimportant, or if a known advocate of gender equality speaks in favor of some gender-based distinctions. Alternatively, the contrast might be between the speaker and other elements in the situation. If you were to be the fifth speaker after four classmates had all discussed similar topics in the same way, you might deliberately modify your speech to do something different. Or the contrast might be within the speech itself, such as changes in pitch, volume, or rate of delivery.

A word of caution is necessary regarding the use of contrast. Any contrast effect you use should be closely related to the purpose of your speech; contrast for its own sake draws attention to itself and distracts from the message. Avoid attention-getting gimmicks, whether in the introduction or anywhere else in the speech. Even if you succeed in getting attention, the audience will remember the trick, not your message.

Make the Message Easy to Follow. Paying careful attention is work for listeners. The more you do to minimize their task and to motivate them to make the effort, the more likely it is that they will be attentive.[7]

Speakers can do several things to make their message easier to follow:

- Strategically plan the organization of the speech in a way that makes your thesis and overall argument clear to listeners.

When this father of one of the 1999 Columbine school shooting victims brought his slain son's shoes to the rally where he spoke at the steps of the state capitol building, he was able to make his point about gun control stand out clearly to his listeners.

- State your main ideas explicitly so that listeners can easily identify them.
- Speak at a rate that sustains listeners' interest but is not so rapid that they have to struggle to keep up with you.
- Repeat your main ideas and key points, signaling to the audience that these are important.
- Use pauses to mark the transitions in the speech.
- Summarize your thesis and main ideas memorably.

Perception

An audience is asked not only to listen carefully to a speech but also to *interpret* it as the speaker intends. **Perception** is the particular interpretation or understanding that a listener gets from a speech. When listeners decide what a speech "means," they are perceiving it in a particular way. Unfortunately, a speaker cannot ensure that the audience perceives the meaning of the speech in the same way that the speaker does. Even individual ideas may be interpreted differently by speaker and audience.

Any message is open to different interpretations and can result in different perceptions. Suppose, for example, that early in an election year, the current president predicts economic growth over the next several months. Should you interpret that message as economic forecasting, or as a political appeal designed to win votes, or as wishful thinking by a candidate who does not really understand the economy? Or is it all of these? Clearly, speakers need to understand how most listeners perceive things.

Recall that perception, like attention, is selective; we interpret messages in ways that render them simple, stable, and consistent with our expectations. Complex or conflicting messages are simplified; qualifying statements and subtle distinctions may be lost. The following examples of how people perceive messages selectively are generalizations and obviously do not apply in every case. But they are based on research, and they can help

perception
The interpretation or understanding given to a speech; the meaning it has for a listener.

Adapting to Your Audience

The Situation

Over the last few months, your town has seen a rise in accidents related to underage drinking. Your local government is starting a campaign to crack down on underage drinking. You have decided that you want to support this cause and volunteer your time. Your first job is to speak to a group of students at the local college about this community problem.

Making Choices

1. How might you determine your audience's likely reaction to your message?

2. If you find that some of your audience members are hostile to your message, what strategies can you utilize to reduce the hostility of your audience and to gain their support and acceptance?

What If . . .

How would your choice of strategies vary if you were speaking to the following audiences who likely would be more supportive of your message from the start?

1. The local campus administration

2. The general audience at the next town meeting

3. The families of students who have been involved in drinking-related accidents

you plan your speech. If applied *too* rigidly, however, they can result in stereotyping, which speakers should always avoid.

1. People tend to view their experiences as structured, stable, and meaningful rather than random, chaotic, or pointless. Seeking order, listeners are predisposed to accept any pattern that the speaker can offer to explain seemingly unconnected facts.

2. People tend to view events not as accidental but as having causes; they also tend to simplify the web of causal connections and sometimes even seek a single cause to explain complex effects. Given that the brevity of a speech also leads to simplification, speakers must be careful not to allow listeners to oversimplify the relationships among events.

3. People tend to view individuals as being responsible for their own actions and to assume that actions reflect a person's intentions.

4. People tend to view others as being basically like themselves. When a speaker discusses personal experiences, listeners often assume that the speaker thought and acted just as they would have in the same circumstances. And if the audience is heterogeneous, different kinds of listeners may perceive the speaker differently.

5. People tend to interpret things in the way that their reference groups do. The desire to fit in and to be accepted by important peers may cause some people to accept the group's perception as their own—without even being aware that they are doing it.

6. People tend to perceive messages within the framework of familiar categories, even at the risk of distorting the message. For example, if someone

believes that Democrats generally favor government intervention in the economy and that Republicans do not, that person is likely to perceive any pro-Democratic message as calling for government involvement in the economy.

Although the tendency of listeners to perceive selectively can distort the speaker's message, knowing about selective perception can help the speaker to plan the speech so that it will be interpreted as desired. Selective exposure, attention, and perception are characteristic of almost all listeners. Whenever you plan a speech, design strategies to overcome these tendencies.

Strategies for Analyzing the Audience

Knowing that audience analysis is so important to your success as a speaker, how do you go about it? Various methods are available, ranging from the highly formal to the frankly speculative.

Formal Methods

Companies developing a new product typically engage in market research. They conduct surveys to learn the needs and desires of consumers (their "audience"); they ask the target group to select adjectives to describe a concept or product; they may convene small discussion groups (focus groups) to probe people's feelings about a product. In principle, methods like these are available to speakers, too, and such formal analysis often is used in large-scale efforts such as a political campaign. Focus groups might also be used in a public speaking class if several speeches were going to focus on the same subject. But for most speeches this approach is impractical. You will have neither the time nor the resources to conduct formal surveys or in-depth interviews of classmates in preparation for a speech. Instead, a general audience survey like the one in Figure 3.2 can be invaluable. Your instructor might ask the class to complete such a survey and then might make the results available to everyone.

Informal Methods

Even if you can't conduct a formal audience survey, you still can learn quite a bit about your listeners. Here are some ideas:

1. Think back to what classmates said about themselves in their introductory speeches. They may have given you clues about their interests, their political leanings, their attitudes toward higher education, their family backgrounds, and other key aspects of audience culture.

2. In preparing to speak to an unfamiliar audience, ask the host or moderator some questions ahead of time. You may be able to find out which topics most interest audience members, who else was invited to speak to them recently, how attentive they are, and perhaps what their motives are for coming together to hear you.

3. If you know the demographic composition of your audience—its size, its average age, and the occupation of most members, for instance—interview people who represent this mix of variables. Although talking with just a few

Figure 3.2
Audience survey.

Audience Survey

Age _____   Gender _____   Year of Graduation _____

Home town _____

High school attended: Public   Private

Parents' occupation(s) _____

Taking course as: Requirement   Elective

Politically, I would describe myself as:

strongly	moderately	middle of	moderately	strongly
conservative	conservative	the road	liberal	liberal

In general, where do you fall along the following scale:

_____

Prefer the familiar   Prefer the new

What three adjectives most accurately describe you?

_____

What three adjectives would you most like to describe you?

_____

I regard college primarily as a time for:

_____

What are the three most pressing problems confronting you in the next five years?

_____

What are the three most pressing problems confronting the country or the world in the next five years?

_____

[NOTE: The survey might well contain additional questions.]

people is not a scientific sample, you may still get clues about the interests, beliefs, and values of the kind of people who will be in your audience.

4. If you know other speakers who have addressed an audience like the one you will face, talk with them ahead of time to learn what they encountered and what they think your audience will be like.

5. If you know which newspapers or magazines your listeners are likely to read, examine some recent copies before you speak. Besides getting a sense of what interests your listeners, you may locate allusions that will be especially meaningful to them.

6. Sometimes library research can help you analyze an audience. In Chapter 5, you will learn how to investigate your topic, and the same methods can help you investigate your audience. For example, you can find recent periodicals with surveys about the political attitudes of college students, or polls showing how older Americans feel about health care, or articles about how gender differences influence how people think or feel.

7.   Don't overlook the most obvious method of audience analysis: direct observation. As your listeners assemble, size them up. About how many people are there? Are they all about the same age? What is the ratio of men to women? How are they dressed? Are they interacting or sitting apart? Do they seem enthusiastic? Such questions cannot give you perfect information about the audience, because they are superficial first impressions, but they often provide valuable insights that allow you to adapt your message appropriately and effectively.

Simplifying Devices

Although it seems desirable to get all the information you can about an audience, having *complete* knowledge is impossible. After all, audiences are often composed of people who are strangers both to each other and to the speaker. Their common interest in the speech may be all that brought them together, and the speaker often does not know who the specific audience members are.

In these respects, speaking in the classroom is atypical. You and your classmates get to know quite a bit about each other by giving and hearing multiple speeches. You may even have conducted formal audience analysis through a survey like the one in Figure 3.2. Given this depth of information, it is not very difficult to craft speeches that recognize the audience's position. Outside the classroom, however, detailed audience analysis is much more difficult, and many speakers employ simplifying devices to make the task easier.

Focus on the General Public. For example you might imagine your specific audience as the **general public**—listeners who share the characteristics of people in general, such as common sense, self-interest, sensitivity to others, and enthusiasm for a good story. The general public might be imagined as the readership of *Time* or some other mass-circulation magazine. In addition, this audience can be assumed to share whatever specific concerns or beliefs are reported in recent surveys of the population. Such surveys may show that people generally regard inflation as a serious problem, or that they oppose U.S. military involvement in other lands, or that they favor tax cuts to stimulate the economy. Not every member of any specific audience will share all these beliefs and values, of course; but the general public may be a reasonable substitute for the specific audience when you lack more precise information.

Focus on Audience Roles or Topic Fields. Another way to simplify audience analysis is to focus on the particular roles that you think your listeners play or on a particular field in which to place your topic. As we have seen, everyone occupies many different roles in society. A person may simultaneously be a parent, child, sibling, student, classmate, employee, coworker, manager, and so on. Each such role may involve basic values and beliefs that are

general public
Listeners who share the characteristics of people in general.

not as relevant to the other roles the person occupies. For instance, the standard of efficient communication that a woman uses at work is not the same standard that she uses as a wife or mother at home.

Similarly, we may think of speech topics as representing different **fields,** or subject-matter areas with different norms and assumptions. For example, most of us regard religion, politics, science, and art as distinct fields. We would not expect an audience to listen to a political speech with the same standards in mind that they would use in assessing a religious discourse. Nor would we expect science and art to evoke the same standards of quality.

In using roles or fields to simplify audience analysis, you should emphasize the particular role or field that seems most relevant to your speech. When addressing an audience at your church, for example, focus on members' moral and religious commitments. When speaking at a rally for student government candidates, focus on the common field of campus politics rather than on the many other topics about which listeners might disagree. And when giving a speech to the local Parents and Teachers Association, focus on listeners' common concerns for children rather than on their highly diverse concerns as public employees and taxpayers, men and women, and people of different ages.

In using simplifying devices to analyze an audience, keep in mind that generalizations often lead to stereotyping. Whether your assumptions about listeners' shared characteristics are true or not, you also want to show sensitivity to the many differences among audience members.

Critical Appraisal

Much of the information you have gained from these methods of audience analysis is inexact, even though you have done your best. For this reason you need to think critically about what you have learned. Ask yourself:

- How reliable, precise, and authoritative is your information about the audience? If the information seems questionable, can you devise strategies that compensate for error?
- Can you craft the speech so that it will be appropriate for listeners who are knowledgeable about the topic and yet can be modified easily if listeners know less than you thought?
- Is your information about the audience really based on analysis, or might you be jumping to conclusions or relying on stereotypes?
- How much can you adapt to your audience without sacrificing your own beliefs and values?

One way to avoid jumping to conclusions is to view your listeners as representative of the **universal audience**—an imaginary audience made up of all reasonable people. No such audience exists, of course. The speaker constructs this image of an audience that accepts only those beliefs and values that no reasonable person would doubt.[8] Precisely because people are different, this is such a rigorous test that it could probably never be achieved. Yet it provides a norm or standard against which to assess your speech. It should prevent you from simply appealing to what you think are the audience's prejudices or indulging in false stereotypes.

You also want to guard against **pandering** to the supposed beliefs of your listeners and losing track of your own. One test is to ask whether your

fields
Subject-matter areas with distinct norms or assumptions.

universal audience
An imaginary audience made up of all reasonable people.

pandering
Saying whatever will please an audience even if it is not what the speaker really believes.

basic message to an audience that disagrees with some of your beliefs is consistent with what you might say to people who believe exactly as you do. Obviously, there will be *some* differences, because audiences are different, but the messages should not be contradictory. A speaker who is thought to be willing to say anything just in order to please an audience is not likely to be believed. During the 2000 presidential campaign, Texas Governor George W. Bush asserted that his opponent, Vice President Al Gore, was such a person. Even Abraham Lincoln was accused of pandering to his audiences, speaking differently to committed antislavery listeners in northern Illinois than to more moderate audiences in the southern part of the state. Although there were obvious differences in tone and emphasis, Lincoln insisted that his basic message was the same. You should be able to reach the same conclusion about your speech.

Thinking critically about your audience analysis will also promote your strategic planning. It will help you determine what you know that is useful to your speech and what questions remain unanswered. Although your knowledge of the audience will never be complete, critical thinking will help you decide whether you can afford to take chances and make guesses about the audience. And in planning strategies for presenting the speech, critical thinking will show you where you need to be especially sensitive to audience reactions.

Audience analysis is more an art than a science. As with every other aspect of public speaking, however, critical thinking and strategic planning will improve your information about the audience and will make your communication more effective.

Checklist 3.1 How To Do Audience Analysis

1. **Formal methods**
   - Surveys
   - Focus groups
2. **Informal methods**
   - Prior knowledge of audience members
   - Interviewing
     The host or moderator
     People similar to the audience members
     Others who have spoken to similar audiences
   - Reading materials that the audience probably reads
   - Library research about the audience
   - Direct observation of audience members
3. **Simplifying devices**
   - Focus on the general public
   - Focus on specific audience roles or topic fields
4. **Critical appraisal**
   - What do you know? How reliable is the information?
   - What gaps remain? How important is it to fill them?
   - Are you relying on stereotypes or jumping to conclusions?
   - Would the speech satisfy a universal audience? Does it avoid pandering to a specific audience?

Analyzing Your Own *Ethos*

In Chapter 1, we introduced the concept of *ethos*, the character that an audience attributes to a speaker. In thinking about your audience, you also want to think about how its members are likely to characterize you.

To begin with, you should determine similarities and differences between you and the audience with respect to demographics, cultures, and psychology. Are you older or younger than most of your listeners? Is your ethnic, cultural, or economic background different? Are your personal interests similar to theirs? Do you have different general orientations toward change? If listeners judge you to be very different from themselves, they may be less likely to respond positively to your message. You will want to plan the speech so that you either minimize perceptions of difference when that is appropriate or acknowledge and compensate for differences when that is desirable.

Knowing what you know about yourself and having thought about the similarities and differences between you and your listeners, consider how the audience members are likely to perceive you. Will they see you as knowledgeable and competent or as arrogant and condescending? In the first case, you can expect listeners to welcome your efforts to share information and ideas; in the second case, expect them to resent your seeming to tell them what to do.

Critical self-assessment should point you to modifications that might improve your *ethos*. Sometimes, minor changes will do the trick. Something as slight as different wording—"We all need to remind ourselves" rather than "I want to remind you," for instance—may help build a sense of community between you and your listeners rather than emphasize your superiority and their dependence. Attention to this aspect of *ethos* is especially important when your audience is culturally diverse. What seems like a straightforward presentation to listeners from a single cultural background may be seen as patronizing to listeners whose backgrounds are different.

You also should think critically about your own beliefs and values. It is tempting to assume that they are self-evidently correct and hence should be accepted by everyone. But that assumption may misfire; if audience members question or reject your values, they may also question or reject your message. Although *you* may believe that our society offers economic opportunities to all, listeners who have recently lost their jobs, are struggling to make ends meet, or are victims of discrimination will probably see things very differently. If you take your personal values for granted in this situation, your speech will fail. The audience will judge you to be

---

WWW. Using the Internet

The Audience as a Constraint

Listen to and/or read one of the following speeches for critical analysis:

- Queen Elizabeth II addressing a worldwide audience on the death of Diana, Princess of Wales. Go to **http://archive.abcnews.go.com/sections/world/diana904/index.html/**, provided by ABC News.
- Secretary-General Kofi Annan, speaking at Georgetown University in Washington, D.C., on February 23, 1999, about "The Future of United Nations Peacekeeping." Go to **http://www.un.org/Overview/SG/sg990223.html**.
- Gunter Grass, receiving the Nobel Prize in literature on December 7, 1999, before the Swedish Academy. Go to **http://www.nobel.se/literature/laureates/1999/lecture-e.html**.
- Kate Michelman, president of the National Abortion and Reproductive Rights Action League, speaking before the 1996 Democratic National Convention. Go to **http://gos.sbc.edu/m/michelman4.html**.

To evaluate how the makeup of the audience was a constraint that influenced what the speaker said, consider some of the following:

- How did the speaker address the listeners as a particular audience?
- How did the speaker address the listeners as part of a universal audience?
- Form a judgment as to how well you think the speaker adapted to the audience.

---

naive, if not misguided, and you will think them ungrateful or unmotivated.

Similarly, you may find that you and your audience have different role models, different common knowledge, and different life-shaping experiences. On each of these dimensions, it is important to think critically about yourself and about how the audience is likely to perceive you. Then you can determine whether you want to make any adjustments in how you present yourself. As always, the goal is to remain true to yourself while also taking the audience's characteristics into consideration.

Adjustments in these areas are not so difficult to make, because the speaker controls much of the behavior by which an audience assesses *ethos*. After all, you can choose whether or not to establish eye contact, whether to smile or frown, whether to pause at the podium before returning to your seat, and so on. You decide which supporting materials to use, how to organize them, and which words and gestures to convey. All these aspects of presentation are under your control, and you can use them to influence how the audience judges you.

You want listeners' assessments of your *ethos* to be positive, and not only because you like to have others think well of you. Your concern goes back to the belief, first articulated by Aristotle, that a speaker's apparent character may well be the most important resource to use in persuasion. How listeners perceive your *ethos* will affect what they think about your speech.

Strategies for Speaking to Diverse Audiences

Respecting Diversity Through Analyzing Your Audience

Audiences are never completely heterogeneous. Careful analysis will help you to identify how the audience is diverse. Then these strategies will help you to plan your speech with audience diversity in mind.

1. Avoid stereotyping.
2. Consider both the distinctive culture of a particular audience and the multiple cultures of audience members.
3. Pay attention to cultural facts.
4. Employ examples from different cultures to appeal to your audience.
5. Consider using universal appeals that transcend cultures.

Summary

In this chapter, we examined ways to analyze an audience in order to develop a sense of how listeners are likely to approach your message. The most important dimensions of audience analysis are demographics, culture, and psychology.

Demographic variables that affect an audience include size, heterogeneity, whether listeners are captive or voluntary, and composition in terms of age, gender, occupation, religion, economic status, and similar criteria. The assumption is that differences in these dimensions may result in different patterns of thought and action.

Audience cultures include elements that are more subjective. One of these is interest, both the listeners' self-interest and the topics that they find personally interesting. Other cultural factors include listeners' beliefs and values, their prior level of understanding about the topic, their common knowledge and experiences, and their roles and reference groups. Cultural diversity characterizes many audiences today, and speakers need to be sensitive to how listeners from different cultures might react to a speech.

Audience psychology involves matters of exposure, attention, and perception—all of which listeners do selectively. Because the audience's presence and attention are not guaranteed, you must make every effort to motivate the audience to listen. You should try to make your message personally relevant and important to listeners, to make your message stand out, and to make your message easy to follow. Even if the presence and attention of an audience are achieved, you must design the speech in ways that discourage distortion of the message through selective perception.

As important as audience analysis is, procedures for doing it are usually inexact. Large-scale campaigns use surveys, focus groups, and other research techniques. But audience analysis is less precise in most situations. You can read newspapers or magazines that your audience is likely to read, interview people who represent the makeup of your audience, talk with other speakers about what to expect, do library research about your audience, and observe the audience as it assembles. You also can simplify your analysis by thinking of the audience as the general public or by focusing on listeners' roles and specialized fields. Because audience analysis is imprecise, you need to think critically about your information and to plan strategies that let you adjust your message effectively.

The final step in audience analysis is to analyze yourself to determine how listeners are likely to judge your *ethos*. Consider any significant similarities and differences between you and your listeners that may affect how they will perceive you. Then make any adjustments that might improve their perceptions of your character, but remain true to yourself. The fact that you control much of the behavior that influences judgments of *ethos* is a strong reason to undertake careful self-analysis.

Discussion Questions

1. In preparing a speech about the dangers of smoking, how might your strategies differ for an audience of fourth-graders, an audience of college students, and an audience from a retirement community? Would you make different appeals to an audience of men and an audience of women? What changes would you make in presenting this speech to an audience of Caucasians and to an audience of Mexican Americans? How might these modifications draw on stereotypes that could offend your listeners?

2. Has culture been enriched or impoverished by the fact that its basic store of allusions often comes from popular culture rather than, as in

the nineteenth century, from classic literature and the Bible? Does this difference really matter? Why or why not?

3. In 1997, Republicans in Congress proposed to overhaul the Internal Revenue Service. President Clinton first opposed this plan but changed his mind when he realized it would pass. He said that alterations in the proposal now made it possible for him to support it. In what way did Clinton use his audience's beliefs and values to reach his goal? Do you believe that this was an honest presentation of his beliefs, a strategic appeal to the audience, or both?

4. Identify some universal values that you could use in a speech to a diverse audience. Challenge your most fundamental beliefs as you and your classmates try to determine whether or not the values truly are universal.

Activities

1. In one page, explain how you would use the strategies of making the message personally important to listeners, making the message stand out, and making the message easy to follow to motivate your audience to pay attention to the message in your next speech. In what ways are you planning to appeal to the self-interest and personal interest of your audience?

2. Complete the audience survey in Figure 3.2, make copies of your answers for your classmates, and exchange them so that each person in the class has a booklet of questionnaire responses. Use this booklet to make a list of the commonalities and differences among audience members that you are likely to encounter when presenting a speech in this class.

3. As a follow-up to activity 2, compare your questionnaire answers to those of your classmates. In what ways are you similar to your audience members? In what ways are you different? How will this affect how your audience perceives you? After critically analyzing your own *ethos*, create a short speech designed to develop a positive *ethos* for you as a spokesperson for a particular topic.

4. Using more informal modes of audience analysis, answer the following questions:
   a. What beliefs and values do your classmates hold regarding the topic you have chosen for your next speech?
   b. What do your classmates know about your topic?
   c. What common experiences do you and classmates share with regard to this topic?
   After answering these questions, write a short essay explaining the specific ways that you plan to use this information in developing strategies to maximize attention and to help the audience perceive your message in a way that advances your goal.

5. Identify several prominent public figures in entertainment, business, sports, politics, and the arts. For each figure, characterize the person's *ethos* and then identify the grounds on which you based your judgment.

1. Joshua Meyrowitz makes the argument that traditional social differences between gender and age groups have been eroded in postmodern culture by the backstage information provided through television. See *No Sense of Place: The Impact of Electronic Media on Social Behavior*, Oxford, England: Oxford Univ. Press, 1985.

2. See E. D. Hirsch, Jr., *Cultural Literacy*, Boston: Houghton Mifflin, 1987.

3. Cultural differences may even influence expectations about the form and purpose of a speech. See Alessandro Duranti, "Oratory," *International Encyclopedia of Communications*, New York: Oxford Univ. Press, 1989, vol. 3, pp. 234–236. Components of *ethos* are also understood differently in different cultures. See, for example, Masami Nishishiba and L. David Ritchie, "The Concept of Trustworthiness: A Cross-Cultural Comparison Between Japanese and U.S. Business People," *Journal of Applied Communication Research* 28 (November 2000): 347–367.

4. To get an idea of the different words and phrases used in regional dialects, see Eric Partridge, *A Dictionary of Slang and Unconventional English: Colloquialisms and Catch-Phrases, Solecisms and Catachreses, Nicknames, and Vulgarisms*, New York: Macmillan, 1984.

5. To gather examples that include the concerns of different cultural groups, you might want to examine some speeches created by and directed toward those different cultural groups. One compilation of culturally diverse speeches is *American Public Discourse: A Multicultural Perspective*, ed. Ronald K. Burke, Lanham, Md.: University Press of America, 1992.

6. Michael Osborn has written about how language is often used to appeal to universal themes. See "The Evolution of the Archetypal Sea in Rhetoric and Poetic," *Quarterly Journal of Speech* 63 (December 1977): 347–363.

7. Another list of guidelines for overcoming selective attention can be found in Howard W. Runkel, "How to Select Material That Will Hold Attention," *Communication Quarterly* 8 (September 1960): 13–14.

8. The concept of a universal audience is discussed in more detail by Chaim Perelman in *The Realm of Rhetoric*, translated by William Kluback, Notre Dame, Ind.: Univ. of Notre Dame Press, 1982.

Chapter Four

Choosing a Topic and Developing a Strategy

In this chapter, we will:

- Consider when it is appropriate for you to choose the topic of your speech and when the choice is beyond your control.

- Learn how the audience, the occasion, the speaker, and the speech together determine the rhetorical situation.

- Identify the characteristics of a good topic and the steps involved in choosing a good topic.

- Examine how to determine the specific purpose of a speech and how to identify the constraints and the opportunities you face.

- Explore what is meant by strategic planning in preparing a speech and how your constraints and opportunities can be used to achieve your purpose.

- Discover how to formulate statements of the specific purpose and thesis of your speech and how these statements will influence other strategic decisions.

- Determine how to analyze your thesis to figure out which issues you need to discuss and which ideas need support.

From your audience analysis, you know as much as you can about your listeners, and now you are ready to make the choices that will shape your speech. Since ancient times, a speaker's choices and activities have been grouped under five major headings:

- **Invention** is the generation of materials for the speech. You produce (or "invent," to use the classical term) these materials through a combination of analysis, research, and judgment. You begin by identifying what *could* go into the speech, then you conduct research to determine what ideas are supportable, and then you select the most effective materials for your purpose and audience.
- **Arrangement** is the structuring of ideas and materials in the speech. This includes the organization of materials for each main idea, the ordering and connecting of main ideas within the body of the speech, and the overall structure of the introduction, the body, and the conclusion.
- **Style** is the distinctive character that may make a speech easily recognizable or memorable. Style is achieved primarily through language, and it reflects the speaker's awareness of how language can be used both to "show" and to "tell"—both to evoke emotions and to convey descriptive meaning.
- **Delivery** is the presentation of the speech. Whereas the preceding activities are performed by the speaker alone, delivery involves actually sharing the message with the audience. Skillful delivery involves the effective use of voice, gesture, facial expression, physical movement, and visual aids.
- **Memory** was an extremely important category of skills at a time when most speeches were memorized. Today, however, most speakers use either **extemporaneous presentation** (referring to an outline) or **manuscript presentation** (reading a written script). Even so, some dimensions of memory are still very important—for example, keeping track of your main ideas, phrasing ideas so that listeners will remember them, and precisely wording an effective introduction and conclusion. Memory skills also are critical in rehearsing your speech mentally and in practicing it aloud before presentation.

In this chapter and the next two, we will address matters of invention. Then, in Parts 3 and 4, we will study the skills of arrangement, style, and delivery. Although no chapter focuses solely on memory skills, those concerns will surface throughout our study.

All your decisions as a speaker should be made *strategically,* that is, with a view to what will best achieve your purpose. But first you need to know what your purpose is; and to decide that, you need to know what your **topic** is.

For many students, deciding what to talk about is the hardest part of a speech assignment. Fortunately, when you speak outside the classroom, elements in the situation will often make that decision for you. Suppose, for example, that you are committed to a specific public issue, such as protecting the ozone layer against further depletion. The issue itself defines your topic, and *personal commitment* determines why it is important for you to speak. Or your *experience and knowledge* may lead to an invitation to speak about a specific topic. If you are an expert on bicycle safety, for example, a group of amateur cyclists might invite you to speak about safety tips. If you

invention
The generation of materials for a speech.

arrangement
The structuring of materials within the main ideas, the organization of main ideas within the body of the speech, and the overall structure of introduction, body, and conclusion.

style
The distinctive character that may make a speech recognizable or memorable.

delivery
The presentation of the speech to an audience.

memory
Mental recall of the key ideas and the basic structure of the speech.

extemporaneous presentation
A mode of delivery in which the speech is planned and structured carefully but a specific text is not written in advance nor memorized.

manuscript presentation
A mode of delivery in which the speaker reads aloud the prepared text of the speech.

topic
The subject area of the speech.

instead discussed U.S. foreign policy, or the pleasures of sailing, or the need for reform in the university, you would not be meeting your responsibility to the audience.

Sometimes the *occasion* will determine your choice of topic. Many speeches are delivered on ceremonial occasions. If you are accepting an award, the award and what it represents will decide your topic. If you are delivering a eulogy, the achievements of the person who died become the subject of the speech. If you are roasting a coworker who is about to retire, your subject matter will be humorous traits or events involving that person.

Sometimes, a classroom speaking *assignment* will specify the topic. More typically, the choice of topic will be left to you, with the understanding that you will address an audience of people your age, in your school. Selecting a topic is an important step in creating a speech, and you need practice in matching your topic to the situation. In addition, you probably will be more effective if you talk about something that interests you rather than an assigned topic that has been chosen by someone else.[1] In the classroom, it is particularly important that you size up the situation and then stand up for what interests you, for what you believe and can share with others.

Outside of class, the primary occasion when you will have freedom in choosing your topic occurs when the audience is interested in hearing *you*, almost regardless of what you have to say. Such an open-ended invitation may arise out of respect for your achievements, interest in your experiences, curiosity about your personality or general approach, or the desire to learn whatever is on your mind.

Understanding the Rhetorical Situation

Whether your topic is determined by the occasion, assigned by your host, or selected by you, you will not begin in a vacuum. Your speech will be influenced by the **rhetorical situation** to which it responds. We introduced this concept in Chapter 1; now it is time to explore it in much more detail. No two speeches are exactly the same, because the rhetorical situations are not identical. Moreover, your speech not only responds to the situation but also modifies it. In doing that, you face opportunities as well as constraints. Your goal is to devise a **strategy**—a plan of action—that will respond to the constraints and take advantage of the opportunities.

The following example illustrates the double-sided nature of the rhetorical situation. On September 11, 2001, the nation watched in horror as two commercial airplanes crashed into the World Trade Center in New York City. A third plane crashed into the Pentagon in Washington, D.C. A fourth plane, thought to be headed for another national landmark, crashed in a field in Pennsylvania, following heroic efforts by the passengers to thwart the hijackers' plans. Thousands of lives were lost in the crashes and the destruction of the twin towers of the World Trade Center, from office personnel to rescue workers. This was the single deadliest act of terrorism on American soil in history. Americans needed to know what their government was doing to protect them.

This context defined a rhetorical situation. The audience was the American people, who needed to be consoled and protected. The occasion was one of collective grief, uncertainty, and fear. In times of national crisis,

rhetorical situation
A situation in which there are challenges or needs that can be met through effective messages.

strategy
A plan of action to achieve stated goals.

President George W. Bush addresses a joint session of Congress and the nation after the terrorist attack on the World Trade Center on September 11, 2001. How would you describe this specific rhetorical situation? What needs were posed by the audience, occasion, speaker, and speech?

people look to the president for leadership. President George W. Bush was still in his first year of office after the contested vote count of the 2000 election. He needed to prove that he could handle the crisis and lead the nation.

On the evening of September 20, 2001, President Bush spoke to a joint session of Congress and to the nation. His speech consisted of both the prepared text and its oral presentation by the President. His text, prepared by lead speechwriter Michael Gerson and other staff members, began responding to the situation by honoring those who had died in the terrorist attacks. He said that the courage of those who died spoke for the strong "state of the union." At the same time, the speech set forth plans to calm fears and prevent further attacks. President Bush set out his new foreign policy to combat terrorism around the world and also announced a new administrative position of coordinator of homeland security to strengthen domestic defenses.

The speech responded to the immediate situation of the terrorist attacks and created a new situation of a war on terrorism, refocusing Americans' attention from fear, grief, and mourning to indignation, resolve, and unity. (You can read the text of this speech in Appendix B.) In short, although President Bush was *constrained* by the needs to provide meaning, reassurance, and focus, he made the choice to characterize the situation as a war on terrorism, and by doing so he took advantage of an *opportunity*. Every rhetorical situation consists of a mix of constraints and opportunities.

Similarly, when you give a speech in class, your rhetorical situation is influenced by the audience and by the values its members hold. These are constraints within which you must work. At the same time, you have the opportunity to modify listeners' beliefs and values by what you say. You want to understand the constraints and the opportunities in a rhetorical situation so that you can use both to achieve your purpose.

As we noted in Chapter 1, the key elements that create the rhetorical situation for any speech are the audience, the occasion, the speaker, and the speech itself. Each element warrants further brief discussion now.

The Audience

Unlike a poem or a novel, a speech is presented for a specific audience, and its success in achieving its goals depends on the reactions of those listeners. This is why audience analysis, discussed in Chapter 3, is so important. The audience helps to create the rhetorical situation by affecting, among other things, your choice of what to emphasize in the speech, what level of knowledge to assume, how to organize the speech, and what your specific purpose will be.

Most speakers, most of the time, want to present their ideas in ways that achieve **identification** with the audience; that is, they try to find common ground between what they know about the audience and what they want to say.[2] Without distorting their own message, they try to emphasize the elements that are most likely to strike a responsive chord among audience members. Thus, an African American speaker who is addressing a mostly white audience might emphasize their shared American dream.

Sometimes, though, a speaker may deliberately *avoid* identification with the audience and may even try to antagonize listeners. The same African American might point out that the American dream is *not* shared equally by all citizens. Such a tactic may suggest that the speaker is a person of high integrity who will not hold back punches simply to gain the audience's approval. Or the strategy may be intended to influence some other audience that is overhearing the speech.[3] Whether the goal is to identify or to criticize, however, knowledge of the audience is critical in assessing the rhetorical situation.

The Occasion

Some speech occasions are **ceremonial,** such as presenting or accepting an award, introducing someone, delivering a eulogy, or commemorating an event. Others are primarily **deliberative,** such as making an oral report, delivering a sales presentation, advocating a policy, or refuting another person's argument. Ceremonial speaking focuses on the present and is usually concerned with what is praiseworthy in the subject. Deliberative speaking focuses on the future and is usually concerned with what should be done.

Many occasions combine ceremonial and deliberative elements. For example, the manager of a firm that is losing money during a recession might speak to employees. The occasion is deliberative in that the manager informs workers about the company's financial circumstances, announces new policies, and seeks reactions to proposed changes; but the occasion is also ceremonial because the manager's presence demonstrates a personal interest in workers' well-being and because the speech provides reassurance and motivates workers to do their best.

Similarly, the president's State of the Union address is a ceremonial ritual prescribed by the Constitution of the United States. But, especially in recent years, it's the occasion when the president is expected to persuade

identification
Formation of common bonds between the speaker and the audience.

ceremonial
Speaking that focuses on the present and is usually concerned with praise.

deliberative
Speaking that focuses on the future and is usually concerned with what should be done.

the public to support and the Congress to enact the administration's legislative proposals. This expectation makes the State of the Union a deliberative occasion as well.

A third category of speech occasion, traditionally known as **forensic,** is concerned with rendering judgments about events in the past. Although this is the dominant form of speaking in courts of law, it plays only a small role in public speaking elsewhere.[4]

Each type of occasion raises certain expectations about what is appropriate behavior, and these expectations help to define the rhetorical situation. For example, if an engineer is presenting the features of a new product to the marketing group, everyone will be focused on the product's best features and how to make them more salable. The occasion will be deliberative. Unlike a ceremonial occasion, it will not emphasize good wishes or feelings about the product or the staff. And unlike a forensic occasion, it will not concentrate on the company's past sales performance with other products. Rather, the focus will be on how best to design the new product to achieve a strong sales record in the future.

The Speaker

The same speech delivered by different speakers can produce quite different reactions and effects. Your interest in the subject—as made evident through voice, delivery, and the vividness of your imagery—helps to determine how the audience will react to the speech. Your *ethos* affects whether or not listeners will pay attention and will regard you as believable. This is why we stressed the goal of developing a positive *ethos* in Chapter 1 and why audience analysis, detailed in Chapter 3, includes the important step of analyzing your own *ethos*.

Fortunately, many of the skills that enable speakers to contribute positively to a rhetorical situation can be learned. Previous public speaking experience will also affect your comfort level, and the ability to respond to audience feedback will make you more flexible in any rhetorical situation.

The Speech

Although we tend to think of the rhetorical situation as predating the speech, the message itself works to shape the situation. The length of the speech, the clarity of its structure, the variety of supporting materials used, the degree of formality, the extent to which the speech tells a story, and the degree to which it is adaptable in response to feedback—all will affect its power in the rhetorical situation. In general, a speech is more likely to contribute positively to the situation when its structural pattern is simple and clear, when it is engaging to the audience, when its approach is informal, and when it is adaptable during delivery.

forensic
Speaking that focuses on the past and is usually concerned with rendering judgment.

What Makes a Good Topic?

If the topic of your speech is dictated by the issue, occasion, or audience, it is easy to decide what will make a good topic: whatever is pertinent and appropriate to the situation. You talk about what you were asked to discuss or about what the issue or occasion seems to require.

But what should you talk about if you have complete freedom to select the topic? Figure 4.1 identifies some potential speech topics, and the following criteria will help you to decide whether the topic you have in mind is a good one. (As you read, you might want to apply these criteria to the topics listed in Figure 4.1.)

Importance to the Speaker. A good topic is one that matters to you. If you do not care about the subject, it will be very hard to make it interesting or important to the audience. Consider how the following three students used their personal interests to develop good speech topics:

- Melody Barron is a passionate volunteer for her school's blood drive. She used her public speaking opportunity to refute perceptions that blood banks were full after the donations that were made following the September 11 terrorist attacks. She wanted to convince her class to donate blood in the upcoming blood drive.
- Elisabeth Pinkerton was at a movie theater with friends when someone's cell phone began ringing during the show. This was not the first time this had happened. Elisabeth was appalled by this person's rudeness and lack of consideration for others. She used her speech class to share information about cell phone etiquette with her classmates.
- Phillip Marcus was angry. During a closed-book exam in a sociology class, he saw another student copying answers from a sheet of paper. Phillip had heard that cheating on exams had become a serious problem, but until now he had not seen such a blatant example. At first he was stunned by what he regarded as outrageous conduct; then he became upset that his work and the work of other honest students was devalued by this incident. He decided to give a speech in his public speaking class

Figure 4.1 Sample speech topics.

Public Issues	Personal Experience	Occasions
Stem cell research	Lifeguarding	Commencement
Gun control	Snowboarding	Death of friend
Video game violence	Sign language	Wedding
Northwest logging	Yoga	School election
Gay rights	Poetry writing	Presentation of award
Internet Privacy rights	International travel	Office party
Affirmative action	Volunteering at a homeless shelter	
Euthanasia	Digital filmmaking	
AIDS epidemic	Political campaigning	
Third World debt	Hot-air ballooning	
Dependence on fossil fuels	Tutoring	
Terrorism		

to make others aware of what was happening, to evoke in them similar feelings of anger, and to channel their emotions toward doing something about cheating. How Phillip chose his topic and developed his strategy will be seen throughout this chapter.

In speaking about a topic of personal interest, you must be careful that your own interest does not harden into bias. You must be able to discuss the subject impartially and must recognize the value of other people's points of view.

Interest to the Audience. Even though the topic matters to you, you still must gain the interest of the audience. Audiences will be interested if your topic provides new information they can use, if it offers a solution to a puzzle or problem that affects them, if it connects what is unfamiliar to what they know, or if it reports stories or experiences similar to their own. Phillip Marcus decided that his story of the student who was cheating on the exam would interest others and also would arouse their anger.

Keep in mind as well that an audience's strong interest in the topic potentially may lead to *mis*communication as a result of selective perception. For example, when a manager addresses employees to describe the company's new policy about personal telephone calls, the audience has a strong interest in the message because it clearly will affect them. But there is also a risk that the audience will feel threatened or will believe that the company has become less friendly. Thus, even when listeners are strongly interested in the topic, they may resist the message related to it. Their personal interest may actually weaken their ability to listen critically.

Worthy of Listeners' Time. A related criterion is that the topic should be something that listeners regard as worth hearing about. If the topic is frivolous or trivial, they may feel that they have wasted their time by listening to you, especially if they came voluntarily and could have been doing something else. Unless there is something unique about the approach, a topic such as "How to open a beer can" probably would not meet this test. This does not mean that your topic must be profound or deadly serious; lighthearted humor or new insights on familiar subjects can work very well in a speech. The question to keep in mind is whether the audience will feel that what you have had to say was worth their attention and time.

Appropriateness of Scope. A speaker has to cover the topic to an appropriate degree within the time available. A topic that includes a very large number of points that can be covered only superficially—for example, a five-minute analysis of U.S. foreign policy—should probably be avoided. Similarly, a very narrow topic that can be covered completely in a short time—such as a description of how to stop when skating in-line—is probably not a good choice either.

Even in a five-minute speech, you might discover that you are repeating yourself several times. Although the topic of cheating on exams might invite a long philosophical discussion of ethics and morality, it also could be focused enough to be covered in a short speech. It is a good topic because it offers rich possibilities for the development of ideas without excessive repetition.

Appropriateness for Oral Delivery. Sometimes, a topic can be developed better in an essay than in a speech. Because readers proceed at their own pace, they can reread any passage that is difficult to understand. But a speech is delivered in real time and at the same pace to all listeners, some of whom will not be able to recall it after delivery. Listeners who miss a particular link in a speaker's chain of ideas cannot rewind the live speech and replay it; if the link was critical, the rest of the speech might become meaningless.

Topics that depend on technical formulas or elaborate arguments are usually better presented in print than in oral delivery. Still, if a speaker's main ideas and examples are planned carefully and presented clearly, even technical and complex topics can be understood by a nonspecialist audience.

Clarity. Finally, of course, the speaker should make it clear to all listeners what the topic is. Speakers often fail to refine their topics sufficiently, and the result is a confused jumble of poorly connected ideas. If you are confused about the ideas in your speech, you can be sure that your audience will be confused too. Even if you think you understand the topic, the fact that you know more about it than the audience does may lead you to present it in a way that is beyond comprehension. For this reason, you should always strive to understand and be sensitive to the audience's level of knowledge.

Checklist 4.1 Characteristics of a Good Topic

1. **Importance to the Speaker: A good topic is one that matters to you.**
2. **Interest to the Audience: A good topic will gain and hold the audience's interest.**
3. **Worthy of Listeners' Time: A good topic is one that listeners feel is worth their time to hear about.**
4. **Appropriateness of Scope: A good topic is manageable within the time available.**
5. **Appropriateness for Oral Delivery: A good topic is one that can be understood from a speech, without having to go back over the ideas.**
6. **Clarity: A good topic is one that audience members can easily identify.**

How to Choose a Good Topic

The preceding discussion of the general characteristics of a good speech topic may still leave you wondering what is the right topic for you. This section offers some suggestions to help you identify a good topic.

Conduct a Personal Inventory

In Chapter 3, you learned how to ask questions to analyze your audience. Now it is time to ask some questions about yourself.

What Public Issues Do I Care About? Public issues are those that concern people generally. Because most audience members are likely to be affected by these issues, they often make good speech topics—but only if you yourself also care about them. It is important, then, to be aware of current events and to think about how you and others are affected by them.

Suppose you decide that animal rights, homelessness, child abuse, and shifting ethical standards really matter to you. These are topics about which you feel strongly. On the other hand, to be perfectly honest, you are not very interested in international trade, health-care financing, and school voucher systems. You probably could develop the first group of topics into effective speeches; the second group would probably not inspire you.

Which of My Experiences Might Be Generalizable? Everyone has had unique experiences, but these do not always make good speech topics. If audience members do not believe that your experience could happen to them, they may react to your speech with the same boredom that many people feel when watching someone else's home videos. On the other hand, if something about your experience can be generalized so that others can imagine themselves in the same situation, you may be onto a good topic.

The fact that your car broke down on the highway on a dark rainy night might matter only to you. But if you can generalize the experience—for example, to the fear that many people share of being overwhelmed by technology or to the advantages of carrying a cell phone for emergencies—your experience might make a good topic. Audience members who don't care at all about your car might still become interested in a speech about a more general problem that they share. Likewise, Phillip Marcus's anger at seeing a classmate cheat could be generalized if he relates the experience so that listeners can imagine how they would feel if it had happened to them.

Which of My Interests Overlap with Those of the Audience? Another question to ask in your personal inventory is whether you and your listeners share a common interest in any topic. If so, you'll have a good match. You will have an incentive to speak about the topic, and they will be motivated to listen.

Sometimes, the match may be exact. For example, you may find that both you and your audience are interested in the Beatles. At other times, you will have to match a specific interest with a more general category. For example, you are interested in the Beatles, and your audience is interested in rock stars of the more recent past. In that case, you'll want to relate the more specific to the more general, explaining how the Beatles exemplify the general subject of rock stardom. If you can do that, you have a good topic.

Use Finding Aids

If your personal inventory did not uncover a good topic for your speech, you can use certain procedures and sources to find a topic. One such finding aid is **brainstorming,** a mental exercise in which you identify the first things that come to mind when you are presented with a given term or category. Do not censor your thoughts; just record them without evaluation. For example, you might divide a sheet of paper into columns with such category headings as "Heroes," "Places to Visit," "Hobbies," and "Favorite Books." (These are just examples, of course; pick whichever categories you want to explore through brainstorming.) Under each heading, jot down the

brainstorming
A mental free-association exercise in which one identifies, without evaluation, the first thoughts that come to mind when one is presented with a given term or category.

first five things that occur to you. For example, you might list five heroes or five characteristics of a hero, or you might name five places you have visited or five places you hope to visit. Do not stop to evaluate your ideas; write down whatever first comes to mind. Then study the list to see whether you can find any patterns. You may discover, for example, that your lists of heroes, places to visit, hobbies, and favorite books all include items related to the Civil War. Since you seem to have an interest in the Civil War, some aspect of that could become your speech topic.

Brainstorming works well when you can identify a group of categories, as in the previous example. *Topoi* (a Greek term meaning "commonplaces" or "common topics") can be used to form the categories in the first place. As the term suggests, *topoi* are general headings for subject matter. Among Aristotle's *topoi* were "war and peace" and "legislation." Today, the *topoi* of public life might include the economy, science and technology, public finance, social policy, education, and the environment, among others. The *topoi* of the college experience might include classes, residential life, social activities, extracurricular organizations, independent study, and community service. Under each of these categories you can identify potential topics for speeches.

WWW. Using the Internet

Choosing Your Topic with Online Resources

Is your intention to share information or to persuade? Use the "Assess Your Speechmaking Situation" page from the **Allyn & Bacon Public Speaking Web Site** to consider topic ideas and to clarify your purpose. Point your browser to **http://www.abacon.com/pubspeak/assess/topic.html.** From there, you can sort out a range of topic choices and subject areas that might be fruitful starting points for planning your speech.

Do a personal inventory and analyze your audience:

- Which topics on this list are meaningful and interesting to you?
- How do you assess your audience's interest level?
- Which of your interests overlap with those of your audience?
- How can you narrow your topic to fit the constraints of the situation?

Some of the sources on this page are general search tools. You can learn more about using search tools by clicking on the link for "Notes on Using Search Tools." It is identified by the blue icon for "Notes from the Instructor." You may also go directly to that source by pointing your browser to **http://www.abacon.com/pubspeak/research/notetool.html.**

Another kind of finding aid is printed source materials, such as newspapers, magazines, encyclopedias, dictionaries, and atlases. Browse through these materials, and jot down notes about topics that interest you. Even if you have not given much thought to these topics before, perhaps now you can see how they could lead to a good speech.

Narrow the Topic

The final step in selecting a good topic is to narrow it so that it fits the situation. If your speech is limited to only ten minutes, for example, you could not begin to explore a topic like "America's Shifting Ethical Standards." But suppose that you narrowed the topic down to the specific standard of honesty, then narrowed that to cheating as an example of dishonesty, and then narrowed that to cheating by college students and finally to "Cheating on This Campus." *Now* you could cover the topic within the allotted time, and your topic would relate to the broader subject that caught your interest in the first place.

Narrowing the topic is like pouring it through a funnel: What goes into the large end is too much to manage, but what comes out the small end can be focused effectively. Time constraints are one obvious reason to narrow the topic. But you also should narrow it to be sure that you can learn enough about the topic before your speech is due and to be sure that the topic fulfills your specific assignment.

topoi
Common or typical categories for organizing subject matter.

Whatever else you do, resist any urge to postpone selecting a topic. If you wait until the last minute, you won't have time to inventory your interests, to use finding aids, and to narrow the topic appropriately.

Checklist 4.2 Steps in Choosing a Good Topic

1. **Conduct a personal inventory.**
   - What public issues do I care about?
   - What experiences have I had that might be generalizable?
   - Which of my interests overlap with those of the audience?
2. **Use finding aids.**
   - Brainstorm.
   - Browse through printed materials.
3. **Narrow the topic so that it can be covered adequately within the time available.**

Developing a Strategic Plan

So far, we have examined the elements that *create* a rhetorical situation (audience, occasion, speaker, and speech). And now that you understand how to select a topic, it is time to consider how your speech will *respond* to the rhetorical situation.

Because any speech will affect or change the situation in some way, giving a speech may be thought of as intervention in the rhetorical situation. This intervention should be strategic, not random; the speech is planned so that it becomes the means to a desired end. Consequently, a crucial early step in preparing to give a speech is to discern your purpose, any factors that might limit your strategies, and the options and opportunities available.

In preparing to respond to and intervene in the rhetorical situation, you need to develop a **strategic plan** that identifies the purpose of your speech, the constraints on it, and the opportunities it provides (see Figure 4.2). Then you select the best means to achieve your purpose. Ideally, the strategic plan also should indicate how you will know whether your purpose has been achieved.

strategic plan
An identification of the objectives to be sought in a speech and the means for achieving them.

purpose
The outcome the speaker wishes to achieve; the response desired from the audience.

Figure 4.2
A strategic plan for intervening in the rhetorical situation.

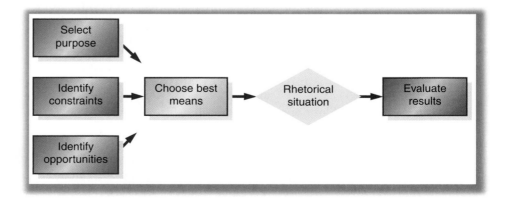

Choosing an Appropriate Topic

Tim Ortiz

Choosing a topic is absolutely painful! I suppose it might not be so difficult if I didn't believe that most every topic has some level of interest to someone. I believe that everything should be given a chance, and with an attitude like this, you can see how difficult making a choice might be. The topic I finally chose was also an important personal issue to me.

Priya Mydur

I am one of those people who really dislikes conventional topics that are always in the news. I prefer being distinctive, giving something for others to be entertained by and have some interest in. I chewed through about ten topics until I finally picked the one lingering in the back of the "refrigerator" (my head).

Prof. Blivens

Personal interests and your personality should guide you to your topic. If you pick a topic that you're personally interested in, it has several impacts. First, if you're interested in it, chances are your classmates will be, too. Second, it makes the research and writing part easier for you. Another strategy outside of personal interest would be your personality. Priya, your personality always comes through in your speeches, and you effectively took a topic that sounded too light-hearted for a persuasive speech and made it work. Brainstorming seemed to work for both of you. Tim, make sure to not critique your topics while you're brainstorming; just write everything down. Then come back and sort through your ideas. If your interests are very diverse, consider other things, like what types of sources you will require. Will I have enough time to research this topic thoroughly enough to make arguments and explain it? Can this topic be thoroughly explained in the amount of time I have to speak? Brainstorming will give you many topics to choose from, but it's always easier to narrow the list down and pick one than it is to just have one topic in mind initially, then find, for some reason, that it won't work for your speech. Look for trends and common areas, Tim, if you're still having difficulty. Outside of brainstorming, consider the news, magazines, and the environment around you. Chances are if you pick a topic you hear about on the news or in a magazine there is plenty of other research on it. This is the best way to find societal topics. Also, look in magazines that are not mainstream. Instead of *Cosmopolitan* try *Mother Jones*. That's where I found out about the Nestle Corporation boycott and the Wal-Mart employee violations topics we discussed and did outlines for in class. The main issue with topics is to find one that you feel like you could give a well-organized and supported speech on.

Identifying the Purpose

The classroom assignment to "make a speech" may mislead you into thinking that fulfilling the assignment is an end in itself. That approach courts disaster, however, because strong public speeches have a clear sense of **purpose.** The speaker plans to achieve a particular goal and wants the audience to respond in a specific way. A speaker's purpose provides the criteria that determine whether the speech was successful or not.

We saw earlier that speeches traditionally are classified as ceremonial, deliberative, or forensic, depending on their purpose. Ceremonial speeches entertain but also celebrate shared values and strengthen commitments to them. Deliberative speeches explore what public policy ought to be. And forensic speaking seeks justice with respect to past events. In addition, recall that in Chapter 1 we described the purposes of a speech in terms of informing, persuading, and entertaining.

Both of these conceptions of purpose are of some use, and yet both are limited. For example, many speeches combine deliberative and ceremonial elements, and it is not uncommon for a single speech to both inform and persuade. For the rest of our study, then, we will use a more precise classification that identifies seven common speech purposes.[5]

1. Providing new information or perspective
2. Agenda setting
3. Creating positive or negative feeling
4. Strengthening commitment
5. Weakening commitment
6. Conversion
7. Inducing a specific action

Providing New Information or Perspective. Sometimes, the audience generally knows about a topic but is unfamiliar with its details. Your goal as speaker may be to fill in such gaps by providing new information. For example, listeners may be aware that U.S. political campaigns are expensive, but they may not know that costs are escalating, or the reasons for this trend and its implications, or whether there are practical alternatives. Thus, the purpose of a speech about campaign finance might be "to deepen and enrich the audience's understanding of campaign costs."

Alternatively, listeners may be accustomed to thinking about a topic only from a certain **perspective,** or point of view. Commuting to work, for instance, might be seen only as a source of tension, frustration, and lost time—all outcomes that make commuting seem negative. But commuting can be viewed much more positively—as "buffer time" to prepare for the workday or to "decompress" before returning home, as a time to catch up on news with the help of the car radio, or as time to handle paperwork while on the bus or train.

Changing listeners' perspectives about a subject may alter beliefs and values relating to it. At the very least, it may convince listeners that the subject is more complicated than they thought and that how they think about the topic is affected by the perspective from which they view it.

Agenda Setting. One purpose of a speech is **agenda setting,** causing people to think about a topic that they previously knew little about or ignored. The goal of the speech is to put the topic "on the agenda," to draw attention to it. Many environmental threats, for example, were not taken seriously until advocates put them on the agenda by speaking about them.

Maria Rogers, a first-year college student, heard a report on the news that sport utility vehicles (SUVs) were fast becoming the number one vehicle of choice in the United States. She also learned that, because of their design, SUVs were more likely than cars to roll over and that they pollute the air at a rate three to five times higher than cars. She carried out a two-week survey of the student parking lots on campus and discovered that almost one-third of the vehicles there were SUVs. She used all this information to create a speech to alert her fellow students about SUVs, safety, and the environment:

> Did you know that with the growing popularity of SUVs, more people are dying from accidents that lead to rollover crashes? Almost 9,500 people die every year in rollover crashes, and government auto-safety regulators believe this has

perspective
The point of view from which one approaches a topic.

agenda setting
Causing listeners to be aware of and to think about a topic that previously had escaped their attention.

something to do with the unique design of SUVs. And did you know that SUVs emit tailpipe pollution three to five times as much as passenger cars do? By telling you about the safety and pollution hazards of SUVs, I hope to draw your attention to a serious and growing concern.

Creating Positive or Negative Feeling. Sometimes a speaker's goal is more general: to leave the audience with a positive or negative feeling about the occasion, the speaker, or the message. Political candidates, even as they discuss specific policy issues, are often really more interested in making listeners generally feel good or bad about themselves or the world.

Student speaker Craig Hinners prepared a speech of this type when he took a short, nostalgic look at the Chicago elevated train, called the El by locals:

> On the El, you are always entertained. If you gaze out the window, you are treated to an intimate look at the lives of people whose backyards and windows face the tracks. If you set your sights inside the train, you can see and hear the stories of people from all walks of life—office workers, mothers with children, old men. You glance at the bright color of gum casually placed on the back of the seat by a teenager who no longer tasted its flavor, and hear the sound of old vehicles and snow-damaged tracks.

Craig's purpose was not to get listeners to do anything about the El, or even to change their beliefs about its run-down condition; he wanted to share a wistful, comfortable feeling with them.

Likewise, many ceremonial speeches aim to evoke or strengthen common bonds by reference to a shared event or experience. The speakers wish to have the audience feel as they do, most often in a positive way. The audience's general attitude, not a belief or action, is the measure of success.

Strengthening Commitment. Many speeches are like "preaching to the converted"; they are delivered to listeners who already agree with the speaker. In such cases, the goal is to motivate audience members to become even more strongly committed. It is one thing to casually favor a candidate's election to office, but it is quite another thing to contribute money to the candidate's campaign, to display the candidate's poster on one's lawn, or to mobilize friends to vote for the candidate on election day. Increasing the intensity of listeners' commitment makes them more likely to act on their beliefs.

Defeated in the presidential primaries in early 2000, and soon to suspend his campaign, Bill Bradley sought to strengthen the commitment of his supporters to his goals even in the face of his own election losses. He offered his campaign staff, supporters, and contributors these words:

> Above all, we must remember that the fact that we've not succeeded in winning tonight's primaries makes the cause no less just, the fight no less honorable, the goal no less reachable. Some have called our goals unrealistic. I call

This speaker knows that her audience already shares her commitment to Native Americans. Now she must figure out how to convince her audience to take that belief to the next level, where they contribute money or actively rally for the cause.

them common sense. I call them democratic, I call them American, and I'm going to work for them until we win—and we will win!

These sentiments helped convince listeners to rededicate themselves to Bradley's goals, even if doing so meant supporting a different candidate in the election of 2000.

Weakening Commitment. Speakers also sometimes want to reduce the intensity of listeners' commitment to a belief—not so much to get them to change their minds as to acknowledge some sense of *doubt.* Recognizing that an issue has more than one legitimate side may be the first step in *eventually* changing people's minds. Even if listeners remain committed to their position, a reasonable but contrary argument may weaken their support for it. Although you may believe, for example, that higher defense spending is necessary, you may at least think twice about it after hearing a speech that argues that much defense spending is wasted.

Dorte Hoerst knew that her listeners strongly believed that the United States should continue the search for weapons of mass destruction in Iraq. She also knew that a single ten-minute speech was unlikely to change their belief. But she might be able to chip away at their position if she could show convincingly that the search was preventing the reconstruction of Iraq, a goal on which both she and the Bush administration were agreed.

> I know that most of you think the United States should keep looking for weapons of mass destruction in Iraq. But some in our own government are having second thoughts. Continuing the search puts the U.S. military in the role of the police, for which they are not qualified, and it prevents the return of civilian government to Iraq—precisely the goal that all U.S. factions in this dispute claim to favor. At least consider the risks of continuing this search; they may be greater than the risks of calling it off.

Conversion. Although it happens rarely on the basis of a single speech, sometimes listeners actually *are* persuaded to change their minds—to stop believing one thing and to start believing another. In short, listeners are converted. **Conversion** involves the replacement of one set of beliefs with another set that is inconsistent with the first. For example, a listener who believes that homeless people are themselves to blame for their condition might be persuaded by a speaker that homelessness reflects faulty social policy, not faulty individuals.

Student speaker Rachel Samuels converted some of her audience by explaining the need for adult teachers to act as editors to censor high school newspapers. Her classmates initially bristled at the idea of curtailing students' freedom of speech. But when Rachel demonstrated that libel lawsuits could bankrupt the public school system, they began to understand her position:

> The editing of high school newspapers is not government censorship of political or religious speech. Rather, it is editing by an authority to avoid the danger of libel lawsuits. In the world outside high schools, editors often keep journal-

conversion

The replacement of one set of beliefs by another that is inconsistent with the first.

ists from printing the whole story in order to protect citizens' privacy. High school newspapers should be no different.

Inducing a Specific Action. The last purpose we will consider is the most specific and most pragmatic. Often, speakers do not really care about the beliefs and attitudes of individual listeners, as long as they can persuade people to take a specific action—to make a contribution, to purchase a product, to vote for a specific candidate, and so on.

When the goal is action regardless of the reason, the speaker may use widely different appeals. One listener may be induced to vote by the argument that it is a civic duty; another may favor a particular candidate's economic proposals; a third may know one of the candidates personally. The speaker does not care whether listeners have the same reasons for voting; all that matters is that they be prompted to take the same action.

Linda Morales, a student in charge of a new recycling program at the university, gave a speech urging students to recycle paper, bottles, and cans. She started with an appeal to the audience's social consciousness:

> We must recycle if we want to preserve the world in which we live. It takes work to ensure a clean and unpolluted environment. But it is our responsibility to ourselves and to our future.

Although this was a strong argument, it was unlikely to motivate all students. Knowing that others might be moved more by an appeal to school spirit, Linda described a recycling competition against their collegiate rivals:

> Students at other universities in town have already recycled thousands of pounds of newspapers and bottles this year. Our rivals to the south have pulled ahead of us with a vigorous recycling effort. Are we going to allow ourselves to be left in the dust?

Linda figured that still other listeners might recycle if they thought they could gain something immediately. To appeal to them, she also talked about a promotional contest among dormitories:

> And don't forget the prize money! The dorm that gathers the most junk gets $500 to spend on food, drink, and music at the end of the year.

Linda's only real concern was whether audience members would participate in this recycling program. She didn't care whether they were motivated by social consciousness, by school spirit, or by personal gain. She used multiple appeals to achieve her purpose with as many listeners as possible.

These seven categories of purpose certainly do not exhaust the possibilities, but they illustrate some common reasons why people give a speech.[6] Identifying your purpose is a critical step because that will help you to plan strategies which accomplish your goal.

Identifying the Constraints

After you identify the specific purpose of your speech, the next step in developing a strategic plan is to identify the constraints within which you must maneuver. As noted earlier, constraints are factors beyond your control that limit your options. Constraints may arise from:

- Audiences in general.
- Your specific audience analysis.

- Your *ethos* as a speaker.
- The nature of your topic.
- The rhetorical situation.

From Audiences in General. As we learned in Chapter 2, the attention span of most listeners is limited, and it has shrunk over the years. Today, most audiences begin to get restless when a speech exceeds 20 or 30 minutes. And even when listeners are generally attentive, the degree of attention varies. At one moment, your speech may be the most important thing on their minds; at another moment, something you say may trigger an unrelated thought; and at yet another moment, listeners may be distracted by something else altogether.

Knowing that attention spans are so limited, you will want to help the audience remember your main ideas by phrasing them simply, organizing them in a structure that is easy to follow, and repeating them during the speech. Another strategy is to use interesting examples and to choose language that captures attention.

Besides having limited attention spans, audiences tend to have a high opinion of themselves and naturally resist being talked down to. They may believe that they have exerted great effort or even done you a favor by coming to hear you speak. You should always show respect to the audience and recognize that they will be the ultimate judges of your speech.

From Your Specific Audience Analysis. You also will be constrained by the analysis you performed of your specific audience, as described in Chapter 3. Your audience analysis may tell you that some appeals are out of bounds and that others are far more likely to succeed. For example, the manager who speaks to employees about the company's strained economic conditions has many choices; to succeed, however, she or he *must* deal with the fact that workers are worried about losing their jobs. This fear, identified through audience analysis, is an important constraint on what the manager can say.

From Your *Ethos* as a Speaker. The audience's perceptions of the speaker's character, or *ethos,* are another important constraint. If listeners see you as competent to discuss the subject, as trustworthy, as dynamic and energetic, and as having goodwill toward them, you enjoy a positive *ethos.* As we saw in Chapter 3, you want to evoke positive assessments of your *ethos* because an audience's perceptions of your character strongly affect whether that audience will be influenced by what you say.

Even a generally positive *ethos* can constrain you, however, because then you must craft a speech that sustains or builds on the audience's high expectations. When well-loved comedian Bill Cosby gives a speech, the audience expects lighthearted humor and would be confused if he presented a serious lecture. Even when he resumed speaking after the tragic death of his son, people expected him to be good-natured and funny. Although his *ethos* is positive, he must work within its constraints.

If, for whatever reason, your *ethos* is generally perceived as negative, then your challenge is either to change it or to overcome it. When President Bill Clinton acknowledged that he had been involved in an inappropriate sexual relationship with a White House intern, after having earlier denied it, he found subsequently that many people suspected him of dishonesty whenever he spoke. His negative *ethos* was a constraint on his effectiveness. He tried to overcome it by focusing his speeches instead on the strength of the economy and society during his administration.

From the Nature of Your Topic. Some topics constrain a speaker more than others do. A highly technical subject that is difficult to make interesting strains the audience's attention span even more than usual. And a topic that seems far removed from listeners' concerns is unlikely to spark and hold their interest.

In such cases, the challenge is to plan strategies that evoke and heighten interest. This is what student John Casey did in speaking about the research under way in the university's laboratories. Rather than droning on about details of antibodies and peptides, he made the topic interesting by describing the scientific community's quest for a "magic bullet" to cure cancer.

From the Rhetorical Situation. Every speech is a one-shot effort to influence the audience, but the occasions when a single message will change anyone's attitudes are few. For example, a classroom speech about abortion is unlikely to convince strong believers on either side to switch allegiance. Moreover, a speaker's range of stimuli is limited to only words and, sometimes, visual aids. Yet most cases of successful persuasion involve multiple messages and a variety of stimuli—verbal, visual, and experiential. Of course, a one-shot effort may be more likely to succeed when your goal is to reinforce the commitment that listeners already feel. Even so, a speaker should never overestimate the effect that a single speech can have on an audience.

We see, then, that a speaker cannot plan a speech with complete freedom. The constraints imposed by the audience, the audience analysis, the speaker's *ethos*, the topic, and the rhetorical situation must all become part of the strategic plan. Then the challenge is to be creative and find opportunities within these limits.

Identifying the Opportunities

Your opportunities as a speaker result from the special assets that you bring to the situation and from the choices that you *are* able to make. But to take advantage of the opportunities in developing a strategic plan, you first need to be aware of them.

Probably your most important asset is that you have an *information advantage* over listeners; you are likely to be better informed about the topic than they are. This may offset the constraints that the audience imposes. After all, you selected the topic because it matters to you, and you have researched it, as we will describe in Chapter 5. You have given the topic sustained attention, and so you should be able to awaken interest in it, to provide new information about it, and to explain difficult concepts.

A second opportunity arises from your *audience analysis* (see Chapter 3). It will tell you something about the composition and attitudes of your specific listeners. Furthermore, almost any topic can be presented in various ways; there is no single "correct" approach but many different paths to the same goal. Your audience analysis will enable you to select which path to pursue and to plan strategies that are most likely to succeed.

For example, suppose that you know that, despite threats of legal penalties, large numbers of college students use the Internet to copy MP3s. These are compressed audio files that allow music lovers to store on their computer hard drives music that was transferred from store-bought compact discs, without permission and without any payment to the artist who created the music. You want to persuade your fellow students that they should not copy MP3s, and you expect strong opposition from students who would see your proposal as a limitation of their freedom. So you might suggest that this limitation is justified:

> College students today hook up to the Web and copy MP3s from each other's hard drives quickly and with little effort. At the click of a button, we can get the music of 'N Sync, Lauren Hill, and Rage Against the Machine—all for free and, yes, all without the artist's permission. When we do this, we're breaking the law and preventing artists from getting paid for the use of their work. We have a responsibility to support these artists and to uphold the copyright laws.

While these justifications seem reasonable, they depend on values such as sympathy for artists and respect for the law. This argument probably would be more effective in reinforcing the commitment of listeners who already believed in upholding copyright laws than in converting people who are not particularly bothered by this legal transgression but are disturbed by what they see as limitations on their freedom. To reach these listeners, a strategy of stressing the personal benefits of not copying CDs might be more effective. For them, you might add:

> And not only that, we ourselves will benefit from our restraint. How? By contributing to the development of the music industry and by promoting future creativity. So this is not really a curtailment of freedom; it's an opportunity for us to hear more and more music from artists who will be secure in their ability to make music and make a living too.

Speakers sometimes choose their means without much thought, but, as this example shows, attention to the specific audience can help you plan strategies that will advance your ideas effectively.

Selecting the Means

If you have been thinking strategically, by this point you have articulated the purpose of your speech and have identified your constraints and opportunities in proceeding toward that goal. The final step in strategic planning is to select the means that you will use to achieve your purpose.

In many respects, this decision is the most important, because it touches on virtually every aspect of your speech. How will you lead your audience in reasoning through to the conclusions you want to establish? How will you structure the speech? What supporting materials will you use? What choices will you make about wording, emotional language, and repetition? How will you actually present the speech? All these matters will be explored in later chapters, but here you should recognize that each of them involves a choice that can be made either by accident or by design. The essence of strategic planning is to avoid accident and to design means that are most appropriate for achieving your purpose.

Developing the Purpose Statement and the Thesis Statement

From this understanding of strategic elements—purpose, constraints, and opportunities—you can begin to construct the skeleton of your speech. You have already determined the topic. The next steps are to formulate a clear statement of purpose and a thesis for the speech.

The Purpose Statement

Our earlier discussion suggested seven general categories of purpose: agenda setting, providing new information, weakening commitment, and so on. Review those categories to determine which one best describes the overall purpose of your speech. That description is your **general purpose statement.** Then you need to develop a **specific purpose statement.** This focuses on the outcome of your speech by specifying what you want to achieve, and for that reason it is audience centered. It follows from the seven general purposes described earlier; those general purposes are made more specific by relation to a particular topic.

For example, if you were going to discuss cheating at the university, you might proceed as follows:

TOPIC: Cheating at the university

GENERAL PURPOSE: To provide new information

SPECIFIC PURPOSE: To inform listeners of widespread cheating on this campus

The specific purpose is an instance of the general purpose, to provide new information.

Notice that the specific purpose statement has several important characteristics. First, it focuses on the audience rather than on the speaker. It identifies the outcome you seek, not how you will achieve that outcome. Second, it summarizes a single idea. Although some speeches are complex and have more than one purpose, you are likely to be more effective if you can state your purpose as a single succinct idea. Third, the specific purpose statement is precise and free of vague language. It tells exactly what you are trying to achieve, and so you can determine whether or not you succeed.

Next, think critically about your specific purpose statement. Remember that listeners are giving their time and energy to hear you speak, and ask yourself whether your specific purpose is worthy of their efforts. If you are telling them only things that they already know, if your purpose is too grand to be achieved in the time available, if the topic is too technical or seems trivial, listeners are unlikely to pay close attention. In that case, of course, you cannot achieve your purpose.

The Thesis Statement

The final step in preparing the overall design of the speech is to identify the **thesis,** a succinct statement of the central idea or claim made by the speech. Whereas the specific purpose statement indicates what you want the audience to *take from* the speech, the thesis statement indicates what

general purpose statement
Statement of the overall goal of the speech: providing new information or perspective, agenda setting, creating positive or negative feeling, strengthening commitment, weakening commitment, conversion, or inducing a specific action.

specific purpose statement
Statement of the particular outcome sought from the audience; a more specific version of a general purpose.

thesis
The central idea or claim made by the speech, usually stated in a single sentence.

The thesis statement sums up what you most want listeners to remember. It should be possible to translate the thesis statement into a slogan for a poster.

you want to *put into* it. The thesis sums up the speech in a single sentence that you most want listeners to remember. Here is how the thesis statement about campus cheating might evolve:

TOPIC: Cheating at the university

GENERAL PURPOSE: To provide new information

SPECIFIC PURPOSE: To inform listeners of widespread cheating on this campus

THESIS STATEMENT: Far more students engage in cheating than most of us think.

Notice how the topic (itself the result of a narrowing process) has been narrowed into a thesis statement that summarizes exactly what the speech will say.

Many of the tests of the specific purpose statement also apply to the thesis. Both should be stated in a single phrase or sentence. Both should be worded precisely. And both should fit the time available and other constraints in the situation.

Occasionally, a speaker does not state the thesis explicitly, relying instead on all the supporting ideas to imply it. There are advantages and disadvantages to letting the audience determine the exact thesis. If listeners participate actively in figuring it out, they are likely to stay interested in the speech and perhaps may even be more likely to accept the thesis. On the other hand, if the thesis is not stated, the audience might not identify it accurately, or different listeners might identify different theses. Even though accomplished speakers sometimes trust the audience to identify the thesis, students of public speaking are well advised to state it explicitly.

Analyzing the Thesis Statement

The thesis statement governs various choices about the content of a speech. By analyzing your thesis statement, you can determine just what your choices are.

Identifying the Issues

First, you must identify the issues contained within the thesis statement. People often use the term *issue* quite loosely, as when they say, "Don't make an issue of it." But the term has a more precise meaning. An **issue** is a question raised by the thesis statement that must be addressed in order for the thesis itself to be addressed effectively.

Issues are identified by posing questions about your thesis statement. Because the statement is so simple and brief, it always leaves much unsaid. By raising questions about the thesis statement, you'll discover what it seems to take for granted. Then your speech can flesh out these underlying assumptions and show that they are correct, giving listeners reason to accept the thesis statement itself.

Consider the thesis statement in the example above: "Far more students engage in cheating than most of us think." It seems straightforward. But notice what happens when we ask questions about the statement:

"Far more students"	→	How many? Is that number more than we think? Is it "far more"?
"Engage in cheating"	→	What is covered by the term *cheating?* And what must one do to "engage in" it?
"Than most of us think"	→	Who are "most of us"? What do "most of us" think? Why do we think this?

These questions identify the issues in the thesis statement. You may decide that some of the answers are obvious or that some can be covered together. You may decide not to take them up in the same order in the speech. But these essentially are the questions you'll need to answer if you want listeners to accept that "far more students engage in cheating than most of us think."

Now consider a thesis that is not yet well formed. Bill Goldman wanted to explore whether "voting in local elections is a worthwhile effort for me as a student." He had not yet framed an explicit thesis, but even this more broadly phrased statement can be questioned to discover the issues. Bill had to think about what "worthwhile" means for a student, whose stake in local elections is usually small; he also had to think about what "effort" is required to vote and why even that is an issue. He then began to question whether it was "harder" for him to vote than for others or harder than it "should" be. Gradually, he came to believe that low voter turnout can be explained by the fact that voting is inconvenient. This process of discovering issues helped Bill both to refine and to test his thesis statement.

Finally, consider the example of Angela Peters, who wanted to talk about the college admissions process. After doing some research, she might begin to develop her speech like this:

TOPIC: The college admissions process

GENERAL PURPOSE: Weakening commitment to a position

issue
A question raised by the thesis statement that must be addressed in order for the thesis itself to be addressed effectively.

SPECIFIC PURPOSE: To cause listeners to doubt their belief that admissions decisions are made rationally

THESIS STATEMENT: Most colleges and students lack clear criteria for making admissions decisions.

ISSUES:

1. What are "most colleges"? Who are "most students"? How do we know?
2. What makes the criteria for admissions clear or unclear?
3. What are a college's or a student's criteria? Are they "clear" or not?
4. What are the admissions decisions about which we are concerned?

Now Angela can complete her research by looking for the answers to these specific questions. When she speaks about "the college admissions process," she will know what she wants to say, and she will have the supporting material she needs to weaken listeners' commitment to the belief that admissions decisions are made rationally.

Why Identify the Issues?

Analyzing the topic to identify the issues is important for several reasons. First, it enables you to determine what the speech must cover. Without knowing the issues, you risk giving a speech that listeners will dismiss as being beside the point.

Recall that Bill Goldman initially wanted to explore whether "voting in local elections is a worthwhile effort for me as a student." Through the process of discovering issues, he eventually came to believe that low voter turnout reflected the fact that voting is inconvenient. At this point, his topic became "Why Americans don't vote," and his thesis was "Because voting is inconvenient, many people don't vote." He was able to document that even in presidential elections voter turnout is low and that it is declining. He also was able to show that polling places may be inconvenient to get to, that people don't like waiting in line, and that the form of the ballot is often complex. He proposed as his solution that people be allowed to vote from home through the use of a touch-tone telephone. This solution seemed appropriate *as he described the problem*, but he did not really analyze the issues and causes fully. His thesis statement was too vague and did not consider alternative explanations.

After the speech, an audience member challenged whether Bill had really thought through the problem. The listener pointed out that, because people will endure inconvenience if they believe that the rewards justify it, perhaps a more significant cause for failing to vote is the belief that one's vote will make no difference or that the voter will have nothing to show for the effort. Although the "costs" of standing in line at an inconvenient location and being confronted by a confusing ballot may explain why many citizens do not vote, a deeper reason may be that they see no real "benefit" from casting their votes. If so, then voting by telephone is unlikely to improve the turnout rate. Had Bill analyzed his thesis more carefully, he might have seen that the costs and benefits of voting were likely to be an issue, and he would have been prepared to address this.

A second reason to analyze the thesis statement is to direct your research, which otherwise could be endless. Combing your own experience and ideas, talking with others, and investigating library resources could go on indefinitely. A search of books and articles in just a single library will probably turn up hundreds of sources that have something to say about voting rates (and on the Internet, an unfocused search will yield truly unmanageable results).

One way to make your research task manageable is to focus your inquiry. By analyzing your thesis to determine the issues, you can better decide what and how to research. For example, in giving a speech about voting rates, you may decide that the key issue relates to voting at state and local levels. As a result, you would not pay much attention to the vast literature comparing turnout rates among countries or turnout rates in national elections. Your research would be directed to the questions that bear on the issues you have identified.

A third reason to identify the issues is that doing so may lead you to modify your thesis. If your initial thesis is "Americans are too busy to vote," analyzing the issues might convince you that your thesis should be "Americans are too lazy to vote" or "Americans are too confused to vote" or "Americans feel that they have no reason to vote." The differences among these statements are obvious. Which one (or more) claim you try to develop and defend in the speech will be influenced by your analysis of what the issues really are.[7]

Finally, as you will see in Chapter 7, analyzing your thesis is also helpful when you turn to organizing your speech.

Strategies for Speaking to Diverse Audiences

Respecting Diversity Through Your Topic Selection and Strategy Development

Some topics work better than others for a diverse audience. Likewise, identifying your purpose and selecting a strategy are affected by the need to reach listeners with diverse backgrounds and perspectives. These strategies will help you to consider diversity at these key stages of speech planning.

1. Select a topic that is important to both you *and* your audience.
2. Consider a topic that reduces cultural stereotypes or emphasizes points of commonality in your audience.
3. Evaluate your audience's prior commitment to your topic.
4. Identify the constraints and opportunities posed by the diversity of your audience.

Summary

In this chapter, we investigated the initial steps in preparing a speech: understanding the rhetorical situation, choosing a topic, and developing a strategic plan—an action plan that reflects a clear sense of purpose and that identifies your constraints and opportunities.

Whether or not you choose your own topic, it is important to understand the factors that determine the rhetorical situation: the audience, the occasion, the speaker, and the speech. Sometimes, speakers do not choose their own topics, which instead are determined by the issue, the occasion, or the audience. But in situations where you do choose the topic, your speech will be more effective if the topic matters to you, if you can make it interesting to the audience, if its scope fits the time available, if it is appropriate for oral delivery, and if it is clear.

When you are able to choose your own topic, you should follow certain steps. Conduct an inventory of your interests and those of the audience, use finding aids such as brainstorming and general reading, and narrow the topic so that it can be addressed adequately within the time available.

With a topic in mind, speakers formulate an overall strategy for responding to the rhetorical situation. Strategic planning is guided especially by the purpose of the speech: whether to provide new information or perspective, to raise issues, to create positive or negative feeling, to strengthen or weaken commitment to a position, to change listeners' minds, and/or to induce a specific action by audience members.

Achieving your purpose depends in part on the constraints and opportunities in the rhetorical situation. Constraints limit what you can do and may result from what you know about audiences in general, from your analysis of the specific audience, from your *ethos* as a speaker, from the nature of your topic, or from the fact that a speech is a one-shot appeal that is primarily verbal. Opportunities arise from the fact that you probably will know more about your topic than listeners do and from the fact that you may draw on and respond to the audience's attitudes and values. Your strategy should use constraints and opportunities to achieve your purpose.

The process of identifying your topic, your general and specific purposes, and your thesis statement allows you to focus on the strategic development of the speech. You know what you want to say and what effect you want to achieve. You might modify these ideas as you learn more about the subject or refine your audience analysis, but the purpose and thesis statements will influence the following strategic decisions:

- What you need to know about the topic in order to establish that the thesis is true
- Which main ideas you need to develop to establish the thesis
- Which inferences must be made to link the main ideas to the thesis
- How best to organize your development and support of the thesis
- Which elements in the design of the speech will make listeners most comfortable about accepting the thesis statement

We will focus on these important strategic choices in the next several chapters.

Discussion Questions

1. When a small liberal arts college decided to change its core curriculum, the issue of core requirements became important to students in a public speaking class, many of whom spoke about that topic. Discuss the issues in this rhetorical situation that seemed to call for speech.
2. How do the purpose of a speech and its subject matter relate to one another? Discuss the speech purposes described in this chapter, and identify some potential topics for each purpose.
3. Imagine that you are giving a six- to eight-minute speech to a group of fraternity members in which your purpose is to weaken their commit-

ment to the idea that alcohol is desirable at parties. What constraints and opportunities do you face in this situation? How will you use those constraints and opportunities in your strategic plan for this speech?

4. Now imagine that you are giving a six- to eight-minute speech to a meeting of Students Against Drunk Driving in which your purpose is to strengthen their commitment to the idea that alcohol is dangerous at parties. How do the constraints and opportunities of this situation differ from those in item 3? In what ways would your strategic plan for this speech be different?

1. Choose a good topic for a speech in this class. In doing so, conduct a personal inventory and use finding aids such as brainstorming and source browsing. Make sure that you narrow the topic so that it is appropriate for the time available.

2. Produce a list of constraints and a list of opportunities for the topic you have chosen (in activity 1). Consider the audience, the occasion, the speaker, and the speech. In a few paragraphs, describe your purpose and how you are going to achieve it within the bounds of these constraints and opportunities.

3. Provide the following information about your speech:

   TOPIC:
   GENERAL PURPOSE:
   SPECIFIC PURPOSE:
   THESIS STATEMENT:

   Evaluate each of these decisions, explaining why you made the choices you did.

1. See Craig R. Smith and Paul Prince, "Language Choice Expectation and the Roman Notion of Style," *Communication Education* 39 (January 1990): 63–74.

2. *Identification* is a rhetorical concept treated by Kenneth Burke in *A Rhetoric of Motives*, Berkeley: Univ. of California Press, 1969.

3. The strategy of speakers who do not seek identification is examined in Robert L. Scott and Donald K. Smith, "The Rhetoric of Confrontation," *Quarterly Journal of Speech* 55 (February 1969): 1–8.

4. These three categories are described in Aristotle, *The Rhetoric*, translated by W. Rhys Roberts, New York: The Modern Library, 1954, Book I, Chapter 3.

5. This classification system is original. Although the broad categories served our purposes in Chapter 1, we will use this more precise system of purposes for the remainder of our study.

6. For another list of purposes, see Sonja K. Foss and Karen A. Foss, *Inviting Transformation: Presentational Speaking for a Changing World*, Prospect Heights, Ill.: Waveland Press, 1994, pp. 10–16.

7. Classical rhetoric addresses the subject of issue identification as "stasis theory." For more on this theory, see Otto Alvin Loeb Dieter, "Stasis," *Communication Monographs* 17 (November 1950): 345–369; Ray Nadeau, "Classical Systems of Stases in Greek: Hermagoras to Hermogenes," *Greek, Roman, and Byzantine Studies* 2 (January 1959): 51–71; and Ray Nadeau, "Hermogenes on Stases: A Translation with an Introduction and Notes," *Communication Monographs* 31 (November 1964): 361–424. For a modern approach to classical stasis theory, see Lee S. Hultzen, "Status in Deliberative Analysis," *The Rhetorical Idiom: Essays in Rhetoric, Oratory, Language, and Drama*, ed. Donald C. Bryant, Ithaca, N.Y.: Cornell Univ. Press, 1958, pp. 97–123; Sharon Crowley and Debra Hawhee, *Ancient Rhetorics for Contemporary Students*, 2d ed., Boston: Allyn and Bacon, 1999.

Chapter Five

Researching
the Topic

**In this chapter,
we will:**

- Understand how research requires strategic choices in light of your audience and your purpose.

- Identify the kinds of material that are available to support the ideas in your speech.

- Explore how to find supporting materials through your personal experience, interviews with others, library research, and electronic searches.

- Describe a strategy for conducting research efficiently and productively.

- Explain how to cite sources and how to take notes about your research.

In this chapter, you will learn how to investigate your topic so that you can speak about it intelligently. Because you are making claims on listeners' time and attention, both you and they will want to be confident that you know what you're talking about.

The process of finding supporting material for your speech is called **research.** It is closely linked to the process of **analysis** that you studied at the end of Chapter 4. Indeed, the available materials guide you in identifying the issues related to your topic, and searching for material without knowing which issues you need to investigate would be pointless.

Sometimes, analysis precedes research. This is the right sequence when you already know what your thesis statement is. You then determine which questions must be answered in order to make that statement, and you go to find the answers. Sometimes, though, you don't yet know your thesis statement; you know only the topic. Angela Peters wanted to talk about the college admissions process (topic), but she didn't know enough about it to be sure what she wanted to say (thesis). In this case, she should begin not with analysis but with research. She needs a general understanding of the topic before she can frame the thesis statement. Then she should analyze her thesis statement as described in Chapter 4 and, finally, return to research for answers to the specific questions she identified.

Strategic Perspectives on Research

Whether your research precedes or follows your analysis, you will want it to accomplish three basic goals:

1. To develop or strengthen your own expertise on the topic
2. To find the evidence that will support your ideas
3. To make your ideas clear, understandable, and pertinent to your audience

Keep in mind that these different goals may not all be achieved by the same kind of material. If you conceive of the research process too narrowly, you may find that you have obtained great background knowledge but have no specific material to include in your speech. Or you may find that your evidence is clear and meaningful in the context in which you found it, but it may mean little to your audience without that context.

Like every other aspect of public speaking, research involves strategic choices. You simply cannot find out all there is to know about every possible aspect of your speech topic. Consequently, you will have to decide:

- How much general background reading to do and what sources to select for this purpose.
- What issues in your speech will require specific supporting material.
- What types of supporting material you will need and where you should go to find it.
- How much supporting material you need to find.

These choices often are made haphazardly. A library or Internet search yields a large number of source citations, the speaker tracks down the first two or three she can find, and she stops as soon as she has enough to fill the speaking time she has been allotted. Whether she has the best kinds of support or the right amount of it are questions never considered. Or, be-

research
The process of looking for and discovering supporting materials for the speech.

analysis
Exploration of a speech topic to determine which subordinate topics must be covered.

cause another speaker's personal experience is relevant to his topic, he does not bother looking for other types of supporting material. Whether an audience will find his personal experience adequate or credible is never considered.

Instead of acting in such an unplanned way, you should make these choices—like all others—in light of your audience and your purpose. What will your audience expect of you? What claims might listeners be expected to accept without evidence? Will examples or statistics be more likely to lead them to accept your thesis? At what point would you provide so much evidence that it overwhelms them? Carefully considering questions like these will help you approach research strategically.

In the classroom, this thought process may be simplified by the details of the speech assignment. You may be asked, for instance, to give a speech with at least five pieces of supporting material of at least three different types. These are arbitrary instructions, not an all-purpose formula. Their purpose is to expose you to the range of possible supporting material and to give you practice using it. That is valuable, of course. But outside the classroom, you will have to make these choices based on the particular rhetorical situation you face, not by adhering blindly to what was appropriate for your assignment in this course.

Types of Supporting Material

To do research for your speech, you first have to decide which types of supporting material you need. The following seven types illustrate the array of possibilities:

1. Personal experience
2. Common knowledge
3. Direct observation
4. Examples
5. Documents
6. Statistics
7. Testimony

Personal Experience

Sometimes, you can support your ideas on the basis of your own experience. Suppose your topic concerns the difficulties that first-year students have in adjusting to college life. You might well illustrate your main points by referring to your own first college days. If you were speaking about volunteerism, your experience in tutoring elementary school students or working in a soup kitchen would certainly be relevant. Student speaker Mitch Apley used a personal story to introduce his speech about the need to teach children that getting drunk is not a social coup:

> Last quarter, I went out with some buddies of mine to have a good time. We were partying hard, and I got really wasted. I mean, I've never been so trashed in my life! A few weeks ago, I saw some pictures of myself that I don't even remember being in. It was great! That is—until I rolled my new sports car. The police tell me that I was lucky to walk out of there alive. I was even more lucky to avoid hurting someone else. Many drunk drivers aren't so lucky.

Mitch gained credibility—and the audience's attention—because he knew what he was talking about. He used his experience to illustrate his main points, and because his listeners could relate to him, they found his experience pertinent to them as well.

Those are the strategic benefits of using personal experience to support your ideas. Of course, audience members must be able to relate to your experience or they will not think it meaningful to them. For this reason, only rarely should a speaker rely on personal experience as the *only* type of supporting material.

Common Knowledge

An often-overlooked type of supporting material is **common knowledge,** the understandings, beliefs, and values that members of a society or culture generally share. Such beliefs are sometimes called "common sense." Some writers use the term *social knowledge* to emphasize that we know these things to be true on the basis of broad social consensus.[1]

Common knowledge is often expressed in the form of *maxims,* such as "Work expands to fill the time available for its completion," "You can't trust the people who made the mess to clean it up," "Nature abhors a vacuum," or "If you want something done right, do it yourself." Sometimes, common knowledge takes the form of *generally held beliefs.* For example, whether correctly or not, most Americans believe that large government programs don't work, that taxes are too high and definitely should not be increased, that the Cold War is over, and that God plays a role in their lives. Common knowledge also is expressed in *value judgments,* such as the importance of protecting the environment, the commitment to a right to privacy, and a preference for practical solutions over ideological disputes.

One student speaker used common knowledge as supporting material when he said:

> Everybody knows that youth is a time for experimenting, for doing adventurous things. That's why you should consider signing up for study abroad.

When asked later, audience members agreed with the speaker's assertion that young people are adventurous and willing to try something new.

Common knowledge is not always correct, of course; people certainly can believe things that "ain't so." But common knowledge has the status of **presumption**—that is, we consider it to be right until we are shown otherwise. Precisely because the knowledge is "common" and widely shared, it can often be strategically useful as supporting material.

Direct Observation

Sometimes, you can support your claim on the basis of simple, direct observation—the heart of the scientific method. If you are speaking about whether drivers obey basic traffic laws, you can stand near a traffic light or stop sign and count how many drivers ignore these signals. If you are speaking about the widespread use of telephone answering machines, you can call various friends and organizations and observe how often the calls are answered by a machine. Student speaker Susan Anderson used direct observation to support her claim that students are taking unnecessary risks by not wearing bicycle helmets.

common knowledge
The beliefs and values that members of a society or culture generally share.

presumption
The assumption that a statement or claim is true until shown otherwise.

You've seen them. They're big, oval-shaped, and odd-looking. And they sit on top of bicyclists' heads to reduce the risk of head injury in the unfortunate event of an accident. At least, that's what they're intended to do—but only if you wear them. Today I saw twenty-seven students on bicycles, but only five— that's right, five—of them were wearing helmets. The other twenty-two students may not know this, but they were unnecessarily risking their lives.

This form of evidence appeals to the common cultural value that "seeing is believing." Susan's point gained credibility because she was reporting what she had seen with her own eyes. And direct observation is not just a recollection of personal experience; it can be verified by others. Usually, direct observation results from a deliberate decision to gather evidence that might support your point, but occasionally it is powerful because you saw something by accident—such as an act of crime—while you were doing something else.

Examples

When you offer an example, you make a general statement more meaningful by illustrating a specific instance of it. This form of supporting material helps to make an abstract idea more concrete. You can provide this kind of support for a claim by using a brief example, a hypothetical example, an anecdote, or a case study.

Brief Example. If you wanted to support the claim that the structure of the United Nations does not adequately reflect the current balance of power in the world, you might cite as an example the fact that Germany and Japan— despite their economic strength—do not have permanent seats on the Security Council. You might cite as another example the dominance of the General Assembly by "third world" nations. And you also might cite the United Nations' inability to compel member nations to pay their assessments. You would not develop any of these examples in detail, however; they are important because *together* they support your claim that the structure of the United Nations is outmoded.

Hypothetical Example. In using a hypothetical example to support a claim, you ask listeners to *imagine* themselves in a particular situation. You might say, "Suppose that year after year you spent more money than you took in. What would you have to do about that?" Listeners might conjure up images of severe cuts in their budget, selling their home or car, or even bankruptcy. You then could use this example to help the audience understand the difficult choices Congress makes in fashioning the federal budget.

Anecdote. An anecdote, or story, allows you to develop an example in greater detail. If your topic is the frustration of dealing with a bureaucracy, you might tell a story about someone's failure to get a problem resolved within the system. You could describe the maze of telephone inquiries and form letter replies and your hero's trek to the seat of power, only to be directed to the wrong office. Finally reaching the appropriate official, the person is patronized by a clerk who says, "According to our records, you are dead." Such an extended, engaging story would illustrate your point and help the audience relate to the issues.

Referring specifically to key documents can be a good way to show authoritative and specific support for your claims.

Case Study. You often can support a general claim by zeroing in on one particular true case and discussing it in detail. If your topic is about whether or not campus codes to regulate offensive speech can be effective, you might describe one or two campuses that have tried this approach and then argue that their experiences illustrate whether such codes are workable in general. If you believe that making Election Day a national holiday would increase voter turnout, you might support your claim by drawing on case studies of nations where Election Day is a holiday. During recent political campaigns, candidates frequently have used this form of support when they showcase specific families they said would benefit more from their tax and spending proposals than from their opponent's.

Notice that all these types of examples work by relating a part of something to the whole. By examining a particular instance of whatever is being discussed, you may be able to support claims about the topic as a whole.

Documents

Word processing programs often identify anything they produce as a document, and Web pages are also sometimes called documents. As a type of supporting material, the term **documents** has a more specific meaning. It refers to primary sources that can establish a claim directly, without the need for opinion or speculation.

A person's will is a document specifying what will happen to his or her possessions after death. This document takes priority over someone's opinion about what the deceased "really wanted." Likewise, a lawyer who wants to know what the copyright law is will not ask for a colleague's opinion; he or she will look up the text of the act passed by Congress. If you want to know who has the authority to set the dues for the campus film society, you'll consult the society's bylaws—another example of a document.

Documents can be a valuable source of supporting material. The Declaration of Independence is often quoted to support the belief that there are natural rights. For many people, the Bible is the document most often quoted. In the investigation of Watergate, the key documents were White House tape recordings in the investigations of the 1972 break-in at the offices of the Democratic National Committee in the Watergate complex in Washington, D.C. One recording has been called the "smoking gun" of the Watergate scandal because it provided evidence that President Nixon knew about the break-in and had participated in covering up the crime until 1974.

The student who spoke about cheating on campus referred to a university document to show that academic dishonesty would not be tolerated:

documents
Primary sources that can establish a claim directly, without opinion or speculation.

According to the student handbook we got as freshmen, cheating is "a serious breach of our commitment to ethical behavior as students" and will be punished with "a failing grade in the class and possible expulsion from the university."

Documents can be a solid form of evidence if your audience regards them as trustworthy—and if you quote them accurately. The exact words of a document provide a record that is not skewed by the opinions and interpretations of others.

Statistics

Supporting materials presented in quantitative form, as statistics, are especially useful when the scope of the topic is vast. They make it possible to generalize beyond a few specific examples and hence to make a powerful statement about larger populations. If you are speaking about your family or your college class, the scope of the topic is narrow enough that you probably don't need statistical support; you can just provide a set of examples or case studies. When your topic involves the state or the nation, however, one or two examples are unlikely to represent the diversity of the population.

Statistics are numbers that record the extent of something or the frequency with which something occurs; they take such forms as medians, averages, ratios, indices, and standardized scores. Such numbers become meaningful when they are compared with some baseline or other pattern to permit an inference about the relationship between the two. For example, you might support a claim by comparing the median family income for different professions or different ethnic groups or different nations.

Although statistical statements take a great variety of forms, the following four types are especially valuable for supporting material in speeches.

Simple Enumeration. The most basic form of a statistic is a single number. "A total of 35 faculty members on our campus have won teaching awards" is an example of such a statistic; it merely reports the result of a counting exercise. Such statistics have the virtue of simplicity, but they actually may be difficult to interpret without more knowledge of the context. Having 35 winners of teaching awards on the faculty means one thing at a small college with only 60 faculty members, but it means something different for a large public university with 3,000 people on the faculty.

Interpreting simple enumerations can be tricky. In a speech in the spring of 2003, President George W. Bush said that, under his tax cut proposal, "92 million Americans would receive an average tax reduction of $1,083" and "that 1.4 million new jobs would be created by 2004." The figure for the average tax reduction was mathematically correct, but the figure meant something different when it became clear that the average was skewed by a small number of very large reductions. Indeed, 50 percent of all taxpayers would see a tax cut of $100 or less. And the same forecaster who predicted the short-term job growth also predicted that the tax cut would harm the economy in the long run.[2] Because context shapes our understanding of simple enumerations, you want to be very careful not just to accept them at face value, but to place them in appropriate contexts.

statistics
Numbers recording the extent of something or the frequency with which it occurs.

Surveys and Polls. Suppose your topic was about how most Americans regard the public education system. In theory, you or someone else could interview all Americans and then tabulate the results. But that approach is doomed to fail. Not even the Census Bureau has been able to find and count all Americans, and the time and expense involved would make the task impossible. Moreover, the data would be obsolete by the time you completed your survey.

Instead, you can *infer* the attitudes of the people as a whole from the attitudes reported by a sample of the population, as long as the sample is representative of the whole. In the case of public opinion about the U.S. education system, a 1992 Gallup Poll reported that 68 percent of the sample interviewed believed that public schools fail to educate the nation's children. That statistic would be used to suggest that the general public—not just the people interviewed in this survey—give American public education a vote of no confidence.

Surveys and polls are widely used in the physical and social sciences and to gain information about public opinion on matters of policy.

Rates of Change. Often, what is noteworthy about a statistic is not its absolute size but its rate of change. For instance, it may be more important to know that the national debt doubled during the 1980s than to know the total dollar amount of the debt. Similarly, knowing that medical costs have increased at a much faster rate than personal income may be more useful than knowing either of the exact amounts. And knowing that the world's population is doubling faster and faster may have greater implications than knowing what the total population is. Speakers often can illustrate and emphasize such dramatic rate changes through visual aids.

Rates of change show what is happening and can help an audience compare the situation to some known benchmark. By themselves, however, statistics may not tell much and may easily mislead.[3] For example, one student speaker supported the claim that the university was not promoting affirmative action by citing what seemed like an important statistic:

> Did you know that fewer African Americans were admitted to this school this year than last year? There's no excuse for that! It proves that this school has no commitment to diversity.

The speaker had fallen into a statistical trap, however, by failing to note that the *total* number of students admitted was lower this year than last. The percentage of African American students in the entering class was actually slightly higher and had increased for three years in a row.

Experiments. Experiments are controlled tests of the effect of one thing on another. They are conducted by comparing situations that are essentially similar except for the factor being tested. A claim that secondhand smoke leads to lung cancer, for example, would be supported by comparing the cancer rates of two groups that were similar in all essential respects except that one had been exposed to secondhand smoke and the other had not. Similarly, the claim that African American drivers are stopped by police officers in a particular neighborhood more often than are Caucasian drivers could be tested by sending the same model car through the same neighborhood at the same time of day at the same speed with drivers who differ only in the color of their skin.

Using Research to Support Your Speech

The Situation

The industrial area in the town where you live is undergoing substantial growth and change. Several warehouses have already been torn down, and high-rise office buildings have gone up in their place. You believe that a direct result of this development is increased traffic on the local streets by commuters, which is causing massive traffic jams and having an impact on the quality of life in your town. In addition, the removal of what had been green space leads to increased water runoff and pollution, and also to the elimination of a habitat for wildlife. These dangers do not seem apparent to the town planners, though, especially when they can point to the economic benefits of new construction. Now another major office complex is being planned for the only remaining open space in town. You and several other residents have formed a grassroots community organization to fight this development. Your group is planning to present your case at the next meeting of the municipal planning board, and you have been appointed spokesperson.

Making Choices

1. What questions do you need to answer in order to provide evidence to back up your belief that the development is responsible for many problems?

2. What sources of information will you use to research your cause?

What If . . .

Suppose that your research shows that a new direct exit from the highway to the office park is being planned to alleviate the traffic tie-ups on local streets.

1. With one of your key arguments lacking support, what additional information should you get to support your overall case?

2. What other arguments might you make based on the evidence, and how might you support them?

3. What will you do with information that does not support your case?

Testimony

Testimony is information or an opinion that is expressed by someone other than the speaker, who uses the testimony to support some claim. When using testimony, you rely on someone else's judgment, and so you need to assess that person's competence and credibility. You may also need to convince the audience that your source is knowledgeable and trustworthy.

Factual Testimony. *Facts* are pieces of information that can be proved true or false. Speakers often support ideas by reporting facts that were gathered by others, such as quoting the secretary of state about developments in the Middle East, or quoting a public health expert about the dangers of secondhand smoke, or quoting a campus security officer about the number of crimes reported last year. When you quote facts, you are implying that you cannot verify the information yourself but are willing to accept it because you think the source is credible.

Opinion Testimony. *Opinions* are beliefs formed from experience and judgment. When you offer another person's opinion to support a claim, you are indicating that someone whose judgment is trusted, whose expertise is val-

testimony
Information or an opinion expressed by someone other than the speaker, cited to support some claim.

ued, or who is in a better position to know than most people are has reached a certain conclusion. You are asking the audience to accept that conclusion because of the person's expertise, judgment, or knowledge, not because you can verify the statement. Thus you might quote an expert in Middle Eastern politics to support a point about the peace process in that region, or you might quote campus security officers about whether the campus is a safe place to be after dark.

When using opinion testimony for support, consider whether the audience will know and trust the person you are quoting. You may have to establish why your source's opinion is more valuable than the average person's.

Checklist 5.1 Testing the Strength of Supporting Material

1. **Personal experience**
   - Are you sure your memory is reliable?
   - Is your experience generalizable?
   - Will others interpret it the same way?
2. **Common knowledge**
   - Are you sure the audience shares it?
   - Are you sure it is correct?
3. **Direct observation**
   - Are you sure of what you saw?
   - Might you have any bias?
4. **Examples**
   - Are they representative?
   - Are there enough of them?

5. **Documents**
   - Can they be trusted?
   - Are they properly interpreted?
   - Is the context made clear?
6. **Statistics**
   - Are appropriate measures used?
   - Are they reliable and valid?
   - Have they been interpreted properly?
7. **Testimony**
   - Does the person have access to the data?
   - Is the person expert on the subject?
   - Is the person reasonably objective?

Finding Supporting Material from People

The word *research* conjures up images of the scientist in the laboratory, the solitary scholar in a musty library, or the introvert peering for hours into a computer screen. Although laboratories, libraries, and computers are indeed places where evidence can be found, do not overlook your memory and interviews with others as potential sources of support.

Whereas the previous discussion dealt with *types* of supporting material, we now will consider the *sources* of supporting material—the places where you could find it.

Memory

Your memory is an important source of evidence. Experiences you've had, events you've observed, and things other people have said to you all become part of your personal stock of supporting material.

Besides the things you remember, your own observations may be a source of evidence. If your topic is about the quality of campus housing, you might visit a variety of living units and observe what conditions are like. In your speech you then could state, "I visited six kinds of living units on campus, and here is what I found." Your reported observations would become evidence.

Interviews

Sometimes, the best source of supporting material is other people. Interviews enable you to ask exactly the questions that you need to have answered, and the give-and-take of the interview routine permits follow-up discussion. Moreover, people sometimes will make statements in an oral interview that they would not be willing to make in print.

It is not only national and international experts who provide valuable interviews. The manager of the local department store has a perspective on how economic conditions affect consumer confidence. Faculty members have expertise on a variety of issues in every academic discipline. And fellow students can tell you about all aspects of campus life, including, say, how changes in funding for student loans may affect their educational plans. Clearly, potential interviewees are everywhere, and your strategic planning should consider all options.

If distance or time constraints prevent you from conducting face-to-face interviews, you can question sources by telephone, mail, or the Internet. However you actually contact your sources, the following guidelines will help make your interviews effective.

Prepare for the Person. Learn as much as you can about the people you plan to interview. How long have they held their current position? What experiences have they had with the subject? Are they prominently identified with some issue or aspect of your topic? Are they well known, or will you need to establish their credentials? Thinking about such questions in advance of the interview process will allow you to derive the greatest benefit from your sources' expertise in the time available.

Prepare for the Subject. It is a waste of your sources' time if you ask them very general questions or seek information that you can get easily in other ways. Don't let the interview substitute for your own background reading and research. Be familiar with general aspects of the subject, including its history, its current status, and relevant issues. Make sure that you understand basic concepts that are likely to come up in the interview so that you can focus your questions on unique information that your source can provide.

Prepare for the Format. An interview is a particular kind of communication event that proceeds through questions and answers. Before the interview, formulate your questions carefully so that they are not vague and not leading or hostile. Your questions should be simple and direct and should not anticipate answers or favor any particular viewpoint. Instead, you should give your sources the opportunity to make their own judgments, to explain why they think as they do, and to comment on different points of view that others may have expressed.

Also be aware that different types of questions elicit different types of information. A **closed question** limits the respondent to a fixed number of choices, such as "Would it be more efficient for campus security to invest in (1) an escort system or (2) a shuttle bus?" This type of question directs the respondent to pick one option from those you have offered, which is helpful when you want to commit the person to a definite position. A closed question also allows you to count and compare the answers of different respondents, since they all choose from the same optional answers. But closed questions do not reveal much about respondents' thinking and opinions.

In contrast, an **open-ended question** does not limit or direct the person's response, as in "What do you think should be done to enhance campus security?" Although an open-ended question does permit full expression of opinions, the answer may stray far from the information you most need for your speech, and you may have to refocus the interview repeatedly.

Time is another factor to consider in formulating questions. A closed question can be answered quickly and may allow you to interview more respondents; but you will need time to collect, tabulate, and analyze responses before you can use the information in developing your speech. Open-ended questions take more time to answer, which may limit how many respondents you can interview (and how many are willing to be interviewed). Also, respondents often introduce important matters that you did not consider in your original questions, and you should allow time to pursue them.

Conduct the Interview Competently. Being a competent interviewer includes such basic matters as arriving on time, reminding the person who you are and the purpose of your interview, and thanking him or her for taking the time to help you. But competence also includes the ability to adjust your questions in response to the flow of the interview itself. The person may say something that answers several of your questions or parts of them, or a comment may bring up a question that you had not planned on asking. Do not regard your questions as rigid and inflexible; adjust them as the interview evolves. On the other hand, if the interviewee seems to ignore a question, you may need to ask it again, perhaps phrasing it differently. Or, you may need to ask a **follow-up question** that explores the implications of a previous response. Finally, you must take care to reach an agreement with the respondent about what information, if any, you can quote directly and what information is solely for your own use. If you do intend to quote directly, be sure that your understanding of the person's answers is accurate and exact.

Take Notes or Record the Interview. Don't assume that you will remember everything important that is said during an interview. Arrive prepared, with notebook in hand, so you can keep track of important points. If you prefer to record the interview, be sure to ask ahead of time whether that will be all right; no one should be recorded without permission. Think carefully about recording the interview, however. Although it does free you from the burden of note taking and ensures an accurate record of the interview, it also may make the respondent more guarded and less candid, knowing that every

closed question
A question with a finite number of choices from which the respondent must pick.

open-ended question
A question that does not restrict the range of possible responses.

follow-up question
A question that explores the implications of a previous response.

word is being "recorded for posterity." Besides, later on you'll have to transcribe the entire recording in order to organize notes for your speech. It may be more practical and more effective to take notes during the interview itself, while you have the opportunity to follow up and clarify the person's remarks.

Determine What to Use in Your Speech. Not everything that you obtain in an interview will be useful in your speech; nor should the interview be your sole source of information. As you assemble materials for the speech, ask yourself which points can be supported most effectively by the interview and which points can be supported just as well by other sources. For example, you may decide to rely on printed sources for general or statistical information about your topic and then draw on the interview for opinion testimony and for real-world examples.

Checklist 5.2 Guidelines for Interviewing

1. Prepare for the person.
2. Prepare for the subject.
3. Prepare for the format.
4. Conduct the interview competently.
5. Take notes or record the interview.
6. Determine what to use.

Finding Supporting Material in Print

Although your personal knowledge and experience with others are valuable sources of evidence, you probably will need to rely heavily on printed material—especially when your topic is of public significance. In that case, you'll want material of broader scope than what you have experienced or what people have told you. The library is the best source of printed material, and often of audiovisual material as well. An added benefit of doing library research for your speeches is that you will learn much about how to use the library and will probably discover that it is an inviting rather than a forbidding place. And you will gain access to the many printed materials that do not exist in electronic form and hence are not accessible through the Internet.

Books

When you think of printed materials, you probably think first of books. Both general and specific books about your topic—as well as anthologies of essays by different authors—can be valuable sources of supporting material. In most libraries, the fastest way to locate relevant books is to consult the online index, which has largely replaced the card catalog. Today's computerized catalogs are easy to use and make research remarkably efficient and productive. Don't hesitate to ask a librarian for help in using a computerized catalog.

The subject entry will give you important information about a book: its author, title, length, date and place of publication, other subjects under which the book is listed, and its call number (see Fig. 5.1). The entry also may guide you to other closely related subjects. For example, the subject heading "labor unions" may direct you to such categories as "trade associations," "labor-management disputes," and "collective bargaining." Don't hesitate to explore these headings as well.

The book's call number will tell you where to find the book on the library's shelves. If the stacks are "open," meaning that you have access to them, browse the books with call numbers near to the book that you want. You may discover related titles that you hadn't identified by other means.

Sometimes, particularly if your library is small, you may run across a citation to a book that cannot be found. Fortunately, most libraries can arrange an interlibrary loan, using specialized indexes to help you identify other libraries that have the book and arranging to borrow it for you. Be aware, however, that this takes time. If you anticipate needing books that your library doesn't have, request them far ahead of when you will need them for your speech. The librarian in charge of interlibrary loans can explain the procedure and time frame to you.

Reference Works

Although usually published in book form, reference works are a special category of printed sources. They are seldom intended to be read from cover to cover; they do not develop a sustained argument or claim; and they usually are not written in narrative form. Rather, they are convenient collections of facts and information. Typically, reference works are shelved in a special section of the library, where a reference librarian can help you find and use the following common types of materials.

Dictionaries not only tell you the definitions of a word but also trace its origin and usage. Besides general dictionaries, you can find specialized dictionaries that identify the terms and usage within particular fields.

Encyclopedias are either general—the kind found in many homes—or specialized in particular subjects, such as *The Encyclopedia of Philosophy* and the *International Encyclopedia of Communications*. Encyclopedias contain brief essays that will give you an overview of a subject. If that subject is incidental to your speech, this level of understanding may be all you need. If you need a deeper understanding, the encyclopedia will give enough background information to steer you to more specialized sources.

Author Card—Computer Display

Search request:	F PA MISHARA, BRIAN
Search result:	5 records at all libraries
Type HELP for other display options.	
1.	
Author:	Mishara, Brian L.
Title:	Alcohol and old age / by Brian L. Mishara and Robert Kastenbaum. New York : Grune & Stratton, c1980.
Description:	ix, 220 p. ; 24 cm.
Series:	Seminars in psychiatry.
Notes:	Includes bibliographical references and index.
Subjects:	Aged -- Alcohol use. Alcohol -- Physiological effect. Geriatric psychiatry.
Other entries:	Kastenbaum, Robert, joint author. Seminars in psychiatry (New York, N.Y. : 1975) (Record 1 continues on the next screen.)
Press RETURN to see the next screen.	
- > f su aged alcohol use	

Figure 5.1 Library card catalogs are often computerized, making it easier and more efficient to locate research materials.

Abstracts are short summaries of articles or books related to a particular discipline. Many academic and professional groups publish abstracts of the articles appearing in their current journals. By reading abstracts instead of entire journals, you can discover which articles include material that may be useful.

Fact books are compilations of statistical information that you can consult when you need specific data to support a point in your speech. Almanacs, for example, are published every year and supply up-to-date facts about an enormous range of subjects.

Biographical references identify particular individuals and outline their backgrounds and achievements. *Who's Who* is the best-known biographical reference, but a vast number of such sources can tell you about both contemporary and historical figures.

Compilations and yearbooks are edited collections of material of a given type. For example, *Editorials on File* is a digest of selected newspaper editorials arranged by topic; it is published regularly and then compiled into a yearbook each year. Other examples of such compilations are *Facts on File* and *Congressional Quarterly Almanac,* an especially useful guide to the status of issues currently before the U.S. Congress. *Congressional Quarterly* also publishes a pamphlet called *CQ Researcher,* which examines a different issue of public interest each week. This compilation of facts and opinions includes background information, editorials about each side of the issue,

and a bibliography of important books and articles to help you start researching the issue.

Atlases provide geographical information, including the exact location and physical characteristics of specific sites, cities, and regions.

Collections of quotations are useful both for tracking down the origin of popular sayings and for finding maxims or brief quotations related to a particular topic.

Periodical indexes, found in the reference section of the library, are described in the next section.

Periodicals

Periodicals (sometimes called *serials*) are published at regular intervals—usually weekly, monthly, or quarterly—and have the advantage of being more up to date than books.

General-Interest Periodicals. These are usually sold on newsstands and by subscription, and they thus circulate widely; examples include *Time,*

Newsweek, U.S. News & World Report, and *People.* Periodicals such as these may have useful information about current events, but their coverage of issues is fairly brief and not deep, with the exception of feature articles. Given their mass circulation, they may be useful in identifying topics of interest and prevalent attitudes among many readers.

Other general-interest periodicals are more focused journals of opinion that delve more deeply into issues and often espouse a particular point of view. Examples include *The American Prospect* and *Progressive* (liberal) and *Commentary* and *National Review* (conservative). Consult sources such as these when you are interested in a particular political perspective on your topic. Other opinion journals, such as *Atlantic* and *Harper's,* tend to represent more diverse and eclectic viewpoints.

Special-Interest Periodicals. These are intended for readers who have particular interests, which may be as broadly defined as business (*Fortune* and *Business Week*) or rock music (*Rolling Stone* and *Spin*) or may be as narrowly focused as snowmobiles, digital imaging, or coin collecting. Whatever your topic is, you probably can find a periodical that is devoted to it. Some are aimed at specific demographic groups—based on age, gender, ethnicity, and so on—and even cities, for that matter, are the focus of magazines named after them.

Technical Periodicals. These are written primarily for specialists in a given field. Scholarly journals are the obvious example, with one or more publications dedicated to most academic disciplines: *American Political Science Review, Journal of the American Medical Association, Journal of American History, American Bar Association Journal, Quarterly Journal of Speech,* and so on. Colleges and universities also sometimes publish scholarly journals, such as *Critical Inquiry* and *Yale Review.* Law reviews also fit into this category. Although journals such as these are intended mainly for subject-matter specialists, they sometimes include material that can be very helpful for a speech, such as the results of surveys, experiments, and historical and critical analyses conducted by experts in various fields.

Indexes to Periodicals. You can locate periodical articles by consulting published indexes, the most common of which is the *Reader's Guide to Periodical Literature.* This easy-to-use subject-matter index can be found in virtually every library, and you probably have used it in the past. With few exceptions, however, it indexes only popular, general-interest periodicals.

To locate articles in special-interest and technical periodicals, consult the large number of specialized indexes that are available. The *Bulletin of the Public Affairs Information Service* is useful for many topics dealing with public policy issues. The *Social Sciences Index* and the *Humanities Index* can point you to journals and periodicals relating to those many disciplines. The *Business Periodicals Index* can help you research topics about the economy and business conditions, and the *Index to Legal Periodicals* covers law reviews and journals. Finally, the *International Index to Periodicals* can guide you through journals published in other countries. If the subject of your speech falls outside these categories, ask the reference librarian to suggest appropriate periodical indexes.

Newspapers

Newspapers are the most important source of ongoing current information. Besides reporting the latest news, many newspapers analyze and interpret it and publish related feature articles. Your own daily newspaper will be a valuable source of information for speeches. If you do not already do so, develop the habit of reading the paper regularly and clipping material that you think may be useful in developing a speech.

Especially if you live outside a major metropolitan area, it's a good idea to consult newspapers that cover current events and opinions more comprehensively than your local paper does. Many of these have their own indexes, including the *New York Times* (probably the most comprehensive), the *Wall Street Journal* (especially good on business and economic issues), the *Christian Science Monitor,* the *Washington Post* (particularly on matters of national politics), the *Chicago Tribune*, and the *Los Angeles Times.*

Like most of us, libraries discard all but the most recent newspapers, but first they usually record them on microfilm. You can read the film on machines designed for this purpose, and you can take notes or make photocopies of material that you want to use in your speech.

Government Publications

Another often-overlooked source of supporting material is the vast range of publications by state and national governments. Many college and university libraries are government depositories, which means that they regularly receive copies of most federal (and sometimes state) government publications. Some also include the publications of foreign governments and of the United Nations.

Covering virtually every public issue, government publications include bulletins, reports, pamphlets, research studies, congressional deliberations, judicial opinions, and agency publications. Often, however, these are not indexed in the card catalog or general periodical indexes. If your speech topic is of concern to government bodies, you are well advised to visit the government publications section of your library and to consult with the librarian in charge. Although government documents may seem intimidating at first, you can learn to use them effectively by following their few printed directions and seeking the help of the librarian if necessary.

The most comprehensive federal index is the *Monthly Catalog of U.S. Government Publications*, in which titles are arranged alphabetically under the government agency that published them. The subject index is probably the best place to start. When you look up the subject of your speech, you will find a series of entry numbers, one for each document in the alphabetical listing. When you find the entry number, return to the front of the index and locate the document with that entry number. You will then be able to identify the issuing agency, title of the document, call number, and Superintendent of Documents number. Although the *Monthly Catalog* is the most comprehensive index, it is not annotated. You will have to guess from the issuing agency and the title whether the document will be useful to you.

The *Congressional Information Service* is an especially valuable index to congressional publications because it includes abstracts, or brief summaries, of their contents. Again, the subject index lists entry numbers that you can use to look up the abstracts. This is particularly useful in approaching multivolume transcripts of congressional testimony. The *Congressional Information Service* includes all the publications of the legislative branch: hearings, committee reports, commissioned studies, and other documents. It does not index the executive or judicial branches, and it does not cover years before 1970. Nonetheless, for matters that are currently before Congress or that have been considered in the recent past, it is an invaluable reference source.

Other indexes to federal government publications include the *Congressional Record Index*, the *American Statistics Index*, and the *Index to U.S. Government Periodicals*. The librarian in charge of the government periodicals section can help you locate and use these. Similarly, because state and international documents are indexed in a variety of ways, ask the librarian for help.

Finding Supporting Material Electronically

The development of the Internet, and especially the World Wide Web, has made a wealth of supporting material available. Some of the material is very useful, such as online library card catalogs, information from organizations, and subject-specific information that you can't find anywhere else. Properly used, the Web can be a valuable supplement to library research. Keep in mind, though, that *anyone* can publish on the Web; with no assurance of quality control, you also will find information that is inaccurate, useless, tasteless, or even willfully misleading. For this reason, no matter how critically you assess information on the Web, you should not rely entirely on it for your research but should use electronic sources in *addition* to sources you find from people or in print.

The Web got its name because each site on it usually contains *links* to other related sites, thus forming a kind of web. Having found a site that contains useful information, you can follow its links to other sites that seem interesting. This is

WWW. Using the Internet

Finding and Citing Online Research Sources

Do an interactive exercise from the **Allyn & Bacon Public Speaking Web Site** that guides you through the process of doing a variety of types of online research. You will also learn how to cite an online source using the MLA (Modern Language Association) guidelines. Go to **http://www.abacon.com/pubspeak/exercise/mlaexer .html/**.

Note that you have the option of sending a copy of your results page to your professor or to yourself. You may also print a hard copy. Click on the various links to pages that will take you step by step through:

- Using search engines such as AltaVista, and Yahoo!, and Google
- Sources for finding and citing online periodicals and journals
- An exercise for finding an online speech text and citing it
- You can also locate a Web version of a magazine or journal. To find articles online, point your Web browser to **Find Articles.com** (**http://www.findarticles.com/ PI/index.jhtml**).

like using the bibliography of one book to find other books, only much faster.

Types of Information on the Web

Just as there are different types of print materials, you can find many kinds of supporting material on the Web. Here are some of the major categories.

Electronic Versions of Printed Publications. Newspapers, magazines, and journals often publish electronic as well as print versions. The two versions may be identical, but often the electronic version will contain more detailed information or be updated more frequently. In addition, of course, the electronic version is more convenient because you can access it from your computer without having to go to the library and hunt for the printed publication. In general, electronic versions of printed material should be treated with the same authority that you give to the printed material itself.

Fugitive Materials. Many documents that are hard to find (hence the term *fugitive*) are posted on the World Wide Web. These include papers presented at professional meetings, conference proceedings, position papers, working documents and archives of groups and organizations, and unpublished essays and manuscripts. These can often provide valuable background, give you a behind-the-scenes perspective on a topic, and give you access to specialized information. They should be viewed with some caution, however, as there is significantly less quality control in the selection of materials to post.

Electronic Journals. As the cost of printing increases, a growing number of journals—especially those with high production costs or limited circulation—are being produced only in electronic form. Electronic publishing also allows readers to have research results much earlier, an important consideration for scientific journals. Some electronic journals have editorial review procedures just like those for print journals, whereas others are open to anyone who wishes to "publish" an article by posting it to the journal. When you seek evidence from electronic journals, it is very important to know whether submissions to the journal are subject to editorial screening and review.

Web Pages. Millions of individuals, companies, associations, professional organizations, and government agencies maintain Web pages. When a magazine advertisement says, "Visit us at . . ." followed by an Internet address, you are being invited to view the organization's home page. The home page provides you with information about the person or organization, usually in more detail than you can find in print, and usually will provide links to more specialized pages. The home page for a university, for instance, might contain links to such topics as admissions, degree requirements, departments and curricula, events and activities, and recent news. Because Web pages are self-published, they will vary greatly in quality and should be used with caution. Later in this chapter, we will consider how to evaluate the strength of Internet evidence, including that on Web pages.

Searching for Information on the Web

Browsers. To navigate through the links on the Web, you need a *browser*, a computer program that keeps track of where you are on the Web and of the path you took to get there. The browser also displays a particular site's information on your computer monitor. The two most widely used browsers are Netscape Navigator and Microsoft Internet Explorer.

A browser will enable you to:

- *Go to a specific site by entering its address into the computer.* Each site has a distinct address, called a *Uniform Resource Locator* (*URL*). This always begins with the letters http://. The colon and the two slash marks are required and are followed by the specific URL. For example, the Web site for Allyn & Bacon, the publisher of this book, is http://www .ablongman.com.
- *Move to a new site by selecting an on-screen link.* When you look at a page displayed by the browser on your monitor, you'll often see words and phrases that are highlighted, usually by being underlined and appearing in a different color from the main text. Highlighted phrases are the links to other pages on the Web. Click your mouse on a highlighted phrase, and the browser will jump you to the selected location. Some links lead to programs or data files that you can download to your computer.
- *Return to previous sites.* Clicking the mouse on the "Back" button retraces your path through the linked pages of the Web. Clicking on the "Forward" button returns you to the site you left when you began retracing your path.
- *Go to your home page.* When you start your browser, it always brings you to the same starting point, or *home page.* Clicking the mouse on the "Home" button returns you to that page.
- *Set bookmarks to locate specific sites.* A *bookmark* brings you directly to a Web page without having to go through the other links. This is useful when, after dozens of links, you finally find what you were searching for or when you discover a site that you may want to explore later. Netscape Navigator files bookmarks under the "Bookmark" menu, and Microsoft Internet Explorer files them under "Favorites." In either case, when you reach a site that you want to bookmark, select the "Add" option under those menus; to return to a bookmarked site, pull down the menu and select the name of the bookmark. Figure 5.2 lists some subject-specific sites that you might want to bookmark.

IdeaList	http://www.contact.org
Google	http://www.google.com/
Thomas, Legislative Information on the Internet	http://thomas.loc.gov
Yahoo! Events	http://www.broadcast.com
ForumOne	http://www/forumone.com
Real.com	http://realguide.real.com

Figure 5.2 Frequently used subject-specific sites.

- *Revisit any recent site.* The browser creates a *history file* that records the name of every site you visit as you surf the Net. This lets you return to any recently visited site. In Netscape Navigator, you'll find the history file in the options under the "Windows" menu, and in Microsoft Internet Explorer, it is under the "Go" menu.

- *Print the currently displayed page.* When you find information that you want to keep, you can print it out by clicking the "Print" button.

Search Engines. There is no overall organization for Web sites that is similar to a library's card catalog. Thus, when you are researching a speech, it is difficult to know where to look for useful information. You have to roam the Web until you happen to find what you're looking for. With a browser, your search might be immediately productive or it might take a good deal of time and still you might miss key sites altogether. With so many diverse sites on the Web, it's impossible to visit them all yourself in search of information.

To solve this problem, you need a kind of program called a *search engine,* which scans a gigantic index that is created by robot programs that roam the Web collecting and indexing its pages. One of the most popular search engines is Google (http://www.google.com) (Figure 5.3). It can access more than three billion Web pages, searching its index in a fraction of a second to find key words and phrases.

Another popular search engine is maintained by Yahoo! (http://www.yahoo.com). Founded in 1994 by two Stanford University doctoral students, Yahoo! was the first online navigational guide to the Web. The Yahoo! Web site claims that it has the largest number of users worldwide.

Search engines use different searching strategies and slightly different approaches to cataloging the Web. No one search engine does a perfect job

Figure 5.3 Search engines such as Google and Yahoo! are good places to start if you are having difficulty locating information for your speech. Remember, however, that the search engines do not evaluate the reliability of Web sites—they only identify their availability.

all the time, so serious researchers will always use more than one search engine.

Electronic Databases. Such databases are more specialized research tools. Rather than guiding you to everything online that contains the key words you select for a search engine, they index online documents of a given type or on a given subject. If you already know the category of material you are looking for, they can help you find it efficiently. In this sense, they are like specialized periodical indexes. Figure 5.4 lists some especially useful electronic databases.

Avoiding Information Overload

Because search engines have massive indexes, they are likely to give far more information about sites than you can absorb, much less use. By mak-

The Internet Public Library	Indexes online newspapers.	http://www.ipl.org/reading/news
FedWorld Information Network	Index of local, state, and federal agencies.	http://www.fedworld.gov
Libweb	Links to library collections around the world.	http://sunsite.berkeley.edu/Libweb
News Directory.com	Links to worldwide media sources.	http://www.newsdirectory.com
Electronic Journals in the World Wide Web Virtual Library	Electronic journals organized by topic.	http://www.edoc.com/ejournal/
Biography.com	Database of famous people.	http://www.biography.com
Douglass	Texts of famous American orators.	http://douglass.speech.northwestern.edu/
Government Xchange	Access to government documents.	http://www.info.gov/
THOMAS, Legislative Information on the Internet	Library of Congress site for learning about Congress and government.	http://thomas.loc.gov/
State and Local Governments on the Net	Servers for each of the 50 states, with links to various branches of state government agencies, county or city servers.	http://www.piperinfo.com/index.cfm
E-journals	Electronic journals organized by topic.	http://www.e-journals.org
White House	Links to White House documents.	http://www.whitehouse.gov
Fed Stats	Links to statistics from over 100 Federal agencies.	http://www.fedstats.gov
Arts and Letters Daily	Media links, including magazines, newspapers, and wire services.	http://www.aldaily.com

Figure 5.4 Electronic databases.

ing your search as specific as possible, you can trim down the number of sites returned. Suppose that your topic is about drunk driving.

Using Google, type "drunk driving" into the search box and click "Search." Google will search its index for all the Web pages that have the words *drunk* and *driving*. Within seconds you will see that Google located 848,000 sources. There is no way you can consult all of these sources, even if you had weeks to prepare your speech. And even if you could, you would find that most of the pages are not pertinent to your topic. How can you avoid this problem?

Try again, but this time narrow your focus. If you are interested in drunk driving laws, try "drunk driving laws" in the search box, placing quotation marks around the phrase. The quotation marks tie the three search words together, so Google will locate only sites that contain these words as a phrase. The new search results in 6,070 sites. (Without quotation marks, the search would result in 201,000 sites.)

Now conduct the same search using Yahoo! Instead of "Searching the Web," scroll down to the Yahoo! directory. The directory organizes Web pages into categories. If you click on the "Society and Culture" category and type "drunk driving" in the search window, the search results in 63 sites. If you narrow your focus to "drunk driving laws" in the "Society and Culture" directory category, your search will produce five sites, which is much more manageable for your research.

This distinction illustrates the difference between a search engine that is looking for *key words* and one that is looking for *categories of sites*.[4] Despite this distinction, in recent years search engines have become more similar in their operations. Both Google and Yahoo! are searchable using key words or categories.

Here are some other search engines that you might want to explore:

Dogpile	http://www.dogpile.com
Excite	http://www.excite.com
AltaVista	http://www.altavista.com
Info Seek	http://www.GO.com
Lycos	http://www.lycos.com
WebCrawler	http://www.webcrawler.com

Using quotation marks around words is one way to narrow the scope of a search by directing the search engine to find only cases where the entire phrase appears. Here are some other ways to narrow your search:

- **The + Sign** Using the + sign between words accomplishes about the same thing as placing quotation marks around a phrase—it directs the search engine to look only for cases in which the terms appear together, although they can be in any order.
- **AND** This command causes the search engine to find only Web pages that include *all* the key words you specify (but not necessarily together). For instance, if you entered "drunk AND driving," the search engine will find only Web pages that use both words.
- **NEAR** This command is used to find Web pages on which two words are close to each other. For example, "drunk NEAR driving" will lead you

to pages that include such phrases as "driving while one is drunk." Various search engines have different tolerances for "closeness," but usually the search terms must be within six or eight words of each other.

- **NOT** The NOT command allows you to make a distinction between closely related terms when you know which key words you want to eliminate. For example, "DWI NOT DUI" will locate pages with the term *DWI* (driving while intoxicated) but not any related pages that use the term *DUI* (driving under the influence).

Finding Useful Information

Because anyone can construct a Web site for any reason, the Web includes information that is biased, out of date, or simply inaccurate. But it also contains the most recent information about topics of current interest. You have to figure out where to look.

Pay special attention to the home pages of government agencies and think tanks. These organizations conduct extensive research and release policy papers on a range of issues. One of the most comprehensive is the Electronic Policy Net, http://www.epn.org/, which includes an easily navigated image map. Clicking a location on this map brings you to the home page for a particular subject, such as "Health Policy." When you arrive at the page for health-related issues, you will see a variety of specific subjects. Click on one of these, and you will enter a hypertext analysis of the issue.

Think tanks are often not neutral but supported by organizations with a particular ideological perspective. The Electronic Policy Net, for instance, labels itself a progressive organization. You can find a wide range of think tanks at Allyn & Bacon's Public Speaking Web site under the link for "Social Problems and Social Policy" (http://www.ablongman.com/pubspeak/topic.html).

Evaluating Internet Evidence

In Chapter 6, we will consider how to decide whether your supporting materials are of good quality and really do support your claims. Before we get there, however, there are special issues regarding Internet evidence that we need to consider.

The Internet has been described as the most democratic means of publishing there is. Virtually anyone can post virtually anything on the World Wide Web. As a consequence, there is almost no editorial or quality control except whatever is exercised by the producer of the site. An online version of a printed publication—an electronic copy of a print journal article, for example—can be assumed to reflect the same editorial judgment as the printed publication itself. At the other extreme, an individual's personal Web site may not have been checked at all. And some organizations whose mission is to promote a particular viewpoint can be deceptive, presenting propaganda as if it were scholarship.

Search engines looking for key words will not distinguish between reliable and unreliable Web sites. And whether the site looks "professional" is not a reliable indicator either, because it is easier to design a sophisticated-looking site than it is to produce a book. In fact, sophisticated Web sites

Evaluating Sources

Excerpts from Priya's Bibliography for her Persuasive Speech on "The Health Benefits of Chocolate"

Cortright, Susie. "Candy is Dandy: The Health Benefits of Chocolate." 1 March 2003. **<http://www.momscape.com/articles/chocolate.htm>**.

Holt, Roberta R., et al. "Chocolate Consumption and Platelet Function." *JAMA* 287 (2002): 2212–13.

Mason, Ian. "Benefits of Chocolate." Medical Science Society. 9 February 2003. **<http://www.medscicommunications.com/just_for_fun.htm>**.

Rauch, Catherine. "The Melt in Your Mouth Mystery." 9 February 2003. **<http://my.webmd.com/content/article/11/1671_50538>**.

Twesky, Ori. "Chocolate—and Your Health." 6 February 2003. **<http://my.webmd.com/content/article/8/1619_84752>**.

Prof. Blivens

Make sure you get full use of all your sources. It's important not only to use a source's statements and evidence to support your own, but to use the source's credentials and viewpoint to lend your speech credibility. Instead of just saying "according to" and listing the information in the article, give us some preliminary information about the citation. For example, if Roberta Holt is a doctor, tell us that. Who is Catherine Raunch, and what research did she do? For information from the Web, this is especially important; include who or what organization runs the Web site, when the site was last updated, and whether the site owners are a special interest group. Look for this information to test a Web site's credibility. If it's not listed, or they give no background on the author, skip it and look for other sources. Also, it seems like your bibliography is Internet-heavy. The library has several databases that include a wide range of source material. Use those to help diversify your sources. The wider your range of research material, the more weight your argument will carry.

that look like those of easily recognized organizations have been created for the purpose of coaxing individuals to reveal their Social Security and credit card numbers in order to facilitate identity theft. This, of course, is fraud.[5] Extra vigilance is needed to be sure that you take only reliable evidence from the Web. For these reasons, the responsibility to evaluate Internet evidence rests with you. We need, therefore, to note some special precautions about supporting materials from electronic sources. The following questions are especially pertinent.[6]

- *Does the site meet the basic standards of credibility?* At a minimum, a credible Web page should contain the name of the sponsor, identification of expert and believable author(s), and information that is current, appropriate, and capable of being checked for accuracy.
- *Who set up the Web site?* If you cannot tell who sponsors the site, be suspicious of its contents. People or organizations with an ax to grind can disguise their motivations or identity, leading you to regard biased information as though it were neutral. One clue to a site's reliability is its *domain name*—the last portion of its URL. As a general rule, URLs that end

in .gov (government agency) or .edu (educational institution) may be more reliable sites than those ending in .org (organization) or .com (commercial source).

- *What are the source's credentials?* To determine whether the author has expertise on the subject, you should check a credentials page. You may need to trace back in the URL (Internet address) to find one. If the author has a specific agenda or ideology, take that into consideration when you evaluate the source.

- *What is the purpose of the Web site?* If the goal is to sell a product or service or to campaign for an individual or a point of view, you should examine the content more skeptically than if the goal is simply to provide information. Sometimes, the site's purpose will not be apparent from its title and the name of the source. You will need to read through the material on the site in order to form a judgment.

- *Does the content appear to reflect scholarship?* Scholarly work generally provides documentation for claims, indicates where information was obtained, describes limits of the data and does not overstate claims, considers alternative viewpoints on matters of opinion and describes these alternatives accurately, honors context, and relies on critical thinking skills (such as those discussed in Chapter 1). If the site contains excessive claims of certainty, presents ideas out of context or without documentation, and suppresses alternative views, it is more likely to be biased advocacy or propaganda.

- *Can you confirm the information?* If something seems too good to be true, it probably is. And if you find information on the Web that seems to make your case airtight or to refute someone's ideas conclusively, be careful. A good general rule is to check electronic information against other sources. Even if you can't find the exact same facts or ideas, what you obtain from the Web should be compatible with what you learn from people or in print.

- *When was the site last updated?* The value of the World Wide Web is that it can supply up-to-the-minute information about current topics. Often, however, sites are not updated regularly, and the information becomes obsolete. If you cannot tell when a site was last updated, that may be a reason to be wary of its content.

A Strategy for Research

Researching for a speech can seem overwhelming. At first, the topic may seem so vast that you don't know where to begin. You may not be able to think of any people you should interview, or you may identify so many people that you don't have time to question them all. The resources of a major library can be daunting, and specialized indexes and finding aids may only compound the problem by revealing an even larger mass of material to consider. And the Internet sources you checked might include literally thousands of citations. How can you possibly go through them all?

A research strategy can make these burdens manageable. Just as you need to understand your speech goals and the means to achieve them, you need to approach research strategically. The following suggestions will help you devise a research strategy.

Start Early. Your instructor no doubt has warned you not to wait until the last minute to begin preparing your speech. This is sound advice. Research does take time and involves a certain amount of trial and error. The sooner you begin thinking about and working on the speech, the better.

Determine Where You Need to Go. Your topic may require you to do research in the field, in the library, on the Internet, or by a combination of methods. The analysis of the issues related to your topic, described in Chapter 4, should help you determine which questions you need to answer and which kinds of research will help you answer them. Keep those questions in mind as you do your research.

Bring Necessary Materials and Supplies. It's frustrating (and often embarrassing) to arrive at the research site and discover that you don't have the materials you need. For example, if you are conducting interviews, you may need a tape recorder, tapes, and batteries or an extension cord as well as a notebook and pen. In the library, you may need notecards, pencils or pens, computer disks, and correct change for the photocopying machine. Think ahead, and be prepared.

Learn the Library's Layout. You do not want to waste valuable research time figuring out how the library is arranged and where things are. You should know your way around. Learn where to find the computer catalog, the reference room, and the stacks. Find out where periodicals, newspapers, and government publications are kept. Learn whether copying and computer equipment is available and what the library's hours and procedures are. If your library offers an orientation tour, arrange to take it even before you begin intensive research for your speech.

Develop a Preliminary Bibliography. Consult the various indexes and reference works described in this chapter to develop a list of potential sources. To save time later, this preliminary bibliography should include the call numbers or other identifying numbers you will need to locate the material.

Set Priorities Within the Bibliography. The order of items in your bibliography will probably not reflect the order in which you want to read the materials. Decide what is most important to locate right away. It may be a particular aspect of the topic or a certain kind of source.

Read Progressively. If you are not yet very familiar with your topic, begin by reading general works to gain a background understanding of key terms, major issues, and the origins and development of the subject. This background will prepare you for in-depth reading about the specific issues that you will highlight in your speech. Finally, there probably are particular claims or arguments for which you will need support: a specific example, a particular statistic, or a certain piece of testimony. As you proceed through your research, be clear about what level of understanding you seek. In general, if you find yourself reading about the same points repeatedly in different sources, it is time to move on to a more specialized level of research.

Read Selectively. Very likely, you will discover far more information than you can read—or even skim—in the time you have to prepare your speech. The key is to be selective in what you read. For example, check the dates of available sources. For some topics, such as whether a recession is likely to occur in the next year, very recent material is crucial. For other topics, such as the origins of the Social Security system, older material may actually be more valuable. If the date seems inappropriate for your purpose, don't bother consulting that source.

Read Efficiently. Doing research is not like reading a novel; you want to read quickly and efficiently, not from cover to cover. The goal is to identify which elements of a document or source are most pertinent for your speech. Skim material, looking for key words and a general sense of the context. Use guides—such as a book's table of contents, index, and headings—to determine which sections to read carefully and which you may skim or skip. Stay alert, however; efficiency is not haste, and you do not want to make a wrong turn somewhere that causes you to misunderstand the context of key points.

Be Open to New Ideas. Even though you are reading with a particular goal in mind, keep open the possibility that your research may change your perspective or uncover something about your topic that you had not considered. You might discover issues that you did not originally anticipate, and you might even decide to change your thesis statement.

Use Multiple Sources and Evidence of Various Types. Your speech will be less credible if all the supporting material comes from a single source or is of one type. If you use a single source to support your claims, the audience may think that you are simply parroting the thoughts of someone else. For example, one student's speech about recycling presented the same information, in the same order, as did a pamphlet that had been distributed to every student on campus. Not only did this student bore the audience with information they already had, but she made them angry, since they thought she was trying to avoid the work of amassing evidence from different sources and arranging it creatively for their benefit.

Likewise, the speech will be less interesting if all your evidence is of the same type. A mix of examples, testimony, statistics, and other types of support not only will hold the audience's attention but also will add credibility to your claims by suggesting that the same conclusion was reached through several different methods.

plagiarism
Using someone else's words or ideas as though they were your own.

Protect Against Plagiarism. In Chapter 1, we were alerted to avoid **plagiarism,** which is usually thought of as the use of someone else's words as though they were your own. But the same warning applies to using someone else's *ideas* as though they were yours. In either case, the plagiarist both misrepresents himself or herself and steals the intellectual property of another.

Most people recognize that plagiarism is wrong. When it happens, it usually is unintentional. A student organizes her speech in exactly the same way as a magazine article on the same subject without identifying the article and either doesn't realize it happened or doesn't recognize that it is a form of plagiarism. Another student thinks he is paraphrasing his source, but in fact is engaged in almost direct quotation without saying so. Because he identified the source, he may not think this is plagiarism, or he may not realize how close his speech stays to the original. A third student gives a speech basically reporting what a single source said without identifying the source because the student's speech was not a direct quotation. He, too, has misrepresented another person's thinking by treating it as his own idea. Each of these examples is a form of plagiarism.

How can you protect against plagiarism while doing your research? First, don't limit yourself to a single source. The need to bring together several different sources should reduce any unconscious tendency to stick too closely to the text. Second, as you take notes, paraphrase except when the exact words of the source are important to quote. In this way, you'll cast your notes in your own words right from the beginning. Third, organize your notes without any of the sources immediately at hand, so you won't be tempted to follow someone else's organizational structure. Finally, whenever you draw upon one of your notes to use it in the speech, be sure you identify the source.

Keep a Speech Material File. Sometimes, you will find materials that could be useful in a speech while you are doing something else—reading the newspaper, watching television, conversing with others, or studying for other courses. Don't lose track of this material or assume that you can find it when you need it. If you think that you may want to talk about a subject later in the term, begin now to save relevant material as you come across it.

Experienced speakers develop a **speech material file.** The file might be a notebook in which you jot down ideas, quotations, stories, poetry, or interesting examples. It might be a file of clippings from newspaper or magazine articles. The form of the file is not as important as the habit of keeping one. You will be pleasantly surprised by how much easier it is to prepare a speech when you do not have to start literally from scratch, when you already have materials about topics that interest you.

Know When to Stop. Research is an ongoing activity, and you can always learn more about any topic—especially if you enjoy the subject and like doing research. But there comes a point at which you must stop collecting evidence and assemble the speech, which, after all, has limits of time and scope. Besides, you want to leave enough time for the other steps of preparation; further research will only tell you more about what you already know—and more than you can possibly tell the audience. Considerations such as these should help you to determine when it is time to move on to the other steps of speech preparation. As you develop the speech, you can return to research as needed to fill specific holes.

speech material file
A file of clippings, quotations, ideas, and other gleanings on a variety of subjects that may be used as supporting materials.

Note Taking and Filing

No matter how thorough or extensive your research is, it will do you little good if you forget what you learned or where you learned it. Sometimes, something will seem so vivid or so obvious that you cannot imagine forgetting it, but most people remember far less than they think they will. Experienced speakers have learned to keep track of their speech material by establishing some system of note taking. Be guided by whatever works best for you, but the following suggestions should help you to establish an effective note-taking system.

Use a Flexible System. Recording each idea, statistic, example, quotation, and the like on an individual notecard or sheet of paper is better than taking continuous notes about different topics or taking notes in a spiral notebook or other bound book. A flexible system is one that makes it easy to sort and rearrange material in organizing the speech, to locate related materials, and to discard items that you decide not to use. Taking notes on a computer may be the most flexible system, as long as you can rearrange the notes easily in developing the speech.

When taking notes from electronic sources, you can follow the same methods described here—copying material from the monitor onto notecards or sheets of paper. But there are also programs that enable you to take notes electronically. One such program, distributed by Allyn & Bacon, is Q•Notes. It enables you to select electronic information for later reference and to capture the source information. The program creates notecards with the information, allows you to add comments to each card, and organizes and files the notecards for later use. It also allows you to keep track of sources and to build references and footnotes.

Include Full Bibliographic Citations. A "full" citation contains all the material needed to find the source from which you took notes. This step may seem time consuming, but you can make it more efficient through careful use of abbreviations. In any case, it should not be omitted. First, you often will need to go back to the original source to verify your notes, to check their context, or to compare them with other sources. Second, the bibliographic information will often be helpful in evaluating the strength of evidence or in choosing among different sources of evidence. It takes far more time and effort to find the source a second time than to note its full bibliographic citation while doing research.

Because standard guides for citing sources often neglect electronic material, the following suggestions should be helpful for knowing what constitutes a full citation of an Internet source:[7]

- If the Internet material has a print equivalent, begin with the citation for the hard-copy version, and then cite the online version.

- A complete online reference contains the title of the project or database (underlined); the name of the editor of the project or database (if given); electronic publication information, including version number (if relevant and if not part of the title); date of electronic publication or latest update; name of any sponsoring institution or organization; date of access; and electronic address.

- The electronic address (known as URL, for Universal Resource Locator) is enclosed in angle brackets (< >) and contains all the parts necessary to identify the file or document being cited—for example, <http://www.cats .org/docs/primary/index.html>. Some computer programs automatically convert the angle brackets to an underline. If a URL must be split across two lines, break it only after a slash (/). Do not introduce a hyphen at the end of the first line.

- If you cannot find all of the information, include whatever is available.

The purpose of citation is to allow someone to obtain information from the sources you used. Unlike print materials, a document on the Internet can appear, disappear, or be revised without any warning. For this reason, you need to include information on when a source was posted on the Internet (if that is available) and when you obtained the information. If you think that the Internet source may play a large role in your speech, it is a good idea either to print or to download the electronic document, preserving it in the form in which you consulted it.

Citing sources in notes or a bibliography is an essential part of your research. When you cite the source orally, during the speech itself, the process is a bit different. We will consider that issue in Chapter 7, when we discuss incorporating supporting materials into the speech.

Decide Whether to Quote or to Paraphrase the Source. It takes less thought but more time simply to copy the exact words of the source. Unless an exact quotation is necessary, it is more efficient to paraphrase, to summarize the gist of the idea in your own words. Obviously, your note-taking system should signal to you at a glance whether a note is quoted or not. A good method is to enclose the words of others in quotation marks but to omit them from your own paraphrases or summaries.

Clearly Identify Deletions and Additions in Quoted Material. Sometimes, the quotation you want to use is interspersed with other material that is unrelated to your purposes or is longer than you want to quote. At other times, the quotation may not be clear unless you add some words—for example, to identify the reference of a pronoun in the quotation.

When you use a quotation, you must make certain that all deletions and insertions are faithful to the context of the original source. Your notes should identify any variations from the exact text of the quotation. The most common practice is to identify deletions in your notes with an ellipsis (a series of three dots, like this: . . .) and to identify insertions in notes with brackets (like this: [ ]). It is important to use brackets rather than parentheses, because parentheses would indicate that the inserted words were in the original source. (In the speech itself, use changes in pitch or rate to identify insertions or deletions.)

Take Notes Only Once. If you take notes in longhand, be sure that you write legibly so that you do not have to recopy or type the notes. Duplicate note taking is a waste of time. Increasingly, laptop computers are used for note taking, which overcomes the problem of unclear handwriting. A computer also lets you take notes in continuous fashion and later print them out on separate sheets of paper, as recommended earlier. Or you may keep your notes in electronic files that you can search and manipulate as needs arise.

Strategies for Speaking to Diverse Audiences

Respecting Diversity Through Research

Using a variety of research sources will help you to find and to recognize diverse perspectives on your topic. These strategies will help you to do appropriate research in light of the diversity of your audience.

1. Go beyond U.S.-based media sources, particularly if your topic is international in scope.
2. Be aware of the partisanship of your media sources. Include both "liberal" and "conservative" perspectives on your topic.
3. Consider the "voices" you quote in your speech. Are they all male? American? Over age 55?

Summary

Research locates the supporting materials to be used in the speech. Because a speaker cannot find out everything there is to know about a topic, he or she must make choices about the amount and kind of supporting material and about the places to look for it. These decisions should be made in light of the audience and the purpose. Supporting materials are of many types, including personal experience, common knowledge, direct observation, examples, documents, statistics, and testimony. They can be found from people, in print, and electronically. Supporting materials from people include personal experience and interviews. Among printed sources of supporting material are books, reference works, periodicals, newspapers, and government publications. There are special indexes and finding aids for many of these sources of supporting material.

Computer technology makes it possible to find supporting material on the World Wide Web by using a browser or a search engine. With appropriate search strategies, you can avoid information overload and find useful material. Because few if any restrictions govern Internet publication, electronic evidence must be evaluated with special care.

Although the process of researching a speech can seem overwhelming, it can be managed by developing a research strategy. Such a strategy includes beginning early, being clear about what is needed and where it can be found, setting priorities and reading materials progressively and efficiently, taking useful notes, and developing the habit of maintaining a speech material file.

Discussion Questions

1. Which types of supporting material would you need to back up the thesis "Television programs have too much violence"? Evaluate each type of supporting material, and determine which part of the thesis each type would best support.
2. With a group, discuss the pros and cons of the following sources of supporting material, including the situations in which each type would be most appropriate:

   Personal experience
   Interviews
   Library research
   The Internet

Activities

1. In researching a thesis of your choice, find an example of each type of supporting material. Test the strength of each type to determine which material would best support your thesis.
2. Conduct an interview, following the guidelines offered in this chapter.
3. Follow the directions in this chapter for using the Internet to research your speech. Did the browsers and search engines work effectively? Did you find relevant information without being swamped by irrelevant material? How did you determine which material was relevant and trustworthy?

Notes

1. Thomas B. Farrell, "Knowledge, Consensus, and Rhetorical Theory," *Quarterly Journal of Speech* 62 (February 1976): 1–14.
2. David E. Rosenbaum, "The President's Tax Cut and Its Unspoken Numbers," *The New York Times,* February 25, 2003, p. A23.

3. For more on the misuse of statistics, see John Allen Paulos, *Innumeracy: Mathematical Illiteracy and Its Consequences*, New York: Hill and Wang, 1988.

4. Search strategies are considered much more thoroughly in Mary McGuire, Linda Stilborne, Melinda McAdams, and Laurel Hyatt, *The Internet Handbook for Writers, Researchers, and Journalists*, New York: Guilford, 2002, pp. 44–71.

5. For an example of this problem, see Jon Swartz, "Spammers' Fake Sites Dupe Consumers," *USA Today*, July 7, 2003, p. B1.

6. Some of the problems with doing electronic research are explained in Steven B. Knowlton, "How Students Get Lost in Cyberspace," the *New York Times*, "Education Life" section, Nov. 2, 1997: 18, 21. There are also online sources offering good suggestions for evaluating Internet evidence. Two examples are the site at the State University of New York at Albany (http://www.albany.edu/library/internet/evaluate.html) and the site at Illinois State University (http://www.mlb.ilstu.edu/ressubj/subject/intrnt/evaluate.htm).

7. For more information about how to cite electronic sources, see Janice R. Walker and Todd Taylor, *Columbia Guide to Online Style*, New York: Columbia Univ. Press, 1998. See also Terrence A. Doyle and Doug Gotthoffer, *Quick Guide to the Internet for Speech Communication*, Boston: Allyn and Bacon, 2000, pp. 127–133.

Chapter Six

Reasoning

In this chapter, we will:

- Examine the nature of rhetorical proof in public speaking and learn how it differs from proof in formal logic or mathematics.

- Identify the three components of rhetorical proof: claim, supporting material, and reasoning.

- Explore six basic patterns of reasoning, focusing on their types, appropriate tests of their soundness, and how to use them in a speech.

- Learn what a fallacy is and identify both general fallacies and fallacies that correspond to particular patterns of reasoning.

- Appreciate how an understanding of reasoning processes helps in preparing and delivering a speech and in being an active, critical listener.

By now, you have analyzed your situation, picked a good topic, and assembled some useful supporting materials. But how do you know whether these materials actually prove the point you want to make? In this chapter, you will learn about proof in public speaking and how to strengthen the reasoning in your speech.

Consider the following claims:

- 2 + 2 = 4
- The sum of the angles of a triangle equals 180 degrees.
- Light travels at about 186,000 miles per second.
- *The Mona Lisa* is Leonardo da Vinci's most beautiful painting.
- The semester academic calendar is best for our university.
- The government's economic policy is bad for the country.

The first three statements are mathematical or scientific claims; they are based on a system of rules by which they can be proved with absolute certainty—as long as you operate within that system. The last three claims are different; they involve beliefs, values, and judgments. Although for any of these three you could find evidence that convinces *you* of their truth, someone else might be unimpressed by your evidence or might find counterevidence to argue an opposing point. Therefore, the "proof" of these claims is not offered with the same level of certainty that supports the first three claims.

Proof, Support, and Reasoning

The ideas in a speech almost never take the form of a fixed mathematical principle as in the first three claims above. Instead, the basic material of public speaking is like the last three claims, involving matters of belief or value, judgments about what ought to be, norms of conduct, or predictions about the future. Such statements require agreement between the speaker and listeners, not only about the truth of the claim but also about what should count as proof in the first place.[1]

Rhetorical Proof as Support

Rhetorical proof is established through interaction in which the speaker and listeners reason together. This type of proof does not *ensure* that a conclusion is correct, but it offers *support* for a conclusion. It gives listeners confidence that the conclusion is probably correct and that they can share it, make it part of their working knowledge, and act on it if they are able to do so.

Suppose you are speaking to first-time employees about how they should save and invest their money. Research and analysis have convinced you that buying stocks is the best investment, but you can't be absolutely certain of that conclusion because it involves value judgments, predictions, and speculations. To help listeners reach the same conclusion, your speech might draw on statistics, historical accounts of the growth of the stock market, and examples of successful investors. These are called "supporting materials" precisely because their function is to *support* your conclusion. They do not guarantee that your conclusion is correct, but they give listeners good reasons to accept what you say and to act on it.

rhetorical proof
Proof established through interaction between the speaker and the listeners; provides support for a conclusion but not assurance that it is true.

Unlike mathematical proofs, then, rhetorical proofs have degrees of support ranging from strong to weak. As a result, both speakers and listeners must evaluate rhetorical proofs critically, testing them rather than taking them for granted. Your goal as a speaker is to provide the strongest support possible for your conclusion. What factors make rhetorical proof strong?

Proof and the Audience

The overriding factor in supporting a claim is, of course, the audience. Listeners who pay attention to the reasoning in a speech are critical and active; they are willing to be convinced but are skeptical enough to ask whether the speaker's reasoning withstands scrutiny. Critical listeners will ask whether your causal links are valid, whether your comparisons are apt, and whether the people you quote are authorities in the subject—all tests that you will study in this chapter. Knowing that you will face a critical audience helps you as a speaker, because you will make sure that your reasoning is strong. In this way, you and your listeners work together to achieve the highest possible standard of rhetorical proof.

Audiences differ, of course, and so you might need different proofs to convince, say, an audience of Democrats that the administration's economic policy is flawed than you would need for an audience of Republicans. But if you focus too narrowly on the immediate audience, you could run into a serious ethical problem: Yes, you may be *able* to convince the audience, but *should* you? Not all audiences are made up of critical listeners (as advertisers know only too well). Indeed, some listeners probably would accept just about any conclusion.

When Adolf Hitler's devoted followers accepted his claims about German racial superiority, did that prove his statements true? The answer to this difficult question turns out to be "yes and no." In a purely functional sense, yes: For those people in that situation, Hitler's claims could be considered proved; believers made the claims part of their working knowledge and acted on them. But in a larger sense, no: Regardless of what Hitler's supporters did or did not believe, they *should not have* accepted his claims, because his reasoning and evidence were flawed.

Speakers need to focus not only on proofs that listeners *actually do* regard as solid but also on proofs that they *ought* to regard as solid. Generally, a proof is **reasonable** if it would be taken seriously by a broad and diverse group of listeners exercising their best critical judgment.[2] Such an audience includes people who actually hear your speech as well as a larger, more culturally diverse audience who might "overhear" it through word of mouth or the media. When you offer rhetorical proofs, you are making strategic choices about the reasoning patterns that your immediate audi-

WWW. Using the Internet

Using Effective Rhetorical Reasoning

Effective reasoning must be based on evidence that is carefully gathered and analyzed critically. In addition, we can engage in further critical thinking about a piece of evidence or the claims we infer from it by taking part in discussions. This exercise uses critical thinking on four levels:

- Gathering evidence
- Selecting evidence
- Forming inferences
- Testing evidence and inferences through discussion

The effective use of reasoning depends on solid critical thinking as one makes inferences through the use of examples, analogy, signs, causality, testimony, and narratives. Examine how some of these types of inferences were made through a historic case study of the Salem witch trials. How did reasoning go awry? Go to the site created by *National Geographic* entitled **"Salem, Witchcraft Hysteria"** by pointing your browser to **http://www .nationalgeographic.com/features/97/salem/.** After taking part in the hypertext, go to the forum created by *National Geographic* at **http://www.nationalgeographic .com/features/97/salem/newdiscussframe.html/.** There you can see how other people have responded to the situation.

reasonable
Would be inferred by most people when exercising their critical judgment.

ence and this larger audience would accept. Think of a well-selected jury of peers in a well-run courtroom as your audience; if such a group of critical listeners would accept your proof, the inference is reasonable.

Even if your actual audience does not resemble such a group, do not abandon your standards. In offering a rhetorical proof, you must satisfy the immediate audience and also must meet a broader standard of reasonableness that would satisfy a larger imagined audience of critical thinkers.

Components of Proof

Any idea in the speech—whether a main point or a subordinate point—can be regarded as a *unit of proof* that has three principal components: the claim, the supporting material, and the reasoning.

Claim. The **claim** is the statement that you want the audience to accept; it is what you are trying to prove. The claim could be your broad thesis ("Popular music has changed greatly since 1960"), or one main idea ("Music videos have added a new dimension to popular music"), or a specific subpoint ("Having a video aired on MTV is now as important as getting radio time").

Supporting Material. This second component of a proof, examined in Chapter 5, provides *evidence* for your claim. To prove your claim, you must show that evidence supports it.

Reasoning. It is reasoning that links the supporting material to your claim so that you and your listeners together can decide whether the evidence really does support the claim.

Usually, the claim and the supporting material are stated explicitly in the speech and are easy to identify. But the essential link, reasoning, is usually implied; it involves a mental leap from the supporting material to the claim. This leap is called an **inference.** The inference enables us to say that, even though we are going beyond what the supporting material literally says, we feel justified in doing so because similar inferences in the past have usually led to acceptable results.[3]

An Example of Rhetorical Proof

After introducing a speech about the effect of tax increases on a family's budget, student Catherine Archer claimed:

> Taxes have taken a bigger bite out of the average paycheck each year. Just look at the record. Our state sales taxes have gone up faster than our income. Local property taxes have gone through the roof. And now the federal government is proposing to raise gasoline taxes again. Where does it all stop?

After the speech, she invited questions from the floor. "What about Social Security?" one woman asked. Catherine replied:

> Thank you. That's still one more example of a tax that has gone up faster than income. In fact, many people today pay more in Social Security tax than in their income tax.

claim
A statement that a speaker asks listeners to accept and that the speaker tries to prove.

inference
A mental leap from the supporting material to the claim.

Then a man in the audience said, "Since you mentioned income taxes, I want to remind you about the significant cuts in income tax rates that were passed by Congress and signed by President Bush in 2001 and 2003. Congress also has cut taxes on capital gains and on dividends."

This man seemed to imply that Catherine had not considered all the possible taxes and had jumped to a conclusion. She didn't disagree with the man but restated her claim: "You're right about capital gains, but other taxes have gone up so much that my main point is still true and the new proposals haven't been fully implemented yet."

This example illustrates five important aspects of rhetorical proof:

1. Reasoning plays the crucial role in linking supporting material to the claim. Catherine's reasoning connected specific examples to her claim that taxes take a larger share of the paycheck each year.
2. Reasoning depends on an inference but cannot guarantee that the inference is "right." Nonetheless, we still can apply tests of soundness. In this case, for instance, do the examples really represent the overall tax picture, or has Catherine left out some important categories?
3. An inference often takes the form of an implicit statement that some general rule is being followed. Catherine's reasoning implied, "These examples of tax increases are significant and representative."
4. The speaker and listeners together decide whether the inference is sound. This audience participated by asking questions that helped to identify possible problems with Catherine's inference, and she had a chance to address their concerns. Together, speaker and audience probably became more confident about the inference.
5. Nothing can guarantee that the inference of a rhetorical proof is correct, but tests have evolved over time to distinguish between good and bad inferences. Asking whether Catherine's examples represent all categories of taxes is one such test.

Using Rhetorical Proof in Your Speech

Figure 6.1 shows the relationships among claims, supporting material, and reasoning. It shows the "inner workings" of the speech. This is an adaptation of a model developed by a contemporary British philosopher, Stephen Toulmin. The other elements of the rhetorical situation are also shown, to remind you that the speech interacts with the speaker, the audience, and the occasion. Choices of reasoning patterns are influenced by each of these other elements.

The best time to construct effective reasoning relationships is after you research the speech. Your outline (discussed briefly in Chapter 1 and fully in Chapter 9) will help you to see what is used as supporting material for each claim. As Figure 6.2 shows, each Roman numeral in the outline identifies a main idea that supports your thesis statement, and each capital letter represents supporting material for that main idea. At a smaller level, each capital letter marks a claim that is supported by all the Arabic numerals under it, which, in turn, are supported by the lowercase letters, and so on.

Beginning with the smallest claims in your outline, examine the supporting material for proofs; then identify what kind of link (inference) will best connect the supporting material to each claim. In this chapter are prac-

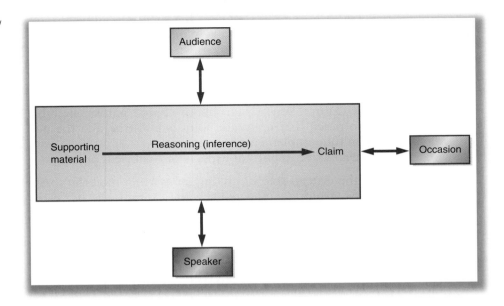

tical methods to help you discover appropriate links and to test whether they will make the connection that you want to make with your audience.

To help you develop convincing rhetorical proofs, next we will discuss six broad categories of reasoning: example, analogy, sign, cause, testimony, and narrative. For each category, the discussion first will focus on the variety of types, then on some tests to discover errors in reasoning, and finally on suggestions for using each reasoning pattern in a speech.

It may seem confusing that some of the reasoning patterns have the same names as types of supporting material (reasoning through example, for instance). However, the reasoning pattern is not the same thing as the supporting material. Rather, it explains why the supporting material should count as support for the claim. Suppose you were to say, "Politicians are corrupt; just look at Smith, Baker, and Jones." The presumably corrupt politicians Smith, Baker, and Jones would be your examples (supporting material), and the inference that the three of them are representa-

Figure 6.2 An outline reveals links in reasoning.

II. Lack of variety is not a valid complaint against Campus Food Service.
    A. You get more choices than you would at home.
        1. Each day, there are three main entrees and a vegetarian meal.
        2. There also are other options.
            a. A salad bar
            b. Cereals
            c. Breads
            d. Soups
    B. A special dinner is offered once each month.

tive or typical of politicians would be your reasoning (reasoning through example).

These categories were chosen because, at least in Western culture, they have been found over time generally to yield reliable results. Not all cultures will share all these norms of reasoning or give them the same emphasis. For example, some Eastern cultures are easily able to embrace contradictory positions. Western culture, on the other hand, usually adheres to the "law of noncontradiction": that something cannot have one feature (call it x) and its opposite (*not-x*) at the same time. Likewise, some cultures prize storytelling and therefore would give more weight to narrative inferences, whereas others are more concerned with prediction and control and hence give more weight to inferences from cause. When speaking to a culturally diverse audience, you will want to use multiple reasoning patterns in order to take these differences into account. Still, most of these reasoning patterns will be applicable across cultures, even if the emphasis differs.[4]

Strategies for Reasoning through Example

Probably the most common reasoning pattern in public speaking is inference from example. **Examples** are specific instances that are used to illustrate a more general claim; the inference is that the specific is typical of the general. For *example:*

- A tourist notices that three downtown streets are deserted at midday and infers that businesses in that town are not doing well.
- On four occasions, a student succeeds in visiting faculty members during their office hours and infers that instructors are conscientious and accessible.
- A researcher discovers that 15 percent of the people in one community lack health insurance and infers that about 15 percent of the country's population has no health insurance.
- Believing that most politicians cannot be trusted, a citizen infers that neither of the candidates for mayor can be trusted.

In each example, someone has brought together a statement about a particular situation and a statement about a general claim and has attempted to relate the two. Whether proceeding from specific to general (the first three examples) or from general to specific (the last example), the inference is that particular cases are **representative** of the general category. To say that they are representative is to say that they are typical cases, that there is nothing unusual about them.[5]

A moment's thought shows why representativeness is important. Suppose that, although three downtown streets were deserted, traffic jams occurred near all the city's shopping malls; then, the tourist would not be justified in drawing a general conclusion from the specific case observed. Or imagine that the student's four successful visits were all on days when faculty members were careful to hold office hours because they were advising majors for next semester's registration; then, it would not be valid to infer that instructors are accessible at other times.

examples
Specific instances used to illustrate a more general claim.

representative
Typical of the larger category from which a case is selected.

Logic and Reasoning

Excerpt from Darbi's Persuasive Speech on "The Place of Religion in Schools"

Darbi Howard

Religion creates passion, love, and hope. I believe taking religion out of school was a big mistake, something that may have caused irreversible effects. Maybe, just maybe, if religion hadn't been taken out of schools, we as a nation could have avoided school shootings such as Columbine.

I believe religion being in schools provides more benefits than does cause problems. I am here today to inform you of some positive reinforcements of religion in school long forgotten, and to help you as a new generation of influential decision makers for this country to make beneficial choices for your children.

Our country was first built on the pillars of religion. Religious persecution is the reason that the Puritans first left England in the first place. They wanted citizens of the new country to be able to make their own choices on what to believe.

"Four score and seven years ago, our forefathers brought forth a new nation under God" is a well-known quote from the Gettysburg Address. This country was originally created on the basis of religious tolerance. The Ten Commandments are carved on the Supreme Court wall, but they are not even allowed to post the Ten Commandments on bulletin boards at public schools, which are government funded.

The Constitution provided for a secular state, one based not on religion, but on toleration and liberty of conscience. Amendment One states, "Congress shall make no law respecting the establishment of religion, or prohibiting the free exercise thereof, or abridging the freedom of speech, or of the press, or the right of the people peaceably to assemble and to petition the government for a redress of grievances." The phrase "under God" was added to the Pledge of Allegiance in the 1950s, so the public would commit themselves in public events to living in "one nation under God, indivisible, with liberty and justice for all."

Ignorance of religion causes hate. Many people say and believe ignorance is bliss. But I believe that's an over-simple copout to excuse someone from having certain responsibilities. Emily Bea, a high school student, spoke out about her feelings about the Holocaust. "It is so essential that society learns about the Holocaust. Ignorance is worthless. We must educate ourselves to prevent such a devastating event from ever happening again." The world should know all about the Holocaust. The Holocaust is very important to our world today. The Holocaust can happen in places where people are prejudiced and don't understand each other. It is good to learn about things that happened millions and millions of years ago, or just recently. The events in the Holocaust were the result of ignorance.

Taking religion out of school has affected public education in many negative ways. Safety is a huge issue. To

In short, if the particular cases are *not* typical (not representative), we cannot confidently infer that what is true of them is true in general. Again, inferences cannot be guaranteed as mathematical proofs can be. But even if we can't be absolutely certain that examples are representative, we can still try to select them in a way that removes all known causes of distortion or bias.

The strategic advantage of inference from example is that it makes a general or abstract statement more concrete and tangible. The politician who says, "My economic program will benefit middle-class families," may help her audience to accept her claim by talking about specific families—preferably people with whom listeners can identify—who will gain from the program. Of course, the power of the appeal depends on whether the specific cases will be accepted as representative.

some people, when considering religion at schools, there are lots of people who believe school shootings such as Columbine could have been avoided if religion remained in schools.

Representative Bob Barr voted for a bill in Congress that would permit states to mandate the posting of the Ten Commandments in offices in public schools. He suggested that the Columbine tragedy might not have happened if the Ten Commandments had been displayed.

Clarence Thomas' mom once said, "Taking religion out of schools has made the schools go to hell." I believe she has a very good point since much of the evidence I have provided says the same thing. I don't stand here before you to say that everyone in public schools should become Christian or Jewish or Muslim.

I'm not here to be a missionary. I don't believe that all children should have to pray every day at school or attend bible studies regularly. But I am here because I believe religion has a great many benefits. I want America to be educated and open minded. I want our heritage and our past not to be forgotten. I want our future always remembered as a time of tolerance and hope.

Prof. Blivens

Logic and reasoning in persuasive speeches is important if you want to successfully persuade your audience. Throughout the speech and in the introduction, you allude to the Columbine school shooting and indicate it might not have happened if religion had been allowed in schools. You base this claim on quotes from a representative and Clarence Thomas' mom. There is no foundation for this claim and no direct link between religion and the Columbine shootings. It starts and ends the speech on a weak claim. I would consider taking it out entirely or supporting it with evidence. Next, there are several assumptions you make that are not accurate. For example, the Puritans sought freedom from religious persecution, but you can't assume that they wanted religious freedom for all. Also, you make assumptions about the First Amendment. Does it provide for religion in schools? It does mention "free exercise," and currently students are allowed to freely meet if they choose. In the next main point, you assert that ignorance of religion led to the Holocaust. This needs a stronger link to your overall argument. What are you trying to support by this example? Are you saying that if we don't have religion in schools this could happen again? The point seems out of place with the rest of the speech. To strengthen your speech, I would first discuss the status quo. You mentioned that teachers couldn't post the Ten Commandments. Explore this area more. I would go back and do research over your current main points. Then, when you have your research to support all of your claims, begin to write your speech. Remember that all of your evidence should have a direct link to the claim, and you have to explain that link in detail to prove your point.

Figure 6.3 maps an inference from example, applying the general pattern shown in Figure 6.1. A student speaker says, "I learned to be a good driver after taking driver's education; others will also become good drivers if they are forced to take driver's education."

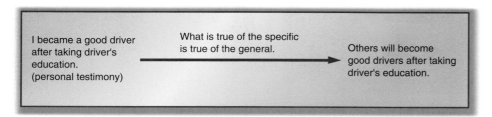

Figure 6.3 Inference from example.

Notice something else about Figure 6.3. This student is offering herself as an example, but her supporting material is personal testimony. *Example*, as we have said, refers to *both* a reasoning pattern *and* a type of supporting material, but these are not exactly the same thing. *Any* type of supporting material could provide the specific cases you use when you reason from example.

Types of Inference from Example

Speakers use many different types of examples, depending on their purposes. The following three considerations are especially pertinent in selecting examples.

Individual Versus Aggregate Examples. Sometimes, a speaker describes individual occurrences of an example. John, Martha, and Claude, for instance, are all friends of the speaker who had to interrupt their education for financial reasons; by talking about each of them, the speaker supports the inference that the cost of a college education is a serious concern.

At other times, individual cases will be less convincing than an aggregate statistical example. Because 50 percent of students in a national survey report that they have seen someone cheat on an examination, the speaker infers that probably half the students on campus have witnessed such behavior.

Factual Versus Hypothetical Examples. Factual examples are actual occurrences; whether individual or aggregate, they are "real." In contrast, a speaker may construct hypothetical examples, creating a vivid (but imaginary) illustration of something abstract. To describe the problems of home-

When your argument is based on quite specific examples, you must try to show that these examples are typical. This speaker uses aggregate examples to support her claim.

lessness, for example, a speaker might invent a hypothetical character whose daily experiences are typical of homeless people generally.

A speaker may have good reasons to offer a hypothetical example rather than a factual one, but the invention should be acknowledged and should never be treated as fact. One journalist received a Pulitzer Prize for a series of stories describing the plight of a child who was addicted to drugs; when it came to light that this child was hypothetical rather than a real person (as the stories had intimated), the prize was withdrawn.

Brief Versus Extended Examples. Sometimes, a quick list of examples is effective because the speaker's emphasis is on the existence and number of cases rather than on their details. Thus, to establish that many students are worried about the cost of education, a brief mention of John, Martha, and Claude should support the claim.

But suppose the speaker wants listeners to understand what students go through when financial problems make them leave school. It would then be more effective to offer a more complete description of just one case. Better than to simply report that John had to leave school for financial reasons would be to describe the events that led to his decision—the conversations between him and his parents, how he broke the news to his friends, and what his life has been like since leaving.

Tests for Inference from Example

Inference from example will be accepted as reasonable if listeners have no reason to doubt it. Ask yourself these questions when using inference from example to support your claim:

1. *Are there enough examples?* If the number of examples is very small, particularly in making a statistical generalization, the sample may not include significant features of the population as a whole. If you claim that more students are graduating from high school than ever before because *your* high school graduated a record number of students, the audience may doubt your inference; your high school is only one of thousands.

2. *Do the examples represent the whole category?* If all the cases you cite are alike in some way that distorts your inference—say you use only fraternity members as examples to support some point about *all* college students—your claim will be weakened.

3. *Are the examples ambiguous?* Sometimes a single example can support different inferences, making it a poor example. If 70 percent of employees are dissatisfied with the company's new computer system, one speaker may claim that the new system is flawed; but another speaker may claim that employees need more training to understand the new system. Which claim is the audience to believe?

4. *Are the examples fallacious?* A **fallacy** is an inference that appears to be sound but that, on inspection, contains a significant flaw. In the case of inferences from example, which relate parts to wholes, the flaw is that the whole is not always the same as the sum of the parts. The **fallacy of composition** results from assuming that what is true of the part is automatically true of the whole. ("The instructor enjoys this class very much, and so

fallacy
An inference that appears to be sound but that, on inspection, contains a significant flaw.

fallacy of composition
Assuming that what is true of the part is automatically true of the whole.

the students must enjoy this class, too.") Conversely, the **fallacy of division** results from assuming that what is true of the whole is automatically true of the part. ("The campus is excited about the homecoming game, and so the instructor must be excited, too.")

Checklist 6.1 Tests for Inference from Example

1. **Are there enough examples?**
2. **Do all the examples represent the category?**
3. **Are the examples ambiguous?**
4. **Are the examples fallacious? Do any examples assume that:**
   - What is true of the part must be true of the whole (fallacy of composition)?
   - What is true of the whole must be true of the part (fallacy of division)?

Guidelines for Reasoning through Example

1. *Limit the number of examples.* You want enough examples to indicate a pattern that supports your inference, but you don't want to risk boring the audience with unnecessary examples. Consider your purpose and audience carefully; a single example may be enough.

2. *Make sure each example is believable.* Even one unbelievable example can undermine your inference—and your entire point.

3. *Avoid obvious, overused examples.* If you tell listeners what they already know, your inferences may seem trivial or trite. Seek novel examples that might surprise the audience. Arguing against censorship, for example, student Sarah McAdams skipped the standard example of book burning in Nazi Germany; instead, she surprised listeners by citing examples of U.S. censorship:

> In 1925, anyone caught teaching Darwin's *Origin of Species* in a Tennessee public school was fined. In 1933, a young actor was arrested for smuggling an illegal item into the United States. That item was James Joyce's *Ulysses*—a book that is now considered a literary masterpiece. In 1980, some high school students were forced to read an edited version of Shakespeare's *Romeo and Juliet* because parents and teachers thought the original play was too racy.

4. *Match the details of examples to your purpose.* If your main point is the very existence of the example, few details are needed. But if you want to show the audience exactly how the example illustrates your inference, supply more detail.

fallacy of division
Assuming that what is true of the whole is automatically true of the part.

5. *Make the examples memorable.* After selecting enough believable, fresh examples, bring your inference to life for the audience by carefully selecting details and describing the examples vividly. We will pursue this goal in Chapter 10, "Achieving Style through Language."

Strategies for Reasoning through Analogy

An **analogy** is a comparison of people, places, things, events, or more abstract relationships. Whereas the key feature of inference from example is the link between the parts and the whole, the key feature of inference from analogy is a comparison between the known and the unknown.

Suppose your college is considering a major investment in the athletic program, hoping to increase alumni contributions through successful athletic competition. You don't know whether that will happen, but you do know that a similar school increased alumni contributions after overhauling its athletic program, and so you infer that your school will benefit similarly.

An inference from analogy asks the audience to accept the idea that items that are basically alike in most respects will also be alike in the particular respect being discussed. Figure 6.4 offers a map of an analogy. In a speech on gun deaths, a student speaker said, "The United States would have fewer gun deaths if it made guns illegal because Japan has few gun deaths and guns are illegal there."

Analogical inferences are prominent in public speaking because they are psychologically appealing to an audience. They enable us to accept something that is unknown because it is similar to something that we do know.[6]

Types of Inference from Analogy

Depending on whether the comparison between things is direct or concerns their relationships, an analogy is either literal or figurative.[7]

Literal Analogies. A **literal analogy** is a *direct* comparison of objects, people, or events. A speaker who says, "Illinois will not be able to escape the recession, which has already hit Michigan—another Midwestern industrial state," is directly comparing Illinois to Michigan. The inference is that, because Illinois is basically like Michigan, it, too, will probably face recession.

Speakers often use literal analogies to suggest that one action or event is a precedent for another—that actual experience with one enables us to predict what will happen with the other. Senator Charles Robb of Virginia took this approach in arguing that a proposed law to prohibit the federal government from recognizing same-sex marriages was discriminatory:

analogy
A comparison of people, places, things, events, or more abstract relationships.

literal analogy
A direct comparison of objects, people, or events.

Figure 6.4 Inference from analogy.

Until 1967, 16 states, including my own state of Virginia, had laws banning couples from different races to marry. When the law was challenged, Virginia argued that interracial marriages were simply immoral. . . . The Supreme Court struck down these archaic laws, holding that "the freedom of choice to marry" had "long been recognized as one of the vital personal rights essential to the orderly pursuit of happiness by free men."

Today, we know that moral discomfort—even revulsion—that citizens then felt about legalizing interracial marriages did not give them the right to discriminate 30 years ago. Similarly, discomfort over sexual orientation does not give us the right to discriminate against a class of Americans today.

Figurative Analogies. A **figurative analogy** compares the *relationships* between objects, people, or events in order to make complex or abstract statements more vivid and more concrete. Again, the comparison begins with something the audience already knows.

Suppose you wanted to claim that the Social Security System will face financial problems around the year 2020 as "baby boomers" reach retirement age. You could support your claim with only statistics, of course, but that could be tedious and would work far better in print than in a speech. But if you said, "Depending on Social Security for your retirement income is like playing Russian roulette with your future," your comparison would make the statistics—and your point—clear: Social Security is a gamble.

Similarly, the speaker predicting a recession in Illinois might add, "Trusting the politicians to find a way to avoid it is like putting the fox in charge of the chicken coop." This speaker is not directly comparing politicians to foxes or the recession to a chicken coop. Rather, the comparison is figurative; it points to *relationships*. The politicians stand in the same relationship to the recession that the fox does to the chicken coop. In both cases, those who supposedly are protecting something are really a grave threat to it.

Tests for Inference from Analogy

As we saw concerning inferences from example, things may be *similar*, but they are never completely *identical*. Thus, as with examples, we can never be sure that an analogy is completely valid. No matter how similar things are, they are also different in some respects.

For an analogy to be strong and compelling, listeners have to believe that the basic similarities between two items outweigh their basic differences. An analogy raises two closely related questions:

1. *Are there basic differences as well as similarities?* Suppose a speaker claims that Detroit and Chicago have similar economic concerns because they are alike in so many ways: Both are northern metropolitan areas, both have large populations, both are surrounded by suburbs that erode the tax base, and so on. Besides these similarities, however, there is an obvious and important difference between the two cities: Detroit's economy has depended on one industry, automobiles, whereas the economy of Chicago is more diversified.

2. *Do the differences outweigh the similarities?* The discovery of differences between items being compared is not, in itself, reason to question the analogy. One has to demonstrate that the differences really do matter. For in-

figurative analogy
A comparison of the relationships between objects, people, or events.

stance, if a diversified economy protects a city better against recession because workers who lose jobs in one industry can find new jobs in another, then this difference outweighs the similarities between Detroit and Chicago, and the analogy is questionable. But if a weak national economy hurts cities in general—whether or not they have a diversified economy—then this difference between Detroit and Chicago would not matter much, and the analogy would stand.

Checklist 6.2 Tests for Inference from Analogy

1. **Are there basic differences as well as similarities?**
2. **Do the differences outweigh the similarities?**

Guidelines for Reasoning through Analogy

1. *Avoid analogies that are trite or farfetched.* An overused analogy will lose the audience's attention and make the entire speech seem stale, while an analogy with no basis in common sense may call so much attention to itself that it distracts from the point it is supposed to prove. Recently, a televised public service announcement (PSA) compared the brain to an egg and heroin to a cast-iron frying pan that "smashes" the brain. The PSA also compared the heroin user's family, friends, job, and future to various kitchen utensils and appliances and implied that heroin also "smashes" the user's relationships and life. Though its shock effect gained it attention, the PSA was viewed by many as farfetched and trite. Its target audience of young people knew that their friends who use heroin did not immediately and irreversibly "smash" their brains and everyone and everything around them. The comparison was exaggerated and, consequently, the target audience dismissed it.

Financial manager Manuel Gonzalez was more effective in using an analogy to convince operations managers that the company was overextended and risked being bogged down by a product competition it could not win. He compared the company's situation to that of the United States trying unsuccessfully during the 1960s to win the war in Vietnam. He fleshed out the analogy by showing how a lack of understanding of local conditions in each market, plus an unmeasured outpouring of resources in pursuit of vague objectives, was putting the company in the kind of no-win situation that the United States faced in Vietnam. Because the comparison of a company's sales and a nation's military strategy was fresh and because Mr. Gonzalez developed it in detail, the audience paid attention and did not find it farfetched.

2. *Analyze what you are comparing.* Make sure that you understand the essential similarities and differences of the items in your analogy so that you can argue convincingly that their similarities outweigh their differences and will not be surprised if a listener suggests otherwise. The speaker who compared Detroit's and Chicago's economic outlooks must be ready to respond to a listener's observation that the cities differ in the important factor of economic diversification. If that difference wasn't important to the speaker's main point, the analogy could be defended.

3. *Use analogies sparingly.* Although analogies are a form of inference, they also are like ornaments (to use an analogy of our own). Too many ornaments may hide what they are intended to decorate, and too many analogies in a speech may obscure the main point. Political speaker Ross Perot, for example, uses so many attention-grabbing figurative analogies that they sometimes overwhelm the audience.[8]

Strategies for Reasoning through Signs

A **sign** is something that stands for something else—which is usually an abstraction or something that we cannot observe directly. The presence of the sign causes us to infer the existence of what it stands for.

If the number of students absent from class increases suddenly, that may be a sign of a flu epidemic. If today's average grades are higher than 10 years ago, that may be a sign that grading standards have changed. If homeless people are living on the streets, that may be a sign that public policies are not meeting the needs of the disadvantaged. If wages differ for male and female workers doing similar jobs, that may be a sign of gender discrimination. In each case, we infer that something exists based on something else that presumably is a sign of it. The strategic benefit of inferences from sign is that they enable listeners to reach a conclusion about something that they don't know by linking it in this way to something that they do know.

Figure 6.5 offers a map of an inference from signs. A newspaper reporter covering a political campaign writes, "The Governor is doing well in his quest for votes since his crowds are large and enthusiastic."

Types of Inference from Signs

In theory, anything can stand for anything else. In practice, however, inferences from signs fall into several types:

- Physical observation
- Statistical indexes
- Institutional regularity

sign
Something that stands for something else.

physical observation (as a sign)
Regarding something that can be observed as a sign of something that cannot.

Physical Observation. If the alarm goes off and you don't check the time but you look out the window and see a bright sun, you probably infer that the sun means it's morning. Similarly, through **physical observation** of a bulldozer on an empty campus lot, a student inferred that the university was about to construct a new building. The sun and the bulldozer were observable signs of other things that could not be observed.

Figure 6.5 Inference from signs.

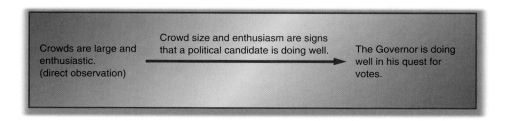

Crowds are large and enthusiastic. (direct observation)

Crowd size and enthusiasm are signs that a political candidate is doing well.

The Governor is doing well in his quest for votes.

Statistical Index. Many statistical measures are taken as signs. High scores on exams, for instance, are widely accepted as a sign of intelligence. Similarly, the ups and downs of the Dow-Jones Industrial Average are seen to indicate the health of the economy, and a rising Consumer Price Index is regarded as a sign of inflation. Intelligence, economic health, inflation—these are all abstract concepts that cannot be observed directly. But in each case, some **statistical index** that we *can* see is regarded as a sign of something that we cannot observe.

Institutional Regularity. **Institutional regularity** is an observable pattern that results from some norm or social convention. For example, because athletic competitions usually begin with the singing of the national anthem, if you turned on your TV and heard people singing it, you might infer that a game was about to begin. In the same way, because diplomatic disagreements often are described by such polite phrases as "They had a frank exchange of views," that phrase in a news story about international negotiations might be a sign that discussions had reached an impasse.

Tests for Inference from Signs

If a sign *always* stood for the same thing, then whenever we observed the sign, we could infer that the abstract concept was present as well. Thus, *whenever* someone scored high on a test, we could infer that the person was intelligent; and *whenever* we heard the national anthem, we could expect a sports event to follow. So certain a sign would be said to be *infallible,* meaning that it predicts with certainty the existence of the thing it signifies.

Reality offers few (if any) infallible signs. To say that something is a sign, then, means that it *usually* signifies something else, although in a given circumstance it might not. The high rate of absenteeism from class may well signify an epidemic, but are students suffering from the flu or spring fever? Because most signs are *fallible* and can be interpreted variously, critical listeners and speakers will subject them to the following tests of reasonableness.

1. *Is an alternative explanation more credible?* Is it more reasonable to suppose that today's higher grades signify harder-working students, or changes in grading standards, or changes in admissions policies? The question can be resolved by gathering other information. If the credentials of entering students have been similar for the past ten years, then it is more reasonable to infer that the higher grades signify changes in grading standards. Examine alternative explanations for a sign before accepting inferences based on it.

2. *Can the alleged sign be found without the thing for which it stands?* Although the national anthem is often sung before an athletic contest, it also is sung on many other occasions—at the opening of a patriotic rally, for example, or at the end of a television station's broadcast day. A sign that can be found in a variety of circumstances is not a solid basis for an inference.

3. *Is the sign part of a pattern, or a single unusual case?* If only one instance of gender-based wage differences can be found, that is not a strong sign of discrimination. But if a *pattern* of wage differences can be identified, it is more reasonable to see that as a sign of gender discrimination.

statistical index (as a sign)
A statistical measure that is taken as a sign of an abstraction.

institutional regularity (as a sign)
A sign relationship that results from norm or social convention.

> ### Checklist 6.3 Tests for Inference from Signs
>
> 1. **Is an alternative explanation more credible?**
> 2. **Can the alleged sign be found *without* the thing for which it stands?**
> 3. **Is the sign part of a pattern, or a single unusual case?**

Guidelines for Reasoning through Signs

1. *Use sign inferences to link the abstract with the concrete.* Keep in mind that the primary purpose of a sign inference is to predict the existence of something that cannot be observed on the basis of something that can be. Use sign inferences to convince listeners that something they cannot see does, in fact, exist.

2. *Explain the sign relationship clearly.* Make sure your listeners understand exactly *what* you are alleging to be a sign of something else and *why* you think it predicts what you claim. The student speaker who said, "All we have to do is turn on the television set to see signs of the glory of modern civilization," left the audience wondering. Was she referring to the technological achievements of broadcasting? Did she believe that the content of television programs showed the triumph of the human spirit? Or was she actually being sarcastic and preparing to criticize typical television fare?

3. *Point to multiple signs of what you want to infer.* Student Roger Berkson used several signs in a speech. Alone, each sign could be fallible, but together they all pointed in the same direction and gave his inference credibility:

> When I saw that many more students were absent from class lately, I wasn't sure that it meant that they were sick. After all, it was close to midterm exams, and everyone could use more time to study. But then I found out that visits to the infirmary went up, sales at the pharmacy were on the rise, and more beds were in use at the city hospital. Those signs suggest to me that we have a flu epidemic on campus.

4. *Do not claim more for a sign inference than it can establish.* A sign inference claims a predictable relationship between the sign and the thing for which it stands, but it does *not* establish that either one affects the other. Although a rise in the Consumer Price Index may predict inflation, it certainly does not influence, cause, or lead to inflation. This last point highlights an important distinction between sign inferences and our next form of reasoning: inference from cause.

Strategies for Reasoning through Cause

Unlike a sign inference, a **causal inference** explains the relationship between things by pointing to the influence of one thing on the other.

Suppose the state legislature significantly raises the gasoline tax, which service stations pass along to consumers by raising the price of gasoline, and sales then decline. Is this chain of events a coincidence? We can never know for sure. But it may be reasonable to infer that the price increase af-

causal inference
A pattern of inference that suggests that one factor brings about another.

fected consumption patterns—that as the cost of gasoline rose, more consumers decided to limit their driving and to conserve gasoline as well as their money.

A causal inference relates things by identifying one as the cause (higher price) and the other as the effect (lower sales). The cause, of course, must both precede and lead to the effect. The scientific method offers procedures for deciding whether to infer such a cause–effect relationship, or *causality*. Researchers devise controlled testing situations that are alike in every respect and are held constant; the researchers then vary the one factor that they think is the cause. If they get different results, they infer that the difference was caused by the one factor that they changed.

This method of inferring causality is not available to public speakers, who deal with subjects on which a "laboratory" cannot be controlled. The speaker must examine the subject as it is and cannot possibly hold constant its many complex variables. The method for inferring causality, then, is to demonstrate reasons why the cause–effect relationship makes sense and to ask whether any alternative explanation is more plausible.

The strategic advantage of inferences from cause is that they enable listeners to see a pattern among what otherwise might be unconnected events. Recognizing the pattern, they can predict what will happen next or they can determine what must be done to avoid that outcome. Listeners are made to feel that they know "what is going on" and that they can do something about it.

Figure 6.6 maps an inference from cause. When California eliminated affirmative action in college admissions, some higher education officials alleged that the end of affirmative action would drastically reduce the number of minority students.

Types of Inference from Cause

There are several types of causal inference. Among the most common are prediction, assignment of responsibility, explanation, and steps to a goal. Each of these types is a different use you can make of the inference from cause.

Prediction. Some causal inferences explain changes by predicting what leads to what. In a speech about the loss of the ozone layer over the South Pole, a speaker might say, "When we release fluorocarbons from aerosol cans and air conditioners, we cause the thinning of the ozone layer"; the inference is that fluorocarbons in the atmosphere destroy the layer of ozone that shields us from the sun's ultraviolet rays.

Assignment of Responsibility. Another common use of causal inferences is to assign responsibility for something, to explain why it occurred. Suppose

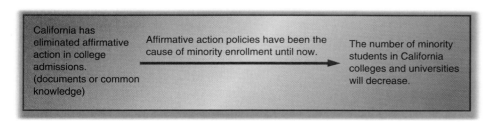

California has eliminated affirmative action in college admissions. (documents or common knowledge)

Affirmative action policies have been the cause of minority enrollment until now.

The number of minority students in California colleges and universities will decrease.

Figure 6.6 Inference from cause.

you were asked to speak about the question "Why would someone run for president if there were no chance of being elected?" In thinking about the question, you may see other reasons to run for office: to get publicity, to establish political relationships, to add certain issues to the agenda for public discussion, to position oneself to run for vice president, to have a good time, and to be ready in case leading candidates falter. Through a causal inference, you could present these as reasons or motivations—as causes—for the decision to run.

Explanation. A causal inference also can be used to explain something that otherwise doesn't make sense. Consider this paradox: Why, in the richest nation on earth, are there shortages of funds for virtually every social program? Answering such a question involves finding some element—often unexpected or obscure—that explains the situation. If your inference explains that Americans strongly prefer private over public investment, you would have identified a possible cause of the paradox.

Steps to a Goal. A causal inference also can relate the means to the ends, as when we know our goals and want to determine the best way to attain them. This form of reasoning is used often in problem–solution speeches. If you advocated the development of solar power in order to avoid risking an energy shortage, you would be employing this type of causal inference.[9]

Tests for Inference from Cause

As with the other patterns of reasoning, the rhetorical proof in a causal inference is not ironclad. We may think we understand how one aspect of a

Politicians often use causal inferences in their campaign rhetoric. For example, one of Al Gore's promises in the 2000 presidential campaign was to strengthen Social Security, which would have the effect of assuring a decent standard of living for the millions of "baby boomers" who soon will retire.

situation influences another and yet may be mistaken—as examples throughout this chapter have shown. In the case of Figure 6.6, for instance, some people have maintained that, except for an initial drop, the number of minority students did *not* decline after affirmative action was abolished. (There was considerable disagreement about whether this was true and what these results meant, but that is another story.) Any of the following analytical errors will make a causal inference less reasonable:

1. *Has a sign relationship been confused with a causal relationship?* Because we know that two things are somehow related, we mistakenly assume that one causes the other. Student Michael Leu, for example, let enthusiasm for his subject overpower his ability to test inferences when he made the following argument:

> Only the best professors on this campus teach their classes at noon. If Professor Walker really wanted to be a better teacher, he would change the time of his class so that it met at noon instead of 10.

Had Michael tested his inference carefully, he might have recognized a serious flaw in his reasoning. Teaching at noon might be a *sign* that one was a good teacher, because only the best professors teach at that hour right now. But there is no reason to believe that teaching at noon *causes* anyone to be a good teacher. Professor Walker's changing his class time won't make him a better teacher; instead it will make Michael's first sentence no longer true.

2. *Does some common cause of both factors make it seem that they have a cause–effect relationship?* This reasoning error alleges that one factor is the cause of another, although in fact *both* manifest some third cause. If you fall prey to the **common cause fallacy,** you may mistakenly remove what you think is the cause of a problem, only to discover that nothing changes.

For example, the fact that students in wealthy school districts generally score higher on standardized tests than do students in poorer districts may seem at first glance to prove that higher spending for education results in higher test scores. But some have argued that the real reason why wealthy districts score better is that the families who live in them can afford to give their children reading and travel experiences and even personal computers—and that this enrichment at home leads *both* to higher test scores *and* to pressure on school districts to spend more for education.

3. *Is there a* post hoc *fallacy?* In Latin, *post hoc* means "after this"; thus a ***post hoc* fallacy** occurs if you assume that, because one event occurred *after* another, it was *caused* by the earlier event. This reasoning error comes up often in political speeches. Republicans observe that the Cold War ended after President Reagan took office and assume that he should get credit for it; Democrats point to a strong economy while President Clinton was in office and credit him for it. Can we reasonably infer that the end of the Cold War and the sustained economic growth were caused by these two presidents?

4. *Have important multiple causes or multiple effects been overlooked?* If a problem has multiple causes, acting to remove a single cause is unlikely to solve the problem. Consider the high cost of health care. One important cause is the inefficient distribution of doctors—most practice in large cities rather than in smaller communities and rural areas. But forcing doctors to move will not solve the problem, because other factors also cause health costs to rise: the small total number of doctors, their inability to control fees,

common cause fallacy
Assuming that one thing causes another when in fact a third factor really is the cause of both.

***post hoc* fallacy**
Assuming that, because one event occurred before another, the first is necessarily the cause of the second.

Responding as a Critical Audience Member

First, review a transcript of one of the presidential debates by going to the page for the **Commission on Presidential Debates** at **http://www.debates.org/.** Click on "Debate History" to locate transcripts.

Select one of the transcripts and identify one of the central arguments made by a presidential contender. Next, assess the quality of the rhetorical proof that was offered:

- Which reasoning pattern was used?
  Example
  Analogy
  Sign
  Causation
  Testimony
  Narrative

- Apply one or more of the general tests of inference:
  Did the speaker's claim follow from the supporting material?
  Did the claim advance the audience's understanding beyond the supporting material?
  Was the claim relevant to the issue?
  Was the language clear and unequivocal?
  Was probability distinguished from certainty?
  Was the emotional response of the speaker appropriate to the situation?

the costs of advances in medical technology, and changes in the insurance industry.

Likewise, a particular action may have multiple effects, some of which may be undesirable. Student speaker Demetris Papademetriou overlooked this when he used a causal inference to argue for the legalization of marijuana:

> No one wants to lose the forests of America. But in our modern society, we need paper, and wood is an essential ingredient in paper. Even with recycling, we are forced to cut trees at an alarming rate. But we shouldn't lose all hope. There is a type of plant that could save our trees. By legalizing marijuana, we could use the hemp to make paper, just as our forefathers did when they produced the paper on which the Constitution is written.

Talking with classmates after his speech, Demetris found that he had not convinced them because he had neglected another possible effect of legalizing marijuana. Besides producing more paper, his "solution" could lead to increased use of other drugs—an effect the audience wasn't willing to risk.

5. *Is there a likely alternative cause?* Sometimes what appears to be the cause really isn't. Things may be related, but for a reason different from the one the speaker suggests. Student Muhammad Gill pointed out this mistake in arguments that endorse racial profiling (the practice of making traffic or other investigative stops on the basis of a person's race or ethnicity):

> Some people argue that racial profiling is justified. And in rare cases, such as those involving suspected terrorists, it may be. But it is wrong when people look at the high arrest and conviction rates for illegal drug possession among African Americans and they infer that the reason that there are more blacks in court and more blacks in jail is that blacks are more likely to commit crime. The real reason our courts and jails are disproportionately black is that there has been long-standing racial discrimination in both arrests and sentencing.

Checklist 6.4 Tests for Inference from Cause

1. **Has a sign relationship been confused with a causal relationship?**
2. **Does some common cause of both factors make it seem that they have a cause–effect relationship?**
3. **Does the fact that one event occurred after another falsely signify a cause–effect relationship?**
4. **Have important multiple causes or multiple effects been overlooked?**
5. **Is there a likely alternative cause?**

Guidelines for Reasoning through Cause

1. *Analyze what the alleged cause is and how it exerts its influence on the effect.* A student speaker who ignored this advice argued that the position of the stars on a person's birthday causes that person to show certain personality traits. When listeners asked questions, though, the speaker was unable to explain the astrological cause or how it worked its influence.

2. *Realize that causal relationships are often complex and subtle.* A cause can have multiple effects, and an effect can have multiple causes. Be sure that your analysis of the cause–effect relationship is plausible and that your inference will be accepted as reasonable.

Strategies for Reasoning through Testimony

When you rely on other people for the accuracy of supporting materials, their *testimony* stands in for your own direct encounter with the materials. You have confidence in their judgment and are willing to argue that the claim is true because they say so.

When a claim involves, for example, various economic indicators, or the long-term significance of a Supreme Court decision, or adequate safeguards for removing toxic waste, few speakers know enough to support the claim based on their own knowledge. In such cases, both speaker and listeners are usually willing to defer to the judgment of someone whose training, experience, or esteem might all be reasons to trust that person's judgment.

Using testimony, like any other form of reasoning, is a strategic choice. The benefit of inferences from testimony is that they make use of the source's authority in two ways: her expertise makes the audience more disposed to accept the claim and her *ethos* becomes associated with that of the speaker.

Figure 6.7 offers a map of an inference from testimony. It is based on an event that occurred in late 1998 when the House of Representatives was considering the impeachment of President Clinton. A large group of professional historians published a newspaper ad contending that the president's actions were not "high crimes and misdemeanors" as that term was understood in historical context and, therefore, that he should not be impeached. Citing this ad, Clinton's supporters urged that we take the historians' judgment seriously because of their professional expertise.

Types of Inference from Testimony

In Chapter 5, you learned that testimony can be either fact or opinion. Each of these forms of testimony can be classified further according to (1) the type of person who offers it and (2) whether it is quoted or paraphrased.

Expert Versus Lay Testimony. In most cases, we seek **expert testimony**—the support of someone who is recognized as an authority on a particular subject, who has studied the subject in detail, and whose knowledge and interest in the subject far exceed the average person's. It is not unusual, however,

expert testimony
Testimony from a person who is generally recognized as an authority on a particular subject.

Figure 6.7 Inference from testimony.

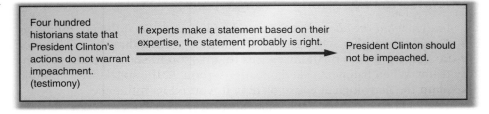

for an expert in one field to make judgments about another field, as when a sports figure endorses a breakfast cereal or an economist comments on fashion trends. When experts testify about matters outside their field of expertise, we should examine their claims closely.

Although expert testimony usually provides stronger support for a claim, speakers sometimes deliberately use **lay testimony,** citing the opinions of "ordinary people" to show what nonexperts think about the subject. President Reagan's speeches often cited ordinary citizens as heroes to make the point that patriotism is not abstract or complex and can be expressed by anyone in daily life.

Quoted Versus Paraphrased Testimony. Quoted testimony repeats the exact words of the source, whereas paraphrased testimony gives only a general idea of what the source said. The statement "Police Chief Walters said, 'The rate of burglaries in our town is an embarrassment to civilized society' " is quoted; to paraphrase this, you might say, "Police Chief Walters said that the burglary rate was unacceptably high."

Although quoted testimony usually provides stronger support, at times a quotation is too long, too confusing, or too technical for listeners to follow. In that case, a paraphrase may allow you to cite what the source said without losing the audience's attention. The paraphrase, of course, must render the quotation accurately, or else you will *misquote* the source.

Tests for Inference from Testimony

Enticed by fame or fortune, some people will say just about anything. Therefore, even the quoted testimony of an expert is not always strong support for a claim. Like other forms of reasoning, inferences from testimony must meet certain tests.

1. *Does the statement accurately reflect the source's views?* Imagine that a student, in arguing that creationism should be taught in public schools, paraphrased a well-known paleontologist as saying that Darwin's theory of evolution is wrong. Listeners could find this hard to believe, and their doubts would turn out to be well-founded if the paleontologist actually said:

> Darwin was wrong. Natural selection is not the most important way in which evolution occurs. Other mechanisms that Darwin did not consider play a role just as crucial to the evolution of species.

This exact quotation shows that the scientist would not have questioned Darwin's theory but only the importance of one proposed means of evolutionary change. The speaker's paraphrase of the statement as an attack on

lay testimony
Testimony from a person who is not an expert.

the theory of evolution was not accurate, and the audience rejected the claim.

2. *Is the source an expert on the topic?* As noted earlier, an expert in one field sometimes offers opinions about other fields. But a physicist is not necessarily an expert on international relations, nor is an actor the most credible source for a claim about nuclear energy. It is not enough that a source be regarded as *generally* well qualified; the source needs to be an expert in the *particular* subject about which you are making a claim. (This test was discussed in Chapter 5. Although it always applies to expert testimony, adapt it to assess lay testimony by asking, "Does this person have experience relating to the claim?")

Student speaker Trisha Butcher gave a speech about the benefits of building more prisons as a way to reduce crime. She based many of her arguments on what she had heard from her father, the owner of a company that specializes in large-scale industrial construction projects and that had received several contracts to build new prisons:

> During a personal interview with my dad, I learned that building more prisons is an effective way to reduce the crime rates in our cities. My father also assured me that, compared to other methods of rehabilitation and punishment, prisons will prove the most economically feasible for the country in the long run.

Listeners were unconvinced—as they should have been, since this testimony failed several tests. As the owner of a construction company, Trisha's father was hardly in a position to compare approaches to reducing crime; nor was he qualified to make national economic forecasts. And because he earned money from industrial construction, and specifically from building prisons, his opinions were likely to be biased. But Trisha recovered when she revised this speech for her final class project. She found a criminologist to comment about how prisons might deter crime and an economist to assess the economic effects of prisons. Then she used her father's testimony to illustrate the personal experience of someone involved in building prisons—a point on which he *was* well qualified to speak.

3. *Is there a basis for the source's statements?* A speaker who offers judgments without providing any basis for them is said to **pontificate.** Unfortunately, experts as well as lay people can do this. But if the source is offering judgments, listeners need to be confident that he or she is familiar with all aspects of the topic and has reasons for making the claim.

4. *Is the source reasonably unbiased?* No one is completely free of bias, of course, but if a source has a vested interest in a claim, the pressure will be strong to offer testimony consistent with that interest. An environmental engineer who owns land at a particular site, for example, may be more likely to downplay hazards on the site than would an engineer who has no economic interest in the matter. Similarly, claims by industry experts— whether automakers, cigarette manufacturers, or health-care providers— should be scrutinized. On the other hand, just because an expert stands to gain from the consequences of his or her testimony does not mean that the testimony itself is wrong. When expertise and self-interest are mixed, however, you need to be a skeptical, critical listener.

pontificate
To offer judgments without providing any basis for them.

5. *Is the testimony up to date?* Some issues are truly timeless, and so it will not matter when a person's testimony was offered. Moral and philosophical principles may be timeless matters, although even here advances in knowledge and technology may affect what once seemed settled matters. On most matters, though—and particularly when data and statistics are involved—recent testimony may be more valuable than older support.

Even when testimony meets all these tests, you still may have to choose among the conflicting claims of qualified experts who disagree. Do not simply pick what supports your thesis and ignore other testimony. Instead, (1) ask what each expert's record of previous statements may imply about the quality of judgment in this case; (2) ask which expert's testimony is closest to consensus in the field; and (3) ask which expert's statement is most consistent with other things you already know or believe.

Checklist 6.5 Tests for Inference from Testimony

1. **Does the statement accurately reflect the source's views?**
2. **Is the source an expert on the topic?**
3. **Is there a basis for the source's statements?**
4. **Is the source reasonably unbiased?**
5. **Is the testimony up to date?**

When qualified experts disagree, ask:

1. **What does each expert's record of previous statements imply about the quality of judgment in this case?**
2. **Which expert's testimony is closest to consensus in the field?**
3. **Which expert's statement is most consistent with other things you already know or believe?**

Guidelines for Reasoning through Testimony

1. *Be sure you quote or paraphrase accurately.* Obviously, a direct quotation must be exactly what the source said. But it is equally important that a paraphrase be faithful to the context and meaning of the original statement and that it fairly reproduce its subtleties. Thus, if the context suggests that the source favors an action but has reservations about it, you would not paraphrase accurately if you suggested that the source wholeheartedly supports the action.

2. *Usually, draw on multiple sources of testimony.* If all your testimonial evidence comes from a single source, listeners may infer that no one else agrees or that your research is shallow; this could undermine even an authoritative source's credibility.

3. *State the credentials of your source.* Because an inference from testimony depends on listeners accepting the source as an authority, you should specify whom you are quoting or paraphrasing. Don't include every credential of the source, but list qualifications that support the claim in the quotation. Similarly, in selecting sources to quote, focus on people whose credentials are pertinent to your subject. The endorsements of celebrities who lack subject-matter expertise carry little weight.

4. *Your own* ethos *affects the credibility of testimony you cite.* If listeners regard you as highly credible, they will be more likely to accept what you say; they will make inferences about the truth of your claims based on your own credibility. When basketball star Magic Johnson, after being diagnosed HIV-positive, urged others to avoid contracting the virus, he was a highly credible source because he was directly affected. Beyond that, if listeners love basketball and admire Magic Johnson, your use of his testimony will be more credible than it would be if they had no apparent interest in him or the sport.

Strategies for Reasoning through Narrative

This final category of inference, called *narrative,* comes into play when a speaker tells a story. A story is often more powerful than other ways of developing an idea. First of all, it is *personalized;* it presents a broad, general, or abstract idea as a specific situation involving particular people. Listeners become involved in the action and wonder what will happen; the story thus adds an element of suspense. A narrative works just like an extended example, and so *representativeness* serves to test the inference, just as it does for inference from example.

The dramatic structure of a narrative inference makes it powerful, which is apparent to anyone who reads novels or watches television and movies. The narrative structure consists of *characters,* a sequence of episodes or moves (often called a *plot*), the resolution of some sort of *conflict* (broadly defined), and an *ending* to which the resolution points. But the ending—the "moral of the story"—often is not stated explicitly. Audience members infer it for themselves.[10]

Narratives take many forms in speeches and have many uses. They may be personal—a story in which the speaker is the main character—or they may be about other people. They may describe real events or a hypothetical situa-

A speaker may use narrative reasoning to talk about hypothetical, real, or fictional events. To be effective, the story should be coherent, plausible, and consistent, and should resonate with the listeners.

Figure 6.8 Inference from narrative.

The Kansa–Nebraska Act, the president's statements, and the *Dred Scott* decision all prepared the way for the next advance of slavery. (examples)	A coherent story contains a pattern that enables prediction of what will come next. ⟶	The way is now being prepared for another *Dred Scott* decision that would make slavery legal everywhere.

tion; fictional narratives are also common in speeches, as in the retelling of children's stories, fables, biographical accounts, and historical scenarios.[11]

Figure 6.8 maps a famous historical case of inference from narrative. During the 1850s, some Northern politicians, including Abraham Lincoln, believed that a group of Southern supporters were plotting to extend slavery over the entire country. In the "House Divided" speech, Lincoln arranged a series of recent events into narrative form so that they told a story of the work of this "slave power." Each of these events, such as the Kansas–Nebraska Act opening formerly free territories to slavery and the *Dred Scott* Supreme Court decision preventing Congress from outlawing slavery in the territories, prepared the way for more drastic action to extend slavery. Lincoln used the coherence of the story to predict what these plotters would do next: bring about a second *Dred Scott* decision that would prevent *states* from outlawing slavery anywhere. Figure 6.8 paraphrases his argument.

We have referred to narrative as a kind of verbal storytelling. But narrative inferences can also be made from visual evidence. Interpreting a picture, for instance, one might reveal the "story" that the picture tells.

Tests for Inference from Narrative

To test whether a narrative inference is sound, examine various elements of its structure. Some important questions follow.

1. *Is the narrative coherent?* Does the story hang together and make sense? Is everything tied together at the end? Or do unexplained factors and loose ends make the story seem "unfinished" and its point seem unclear?

2. *Is the narrative plausible?* Is the story realistic, or is it farfetched? Because the narrative is offered to explain or support some claim, an implausible narrative will call that claim into question as well.

3. *Are characterizations consistent?* Do individuals in the story act as the audience has been led to expect? Just as you must be credible as a speaker and just as the experts you quote must be credible as authorities, so the characters in a narrative must be credible. If they are not, the audience will question the story—and the claim.

4. *Does the narrative have resonance?* **Resonance** is a feature that makes a narrative strike a responsive chord with listeners, allowing them to identify with the story and to relate it to their own experience. If your narrative has resonance, listeners will realize that you are telling the story not for its entertainment value but to speak directly to them and to make them understand your point.

---

resonance
The quality of striking a responsive chord with listeners, causing them to identify with what one is saying.

1. **Is the narrative coherent?**
2. **Is the narrative plausible?**
3. **Are characterizations consistent?**
4. **Does the narrative have resonance?**

Avoiding Errors in Reasoning

We have examined a variety of inferences and some tests for each of them. The best way to ensure that your reasoning is sound is to apply those tests to specific inference patterns. But there are also some general errors in reasoning. As we have seen, these are called *fallacies.* The inference appears at first to be sound but, on inspection, it contains a major flaw. Although fallacies often seem persuasive, critical listeners quickly realize that the reasoning goes astray.

Sometimes, the term *fallacy* refers very broadly to any claim that people disagree with or any statement that they do not like. At other times, the term refers very narrowly to defects in formal logic only. In public speaking, however, fallacies are inferences that would generally be regarded as unreasonable by a broad and diverse audience of listeners exercising their best critical judgment.[12]

Six General Tests of Inferences

1. *Does the claim follow from the supporting material?* This is the most basic question. If a speaker stated, "Because our school is 100 years old, it needs higher academic standards," we would be hard pressed to find any relationship between the supporting material (the age of the school) and the claim (that higher academic standards are needed). The claim might be correct, but it probably could not be inferred from *this* supporting evidence. The technical term for an inference in which the claim does not follow from the supporting material is **non sequitur** (Latin for "It does not follow").

2. *Does the claim advance our understanding beyond the supporting material?* Because we reason from what we already know (the supporting material) to what we wish to establish (the claim), an inference moves beyond the supporting material. But sometimes an inference has no real movement; the claim simply restates the supporting material in slightly different words. Such an inference is said to be a **circular argument,** as in this statement: "Freedom of speech is for the common good [claim] because the expression of opinions is ultimately in the best interest of all [supporting material]."

3. *Is the claim relevant to the issue?* Sometimes, a speaker makes a claim that is not pertinent to the topic at hand. Consider the following argument from a student who was claiming that the Scholastic Assessment Test (SAT) does not predict academic success:

> The test numbers do nothing to measure a student's potential for success in college. I am so tired of the way the modern world reduces us all to numbers. The college admissions process has become a clear example of this. When students

non sequitur
A claim that, on its face, is unrelated to the supporting material.

circular argument
Only restating the claim in slightly different words, rather than supporting the claim.

want most of all to be seen as unique persons, they are instead reduced to an SAT quotient.

By noting the dehumanizing effect of using test scores to assess college applicants, the speaker *was* making a claim about modern life, and supported it with reference to the SAT, but the claim had nothing to do with the issue of whether the exam is a poor measure of students' potential. Whereas test number one refers to the relationship between the supporting material and the claim, this test concerns the relationship between the claim and the issue. An inference that diverts attention from the issue is said to be **ignoring the question.** (More commonly it is called a *red herring*, from the practice of dragging a smoked fish along a trail to confuse hunting dogs.)

4. *Is the language clear and unequivocal?* In Chapter 10, we will study the specific roles of language in a speech. The important point here is that the clarity of language may affect the quality of an inference. When the language of a speech can have multiple meanings, it is said to be **equivocal;** and any inferences based on that language will also be open to interpretation.

Suppose that a politician promises "no tax increases." This sounds straightforward but can be interpreted in many ways. Is the politician promising that there will be no new taxes? Or that the current tax rate will not increase? Or that the percentage of a family's income paid in taxes will not change? Or that the family will spend no more on taxes this year than last year? Furthermore, what is a "tax"? Is it limited to such obvious categories as income, sales, and property taxes, or does it also include fees for driving on toll roads or camping in national parks?

5. *Has probability been clearly distinguished from certainty?* Speakers sometimes forget that inferences cannot be guaranteed, and they regard as *certain* what is really only *probable*. A speaker might argue, for example, that viewing violent television programs unquestionably inspires people to act violently. But this claim is hardly a sure thing; some researchers suggest that television violence may have little or no effect on behavior, and some even argue that television violence reduces aggression by providing a relatively harmless outlet for it. When a speaker suggests that all the evidence is clear-cut in one direction, listeners will do well to be wary that he or she is overstating the case.

6. *Is the speaker's emotional response appropriate to the situation?* During the 1988 presidential debates, Democratic candidate Michael Dukakis, who opposed capital punishment, was asked whether he would favor it were his wife raped and murdered. Dukakis virtually ignored the hypothetical situation posed by the questioner and proceeded in analytical fashion to restate his position on capital punishment:

> I think you know I've opposed the death penalty during all my life. I don't see any evidence that it's a deterrent, and I think there are better and more effective ways to deal with violent crime. We've done so in my own state. And that's one of the reasons we have had the biggest drop in crime of any industrial state in America.

ignoring the question
Making an inference that diverts attention from the issue at hand.

equivocal
Having multiple meanings.

Many viewers reacted negatively to this response because Dukakis seemed to show no emotion; nothing in his answer suggested the rage people might expect from a husband in this situation. As a result, many listeners both discounted Dukakis's views on capital punishment and decided that he was not credible. Both conclusions were reached by inference from the mismatch between Dukakis's emotional reaction and what would be expected.

As this example illustrates, appropriate emotional response sometimes is more important than the details of the inference. This point was made vividly in August 1998 when President Clinton spoke to the nation about his improper relationship with Monica Lewinsky. Although many people believed that an overzealous special prosecutor was the real cause of his problems, Clinton's use of that claim in his speech did not go over well. At that point, the audience was expecting to see the emotions of contrition and remorse, not causal arguments.

The key issue is the *appropriateness* of the speaker's emotional response. Some situations, such as the presentation of scientific research, call for straightforwardness and calm; others, such as the ones Dukakis and Clinton faced, call for a passionate response. But because the meaning of situations is not given and because inferences from emotions—like other inferences—cannot be guaranteed, how do we know what a particular situation calls for? The real point is that most people in a given audience or even a given culture will regard a situation in a certain way, and a speaker should analyze the norms of appropriate emotional response as part of the audience analysis.

Second, should speakers *always* respond in the "appropriate" way? Like other principles of public speaking, this one is not universal. At times, a speaker deliberately violates listeners' expectations by making an "inappropriate" response, perhaps becoming emotionally aroused about a subject that the audience regards as "no big deal" or finding humor in a subject that the audience takes seriously. Usually, when a speaker violates norms of appropriateness, the purpose is to shock listeners, to make them sit up and take notice, and to convince them to reexamine their ideas about the situation. But such a strategy is risky, because the discomfort produced by an inappropriate response may turn the audience against the speaker instead of stimulating analysis.

Finally, be aware that emotional responses are sometimes misused, as when a speaker labels ideas he or she does not like as "anti-American" or "sexist" or "racist." Unsupported appeals to fear, to prejudice, or to pride are actually devices to *prevent* inference, an attempt to substitute emotional reactions for substantial proof.

Checklist 6.7 General Tests for Inferences

1. **Does the claim follow from the supporting material?**
2. **Does the claim advance our understanding beyond the supporting material?**
3. **Is the claim relevant to the issue?**
4. **Is the language clear and unequivocal?**
5. **Has probability been clearly distinguished from certainty?**
6. **Is the speaker's emotional response appropriate to the situation?**

Reasoning in Public Speaking

It is time to apply our exploration of the reasoning process to preparing, delivering, and listening to speeches.

When preparing a speech, ask yourself why listeners should regard the supporting material as grounds for your claim. Then apply the tests for the particular kinds of inferences (Checklists 6.1 to 6.6) and the general tests for inferences (Checklist 6.7) to determine whether your reasoning seems sound. Then imagine a relatively skeptical listener—not someone hostile to the topic but someone who really does need to be convinced. Would that person regard your reasoning as sound?[13]

Proceed to higher levels of claims and repeat this process. Finally, ask whether all the statements marked by Roman numerals in your outline taken together provide a basis for inferring your central claim. If so, then you have done a good job in working with your speech materials. But if you find any questionable inferences, your listeners are likely to find them, too.

When presenting a speech, remember that the audience is a critical factor in establishing rhetorical proof; the speaker and listeners reason together. As we have seen throughout the chapter, your selection of one reasoning pattern rather than another is a strategic choice, because each pattern reflects a different aspect of how listeners think along with you. Moreover, you will not always make every step in your reasoning explicit; sometimes, the supporting material or, more likely, the inference will seem to be assumed. This means that you are drawing on the audience's knowledge and expectations to establish the inference.

For example, audience analysis might suggest that your listeners believe that mergers of media companies threaten the ability of the press to be both a government watchdog and a guardian of democracy. You might never mention that inference explicitly in your speech, instead saying, "This week we heard news reports of yet another media corporation merger. We know what that means for the strength of American democracy." Occasionally, of course, the audience analysis will be mistaken. Suppose that the last statement was met by blank stares—or, worse, by frowns. Such feedback signals that the audience is not ready to participate in this inference. Even while giving the speech, you may modify your strategic plan, deciding in this case to make the inference explicit—not only stating that media mergers threaten democracy but also giving evidence to support your claim.

You can help listeners follow your reasoning process by signposting its steps and inferences. Saying, "Let me provide three examples," or, "An analogy is in order here," will prompt listeners to anticipate the inference and its appropriate tests. Asking (and later answering) such a question as "How do we know that the statistical sample was representative?" will suggest that you know the relevant tests of reasoning and are confident that your speech satisfies them. Even the use of reasoning terms (*consequently, therefore, the premise is, the implied conclusion is,* and so on) will help listeners understand where you are in reasoning through the speech. Not only that, but your care in reasoning appropriately from supporting material will help to promote your audience's critical thinking and listening skills—just as their critical listening will provide you with an incentive to reason carefully.[14]

Respecting Diversity Through Reasoning

Not all individuals or cultures reason in the same way. The following strategies will help you to ensure that you do not unconsciously assume that all audience members reason in the same way that you do.

1. Use a variety of inferences to appeal to all members of your audience.
2. Be sure that your inferences (from example, analogy, sign, cause, testimony, and narrative) avoid stereotypes of people or cultural groups.
3. Check especially to avoid fallacies that could offend your audience.

Summary

In this chapter, we have seen that rhetorical proof in public speaking is different from proof in mathematics or science. Rhetorical proof depends on an interaction between the speaker and the audience; although their joint conclusions cannot be guaranteed absolutely, they can be supported and shown to be probable.

A rhetorical proof includes three components. The claim is the statement that listeners are asked to accept. Supporting material provides the foundation for the claim. And reasoning links the supporting material to the claim; it involves making an inference—a mental leap—that the supporting material really does support the claim. Although inferences cannot be guaranteed, certain patterns of inference can be shown to be generally reliable. An inference is reasonable if it would be made by most people when exercising their critical judgment.

We distinguished among inferences from example, analogy, sign, cause, testimony, and narrative. Each of these reasoning patterns has several different types, and for each certain tests are appropriate. In addition, we studied six general tests of reasoning to help you avoid such fallacies as the non sequitur, circular argument, ignoring the question, equivocal language, confusing probability with certainty, and inappropriate emotional response. These are fallacies because their inferences seem to be sound but actually are seriously flawed.

The chapter concluded with suggestions for using your understanding of the reasoning process in preparing, delivering, and listening to speeches.

Discussion Questions

1. In class, watch a videotape of a recent political speech and discuss its reasoning process. What patterns of inference were used? Why do you

think the speaker chose to use those patterns? Did they work? Did you recognize any fallacies?

2. If you knew that your audience would be uncritical, why would you still take time to test your inferences before speaking? With a group of peers, discuss the ethics of proper reasoning.

3. In what ways might emotion help someone or prevent someone from making a proper inference? Discuss situations in which particular emotions (love, fear, hate, anger, boredom) might advance or detract from the reasoning process.

Activities

1. In Chapter 2, you studied how to listen critically to a speech and to develop a map of what was said, evaluating each link between support and claim with a plus or minus sign. Now expand your evaluation of each link on that map. Identify each type of inference, and conduct appropriate tests to understand why each link is positive or negative.

2. Identify examples of each type of inference that you plan to use in your next speech. Which reasoning patterns are most appropriate for your topic? Which do you think will be most effective with your audience? Which types of inference are you most comfortable using?

3. For the next few days, think critically about the everyday communication events around you. Using Checklist 6.7 as a guide, identify a recent claim that fails one of the general tests, and explain its fallacy. Pay close attention to television commercials, news editorials, and "heat of passion" arguments.

4. Find a letter to the editor in the campus or local newspaper. Identify and analyze the inferences the writer makes. What patterns are employed? Are the tests for each pattern satisfied? Are there any general errors in reasoning?

Notes

1. Although scientists and mathematicians may argue about what counts as proof, their institutional standards for agreement are usually clearly defined. See Philip J. Davis and Reuben Hersh, "Rhetoric and Mathematics," *The Rhetoric of the Human Sciences: Language and Argument in Scholarship and Public Affairs*, ed. John S. Nelson, Allan Megill, and Donald N. McCloskey, Madison: Univ. of Wisconsin Press, 1987, pp. 53–68; Gyorgy Markus, "Why Is There No Hermeneutics of Natural Sciences? Some Preliminary Theses," *Science in Context* 1 (Spring 1987): 5–51.

2. See the discussion of "universal audience" in Chapter 3. See also Chaim Perelman and Lucie Olbrechts-Tyteca, *The New Rhetoric: A Treatise on Argumentation,* translated by John Wilkinson and Purcell Weaver, Notre Dame, Ind.: Univ. of Notre Dame Press, 1969, pp. 31–35.

3. For a more detailed map of the reasoning process, see Stephen Toulmin, Richard Rieke, and Allan Janik, *An Introduction to Reasoning,* 2nd ed., New York: Macmillan, 1984. See also J. Ramage and J. Bean, *Writing Arguments,* 3rd ed., Boston: Allyn and Bacon, 1995.

4. For recent research on the influence of culture on reasoning patterns, see Erica Goode, "How Culture Molds Habits of Thought," *New York Times* (Aug. 8, 2000): D1, D4.

5. Also consult a theoretical discussion of inferences from example in speeches, such as Scott Consigny, "The Rhetorical Example," *Southern Speech Communication Journal* 41 (Winter 1976): 121–134.

6. Researchers have shown that both figurative and literal analogies are persuasive for audiences. See James C. McCroskey and Walter H. Combs, "The Effects of the Use of Analogy on Attitude Change and Source Credibility," *Journal of Communication* 19 (December 1969): 333–339.

7. Our modern understanding of literal and figurative analogies developed from the classical tradition. For more on the genesis of analogical reasoning, see James S. Measell, "Classical Bases of the Concept of Analogy," *Argumentation and Advocacy* 10 (Summer 1973): 1–10.

8. For more on the use of analogies in speeches, see James R. Wilcox and Henry L. Ewbank, "Analogy for Rhetors," *Philosophy and Rhetoric* 12 (Winter 1979): 1–20.

9. For a more detailed theoretical discussion of inferences from cause, see David Zarefsky, "The Role of Causal Argument in Policy Controversies," *Argumentation and Advocacy* 13 (Spring 1977): 179–191.

10. According to some, storytelling is the most important aspect of speechmaking. See Walter R. Fisher, "Narration as a Human Communication Paradigm: The Case of Public Moral Argument," *Communication Monographs* 51 (March 1984): 1–22.

11. For a good practical discussion of the power of narrative in speeches, see A. Cheree Carlson, "Narrative as the Philosopher's Stone: How Russell H. Conwell Changed Lead into Diamonds," *Western Journal of Speech Communication* 53 (Fall 1989): 342–355.

12. Several books explore fallacies in detail. See Alex C. Michalos, *Improving Your Reasoning*, 2nd ed., Englewood Cliffs, N.J.: Prentice-Hall, 1986; T. Edward Damer, *Attacking Faulty Reasoning*, 2nd ed., Belmont, Calif.: Wadsworth, 1987; Howard Kahane, *Logic and Contemporary Rhetoric*, Belmont, Calif.: Wadsworth, 1980.

13. It has been said that "arguments are found in people," meaning that listeners are responsible for making the inferential leaps between supporting material and claim. See Wayne Brockriede, "Where Is Argument?" *Argumentation and Advocacy* 11 (Spring 1975): 179–182.

14. For a more detailed discussion of how speakers (and audiences) develop skill in reasoning, see Dale Hample, "Arguing Skill," *Handbook of Communication and Social Interaction Skills*, ed. John O. Greene and Brant R. Burleson, Mahwah, N.J.: Erlbaum, 2003.

Chapter Seven

Organizing the Speech: The Body

In this chapter, we will:

- Explain why the organization of a speech is important for both the speaker and the audience.

- Identify criteria for selecting the main ideas to include in your speech and the characteristics that a main idea should have.

- Learn how to arrange the main ideas into recognizable patterns and which patterns of arrangement you might use.

- Examine ways to decide how much and which kinds of supporting material you need and how to arrange the support for each idea.

If you have used all the strategies suggested in Chapters 4 and 5 for investigating your topic, you now should have a better understanding of the issues that are implicit in your thesis. You also should have located a variety of supporting materials for your ideas—examples, statistics, testimony, and so forth. You have probably investigated many more ideas than you can discuss in the time available, and you very likely have located far more supporting materials than you can use, even after applying the tests of reasoning that we examined in Chapter 6. For all this effort, your ideas and materials may show no evident pattern and may not seem to fit together well. What, then, do you do with all the ideas you have explored and all the evidence you have gathered?

Identifying and locating material for the speech is not enough; you also need to organize it in strategic ways that advance your purpose. **Organization** is the selection of ideas and materials and their arrangement into a discernible and effective pattern. This process is so crucial that we will discuss it in three chapters. Here, we will focus exclusively on the body of the speech. Then, in Chapter 8, we will consider introductions, conclusions, and transitions. Finally, in Chapter 9, we will learn how to apply the principles of organization in outlining your speech.

Why Is Organization Important?

To help orient new students to the college, the Counseling Office offers a program in which seniors give speeches about how to develop good study habits. The first speaker, Burt Wilson, maintained that "good habits depend on several important factors. For one thing, you have to avoid procrastination. Good reading skills are also helpful to college students. Oh yes, and by the way, you also need to be self-motivated." The incoming students looked puzzled and unconvinced; they stopped taking notes, and no one asked questions. The very next speaker, Laura Simmons, covered the same ground, but she said: "Good study habits depend on a balance of skills plus motivation. On the one hand, you have to develop good reading skills; on the other hand, you need to overcome procrastination. You can do both if you focus on the priorities that motivate you to study." The audience responded very differently to Laura's speech; they took notes and asked a number of questions when she finished.

This example illustrates that audiences will understand, remember, and be influenced by an organized message more than by a disorganized one. The reason is obvious. Careful listening is difficult under any circumstances, and it is even more difficult when listeners cannot tell where the speaker is going or how the parts of the speech relate to one another. An idea or example that is not connected to anything else is easy to forget.[1] The mental energy that listeners use in reconstructing a confused or disorganized speech is not available for absorbing and reflecting on its main points.[2] Moreover, listeners may resent this additional work and may express their resentment by resisting the message.[3]

Beyond such basic considerations about the audience, a speaker should recognize that organizational pattern, or form, itself is persuasive. If listeners can identify a clear pattern in the speech, they can anticipate what idea is coming next. If a speaker describes the development of intercollegiate athletics by talking first about the past and then about the present, listen-

organization
The selection of ideas and materials and their arrangement into a discernible and effective pattern.

ers reasonably can expect to focus next on the future. As the speaker develops the main ideas aloud, listeners follow along and develop the ideas in their minds.

The ability to follow a speaker's organizational pattern is important for several reasons:

- An audience can better remember the main ideas of a speech when the speaker presents them in a recognizable pattern. For example, the past/present/future pattern is one category of arrangement that prompts the recall of specific ideas. Listeners are more likely to remember the first idea if they can connect it mentally to the heading "past."
- Effective organization encourages active rather than passive listening. It engages listeners' attention and helps them to ignore or override distractions.
- Being able to anticipate what's coming next makes listeners feel that they are "in the know." They may believe, for example, that the next natural step in the speaker's organizational pattern is to discuss the present influence of television revenues on college sports. If that is indeed the next main idea, listeners are likely to feel personal satisfaction at having "called it right."[4]

In short, form is persuasive because listeners are more likely to be disposed positively toward ideas that they have helped to shape, that they can remember well, and about which they feel personally satisfied.

Organization is important for the speaker as well. In Chapter 4, you were introduced to the idea of *strategic planning* for a speech. In any rhetorical situation, the goal is to respond to your constraints and to take advantage of your opportunities to achieve your purpose. Organization is a major strategic resource that greatly affects the outcome of a speech. You need to bring critical thinking and reflection to such organizational decisions as the number and order of ideas, how you group them, what you call them, and how you relate them to the audience. In devising your strategic plan, you should question what your options are, how each option relates to your purpose, and how different choices are likely to be perceived by listeners.

Moreover, in planning your speech, organization can be a guide to check that you haven't accidentally left anything out. For example, noticing that your speech covers both the past and the present of your topic, you recognize that the audience will be likely to think, "But what about the future?" This prompts you to find the materials needed to discuss the future as well. During your presentation, too, keeping the organization in mind can prevent the embarrassment of suddenly forgetting what the next point should be.[5]

Organization has two basic components: *selection* and *arrangement*. We will discuss each component with respect both to the main ideas of the speech and to the supporting materials.

Selecting the Main Ideas

As you remember from Chapter 4, the thesis statement is the principal claim of your speech, the statement you want listeners to accept. When you ask questions about your thesis statement, you identify the issues that you must address in order to establish the thesis. **Main ideas** are the claims that

main ideas
Claims that address the issues in the thesis statement; the primary divisions of the speech.

address the issues in your thesis statement, and they are the major divisions of the speech. In Chapter 9, you'll see that main ideas are signaled in the speech outline by Roman numerals.

Identifying Your Main Ideas

The first step is to identify what the main ideas in your speech will be. To do that, you must determine the possible main ideas from which you could choose. You can do that either (1) from your thesis or specific purpose or (2) from patterns in your research.

From Your Thesis or Specific Purpose. Stuart Kim used this approach to identify his main ideas in a speech seeking to persuade the audience to contribute to the United Way. Like many college students, Stuart was a community service volunteer; he tutored reading and math at an after-school center for children from low-income families who had no parent at home during the day. Stuart enjoyed the work and felt that he was really helping the children, but toward the end of the year he was startled to learn that the center would have to close. It was funded by the United Way, and contributions were down. Appalled that "his" children would have nowhere to go, Stuart decided to speak to community groups and urge them to support the United Way. He used his public speaking classmates as a test audience to practice the speech.

Because Stuart's purpose was to persuade the audience to contribute to the United Way, he thought immediately of several ideas that he needed to address. He would have to tell listeners what the United Way is, that the agencies it supports (such as Stuart's after-school center) were important and valuable, that other sources of funding were not readily available, and that the United Way needed and merited *their* support. If the speech failed to address any of these elements, the audience was unlikely to be persuaded to donate money. Stuart regarded these as the main ideas, and he divided the speech into corresponding sections:

I. The United Way is a federation of health, recreational, and social service agencies.
II. The activities of these agencies are important and valuable to our community.
III. These activities cannot be continued unless we support the United Way.

In this example, Stuart was able immediately to see the main ideas that derived from his thesis and purpose. But sometimes, the connection is not so obvious. If Stuart had not identified his main ideas at once, he might have worked them out by quizzing his thesis statement, using the method you learned in Chapter 4:

TOPIC: The United Way

GENERAL PURPOSE: Inducing a specific action

SPECIFIC PURPOSE: Convincing listeners to give money to the United Way

THESIS: Everyone should contribute to the United Way.

ISSUES:

1. Everyone   →   Why me?
2. Should contribute   →   Why? What does it do?
3. The United Way   →   What is it?

MAIN IDEAS:

1. The United Way needs and merits your support.
2. The United Way supports important and valuable programs.
3. The United Way is an umbrella organization to raise money for social service programs.

Looking over this list, Stuart would probably decide to put main idea 3 first in the speech and to end with main idea 1. Why? Because listeners need to know what the United Way is before they can decide whether to support it and because the direct appeal in main idea 1 provides a strong conclusion. Applying these analytical steps, Stuart would derive the same main ideas that he was able to recognize instinctively.

Checklist 7.1 contains some of the standard questions to ask about a thesis statement in order to identify your main ideas.

From Patterns in Your Research. Another approach to identifying main ideas is to observe patterns in the research that you have completed. If the people you interview and the literature you read repeatedly mention certain subjects, those may well be the main ideas about your topic.

For example, suppose that almost everything Stuart Kim read about the United Way mentioned its low administrative costs and suggested that its reliance on volunteers meant that most of the money raised can be spent directly on providing services. This idea may not have emerged from Stuart's initial conception of a strategy to meet his purpose, and yet it may be very important to include the idea in the speech. It suggests that it is better for people to contribute to the United Way than to support a host of individual charities that do not use their funds as efficiently.

Checklist 7.1 Questions to Help Identify Main Ideas

1. What does it mean?	11. How will it happen?
2. How to describe it?	12. Who is involved?
3. What are the facts?	13. What are some examples?
4. What are the reasons?	14. Why is it strange?
5. How often does it occur?	15. What are the objections?
6. What is my view?	16. Compared with what?
7. What are the parts?	17. What is the effect of this?
8. What is the reasoning?	18. Any stories to tell?
9. What is the cause?	19. How often?
10. Which ones?	20. What is preventing it?

Choosing Among Main Ideas

The thesis and purpose of a speech as well as the process of research are sources of main ideas. Often, however, you'll have more ideas than you have time or energy to pursue—and more than your audience will be willing and able to consider.

Suppose, for example, that Stuart's research suggested all the following points:

- The administrative costs of the United Way are low.
- Organizations in the United Way must be nondiscriminatory.
- The United Way had its origins in charitable organizations of the late nineteenth century.
- Some groups within the public object to the programs of certain United Way organizations.
- The United Way is staffed largely by volunteers.
- It is not clear whether someone who lives in one community but works in another should support the United Way at home or at work.
- The United Way substitutes a single annual campaign for what otherwise would be continuous solicitation for each of the member agencies.
- The alternative to supporting the United Way is to expand the government's social welfare programs.

Each of these topics could be discussed at length, and each might be supported by a variety of materials. Yet no speech of reasonable length could address them all. Therefore, like most speakers, Stuart will need to select from among the possible main ideas which ones to use in the speech.

Criteria for Selecting the Main Ideas

Most speeches cover between two and five main ideas. Although there is no magic to these numbers, they do generally represent what an audience expects and can likely follow and remember.

If you have derived more than five main ideas from your thesis and purpose and from your research, you can reduce their number and select which ideas to include by asking two questions:

- Is this idea really essential to the speech?
- Can a more general statement combine several ideas?

Is This Idea Essential? In researching a speech, you may discover many interesting things about your subject that are, frankly, sidelights. Although they may be fascinating to you, they distract from your specific purpose. For example, knowing that the United Way developed from nineteenth-century charitable organizations may reveal quite a bit about American attitudes toward charity or about how organizations evolve. But remember that Stuart Kim's purpose is to persuade audience members to donate money. Most people don't need to know about the United Way's origins and history in order to decide whether to contribute. Likewise, if Stuart's goal is only to persuade people to give, it may not matter whether they do so at work or at home.

This first criterion is often difficult to apply. Speakers are reluctant to omit ideas that interest them, and valuable research time seems wasted if the results do not find their way into the speech. But including nonessential material may distract the audience and prevent you from achieving your ultimate purpose. It is necessary, then, to be hard-nosed and to subject all potential main ideas to this rigorous test: If an idea—no matter how interesting—is not essential to your specific purpose, it does not qualify as a main idea and should be excluded.

Can Several Ideas Be Combined? When you find yourself considering a large number of main ideas, consider whether some of them are not main ideas at all but illustrations of, or support for, more general statements. You may be able to combine what you thought were distinct main ideas into one general statement, thereby reducing the number. Your thesis should suggest these more general statements into which you could combine elements.

In the United Way example, the low administrative costs, the nondiscriminatory policies, and the convenience of a single annual campaign might turn out not to be separate main ideas but examples to support a general statement such as "The United Way is the best way to contribute to charity." The three statements all answer the question "Once I've decided that it's important to make a charitable contribution, why should I do so through the United Way?" That question is a longer form of "Why me?" which was derived from the thesis statement. All these examples thus could support the main idea, "The United Way merits *your* support." By referring to the issues suggested by the thesis statement, or just by asking whether a more general statement could be made, we reduced three statements of main ideas to one.

Characteristics of the Main Ideas

Unfortunately, just cutting the number of main ideas—as difficult as that is—may still result in a speech that does not seem complete, coherent, or persuasive. It is also important that the selected main ideas have the following characteristics.

Simplicity. Because the main ideas serve as memory aids for both speaker and audience, they should be stated simply and succinctly so that they can be remembered. "The United Way is efficient" is a better statement of a main idea than is "The United Way has low administrative costs, economies of scale from combining campaigns, and simple distribution mechanisms." As a general rule, a main idea should be stated in a single short sentence.

Discreteness. Each main idea should be separate from the others. When main ideas overlap, the structure of the speech becomes confusing, and it is difficult to remember what was said under each main heading. For example, if one main idea is "The United Way supports agencies that meet social needs" and another main idea is "The United Way supports health and recreational agencies," the two ideas overlap; they are not discrete. After all, health and recreation are also among our social needs. Such a structure will not be clear to listeners, and the speaker will not know where to put supporting material.

Parallel Structure. When possible, main ideas should be stated in similar fashion. Sentences should have the same grammatical structure and should be of approximately the same length. This principle, known as **parallel structure,** makes the pattern easy to follow and to remember. For example, Stuart Kim might use this pattern:

> The United Way is effective.
> The United Way is efficient.
> The United Way is humane.

In this example, *effective, efficient,* and *humane* are the key terms that listeners are asked to remember. Each of these value judgments can be supported with different types of evidence, but the basic structure of the speech is parallel.

Balance. Taken together, the main ideas should not be loaded toward one particular aspect of the subject. Rather, they should add up to a balanced perspective. In the preceding list, each of the three key terms refers to a different aspect of the United Way: what it accomplishes, what it costs, and what values it represents. These are three different factors that would affect the decision to contribute, and together they offer a balanced perspective. If, on the other hand, three or four main ideas related to the United Way's finances and only one dealt with its underlying values, the organization of the speech would appear unbalanced. Finances would be covered in detail, but other important aspects of the topic would be treated superficially or ignored.

Coherence. **Coherence** means that the separate main ideas have a clear relationship and hang together; listeners can see why they appear in the same speech. If Stuart Kim wished to persuade listeners to contribute to the United Way but offered one main idea about the origins of charitable organizations, another about efforts to extend the United Way to Eastern Europe, another about controversial agencies that the United Way supports, and another about accounting procedures, it is hard to imagine how the speech could be coherent. These topics are not clearly related to each other (except that they all involve the United Way), and they do not come together to support any conclusion—certainly not the ultimate claim that "you should contribute to the United Way."

Completeness. Finally, the main ideas taken together should present a complete view of the subject, omitting nothing of major importance. If Stuart wants to convince the audience to contribute to the United Way but fails to explain what the organization does with the money it receives, the pattern of main ideas would not be complete. Most people who make charitable gifts want to know how their contributions are used.

parallel structure
Structure in which phrases are of similar syntax and length.

coherence
Clear relationships among ideas and topics so that the speech appears to hang together as a natural whole.

Checklist 7.2 Characteristics of Main Ideas

Taken together, the main ideas of the speech should be characterized by:

1. Simplicity
2. Discreteness
3. Parallel structure
4. Balance
5. Coherence
6. Completeness

Arranging the Main Ideas

Having selected the main ideas for your speech, the next step is to decide upon their order—which ideas to put first, last, or in the middle. We'll look at the factors you should consider in arranging your main ideas and then at a variety of organizational patterns that you can use.

Factors Affecting Arrangement

Are the Main Ideas Dependent? Ideas can be arranged in a pattern that makes them either *dependent* or *independent*.

Logically dependent ideas are like links in a chain, because the strength of each depends on all the others. If one link is broken, the chain is destroyed. This organization of ideas is called a *series* or *subordinative* structure. Here is such a chain of logically dependent main ideas:

> If we develop regulations for campus speech, they will necessarily be vague.
> If regulations are vague, people will not know whether or not the regulations apply to them.
> If people are unsure whether regulations apply to them, they will hesitate to speak out about controversial issues.
> If people do not speak out about controversial issues, intellectual debate is undermined.

This speaker, obviously, would argue that codes to regulate speech would undermine the vital intellectual exchange of campus life. The links in this argument need to be arranged precisely as shown if the audience is to follow the speaker's reasoning.

Logical dependence is common in telling a story. With obvious exceptions (such as flashbacks), you should relate events in the order in which they occurred so that listeners can follow the plot. Likewise, if you arrange ideas in a spatial pattern—talking, for example, about colleges in different regions of the country—then you need to maintain that pattern of geographical movement. You might move from east to west or from west to east, but you would not want to zigzag from New England to the Southwest and then to the mid-Atlantic states.

In contrast, **logically independent ideas** stand alone, and the truth of each in no way rests on the others. This organization of ideas is called a *parallel-* or *multiple-argument* structure. Again using the example of a proposed code to regulate campus speech, here is a logically independent pattern of reasoning:

logically dependent idea
Cannot stand on its own but requires that some other claim or statement be true.

logically independent idea
Does not require the truth of any other claim or statement as a condition for its own truth.

Organizing Your Speech

Priya Mydur

Priya talks with Prof. Blivens about difficulties she had organizing her persuasive speech on "The Health Benefits of Chocolate."

Writing the speech was not as complicated as organizing all my information. I could not decide what exactly I wanted to speak about and how I wanted to arrange the outline. I continuously changed my headings and subheadings, thinking that the speech would not flow well because many of the aspects depended on each other, so I had to introduce it, so that I could discuss it later in the speech.

Prof. Blivens

It's important to organize your evidence into categories based on what you found. The amount of evidence in one area could indicate a main subheading that should be included in your speech. Once that's completed, look at the categories the evidence falls in, then pick what are the "main" categories that should be discussed. At this point, you might have to do more research in one area or downsize another to balance evidence in the main points. What strategy did you use to finally pick your main points?

Priya Mydur: Finally, I decided I would speak about chocolate's effects on three different parts of the body: the cardiovascular system, the central nervous system,

and the mouth. I had about twice as much information for the cardiovascular system as I did for the mouth, so my speech was very imbalanced.

Prof. Blivens: Imbalanced speeches are something that I see a lot of from students. When that happens, review the smaller areas and consider doing more research. If there is not enough research on it, consider whether or not it should be a main point. Don't forget to be critical of your evidence under the cardiovascular section. Does it support your argument? Does it come to similar conclusions? Is it all needed to support your claim? Once you had completed all your research, how did you choose to organize it?

Priya Mydur: I had gone through all my notes and numbered them so that I could refer back to write my speech. For example, since the nervous system was my second heading, any information dealing with it that I would use in my speech had a "II" by it, and if it was about caffeine, which was the first subheading, then it had "II a" by it. So, it was quick to flip through the pages and find specific pieces of information.

Prof. Blivens: Some final things you could have done were to have an outsider look over your research and offer a second opinion. Having someone else discuss your evidence can help you decide what to cut and what to develop. Marking your evidence is an effective way to keep everything organized. I would like to hear more comments about the strategic selection and critical evaluation you did for each piece of evidence.

Campus speech codes are unacceptably vague.
Campus speech codes discourage the airing of controversial issues.
Campus speech codes bring bad publicity to the college.

This speaker also wishes to oppose campus speech codes, but notice the difference in the structure of main ideas. In this case, each idea bears *independently* on the conclusion. Any one of these claims by itself could give the audience good reason to oppose speech codes, regardless of the other claims. Speech codes are undesirable if they are too vague, *or* if they chill the discussion of controversial issues, *or* if they bring unfavorable publicity.

A dependent pattern of reasoning can be risky, because the defeat of any one link will cause the chain to break. For this reason, some writers advise the use of an independent pattern whenever possible. But a dependent pattern also offers advantages. It is highly coherent and easy to follow. And if each link is established successfully, the force of the overall pattern may cause the whole chain to seem even stronger than the sum of its links.

A *convergent*, or *coordinative*, arrangement of ideas uses both logically independent and dependent ideas. The points are presented as independent ideas, but all the points are needed in order to support the main argument. This is different from a series arrangement in that the ideas are not dependent on each other in an ordered series. A convergent arrangement is different from a parallel structure in that each point is needed to support the argument adequately. Here is a convergent arrangement of ideas that support the claim, "Campus speech codes discourage talk about many controversial issues."

> Campus speech codes discourage talk about affirmative action policies.
> Campus speech codes discourage talk about abortion rights.
> Campus speech codes discourage talk about U.S. foreign policy in Iraq.

The ideas appear to be independent, but all are needed to support the claim that the discussion of many controversial issues is discouraged by campus speech codes.

The choice of a dependent or an independent pattern is influenced most strongly by your thesis statement. Use whichever pattern is more effective in establishing your claim for your audience. But one thing is certain: If your main ideas are dependent on each other, their arrangement is virtually decided. You can begin at either end of the chain, but you must connect the ideas in order, link by link. With an independent pattern, however, you do not have to present the main ideas in any particular order. In that case, additional questions will arise.

Are Some Main Ideas Relatively Unfamiliar? Because most people comprehend unfamiliar ideas by linking them to familiar ideas, you may wish to begin your speech with a main idea that is already familiar to listeners. This will attract their interest and get them thinking about your topic. Then you can move to the less familiar ideas, knowing that the audience is working with you.

Your audience analysis may suggest that most people realize that campus speech codes attract adverse publicity but that they may not be familiar with the vagueness of such codes and may not have thought about their effect on the airing of controversial issues. You therefore might begin with the familiar idea that campus speech codes attract negative publicity, making the point that this is just the tip of the iceberg. Speech codes also have two less obvious problems: They are too vague to be administered fairly, and—even worse—they stifle discussion of controversial issues. If your audience analysis is correct, you have succeeded in arranging the ideas from most familiar to least familiar.

There is another reason to begin with the familiar. If your first main idea were completely unfamiliar to the audience, it would be much more difficult for listeners to grasp. You might distract them by making them stop to think about what you mean by "the inherent vagueness of speech codes," and they might miss your next point. On the other hand, discussion of a familiar main idea can be used to explain a less familiar idea. For example,

When you have a strong idea that you plan to present emphatically, as this speaker does, should it be placed first or last in your speech?

knowing that listeners might quickly recognize that campus speech codes cause adverse publicity, you might ask why the publicity is so adverse. This question would provide a natural transition into your second, less familiar idea.

Should the Strongest Idea Come First or Last? This question comes into play when two conditions are met: when the main ideas are independent and when they are not equally strong. (A "strong" idea is one that will seem compelling to an audience of critical listeners. An idea is not considered to be strong if it does not make much difference to listeners—even if it is true and well supported.)

Should you present your strongest main idea first in order to make a strong first impression on the audience? Or should you present it last, to end with a bang and leave the audience on a positive note? Many researchers have studied the relative merits of a **primacy effect** (strongest idea first) versus a **recency effect** (strongest idea last), but the results are inconclusive.[6] Too many other factors also influence the impact of arrangement. However, if one idea seems weaker than the others, you should present it in a middle position rather than either toward the beginning or toward the end.

Often, the strength of an idea depends not on any inherent feature of the idea itself, but on how well the idea sits with the audience. This involves such factors as whether the idea relates to listeners' experience, whether it strikes most people as being consistent with common sense, and whether— if it is true—it makes a major or only a minor contribution toward the overall goal of the speech. Because the strength of an idea depends on listeners' perceptions, your audience analysis is not finished when you first select a

primacy effect
A tendency for what is presented first to be best remembered.

recency effect
A tendency for what is presented last to be best remembered.

topic, purpose, thesis, and strategy; the audience affects all major decisions about speech preparation and delivery.

Patterns for Arranging Main Ideas

In theory, you can arrange main ideas in an infinite number of patterns. But several common patterns are easy for an audience to follow, and they work well for a variety of topics. You first should focus on these general patterns, which are described next. Then, if your topic, purpose, or audience seems to call for a different pattern, you can develop your own.

Chronological. The passage of time is the organizing principle in the chronological approach. The units of time (most often the past, the present, and the future) become the main ideas. For example, in discussing the topic of "Discrimination Against Female Sports Reporters," student Jordan Breal organized her speech this way:

I. Female sports reporters received little credit for their work until the 1930s.
II. Female sports reporters were not allowed into press rooms until the 1970s.
III. Female sports reporters were not allowed into locker rooms until the late 1970s.
IV. Treatment of female sports reporters leaves much room for improvement in the future.

This example proceeds in normal chronological order, beginning with the past and ending with the future. But you can start at any point in the chronology. For example, you might decide that a speech about AIDS should begin with a discussion of the current crisis of AIDS in Africa, then move backwards in time to examine the origins of AIDS, and conclude with a discussion of the future of AIDS research and possible cures.

Spatial. Whereas chronological order organizes main ideas according to time, spatial order arranges them according to place or position. A speech might begin with the aspects of the topic that are nearest and then proceed to the aspects that are farther away. This pattern might work well for a speech about the effects of a strong national economy, in which the main points are:

I. A booming economy increases the individual's spending power.
II. A booming economy supports state and local projects.
III. A booming economy improves the federal budget.

Another common spatial arrangement would be to present ideas literally in geographic order:

I. A booming economy helps farmers in the South.
II. A booming economy helps manufacturing in the Midwest.

WWW. Using the Internet

Finding Patterns of Arrangement

Observe the pattern of arrangement used in speeches by listening to RealAudio files or by reading texts of speeches. Go to the **Allyn & Bacon Public Speaking Web Site** link "Develop an Organizational Pattern" by pointing your browser to **http://www.abacon.com/pubspeak/organize/patterns.html**. After listening to the speech, assess the organization critically:

- Do the main ideas satisfy the criteria of simplicity, discreteness, parallel structure, balance, coherence, and completeness?
- Is the organizational pattern chosen appropriate for the purpose of the speech and the audience?
- Does the speaker use supporting material to develop each main idea?

III. A booming economy helps the oil industry in the Southwest.
IV. A booming economy helps technology industries in the Northwest.

Categorical (Topical). In the categorical pattern, each main idea that you identified in analyzing your topic becomes a major division of the speech. For example, in researching the Hindu religion, student Anuj Vedak learned that Hindus hold many distinct beliefs, including a belief in karma as a guide to treating others ethically, a belief in reincarnation for those who have died, and a belief in nirvana as the soul's act of attaining salvation. Each of these topics can become a major heading in a speech. Because a categorical pattern has no required order (e.g., from past to present or from left to right), it is important that main ideas be stated in parallel fashion and that they be easy to recognize and remember. The major headings for a speech on Hinduism might be:

I. Hindus believe in karma as a guide to ethical behavior.
II. Hindus believe in reincarnation as the process of rebirth for the deceased.
III. Hindus believe in nirvana as the soul's act of attaining salvation.

This pattern is also called *topical* because it derives from the *topoi.* As we saw in Chapter 4, these are obvious or typical categories for organizing subject matter. They usually will have an obvious or standard structure. "People, places, and events" is an example of a set of *topoi,* as is "economic, military, and political aspects."

Cause–Effect. In Chapter 6, you learned how to infer causes and effects. Cause–effect is also an organizational pattern, and it can proceed in either direction. You can focus on causes and then identify their effects, or you can first identify effects and then try to determine their causes. For example, a speech about the depletion of the ozone layer might proceed like this:

I. Society has increased the use of aerosol spray cans.
II. These release fluorocarbons into the atmosphere.
III. Fluorocarbons erode the ozone layer surrounding the earth.
IV. Depletion of the ozone layer exposes people to additional ultraviolet radiation.

Or, rather than moving from cause to effect, you might proceed from effect to cause:

I. We are becoming more vulnerable to ultraviolet radiation.
II. This effect results from the release of fluorocarbons into the atmosphere.
III. Widespread use of aerosol cans is one source of the problem.

The choice between these two arrangements would be governed by which topics you wanted to present first and last, not by anything intrinsic to the cause–effect organizational pattern.

Problem–Solution. A variation of the cause–effect pattern is one that focuses on problems and their solutions. A speech using this pattern first lays out the dimensions of the problem and shows why it is serious; then it considers one or more potential solutions. It may simply report on the various

You can use a variation on cause–effect organization when your speech describes a problem for which you offer a solution. South African President Nelson Mandela often used this approach throughout his efforts to end apartheid in South Africa.

possible solutions or it may proceed to explain why a particular solution is best. For example, a speech about the difficulties of the college registration system might be structured something like this:

I. The current registration system is both inefficient and unfair.
II. Registration over the Internet or by touch-tone telephone would solve these problems.

The development of the first major heading might claim that the current registration system does not match students with their preferred courses as well as possible and that it gives an unfair advantage to students who happen to be first in line. Perhaps after considering some other solutions, the speaker would then claim that these problems can be overcome by using computer and telephone technology.

Often, problems are not self-evident to an audience. A speaker has to motivate listeners to feel that some important need is not being met before they will regard a situation as a problem. A variation on the problem–solution pattern, then, is to emphasize *psychological order*. The speaker first motivates listeners to perceive a problem and then provides the means to satisfy that feeling by identifying a solution. If Stuart Kim had chosen this approach in speaking about the United Way, his speech might have been organized as follows:

I. We all have a responsibility to others.
II. This responsibility includes financial support for the social service organizations that help others.
III. Giving to the United Way helps us to meet our responsibilities.

In this example, the first step is to arouse an attitude, motive, or desire among the audience members. Subsequent steps then refine that motivation and show how it can be satisfied by a particular action. In Chapter 14, we will examine an elaborated version of this organizational pattern, called the "motivated sequence," that is especially useful for persuading.

Comparison and Contrast. Sometimes, it is easiest to examine a topic by demonstrating its similarities to, and differences from, other topics with which the audience is likely to be familiar. From your studies of American history, for example, you know that women and racial and ethnic minorities have sometimes been subjected to prejudice and discrimination in the workplace. Your speech might be organized to compare the experiences among these groups:

   I. Women often are not promoted to senior positions because executives do not think they will remain on the job while raising children.
  II. Mexican Americans, in many parts of the country, are hired only for the most menial jobs.
 III. Earlier, German Americans and Japanese Americans were fired from their jobs because employers thought them to be unpatriotic.
  IV. Today, immigrants from the former Soviet Union are at risk because they are seen as competing for existing jobs.
   V. African Americans have been limited in work opportunities because many whites believe that they do not want to work.

Now the question is whether you want to highlight the differences or the similarities among these groups. You might select either of the following as your last main idea:

  VI. Although some groups have managed to overcome the effects of discrimination and have succeeded in the workplace, others have not been so lucky.

or

  VI. Although the experiences of these groups are very different, they have one factor in common: Society's prejudice places an artificial ceiling on their economic opportunities.

In either case, the earlier main ideas are brought together in the last one, which shows either how differences outweigh similarities or the reverse.

Residues. A final organizational pattern is to arrange the speech by process of elimination. This pattern works well when there are a finite number of possibilities, none particularly desirable, and you want to argue that one of them represents "the least among the evils." For example, in a political campaign in which you find no candidate particularly appealing, you could use this pattern to rule out all but one candidate, whom you then support as being the least objectionable.

Student speaker Jennifer Aiello used organization by residues to get her classmates to consider seriously the proposal that gun manufacturers should be required to install locks on guns. She arranged her main ideas to rule out the other options available to society:

No one wants freedom infringed upon. And no one wants to have to pay more for a gun. But let's consider the alternatives. Does anyone want more children to have in their hands guns that take virtually no effort to use? Does anyone want to attend more funerals of children shot dead while at school? Does anyone want to see more six-year-olds lying in critical condition in hospital beds because they were shot during a trip to the zoo? Does anyone want to see parents, friends, and family mourning another unnecessary death?

By ruling out each of these other alternatives, Jennifer was able to convince many of her audience members that putting locks on guns was a proposal worthy of their reflection.

Checklist 7.3 Basic Organizational Patterns

1. Chronological
2. Spatial
3. Categorical (topical)
4. Cause–effect

5. Problem–solution
6. Comparison and contrast
7. Residues

Choosing the Organizational Pattern

The organizational patterns described here do not exhaust all the possibilities, but they illustrate that you have many options from which to choose.[7] How should you decide which organizational pattern to use in your speech? Does it matter, for example, whether you use a cause–effect pattern or a comparison and contrast pattern? How do you know whether, say, the costs and benefits of voting are more important than the convenience of voting? Questions like these require you to think strategically. The answers are complex and must take into account your subject, your purpose, your audience, and your culture.

Based on Your Subject. Certain subjects lend themselves to particular organizational patterns. For example, because the collapse of communism in Eastern Europe is a historical event, it has a dramatic structure that would be emphasized by telling a story in chronological order. On the other hand, a speech about the components of air pollution would more likely suggest a topical pattern—unless, perhaps, it was being delivered to an audience of environmental historians who would be more interested in understanding when and how these components became serious national problems.

Based on Your Purpose. Your purpose or strategy also influences the selection of an organizational pattern. For instance, if you want to urge the audience to lobby for the regulation of cable television, an analytical pattern that emphasizes problems and solutions will be especially appropriate because it will focus attention on the specific proposal for which you want listeners to lobby. In contrast, if your purpose is to show that cable presented regulatory issues different from those presented by television, a comparison–contrast pattern probably would make more sense.

Based on Your Audience. Your audience is another influence on the arrangement of your speech. For example, listeners who have paid little at-

Organizing Your Speech

The Situation

You and a number of other students are dismayed by the administration's recent choice to build a monument in tribute to a famous alumnus, who—although he accomplished many admirable things and provided benefits and financial assistance to the university—is rumored to have died of a drug overdose. You've been attending the rallies against building the monument, and the antimonument group has selected you and two fellow students to speak to the university administration about your objections.

Making Choices

1. How should you decide what main points you want to relay to your audience, and in what order should you present them?

2. What do you know about the administration's position that would affect your organizational choices?

3. What kind of supporting material would be important to include—and where in the speech should you include it?

What If . . .

How would your organizational decisions change if the following were true?

1. The alumnus left a great deal of money to the university, on condition that a monument in tribute to her be built.

2. The administration had not already decided to build the monument but was instead seeking feedback from both supporters and opponents of it.

tention to developments in Eastern Europe would probably be more interested in an overview of the collapse of communism since 1989 than in a country-by-country analysis. But an audience composed mostly of people with Eastern European origins might be strongly interested in hearing about events in their "old countries." And listeners who are involved in foreign policy issues would probably be most interested in the implications of changes in Eastern Europe. These differences can help you decide which points to put first and last.

Based on the Culture. Finally, the culture will affect your organizational pattern. For example, mainstream American culture is strongly oriented toward pragmatism, and so a pattern that focuses on problems and solutions would resonate well for many listeners. But other cultures and subcultures have a much greater concern for ideology, for myth and ritual, for narrative, or for authority; the preference for these values would affect the pattern of analysis.

Joanna Watkins was about to address an audience with a high proportion of Asian students. She had studied some Roper Poll surveys about dominant values among various cultural groups in the United States and had learned that many Asians value family and group loyalty and mutual support more than such mainstream American values as competitiveness and individual achievement. Because Joanna's topic was about how to get ahead in college, she needed to arrange her speech carefully. In this case, a highly pragmatic cause–effect pattern—which might be just right in other situations—would probably be inappropriate.

Joanna chose to include material about the value of close friendships and the sense of community that often develops among Asian college students. At the same time, she was careful not to stereotype her audience or to assume that "all Asians think alike." She did not say, "Since most of you are Asian, let me talk about group loyalty," and she was careful also to include at least some appeals based on pragmatic values, too.

Clearly, no organizational pattern is automatically "right" for any given speech. You need to think critically about the implications and effects of any pattern and choose an arrangement that suits your strategy. Moreover, although we have considered these basic patterns as though they were mutually exclusive, you obviously can combine them. For instance, you could use a chronological pattern but at each step in the chronology you might examine developments topically or by reference to causes and effects. Or you could organize your speech using both a topical pattern and comparison and contrast. In theory, the potential combinations of patterns are limitless. Particularly when audience members have different cultural backgrounds, value systems, and priorities, a creative combination may be most effective.

WWW. Using the Internet

Assessing Principles of Organization on Web Pages

What principles of organization work best for a Web page? Use the questions outlined below to assess the organizational strategy used in each of the following Web addresses:

The World Wide Web Virtual Library: http://www.vlib.org
State and Local Government on the Net: http://www.statelocalgov.net/index.cfm
Yahoo! News: http://dailynews.yahoo.com/headlines/ts/
The Federal Court Locator: http://www.infoctr.edu/fwl/fedweb.juris.htm
HotWired Magazine: http://hotwired.wired.com/
The Washington Post: http://www.washingtonpost.com
Virtual Tourist: http://www.virtualtourist.com

- To enable a user to navigate from one main idea to another, does the Web page designer use the criteria of simplicity, discreteness, parallel structure, balance, coherence, and completeness?
- Is the Web page effectively organized by using one of the patterns of arrangement used in speechmaking: chronological, spatial, categorical, cause–effect, problem–solution, comparison and contrast, and residues?
- Does the organizational strategy for the page seem to work for the type of content on it and for the audience for whom the page is written?

Selecting and Arranging Supporting Materials

This discussion has focused on the selection and arrangement of main ideas. Most main ideas are sufficiently complex that they involve several supporting ideas or **subheadings**. The supporting material that you located following the guidelines in Chapter 5 will usually support these subheadings, which in turn will support the main ideas. Subheadings are chosen and arranged using the same methods that we have described for main ideas. Moreover, many of the same considerations also apply to the materials you will use to support your main ideas and subpoints. In Chapter 5, you studied research techniques to help you locate supporting materials; now, you should consider which materials to select and how to arrange them.

subheadings
Ideas that are components of or support for the main ideas in the speech.

Selection of Supporting Materials

How Much and What Kind? Probably the most important question, and the hardest to answer, is "How much support is enough?" You need to offer enough evidence to establish your claims but not so much that the speech becomes repetitive and boring. But how do you know what is the right balance?

The only all-purpose answer to this question is, "It depends."[8] It depends, most of all, on your audience analysis. In examining listeners' prior understanding of your topic, you may find that your main idea is one with which they are likely to agree. If so, a relatively modest amount of support will be enough. But if the audience is likely to find your main idea controversial, you will need more support to convince doubters.

For example, a speaker who tells a college audience that the legal drinking age should be lowered to eighteen is probably "preaching to the choir." These listeners have likely already accepted the claim, and so the speaker needs only a few pieces of reliable supporting material. But a speaker who tells the same audience that the legal drinking age should be kept at twenty-one will probably need to supply much more evidence to convince listeners that the disadvantages of change would outweigh the benefits. In contrast, if the audience were composed of older people, the reverse would likely be true: The speaker who wants to raise the drinking age might need less supporting material than the speaker who wants to lower it.

Besides listeners' beliefs about the specific topic, their common knowledge and experience will affect how much supporting material you need. Also, if they are skeptical by nature, you will want to add more support. If they are impatient or are not good listeners, you will want to keep the speech short and the supporting materials simple. If they are accustomed to asking questions after a speech, you will want to anticipate their major questions and to incorporate supporting material that prepares you to answer them.

The general principle to follow is: The greater the distance between the audience's current views and the position you wish listeners to adopt, the more supporting material will be required. Conversely, a position only slightly different from the audience's own may not require extensive support or justification. Audience analysis, of course, is important so that you will know the audience's current position. You also must be careful not to stereotype or to assume that all listeners would identify their position on an issue in the same way.

In any case, supporting material should not be redundant; each piece of evidence should add something new to the speech as a whole. The testimony of three different people who say exactly the same thing is not likely to be higher in value than one person's testimony. Nor will you strengthen the speech by citing the same example from multiple sources.

WWW. Using the Internet

Analyzing the Components of a Speech

Some topics seem to demand only one organizational pattern; however, topics often can be organized based on more than one pattern. Read or listen to a speech from the **History Channel Speech Archives** Web site (**http://www.historychannel.com/speeches/**).

- Identify the thesis and main points of the speech.
- What organizational pattern was used to design the speech?
- How could the main points of the speech be reorganized based on a different pattern?
- Would the speech be as effective using a different pattern of organization?

Regarding the types of supporting materials to use, the general goal is to aim for *variety*. The speech should not depend entirely on statistics, on testimony, on examples, or on primary documents. The reasons are simple. First, you are more likely to hold the audience's interest by varying the types of evidence you offer. Although it is important that the audience be able to anticipate your general pattern, too much repetition induces boredom. Second, different listeners will be persuaded by different kinds of evidence. If your audience is heterogeneous, then using a variety of support helps you to strike a responsive chord among many different listeners.

What Criteria? Having decided how much and what types of support you need, you still face other choices. For example, you may have decided that testimony is the form of support you need and that one quotation from an expert will be enough. But your research may have accumulated the testimony of four or five experts. How do you decide which one to use? Similarly, you may have found multiple examples, various statistical measures, or more primary documents than you might need.

What criteria can you use to assess these supporting materials? Obviously, your choices should not be random. The following guidelines will help you to select supporting materials that will contribute the most to your speech:

1. Apply the criteria for strength of supporting material that were given in Chapter 5. For instance, with regard to testimony you should ask which authority has the greatest expertise on the subject, which statement is most recent (if timeliness is a factor), and so on. With respect to examples, you want to use a case that is representative. And if you are choosing among pieces of statistical evidence, consider the reliability and validity of each.

2. Select the supporting material that is easiest to understand. Remember that you want to direct the audience's thinking toward your main ideas. If listeners have to work hard to understand and remember your supporting material, they will be distracted from the focus of your speech.

This can be a special concern with respect to statistical evidence. Complicated or overly precise statistics may be hard to comprehend orally, and using them may require some minor editing. For example, rather than reporting that the federal budget surplus is projected to be $4,267,153,697,000 over a 10-year period, you might report the projection as "more than $4 trillion." Rather than "significant at the .001 level," you might say, "These are results we would get by chance only 1/1000 of the time."

3. Select vivid or interesting supporting material when you can. Not every piece of evidence will be graphic and easy to remember, of course. But when you have a choice, select supporting material that will interest listeners and will hold their attention. Less interesting material requires the audience to give it greater concentration, which again will distract from your main ideas.

Again, how you present the supporting material can make a difference. Having trouble explaining to audiences why there was suspicion that President George W. Bush had exaggerated Iraq's potential for weapons of mass destruction, a speaker might simply invoke the familiar question, raised first in the early 1970s with respect to Watergate, "What did the President know and when did he know it?"

4. Select supporting material that is consistent with other things you know. It is always possible, of course, that your prior beliefs and the audience's common sense will turn out to be mistaken. But a useful test of supporting material is whether it is consistent with what you already know to be true. If you use material that challenges commonly held beliefs, you should be prepared to defend it and explain why the audience should not reject it out of hand.

5. When you have a choice, select supporting material that will be efficient to present. In general, a short anecdote is better than a long narrative, if they make the same point. And a statistical measure with categories that are clear is more useful than one that needs lengthy explanations.

6. Other things being equal, select supporting material that can be cited easily in the speech. Unlike a written mode, you cannot supply a full bibliographic citation orally. Listeners probably would not remember it, and it would interfere with the progression of your thought. But you do want to give enough information so that a listener knows where you got the material. An "oral footnote" that refers to "Secretary of State Powell in last January's issue of *Foreign Affairs*" is a good example.

Checklist 7.4 Selecting Supporting Materials

1. **Does the supporting material meet tests of strength for its type? (These are given in Chapter 5.)**
2. **Will the supporting material be easily understood?**
3. **Is the supporting material vivid and interesting?**
4. **Is the supporting material consistent with other things you know?**
5. **Will the supporting material be efficient to present?**
6. **Can the supporting material be easily cited in the speech?**

Arrangement of Supporting Materials

Just as the main ideas of a speech can be arranged according to a variety of patterns, so, too, can the supporting materials that establish each main idea. The same considerations—your purpose and your strategy—govern the arrangement of main ideas and of supporting materials.

Suppose, for example, that for a main idea you want to demonstrate that the percentage of deaths from car crashes linked to alcohol use actually has declined over time. Because your objective is to demonstrate a rate and direction of change, a chronological pattern might serve best. It would enable you to "take a snapshot" of how many crash fatalities were linked to alcohol at different points in time. You could show your audience that in 1985,

Year	Percent
1980	41.3
1985	41.2
1990	41.0
1991	39.1
1992	37.4
1993	35.5
1994	33.6
1995	33.2
1996	32.4
1997	30.6
1998	30.5
1999	30.1
2000	31.1

Figure 7.1 Alcohol-related traffic crash fatalities as a percentage of all traffic crash fatalities.

Source: National Institute on Alcohol Abuse and Alcoholism, 2002.

over 40 percent of accident fatalities were linked to alcohol, that it was down to 33 percent by 1994, and that by 2000 it was 31.1 percent (see Figure 7.1). By arranging these "snapshots" in chronological order, you can convey the message of ongoing progress.

For another example, suppose you want to establish that alienation from politics is a nationwide occurrence. You might use a spatial pattern, drawing on examples from the East, the Midwest, the South, and the West. In yet another speech, you might want to emphasize trends in the training and preparation of popular music singers. You could use a topical pattern to focus on each singer you want to discuss or a comparison and contrast pattern that would let you demonstrate important similarities and differences among the singers.

You also can combine the patterns of arrangement in a single speech. In discussing the apathy of American voters, you might use both a chronological and a spatial pattern, as follows:

I. Voter apathy has become a growing concern.

   A. During the years before World War I, voter turnout was high.

   B. In the modern age, the height of voter participation came in 1960.

   C. Since 1960, there has been a slow but steady decline in political participation.

   D. By 1996, voter turnout was at the lowest level since 1924.

   E. Even in the razor-thin election of 2000, turnout rose only slightly.

II. Voter apathy is widespread.

    A. It can be found in the East.

    B. It can be found in the Midwest.

    C. It can be found in the South.

    D. It can be found in the West.

Such a combination, aside from clarifying each main idea in the most appropriate way, also brings variety to the speech—a desirable objective in itself.

Strategies for Speaking to Diverse Audiences

Respecting Diversity Through the Organization of the Body of Your Speech

A sense of form is achieved in different ways for different cultures. Here are strategies to respect the diversity of the audience when organizing the body of the speech.

1. Acknowledge the presuppositions of your audience members and organize your points accordingly.
2. Consider cultural differences in organizational patterns. Do cause–effect structures hold more legitimating power, or do narrative and myth?

Summary

Organizing the body of the speech involves two sets of choices: what to include and what pattern of arrangement to use. Both decisions relate to the main ideas of the speech as well as to materials that support those ideas.

Organization helps both the audience and the speaker. A well-organized speech is more persuasive and more easily remembered—partly because form itself is persuasive, partly because a recognizable form makes content easier to remember, and partly because listeners can anticipate what is coming next. For the speaker, organizational structure is an aid in preparing the speech, in evaluating its main ideas, and, when presenting, helping you remember what comes next.

Main ideas are chosen by reference to the speaker's strategy and purpose and also by reference to the themes that are most frequently identified through research. Main ideas should be relatively few in number, simple in phrasing, parallel in structure, coherent, and complete in their treatment of the topic.

Arranging the main ideas raises such considerations as their dependence on one another, the value of beginning with the familiar, the importance of first and last impressions, and especially the nature of the audience. Speakers should be familiar with seven general patterns of arrangement: chronological, spatial, categorical (topical), cause–effect, problem–solution, comparison and contrast, and residues.

Selection criteria are also invoked with respect to supporting materials for the speech. These criteria begin with audience analysis, which helps to determine how much and, perhaps, which types of supporting material are needed. Supporting material should be easy to understand, interesting, varied in type, representative of the available evidence, easy to present, credible, and consistent with what already is known. The same factors that affect the arrangement of main ideas also affect the arrangement of supporting material. Materials that support different main ideas may be arranged in different patterns.

From this discussion of how to organize the body of the speech, we move next to focus on the introduction, the conclusion, and transitions. Then we will examine the organization of a complete speech.

Discussion Questions

1. In this chapter, we examined Stuart Kim's strategic plan to select and organize main ideas for a speech to convince listeners to donate to the United Way. But what would Stuart's speech be like if he faced a different rhetorical situation? Imagine that he is planning to speak to fellow volunteers at a year-end gathering to celebrate the United Way. Using the list of ideas that Stuart developed in his research, and drawing on your own imagination, discuss the selection and arrangement of appropriate main ideas for such a speech.

2. Which organizational pattern would you recommend for each of the following rhetorical situations? Why?

   To inform an audience of high school students about their college options

   To explain the historical development of baseball to a group of British tourists

   To teach a group of coworkers how to use a new computer program

   To strengthen the commitment of fellow party members to a candidate's campaign

   To persuade a hostile audience that cigarettes should be regulated more strictly

   To introduce an award-winning journalist who is about to give a lecture at a school assembly

3. What is the best organizational strategy for your next speech in this class? Gather in groups of four or five, and discuss your strategic plan with your classmates. Answer the following questions about each group member's strategy:

a. Do the main ideas satisfy the criteria of simplicity, discreteness, parallel structure, balance, coherence, and completeness?
b. Which other organizational patterns might be more suitable for the purpose and audience of this speech?
c. Which type of supporting material is needed to develop each main idea in the speech?

Activities

1. Select the main ideas for your next speech.
   a. Use Checklist 7.1 to generate a list of potential main ideas.
   b. Subject each idea in the list to the tests described in this chapter: Is the idea essential? Can a more general statement combine several main ideas?
2. Arrange the main ideas for your next speech.
   a. Identify the pattern of arrangement that you have chosen.
   b. Write a paragraph or two to justify the pattern that you have selected. In doing so, ask yourself the following questions:

   Are the ideas dependent on or independent of one another?
   Are you beginning with the familiar or with the unfamiliar?
   Are the first and the last ideas strongest?
   Why is this pattern most appropriate for your audience and purpose?
3. Select the supporting material for your next speech.
   a. Apply the general principle described on page 212 to determine how much supporting material you need.
   b. Choose the supporting material that you will use to develop each main idea in the speech.
   c. Using the criteria in Checklist 7.4, write a sentence or two to explain why you have chosen each piece of supporting material.

Notes

1. Experiments show that an audience retains more of a message that is organized than of one that it is not. See Ernest C. Thompson, "An Experimental Investigation of the Relative Effectiveness of Organizational Structure in Oral Communication," *Southern Speech Communication Journal* 26 (Fall 1960): 59–69.
2. Research confirms that organized speeches are comprehended more fully than unorganized speeches. See Arlee Johnson, "A Preliminary Investigation of the Relationship between Message Organization and Listener Comprehension," *Communication Studies* 21 (Summer 1970): 104–107.
3. One study suggests that an unorganized persuasive message may actually produce an effect that is opposite to what the speaker intended. See Raymond G. Smith, "An Experimental Study of the Effects of Speech Organization upon Attitudes of College Students," *Communication Monographs* 18 (November 1951): 292–301. Another study simply concludes that an extremely unorganized speech is not very persuasive. See James C. McCroskey and R. Samuel Mehrley, "The Effects of Disorganization and Nonfluency on Attitude Change and Source Credibility," *Communication Monographs* 36 (March 1969): 13–21.

4. Rhetorical theorist Kenneth Burke envisions form as "the creation of an appetite in the mind of the auditor, and the adequate satisfying of that appetite." See "Psychology and Form," *Counter-Statement,* Berkeley: Univ. of California Press, 1931.

5. One study demonstrated that speakers who have a plan and practice that plan have fewer pauses in their speeches. See John O. Greene, "Speech Preparation and Verbal Fluency," *Human Communication Research* 11 (Fall 1984): 61–84.

6. See Howard Gilkinson, Stanley F. Paulson, and Donald E. Sikkink, "Effects of Order and Authority in an Argumentative Speech," *Quarterly Journal of Speech* 40 (April 1954): 183–192; and Halbert E. Gulley and David K. Berlo, "Effect of Intercellular and Intracellular Speech Structure on Attitude Change and Learning," *Communication Monographs* 23 (November 1956): 288–297.

7. For a few more ideas, see James A. Benson, "Extemporaneous Speaking: Organization Which Inheres," *Argumentation and Advocacy* 14 (Winter 1978): 150–155.

8. Some researchers who have tried to determine experimentally the place of evidence in a speech have concluded that there are just too many variables (such as the prior beliefs of the audience members, the credibility of the speaker, and the different types of evidence) to draw deterministic conclusions. See Kathy Kellermann, "The Concept of Evidence: A Critical Review," *Argumentation and Advocacy* 16 (Winter 1980): 159–172; and Richard B. Gregg, "The Rhetoric of Evidence," *Western Journal of Speech Communication* 31 (Summer 1967): 180–189.

OCCIDENTAL

COLLEGE

Chapter Eight

Organizing the Speech: Introductions, Conclusions, and Transitions

In this chapter, we will:

- Discover why an introduction and a conclusion are needed to complete a speech and give it a satisfying sense of form.

- Examine the main purposes and some common types of introductions and conclusions.

- Offer strategies for preparing an introduction and a conclusion.

- Explore how speakers use transitions to connect the elements of a speech and give its structure a dynamic quality.

- Determine the elements of a transition, which may be either explicit or implicit.

The body of the speech (Chapter 7) is certainly its most important part; it takes up the most time, and it expresses and supports the main ideas. But if a speaker launches directly into the first main idea and ends abruptly after the last, you probably would think something was strange, perhaps even insulting, about the speech. It would be like joining a conversation that was already well along, having missed the beginning completely. The ending would seem abrupt, too—like reading a book that was missing its last few pages or walking out of a movie in its last minutes. You would be surprised that the speaker had stopped, because the speech would not seem "finished."

An audience reacts this way because a speech that is composed only of its body is not really complete. It does not satisfy listeners' expectations about form. Listeners expect a beginning, a middle, and an end. They expect to be guided into a topic, not dropped in its midst, and they expect the discussion to conclude naturally. Audiences notice when a speaker departs from this customary sense of form; if they are not disturbed by it, they at least are likely to be distracted.

In this chapter, we will explore the two elements of a speech that surround its body: the introduction and the conclusion. We will focus on the purposes of these elements, some common types, and strategies for preparing them. Finally, we will look at how speakers use transitions to connect the introduction, body, and conclusion and thus give the speech a dynamic quality.

Introductions: Beginning the Speech

Both daily life and studies in the psychology of persuasion tell us that first impressions are extremely important. When you meet someone new, you quickly form impressions about that person, often based on little more than superficial characteristics such as the person's clothing and hairstyle, or car, or way of speaking. Moreover, many first impressions are likely to prove durable; they will influence how you interpret what this person says and does.[1]

The Purposes of an Introduction

The **introduction** to a speech powerfully affects the audience's first impressions of the speaker. It gives the audience clues about the speaker's personality, intentions, style, and overall perspective. These first impressions shape how the audience will perceive the entire speech.

The introduction also prepares the audience for the speech by giving clues about what will follow. It establishes the context for the speaker's ideas, thus putting listeners in the right frame of mind to attend to those ideas.

The overall purpose of using your introduction to prepare the audience can be broken down into four specific goals:

1. To gain the attention and interest of your audience
2. To influence the audience to view you and your topic favorably
3. To clarify the purpose or thesis of your speech
4. To preview the development of your topic

introduction
The beginning of the speech, which affects listeners' first impressions of the speaker and prepares them for the speech.

Gaining the Attention and Interest of Your Audience. The introduction should make the audience want to hear what will follow. Accomplishing this goal is critical because, like someone switching television channels, listeners can choose whether or not to pay attention. Even when the audience cannot escape a speaker physically, individuals can decide whether or not to be active listeners. They can pay careful attention and follow the speaker's thought process, or they can fidget and daydream until the speech ends—unheard.

The primary way to make listeners pay attention is to convince them that what follows will be interesting. An effective introduction suggests to listeners that they will be stimulated by the speech. The suggestion may be explicit, as when a speaker says, in so many words, "This concerns you." But often, it is the form of the introduction as much as its content that captures the audience's interest. A lively narrative, startling or unexpected information, or a personal experience that listeners can identify with obviously has content; perhaps more important, however, is that such introductory techniques suggest that the speech will be interesting and thus warrants attention.

Influencing the Audience to View You and Your Topic Favorably. It is not enough merely to get the audience's attention. Indeed, a speaker can easily gain attention by turning the audience hostile, but such an introduction would be counterproductive. No one likes to be assailed by a speaker, and few listeners will respond positively to someone they distrust or someone who seems to know little about the topic. How much energy would you invest in following a speaker who is overbearing, pompous, or dogmatic?

Beyond sparking attention, then, the introduction aims to influence the audience to view you and your topic favorably so that listeners will be sympathetic and attentive. This is not to suggest that they will listen uncritically and accept whatever you say, but rather that they will be charitable in interpreting and responding to your speech. You can create a favorable first impression not only by being well prepared and confident but also by offering examples and narratives that fit your listeners' interests and perspectives. As you learned in Chapter 3, the audience analysis will indicate the basic predispositions of your listeners. By identifying with these predispositions in your introduction, you make it more likely that the audience will be favorably disposed toward you and your topic.

Like most generalizations, this one needs to be qualified a bit. Sometimes, a speaker will choose deliberately not to gain the audience's favor. For example, a dissenter who feels the need to speak out against the majority opinion may intentionally make an audience hostile by, say, accusing them of denying rights to those who are less powerful. Even though the immediate audience is unlikely to be persuaded by such a direct attack, the dissenter may, in fact, be addressing those listeners primarily to gain the attention and favor of some other audience. The real intended audience is composed of people who will hear about the speech and conclude that the dissenter is a person of courage and principle for venturing into hostile territory. This audience, of course, will then be favorably disposed toward the

WWW. Using the Internet

Exploring Resources Online for Your Introduction and Conclusion

Go to the **Allyn & Bacon Public Speaking Web Site** page entitled "Writing Your Beginning and Ending" at **http://www.abacon.com/pubspeak/organize/ begend.html/** where you will find ideas and examples for being more creative as you write your introduction and conclusion. There are also links to other resources for finding useful material for an introduction or conclusion.

speaker and the topic; the dissenter will have gained both their attention and their goodwill.

Clarifying the Purpose or Thesis of Your Speech. Listeners are more likely to follow your speech and be influenced by it if you clearly identify what you want them to believe or to do. Most introductions include an explicit statement of the speaker's thesis or purpose, such as "I will argue that the United States cannot compete economically without strengthening public education" or "After you consider the facts, I hope you will call the Red Cross and volunteer to donate blood."

Speakers often state their purpose after making introductory remarks that gain the audience's interest and make listeners favorably disposed. But sometimes, speakers can *assume* that the audience is interested and favorably disposed. For instance, a speaker addressing candidates for office in student government, and who discusses the benefits of student government, surely could assume interest and motivation on the part of the audience. In this case, the entire introduction might focus on an explicit statement of purpose.

Previewing the Development of Your Topic. Besides capturing the audience's attention, influencing them to view you and your topic favorably, and clarifying your purpose, the introduction also previews how you will develop your topic in the body of the speech. Classical theorists of public speaking refer to this step as the **partition;** the speaker divides the body of the speech into selected categories for discussion.[2] For example, a speaker might say, "First I will explain how higher education got into financial trouble, then I will describe the consequences of this for students and faculty, and finally I will tell you what we can do about it." Basically, the speaker has revealed the pattern for the body of the speech (in this case, a problem–solution pattern) and what the major headings will be. As we saw in Chapter 7, such a "road map" helps listeners to follow the speaker's thinking and to anticipate what will come next. If listeners recognize the form of the speech early along and participate in following it, they will be more likely to find the speech effective and to be influenced by it.

An Example of an Introduction

Only your own imagination and creativity limit you in devising an introduction that achieves the four primary goals. Even so, several types of introductions show up frequently in successful speeches, and you should be aware of them to decide whether they will be effective for your speech and audience. Before examining them individually, let's look at how one student used her introduction to prepare the audience.

Michelle Ekanemesang was the third speaker in her public speaking class. To gain her listeners' attention (after all, they had already heard two speeches), she walked to the podium, paused, looked at the audience, and then suddenly dropped a large book on the floor. The resounding thud brought all eyes to Michelle as she began to speak: "Just as easily as that book fell to the floor, the innocence of a child can crash." Then, walking around to the front of the podium to retrieve the book, Michelle continued:

However, unlike this book, a child's innocence cannot be picked up and placed back on the pedestal where it was. Children today encounter many experiences

partition
Division of the body of the speech among selected categories for discussion.

that lower the level of their innocence. Along with gangs, guns, and drugs, they also face another monster that is not so well publicized. This monster is sexual abuse. Approximately one child out of four is sexually abused by the age of 18. This means that perhaps four people in this classroom have been abused. Today, I want to give you some insight into the causes and effects of childhood sexual abuse as well as some tips about preventing it and what to do if you or a child you know has been a victim of sexual abuse.

Michelle's book-dropping trick could have turned into a resounding flop if she had not explained how it connected to her speech. She quickly and effectively gained her listeners' attention and then maintained it by saying that some of them might be victims themselves, thereby emphasizing the personal relevance of her topic. From the outset, it was clear that Michelle was going to talk about the horrors of child abuse. She took a serious tone of outrage and influenced the audience favorably toward her treatment of the subject. Her final statement in the introduction then clearly previewed which main topics the audience could expect her to cover: the causes, effects, prevention, and treatment of childhood sexual abuse.

Types of Introductions

In deciding which of the following types of introductions to use, always try to relate the introduction directly to your speech, as Michelle did. If you quote someone famous or tell a joke without showing how that connects to the speech itself, you risk raising the audience's expectations, which your speech may not fulfill. The speech, after all, should be a unified whole. The introduction and the conclusion should work together with the body of the speech to create the response or action that you desire.

Identifying with Your Audience. One obvious way to build goodwill and capture the audience's interest is to draw on something that you share—a common experience, common acquaintances, common values, or common goals. If listeners perceive you as being basically like themselves, they automatically form a good first impression of you. And their interest should be high because, in effect, you may be telling them something about themselves or be speaking on their behalf.

Student speakers often find it easy and effective to identify with their audience because, typically, they do share many common experiences with their listeners. One student began a speech about the disillusionment felt by many of America's less fortunate youth by making a reference to a popular Hollywood movie:

Based on the box-office numbers, many of you have seen the hit movie *The Matrix*. This high-budget film paints America as one huge computerized box in

When George W. Bush speaks, he often tries to identify with his audience during the introduction. By doing so, he is able to build goodwill and capture the audience's attention.

which we all are trapped, with no real control of our lives and no say in our futures. We are just digits in an artificially intelligent matrix—added, subtracted, multiplied, and divided at the will of a supercomputer. When my friends and I walked out of the theatre, we felt strangely numb and powerless, but the feeling only lasted a few minutes. But for many of America's less fortunate youth, this is the only feeling they know.

Having gained the interest and goodwill of the audience by identifying with them, and having stated the thesis, the speaker was then well positioned to complete the introduction by previewing how the feelings of disempowerment among America's disadvantaged youth would be developed in the speech.

Referring to the Speech Situation. Another way to establish common bonds with an audience and to strike an appropriate opening note is to refer directly to the situation. Many speeches are delivered on ceremonial occasions (for example, commencement addresses, wedding toasts, speeches of welcome or farewell), and these often are introduced effectively by an explicit reference to the occasion.

Similarly, speeches that happen to be given on a significant anniversary might make reference to the date. For example, a student scheduled to speak on September 11, 2003, began this way:

> Two years ago today, our generation and our country lost some of its innocence. None of us will ever forget the image of the plane crashing into the World Trade Center. That action started what the president called a war on terrorism. Two years later, do we feel safer or more secure? Can we deter or stop terrorists? In short, are we winning the war?

The speaker went on to state the thesis and preview its development: "I do not think we are. Our airports are safer, but our transportation system and our industrial base are vulnerable." As this example illustrates, sometimes it is the content of the speech, rather than its ceremonial character, that may dictate a reference to the occasion. The student who is speaking about campus bureaucracies, for example, might preview the development of the topic by tying it to the situation: "Since today is the beginning of registration for next semester, it's high time to do something about the inefficient, ineffective bureaucracy that controls our academic destinies."

Other situational factors also can be the touchstone for an effective introduction. For example, the location of the speech might be important, as it was when Martin Luther King, Jr., began his famous address "I Have a Dream." Dr. King's introduction noted that he stood symbolically in the shadow of Abraham Lincoln; he was delivering his address from the Lincoln Memorial.

Referring to a previous speaker might be a natural introduction to your own speech. If your reference endorses or builds on something a previous speaker said, it creates a bridge between the two speeches and a seemingly logical flow to the discussion. And if the previous speaker was competent and credible, you even may inherit the audience's favorable disposition toward that speaker.

On the other hand, your reference does not have to support the previous speaker. In fact, that speech might provide the ammunition needed for you to disagree with something the speaker said. In this case, your introduction is both a bridge that maintains continuity and a stop sign that signals the differences between the two of you. For example, imagine that a student in a public speaking class just spoke about the underappreciated beauty of snow. By coincidence, the next speaker has planned to extol the joys of summertime. Adapting the introduction to fit this situation, the second speaker could say, "Snow is nice if you're looking at it from afar. But speaking as a Midwesterner who is tired of sloshing through an icy mess on my way to school, I celebrate something far more beautiful: summertime."

Stating Your Purpose. Sometimes, an introduction that explicitly states your purpose can be very helpful, especially if the audience is captive or is known already to be favorably disposed to your ideas. This approach is also effective when your thesis is startling or unexpected: "In the next hour, many children in this town will suffer from abuse and neglect. We will see why this happens. Then I want you to volunteer one day a week to help stop this." Your direct challenge will probably make the audience take notice. You've alerted them that you expect something of them, and so they are likely to pay attention in order to decide whether or not to grant your request.

Stating the Importance of Your Topic. Another effective opening device is to alert the audience to the significance of your topic before actually stating what the topic is. For example, a speech about preventing AIDS might begin with the statement "I have information that literally can save your lives." Similarly, a speech about purchasing a home might begin with "Today, I want to discuss the most important financial decision most of us will ever make."

This type of introduction demands the audience's attention. Just by saying that your topic is important, you ask people to take notice. This strategy also has an element of mystery, which leads the audience to wonder just what it is that is so critical. Be aware, however, that this approach has been overused, and audiences sometimes react to such claims by being skeptical. A speaker who opens with "This speech could change the course of your life" may actually prompt listeners to think, "Oh, sure; I've heard that before." Consider your topic and your audience carefully to ensure that this type of introduction will help you and will not backfire. Remember: One goal of your introduction is to dispose the audience favorably toward your point of view. If listeners react skeptically at the outset, you may never regain their support.

If your speech has a formal title, be sure that its specific wording is accurate and complete. Then your introduction can "unpack" the title to forecast what will follow and to highlight your main points. In 1984, Governor

Mario Cuomo of New York illustrated this introductory strategy in a speech at the University of Notre Dame:

> I would like to begin by drawing your attention to the title of this lecture: "Religious Belief and Public Morality: A Catholic Governor's Perspective." I was not invited to speak on "Church and State" generally. Certainly not "Mondale versus Reagan." The subject assigned is difficult enough. I will try not to do more than I've been asked.

Governor Cuomo then proceeded to state his perspective and to indicate how he planned to develop his ideas.

Citing Statistics, Making Claims. Listeners sit up in interest when a speaker cites startling statistics or makes a surprising claim. Their astonishment on hearing the information causes them to pay attention. For example, to introduce the topic of poverty in the Navajo Nation, a student might begin:

> The Navajo Nation is the largest Indian reservation in the United States. It has a population of 235,000 and covers an area of 16.2 million acres. But the largest Indian reservation in America is not thriving as well as some of the country's smallest towns. According to a 1997 Bureau of Indian Affairs report, the unemployment rate in the Navajo Nation was almost 58 percent. Only 22.5 percent of Navajo homes have any telephone service, and many of the lines are too old to support modern Internet communication.

This type of introduction works best when the statistics are accurate but not well known—when there is a gap between what listeners think they know and what is actually the case. Statistics can show that our common assumptions are not accurate, that a problem is greater than we know, that a condition we viewed as worsening is actually improving, and so on. But the risk with this approach is that listeners may become defensive about their predispositions. Rather than considering the possibility that academic dishonesty really is more serious than they thought, for example, they may react by doubting the statistics or by denying the claim. You certainly want to encourage listeners to think critically; but if their very first response to your introduction is to doubt what you say, it will be difficult to build goodwill and regain their interest. Keep your primary purposes in mind when developing your introduction.

Telling a Story. Speakers often begin with an anecdote—an extended illustration or example that is cast in narrative form. In other words, an anecdote tells a story, which may be true or fictional. A speaker introduces the topic by relating a personal experience or something that happened to others. For example, when Elie Wiesel, Holocaust survivor, novelist, and Nobel Peace Prize winner, gave a speech at the White House in April 2000 on "the perils of indifference," he began by relating the story of a young boy who had been rescued from a Nazi concentration camp by American soldiers:

> Fifty-four years ago to the day, a young Jewish boy from a small town in the Carpathian Mountains woke up, not far from Goethe's beloved Weimar, in a place of eternal infamy called Buchenwald. He was finally free, but there was no joy in his heart. He thought there never would be again.
>
> Liberated a day earlier by American soldiers, he remembers their rage at what they saw. And even if he lives to be a very old man, he will always be grateful to

them for that rage, and also for their compassion. Though he did not understand their language, their eyes told him what he needed to know—that they,
too, would remember and bear witness.

The power of an anecdotal introduction lies in its narrative form. The
story is engaging, and the chronological sequence is easy to follow. A narrative is concrete—it involves specific characters in a particular situation—
and therefore listeners can attend to it with less effort than is needed to
follow something more abstract. A narrative encourages the audience to
sympathize and even identify with its characters. In contrast, opening with
statistics or a quotation removed from its context seems less natural to listeners, and they may wonder what your point is.

One potential drawback in using an introductory anecdote is that it may
overshadow the preview of your topic or even the body of the speech. It may
be so interesting that it distracts attention from your main points. To avoid
this, use an anecdote that leads directly into your thesis statement and partition. Try to create unity between the anecdote and the main points so that
each reminds the audience of the other. If you can achieve unity, the anecdote alone will remind listeners later of what you said.

Using an Analogy. Closely related to the anecdote is an analogy, which, as
you learned in Chapter 6, is a comparison. An analogy draws attention to
the similarities or the differences between two objects, events, or situations.
A speaker can use an analogy to clarify an unfamiliar subject by comparing
the subject with something else that the audience already understands. For
example, a speech describing the pros and cons of school vouchers might
compare public and private schools with retail stores and parents and their
children with consumers. In this way, the unfamiliar issue of school vouchers can be explained in the more familiar terms of shopping.

Like anecdotes, analogies help to make abstract concepts concrete. They
are especially useful in introducing technical material to listeners who are
not specialists in the speaker's field. For example, to inform his audience,
consisting of people unfamiliar with the Internet, about search engines,
student Stan Barkers began with the following analogy:

> When borrowing a book from a public library, the first thing you do is consult
> the online catalog. You do this to find out the shelf where the book is located.
> Then you proceed towards the shelf and get the book. The Internet doesn't have
> a catalog, but a search engine serves the same purpose. Instead of looking up
> an author or title, the search engine identifies key words and looks for them in
> millions of documents that are posted on the Internet. So it probably makes
> sense to think of a search engine like Google as the Internet's card catalog.

This analogy translated what could be an unfamiliar process—using a
search engine to research on the Internet—into a process that the audience
easily could grasp.

During World War II, as we saw in Chapter 3, President Franklin D. Roosevelt was gifted at using analogies to explain the complexities of foreign
policy to average voters. Discussing why, in 1940, the United States should
lend (rather than sell) war materials to Great Britain and its allies, he offered the analogy of a man whose neighbor's house was on fire. When the
neighbor ran up to ask for a garden hose, the man did not first demand payment; instead, he gave the hose to the neighbor on the promise that it would

be returned when the threat was past. In just this way, Roosevelt reasoned, the United States should approach lending supplies to cash-strapped allies. This simple analogy both explained and dramatized the president's perspective, and it helped make his case with the public.

Analogies are persuasive (and thus advance the purposes of an introduction) because most listeners find it easy to focus on similarities and differences. To be effective, though, an analogy should be fairly simple and direct, like Roosevelt's. A complex comparison will force your listeners to puzzle out just what it is that you think is similar about the two things, and they will be distracted from the body of your speech. And if your analogy is too farfetched, listeners' first impressions of you may be negative, and they may not take your main ideas seriously. In both cases the analogy would undercut the purposes of the introduction. An analogy should be fashioned with care. If it doesn't advance your purposes, look for some other way to begin your speech. And if your analogy assumes key similarities without considering significant differences (as several audience members thought was the case with Stan Barkers's, because people use online catalogs to find specific books, not to see all the places that a particular word or phrase is used), listeners' first impressions of you may be negative, and they may not take your main ideas seriously. In both cases, the analogy would undercut the purposes of the introduction. An analogy should be fashioned with care. If it doesn't advance your purposes, look for some other way to begin your speech.

Asking a Rhetorical Question. Do you think you need to know what a rhetorical question is? Like the sentence you just read, a **rhetorical question** is one for which no answer is really expected. Instead, simply asking the question will cause an audience (or a reader) to think about the answer.

When a speaker poses a rhetorical question, the real goal is not to come up with an answer but, rather, to make the audience think. This device may prompt listeners to imagine themselves in some other time, place, or situation. For example, in urging white Americans to be sensitive to the role of race in the lives of African Americans, a student speaker might begin by asking, "How would you feel if, at the time you were born, your earning capacity and life expectancy were automatically reduced for no reason but the color of your skin?" Then, to preview the development of the speech, the student might ask, "Why is it that, 40 years after *Brown v. Board of Education*, educational opportunities still are not equal?" The first question gets the audience to empathize with African Americans, and the second question previews the development of the speech. Because the goal is to make the audience think, the speaker in this case would probably not state the thesis explicitly just yet.

The pitfall in asking rhetorical questions is that speakers have overused or misused this device. Some may ask an introductory question merely to ask it, rather than to induce listeners to imagine a situation or to preview the speech. An even greater risk is that listeners will answer the question in their minds—with an answer that is different from what the speaker wants to discuss. In the worst case of all, someone in the audience may offer a response that undermines the entire introduction. One student began a speech about popular films of the 1960s by asking, "What do you think of when you hear the name 'James Bond'?" From the rear of the classroom another student called out, "A third-rate movie." As beginning lawyers learn

rhetorical question
A question for which no answer is expected but which encourages listeners to think.

(sometimes the hard way), you should never ask a question unless you already know the answer.

Quoting Someone. The introductory device of beginning a speech with a quotation is especially common and useful in sermons; the scriptural quotation then serves as the text on which the sermon is based. In secular settings, too, speakers often open with a quotation that captures the essential idea they intend to develop. Besides gaining the audience's attention, the quotation leads naturally into the development of the speaker's main ideas.

For example, student speaker Andrea Richards introduced a speech on cultural diversity by saying,

> In a famous speech in 1963, President Kennedy said, "If we cannot now end our differences, at least we can help make the world safe for diversity." President Kennedy was talking about ideological diversity, but today we need to apply his insight to the growing issue of racial, ethnic, and cultural diversity.

The quotation does not have to come from a famous person. It might be a simple statement such as this one: "My father once told me that when someone says, 'It's not about the money,' then it's about the money. This is how I feel about all the politicians who keep insisting that they won't use negative campaigning."

Quoting an opposing viewpoint is a variation of this type of introduction. Abraham Lincoln did this superbly in a famous speech he made at Cooper Union in 1860. He began by quoting what his political rival, Stephen A. Douglas, had said about the intentions of the country's founders; then Lincoln used the Douglas quotation to highlight and advance his own thesis and main points.

Beginning a speech with a quotation is such a common introductory device that whole books of short quotations are published for this purpose. The warning about introductory quotations, however, is exactly the same as for anecdotes and analogies: Your introduction must relate directly to what you plan to say in your speech. If the audience cannot see the connection clearly, the introduction will seem superfluous and, therefore, will be counterproductive. A good test is to ask yourself whether the quotation will lead naturally to your thesis statement and partition and then to the body of the speech.

Using Humor. Perhaps the most common introductory device is to begin the speech with a humorous reference or a joke. Humor relaxes the audience, influences listeners to view the speaker favorably, and disarms skeptics. It also tells both the speaker and the audience to keep their perspective about the topic and not to take themselves too seriously.

Despite all these advantages of humor, the worst advice for preparing the introduction to a speech is that "every speech should start with a joke." Humor is not always appropriate to the subject (or the occasion or the audience), and the joke does not always relate directly to the speech. Again, unless the connection is clear to the audience, at best a joke delays the "real" speech, and at worst it detracts from the speech.[3]

In 1964, President Lyndon Johnson used the occasion of commencement at the University of Michigan to proclaim the values of the Great Society. Unfortunately, his opening was more of a warm-up of the audience than an introduction to the speech:

It is a great pleasure to be here today. This university has been coeducational since 1870, but I do not believe it was on the basis of your accomplishments that a Detroit high-school girl said, "In choosing a college, you first have to decide whether you want a coeducational school or an educational school."

The president's good humor continued:

I came out here today very anxious to meet the Michigan student whose father told a friend of mine that his son's education has been a real value. It stopped his mother from bragging about him.

These jokes clearly had nothing to do with the Great Society, as was apparent when the president's tone changed abruptly: "I have come today from the turmoil of your Capital to the tranquility of your campus to speak about the future of your country." That was the real beginning of the speech; the humorous references were not developed further. President Johnson's joke got listeners' attention and may have disposed listeners positively toward him, but it did not achieve the other purposes of an introduction.

This survey of the types of introductions is extensive, but it is not meant to be complete.[4] Anything can be used to begin a speech if it will achieve the four purposes of an introduction: gaining your audience's interest, influencing listeners to think well of you and your topic, clarifying your purpose or central theme, and previewing how you will develop the topic. The great variety and range of introductory devices, however, does not mean that you should select one hastily or without care. The introduction is clearly critical in making an effective speech, and you should prepare it as carefully as you do the body and the conclusion.

Checklist 8.1 Types of Introductions

1. Identifying with the audience
2. Referring to the speech situation
3. Stating the purpose
4. Stating the importance of the topic
5. Citing statistics or making claims
6. Telling a story (anecdote)
7. Using an analogy
8. Asking a rhetorical question
9. Quoting someone
10. Using humor

Strategies for Preparing an Introduction

The multiple purposes of an introduction and the great variety of ways to achieve them may seem daunting, but the following strategies and suggestions should help you plan a successful introduction for your speech.

Prepare the Body of the Speech First. Just as this book explains how to organize the body of the speech (Chapter 7) before focusing in this chapter on introductions and conclusions, you should follow that same sequence in preparing your speech. After all, it helps to know what you are introducing. Having already prepared the body, you now know what your main ideas are and how you will develop them. That information will help you craft an appropriate introduction that prepares the audience effectively. Another good reason to follow this strategy is that you will be less likely to delay preparing the entire speech just because you haven't yet thought of the "perfect" introduction.

Relate the Introduction to the Body. Keep in mind that the introduction has to prepare your listeners and then lead them naturally into the body of your speech. The connection between the introduction and the body should be clear and direct. A particular anecdote, joke, or quotation might well arouse your audience's interest, but if it seems unrelated to your main points, it may not lead listeners in the direction you intend. Indeed, some introductions—no matter how engaging—may undercut your purposes, weakening the entire speech. Although this book examines each element of a speech individually, your goal is to convey a satisfying sense of form to the audience. The introduction is the obvious place to start doing this.

Keep the Introduction Brief. Remember that the focus of the speech is on the main ideas that you will develop in the body; the introduction should lead listeners to these ideas, not obscure them. A too-long, too-strong introduction could turn into the tail that wags the dog, running away with the speech and ultimately confusing your audience.

Some speechwriters advocate that an introduction should take 10 to 20 percent of the total time for the speech. Although we resist such precise measurement, the key point remains: Limit the length of your introduction so that it does not become a speech in itself.[5]

Make the Introduction Complete. As you experiment with potential introductions, assess how each one advances (or hinders) the purposes that an introduction serves. Although exceptions exist, most introductions include the following elements: a device to gain your listeners' interest and to dispose them favorably toward you as a speaker, a statement of your thesis or purpose, and a preview of how you will develop the topic.

Keep a File of Potential Introductions. In developing an introduction, you doubtless will run across ideas, quotations, examples, and other materials that are not immediately useful but that you can imagine shaping into an introduction for a future speech. Keep track of such materials. Do not rely on memory to recall them or find them at just the moment you need them. You might make notes on index cards or sheets of paper, just as you did when researching a speech (Chapter 5), and establish a file of introductory material arranged by topic. Then, when you start preparing your next speech, you will already have resources and will not have to depend entirely on either memory or inspiration.

Be Guided by the Examples in This Book. In this chapter, you have studied the most frequently used types of introductions; Appendix B and other speeches in the book also illustrate a variety of introductions. Consider these examples not as models to be followed blindly, but as guidelines to help you think creatively about the best way to introduce your particular speech. Developing an introduction is a creative process; use the examples to spark your own thinking and imagination.

Plan the Introduction Word for Word. Especially in the opening lines of the speech, you want to be sure that you say exactly what you intend. An extemporaneous opening is risky even for very confident, very experienced speakers, unless they have thought very carefully about the introduction first, because no one can entirely control the speech setting and circumstances. Nor is it wise to carry a written script to the podium, planning to read the introduction aloud. A good first impression is unlikely when your face is buried in notes. Instead, prepare and practice your opening words carefully so that you can begin speaking with confidence and good effect even if your listeners haven't quite settled down. Remember that one of your goals is to capture their attention, and you must be ready to do it with your first words.

Preparing and practicing the introduction word for word will enable you to create the clearest, most compelling first impression on the audience. Moreover, knowing exactly what you are going to say at the beginning of your speech will give you greater confidence and a sense of security. So armed, you can overcome the anxiety that even experienced speakers feel when they stand to address an audience.

Conclusions: Ending the Speech

Just as you want to begin your speech on the right note, so do you want to develop an appropriate, effective ending. A speech should neither end abruptly nor trail off into oblivion. As we did with introductions, we will approach conclusions by focusing on their purposes and their types and then looking at some strategies for preparing them.

The Purposes of a Conclusion

Like your introduction, your **conclusion** needs to accomplish several specific goals:

- Signal that the end is coming
- Summarize the main ideas
- Make a final appeal to the audience

Signaling That the End Is Coming. Perhaps the most basic function of the conclusion is to signal to listeners that the speech is ending. No doubt you have heard a speaker who seemed to be finishing several times before the speech actually ended. Such a speech has "false conclusions"—misleading signals that the end is near. Summary statements, the use of the word *finally*, and similar cues alert the audience that the speech is wrapping up. But if you send such signals prematurely, you will confuse listeners and may even arouse their impatience when the speech does not end as expected.

You probably also have heard a speaker who ended so abruptly that you were surprised. Suddenly, although you thought the speaker was still developing a major idea, he or she came to the end of a sentence, said, "Thank you," and sat down. Somehow, that approach did not seem right either.

In both cases, the speakers failed to provide a satisfying sense of form. Listeners notice when a speaker departs from customary form, and they are bothered by it. If you confuse them with false endings or surprise them by stopping abruptly, your conclusion has not completed the sense of form.

conclusion
The closing of the speech, which draws together what the speaker has said and indicates what the audience should believe or do in response to the speech.

Listeners do need to be signaled that it is time to draw together their perceptions about the speech; but you should send this signal only at the appropriate time.

Summarizing the Main Ideas. A second important purpose of the conclusion is to draw together the main ideas in your speech in a way that helps listeners to remember them. Even trained and experienced listeners rapidly forget what they have heard. If you want the audience to remember what you have said, you need to issue reminders at appropriate points throughout the speech. And no place is more appropriate for a **summary** than the conclusion is.

To end a speech about the messages embodied in popular music, for example, you might summarize by saying, "As we have seen, popular music tells us about our own values, about our relationships with others, and about our obligations to nature, society, and the next generation." As this example shows, a summary does not entirely repeat the main ideas, and it certainly does not reprise their development. Rather, it reminds the audience of key points, often by highlighting particular words or phrases in a way that listeners can remember—as in the parallel structure of the three "about" phrases in this example.

An effective summary, then, is an aid to memory. By including a summary in your conclusion, you will increase the chances that listeners will recall your main ideas correctly.

Making a Final Appeal to the Audience. The conclusion is also an opportunity to say exactly what response you want from the audience. It is your last chance to remind listeners about whatever you want them to think or do as a result of your speech.

Sometimes a speaker wants listeners to take a very specific action, such as signing a petition, donating money, writing to their legislators, or purchasing a particular product. At other times, the desired response is a belief rather than an action. For example, suppose you want the audience to agree that the current president and administration have set a correct course in foreign policy matters. You are not asking listeners to take any specific action, but you do want them to be favorably disposed toward the president's international policies. Your conclusion might say, "I hope I've convinced you that the president's foreign policy is on the right track." Although you are not asking for anything directly, you do want to intensify or to change your listeners' beliefs. Either response may lead to actions later, but that is not your purpose in making this concluding appeal.

Sometimes, the response you seek may be even more general, as in these concluding remarks:

> The next time you consider buying running shoes from one of these companies, consider the people working in the sweatshops who make it possible for you to get an affordable deal.

> You may not agree with me that Lance Armstrong is the world's best athlete, but I hope you will appreciate the dedication and perseverance of professional cyclists.

summary
A condensed restatement of the principal ideas just discussed.

During the conclusion of your speech, you have one last chance to convince listeners to act on your message. Ruth J. Simmons, who was named president of Brown University in 2000, emphasizes her appeal to the audience as she concludes a speech.

> There are strong arguments on both sides of the abortion debate. I ask that you think about what I have said and come to your own conclusion about what you believe.

> You may not decide to hop a plane to the slums of Bangladesh as I did, but maybe you will consider other spring break travel alternatives that will make a difference in the lives of the less fortunate.

None of these concluding statements calls for action, and yet each of them asks listeners to "do" something: to become more aware of something they had not recognized or to think critically about something they had accepted.

Virtually any speech—whether or not it is billed as a "persuasive" speech—asks for some response from the audience. In developing the conclusion of a speech, your goal is to make the audience understand exactly what response you seek.

An Example of a Conclusion

Here's how Michelle Ekanemesang ended her classroom speech about the sexual abuse of children:

> Remember that children are our future generation and should be safe from plagues like sexual abuse. Committed by psychologically damaged men and women of all ages, sexual abuse is a crime that leaves a lasting scar on its childhood victims. Through education and knowledge, we can help these children and prevent them from having to encounter experiences which will affect them forever after. I hope that the information I've shared with you today will be passed on to a younger audience and will help to stop sexual abuse in the future. Remember, prevention is always better than cure!

Michelle's first concluding sentence hinted to the audience that her speech was coming to an end. The next two sentences summarized the points she had made in the body of her speech. Finally, she asked the audience to take action and help stop sexual abuse by passing on the information that children need in order to prevent abuse from occurring.

Types of Conclusions

You already know that the types of introductions are bent toward a purpose and can be developed in various ways to achieve that purpose. The same is true for conclusions. Indeed, some of the following types of conclusions mirror the types of introductions you have studied; others introduce new elements into the speech.

Summarizing. We observed earlier that one purpose of the conclusion is to summarize the main points of the speech. Sometimes, summary is the dominant purpose. In that case, the concluding summary would be more extended than in the preceding examples. It would remind the audience not only about major topics addressed but also about the details of your argument, even repeating some memorable thematic phrases. Such an extensive concluding summary may need a "miniconclusion" of its own, to avoid ending abruptly or trailing off into insignificance.

In contrast, sometimes a succinct, bare-bones restatement of key phrases may make the most rousing finish. Consider the following conclusion from a speech by President George W. Bush outlining his strategy for responding to the terrorist attacks of September 11, 2001:

> Fellow citizens, we'll meet violence with patient justice—assured of the rightness of our cause, and confident of the victories to come.

The first part of the sentence captures the essence of Bush's policy, and the two clauses after the dash (note their parallel structure!) are a brief but powerful reminder of the attitudes the president sought to represent and to evoke. (The text of this speech is in Appendix B.)

Quoting Someone. Just as many speeches begin with a quotation, so many end with one. In both cases, remember to tie the quotation clearly to your speech. A concluding quotation, however, may also go beyond your central ideas and give the audience something to think about; the risk of confusing listeners is much lower at the conclusion, because they have already heard your main points.

Student speaker Kim Davis found a quotation that succinctly summed up her ideas in a speech about gays in the military. Quoting a gay soldier who had been discharged for his sexual preference, she read, " 'They gave me a medal for killing two men, and a discharge for loving one.' " Closing quotations should be like this one—a few neatly balanced, memorable words that sum up your central idea or advance your main purpose.

Making a Personal Reference. Particularly if your speech is about impersonal or abstract issues, it may be appropriate in the conclusion to personalize the issues by making reference to yourself. Such a concluding device (1) illustrates your own identification with the subject—you embody the ideas and values in the speech—and (2) encourages the audience to identify with you. In this way, listeners might imagine that they have the same feelings you have about the topic.

Student Romila Mushtaq used this type of conclusion effectively after arguing that hate speech should not be outlawed on campus. She ended the speech by showing the audience a handwritten racist note that had been taped to her locker door. By revealing that she had been victimized by hate speech and yet would defend someone's right to use such speech, she demonstrated a level of integrity that the audience couldn't help endorsing and trying to emulate. Her personal reference made listeners identify with her—and with the ideas in her speech.

Challenging the Audience. Particularly when your speech asks the audience to do something, concluding with a direct challenge may be effective. This type of conclusion not only creates a common bond between speaker and audience but also transfers to the audience some of the responsibility for achieving the speaker's goals. For example, student speaker Cathy Cummins, after summarizing her main ideas, ended a speech about the breaking of gender stereotypes with this challenge:

> Together, we must evaluate the definitions set up for gender in our society and realize that we are limiting ourselves and future generations by continuing to reproduce gender roles. It's time we stopped limiting ourselves and our children. I for one am going to raise my children with the knowledge that boys can play with dolls and that girls can have chemistry sets. I hope you will do the same.

Offering a Utopian Vision. Closely related to challenging the audience is this type of conclusion, which offers an idealized, positive vision of what can be achieved if only the audience will work together with the speaker. Rather than focusing on the challenge itself, however, this approach emphasizes the results of meeting the challenge successfully. The vision is called "utopian" not to dismiss it but to emphasize that it usually transcends the immediate, practical world.

One of the most famous examples of a conclusion containing a utopian vision is Martin Luther King, Jr.'s "I Have a Dream" address, delivered in 1963 at the March on Washington and found in Appendix B:

> . . . When we allow freedom to ring—when we let it ring from every village and every hamlet, from every state and every city—we will be able to speed up that day when all of God's children, black men and white men, Jews and Gentiles, Protestants and Catholics, will be able to join hands and sing in the words of the old Negro spiritual, "Free at last! Free at last! Thank God Almighty, we are free at last!"

Even speeches about less momentous topics may conclude by envisioning how things will be once a problem is solved or a goal is achieved. Offering a utopian vision is particularly effective when the speaker is calling on the audience to make sacrifices or to take risks to achieve a distant goal. By predicting ultimate success, the utopian vision assures listeners that what the speaker is calling for will be worth the efforts they make.

Abraham Lincoln used this type of conclusion often. After warning of the perilous situation facing the Union in 1861, at the time of his first inaugural address, Lincoln confidently predicted in his conclusion that "the mystic chords of memory, stretching from every battlefield and patriot grave to every living heart and hearthstone all over this broad land, will yet swell the chorus of the Union, when again touched, as surely they will be, by the better angels of our nature." Yes, clouds may darken the sky at the moment, Lincoln was saying, but he promised his listeners that together they could achieve positive results in the fullness of time.

Besides these specific types of conclusions, notice that many of the introductory approaches discussed earlier also can be used for the conclusion, including narratives, anecdotes, and rhetorical questions.[6] In the same way, some types of conclusions can be adapted effectively for use in an introduction. A quotation or a personal reference, for instance, can be as powerful at the beginning of the speech as at the end.

Checklist 8.2 Types of Conclusions

1. **Summarizing**
2. **Quoting someone**
3. **Making a personal reference**
4. **Challenging the audience**
5. **Offering a utopian vision**

(In addition, many of the types of introductions in Checklist 8.1 can also be used as concluding devices.)

Strategies for Preparing a Conclusion

Several of the earlier suggestions for preparing an introduction apply as well to preparing a conclusion:

- Work on the conclusion after developing the body of your speech; again, it helps to know what you are concluding.
- Connect the conclusion clearly to the body of the speech so that listeners will grasp how it relates to your main ideas.
- Keep the conclusion relatively brief so that it does not detract from the speech itself.
- Aim for a complete conclusion, including both a wrap-up of your major ideas and a clear indication of how you want listeners to respond.
- Summarize your argument memorably; then tell the audience what belief or action you seek.

The following additional guidelines and suggestions will help you develop an effective conclusion.

Be Sure That It Truly Is the Conclusion. This first principle is simple to state but no less important for that. As you begin to develop the conclusion, take care to put it at the end of the body, and lead the audience naturally into your summary and final appeal.

Recall once more that listeners get distracted or confused when a speech departs from customary form. On the one hand, avoid any wording that might signal a false (premature) conclusion. You certainly do not want your audience to applaud when, after several false endings, you finally say,

Introductions, Conclusions, and Transitions

Tim Ortiz

Excerpts from my speech on "Deciding to Pursue a Graduate Education"

Introduction

What were the reasons you decided to continue your education beyond high school? Why didn't you decide to find a job instead? Most in this class are undergraduate students who will soon have to choose between furthering our education by attending graduate school or entering the real world and working instead.

Transition from Introduction to Body of Speech

According to recent surveys, Americans with a graduate degree earn an average of 35 to 50 percent more than those with just a bachelor's degree.

Transition Between Main Points

Graduate school is a major investment, and many will question whether an increase in future salary exceeds the financial loss incurred during graduate school.

Transition from Body to Conclusion of Speech

Those with a graduate degree, such as a professional degree, master's, or doctorate, will earn an average income that is 1.75 times higher than those with only a bachelor's degree.

Conclusion

While it may be difficult to consider pursuing an advanced degree when the possibility of receiving high wages and signing bonuses exists with only an under-

graduate education, having finished graduate school will make a major difference in your financial worth long-term. Over the course of a career, a master's degree is worth an estimated $248,000 more than a bachelor's, and a doctorate outpaces a bachelor's by $722,000.

Prof. Blivens

Tim, opening with strong rhetorical questions is a great attention-getting device. But there are a number of things that should be in the introduction. First, where is your thesis statement and preview of main points? Your introduction is the groundwork that the rest of your speech builds from, so pay attention to how you set it up.

One strategy to make your transitions smoother is to make sure your main points logically flow before writing the transitional statements. If the progression makes sense, writing transitions is easier. Instead of using supporting material in the first transition, think about the overall goal of both main points. Then write a sentence linking both of the ideas. This will also help avoid repetition in the transitional statements. Are they distinct enough? Should some of them be combined or switched?

The transition into the conclusion works well, but the information should be grouped. The last statement about how much those with bachelor's and doctoral degrees make needs to be a separate main point. A good transitional statement should take you right into the next paragraph; if it doesn't then that's a key that it needs to be changed. The conclusion, like the introduction, is underdeveloped. Here, it's important to summarize your main points and restate your thesis.

"In conclusion . . ." On the other hand, indicate clearly when you are ready to move from the body of your speech to its conclusion.

Return to Your Introductory Device When Possible. One way to enhance the sense of form and unity in a speech is to conclude by referring again to the device you used in the introduction. If you began with a quotation, you may be able to repeat that same quotation in your conclusion, teasing a different meaning from it now that the audience has heard how you developed your topic. If your introductory device was an anecdote or a rhetorical question, your conclusion might return to that same device and embellish it based on the ideas you developed in your speech.

Of course, this suggestion cannot always be followed. The ideas in the speech may have moved far beyond where they were in the introduction, and returning to the introductory device would seem jarring ("Isn't this where we came in?"). But when you can return to the introduction, listeners will feel that the speech hangs together well, that it has a satisfying sense of form.

Practice the Conclusion. The inspiration of the moment is no more dependable at the end of a speech than at the beginning. Just as you developed your introduction word for word, so should you prepare a conclusion by writing out key phrases and sentences that summarize your ideas and make a strong appeal. In addition, practice the conclusion orally. Your speaking rate is likely to slow down by the end of the speech; you probably will pause briefly between the body and the conclusion; and specific words and phrases will need careful emphasis. Practicing the conclusion out loud a few times before you present the entire speech will help you craft both its content and its ultimate effect.

Transitions: Connecting the Elements of a Speech

Introduction, body, conclusion—these structural elements seem so static that, in planning one of them, you can easily forget how dynamic a speech actually is. From beginning to end, the speech represents movement. You begin with a set of ideas and a strategic objective; by moving through the ideas, you also move toward achieving the objective. Similarly, listeners begin with a certain level of understanding about the subject and a certain disposition toward you as speaker; careful listening and thinking move them through the speech as well.

This dynamic movement of both speaker and listeners is achieved by—and depends on—connections that the speaker provides to bridge any gaps between elements. **Transitions** connect the introduction to the body, connect each main idea within the body, and connect the body to the conclusion. Ultimately, transitions create the sense of form that makes a speech successful.

The Purposes of Transitions

The most important purpose of transitions is to create this sense of movement and form; transitions make the speech dynamic and satisfying. Along the way, they also help listeners follow the speaker's movement throughout the development of the speech, and they help listeners remember what the speaker said. Equally important, transitions keep the speaker from lapsing into nervous mannerisms that would accentuate the gaps between ideas, eroding the connections that give a speech movement and form.[7]

transition

A connection, or bridge, between the main elements of the speech and between the main ideas within the body of the speech.

Even accomplished speakers sometimes neglect to think about transitions. They may organize the body of the speech carefully, labor to devise an effective introduction, and craft a compelling conclusion; yet they assume that transitions will spring up spontaneously. Facing the audience, however, their spontaneous connections may be as pedestrian as "My next point is . . ." or "Next, let me discuss . . ." The movement is halting; the sense of form is unclear.

Even worse is a speaker who bridges gaps and moves forward on the basis of sheer nervous energy and repetition. You probably have heard a speaker who punctuated every pause with "Ahh . . ." or who completed every thought with "Okay" or "Right?" or who moved to each new point with "Now, then. . . ." Such mannerisms can become so obvious and distracting that the audience starts counting them rather than listening to the speech.

From your experience as a listener, then, you know that an effective speaker understands the nature of transitions and includes them consciously to create movement and form. The rest of the chapter focuses on how to provide such connections in your speeches.

Elements of Effective Transitions

We cannot list and describe "types" of transitions, as we could with introductions and conclusions. Although the following three elements—internal previews, internal summaries, and links—may seem to be separate types of transitions and can sometimes be found in isolation, they are really three elements that together make up a complete transition.

Internal Previews. A preview is a compressed version of what the speaker is about to develop; it prompts the audience to anticipate what is coming, in terms of both content and form. As you saw earlier, the introduction will probably preview your main points. Beyond the introduction, however, consider whether an **internal preview** will help prepare your audience to follow along every time you move from one main idea to another. Here are some examples of how to do that:

1. If the preview in your introduction suggested that there are three main reasons to abandon the quarter system at your college, an internal preview might point out, "One of the most important reasons is that in a semester system students will have a longer time to learn what is offered in each course."
2. In a speech arguing that both students and faculty would benefit if the school offered more sections of closed courses, an internal preview between the first and second main points might tell the audience, "The second reason to have more sections is that the faculty will be able to give each student more attention."
3. In a speech about the current campaign finance laws, the body of the speech might start with an internal preview of the first major argument: "Some argue that campaign finance laws no longer pose a serious problem. I don't agree, and let me tell you why."
4. In a speech about multiculturalism, an internal preview might signal that you are going to tell a story about how cultural diversity became a concern on campus.

internal preview
A preview within the body of the speech, leading into one of the main ideas.

Whether obviously or subtly, each of these internal previews tells the audience what to expect—each is a kind of early alert system for the audience. An internal preview signals that listeners should get ready to move on to some new aspect of the speech, and it provides clues about the nature of the movement or about the new aspect itself.

Internal Summaries. Just as previews are not confined to the introduction, summaries can appear both in the conclusion and at certain points within the body of the speech. Like a concluding summary, an **internal summary** draws together the central points that were just discussed, serving both to aid memory and to signal closure to those points. An internal summary does not wrap up the entire speech; it reviews only a portion of it. The following simple examples are internal summaries for the internal previews you just looked at:

1. So, as we've seen, abandoning the quarter system would permit students to take classes that last longer, allowing them to learn more about a particular subject and reducing the pressures they face.

2. I hope I've made it clear that one benefit of additional sections of closed courses is more individualized attention. The faculty will be able to answer more questions in class and students will get prompt feedback.

3. So the current campaign finance laws really do pose a serious problem, because they encourage influence peddling, because they encourage legislators to forego their legislative work to engage in time-consuming fundraising, and because they lessen public confidence in government's ability to represent the interests of ordinary working people.

4. As I see it, then, our commitment to cultural diversity came about through this and other key incidents that embarrassed us by showing the limitations of our perspective.

Each of these internal summaries wraps up one main idea of the speech. It gives the audience a brief reminder of the idea and also signals the point of completion.

Whether previewing or summarizing the entire speech or just a part, you can use repetition and restatement to alert the audience that you are beginning or ending one of your key points. For example, the first internal preview described above might be elaborated as follows:

WWW. Using the Internet

Analyzing Overall Organizational Structure

After finding one of the sites below, analyze whether the speech creates a sense of dynamic movement from start to finish. Particularly, consider how the speaker began with a set of ideas and a strategic objective. Did the speaker/writer successfully make the types of connections that move the audience from the introduction to the body and on to the conclusion?

- Martin Luther King, Jr., "Letter from Birmingham Jail," first published in *Atlantic Monthly* in August 1963, now online at **Atlantic Unbound,** the digital version of the magazine, at **http://www.theatlantic.com/unbound/flashbks/black/blahisin.htm/.**
- Abraham Lincoln, "First Inaugural Address," presented in 1861, online at **http://www.bartleby.com/124/pres31.html.** Inaugural addresses by other American presidents can also be found at **http://www.bartleby.com/124/.** This site from Columbia University is the Bartleby collection of inaugurals.
- Remarks by Elie Wiesel at the White House can be found at **http://www.nando.net/Kosovo/story/general/0,2773,37981-61198-444354-0-nandotimes,00.html.**
- Carol Bellamy of the United Nations Children's Fund speaks about children in Africa orphaned by AIDS. **http://www.unicef.org/exspeeches/01esp40.htm**

internal summary
A summary within the body of the speech, drawing together one of the main ideas.

One of the reasons that we should abandon the quarter system is that students will have longer to learn what is offered in each course: more time to learn means less rush. Let me explain why this is so.

Similarly, the second internal summary above might be drawn out in this way:

I hope I've made it clear that one benefit of additional sections of closed courses is more individualized attention. The faculty will be able to answer more questions in class, and students will get prompt feedback. Opening up more sections of closed courses will truly help our teachers to interact more with us and that, in turn, will benefit us.

Links. All these examples illustrate that transitions contain links from one idea to the next. Some links are subtle and are established through careful word choice; others are explicit.

The construction *not only . . . but also* is an example of a subtle link. It moves from the point that was just discussed to the one that is coming up next, as in "Not only are closed classes bad for the students but also they're bad for the faculty." The speaker thus links two ideas that previously were separate in the speech.

Conjunctions such as *in addition, furthermore,* and *moreover* have the same effect. They suggest the cumulation of ideas, linking the ideas by hinting that the one to come will build on the one just considered. In contrast, conjunctions such as *however, nonetheless,* and *on the other hand* signal that the speaker is going to move from one point of view to an opposing viewpoint or in some way will qualify or limit the force of what was just said.

Sometimes links are more explicit. The speaker who finishes one idea with an internal summary and then says, "But here's the proverbial fly in the ointment," is announcing that the point just made is about to be rendered troublesome or problematic or that something calls it into question. And the speaker who says, "It's not enough to focus on the cost of higher education; we also have to be concerned with quality," is telling the audience that they need to consider one more important factor.

How subtle or explicit should a particular link be? That depends on several factors. If the connection seems obvious and listeners can be expected to see it without help, an explicit link may be insulting. But if the connection between points is complex or seems to contradict common sense, an explicit link may be appreciated. Audiences can follow narrative and chronological links more easily than they can follow analytical links. Similarly, links based on "common knowledge" and general understanding do not have to be as explicit as links that require specialized knowledge or training.

Complete Transitions. As we have suggested, not every element of every transition need be made apparent. But a complete transition would include an internal summary of the point being concluded, a link to connect it to the next point, and an internal preview leading into the new point. For example, a complete transition in the speech about abandoning the quarter system might go like this:

So there's no doubt that students will benefit from the change. Abandoning the quarter system will give them more time to write papers and study for final

Colin Powell uses gestures to reinforce the verbal signposts that mark the transitions in his speeches.

exams and will reduce their level of pressure and stress. [Internal summary] But students aren't the only ones who will gain from this change. [Link] The faculty will gain two benefits as well. Let me tell you about them. [Internal preview]

If you think that such a complete transition somehow seems stilted or unnatural, think again after imagining how a speech would be hurt by an awkward transition such as this one:

Uh, okay. Enough about that. Time to move on. What comes next? Uh, okay. Oh yes, let me discuss . . .

This speaker completely sacrificed a sense of smooth progression of ideas, one of the most important contributions that transitions make to the speech.

Strategies for Preparing Transitions

Besides deciding how explicit to make each transition and whether to use repetition to emphasize the transition, consider the following brief suggestions.

Identify Main Ideas Succinctly. In internal previews and internal summaries, quickly and clearly identify the main idea being referred to; that will make it easier to remember. Rather than restating an idea completely, use a memorable word or phrase to highlight it in the transition.

Use Parallel Structure If Possible. When related ideas are identified in a similar or parallel fashion, that repeated pattern may make the link more memorable. Whenever possible, internal previews and internal summaries should use one of the organizational patterns described in Chapter 7.

Use Signposting. **Signposting** alerts the audience to where you are in the speech. If you say that you will discuss three advantages of something, in previewing each advantage it will be helpful to identify it as "first," "second," or "third." Listeners will have no doubt that you have completed the discussion of one advantage and are about to talk about the next; and they also will clearly perceive the structure that you intended. Similarly, you can use pauses, repetition, and changes in speaking rate, pitch, or volume as signposting to guide the audience.

> **Checklist 8.3** Transitions: Critical Thinking and Strategic Planning
>
> 1. **Questions to ask yourself: At this point in my speech:**
>   - Do my listeners need a reminder or an alert about how far I've come?
>   - Do my listeners need a reminder of how my last point relates to my next?
>   - Do I need some verbal markers to help me and my listeners follow my outline?
>   - Will my listeners follow my ideas better if I give them a brief preview?
> 2. **If the answer is "Yes," here are some things worth doing:**
>   - Construct brief phrases that identify main ideas in the speech, and use them as markers and reminders at key intervals.
>   - Set up your points in parallel structure whenever possible. Check your outline to help you do this.
>   - Include verbal signposts that briefly show where you are and what comes next.

signposting
Using verbal cues to indicate to an audience where you are in the structure of the speech.

Strategies for Speaking to Diverse Audiences

Respecting Diversity Through Introductions, Conclusions, and Transitions

Introductions and conclusions are important places to recognize and adapt to the diversity of the audience. Here are some strategies that will enable you to do so.

1. Build good will with your audience by identifying with them early in your speech.
2. Humor that demeans individuals or cultural groups may get attention, but it will alienate your audience.
3. Appeal to your audience members' "better selves."

This chapter has offered a catalog of the purposes, types, and guidelines for preparing introductions, conclusions, and transitions. The introduction shapes the audience's first impressions. Its purposes are to gain attention and interest, to influence the audience to view the speaker and topic favorably, to state the thesis or purpose of the speech, and to preview how the topic will be developed. The types of introductions we examined are identifying with the audience, referring to the speech situation, stating the purpose of the speech, stating the importance of the topic, citing statistics and making claims, telling a story (anecdote), using an analogy, asking a rhetorical question, quoting someone, and using humor. The introduction should be prepared after the body of the speech is well in hand; it should be related to the body, should be brief but complete, and should be worded (and practiced) carefully.

The conclusion completes the speech and gives it a sense of form by signaling to the audience that the end is near. It summarizes the main ideas and may make a final appeal to listeners, asking them for a particular belief or action. Among the types of conclusions are summarizing, quoting someone, making a personal reference, challenging the audience, and offering a utopian vision. Guidelines for preparing the conclusion are similar to those for the introduction. When possible, the conclusion should return in some way to the introductory device; this enhances the unity of the speech.

Transitions give a sense of movement or progression to the speech by guiding listeners clearly from one point to another as the speaker develops the topic. Transitions help the audience remember the main points and the structure of the speech; they also reduce a speaker's distracting nervous mannerisms in trying to move from one idea to the next. A complete transition has three elements—internal preview, internal summary, and link—but not all elements are presented explicitly in every transition. Transitions should be succinct, should use parallel structure if possible, and should provide signposting to guide the audience.

1. a. Which type of introduction would be most effective in each of the following speech situations?

   - A speech introducing the recipient of a lifetime achievement award
   - An informative speech to classmates about how to improve study skills
   - A speech to warn boaters about the dangers of "mixing water and alcohol"
   - A speech to strengthen volunteers' commitment to helping the homeless
   - A speech to reverse opposition to the death penalty

b. In those same speech situations, which type of introduction would be least appropriate? Why?

2. What does an introduction need in order to prepare the audience effectively for the speech? Meet in small groups to answer this question. Each group member will present the introduction to a speech, and the other group members then will guess the speaker's purpose, the rhetorical situation, and the content of the speech. After everyone has made a guess, the speaker will reveal the actual purpose, situation, and content so that the group can compare intent and effect and then discuss ways to improve that introduction.

3. Which factors should a speaker consider when deciding how complete to make a particular transition? Discuss how the following constraints and opportunities might or might not influence your decision:

- Your main points are organized in a dependent pattern.
- Your main points are organized in an independent pattern.
- You are moving between main ideas in the speech.
- You are moving between subpoints within a main idea.
- You are giving a speech that teaches a difficult concept to a group of students.
- You are giving a speech to a group of protesters that enumerates well-known reasons to reinforce their commitment to the movement.

Activities

1. Attend a speech in your community or read a speech manuscript that you have retrieved from the library or the Internet.
   a. Identify the strategies used in the introduction and in the conclusion.
   b. Closely examine at least one complete transition in this speech, identifying the internal summary, link, and internal preview.
   c. Evaluate the introduction, conclusion, and transitions of this speech. Are they effective? If so, what makes them effective? If not, how could they be improved?
2. Create three potential introductions and conclusions for your next speech. Choose the best one of each, and explain why you think it is best.
3. Follow the instructions in Checklist 8.3 to plan strategically transitions for your next speech.

Notes

1. See Norman H. Anderson and Alfred A. Barrios, "Primacy Effects in Personality Impression Formation," *Journal of Abnormal and Social Psychology* 63 (September 1961): 346–350.
2. Classical theorists often used words such as this, from the language of architecture, to describe the organization of speeches. See Leland M. Griffin, "The Edifice Metaphor in Rhetorical Theory," *Communication Monographs* 27 (November 1960): 279–292.

3. For more on the effects of humor in speeches, see C. R. Gruner, "Advice to the Beginning Speaker on Using Humor—What the Research Tells Us," *Communication Education* 34 (April 1985): 142–147.

4. For another list of introduction types, see Richard Whately, *Elements of Rhetoric*, Carbondale: Southern Illinois Univ. Press, 1963, originally published 1828, pp. 170–172.

5. One early study found that, on average, introductions made up 9 percent of the total speech and conclusions made up 4 percent. See Edd Miller, "Speech Introductions and Conclusions," *Quarterly Journal of Speech* 32 (April 1946): 181–183.

6. For a discussion on the use of metaphor in conclusions, see John Waite Bowers and Michael M. Osborn, "Attitudinal Effects of Selected Types of Concluding Metaphors in Persuasive Speeches," *Communication Monographs* 33 (June 1966): 148–155.

7. Research shows that transitions make it easier for listeners to comprehend a speech. See Ernest Thompson, "Some Effects of Message Structure on Listeners' Comprehension," *Communication Monographs* 34 (March 1967): 51–57.

Chapter Nine

Outlining the Speech

In this chapter, we will:

- Explore why outlining is a valuable part of speech preparation and presentation.

- Learn how to create a preparation outline that uses proper principles of subordination and coordination.

- Determine how to adapt the preparation outline into a presentation outline that you can use in delivering your speech.

A speech **outline** is simply a display of the organizational pattern of the speech. It serves several purposes:

- The outline helps you clarify and choose the best organizational strategy for your speech.
- The outline helps you check your organizational pattern to see that it is sensible and consistent. It lets you determine easily whether the main ideas support your thesis statement, whether your reasoning is strong, whether the supporting materials are linked to your claims, and whether the overall design of the speech advances your purpose.
- The outline is a written memory aid that helps you become familiar with the claims you want to make and the order in which you plan to make them.

Speakers depend on outlines at two stages: when they put the speech together and when they deliver it. Each stage requires a different kind of outline. The **preparation outline** is used in composing the speech and is developed in enough detail to show how each idea and piece of evidence fits into the overall structure. The **presentation outline,** or speaking outline, is simpler and briefer and is used as a memory aid while you deliver the speech. Although the character and use of these outlines are different, the preparation outline should lead naturally into the presentation outline.

The Preparation Outline

In making your preparation outline, you pull together many of the subjects you studied in previous chapters. You decide on your purpose and thesis statement; you identify the issues and supporting material; and you organize the introduction, body, and conclusion. As you develop your ideas, you plan a strategy for your speech, thinking about what to put where and why. You map out this plan by testing your thesis against the material that supports it. You think critically, inspecting the outline to ask which sections of the speech are complete and which need further development. Outlining a speech is like exercising; it is a "rhetorical workout" that helps you get in shape.

The preparation outline is relatively formal. If your instructor has asked for an outline of your speech, it is the preparation outline that you should submit. Usually, you should write it in complete sentences so that anyone reading the outline can make reasonable guesses about what your speech includes. Student speakers sometimes think of the preparation outline as drudgery. "After all," they might say, "I took this course to learn how to speak, not how to write outlines." And it is true that some very accomplished speakers can do without a fully developed outline. But for beginning speakers, the preparation outline is extremely important and you should approach it with care. It enables you to clarify your own thinking, to be sure that the structure of your speech is clear, and to rehearse on paper the main ideas you will develop and the relationships among them.

What Does a Good Outline Look Like?

An outline indicates the hierarchy of importance of ideas within a speech. Typically, the main ideas are signaled by Roman numerals, and each succes-

outline
A display of the organizational pattern of the speech.

preparation outline
A detailed outline, usually written in complete sentences, used to develop a clear organizational structure during preparation of the speech.

presentation (speaking) outline
A brief outline, usually containing only key words, used as a memory aid during delivery.

sive level of less important ideas is designated first by capital letters, then by Arabic numerals, and finally by lowercase letters.[1] In short, you proceed from the most important ideas to the least important, indenting each level appropriately. The overall structure of your outline would look something like this:

I. Main idea
   A. Supporting idea (subheading)
   B. Supporting idea (subheading)
      1. Supporting material (evidence)
      2. Supporting material (evidence)
   C. Supporting idea (subheading)
      1. Supporting material (evidence)
         a. Backing for the supporting material
         b. Backing for the supporting material
      2. Supporting material (evidence)
   D. Supporting idea (subheading)

II. Main idea

An outline may extend to additional detail, of course, with deeper indentations for each level of organization. But if the structure of a speech is that complex, the audience probably will not be able to follow it carefully. If your preparation outline needs more than four levels of importance, your thesis is probably too broad and unfocused.

A variation of this common outline pattern is the *decimal outline*, in which numbers and decimal points signal the levels of importance. The main ideas are designated with whole numbers; the next level of importance uses numbers with one decimal place (such as 1.1 and 1.2), then numbers with two decimal places (1.1.1, 1.1.2, 1.2.1), and so on. Again, the levels of the outline are indented to show the relationships among the ideas, like this:

1. Main idea
   1.1 Supporting idea (subheading)
   1.2 Supporting idea (subheading)
      1.2.1 Supporting material (evidence)
      1.2.2 Supporting material (evidence)
   1.3 Supporting idea (subheading)

Constructing the Preparation Outline

Whether you use Roman numerals or decimals, the following principles will help you construct your preparation outline.

Statement of Topic, General Purpose, Specific Purpose, and Thesis. These elements, discussed in Chapter 4, should be displayed above the outline. By keeping them in view as you develop the outline, you can check the emerging plan against the goals it is designed to achieve. For a speech about the quality of Campus Food Service, you might precede the outline with the following:

WWW. Using the Internet

What Does a Good Preparation Outline Look Like?

Use guidelines for creating a preparation outline by doing an outline of a historic speech from **The Douglass Archive of American Public Address.** Point your browser to **http://douglassarchives.org** and select one of the speeches from the archive.

Use the format for a preparation outline that includes:

- Statements of the topic, general purpose, specific purpose, and thesis.
- An outline of the key elements of the introduction.
- An outline of the organizational pattern of the body of the speech, in complete sentences. Be sure to identify subpoints in a way that subordinates them to the main ideas.
- An outline of the conclusion.

Outlining

Prof. Blivens

The strengths of this outline are obvious. The formatting over-all works well, and you have a clear and concise thesis state-ment, general pur-pose, and specific purpose. Very well done. The use of humor was effective in the attention getter.

However, the preview ignores the first main point. It does work for the subsequent main points, but in the first main point you say you're in-forming us of the history of the drug. On the contrary, I think you're telling us the origin of the drug and not the history. Essentially, the his-tory of the drug would describe the year it was first used in this manner, for example. You are explaining where the drug comes from and how it's not harmful.

Logically, in main point II, sub-points A and B should be switched. It's easier for audiences if you first explain what it's used for and then how it works. Point C should be a main point, because basically, your speech is dealing with the pros and cons of using the drug. Point III should be a subpoint under the new main point. This will now group all of the advantages and disadvan-tages together. See? Next, there needs to be another subunit under main point IV. Subpoint B should be after number two. Subpoint A ad-dresses muscles and three and four

Priya Mydur

Priya's Preparation Outline for her Speech on "The Benefits of Botox"

TOPIC: Botox

GENERAL PURPOSE: To provide new information

SPECIFIC PURPOSE: To present audience with the many uses of the drug, Botox

THESIS: Little do people know that Botox relieves numerous muscle prob-lems, making life easier for those with a limited range of movement.

Introduction

I. *Attention-getting device:* If a salesman told you that a single drug could cure headaches, obesity, sore muscles, and even body odor for the extremely low price of $300, would you believe him?

II. *Thesis:* Botox has many uses, even serious medical ones.

III. *Preview:* Most people are just learning what Botox is, but if you've never heard of it, you'll want to know more. Botox is most famous for its ability to reduce the appearance of wrinkles, but little do people know that it also relieves numerous muscle problems, making life easier for those with a limited range of movement.

Body

I. Botox has a history that most people do not understand, thus giving the drug an unwarranted bad name.
   A. Botox is derived from the poison botulinum toxin, which causes botulism.
      1. Botulism is a disease that can sometimes be fatal, but usually causes paralysis because of the *Clostridium botulinum* bacterium.
   B. Botox, however, does not harm the body.
      1. Botox is a diluted form of the toxin.
      2. However, it still has some of the same effects.

II. Botox gained fame for its beneficial effects in diminishing wrinkles.
   A. The region where Botox is injected paralyzes the muscle so that it cannot wrinkle.
   B. Botox is commonly used to treat three types of facial wrinkles.

1. Laugh lines
2. "Crow's feet"
3. Wrinkles between the eyebrows
C. There are several things to consider when deciding to have a Botox treatment.
   1. The procedure is quick.
   2. The benefits and ease of the procedure justify the cost.
   3. It only lasts five months.
III. There are few risks involved in Botox treatments.
A. No anesthesia is necessary.
   1. However, only an authorized doctor should perform the procedure.
B. The recovery time is quick.
   1. A few injections are made to the region, but the needle is relatively small.
IV. Botox is no longer only used for cosmetic purposes.
A. Doctors now use Botox to treat muscle disorders or abnormalities.
   1. Botox treatment works best with early detection of muscle disorders.
   2. Dr. Christina Alvarez performed procedures with Botox on babies with clubfoot by injecting the foot and straightening the muscles.
   3. Obese people who have Botox injections have shown a decrease in food intake because Botox makes the stomach feel full longer.
   4. Botox has also been shown to help sufferers of migraines and muscle spasms.

Conclusion

I. *Summary:* Botox can help people suffering from a wide range of muscle problems by relaxing or calming muscles.
II. *Closure:* People may give up searching for the fountain of youth and simply go out on their lunch breaks and get Botox injections instead.

deal with other ailments. That's why I would put another subpoint in between these.

The summary is there, but it could be clearer. Also, I would push harder for audience adaptation. Most of your classmates are young college students who don't need Botox for cosmetic reasons. Keep developing other advantages, like you did in main point four, to address some needs of your audience.

TOPIC: Campus Food Service

GENERAL PURPOSE: Conversion

SPECIFIC PURPOSE: To convince listeners that the often-criticized Campus Food Service is really quite good

THESIS: Campus Food Service is vastly underrated.

Complete Sentences. One function of the preparation outline is to test the clarity and precision of your claims. Sometimes you may have a general idea of what you want to say but are unsure of the exact idea you want to express. By writing the outline in complete sentences, rather than just highlighting general topics, you will force yourself to specify exactly what claims you want to make. This will make you less likely to "talk around the subject" when you deliver the speech.

For example, if your outline simply says "Voting bad," you would have little idea what you really want to say—other than that there is something negative about voting patterns. In contrast, the complete sentence "Voting in presidential elections has declined over time" is much more precise and focuses your attention on your essential message.

Subordination. A primary purpose of the preparation outline is to map out the relationships between claims and supporting materials. The outline should clearly show **subordination;** supporting materials for a given idea should be outlined as indented under that idea. If you designate the main idea with Roman numerals, for example, then you should identify its supporting ideas (subheadings) with capital letters. It is easy to mistake subheadings for main ideas or for supporting material when your outline does not show their subordinate structure.

Look again at this fragment of an outline from Chapter 7:

I. Voter apathy has become a growing concern.

    A. During the years before World War I, voter turnout was high.

    B. In the modern age, the height of voter participation came in 1960.

    C. Since 1960, there has been a slow but steady decline in political participation.

    D. By 1996, voter turnout was at the lowest level since 1924.

    E. Even in the razor-thin election of 2000, turnout rose only slightly.

II. Voter apathy is widespread.

    A. It can be found in the East.

    B. It can be found in the Midwest.

    C. It can be found in the South.

    D. It can be found in the West.

subordination

Designating the supporting materials for a main idea with the subordinate symbol and indentation system in an outline—for example, supporting materials, indicated by capital letters, indented under their main idea, indicated by Roman numerals.

Details about the voting in different eras would be subordinate to a claim that voter apathy has increased over time. Likewise, information about voting rates in different regions of the country would be subordinate to a main idea about the geographic spread of the problem. Each subheading supports the idea under which it is indented. The distinction between main and supporting ideas helps to make the subordinate structure clear and easy for an audience to follow.

Coordination. Closely related to the principle of subordination is that of **coordination:** Ideas with the same level of importance should be designated with the same symbol series—all with Roman numerals, or all with capital letters, and so on. Items so designated are parallel, or coordinate, statements.

The preceding outline appropriately identifies the two statements "Voter apathy has become a growing concern" and "Voter apathy is widespread" as main headings. These are equally important ideas, and they are both parts of an overall topical organization that coordinates two aspects of the topic: chronology and geography. It would be a mistake to label as main headings "Voter apathy has become a growing concern" and "It can be found in the South." These statements are not united by a topical plan and might even be said to conflict, because the first statement implies a national problem and the second focuses on a single region. In the same way, it would be a mistake to label "Voter apathy has become a growing concern" as a main idea and "Voter apathy is widespread" as a supporting point, because the second point is on equal footing with the first, not subordinate to it.

It is easy to see in the abstract that these patterns are in error. But it is also easy to make these types of errors when you are not consciously thinking about outlining and organizational schemes—especially if, say, you happen to find compelling supporting material about voting rates in the South. As you compose your preparation outline, ask whether the ideas that you have designated with the same symbol series are really *coordinate*—whether they are of the same importance and (often) parallel in structure.[2]

Checklist 9.1 provides an opportunity to practice the principles of coordination and subordination.

Checklist 9.1 Subordination and Coordination

Arrange the following statements into an outline that illustrates subordinate and coordinate relationships:

- Food service responds to students' complaints.
- Variety is not a valid complaint.
- Taste is not a valid complaint.
- Food service offers three main entrees and a vegetarian meal.
- Being ignored is not a valid complaint.
- A special dinner is offered once each month.
- All food on the line is taste-tested.

Outlining Introductions and Conclusions

Including the introduction and conclusion of your speech in the preparation outline is fairly straightforward. They are developed as separate sections of the outline, and the primary numerical divisions identify the

coordination
Designating all ideas that are on the same level of importance with the same symbol series and level of indentation in an outline.

elements of the introduction and conclusion. For the introduction, these elements typically are:

I. Attention-getting device.

II. Statement of thesis or purpose.

III. Preview of the speech.

And for the conclusion, the key elements usually are:

I. Summary of main ideas.

II. Action desired from audience.

III. Closure device.

Here is how you might outline the introduction and conclusion of the speech about Campus Food Service:

Introduction

I. **Attention-getting device:** *[Take on persona of student going through food service line.]* "Oh great! Another meal at Campus Food Service. Let's see . . . what do I want? What is that? Uh . . . no mystery meat tonight, thanks. What? Chicken again. There's some pasta. Ugh, it looks like three noodles and a gallon of water. That's it. I'm ordering in tonight."

II. **Thesis:** Campus Food Service, however, is vastly underrated.

III. **Preview:** By showing how Campus Food Service keeps costs to a minimum, keeps offering a good variety, keeps a democratic system sensitive to the needs of the consumer, and keeps maintaining high quality standards, I am going to prove that Campus Food Service is the best meal program for students.

Conclusion

I. **Summary:** The Campus Food Service plan is a fair way for students at the university to eat. It keeps charging students a low price for meals, keeps offering a wide variety of food selections, keeps trying its best to meet the student's needs, and keeps maintaining freshness and taste standards.

II. **Action step:** The next time you hear people making ill-founded complaints about Campus Food Service, don't hesitate to set them straight.

III. **Closure:** We are just left with one problem, though. Now that we know all the benefits of eating at Campus Food Service, what are we going to complain about at dinner?

At the end of the outlined introduction, before you begin the body, it is a good idea to identify the organizational pattern (such as those in Chapter 7) for the body of the speech. This will help you to plan your structure strategically rather than just list your main ideas in the order that they come to mind. You also can use this notation to check that you actually followed the pattern you chose.

Outlining Transitions

The preparation outline will also help you check the flow of your reasoning and the structural "joints" of your message. Look over the outline to check that the sections naturally link to one another. Is it clear, for example, that B is the next logical step after A? Can you envision how you will wrap up the discussion of idea I and then move to idea II?

If you need to make the transitions of your reasoning explicit, incorporate them into your preparation outline. The easiest way to do this is to make parenthetical notes between the items in the outline that the transition will link. In the example about voter apathy, you might include an explicit transition between items I and II in the body of the speech. The relevant part of the preparation outline might look like this:

   D.

(Transition)

   II.

Citing Supporting Materials in the Outline

You also can use the preparation outline to fit supporting materials into the speech. You can do so physically, by sorting your note cards according to the designations on your outline. For instance, you could put in one pile all the notes that bear on item I-A in the outline; separate piles would contain notes that relate to items I-B, II-A, and so on. This process has two obvious benefits:

1. You can easily evaluate the supporting materials for a given idea in the speech and can select which evidence to include.
2. You will discover which ideas still lack supporting materials, indicating that further research may be needed.

After you have selected supporting materials, incorporate them into the outline. The following three alternative ways to do this all have both benefits and drawbacks:

1. In the outline, reproduce the supporting material immediately below the idea to which it relates. This approach most closely resembles what you will do in the speech and is probably easiest for a reader of the outline to follow; but it will make your outline longer and may disrupt the clarity of its structure.
2. Use footnotes in the outline, and then reproduce the supporting materials at the end. This method preserves the clarity of your structure, but you'll have to flip back and forth between the outline and the supporting materials.
3. Attach a bibliography to the outline indicating the sources of supporting materials. This approach will keep your structure clear and will let a reader of the outline know, in general, where supporting materials came from; but it will not match up specific evidence with specific ideas.

The Presentation Outline

As important as the preparation outline is, you probably will not want to use it during your speech. It is cumbersome and wordy; and it may encourage you to read the outline as though it were a manuscript, rather than speaking extemporaneously and adapting to the situation. Therefore, when you are satisfied with the preparation outline, you should develop a presentation, or speaking, outline. This will be the main source of notes you'll use during the speech itself.

Guidelines for the Presentation Outline

Some basic principles will help you develop a useful speaking outline.

Match Structure of Preparation Outline. This first principle is the most obvious. The whole point of carefully developing the preparation outline is to devise a clear and meaningful structure for the speech. The outline from which you speak, therefore, should follow the same pattern.

Use Key Words. The complete sentences that you used in the preparation outline will distract you in the speaking outline; there will be too much to stop and read while you are speaking. Instead, the speaking outline should use key words that remind you of your ideas. For example, the preparation outline for the speech about voter apathy might be translated into this presentation outline:

I. Growing

    A. Before WWI

    B. 1960

    C. After 1960

    D. 1996

    E. 2000

II. Widespread

    A. East

    B. Midwest

    C. South

    D. West

Each key word should recall to your mind the complete statement that appears in the preparation outline. If a key word does not reliably prompt your memory, change the key word.

Include Introduction, Conclusion, and Transitions. Just as your preparation outline includes entries for the introduction, the conclusion, and transitions, your speaking outline can have separate

---

WWW. Using the Internet

How Do You Cite Sources That You Found on the Internet?

You can look up guidelines for the APA (American Psychological Association) or the MLA (Modern Language Association). For APA guidelines, point your browser to **http://www.lib.usm.edu/userguides/apa.html/.** For MLA guidelines, use **http://cctc.commnet.edu/mla .htm/.** For **Citation and Style Guides,** use **http://juno .concordia.ca/services/citations.html.**

You can also do an interactive exercise at the **Allyn & Bacon Public Speaking Web Site** for finding and citing some of the most common types of online sources, using MLA guidelines. Point your browser to **http://www .abacon.com/pubspeak/exercise/mlaexer.html/.** There, you will find an exercise developed from the *Allyn & Bacon Handbook 3/e.*

Using small note cards is a practical way to keep simple cues in front of you as you speak. This speaker could have placed the cards on the lectern or held them in one hand and kept the other free to gesture.

sections for the introduction and the conclusion and can show transitions as parenthetical notes. In keeping with the key-word nature of the speaking outline, however, state these as briefly as possible, with only enough detail to ensure that you will remember them.

There are two exceptions to this general statement. Because the exact wording of your introduction and conclusion may be important to create the desired initial and final impressions, the attention-getting step in the introduction and the closure-developing step in the conclusion may be written out word for word or even committed to memory.[3]

Your speaking outline may refer to transitions in the form of parenthetical notes, such as "(Cause–effect link here)," "(On the other hand)," and the like. These will remind you of how you intend to signal transitions, thereby making the movement through your outline apparent to listeners.

Use of Note Cards

Most speakers find it better to use note cards than large sheets of paper for the speaking outline. Note cards are more compact, sturdier, easier to rearrange, and less distracting. You can set them on the lectern (if you are using one) or hold them in one hand without limiting your freedom of movement or gesture. You can outline each Roman numeral on a separate note card, or you can put your entire speaking outline on a single card. Some classroom assignments may limit you to a single note card so that you will make your key-word outline as simple as possible.

Reference to Supporting Materials

The speaking outline should cue you about which supporting materials to use. If the actual materials are not simple enough to remember, put them on separate note cards. If you are speaking at a lectern, you can stack the cards in the order you'll use them. If not, you may want to hold them with your speaking outline cards.

Here is a simple illustration of how you might identify supporting materials in your speaking outline:

III. Voting not thought important

    A. Makes no difference—[quot. from Dionne book]

    B. No real choice—[on-campus interviews]

Point A would remind you to read the quotation that supports idea III (you can write the quotation on a separate note card if you don't want to handle a large book). Point B will similarly remind you to recount your informal talks with people on campus who said that there is no real difference between the major political parties and hence no reason to vote.

Use of Stage Directions

Your speaking outline also can include reminders to yourself, as long as they are brief and don't interfere with the structure. Reminders like the following will alert you to things you plan to do during the speech:

Broadcasters may use TelePrompTers to cue themselves. Often, the TelePrompTer will present the text in outline form similar to note cards.

I. Growing [REPEAT]

    A. Before WWI [SLOW DOWN]

    B. 1960

    C. After 1960

    D. 1996

    E. 2000

    [SUMMARIZE/PAUSE]

II. Widespread [REPEAT]

    A. East

    B. Midwest

    C. South

    D. West

    [RESTATE POINT]

In this way, your speaking outline not only will remind you of the structural pattern of the speech but also will help you coordinate your actions during its delivery.

Using an Outline in Rehearsal

In Chapter 11, you will learn how to practice presenting your speech. The speaking outline plays an important role in rehearsal. Be sure that its key words remind you of all the solid thinking you've done and the supporting material you've found. If a key word doesn't immediately prompt you to recall the details, change the key word to one that will. As you rehearse, it will become easier to see and remember the relationship between key words and the overall structure you have devised. Also, keep your preparation outline handy; you'll want to check during rehearsal that you are not leaving any gaps and that all your careful work is included in the speaking outline.

Sample Outlines

The "Applying Strategies" box in this chapter shows a sample student outline with the instructor's comments. Here are two more examples, one of a preparation outline and one of a presentation outline. They are based on a speech by Bree Linck, a student at Northwestern University. Also included are comments, questions, and suggestions. These are actual student outlines. They reflect some of the principles in this chapter more than others, and they offer opportunities for improvement. They are not presented as "perfect" outlines, but as sample student outlines for you to review and analyze. They reflect some, but probably not all, of the principles discussed in this and the preceding two chapters. As you read the outlines, consider what is strong and what is weak and whether you can improve upon these outlines.

PREPARATION OUTLINE

Oil Drilling in Alaska: by Bree Linck

GENERAL PURPOSE: To inform the audience about oil drilling in Alaska

SPECIFIC PURPOSE: To teach my audience about a key political issue

THESIS: Drilling for oil in Alaska's Arctic National Wildlife Refuge has advantages and disadvantages.

Introduction

This may seem to be a trite attention-getting device, because most people's families drive cars, and it might risk embarrassing the few who do not. More important, it is not connected directly to the ideas that follow.

I. *Attention-getting device:* How many of your families drive cars? [ASK FOR SHOW OF HANDS.] Our country uses 16,654 barrels of oil per day for only 287 million people. We use more than China at 3,915 barrels for 1.3 billion people [CITE WEB SITE]. Have you ever stopped to consider where this oil comes from? While the majority of our oil is imported, we do have domestic sources, such as Alaska.

This is a clear statement of the thesis and suggests that the speaker will present both sides of a controversial issue.

II. *Thesis:* Drilling for oil in Alaska's Arctic National Wildlife Refuge has advantages and disadvantages.

This is an unusually long preview. The judgment that gas consumption is "excessive" may be both tangential to this speech and inappropriate in a speech whose aim is "to present both sides of a complex issue."

III. *Preview:* Today I hope to inform you of the ongoing debate over oil drilling in Alaska. This issue is pertinent to all Americans because of our excessive gas consumption. Any American should know where the gas comes from that fuels his or her car. I am going to discuss with you one of our domestic sources, Alaska. Not only is this topic important for your everyday routine, it is also a subject of much debate in the House of Representatives and the Senate at the moment. This debate centers around drilling in Alaska's Arctic National Wildlife Refuge, or ANWR. My first main point will discuss the positives of drilling for oil in this wildlife refuge, and my second main point will discuss the negative aspects. I hope to present both sides of a complex issue.

Body

I. The Arctic National Wildlife Refuge is a protected public environmental park.

Do the items in A, B, and C really *support* the main idea in I? What do they have to do with the status of ANWR as "a protected public environmental park"?

   A. ANWR occupies the northeast crook of Alaska.
   B. It makes up 5 percent of Alaska, with its 1.5 million acre coastal plain, and it is bordered by the Arctic Sea and Canada [CITE SOURCE].
   C. An estimated 10.4 billion barrels of oil lie in this area [CITE SOURCE].

II. The recovery of this oil has two positive aspects: decreased foreign dependency and economic benefits.

A. Increasing domestic drilling would reduce foreign imports, which are subject to political tension.
   1. Over the next 20 years, American dependency on imported oil is expected to increase by 57 percent [CITE SOURCE].
   2. Supporters of drilling in ANWR emphasize a need to decrease this heavy dependency that leaves us vulnerable to high prices or cut-off. Recent events such as September 11 and the war in Iraq serve as reminders of political tension that could serve to disrupt oil trade.
   3. Interior Secretary Gale Norton said, "The ANWR is simply not just a place to drill oil, it is the largest potential domestic source of oil. This is a matter necessary for security and also to enhance economic recovery" [CITE SOURCE].

Notice how two separate points are contained in this subheading: the existence of political tension and the vulnerability it creates.

[TRANSITION: Gale Norton mentions economics, which leads us to the next positive aspect of drilling.]

B. Drilling in the ANWR will be economically beneficial for America.
   1. A study done in 1990 predicts the creation of 750,000 new jobs through ANWR drilling [CITE STUDY].
   2. This drilling project in Alaska would not only provide jobs, but pay taxes to Alaskans. These taxes would promote better civil services, increasing living standards.
   3. As oil prices increase per barrel on the world market, investing in a greater domestic source would save the nation money.
   4. A study says that drilling on Alaska's North Slope from 1977 to 2001 saved America one trillion dollars in foreign oil costs [CITE GOVERNMENT HEARING].

Sections A and B are clearly parallel. Each identifies a distinct advantage of drilling in the ANWR.

Is this point really independent of II A or does it belong there? Is it referring to an absolute saving of money (supporting idea II B) or a shifting of foreign expenditures to domestic (supporting idea II A)? How could Bree clear up this ambiguity?

[TRANSITION: These two benefits of drilling—decreased foreign dependency and economic benefits—may prove convincing, but we also must pay attention to the negative aspects.]

III. Oil drilling in the ANWR has two negative components: damage to the environment and minimal oil production.
   A. Drilling in this national refuge would cause permanent environmental damage.
      1. ANWR is a habitat for caribou, polar bears, muskoxen, seals, bowhead and beluga whales.
      2. The primary concern with oil extraction is caribou. The native people Gwish'in's entire lifestyle is centered around the caribou. ANWR is the caribou's breeding ground. It would be disrupted by drilling, causing a decrease in caribou. Interior Secretary Gale Norton said that oil drilling will cut caribou calves by "about 14 percent" [CITE SOURCE].
      3. A second wildlife concern with the oil proposal is migratory patterns of geese and bowhead whales. These animals have altered their migratory patterns due to the noise of oil drilling.

Notice how this main idea is structured in parallel fashion with the previous one.

Do this and the next two items appear to be as serious as III A 2? Should they be included here? If so, is the order right?

Does this represent supporting material (evidence) for the claim in III B? Does it show that drilling will not result in much oil—or does it show that regulations could result in a saving of much oil, as well?

This point could be shortened: "Daily production of the ANWR is only about 100,000 barrels a day, less than 1 percent of our daily oil use."

Is this point still presenting both sides of a complex issue, or is it arguing in favor of one side?

4. A third wildlife concern is the presence of human food in the refuge, a consequence of workers. This availability of food has led to an increase in animal predators and scavengers.
5. A fourth environmental concern is the use of ice roads and drilling pads. These ice formations remove water and may destroy fish. These manmade creations also alter the natural setting, which affects animal behavior.
6. All of the changes are dangerous to the natural environment of the ANWR.

B. A second discouraging reality of oil drilling in Alaska is that it will not result in a great deal of oil.
1. Senator Barbara Boxer quoted the EPA when she said, "In seven years, we could save the same amount of oil available in the Arctic Refuge by requiring light trucks and SUVs to meet the same efficiency standards as regular cars."
2. Another fact that brings the minimal quantity of oil into the picture is that daily production of the ANWR is about 100,000 barrels a day. This number is less than 1 percent of our nation's daily oil use [CITE SOURCE].
3. Through these two statistics, we can see how little Alaskan oil will offer us and understand that it will have little effect on our foreign oil dependency.

Conclusion

I. *Summary:* Today we have discussed the current political debate over drilling in the ANWR and its positive and negative sides. I have outlined the two positive aspects to drilling: decreased foreign dependency and economic benefits. I have also reviewed the two negative aspects of drilling: damage to the environment and minimal oil production.

II. *Closure:* As we polled in the beginning of this speech, we all drive cars. Oil is an essential part of our daily American lives. You now know a little bit more about where this oil comes from. I challenge you to keep updated about the current situation in Alaska, for the future of oil will greatly influence the remainder of our lives.

Here the conclusion returns to the theme of the introduction, enhancing the unity of the speech. However, the fact that this point is not referred to in the body of the speech makes the unity somewhat misleading.

Notice the number and variety of sources—recent newspaper articles, technical journals, Congressional hearings (though inexactly cited), and Web sites.

Bibliography

"Alaska oil and gas exploration good and bad for area life." *Life Science Weekly,* March 24, 2003.

Arctic National Wildlife Refuge Web site, www.anwr.org/features/api-pros.htm.

Capitol Hill Hearing Testimony, House Resources: Oil and Gas Drilling on Arctic Coastal Plain. Washington, D.C., 2003.

Dinesh, Manimoli. "Experts Say Alaska Oil Drilling Hurts Wildlife, Local Culture." *The Oil Daily,* March 5, 2003.

"Drilling Alaska; Undermining the U.S." *Earth Island Journal,* Fall 2001: 48.

"Ex-Canadian PM Opposes Drilling in Alaska." *United Press International,* April 10, 2001.

"How much would it really help? Alaska's oil." *The Economist,* October 20, 2001.

Knickerbocker, Brad. "New push to pump oil from Alaska Refuge." *The Christian Science Monitor,* November 26, 2001.

Lee, Dwight. "To drill or not to drill: let the environmentalists decide." *Independent Review,* Fall 2001: 217.

Planet Save Web site, www.planetsave.com/ViewStory.asp?ID=3378.

Streetlaw Web site, www.streetlaw.org/youthact/energy/drilling.html.

SPEAKING OUTLINE

Oil Drilling in Alaska by Bree Linck
Introduction
I. Attention-getter: How many of your families drive cars? [ASK FOR SHOW OF HANDS.] Our country uses 16,654 barrels of oil per day for only 287 million people. We use more than China at 3,915 barrels for 1.3 billion people [CITE WEB SITE]. Have you ever stopped to consider where this oil comes from? While the majority of our oil is imported, we do have domestic sources, such as Alaska.
II. Thesis: Drilling for oil in Alaska's Arctic National Wildlife Refuge has advantages and disadvantages.
III. Preview

> Some key words might be in order here so the speaker will recall the key points in the preview.

Body

I. Protected Area
II. Positive Aspects
    A. Reduce foreign imports [CITE OIL DEPENDENCY AND NORTON QUOTE]
    B. Economic benefits [NEW JOBS, TAXES, SAVED MONEY]

> A parenthetical note here (as below) would remind Bree of the specific points to make or evidence to use.

[TRANSITION: from positive to negative aspects]

III. Negative Aspects
    A. Environmental damage [CARIBOU, MIGRATION, PREDATORS, ICE ROADS]
    B. Not much oil [BOXER QUOTE, CITE LOW PRODUCTION FIGURES]

Conclusion

I. Summary
II. Closure: [CITE CAR POLL] I challenge you to keep updated about the current situation in Alaska, for the future of oil will greatly influence the remainder of our lives.

> Notice how the speaking outline follows exactly the structure of the preparation outline, while substituting key words for complete sentences and ideas. This is likely to be a valuable memory aid during the speech without getting in Bree's way.

Summary

We have completed our three-chapter discussion of organization by considering speech outlines, which display the formal structure of the speech in terms of numbers and letters. An outline is important both in preparing and in presenting the speech.

The preparation outline allows you to visualize the form of the speech, providing an opportunity to check your reasoning and organizational pattern. Rules of coordination and subordination should be followed in constructing an outline. Ideas that are equally important should be coordinated at the same level on the outline. Supporting ideas should be outlined as subordinate to the main ideas they demonstrate. The preparation outline is usually written in complete sentences and includes primary sections for the introduction, the body, and the conclusion. Transitions are inserted as parenthetical comments, and citations are included within the outline or at the end in footnotes, a reference list, or a bibliography.

Because the preparation outline can be rather long and cumbersome, a presentation outline, or speaking outline, should be used during delivery. The speaking outline follows the form of the preparation outline but is written in key words rather than complete sentences. It can be reproduced on note cards, with separate note cards for supporting materials. Because only the speaker sees this version of the outline, it may include short notes about stage directions.

The sample preparation outline and speaking outline provided at the end of this chapter show some of the issues to be addressed in order for the parts of a speech to come together into a well-planned, purposeful presentation.

Discussion Questions

1. Many beginning speakers write speeches without first developing an outline. How does the construction of an outline help a speaker to pre-

pare a better speech? What are the disadvantages of creating an outline?

2. When developing an outline, how do you determine which ideas are subordinate to others? How do you determine which ideas are coordinate? As a class, construct an outline of this chapter, and discuss how it demonstrates the principles of subordination and coordination.

3. In small groups, share the preparation outline for your next speech with your classmates. Discuss the following questions:

Do the main ideas support the thesis?
Are the main ideas parallel and on the same level of importance?
Do the subpoints support the claims made in the main ideas?
Are the subpoints parallel and on the same level of importance?
Are there places where transitions are especially needed?

Activities

1. Attend a speech or read a speech manuscript that you have retrieved from the library. Create an outline of this speech, and use the outline to critique its structure.

2. Construct a preparation outline for your next speech. Then, annotate your outline, explaining why you made the decisions that you made. Model the page layout of your outline after the sample preparation outline at the end of this chapter, using marginal notes to describe your strategic choices.

3. Create a speaking outline for your next speech, and use it to rehearse. Practice and modify the speaking outline until your delivery becomes smooth.

Notes

1. For another way of creating preparation outlines, see Collin Rae, "Before the Outline—The Writing Wheel," *Social Studies* 81 (July–August 1990): 178.

2. If you are having trouble with the mechanics of outlining, see James Gibson, *Speech Organization: A Programmed Approach*, San Francisco: Rinehart Press, 1971. Also see the instructions about outlining in the computer program by Martin R. Cox, *Interactive Speechwriter*, Boston: Allyn & Bacon, 1995.

3. It has been shown that apprehensive speakers are less likely to follow the strategy that they had planned for the introduction of a speech. See Michael J. Beatty, "Public Speaking Apprehension, Decision-Making Errors in the Selection of Speech Introduction Strategies and Adherence to Strategy," *Communication Education* 37 (October 1988): 297–311. By including a detailed introduction in your speaking outline, you may be more likely to follow your plan, despite apprehension at the beginning of a speech.

Chapter Ten

Achieving Style Through Language

In this chapter, we will:

- Develop an understanding of style as the personal choices that distinguish or characterize speakers.

- Examine the role of language in contributing to the style of a speech.

- Learn the key differences between oral style and written style.

- Explore how definitions affect the stylistic significance of individual words and phrases.

- Identify means to achieve clarity, rhythm, and vividness.

- Distinguish among levels of style and determine how variety, balance, and conciseness affect judgments of the overall style of a speech.

- Suggest things you can do to enhance the stylistic quality of your speeches.

If you told your friends that a popular singer has an intimate style or that a politician displays a presidential style, they probably would know what you meant. Something about that person stands out and makes him or her easy to describe. There is a pattern in the person's behavior—conscious or not—that you can recognize and that may let you characterize the person as being, say, a folk-rock singer or a "New Age" politician. Or the pattern may be unique, allowing you to distinguish that individual from all other singers or politicians.

What Is Style?

These examples offer a working definition of **style** as the pattern of choices attributed to a person by others to characterize or to distinguish him or her. We can elaborate on several aspects of this definition.

First, style is a pattern of *choices* that are not predetermined.[1] That is, the politician does not *have* to appear presidential. Nor does choice necessarily imply strategic awareness. The politician may or may not be conscious of all aspects of behavior that lead voters to regard one as seeming presidential. Even so, if you set out to cultivate a positive style, you *are* engaged in strategic planning, as we will see in this chapter.

Second, although we commonly say that a singer "has" a certain style, as though that style was possessed by him or her, in fact it is the fans who observe a pattern of choices, who label it as a certain style, and who then attribute the style to the singer. Style is perceived by others whose inferences and judgments attribute it to the person. Style is always audience dependent.

Third, style can be used either to set someone apart from others or to identify someone with a particular group. Some singers, actors, or politicians have a highly individualistic style; their patterns of choices make them unique among all other singers, actors, or politicians. In such a case, we say that the person's choices create a distinct **signature.** Just as your handwriting is slightly different from anyone else's and your actual signature is unique, so, too, can your speaking performance have a unique signature.

On the other hand, when a person's style is identified with a particular group, we say that the style is of a certain **type.** There are at least three ways in which a style may be of a given type:

- *Generic types* are styles that fit into a category, such as mysteries, jazz, or tragedy.[2]
- *Culture types* identify the basic styles of a culture, such as the pioneering spirit or the work ethic.[3]
- *Archetypes* are patterns of basic human experiences that recur across time and across cultures, such as the rhythm of birth and death or of struggle, defeat, and triumph.[4]

Style in a Speech

Even if we understand style in general, two common problems arise when we talk about a speaker's style. First, style is not always a positive attribute. If a politician has a bullying manner or a preacher is known for mumbling,

style
The pattern of choices attributed to a person by others to characterize or to distinguish him or her.

signature
An individual pattern of stylistic choices that characterizes a particular person.

type
A pattern of stylistic choices that characterizes a group with which a person identifies.

style will hurt rather than help their effectiveness. Recognize that the distinctive style of a speech can sometimes be negative, as when a speaker keeps saying, "uh," or peppers the speech with "like," or repeats "you know" so often that listeners start counting the repetitions. These are stylistic patterns, to be sure, but they are also nervous mannerisms; they detract from the message rather than help it. For some speakers, the goal is to *remove* negative characteristics from a speech. In removing them, however, the speaker is not removing style, but is *changing* it from a nervous, unsure style to a smooth, confident one.

The other problem is that we often think of style in a speech as ornamentation that is added to the content rather than as part and parcel of the content. In this view, it is enough just to speak plainly and clearly without concern for style. Abraham Lincoln's Gettysburg Address is often cited as an example of a plain speech that is remembered far better than the highly stylistic two-hour address delivered on the same day by Edward Everett. The mistake is to think that Lincoln's speech was pure, distilled content while Everett's had a great deal of added style. In fact, it simply is not possible for a speech to be "without style." Every speaker makes choices. In Lincoln's case, obvious stylistic features include plainness of structure, simplicity of wording, abstraction, and even brevity.[5]

More recently, style and content were merged inseparably in President John F. Kennedy's inaugural address. Although few can identify the main points in Kennedy's outline or his thesis and supporting materials, the speech is recalled for its well-crafted phrases: "Let us never negotiate out of fear. But let us never fear to negotiate," and "Ask not what your country can do for you—ask what you can do for your country." For most people today, these statements embody what the speech *said*. They are stylistic elements, to be sure, but they also represent the content of the speech.

An even more recent example can be found in President George W. Bush's speech to Congress after the terrorist attacks of September 11, 2001. Bush's style included the use of a series of short phrases delivered in staccato rhythm (with brief pauses between the phrases) to highlight the completeness of each. President Bush said, "I will not yield; I will not rest; I will not relent . . ." The style suggested resolve and determination, which of course was the primary content of the speech as well. (The text of this speech can be found in Appendix B.)

If we avoid viewing style either as distracting mannerisms or as unnecessary ornamentation, we will see that the concept of style in public speaking is the same as in art, music, literature, and politics. With speeches too, style is a pattern of choices—as recognized and interpreted by the audience—that may categorize or distinguish the speaker. Moreover, the choices speakers make about language are not just choices about how to make a speech seem pleasing. Like all other strategic choices, they are decisions about how to accomplish one's purpose in a given situation by taking advantage of opportunities and minimizing constraints. Speeches may have distinctive signatures; may reveal generic types, culture types, or archetypes; or may be a mixture of signatures and types.

Style and Language

Like other aspects of public speaking, style is best approached through strategic planning: identifying your resources and using them to achieve your purpose. The most significant resource for creating an effective speaking style is language. But speakers often take language for granted, paying little attention to the words they choose to express their ideas. This is bad strategy because it surrenders control over a resource that can transform a dull speech into a memorable one. Language exerts such effects by influencing the audience's perceptions of both the speech and the speaker.

Perception of the Speech. A speaker's word choices direct listeners to view the message in one way rather than another. Suppose, for example, that one speaker describes the federal government as "the engine of our economic strength" and that another refers to the federal government as "a cancer destroying our independence." Although both phrases create a concrete image for the abstraction "the federal government," notice the difference in perspective. The first phrase is a *favorable* evaluation; it gives the federal government credit for driving the economy and urges us to view economic regulation positively. The second phrase invites exactly the opposite reaction: The government is evaluated *unfavorably* and is viewed as a threat. The simple matter of word choice signals how each speaker feels about the subject and encourages us to evaluate it in the same way. Notice also that the word choices are inseparable from content; both phrases make arguments and inferences implicitly as well as explicitly.

This brief example illustrates what happens repeatedly throughout a speech. Ideas have meaning for listeners only as those ideas are expressed in language, and the language chosen shapes the meaning of the ideas that are expressed.[6]

Perception of the Speaker. Additionally, language influences how the audience perceives the speaker as a person. And because the appeal of ideas cannot be separated completely from the appeal of the person who expresses them, word choices influence a speaker's *ethos*.

Again, consider some simple examples. The speaker who begins every other sentence with the word *now* will drive the audience to distraction. The speaker who needlessly uses obscure or highfalutin words may impress some listeners but also may seem distant, arrogant, or condescending. The speaker who uses words inaccurately or who mispronounces them may seem ignorant. And the speaker whose language offends listeners—as with racist, sexist, or ethnic slurs—usually loses credibility.

In contrast to these negative examples, if you effectively repeat a key word or phrase, you will actively involve listeners in your speech by helping them to anticipate what comes next. If you use colorful, appropriate language, you can lead listeners to see things from a new perspective, perhaps convincing them that your topic deserves more attention than they thought. If you can create a memorable "sound bite," you can cause listeners to think of you more positively. And if your wording avoids jargon, technical terms, and excess verbiage, you probably will be judged pleasing to hear.

Oral Style Versus Written Style

A situation comedy on television requires different stylistic elements than an opera does, and the same characteristics that make a novel stylistically strong may be unacceptable in a newspaper column. In short, a style that is powerful in one medium may be ineffective in another.

In the same way, the stylistic goals that you might aim to achieve in an essay are different from the goals you would pursue in a speech. Try delivering as a speech what you have written recently as a term paper in another course. Your audience will easily recognize that this "speech" is inauthentic, difficult to follow, and perhaps even boring. Your term paper will not succeed as a speech because you have been trained to write for the eye, not for the ear.

Some differences between written and oral presentations are fairly obvious. You can read written material at your own pace, skimming some sections and reading other parts more closely. If something is unclear, you can go back and reread it. If there's an unfamiliar concept, you can stop and look it up. If you lose track of the author's main argument or organizational structure, you can go back and review it. And if you get tired, you can put the writing aside and return to it later.

A speech offers none of these characteristics. Although you could tape a speech and replay it later, this is rarely done. In most cases, a speech is ephemeral—it is delivered, and then it is gone. Listeners cannot control the pace of delivery; each of them must attend to the same idea at the same time. There's no "pause" button that makes the speaker wait while you consult a source to check something that you don't understand. If you forget the speaker's main points or structure, you can't review them. For all these reasons, listeners are much more dependent on the speaker than readers are on the writer. And because concentration is always important and always difficult, the speaker must make the speech as easy as possible for listeners to follow and remember.[7]

Given these differences between writing and speaking, you will want to consider the following factors when developing an oral style.

WWW. Using the Internet

Assessing Style in a Famous Speech

Analyze President Kennedy's inaugural address for style choices. Point your browser to **http://www.hpol.org/jfk**. Then, after reading or listening to the inaugural address, determine whether Kennedy used the principles of oral style and made effective stylistic choices. Evaluate his language choices in light of the way his words:

- Expressed simplicity.
- Created repetition.
- Achieved an appropriate level of formality or informality.
- Demonstrated reflexivity.
- Achieved accuracy.
- Were appropriate to the audience and situation.
- Expressed clarity.
- Created rhythm.
- Created vividness.

Simplicity. Oral style is simpler than written style. Speakers use shorter and more common words. Descriptions are briefer. Sentences are shorter and less complex. Jargon and technical language are avoided. The organization of the speech is clearly identified through previews, transitions, and summaries. All these features of oral style reflect the fact that, unlike the writer, the speaker must seek instant understanding. If listeners have to puzzle out the speaker's meaning or intention, they have less mental energy for concentrating on what comes next. Because the speech can't be stopped in midstream, the speaker's goal is to avoid distracting the audience from following along.

Repetition. Oral style is more repetitive than written style. A speaker might repeat key ideas for emphasis or to ensure that listeners did not ignore them. A catchy phrase or refrain might recur throughout the speech. Even the structure of the speech might follow a repetitive pattern. (This element of oral style is found in print as well. Notice that each heading in this section is followed by the words "Oral style is . . .")

If not overdone, repetition serves several purposes. It can highlight your main ideas and provide emphasis, much like italic or boldface type in print. Similarly, repetition of a particular sentence structure can help listeners "see" the pattern of your speech, allowing them to follow and anticipate its organization. Repetition is also a memory aid for both speaker and listeners.

Informality. Oral style is more informal than written style. Few of us always speak in complete sentences. Nor do we observe all the grammar rules of standard English. In fact, were you to transcribe and read one of your speeches, you probably would find a number of grammatical errors and incomplete sentences; yet when you deliver the speech aloud, these aren't noticed. Speeches often do not read well, just as essays often do not sound well.

Reflexivity. Oral style is more **reflexive** than written style, meaning that speakers often refer to themselves and to the audience and situation. In contrast, your English composition teachers may have told you to limit the use of *I* in your essays and to avoid statements that—although perfectly clear to you and your classmates—might be unclear to outsiders. Recall that written material is usually composed without a specific audience in mind; indeed, writers often intend to transcend particular audiences. Speakers, on the other hand, usually intend to have an impact on a specific audience, which they analyze as described in Chapter 3.

Speakers are also more likely to make their organizational structure explicit, saying things like "Here's how I'm going to develop my idea," "Let me review my three main points," and "Now we're ready for the conclusion." Because listeners cannot stop your speech to check its organization, or put it aside when their concentration wavers, you must help them follow your train of thought. You do this by referring explicitly to your outline and by such devices as signposting, internal previews, and internal summaries (see Chapter 8).

Potential for Clutter. Oral style is more likely to include clutter, because speakers are thinking on their feet and cannot revise their remarks as writers can. Sometimes the thinking and the speech get "out of sync," and—often unknowingly—a speaker may fill the gap with unrelated and unplanned words until the thinking and the speech are brought back into line. The result is clutter: vocalized pauses (*um, er, ah*), digressions, pointless repetition, and distracting words such as *right, you know,* and *okay.*

Because clutter usually occurs when you need some time to think about what you will say next, the remedy lies in your preparation. Before speaking, make sure that you have a strong sense of your outline, your main ideas, and how you will develop your thesis. Preparation helps you to avoid clutter and makes the speech flow smoothly.

Performative Versus Conversational Style

There is not just one "oral style." A recitation of a Shakespearean sonnet is very different from a speech at a protest rally, and a sermon is very different from a story—even though all of these messages are delivered orally. It is useful to distinguish between a *performative* and a *conversational* style.

---

reflexive
Making self-reference to the speaker or situation.

Performative style, as its name suggests, reminds listeners of a performance for which the audience consists of passive spectators. The performers are concerned primarily with expressing themselves and only secondarily with establishing a relationship with the audience members. Conversely, conversational style suggests that listeners are more active participants in a discussion with the speaker, who wants first and foremost to establish a connection with them. Giving a virtuoso performance is only a secondary concern, if it enters into the speaker's mind at all.

Until the television age, formal speeches at large public gatherings called for a performative style. Political oratory was seen as a performance. In contrast, speeches to small groups or to one's peers were thought to call for a conversational style. But television has changed these norms. The small screen reduces the formal speech from a mass public event to a discussion in your living room. Contemporary politicians often speak with the informality and intimacy that fit a conversational style.[8] Presidents Reagan and Clinton were both effective in establishing bonds with their listeners through a conversational style.

It is tempting to conclude that the day of the performative style has passed and that you should always speak informally, in a conversational style. Certainly most classroom speeches will be more effective if you speak informally and conversationally. But formal sermons, polished lectures, testimony in hearings and committees, and protest speeches are all examples in which a more performative style usually is more appropriate. Some of your assignments may simulate these types of speeches, and you probably will give some speeches outside the classroom that you will prefer to deliver in a performative style. Rather than always preferring one style or the other, you should follow the same advice offered on other topics: Select the style that is most helpful to your strategic purpose and most appropriate to the opportunities and constraints of the situation.[9]

Basic Requirements for Effective Style

Before we examine some specific stylistic resources that are available to speakers, it is important to recognize two basic requirements for effective style in all speaking situations:

- The accuracy of what you say
- The appropriateness of what you say

Accuracy. Some philosophers think that there is no such thing as an "accurate" or "inaccurate" use of words, because the connection between a word and the thing for which it stands is just a matter of social convention, which changes. In everyday usage, however, it is meaningful to talk about using words accurately. Speakers who have no understanding of a word's dictionary definition or who use a word in a way that is significantly different from common usage will appear not to know what they are talking about. Sometimes, this can be funny, as when a student speaking about medical research said, "I know that there is a cadaver shortage, but we can train new ones in two weeks." The student obviously didn't understand what *cadaver* meant. And although his slip delighted listeners, they were not just laughing along with a jovial speaker. At the least, they were distracted. And the impression that the speaker was inept weakened his credibility.

Verbally as well as visually, an appropriate style is one that shows your own personal, social, and cultural identity while also showing respect for those in the audience whose identity is different from your own.

Mrs. Malaprop, a character in an eighteenth-century play, repeatedly misused words and has given her name to another kind of inaccurate usage. A **malapropism** is the seemingly unintentional but possibly meaningful confusion of words or usages. While a presidential candidate, George W. Bush occasionally misspoke in this way. He referred to the danger that others might "hold this nation hostile" (he meant "hostage") and, in a speech on world trade, spoke about "terriers" (he meant "barriers"). An especially famous malapropism from a generation ago came from Chicago Mayor Richard J. Daley. After the 1968 Democratic National Convention broke out in riots that some blamed on the aggressive conduct of the Chicago police, he told a press conference, "The police aren't there to *create* disorder; the police are there to *preserve* disorder." The Mayor obviously meant something different from what he said. But his malapropism caused many listeners not to take him seriously and even to suppose that he had made a "Freudian slip" that revealed his "deeper" thoughts.

The character B. O. Plenty in the "Dick Tracy" comic strip is a constant source of malapropisms; so is Archie Bunker on the 1970s sitcom "All in the Family." Although audiences are delighted by gross usage errors in humorous situations, a malapropism can be devastating to a speaker's credibility.

Appropriateness to the Audience and Situation. The second basic requirement for effective style is that your words be appropriate to the audience and situation. You want to show listeners that you are sympathetic and respectful. If your words make them feel patronized, insulted, or taunted, your style will undercut your message.

Be especially careful of wording when your listeners have different cultural backgrounds. If you are insensitive to how various cultures use language, you may easily offend someone. Also make sure that your overall tone matches what is expected in the situation. Vulgar language, for instance, would be jarring in a formal lecture. And although you may think you have an engaging dry wit, you might be surprised to discover that listeners perceive sarcasm that went beyond the bounds of acceptable irony.

Because every situation is different, it is hard to say just what word choices will make your style seem appropriate. But the following general guidelines can help support your message:

1. *Avoid sounding self-important or pretentious.* Do not use language that will make listeners think you are arrogant. The physics major who made fleeting references to "dark matter" and "superstring theory" without explaining what he meant was probably showing off rather than genuinely trying to communicate. Similarly, when a student speaker argued that the

malapropism
Unintentional but possibly meaningful confusion of words or usages.

Using Appropriate Language

The Situation

You work part time for a local software company and have been asked by your boss to talk to a group of foreign visitors about your experiences working at the company, raising a family, and going to school—all at the same time. Your employer naturally wants you to emphasize the company's flexibility in helping you fulfill your other obligations and the benefits you have received working there. You're aware, though, that this English-speaking group of male and female visitors, from different countries and of different ages, does not necessarily share value and belief systems (either with each other or with you). They may not agree that a "balancing act" like yours is a good thing, or they may think you have divided loyalties. Unfortunately, you do not have the time to investigate all of their backgrounds to determine the best approach to the situation—but you do know that how you phrase the benefits and what language you choose will have an impact on their overall impression of you and the company.

Making Choices

1. How will you phrase the thesis of your speech to avoid any negative reactions from those who don't value education as highly as obligation to family?
2. What language strategies would you employ to make the speech sound appealing to the entire group?
3. How can you use language to establish a common ground with everyone in the group?

What If . . .

How would your language choices change if:

1. You were male instead of female or female instead of male?
2. You were a full-time college student without a family talking to the same group about the benefits of working at this company while going to school?

---

university should require more core courses, her language implied that her classmates were culturally illiterate:

> A broad liberal arts background is essential for our generation to cope with the postmodern condition in which we find ourselves thrown. The fact that most of you cannot name the last ten presidents and that many of you have no concept of even the most basic political, social, or literary theory signals an epistemological breakdown in our culture.

Remember that you are seeking a favorable response from your audience. Usually, the most effective routes toward that goal are to establish common bonds and to stress significant points of similarity between you and the audience. No one enjoys being talked down to or called to account by a speaker. Listeners will resist your message if your language or attitude seems superior.

2. *Avoid signs of disrespect.* Racial slurs, sexist references, and ethnic jokes clearly fall into this category. Because such comments debase and degrade other people, most listeners regard them as inappropriate even if not di-

rected at them personally. The best rule is the simplest: Don't use such language, not even to poke fun at yourself.

3. *Avoid inappropriate emotion.* Just as you obviously would not choose the occasion of a funeral eulogy to speak badly of the deceased, neither would you prepare an after-dinner speech that is somber or gloomy. Cultures vary in what emotions are considered appropriate for a given occasion. Situational expectations also are not absolute, and speakers sometimes deliberately violate them in certain circumstances. But that should happen only for a clear purpose. As a general rule, analyze the nature of the speaking situation, and aim to keep your style and tone within the boundaries of what the audience expects.

Once you are certain that your speech meets these minimal conditions for effective style, you can consider various stylistic resources and make language choices that enhance your appeal. You can choose and arrange words to capitalize on their descriptive or persuasive power; to achieve clarity, rhythm, and vividness; and to create interest and balance in your speech.

As we examine the major resources available, understand that we will not even come close to the limits. Centuries ago, handbooks listed 200 or more variations in word usage that could be adapted by eager speakers.[10] Clearly, in this chapter, we are just beginning to scratch the surface.

Defining Terms Appropriately

One of the most important stylistic resources is **definition,** the process by which you establish the meaning of a word for your audience. In defining a word, your choices range from neutral to persuasive, and your decisions should take into account all aspects of the rhetorical situation.

Neutral Definitions

Sometimes, a speaker defines words in a fairly neutral way, with no goal other than being precise and clear. Although no definition is entirely neutral, in this case the speaker does not really want to change listeners' views about the thing described. The following definitional strategies are relatively neutral.

Replacing a Common Meaning with a More Technical Meaning. A teacher of rhetoric might begin an introductory lecture this way:

> Many people, when they think about *rhetoric,* conjure up images of endless political speeches full of bombast and posturing which really don't end up saying anything. But to the Romans of antiquity, rhetoric was one of the seven liberal arts, a set of skills which was not inherently good or inherently bad, but capable of use for good or evil alike.

In this case, the teacher's goal is to make students equate the term *rhetoric* with classical antiquity rather than with contemporary usage. The common meaning is inadequate for the teacher's purposes because it distinguishes between rhetoric and content—precisely the distinction to which the teacher objects.

definition
The process of giving meaning to a word.

Defining by Similarities and Differences. You can convey to listeners a more precise meaning of a term if you can both distinguish the term and compare it with something the audience already knows. A guidance counselor might say, "Cocurricular activities are a fundamental part of a child's education. They are like the curriculum in the demands they make of students but unlike it in their informality and the degree of control invested in student leaders." Thus the term *cocurricular activities* is defined both by comparing it with the academic curriculum and also by showing how it is different.

Operational Definitions. An abstraction can often be defined by an **operational definition,** which explains the meaning of the term by identifying specific operations to be performed. A speaker might ask, "How will we know when we have dealt effectively with worldwide famine?" The answer to the question—"When we have doubled the amount of food aid and when the rate of death by starvation is cut in half"—makes the abstract concept of "effective famine reduction" concrete by defining it in terms of what must be done to achieve it.

In each of these neutral examples of definitions, any shift in the audience's perceptions and attitudes about the topic is incidental to the speaker's goal of clarifying meaning and usage. Often, however, as shown in the next two sections, speakers use definition *precisely* to change listeners' perceptions and judgments.

WWW. Using the Internet

Using Online Dictionaries

In a library, you will find many different types of dictionaries. You can also do this online. From the **Allyn & Bacon Public Speaking Web Site,** you can access a variety of types of dictionaries at **http://www.abacon.com/pubspeak/organize/dict.html/** or go to **Dictionary.com** at **http://dictionary.reference.com/.** Dictionaries are especially useful for finding denotative meanings of words.

Denotation and Connotation in Definitions

Words have meaning on at least two levels. A word's **denotation** is what it refers to, or "denotes"; its denotation is similar to its dictionary definition. For example, the denotation for *chair* is "a seat with four legs and a back intended for one person." At the same time, a word also evokes feelings. This second dimension of meaning is **connotation.** The connotation of *chair* is relatively neutral. But if a speaker referred to this object as a "throne," listeners might respond with feelings of respect or dignity (unless, of course, the speaker was being ironic or sarcastic).

Moving from physical objects to abstractions, the influence of connotation is even stronger. *Liberal* denotes a person who adheres to a particular political philosophy, but its connotation has changed considerably over the years. During the 1930s, and again during the 1960s, *liberal* typically had positive connotations, suggesting farsightedness, vision, and idealism. During the 1980s and 1990s, however, the same word with the same denotation took on quite different connotations, suggesting poor judgment, impracticality, and waste. Because of these shifts in connotation, someone who might have been proud to be called a liberal in the mid-1960s would probably have preferred a designation such as "moderate" or "progressive" in the late 1990s.

As a speaker, you naturally will want to use words whose connotations are consistent with your goals—positive connotations if you want to praise or advocate, negative connotations if you want to condemn or dissuade. But

operational definition
Explaining what a term means by identifying specific operations to be performed.

denotation
The referent for a given word.

connotation
The feelings or emotional responses associated with a given word.

you also should be careful to select connotations that reflect listeners' views, based on audience analysis. If you choose negative connotations for an idea that most listeners regard as neutral or positive, you may be accused of "stacking the deck," "loading the issue," or "begging the question." All these phrases suggest that you are *assuming* by definition what you really need to *demonstrate* by reasoning and argument.

Consider, for example, the connotations in student Zana Kuljanian's speech about why the death penalty should be abolished. She never used the term *capital punishment,* instead saying:

> There is no reason why we should sanction state-sponsored murder. State-sponsored murder is immoral, unconstitutional, and dangerous. Nevertheless, we allow these organized public assassinations to proceed at an alarming pace.

Because Zana used words such as *murder* and *assassinations,* she was not very successful at persuading listeners who didn't already agree with her. Similarly, the white student who called capital punishment "justice for barbaric criminals" was not well received by black listeners, who saw racism rather than justice behind the fact that black prisoners are executed in disproportionately large numbers. On the other hand, if either speaker had faced an audience of people already in agreement with the message, these connotations would have reinforced their agreement.

Persuasive Definitions

The shifting connotation of *liberal* during the 1990s illustrates the persuasive power of definitions. Its connotation changed not by accident but by the deliberate choice of "conservative" politicians to make *liberal* a word of criticism rather than of praise. To do this, they associated the previously positive word with phrases that have negative connotations, such as "big government," "special interests," and "tax and spend." These new associations allowed them to shift the commonly accepted connotation of *liberal* while preserving its denotation.

Persuasive definition can take two forms. In this example, the denotative meaning of *liberal* remained the same while its connotative meaning changed. The word identified the same people as liberals, but its connotation changed from positive to negative. Alternatively, connotative meaning can stay the same while denotative meaning changes. Consider the phrase "special interests." Its connotations are negative because "special interests" are seen in contrast to the general or public interest. Throughout much of the twentieth century, "special interests" were associated with big business and with people of great wealth. During the 1980s, however, they came to be associated with advocates for women's rights, for multiculturalism, for labor, or for abortion rights. Although the phrase retained its negative connotations, the people to whom it referred were considerably different.

Freedom is a particularly good example of a term that is susceptible to persuasive definition. Unlike "special interests," its connotation is positive. Not surprisingly, it has been used to characterize a variety of objects speakers wanted their audiences to favor, ranging all the way from the Iraqi war of 2003 ("Operation Enduring Freedom") to the purchase of consumer goods and services that promise to give you freedom from drudgery.[11]

persuasive definition
A shift in connotation applied to the same denotation or a shift in denotation applied to the same connotation.

You may be wondering how one goes about persuasive definition. Connotations, after all, are not easily abandoned. How does one break the connection between a word and what it "means"? Often, it's done by finding a different connotation that people will respond to. Affirmative action programs came under assault during the late 1990s because critics called them "reverse discrimination"—suggesting that, far from helping the goal of equal opportunity, they were counterproductive. In order to rally public opinion, anti-abortion advocates began to describe a particular procedure for late-term abortion as "partial birth abortion." Opponents of the estate and gift tax have tried to rally public support by referring to it as the "death tax" and insisting that death should not be a taxable event.[12]

WWW. Using the Internet

When Is an Abortion not an Abortion?

This question was at the heart of an historic court case that was described in the *Atlantic Monthly* in 1975. Observe how the opposing sides in the case used the concept of persuasive definitions. Point your browser to **http://www.theatlantic.com/politics/abortion/myda.htm.** After reading the report in the *Atlantic Monthly,* identify some of the specific phrases that were used on each side of the controversy.

Persuasive definition, as in these examples, occurs not only in public life but also in the public speaking classroom. Student Jon Peterson wanted to convince listeners that licensed deer hunting was not a bad thing. Unfortunately, most of his audience had the image of Bambi's mother in mind whenever he uttered the word *deer.* To alter this connotation, Jon created a different vision of what deer are like:

> The Disney cartoon version of a deer is touching. But the innocent creature portrayed in *Bambi* is just as inaccurate as Disney's version of a mouse called Mickey that stands on two feet and wears gloves. To farmers trying to protect their crops, suburbanites trying to grow shrubbery, even nuns trying to tend their garden, overpopulated deer have become large rats with hooves. They eat everything in sight and leave a wake of destruction in their path.

Every speaker has important resources of definition. If your topic is an unpopular proposal to increase students' tuition and fees, you will induce very different reactions in listeners by characterizing the proposal as "extortion" rather than as "fair pricing." Likewise, even though you cannot affect how society views an issue such as health care, you *can* affect how your audience will view it—by deciding, for instance, whether to define national health insurance as "cost containment" or as "socialized medicine." Your ability to use language in defining a situation will affect how your audience perceives and reacts to it.

Achieving Clarity, Rhythm, and Vividness

Just as you can affect the style of a speech by making persuasive definitions, so you can affect its style through language that creates clarity, rhythm, and vividness. Figure 10.1 lists the strategies that we will consider to achieve these three goals.

Clarity

Because listeners usually cannot replay your speech, you should make the speech as easy to comprehend as is appropriate for the situation. The following stylistic resources can increase the clarity of your message.

Clarity	Rhythm	Vividness
• Concrete words • Maxims • Limiting jargon and defining technical terms • Word economy • Active voice • Careful use of irony • Purposeful ambiguity	• Repetition • Parallel wording • Antithesis • Inversions of word order	• Description • Stories • Comparisons: simile and metaphor • Vivid sounds: alliteration and onomatopoeia • Personification • Reference to hypothetical people: dialogue and rhetorical questions

Figure 10.1 Achieving clarity, rhythm, and vividness.

Concrete Words. If listeners have to puzzle out the meaning of your words, they will be distracted from your train of thought. And if they don't decipher your meaning correctly, your message will not get through to them. Because most people process images more easily than abstract concepts, your message will be clearer if you use concrete words and images. The speaker who tries to help listeners grasp the magnitude of "a trillion dollars" by calculating the length of a line of dollar bills laid end to end may be offering a trite example, but the effort is sensible. Concrete, clear images help an audience grasp and remember a message; as a result, listeners are more likely to be swayed by it.

Maxims. **Maxims,** or aphorisms, are short, pithy statements—often in the form of proverbs—that are familiar to most people and can be used to describe a situation or idea. The speaker who wants to downplay the fears of critics who have suggested obstacles to his plan to reform the fraternity system might say, in the words of a popular commercial for athletic apparel, "Just do it." This maxim succinctly expresses an idea that most people will grasp intuitively: An idea can be talked to death; sometimes, one just has to act. Maxims contribute to clarity by offering listeners a memorable phrase that encompasses a larger argument or theme.

Limiting Jargon, Defining Technical Terms. Virtually every field of knowledge has **jargon**—specialized or technical terms that outsiders find difficult to understand. Lawyers, for example, speak of "torts," "probable cause," and "incompetent testimony," but few who are not trained in law will know exactly what these terms mean. Similarly, when student Tracy Hocutt gave a speech about artificial turf, she tossed around such terms as *turf burns* and *staph infections*. Although this is common language for athletes, Tracy was talking over the heads of most of her audience.

Science, athletics, religion, medicine, music, accounting, and even public speaking have specialized languages that make it easier for people within the field to discuss issues and to understand each other. But because specialized terms and jargon may confuse outsiders, you should avoid using them in a speech. The reason is simple: Unless all your listeners are familiar with the specialized meanings, such terms will make your speech difficult to comprehend. And unless *you yourself* are very familiar with the field and its specialized language, you run the risk of using the terms inaccurately or inappropriately.

maxim
A concise statement of a principle, often in the form of a proverb; also called an *aphorism*.

jargon
Specialized or technical terms within a given field of knowledge.

The listener has just one chance to understand the speaker's message. The successful speaker can help to make that happen by seeking to achieve clarity, rhythm, and vividness while speaking.

Even places can generate a specialized language. Every college campus, for example, has its own terms to designate campus landmarks, types of courses, procedures and rules, and the like. If you're speaking on campus or addressing an alumni audience, you can use these terms freely, especially to help establish common bonds with your audience. Jargon is not a problem when everyone knows what it means. But if you're speaking to a general audience, you should avoid specialized terms for the same reason that you avoid professional jargon—to make your meaning clear.

It's not always possible to rid your speech of every last **technical term.** There may be no easily understood equivalent for the term, or it may be important to distinguish the technical term from a more general, popularized concept. In such cases, use technical terms as needed, but be sure to define them clearly and carefully. Some good strategies are to repeat the definition, to restate it differently, or to offer examples that illustrate it.

Word Economy. You can increase the clarity of your message through **word economy**—using words efficiently and avoiding unnecessary words. Listeners find it difficult and tiresome to follow a speech that beats around the bush, that is cluttered with digressions, extraneous ideas, inexact wording, and nervous asides such as *like, okay, now,* or *right* in nearly every sentence. If you record and listen to one of your speeches, you may be surprised to discover the amount of such clutter and to hear how it obscures the clarity of your message. Try to identify the things you do that create clutter; then, make a conscious effort to reduce it. Especially avoid overly complex sentences, excessive use of adjectives and adverbs, and needless hedging terms or qualifiers.

Active Voice. In writing and speaking, we can distinguish between the **active voice,** which focuses on *who did what;* and the **passive voice,** which

technical term
A term that may or may not be widely used in ordinary conversation but that has a specific meaning within a particular field of knowledge.

word economy
Efficiency in the use of words; avoidance of unnecessary words.

active voice
A word pattern that focuses on who did what and prominently features the agent.

passive voice
A word pattern that focuses on what was done and largely ignores the agent.

focuses on *what was done*. The sentence "John hit the ball" is in the active voice and emphasizes the person performing the action. In contrast, "The ball was hit by John" is in the passive voice and emphasizes the consequences of the action. Notice that the passive voice is much less personal than the active voice.

For clarity, you generally should use the active voice. It makes clear who does what, and it usually requires fewer and simpler words to express an idea. Use the passive voice only when the person really does not matter to your point or when the person might detract attention from the act or consequences you want to emphasize.

How Clear Should You Be?

We began this section by observing that you want to be as clear as is appropriate. That is not always the same thing as saying "exactly what you mean" and being so clear that the speech is transparent. Here are two uses of language that enable you, when circumstances call for it, to be a bit more subtle than that.

Careful Use of Irony. Speakers use **irony** when they say the opposite of what they mean, often with a shift in vocal tone or some other nonverbal clue that they do not intend to be taken literally. If you recite a long list of complaints about the quality of the campus food service and then conclude by saying, "No one, it seems, can find fault with the food on our campus"—while really meaning the opposite—you have made an ironic statement. Listeners may chuckle as they realize the great gulf between what you're saying and the reality that you have just described. The reason to use irony in this situation is that you might not want your criticism to be too harsh. You don't want to seem like you are whining or that you are impossible to please, because either of those reactions would cause the people in charge of food service to dismiss your complaints without acting on them. So you coat what you say in an ironic expression that is like a disarming smile. Listeners hear what you say, figure out what you really mean, and realize that you remained in good humor even while being critical.

Likewise, a speaker once referred to a group of tabloid publications at the supermarket checkout counter as "learned journals" in order gently to make the point that the information in these publications should not be given much weight. Carefully used, irony also can be a way for speakers to signal to the audience that they take their ideas seriously but don't take themselves too seriously.

Be aware, however, that irony can make a speech less clear if listeners cannot recognize it as irony. Student Mark Nielson tried to mock animal rights activists in a speech ironically "praising" them:

> We have come here to praise those brave souls, standing out in the rain with their dogs shivering in the cold as they stand up against the inhumane treatment of animals.

irony
Saying or writing the opposite of what is meant.

Mark thought that his use of irony was clear; to his dismay, however, he learned that most listeners thought he was sincere in commending the activists. If you decide to use irony, be certain to provide enough clues so that listeners will not be in doubt about what you really mean.[13]

Purposeful Ambiguity. Words or phrases that can be interpreted in more than one way are said to be **ambiguous,** and speakers striving for clarity generally avoid them. If you use the word *conviction* in a context in which some listeners think you mean "deeply held belief" and others think you mean "judgment of guilt," you probably will not have everyone understand you. But there are some cases in which a speaker deliberately and purposefully uses ambiguity.

The presidential election of 2000 turned on the vote in Florida, where the outcome was a virtual tie. In contesting the award of the state to George W. Bush, Al Gore alleged that thousands of votes had not yet been counted. Bush insisted that they had been both counted and recounted. The disagreement turned on what it meant to "count" a vote. The ballots in question had been run through counting machines, but no presidential vote had been recorded. Bush thought they had been counted, because they had been processed; Gore thought they had not, because they had not been tallied for anyone. But each found it advantageous to leave the term *count* ambiguous. Bush could portray Gore as persisting beyond reason in his challenge, and Gore could portray Bush as disregarding the wishes of thousands of Floridians. Meanwhile, each speaker could act as though the audience clearly agreed with his interpretation of the term, even though he never made that interpretation explicit.

Public speakers often engage in purposeful ambiguity when they use language to provide a rallying point for listeners who have different interests and agendas. In this case, the ambiguous reference is called a **condensation symbol,** because it condenses harmoniously in one word or phrase a variety of attitudes that might diverge if the reference were more specific.[14]

The phrase "family values" is a good example of a condensation symbol. Virtually everyone can be expected to value families, but "family values" may conjure up an array of very different themes. For example, both pro-life and pro-choice supporters believe that their position on the abortion issue better promotes "family values." Most people—whether loggers protesting the loss of jobs because of laws that protect forests or environmental activists concerned about the future of "the human family"—may view their own position as the one that most values families. Without ambiguity, it would be impossible to enlist the power of family imagery to draw support from listeners with so many different opinions and interests.

Condensation symbols are especially useful when addressing an audience that is culturally diverse. They are **multivocal,** meaning that they communicate on many different levels at once. Diverse audience members hear a condensation symbol as having different denotations but a common connotation, whether positive or negative. When a politician advocates "putting children first," one listener will see the need for new government programs to benefit children. Another, thinking the budget is tight, will want to cut other programs to redirect resources to children's programs. A third, who supports children's legal rights, will want to give priority to their well-being even if it means removing them from abusive adults. The term means something different to each listener, but all three agree that protecting children is a high priority. The multivocal term enabled the speaker to embrace different levels of meaning. The goal, then, is not always to avoid ambiguity altogether but to limit it to the appropriate level for your specific audience and situation.

ambiguous
Capable of being interpreted with more than one meaning.

condensation symbol
A word, phrase, or thing that harmoniously accommodates (condenses) diverse ideas or references within a single positive or negative connotation.

multivocal
Speaking simultaneously with different "voices" or on different levels of denotative meaning but with similar connotations.

Rhythm

Because a speech is heard, not read, the sound of the message contributes greatly to its stylistic effect. Language choices that affect the **rhythm,** or pace, of the speech can help to convey a mood—of loftiness, of momentum, or of equilibrium, for example. Moreover, listeners who grasp the pattern of the rhythm can anticipate what is coming next. This feeling of being in the know makes them more active participants in the speech situation. These effects of rhythm on listeners make clear that it is not just embellishment for the speech; it is integral to the speaker's achieving his or her purpose. The following stylistic resources are especially useful in affecting the rhythm of a speech.

Repetition. Repeating a key idea, argument, or theme is a way to emphasize its significance. The speaker who says, "The incarceration rate in the United States is astonishingly high—higher than Canada's, higher than England's, higher than Singapore's, higher even than China's," has left little doubt that the central point is the magnitude of the U.S. incarceration rate. Properly used, repetition acts like bold or italic type in printed material. It tells the audience, "Here is a really important idea." Use repetition selectively, however, or its power will diminish.

Another kind of repetition is a refrain that the speaker begins and the audience joins in or completes. Knowing that the speaker will be pausing for the refrain holds listeners' attention, and shouting out the refrain involves them actively in the speech. Political speakers often use such a repetitive refrain to rally support, and it is also common in protest rallies. Preachers, too—particularly in some mostly African American communities—are fond of using this pattern of **call and response** with their congregations.[15] This form of repetition helps the speaker and listeners bond as they jointly create the rhythmic pattern.

Parallel Wording. A speaker who uses one of the familiar organizational patterns described in Chapter 7 will find that listeners are following along and can guess what will come next. Assume that your topic is unemployment. If you begin by saying, "Here's how unemployment developed in the past," and then you ask, "What's the nature of unemployment in the present?" a careful listener will guess that your next major organizational unit will have something to do with the future. You can further emphasize this pattern, and heighten its effect, by using parallel wording:

> Unemployment has been a tragedy in the past.
> Unemployment is a tragedy in the present.
> Unemployment will continue to be a tragedy in the future.

Parallel wording is stylistically useful even at levels lower than the statement of main ideas. The challenging candidate who insists that the incumbent is "out of luck, out of touch, and come November will be out of office" has created a parallel pattern that listeners can follow easily and in which many can participate. By the time the speaker says, "come November," most listeners can probably figure out that the last item will be "out of office." The rhythm of the three-part pattern is catchy and easy to remember, and being involved in creating it will make listeners more likely to accept it.

rhythm
The sense of movement or pacing within a speech.

call and response
A pattern in which the audience responds to a speaker's questions or prompts, often with a repetitive refrain.

Antithesis. Another rhythmic resource is **antithesis,** the pairing of opposites within the speech. Besides suggesting to listeners that the speaker is clever, antithesis also creates a kind of equilibrium, or balance, in which competing views are weighed and taken seriously. As was mentioned earlier, President John F. Kennedy was noted for his stylistic effectiveness as a speaker, and most particularly for his use of antithesis. In his inaugural address, for example, he said, "Let us never negotiate out of fear. But let us never fear to negotiate." In promoting individual responsibility and voluntarism, he said, "Ask not what your country can do for you—ask what you can do for your country." The first parts of these statements acknowledge that there are limitations and concerns; the second parts transcend them. The use of antithesis suggests that the speaker is aware of the concerns but is prepared to deal with them.

Inversions of Word Order. Variations from normal word order, even if they are not antitheses, may cause listeners to sit up and take notice because an unusual phrase is memorable. In spoken English, the normal word order is subject–verb–object. A variation on this, if not overdone, will attract notice simply because the sound of the speech is different from what is expected. In Kennedy's speech, the phrase "Ask not" differs from the more normal word order, "Do not ask." This inversion attracts extra attention to the sentence.

Vividness

Beyond clarity and rhythm, a third stylistic resource is the ability to make sentences or paragraphs **vivid**—to present in words what are really compelling visual images, pictures that listeners can see in their mind's eye. Not only does vividness add color and interest, but also it makes the speech easier to understand. Again, a variety of stylistic resources are available to make your speech vivid.

Description. Probably the most common way to paint mental pictures is by **description,** by giving specific details. Nearly every day we describe someone in terms of gender and age, height and weight, color of eyes and hair, occupation and interests, style of dress, characteristic attitudes, relationships with others, and so on. The composite of all these details creates the mental picture or image of that person.

Similarly, a speaker can use an accumulation of details to describe an event, a place, or a situation. Student speaker Jennifer Frantz used that strategy to set the tone for an antidrug speech; she began by describing a Swiss park called the Platzspitz:

> It was once a tranquil park, where families could picnic and children could play. Now it is covered with syringes, infested with rats, and inhabited by addicts who no longer have hope. When you see a mother, a father, and a small child lying on the ground and suddenly the mother wakes up, reaches out, and violently shoves a needle into her leg, you begin to wonder what the world is coming to.

Stories. A story has power not only because of its familiar narrative form but also because it permits listeners to "see" what is going on and to iden-

antithesis
The pairing of opposites within a speech, often to suggest a choice between them.

vivid
Graphic, easy to picture. A speech is vivid if its language enables listeners to develop mental pictures of what is being said.

description
A cumulation of details that suggest a mental picture of a person, event, or situation.

tify with it. An issue such as homelessness, for example, is much more compelling to listeners when the speaker tells a story rather than discusses it in the abstract. The speaker might describe a typical day in the life of a particular homeless person: the contempt in the eyes of passersby, the daily search for food, the difficulty of bathing and grooming, and the cold and dangerous night on the street. The sequence of events will make vivid for the audience what it is like to be homeless even for one day. Listeners will be drawn into the story and will be better able to empathize with the homeless and to understand their problems.

Comparisons: Simile and Metaphor. In Chapter 6, we saw that analogy is a powerful form of reasoning; a comparison can help people to accommodate a new idea or new information by deciding that it is similar to what they already know or believe. Comparisons can be made vivid by using similes and metaphors.

A **simile** is an explicit statement that one thing is like another. Responding to a proposal that the drinking age be reduced to sixteen, a speaker might say, "That's *like* giving a stick of dynamite to a baby." The simile clearly invites the audience to see the new or the unknown in familiar terms. Knowing the obvious absurdity of giving a stick of dynamite to a baby, listeners can see that the proposed lower drinking age is a bad idea.

A **metaphor** discusses one thing *in terms* of another. Rather than stating that one thing is *like* another, it assumes as much and names the thing as though it actually were the other. A speaker who refers to a new dormitory as "the Taj Mahal" is not explicitly saying that the dorm is like the Taj Mahal but is assuming so and is inviting listeners to see it in terms of the Taj Mahal. The metaphor thus makes more vivid the disparity between the new dorm and older, less luxurious housing.

Similarly, when former Vice President Al Gore said while campaigning, "We're going to put the Social Security surplus in a lock box," he was not speaking literally. The Social Security surplus is an accounting transaction; it is not "put" anywhere. The point of Gore's statement is to emphasize to listeners that he will not permit this surplus to be diverted to other spending. Referring to an accounting device as a "lock box" helps to make the point far more vivid.

These examples illustrate how metaphors work. Audiences are familiar with and easily able to visualize one of the terms of the metaphor (called the "vehicle")—the Taj Mahal in the first example, a lock box in the second. The thoughts and emotions that listeners associate with this term are then transferred to the other term (called the "tenor")—the new dormitory or the Social Security surplus.[16]

Vivid Sounds: Alliteration and Onomatopoeia. You also can create vividness in a speech through patterns of sound.

Alliteration is a repetitive consonant sound, as in "Tiny Tim" and "Big Bang." Former Vice President Spiro Agnew reveled in such phrases as "the nattering nabobs of negativism." Another politician called for reform "in our communities, our countryside, and our classrooms," repeating the hard *c*. The value of alliteration is that it makes it easier to remember the items arranged in a parallel pattern.

Onomatopoeia is the use of sounds that resemble what they describe. In the phrase "the hissing of the snake," the *s* sounds simulate the very hissing

---

simile
An explicit statement that one thing is *like* another.

metaphor
Naming one thing *in terms of* another; discussing one thing as though it were another.

alliteration
Repetitive consonant sounds.

onomatopoeia
Use of sounds that resemble what they describe.

---

that the speaker wants listeners to imagine. Similarly, people often describe the slow passage of time simply by saying, "tick-tock, tick-tock."

When used sparingly and purposefully, both alliteration and onomatopoeia add sound to mental images, making them more vivid.

Personification. A powerful means of achieving vividness is through **personification,** the discussion of abstract or complex ideas in human terms. In a speech about homelessness, talking about "a day in the life of Sam Walters" is likely to be far more vivid than talking about homelessness as a set of abstract social problems. Personification makes issues concrete and enables listeners to identify with another specific person.

President Ronald Reagan often used personification in his speeches. In his 1987 State of the Union address, he talked about "the kids on Christmas Day looking out from a frozen sentry post on the 38th Parallel in Korea or aboard an aircraft carrier in the Mediterranean—a million miles from home but doing their duty" and "farmers in tough times, who never stop feeding a hungry world" and "the volunteers at the hospital choking back their tears for the hundredth time, caring for a baby struggling for life because of a mother who used drugs." By using these personifications, the president made the point that Americans are heroes far more vividly than he would have by simply stating it as an abstract proposition. Presidents following Reagan have tried with varying success to use the same technique, most obviously in their State of the Union addresses.

Reference to Hypothetical People. The charge is often made that speeches are one-way communications in which listeners are passive and don't participate in the give-and-take of ideas. A speaker can combat the sense that a speech is unexciting by incorporating hypothetical people into it, either through dialogue or by asking rhetorical questions.

Dialogue draws the audience in by reproducing a conversation within the speech, including what both dialogue partners said. Here's how student Beverly Watson used dialogue in a speech about student government:

> I was discussing campus elections yesterday with my roommate. She said, "People don't vote because the elections are a mockery." But I insisted, "The problem is just that there isn't enough publicity." She said, "You're very naive." I said, "And you're far too cynical." Then she began to defend her position.

Although the listeners are still spectators, to be sure, dialogue lets them witness a lively interaction between people. The "overheard" conversation gets them more involved in the speech.

Sometimes, a speaker uses dialogue to refer to opponents' objections—usually anonymously—and then to answer them. Comments such as "There are those who say . . ." or "And then you might ask . . ." or "I hear it said . . ." allow the speaker to state and refute a variety of arguments. Richard Nixon's famous "Checkers" speech of 1952 (when he was a senator running for the vice presidency) took this approach to respond to charges that he had benefited personally from a secret fund established by his political supporters. Nixon admitted there was a fund but insisted that "Not one cent of the . . . money of that type ever went to me for my personal use." To more fully satisfy his critics, he then engaged in hypothetical dialogue: "But then some of you will say, and rightly, 'Well, what did you use the fund for, Senator? Why did you have to have it?' " Nixon speaks as though "some of you" were actu-

personification
Discussion of abstract or complex ideas in human terms.

dialogue
Reproducing a conversation within a speech.

ally present, talking with him. He states "your" concerns and then proceeds to answer them, and "you" as a listener hear both sides of the dialogue. If the speaker has analyzed the audience well and identifies the real concerns on listeners' minds, this can be an effective way to respond to them.

The use of **rhetorical questions** is another way to involve others hypothetically. As you learned in Chapter 8, a rhetorical question is one for which you do not really expect an answer. You ask the question solely to make the audience think about an issue and to quickly reach the obvious answer, which you already know. The "Checkers" speech illustrates this approach to vividness as well. To talk about why the secret fund was necessary, Nixon first asked listeners some questions:

> Do you think that when I or any other senator makes a political speech, has it printed, [we] should charge the printing of that speech and the mailing of that speech to the taxpayers?

> Do you think, for example, when I or any other senator makes a trip to his home state to make a purely political speech that the cost of that trip should be charged to the taxpayers?

> Do you think when a Senator makes political broadcasts . . . that the expense of those broadcasts should be charged to the taxpayers?

Nixon raised these questions because he assumed that listeners would agree that the answer is "No." That set the stage to say that a special fund was needed because these expenditures should not be "charged to the taxpayers."

Style and the Entire Speech

Having examined a variety of stylistic resources relating to word choice and arrangement, it is time to step back, change our perspective, and consider the style of the speech as a whole.

Choosing the Right Level of Style

Classical writers on public speaking distinguished among three levels of style: The *grand style* is majestic, lofty, and formal; the *plain style* is simple and colloquial; and the *middle style* falls somewhere between those two poles.[17]

Our society has largely abandoned the grand style, but not entirely. African American speakers such as Jesse Jackson often bring the grand style of the church sermon into the political arena. Similarly, speakers from some Latin cultures may use indirection or flowery language that characterizes the grand style, and some speakers from Eastern cultures may use a style that relies more on embroidered narrative than on logical demonstration.

Still, most people in mainstream U.S. society overwhelmingly favor the plain style, viewing the grand style as a relic of nineteenth-century orations that often lasted several hours. Most of us prefer understatement to overstatement. We use figures of speech and other stylistic resources not so much for ornamentation as for how they contribute to the clarity of an argument. It is a serious mistake, however, to confuse plainness with artlessness. The "plain" style is not as plain as it sometimes seems. Nor is it natural. Rather, it is carefully crafted of simple sentences, familiar words, the active voice, and a clear progression from one idea to the next.

rhetorical question
A question for which no answer is expected; it is asked to get listeners thinking so that they quickly recognize the obvious answer.

Using Language Effectively

Excerpt from Darbi Howard's Speech on the Nineteenth Amendment

Darbi Howard

Before women attained the right to suffrage, they were incapable of reaching their potential as citizens, as workers, and as human beings; this right gave women a voice. No longer were elections just about men, jobs, and the economy, but about health, well-being, and the rights of all people. Women transformed from quiet and meek followers to proud and ambitious equals.

Since 1919, women have worked their way up from housewives to business owners. They can make just as much money as, if not more than, any man. Women such as Amelia Earhart, first woman to fly a plane; Dr. Mae Jemison, first African American woman in space; and Oprah Winfrey, media mogul and billionaire have all made huge impacts on the world.

Prof. Blivens

Darbi, the use of juxtaposition of women's roles before and after the Nineteenth Amendment works effectively in the first part of the speech. This reinforces the impact that the Nineteenth Amendment had both for women themselves, and, how others viewed them. Watch using overstatement, though; for example, some women would probably take issue with the last sentence in the first paragraph. Making a bold statement can work to your advantage, but be careful of oversimplifying an issue in doing so. Also, in the second paragraph, good use of parallel wording, naming off women who've been successful continues to show the audience the long term impact of the Nineteenth Amendment. Overall, your language reinforces the impact of this amendment and really brings home why this was such an important piece of legislation!

Finding the Right Pace and Proportion

Variety. Using all the stylistic resources we examined in connection with words, sentences, and paragraphs—or using the same few over and over—will call attention to your style rather than to your ideas. This detracts from the audience's perception of the speech as a unified whole. The alternative is variety—in the resources you use, in how often you use them, and so on. Stylistic variety will keep any particular technique from calling attention to itself and will contribute to a pleasing overall impression of the speech.

Balance. A speech that is uniform in style may not sustain the audience's attention and interest. If the entire speech is concrete and anecdotal, listeners may miss the larger point that the examples are trying to make; but if the speech is completely abstract and theoretical, they may not see how it relates to their own experience. If the speech is entirely intense and gripping, listeners may experience "emotional overload"; but if it is completely dispassionate and low key, they may decide that the speaker does not really care about the subject.

A speech loaded with alliteration and antithesis may call attention to these devices rather than to the purposes for which they are used, but a speech that has no interesting turns of phrase may strike listeners as dull. In these cases and in all matters of style, an effective balance among available resources will enhance the overall style of the speech.

Conciseness. Many writers say that it is easier to write a long book than a short one, because editing one's own thoughts is so difficult. In the same way, it often is easier to speak for thirty minutes than for ten. (Although that may surprise you, it's true. As you research your topic, you'll find more and more material that you want to include, and deciding to omit any of it will be difficult.) Particularly in modern American culture, however, speeches that go on for too long or that lack a clear, compact thesis and structure usually will not be judged as exhibiting good style. Today's audiences tend to value messages that are brief, stripped of adornment, to the point, and concise.

Memorable Phrases

Many classic speeches are remembered because of a particular line or phrase. Examples include William Jennings Bryan's "Cross of Gold" speech; Martin Luther King, Jr.'s "I Have a Dream" speech; and Sojourner Truth's "Ain't I a Woman?" speech. A pithy phrase or quotable quote that somehow captures the essence of the speech is today called a **sound bite,** because it is often the only part of the speech that receives media coverage. Former President Clinton's misleading the public about his affair with a White House intern is remembered for the sound bite, "I did not have sexual relations with that woman, Miss Lewinsky." Similarly, the popular-culture phrase "Show me the money" is a sound bite that conveys a sense of skepticism or distrust. But whether you are addressing 25 classmates or a national television audience, a memorable phrase prevents listeners from forgetting your speech and also enhances their judgment of its style.

Congruence of Language and Delivery

Finally, the language of the speech should match your style of delivery (which we will examine in Chapter 11). If your topic and language are serious and formal, your delivery should not be casual and informal, and vice versa. Generally, classroom speeches are informal in both style and delivery. But you may sometimes speak in a more formal situation, and it is important that your choice of language and style of delivery match.

Achieving Good Style

We have been talking about stylistic choices that involve careful planning and forethought. But if you deliver a speech extemporaneously and cannot labor over each word, how can you possibly pay so much attention to language? And isn't it better, anyway, to focus on the content of your message and just talk naturally? Is it realistic to expect any speaker these days, especially a beginning student speaker, really to focus on style?

These are good questions, and you probably have thought about them. Obviously, no one expects to attain the stylistic talent of Winston Churchill, Jesse Jackson, or Ronald Reagan, at least not right away. But you have to start someplace. And lurking behind those questions are two erroneous assumptions about speeches. If you can correct those errors, you will be on the way to understanding how to develop a good style.

Erroneous Assumptions About Speeches

One mistaken assumption about speeches might be called the "plain-style myth"—the belief that people naturally speak in the plain style and have to

sound bite
A memorable phrase that is recalled from a speech and used to identify the speech.

exert effort only to achieve the grand style. Far from being impromptu, however, the plain style may require several outlines and hours of preparation. Few of us speak extemporaneously as clearly or as precisely as we would like. (To test this claim, record an impromptu speech and play it back; you may be surprised at how unclear or awkward your language usage is.) Most of us have to force ourselves to simplify, to consolidate, to focus, and to delete language in order to make the speech artfully plain. *Any* style requires preparation.

WWW. Using the Internet

Using Language for Effect

Review the **Glossary of Rhetorical Terms with Examples** to explore various language strategies that help make an impression, evoke emotion, and create an impact on listeners. Point your browser to **http://www.uky.edu/ArtsSciences/Classics/rhetoric.html#23**.

Equally mistaken is a second belief: that a focus on style is somehow at odds with attending to the content of the speech. As we've seen in this chapter, "content" and "language" are not completely separate categories. Content becomes meaningful as it is expressed in language, and speakers' choices about style and language affect listeners' perceptions of what the content actually is. When we talk about what a speaker "said," then, we are talking about both content and language. So yes, it pays for speakers—even beginning speakers—to focus on achieving style through language.

Suggestions for Developing and Improving Style

1. Review your preparation outline and your presentation outline from the standpoint of style and word choice. Incorporate key phrases and stylistic choices into the preparation outline so that you won't lose track of them when you speak.

2. Practice composing speeches in writing. Although you will seldom speak from manuscript, actually writing out a speech can help you focus on style; it creates a specific text that you can examine and revise to improve your style. This exercise also will help you make stylistic choices when you speak extemporaneously.

Practicing the speech and then viewing yourself on videotape, trying to anticipate how you look and sound to an audience, can be an important step in achieving an effective speaking style.

3. Be your own toughest critic when revising your outline or manuscript for style. Are key ideas and arguments worded as effectively as possible? Does your language make the message easy or difficult for the audience to remember? Does the speech seem interesting or tedious? Use the stylistic resources discussed in this chapter to modify your speech and enhance your style.

4. Practice your speech, not only to become more familiar with its contents and to gain self-confidence but also to listen to its overall rhythm. Does the speech "move" in the way you would like? Does the climax occur at the place in the speech where you intend it to be? If the answers to these questions are negative, you can revise the speech to make appropriate adjustments.

5. Consider how your speech might incorporate the stylistic resources discussed in this chapter. For example, identify any similes or rhetorical questions that you might use. Then practice the speech, and ask yourself whether the stylistic devices really enhanced the overall quality. If not, be ruthless in omitting them. But if a device seems to work, don't be afraid to keep it in. You can apply this process to each of the stylistic devices in this chapter: Invent alterations, try them out, and assess their contributions to the speech.

6. Raise your awareness of other speakers' styles. Read some classic speeches, and try to identify how each speaker achieved the style for which the speech is known. Watch videotapes of contemporary well-known speakers, and analyze their stylistic choices. Listen carefully to classmates' speeches, and try to characterize each person's style. Listening critically to speeches of the past and present will make you more sensitive to the whole idea of stylistic choices—and also occasionally may give you ideas about how similar choices might enhance your own speeches.

7. Don't work on too many things at once. One advantage of giving several speeches in a course on public speaking is that you can focus on different skills in different speeches. It's unrealistic to expect solid research, flawless reasoning, perfect organization, and effective style all in the same beginning speech. But it's also true that all these elements work together to produce an effective speech. By focusing on and practicing a few skills at a time, you will make gradual progress toward integrating all of them.

Checklist 10.1 Strategic Language Choices

1. **Questions to ask yourself: After outlining my speech . . .**
   - Am I sure this will sound like a speech, not an essay?
   - Will my key terms have the connotations I want?
   - Does the language suggest momentum for the speech?
   - Is the language vivid and interesting?
2. **If the answer is "No," here are some things you might want to consider:**
   - Review your key-word choices, and put them in the speaking outline so you won't lose sight of them.
   - Record as you practice the speech; review the recording, and modify word choices to make the speech clearer and more oral.
   - Identify alternative ways to express your main ideas, and test whether they improve clarity or rhythm.
   - Insert appropriate figures of speech into the outline to make the speech more vivid.

Respecting Diversity Through Style and Language

Because language is so powerful, it sometimes can marginalize or offend listeners even though that was not the speaker's intent. These strategies will help you to avoid this mistake.

1. Avoid language that is vulgar, offensive, or patronizing.
2. Define technical terms so everyone knows what you are talking about and no one will feel ignorant.
3. In choosing between performative and conversational style, consider the cultural backgrounds and expectations of your audience.

Summary

Style is attributed to speakers by listeners, based on the distinctive pattern of choices made by speakers to express themselves. The language of a speech affects listeners' perceptions of both the message and the speaker. Oral style differs significantly from written style in its simplicity, repetition, informality, and reflexivity. Performative style also differs from conversational style. The basic requirements for effective style are accuracy and appropriateness to the audience and situation.

The speaker's powers of definition—particularly the connotative aspect and the concept of persuasive definition—are especially important. Other important considerations are clarity (achieved through the use of familiar and concrete terms, limiting the use of jargon, removing clutter, and employing the active voice); rhythm (including such matters as repetition, parallel wording, antithesis, and inversion of normal word order); and vividness. For the speech as a whole, the important criteria are the stylistic level (grand, middle, or plain), variety, balance, conciseness, memorable phrases, and congruence of language and delivery.

Conscious efforts to improve style may seem at odds with a natural or conversational tone, but the plain style is itself a work of art, not an off-the-cuff presentation as it sometimes may seem. Becoming more sensitive to other people's speeches and practicing composing your own are the recommended routes for enhancing your own speaking style.

Discussion Questions

1. What does it mean to say that content and style are interconnected? Try rewording the following statements. Do they have the same impact when you rephrase them? Discuss the ways in which word choice helped to convey the meaning in these passages.
   a. "I have a dream that my four little children will one day live in a nation where they will not be judged by the color of their skin but by

the content of their character."—Martin Luther King, Jr., "I Have a Dream" Speech

    b. "The mystic chords of memory, stretching from every battlefield and patriot grave to every living heart and hearthstone all over this broad land, will yet swell the chorus of the Union when again touched, as surely they will be, by the better angels of our nature."—Abraham Lincoln, First Inaugural

    c. "I remember: It happened yesterday or eternities ago. A young Jewish boy discovering the kingdom of night. I remember his bewilderment, I remember his anguish. It all happened so fast. The ghetto. The deportation. The sealed cattle car. The fiery altar upon which the history of our people and the future of mankind were meant to be sacrificed."—Elie Wiesel, Nobel Peace Prize Acceptance Speech

2. What connotations do people give for the following words? If you wanted to draw on the positive connotations for these words, what terms would you use?
   - Technology
   - Rhetoric
   - School
   - Marriage
   - Rap music

3. As a class, watch a videotape of a great orator. Discuss that orator's style. In what ways does he or she use language to achieve clarity, rhythm, and vividness? How do the language choices of that orator help achieve the purpose of the speech?

Activities

1. Adapt a written form to an oral form, and vice versa. (Note: To complete this activity, you will need a video or audio recorder.)
   a. Read an essay that you wrote for another class. Then put the essay aside, and with a video or audio recorder capturing the event, describe the information in that essay as though you were making an oral presentation before a class. Do not look at the written essay when you make the presentation. When you are done, play the recording, and compare the written essay to your oral presentation. In what ways are they different?
   b. Record yourself giving an extemporaneous speech. Listen to the recording and transcribe that speech, word for word. Then transform that transcription into a form that is appropriate for a written essay. What did you have to change, and why?

2. Read the manuscript of a speech, and seek to discover which language devices are used to develop the style of the speech. Identify the use of at least five stylistic resources (such as persuasive definition, maxim, irony, purposeful ambiguity, repetition, parallel wording, antithesis, metaphor, alliteration, rhetorical question, and dialogue; see Figure 10.1 for a complete list). What effects do these resources have on the au-

dience? How do they create those effects? Why does the speaker use these resources in the way he or she does?

3. Write out your next speech in manuscript form, whether or not you plan to deliver it in that form. As you write this speech, think carefully about the language you are using. In the margins or in footnotes, annotate your manuscript, identifying the language resources that you chose and explaining why you used them in the way you did.

Notes

1. For more about style as choice, see Geoffrey N. Leech, *Style in Fiction: A Linguistic Introduction to English Fictional Prose*, New York: Longman, 1981; especially Chapter 1, "Style and Choice."
2. For more about generic types, see Kathleen Hall Jamieson, "Generic Constraints and the Rhetorical Situation," *Philosophy and Rhetoric* 6 (Summer 1973): 162–170.
3. For more about culture types, see Michael Calvin McGee, "The 'Ideograph': A Link between Rhetoric and Ideology," *Quarterly Journal of Speech* 66 (February 1980): 1–16.
4. For more about archetypes, see Michael Osborn, "Archetypal Metaphor in Rhetoric: The Light–Dark Family," *Quarterly Journal of Speech* 53 (April 1967): 115–126.
5. The style of Lincoln's Gettysburg Address is discussed in detail in Garry Wills, *Lincoln at Gettysburg: The Words That Remade America*, New York: Simon & Schuster, 1992.
6. Since classical times, rhetorical theorists have commented on the connection between ideas and language. See Marcus Tullius Cicero, *De Oratore*, translated by H. Rackham, Cambridge, Mass.: Harvard Univ. Press, 1982, pp. 23–24.
7. For a more thorough examination of the differences between written and oral forms, see Marcia Irene Macaulay, *Processing Varieties in English: An Examination of Oral and Written Speech Across Genres*, Vancouver: Univ. of British Columbia Press, 1990.
8. For an example of this argument, see Kathleen Hall Jamieson, *Eloquence in an Electronic Age: The Transformation of Political Speechmaking*, New York: Oxford, 1988.
9. This analysis disagrees with the conclusions of Todd S. Frobish, "Jamieson Meets Lucas: Eloquence and Pedagogical Model(s) in *The Art of Public Speaking*," *Communication Education* 49 (July 2000): 239–252, which represents the conversational style as being more universally applicable.
10. A modern handbook of such stylistic tools also exists. See Arthur Quinn, *Figures of Speech: Sixty Ways to Turn a Phrase*, Salt Lake City: Gibbs M. Smith, 1982.
11. The use of the term *freedom* as a persuasive definition is considered in Geoffrey Nunberg, "More Than Just Another Word for Nothing Left to Lose," *New York Times*, March 23, 2003, sec. 4, p. 6. See also Eric Foner, *The Story of American Freedom*, New York: W.W. Norton, 1998.
12. For an analysis of how definitions can affect the course of a controversy, see Douglas Walton, "Persuasive Definitions and Public Policy Arguments," *Argumentation and Advocacy* 37 (Winter 2001): 117–132.
13. For more about irony, see Wayne Booth, *Rhetoric of Irony*, Chicago: Univ. of Chicago Press, 1974.
14. However, it should be noted that ambiguity can have positive immediate effects that are followed by negative long-term effects. See David Zarefsky, *President Johnson's War on Poverty: Rhetoric and History*, Tuscaloosa: Univ. of Alabama Press, 1986.
15. See Jack L. Daniel and Geneva Smitherman, "How I Got Over: Communication Dynamics in the Black Community," *Quarterly Journal of Speech* 62 (February 1976): 26–39.
16. Much has been written about the way in which metaphors work. For a start on this subject, see I. A. Richards, *The Philosophy of Rhetoric*, New York: Oxford Univ. Press, 1965, Chapters 5 and 6; Max Black, "Metaphor," *Proceedings of the Aristotelian Society* 55 (1954–1955): 273–294; and George Lakoff and Mark Johnson, *Metaphors We Live By*, Chicago: Univ. of Chicago Press, 1980.
17. For example, see Marcus Tullius Cicero, *Orator*, translated by H. M. Hubbell, Cambridge, Mass.: Harvard Univ. Press, 1939, pp. 69–111.

Chapter Eleven

Presenting the Speech

In this chapter, we will:

- Identify the desirable characteristics of speech presentation, especially naturalness, support of the speaker's purpose, and empathy with the audience.

- Explore how the aspects of a speaker's voice (volume, pitch, rate, pauses, articulation, enunciation, and pronunciation) can support the presentation, and consider how variety in each aspect enhances the speech.

- Examine how the speaker's body (physical appearance, movement, gesture, and facial expression) can help make the presentation effective.

- Distinguish among four basic modes of speech presentation and explore the advantages and limitations of each.

- Suggest a general procedure for practicing the speech before presenting it formally.

People who fear speaking in public are usually anxious about some aspect of oral presentation. "What will I do with my hands?" "What if I forget my speech?" "How will I know if I'm talking too fast?" "Suppose I start shaking and can't control it?" Concerns such as these often lead people to avoid public speaking altogether.

Characteristics of Effective Presentation

Given this common anxiety about speaking in public, it might seem strange that we haven't focused on presenting the speech until now. We've explored how to analyze the audience, select and research a topic, test reasoning, organize the speech, and use language effectively. Why put off the very subject that so many speakers worry about most?

Well, strange as it seems, one of the *least* effective ways to improve your presentation is to concentrate on it directly. If you are self-conscious about what to do with your hands, for example, thinking about them will make you feel even more awkward—they'll suddenly seem like 50-pound weights. Worrying about using your hands will distract you (and your audience) from the subject of your speech. In fact, the best way to improve your presentation is to keep your attention on the speech and on the audience.

Why, then, should you study presentation at all if it might make you even more self-conscious? Because, by learning about the aspects of presentation and by practicing certain strategies, you can train yourself to speak "naturally" even if you are nervous about facing an audience.

Presentation is also called **delivery;** the two terms are used interchangeably to refer to how the voice and body help create the effect a speaker wants. The same ideas, even the same words, can elicit different reactions from an audience, depending on how you present them. Delivery, then, is much more than simply a way to "embellish" a speech. *How* a speaker says something affects *what* is really said, and so it also affects what listeners actually hear and understand.

Delivery that contributes positively to the overall effect of the speech does not call attention to itself or divert attention from the ideas in the speech. Rather, effective delivery will seem natural and uncontrived.

Moreover, effective delivery helps the audience to listen, understand, remember, and act on the speech. Listening carefully and critically to a speech is difficult; the presentation, if well done, will make it less so. Perhaps, by lowering your voice, you can make the audience listen more carefully when you state your main idea. Or well-timed pauses may signal the transitions in your argument, making it easier to follow. Or a gesture that points to the audience may help you personalize your call for action in the conclusion of the speech. Such examples of effective presentation can help you overcome the hurdles that listeners unconsciously put up to protect themselves from being influenced.

Effective delivery also builds a sense of community between speaker and audience. In most situations, the speaker wants to identify with listeners, wants to symbolize that they are all members of the same speaking/listening community. In other words, the speaker wants to show **empathy** with listeners, to give them a sense that he or she knows what they think and can feel what they feel. Empathy is usually achieved through presentation that

delivery
The presentation of the speech, using the voice and body to create the desired effect.

empathy
Feeling what listeners feel and knowing what they think.

invites audience members to listen and suggests that the speaker cares about them.

Now we will look closely at how both your voice and your body can enhance the presentation of a speech and help you build the desired relationship with listeners.

The Voice in Presentation

Unlike a singer, a speaker doesn't cultivate the voice as an end in itself, just to be expressive. Rather, a speaker uses the voice to advance the overall purpose of the speech.[1] Particularly important to realize is that vocal cues are among the audience's earliest evidence in judging a speaker's *ethos*.

Six dimensions of the voice can be drawn on to enhance your effectiveness as a speaker: volume, pitch, rate, pauses, articulation and enunciation, and pronunciation (see Figure 11.1). Any vocal pattern—no matter how pleasant it first sounds—can easily become monotonous and hence distracting. Therefore, to keep a speech interesting and to keep the audience listening, you want to create variety in the six dimensions of your voice.

Volume

Volume refers to loudness; the higher the volume, the louder the voice. But how loud should you speak? That will depend on the size and the shape of the setting and on whether or not you use a microphone. As a beginning speaker, you probably should err on the side of greater volume rather than of less (as long as you don't scream), in order to help convey a sense of self-confidence. To check and adjust your volume in any setting, watch listeners' reactions carefully when you begin to speak.

Besides regulating the overall loudness of your voice, remember to vary the volume at key points in the speech. You can emphasize an idea either by speaking louder or by lowering your voice. In both cases, listeners renew their attention because the vocal variety signals that they should listen carefully. By changing your volume, you can either understate an idea or overclaim it, depending on your purpose and the situation.

Feedback. Most audiences will let you know quickly if they cannot hear you, and their feedback will help you decide how loudly to speak. Also pay attention to the volume of other speakers and to how the audience reacts to them.

Students Brad Cummings, Alicia Lee, and Rosa Dominguez all gave classroom speeches on the same day. Brad was first, and he began in a very soft voice. Listeners had so much trouble hearing him that they moved forward in their seats and even cupped their ears with their hands. Unfortunately, for the first two minutes of his speech Brad looked only at his notes, and he missed the signal from the audience that he should speak more loudly. Alicia noticed the problem and was determined to avoid it when she spoke. But she overcompensated, speaking in a booming voice that made

WWW. Using the Internet

How Important Is the Voice in a Presentation?
Make that judgment after listening to at least two speeches from the **History Channel Archive of Great Speeches.** Point your browser to **http://www .historychannel.com/speeches/,** where you can find the speech featured for the day. Then, click on the link for "Archive" to browse the whole list of offerings. After listening to the two speeches, draw conclusions about which speaker made the best use of vocal qualities: volume, pitch, rate, pauses, articulation, enunciation, pronunciation, and inflection.

volume
Loudness of voice.

Figure 11.1 Dimensions of vocal quality.

Volume	Loudness
Pitch	Placement on the musical scale
Rate	Speed; number of words per minute
Pauses	Silences for emphasis or transition
Articulation and enunciation	Clarity and distinctness of individual sounds or words
Pronunciation	The accepted way to sound a given word

some listeners so uncomfortable that they actually pushed their chairs farther away and covered their ears. When Rosa's turn came, she knew that her volume should be somewhere between Brad's and Alicia's.

Amplification. Before microphones and electronic amplification, speakers seldom had the option of using a low volume, because they could not be heard by the listeners farthest away. Speakers had to talk loudly and to project the voice from deep in the diaphragm so that it had greater carrying power. Today, if the audience is large, you can choose to use a microphone to amplify your voice; this gives you the option of speaking at lower volumes.

It takes some practice to use a microphone effectively, however. You need to speak more slowly and to articulate words more distinctly so that they will not become slurred through amplification. Position your mouth a few inches from the microphone, and speak directly into it. If you hear static or noises or your voice feeds back to you, move farther from the microphone and speak more softly. Don't wait until the time of your speech to test the microphone, and make sure that it is turned on if you plan to use it. You'll undercut the power of your introduction if you have to stop to ask, "Can everyone hear me?"

Since most classroom speeches are not amplified, you need to learn to project your voice adequately by controlling volume and the other dimensions of vocal quality. But because so many auditoriums, large meeting rooms, and outdoor rallies require the use of amplification, you also should look for opportunities to practice speaking with a microphone.

Pitch

When we say that someone's voice is "high" or "low," we are referring to its **pitch**—the placement of the voice on the musical scale. A soprano has a higher pitch than a bass. The pitch of a voice is determined by the speed with which sound waves vibrate. The faster the vibration, the higher the pitch—and voice.

As shown in Figure 11.2, the normal pitch for any speaker is within a fairly narrow range. But extending higher and lower than normal pitch is a larger range within which both speaker and listeners will be comfortable. You can raise or lower your pitch within this range for emphasis, and listeners will still find it pleasant to hear you. The widest range that the speaker is physically able to produce includes extreme pitches that are difficult for an audience to listen to. Extremely high pitches grate on the ears, like fingernails scratching a chalkboard; and extremely low pitches are distorted and too resonant, which most listeners also find displeasing.

Probably the most distracting pitch range for listeners is a **monotone**—a very narrow, unchanging range that is used for the entire speech. Audiences

pitch
Placement of the voice on the musical scale, ranging from high to low.

monotone
A very narrow, unchanging pitch range.

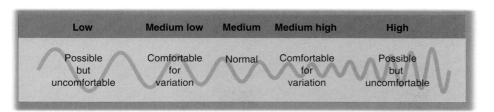

Figure 11.2 Ranges of pitch.

quickly tire of it, and they tune it out; some people even fall asleep, lulled by the droning voice of the speaker. Because most people have a wider range of comfortable pitches than they customarily use, there's no reason to speak in a monotone. By varying your pitch, you can sustain the audience's interest, signal transitions in the speech, and emphasize important ideas.

If you record yourself delivering a speech, you may well discover that your pitch is higher on tape than it sounds to you when you are speaking. Two factors account for this. First, your ability to hear your own voice is always distorted. Second, pitch rises under stress, and giving a speech is stressful for many people. The key to a pleasant pitch is to relax as much as possible. Control your breathing so that you have enough air to complete each sentence; relax your shoulder muscles; and project your voice from deep in your body rather than forcing it from your throat.

Rate

Rate is the speed at which a person speaks. The average rate is between 120 and 150 words per minute, but successful speakers vary considerably. John F. Kennedy typically spoke at a faster rate than did Ronald Reagan, and yet both presidents were immensely persuasive speakers.

Stereotype suggests that there also are distinct regional variations in rate—Southerners talk slower than Midwesterners do, and Easterners talk faster. In fact, regional differences in rate are much less dramatic than they used to be, partly because people move more often and partly because radio and television have created a national audience. Today, for example, many Southerners have just as rapid a speaking rate as anyone else.

Two factors that we considered in connection with pitch—stress and variety—also apply to rate.

Stress. Like pitch, rate goes up when a person is under stress. Students who practice their speech and time it to fill the ten minutes required by the assignment may be surprised that the speech takes only six minutes when they deliver it in class. This happens not because they timed it inaccurately or forgot a large portion of the speech but because they sped up their rate under the stress of presentation.

Racing through your speech makes it difficult for the audience to follow and comprehend your ideas; listeners simply don't have time to process and react to what they hear. The remedy, as with pitch, is to control your breathing and relax. Pause frequently for breath, taking in enough air to complete each statement. And remember to watch for feedback from the audience since you also want to avoid speaking too slowly. A speech delivered at a very slow rate will tire listeners and will give them time to think about things other than your ideas.

rate
The speed at which a person speaks, measured in words per minute.

Variety. Just as a monotonous pitch can seem boring, so a monotonous, un-changing rate can displease listeners. A speaker who utters every word and sentence at the same rate—no matter how significant or suspenseful the ideas are—gives no clues about what's really important. All ideas receive about the same treatment, and listeners tend to tune out.

Beginning speakers sometimes think that the only way to vary rate is to speed up at critical places in the speech. In fact, *both* speeding up *and* slow-ing down can convey movement or suspense and can compel attention and interest. Indeed, the choice of rate may itself communicate a message. Slowing down suggests that the speaker is serious and that every word mat-ters; the audience had better pay attention. It may also create a mood such as calmness or sadness or may suggest that the speaker thinks the ideas are difficult to grasp. Speeding up may propel a narrative forward or may evoke feelings of suspense, excitement, or outrage.

Most speakers vary their rate less than they think they do, and most could benefit by cultivating greater variety. Exercises in which you read a sentence or a list of words at differing rates will help you see how variety in rate can enhance interest in the message. Record yourself reading part of a famous speech at different rates. The playback may surprise you by showing that changes in rate may change meaning as well. This exercise should also give you a sense of which "normal" rate is most comfortable for you personally.

Pauses

Pauses are the brief silences within a speech. Although it may seem strange to include silence among the dimensions of voice, silence as well as speech can be highly communicative. The message in a pause is one of complete-ness and finality.

Properly used, pauses enhance a speech in two ways. First, they empha-size what the speaker said, providing a kind of nonverbal underlining. While the speaker is silent, listeners can think about what they have just heard, storing the thought in memory. A speaker who never pauses will move on to a new idea before listeners can make sense of the last one—and can unintentionally convey that all ideas are equally important or that none is really important. Without pauses, the audience will remember less and will be influenced less.

Second, pauses mark transitions in a speech. Because speaking doesn't have "punctuation marks," pauses—and variety in pitch and rate—can serve that function, telling the audience that the speaker has ended a section and is about to move on to a new topic or idea. This gives the audience time to absorb what was just said before switching again to active listening. It also gives speakers time to collect their thoughts before moving to the next idea.

Simple as the concept of pauses might seem, like the other dimensions of voice, pausing requires practice to be used effectively. You will want to avoid the following common problems.

Pausing Too Often. A pause can signal the end of a paragraph in a speech, but that signal will be undercut if you also pause for every comma or semi-colon. Too many pauses make a speech jerky and make the speaker seem nervous. Use pauses sparingly for effect.

Pausing at the Wrong Places. Because pauses are like punctuation marks, use them at the same places in the text as you would write the marks for

pauses
Periods of brief silence within a speech.

Using pauses to emphasize a parallel speech structure is a good way to let the audience know what to expect next. Rev. Jesse Jackson made especially good use of such pauses in his "Common Ground" speech to the 1988 Democratic National Convention.

which they stand. Pausing in the middle of sentences or ideas can confuse listeners and make comprehension difficult.

On the other hand, powerful effects can result from unusual pausing. One of the most memorable speeches of the twentieth century was delivered by Dr. Martin Luther King, Jr., on August 28, 1963. Standing in front of the Lincoln Memorial in Washington, D.C., he summoned his audience to work peacefully to attain civil rights for African Americans. He inspired listeners with his vision of the American Dream, closing with lines adapted from the song "America":

> So let freedom ring from the prodigious hilltops of New Hampshire. Let freedom ring from the mighty mountains of New York. Let freedom ring from the heightening Alleghenies of Pennsylvania! Let freedom ring from the snow-capped Rockies of Colorado! Let freedom ring from the curvaceous peaks of California!

Instead of pausing after each sentence, Dr. King stopped briefly after each refrain of "Let freedom ring," building intensity and creating the musical effect of a crescendo. His midsentence pauses emphasized the repeating pattern in his examples and let the audience know what to expect next.

Not Pausing Long Enough. Uncomfortable with silence, speakers are notoriously poor judges of how long their pauses are; most imagine them to be much longer than is the case. Again an audio recorder is a valuable aid. Time your recorded pauses, and compare them with how long you *thought* you paused when you spoke. All pauses should be relatively brief, of course, but the effects of a one-second pause and a five-second pause are considerably different.

Using Vocalized Pauses. Sounds such as "uh" and "umm" are **vocalized pauses,** meaningless sounds that a speaker produces during moments of si-

vocalized pauses
Pauses filled with sound, such as "uh" or "umm."

lence. These almost always arise from nervousness and can be highly distracting to listeners. (Have you ever been in an audience that began to count the speaker's "uhs" and "umms"?) Sometimes vocalized pauses are words or phrases such as "like," "you know," "now then," and "okay?" Such repetition is a nervous response; the speaker is uncomfortable stopping for even a few seconds.

Whether syllables or words, vocalized pauses call so much attention to themselves that they interfere with the message. The remedy is easy to state but difficult to carry out: When you pause, *be silent*. Again, an audio recorder is useful, because most speakers are not aware of their vocalized pauses. Listen to yourself, and discover how often you vocalize during a pause. If you do it frequently, make a mental note to *remain silent*.

Articulation and Enunciation

The related concepts of articulation and enunciation have to do with precise, distinct speech. **Articulation** refers to the clarity of individual sounds; **enunciation** refers to the distinctness with which words are sounded.

Articulation. For native speakers of English, common articulation problems include difficulty in forming the *th* sound (saying "dese" instead of "these") and dropping the final *g* from a word ("workin'" and "makin'"). Articulation can be improved through specific vocal exercises for particular sounds. The easiest way to diagnose articulation problems is to have someone else listen with you to a recording of your speech and to identify any sounds that call attention to themselves.

Not everyone articulates in the same way, of course. Speakers whose native language is not English, for example, often have difficulty with standard English articulation. Their goal should be not to articulate like native English speakers but to articulate clearly enough that they can be heard and understood. By the same token, listeners should make reasonable efforts to understand speakers whose articulation patterns are unfamiliar. In our increasingly diverse society, we all meet people who "speak differently." We should not allow cultural differences in articulation to block successful communication.

Enunciation. The distinctness with which words are sounded is another aspect of clarity that speakers need to consider. One specific problem is the tendency to slur words together. This is fairly common in informal settings, where "I'm gonna," "Whaddaya know?" and "Whatcha doin'?" may replace "I am going to," "What do you know?" and "What are you doing?"[2] In a speech, however, such lack of enunciation will seem inappropriate; unless it is being used for effect, it is likely to influence the audience's perception of the speaker.

The other extreme to avoid is being too precise in enunciation, saying each word so distinctly that you seem pompous and condescending to the audience. Speaking too distinctly not only distracts attention from the message but also may arouse negative feelings in listeners, who believe the speaker is "putting on airs."

Pronunciation

Even when a word is familiar to the eye, we sometimes wonder how it should be sounded. Correct **pronunciation** refers to the accepted way to

articulation
Precision and clarity in the production of individual vocal sounds.

enunciation
Precision and distinctness in sounding words.

pronunciation
Sounding of a word in the accepted way.

sound any given word. This includes such matters as which syllable to accent, whether to sound a vowel as short or long, and which optional consonant sound to use (for example, whether to give a *c* a hard sound, like a *k*, or a soft sound, like an *s*).

The Importance of Proper Pronunciation. First, the meaning of a spoken word may depend on its pronunciation, and mispronouncing it may prevent listeners from sensing which meaning you intend. The word *desert*, for example, means something different when you accent the first syllable (noun = "hot, dry place with lots of sand") than when you accent the second syllable (verb = "to abandon"). Second, like some of the other dimensions of vocal quality, mispronunciation calls attention to itself and may overshadow your ideas and message. Third, faulty pronunciation reflects negatively on a speaker's credibility; listeners may (mistakenly) get the impression that the speaker is ignorant or incompetent and hence is not to be trusted.

The phrase "proper pronunciation" may conjure up images of Eliza Doolittle, the British street vendor in *My Fair Lady* who could not speak "the king's English" and was stigmatized because of her lower-class **dialect,** or pronunciation pattern. Today in the United States, however, people are more likely to recognize and to accept that pronunciations vary according to geography (and according to economic and social class, among other cultural factors). We are more likely to hear speakers with a variety of dialects, and so we are less likely to view such differences as highly unusual.

On the other hand, just as slang is sometimes inappropriate, it remains important to speak standard American English in some situations. If the audience is highly diverse, many listeners may be distracted by an unfamiliar dialect. And in highly formal situations, *any* sort of dialect may be seen as a distraction.

Pronunciation and Audience Analysis. In thinking about pronunciation and dialect, analyze your audience in relation to yourself, asking the questions listed in Checklist 11.1. Depending on your answers, design a strategy for your speech as suggested in the checklist.

As you learned in Chapter 3, cultural diversity is a feature of many audiences. Even though dialects have become more familiar and less distinct, the acceptance of cultural diversity (and its variations in the use of language) is still somewhat at odds with the striving for national unity (and its goal of a common mode of speaking). Knowing that, you should plan your presentation in a way that increases the chances of achieving your goals.

Checklist 11.1 Pronunciation and Audience Analysis

Questions to Ask:

- Am I culturally different from most of my immediate listeners?
- If so, how might this affect their impressions of me and my speech?
- How do cultural differences affect my ability to achieve the goals of my speech?
- Does my pronunciation make me vulnerable to stereotyping by the audience? Conversely, is there a danger that I may stereotype the audience?

(continued)

dialect
A pronunciation pattern that characterizes a particular geographic area, economic or social class, or cultural factors.

Inflection. Articulation, enunciation, and pronunciation relate to the sound of individual syllables and words. **Inflection** is a similar concept except that it applies to the sentence as a whole. Appropriate inflection is important for the same reasons we have already discussed: Without it, you risk distracting listeners' attention, distorting your message, and damaging your credibility.

For example, one normal inflection pattern is to raise the pitch toward the end of a question and to lower the pitch toward the end of a statement. Speakers who reverse this pattern sound strange, and the audience may have trouble figuring out what they mean. Some speakers are so unsure of themselves that they raise their pitch after nearly every statement, hoping to discover whether the audience understands and agrees with their point. But this inflection pattern only makes ideas more difficult to follow, because they sound like questions rather than statements. In addition, the speakers appear to be unsure of themselves and overly tentative about whatever they say.

A given sentence may have more than one correct inflection pattern, and yet its meaning will change greatly when an appropriate pattern is used. Student Jeremy Rivers, for example, was extolling the merits of a particular brand of luggage and confidently told the audience, "Nothing could be better than this brand." He thought this statement was strongly positive, and so did most listeners. But Jeremy was surprised to discover that a few audience members understood this remark differently, concluding that they really would be better off with *nothing* than with this brand of luggage. Careful attention to inflection, taking care to stress the word *better* as well as the word *nothing*, would have given the audience a better clue about which meaning Jeremy intended.

In general, think about the audience when you work on improving your speaking voice. Watch for feedback to ensure that your volume, pitch, rate, and degree of pauses are comfortable for listeners and to see that your enunciation, articulation, and pronunciation make your ideas clear. To avoid distracting from your message, aim for a presentation voice that has variety, that seems natural, and that captures and holds listeners' attention.

The Body in Presentation

Just as the voice gives the speaker important *auditory* and *verbal* resources, the body provides equally valuable *visual* resources. Not surprisingly, the same general principles relating to the voice in presentation also apply to the body. The speaker's body is used to enhance the message, not to call attention to itself. The body and its movements influence listeners' first im-

inflection
Pronunciation pattern for a sentence as a whole.

pressions of the speaker and, hence, their willingness to take the speaker seriously. And changes in body placement and movement can mark transitions in the speech and add enough variety to keep the audience interested in and focused on the message.

Physical Appearance

Even before you begin to speak, audience members are forming impressions of the sort of person you are. This happens quickly and on the basis of superficial judgments, but those judgments are durable. (See the discussion of *ethos* in Chapter 1.) Consequently, you want to avoid doing anything that will make you seem unprepared, incompetent, or unreliable.

WWW. Using the Internet

How Important Is Physical Delivery?

Read the article from the *Time* magazine issue of October 10, 1960, entitled "The Campaign Candid Camera," which contrasts the judgments of television viewers with those of radio listeners concerning who won the first Kennedy–Nixon debate.

Point your browser to **http://www.debates.org/pages/debhis60.html**. This is the Web site for the commission on presidential debates. This site features videos and full text transcripts of the Kennedy–Nixon debates.

Which candidate used more effective delivery in the second debate?

Before You Speak. Consider the physical arrangement of the speaking space before deciding such things as how to approach the podium and what to wear. Is the setting large and impersonal or small and intimate? How formal or informal is the setting (and occasion)? Will you be able to establish eye contact with listeners, or will you be far away from them and speaking with a microphone?

Your appearance to an audience at an outdoor rally will be far different from how you appear to the same audience in a cathedral. Similarly, the settings for a retirement banquet, a business meeting, a commencement address, and a medical lecture are all different and can influence how the audience perceives you. Whenever possible, then, you should examine the speaking space and practice in it before presenting your speech.

Approaching the Podium. Your physical appearance begins to create impressions as you walk to the podium. If you start speaking while you walk, before facing the audience, you may seem in a hurry to finish and so unsure of yourself that you won't look the audience in the eye. Likewise, if you shuffle uncertainly toward the podium, the audience may think you lack confidence and don't know what you are talking about. Such assumptions may be wrong, of course, but they affect your *ethos* and can create a "credibility deficit" that you'll have to overcome.

No matter how you feel about speaking, create the best first impression that you can. Walk firmly and purposefully to the podium, pause to collect your thoughts, look directly at the audience, and then begin with confidence. In Chapter 12, you will learn that your body acts as a visual aid for the speech—the audience will be *looking at you*. Try to make your body's message match and reinforce the message of your words.

Clothes and Grooming. What you wear and your personal appearance—everything from hairstyle to footwear—are the stuff of first impressions and will affect your *ethos*. A badly dressed, unkempt speaker easily becomes the focus of attention and distracts the audience from the message. If you constantly push hair out of your face, wear a baseball cap that makes eye contact impossible, or fiddle with keys or jewelry, you practically beg the

Speakers who use natural and relaxed gestures while speaking can enhance listeners' interest in and comfort with the message.

audience to focus on the distractions rather than the speech. Sometimes clothing choices can even send messages that contradict your thesis and tarnish your *ethos*. For example, wearing army fatigues during a speech promoting pacifism or wearing a popular brand of running shoes during a speech about the shoe company's questionable labor practices could send mixed messages to your audience.

Typically, speakers dress a bit more formally than audience members do.[3] The general public may attend a speech in sports attire, but the speaker is a major figure and is expected to look the part. In recent years, this unwritten "dress code" has relaxed considerably. President Jimmy Carter made a point of appearing in shirtsleeves without a tie, and President Bill Clinton's jeans and running clothes became part of his image. Yet both men were well advised to wear suits and ties when addressing the public—when they wanted to project a serious image. So do many speakers in business, the professions, and the entertainment world.

Sometimes, a speaker will want to make a cultural statement through clothing and hairstyle and will resent any advice about adapting to the audience's expectations. But here, as elsewhere, audience analysis is critical; plan your personal appearance to advance your strategic goals.

Movement

How and where you position your body while speaking can also enhance or distract from the message. When student speaker Rachel Samuels stood behind the large, heavy podium in her classroom, only her head was visible. Recognizing the problem, Rachel stepped away from the podium to present her speech.

Even if the height of the podium does not affect your appearance this way, it's a good idea to step away from it occasionally. Many beginning speakers grip the podium as though tensely steering a car that is out of control. This may give you a sense of security, but it also puts a barrier between you and the audience. Instead, if you loosen your grip and step away from the podium at points in the speech, your body language will provide visual cues. For example, you can signal transitions in the speech by moving a step or two forward or to the side. And by moving toward the audience, you can show your trust and break down any imaginary walls between you and listeners.

The 1992 presidential debates among Bill Clinton, George Bush, and Ross Perot were the first that included one format resembling a town meeting in which citizens in the audience asked questions. At one point, when Bill Clinton was asked how the federal budget deficit had affected him personally, he did not respond right away. First he took a few steps toward the questioner and established eye contact. Although he was actually speaking to a television audience of millions, Mr. Clinton seemed to be responding to this citizen one on one. The unstated message was that they had a common bond. And because Mr. Clinton had to face the cameras to answer his questioner, television viewers also felt that he was responding directly to them—and had a bond with them.

Although purposeful, planned movement will benefit your presentation, constant or aimless movement will be a great distraction. A speaker who moves all around the room for no apparent reason puts a burden on listeners; it's up to them to follow the movements and maintain eye contact. Many will simply stop trying—and stop listening as well. Speakers also should avoid shifting their weight from side to side, rocking on their feet. Like vocalized pauses, this nervous response calls negative attention to itself.

Just as you should not begin speaking until you have reached the podium and sized up the audience, so should you not gather up notes and start returning to your seat while you are still speaking. The audience will not have a chance to absorb your final thoughts, and your conclusion will be weakened. You also will give the impression that speaking to them was painful and that you want to finish as soon as possible. Take your time, and take control of the situation. When you do return to your seat, walk confidently without calling attention to yourself.

Gesture

The term **gesture** refers to the movement of hands and arms during the speech as a means of emphasis. Many speakers are especially self-conscious about their hands and what to do with them while they speak. Some put their hands into their pockets—not to create an informal, conversational tone but just to get them out of the way. These speakers usually seem tense, as though they are tightly clenching something buried deep in their pocket. Other untrained speakers fidget, moving their hands and arms aimlessly as a nervous reaction. One nervous student had a tendency to rotate his arms and hands in big circles so that he looked more like an orchestra conductor than a public speaker. Because such movements are not coordinated with the speech, they call attention to themselves and detract from the message.

In contrast, a well-timed, purposeful gesture heightens the power of both your text and your voice. But what is such a gesture like? Centuries ago, theorists of public speaking believed that certain gestures went naturally with particular words or ideas. They wrote manuals illustrating hundreds of gestures and their matching words so that speakers could learn the gestures by rote and perform them automatically when reciting the matching text.[4] Today, this approach is considered nonsense; such a presentation is so artificial and contrived that it seems funny.

Even so, not all speakers are naturally expressive with their hands. Whether you use many or few gestures does not matter; what matters is that your gestures support your message, not draw attention away from it. If you videotaped yourself in informal conversation, you probably would discover gestures that you are unaware of—they simply come out naturally when you talk. A few possible uses of gestures are to emphasize the importance of a point, to suggest balance or opposition ("on the one hand," "on the other hand"), and to position ideas in space and time.[5]

Above all, gestures used in presentation should appear natural. Achieving this is less a matter of memorizing gestures than of becoming familiar

gesture
Movement of hands and arms during the speech as a means of emphasis.

with the general rhythm of gesture. It begins with an **anticipation step,** which simply means that you bring your hands to a position from which a gesture can easily be made. If you are gripping the podium or handling several pages of notes, gesturing will be difficult and awkward. First you need to be in a position that lets you execute a gesture naturally.

Being ready to gesture, you next move to the **implementation step**—the few seconds in which you execute the movement as you intended. Typically, a speaker's gestures occur somewhere between the waist and shoulders, an area that eases natural movement and is also visible to audience members. Perhaps most important in implementing the gesture is to *follow it through.* Untrained speakers often make a half-gesture, raising a hand partway without completing the movement. Such a gesture has little purpose or effect, suggesting instead that the speaker is nervous.

Having implemented the gesture, during the **relaxation step** you return your hands to their normal position, whether at your side, in front of you, or resting on the podium. Without this step, you risk being trapped in continuous gesture. Since your hands are in the visual space where gestures take place, and you haven't returned them to rest, you may find yourself gesturing repeatedly and in the same way for every word or idea. That, of course, dilutes the power of the gesture when you really do want to emphasize something.

Finally, don't worry too much about gestures. Although "what to do with my hands" is a concern for many speakers, the issue is relatively unimportant. Gestures tend to take care of themselves as long as you avoid distracting mannerisms, practice the three steps of gesture, and concentrate on your message.

Facial Expression

The speaker's facial expressions are another powerful element of nonverbal communication that can heighten or detract from the speech. Obviously, a smiling speaker communicates something much different from a frowning one. But someone who smirks or grins throughout the presentation will seem out of place and hence not believable, as will a speaker who delivers a lighthearted message but shows no facial expression at all. Again, it is valuable either to videotape your speech or to have someone observe you practicing it. Discover whether your facial expressions are consistent with and support the message in your text.

Eye Contact. One aspect of facial expression, **eye contact,** deserves special attention. Speakers who do not look the audience in the eye may lose credibility. In mainstream American culture, not looking at someone is widely thought to mean that the person is lying or has something to hide. In fact, speakers from cultures with different norms about eye contact may be misunderstood and misjudged by an American audience.

Another important point is that eye contact lets you see how the audience is responding to the speech; it provides feedback. Listeners' facial expressions often indicate whether the message is clear or needs explanation, whether claims seem persuasive or not, and so on. Such feedback helps you adjust your presentation to fit the audience while you speak. But if you stare at your notes or gaze at the back wall, you cannot make eye contact and take advantage of feedback.

anticipation step
The first step of a gesture; involves bringing the hands into a position from which the gesture can be made.

implementation step
The execution of a gesture, raising the hand and moving it in the intended manner.

relaxation step
Returning the hands to a normal relaxed position at the conclusion of a gesture.

eye contact
Looking directly at members of the audience.

Speaking to a Large Audience. Maintaining eye contact with a large audience presents problems. You can't look at everyone, but if you focus on nearby listeners, those farther away will feel left out. And if you keep turning your head mechanically from side to side, the constant sweeping movements will be a distraction, and you won't really make eye contact with anyone. The remedy is not to fix on particular audience members but to focus on general areas of the audience. Mentally divide listeners into three or four groups, and shift your focus among them to correspond to transitions in the speech. This lets all listeners feel—to some degree—that you are talking directly to them, and you can monitor the groups for feedback. At the same time, your shifting focus helps to signal transitions in the speech.

Eye Contact with Notes. How can you maintain eye contact if you are using notes? It takes practice, but the idea is to glance down at your notes during the brief moments when you pause and then gracefully to resume eye contact when you start to speak again. Having notes that are large and easy to read will help you. What you want to avoid are jerky movements of your head and eyes between your notes and your audience, and you usually want not to have to look down at your notes while you're stating or explaining your main ideas.

Speaking for the Camera. Different problems arise when speaking for the camera. Even though you *are* addressing a very large audience, you are speaking only to a camera—a single "listener" who provides no direct feedback through eye contact. On camera, if you move your head from side to side as you would with a large audience, you create an impression of shiftiness. And because the camera is close in, it exaggerates your shifts in eye contact. You will seem to be rolling your head around, which can only detract greatly from the speech. When speaking on camera, then, it is wiser to imagine only a single listener and to look directly into the camera to address that person. And because you cannot modify your presentation on the spot through feedback, careful audience analysis and strategic planning are extremely important.

Animation. One important component of *ethos* is dynamism. A dynamic speaker is one who appears animated and enthusiastic. Eye contact, smiles, and especially variety in facial response are a few signs of enthusiasm. Although trained actors may be able to "fake" a sense of animation, most speakers cannot. The easiest way to convey the impression that you are animated and enthusiastic about your topic and about speaking to your audience is for you to actually feel that way. As we saw in Chapters 3 and 4, this is an important consideration in audience analysis and topic selection.

Modes of Presentation

Most theorists identify four general modes of presentation: impromptu, memorized, manuscript, and extemporaneous. No matter which mode you choose, you can use voice and body to enhance the presentation. But the modes themselves also involve choices that can strengthen or weaken the speech.

Presenting Your Speech

The Situation

You are a teacher at a grade school and your principal has asked you to present the new curriculum plan to the parents in your community and also to answer any questions they may have regarding these changes. There have been several major additions to the curriculum, and you want to make sure that each change is explained clearly to the parents. You will be presenting in the school gymnasium where a microphone and podium will be set up the evening of your speech—which is two weeks from today.

Making Choices

1. Which presentation mode do you plan to use? Why? What are the benefits and/or drawbacks of this mode?

2. How will you incorporate the podium into your presentation, if at all? Will you use the microphone? Why or why not?

3. How will you prepare for your speech? How will you prepare to answer the audience's questions?

What If . . .

How would your presentation strategies change if the following were true? Would your mode of presenting change? Would your practice strategies change? Why or why not?

1. You are presenting to a group of parents in a small classroom.

2. You have met each of the parents on an individual basis and know that they support the curriculum changes.

3. You have met with each of the parents on an individual basis and know that they do not support the curriculum changes.

4. Your principal planned to make this presentation but has become ill at the last minute. You need to give this presentation tomorrow.

Impromptu Presentation

When you have little or no time to prepare specifically for a speech, you make an **impromptu presentation.** Perhaps someone at a meeting says something that inspires you to respond, and so you raise your hand to offer your views. You thereby give a speech seemingly without any preparation at all. In fact, you may have "spent a lifetime" preparing for that speech. The issues are important to you, and you've thought about them a great deal. But you never imagined that you would be speaking about them on this particular occasion.

Structure an impromptu presentation as simply and clearly as possible. Because you do not have a chance to plan the speech in detail, you may become entangled in the web of your argument. The key is to focus on a very small number of main ideas, previewing and summarizing them so that listeners have no doubts about your thesis or how the ideas develop it. Impromptu speaking also often takes cues from previous speakers, referring to their specific points and suggesting how their message relates to yours.

Memorized Presentation

A **memorized presentation** is the opposite of impromptu; you pay such close attention to your text that you commit it to memory. This mode of

impromptu presentation
A mode of presentation in which the speaker has done little or no specific preparation for the speech.

memorized presentation
The opposite of speaking impromptu; the speaker pays close attention to a prepared text and commits it to memory.

speaking was highly valued in the past. School children studied famous orations and recited them by rote. Great orators often wrote out their entire speeches and then committed them to memory. Such speeches were long; it was common during the early 1800s for a U.S. senator to speak for hours, delivering a memorized presentation.

Today few theorists advise anyone to memorize a speech. Besides the unnecessary investment in energy, speaking from memory has other problems. First, because the text is memorized, the speaker might not take feedback into account and adapt to the audience's needs. More likely, the speaker will ignore the audience and deliver a soliloquy. Second, if you write and then memorize a speech for oral delivery, the recital may be stiff and stilted. It will sound memorized, which quickly causes an audience to lose interest. Finally, a memorized text raises concern about what might happen if you forget a line. Some speakers can ad lib and patch things up quickly, but many become flustered; having forgotten the memorized words, they don't know what to say.

Although memorized presentation has these problems and is generally discouraged, it can be helpful to memorize the first few sentences of your introduction and the last few sentences of your conclusion. Then you will begin the speech confidently and end it solidly, without trailing off. And if you want to use a particular phrase or line in the speech, you might commit that to memory and plan where it would fit best. But the practice of memorizing an entire speech has fallen into disuse—deservedly.

Manuscript Presentation

Like a memorized speech, **manuscript presentation** also involves a text that is prepared word for word, but the speech is read rather than delivered from memory. This speaking mode is useful in highly formal situations, when specific wording is critical. The president of the United States uses manuscript presentation for the State of the Union address and for most speeches about major policies. The risk of saying the wrong thing is too great to rely on other presentation modes.

Manuscript presentation also is useful when precise timing is important, as when speaking on radio or television. This was clearly illustrated in 1952, when vice presidential candidate Richard Nixon appeared on television to defend himself against charges of financial irregularities (the speech is discussed in Chapter 10). He ended by urging listeners to express support for him by writing to the Republican National Committee. But Mr. Nixon was not speaking from manuscript, and he ran out of time as he was telling the audience where to write. Millions of listeners were able to respond anyway, but if you watch that speech on tape, you will see how awkward the ending is.

Although manuscript presentation may be appropriate in these specific circumstances, as a general rule it is not the best mode. First, reading a paper aloud is not the same as speaking directly to an audience. Audiences recognize the difference and are less attentive; the manuscript interferes with direct communication between the speaker and listeners.

Second, very few people are well trained in the art of reading aloud. Even a text that is rich in imagery, that identifies with the audience, and that offers solid argument may be negated if it is read indifferently or with vocal patterns that do not match the intent of the message.[6]

manuscript presentation
A mode of presentation in which the speaker reads aloud the prepared text of the speech.

WWW. Using the Internet

Assess Your Own Delivery Choices

Do an interactive exercise at the **Allyn & Bacon Public Speaking Web Site** entitled "Yeas and Nays of Delivery" to explore common attitudes that speakers have toward delivering a presentation. To do this, point your browser to http://www.abacon.com/pubspeak/exercise/delex.html.

Third, presenting a speech from manuscript makes it difficult to maintain eye contact and profit from feedback. Accomplished speakers sometimes can do it—taking in a sentence or two of their text and then gracefully looking up and speaking to the audience. But many speakers do this awkwardly, which is distracting at best, and they often lose their place in the text.

Extemporaneous Presentation

A speech that is prepared and rehearsed but is neither written out nor memorized is called **extemporaneous presentation.** This mode is recommended for most speakers and speeches, because it encourages a conversational quality and is flexible enough to permit adaptation to feedback. Extemporaneous speaking is not impromptu; the speaker has outlined and planned the speech carefully, has a specific structure in mind, and probably uses prepared notes during presentation. But no word-for-word text exists in advance of delivery, and the speech is not memorized or read aloud.

The advice in earlier chapters that you develop a preparation outline and a presentation outline assumed an extemporaneous mode of presentation. The preparation outline helps you identify your main ideas, their relation to each other and to your thesis, and the order in which to present them. The presentation outline includes enough key words to help you keep the ideas straight and to present them as intended. As you practice the speech, you will try out different ways of verbalizing the ideas, getting a sense of how the speech sounds and what you mean. But you will not memorize or write down the specific wording (other than introductory and concluding sentences). Speaking extemporaneously lets you discuss ideas informally and conversationally. Your focus will be on ideas rather than on specific words, making it easier to maintain eye contact and modify your message in response to feedback.

Practicing for Speech Presentation

The idea of practicing to appear natural may not seem quite so strange, now that we have explored how the speaker's voice and body can be used in a planned way to bring about that result. Yet the easiest way to fail at the goal is to focus too much on your voice or body rather than on what you are going to say and on what you are trying to achieve.

Thinking consciously about your strategic objectives—what you wish to share with the audience, how you want to affect listeners, or what you want audience members to believe or do after hearing your speech—should focus your attention on the purpose of the speech. If you keep content and purpose clearly in mind, then you can practice using your voice and body to *contribute* to those goals rather than to be ends in themselves.[7]

The most important advice about practice is to begin early. Skills of presentation take time to perfect, and you will learn them best when you are relaxed, not tense. Unless the assignment really calls for an impromptu

extemporaneous presentation
A mode of presentation in which the speech is planned and structured carefully but a specific text is not written in advance nor memorized.

A skilled extemporaneous speaker carefully prepares notes to aid in the delivery of the speech, but maintains eye contact with the audience while speaking. Most speeches prepared and delivered in the classroom setting are extemporaneous speeches.

speech, waiting until the last minute is never a good idea. Things will not seem to fall into place. The speech may seem disorganized or not artfully crafted; or the content and presentation may be out of sync; or the gestures, movement, and vocal variations may be distracting. Admittedly, the advice to start early on a task is easier to give than to follow, but it will pay great dividends in the case of speech presentation.

Each person takes a unique approach to practicing a speech, and you should find methods that work well for you. In general, however, a four-step process is likely to be effective:

1. Develop the presentation outline.
2. Mentally rehearse the speech.
3. Practice the speech orally.
4. Simulate the speech setting.

The Presentation Outline

Develop your presentation outline as discussed in Chapter 9, and talk it through several times. By referring only to the outline, you should be able to articulate your main ideas and the links in your thought. Each key word should trigger a more complete thought. If this does not happen, revise the presentation outline to include more key words, different words, or a different structure.

This is also the time to write out or memorize any portion of the speech for which exact language is essential, such as a few introductory sentences or your conclusion. You might include your thesis statement, if you want to have its precise wording in front of you. Although excessive memorization is discouraged, some parts of even an extemporaneous speech depend on exact wording, and this is the time to develop the words you plan to use.

Mental Rehearsal

Picture an imaginary audience, and run through the speech in your mind while holding this image. Try to see yourself in the speaking situation, and think through what you would say. As you rehearse mentally, you may hit upon a particular transitional phrase or may discover the most effective way to express an idea clearly. Speakers who skip the step of mental rehearsal often fail to consider the big picture of how the speech will look and sound when everything comes together. As a result, the speech may seem fragmented or unnatural to an audience.

Oral Practice

Practice the speech orally, several times, under a variety of conditions. **Distributed practice** (brief periods of practice spread over time) is likely to be more effective than **massed practice** (a few lengthy sessions shortly before you speak).

The first few times, deliver the speech with no one else present. Although this will not give you feedback, you will become sensitive to the sound of the speech, to its length and timing, and to opportunities to enhance your use of voice and body. Because you are both speaker and listener, you'll want to satisfy yourself that everything fits together correctly.

Then practice with a small group of friends. Even two or three people are enough, if you trust them to give candid reactions that might improve the speech. This stage of practice will let you actually share your thoughts with others and see how the speech is affected by having an audience present. Use such "early reviews" to check whether the design of the speech will achieve your purpose. Ask especially whether listeners got a clear sense of your thesis, whether the speech moved clearly from one point to another, whether you spent too much or too little time on anything, and whether the speech seemed too slow or too fast. Raise any other specific concerns you have about the speech. The more feedback you get from these first listeners, the stronger your final presentation will be.

Videotape your presentation, if possible, and study the tape to see how the speech looks and sounds to others. This step makes many people uncomfortable, because they think they look and sound different from what the tape reveals. But try to set aside such feelings, focusing instead on what listeners will see and hear. For example, if the tape shows that you are looking only at your notes and are not making eye contact, you can correct this by the time you deliver the speech. The tape also might reassure you about some aspect of performance, such as gestures—perhaps they appear more natural than you thought. Look for positive feedback as well as negative; the tape can build your confidence even as it reveals areas that need improvement.

distributed practice
Brief periods of practice spread over time.

massed practice
A few lengthy practice sessions shortly before delivering the speech.

Simulation

Either practice the speech in the room where you'll speak, or simulate that setting as closely as possible. For instance, if you will be speaking in a large auditorium, practicing there or in a similar space will show you how much you should exaggerate gestures and movement so that they can be seen at a distance. If the setting will be smaller and more intimate, you may need to practice modulating your voice so that you don't seem to be shouting. And if you will be using a microphone, practicing with it will help you control and adapt your voice in ways that avoid distortion and slurring. Finally, this step will make you more comfortable with the setting so that, when the time comes, you can focus on your audience and your message.

Checklist 11.2 Practicing the Speech

1. **Develop the presentation outline.**
   - Talk through the outline several times.
   - Write out or memorize any portion for which exact language is essential.
2. **Mentally rehearse the speech.**
3. **Practice the speech orally:**
   - With no one else present.
   - With a small group of friends.
   - On videotape if possible.
4. **Simulate the speech setting.**

Strategies for Speaking to Diverse Audiences

Respecting Diversity Through the Presentation of Your Speech

Your voice will affect how easily people will hear you, and your gestures will mean different things in different cultures. Here are strategies that will help you to consider audience diversity when presenting your speech.

1. Speak loudly and enunciate clearly so those with hearing impairments can hear you.
2. Avoid gestures that, in other cultures, may have meanings different from what you intend.
3. Avoid the use of slang or false dialects that may stereotype your audience members.
4. Recognize that different cultures have different expectations about appropriate gestures and the physical relationship between speaker and audience.

Summary

The principles and guidelines that we explored in this chapter should be qualified by the important statement that presentation of a speech should appear natural. A speaker's technique should not call attention to itself or in any way distract from the message. But seeming natural is not simple; you must understand the resources of your voice and body and must practice using them.

Besides being a resource for the speaker, voice gives the audience insights into the speaker's personality. Variety in voice keeps listeners interested and adds emphasis to the speech. Six vocal dimensions that a speaker can use to enhance a speech are volume, pitch, rate, pauses, enunciation and articulation of individual sounds, and pronunciation.

Similar general principles apply to the speaker's use of the body. Movement and gestures should appear natural and should contribute to the overall goals for the speech. Resources of the body include physical appearance (posture, grooming, attire, and the like), movement of the body, gesture, and facial expression.

We examined four presentation modes: impromptu, memorized, manuscript, and extemporaneous. Each mode has its strengths and limitations, and each is appropriate for specific speaking situations. For most purposes, an extemporaneous presentation is preferred, although parts of the speech—the introduction, the conclusion, and perhaps the thesis statement—may be committed to memory.

Like most skills, speech presentation is improved by practice, including practicing how to appear natural. Each speaker develops a unique practice routine, but a four-step process is recommended: develop the presentation outline, mentally rehearse, practice orally with feedback, and simulate the speech setting as closely as possible.

Discussion Questions

1. How does delivery vary according to purpose? In what ways might delivery be different for a eulogy, an instructional speech, and a speech of dissent?

2. In what ways does delivery style contribute to or detract from a speaker's strategy? Discuss and compare the strategies and styles of some famous speakers—for example, Ronald Reagan, Bill Clinton, Madeleine Albright, Jesse Jackson, Tony Blair, and Pat Robertson. Discuss both their manuscript delivery in formal televised speeches and their extemporaneous delivery in debates and press conferences.

3. In what ways might you improve your delivery? Each student should present a short introduction to a speech, and classmates should then discuss the strengths and weaknesses of the presentation. Focus especially on aspects of delivery that the speaker is unlikely to recognize by examining a tape, such as articulation, enunciation, and pronunciation.

1. Select a passage from a speech that you can obtain in manuscript form. Record yourself presenting this passage first at a very slow rate, then at a moderate rate, and finally at a quick rate. Then vary the rate *within* the passage, slowing down or speeding up as needed to best convey the message. Repeat this process varying the volume of your delivery. Listen to the tape of these variations, and identify how changes in rate and volume affected the presentation.

2. Write out the introduction and conclusion of your next speech. Before you practice the delivery of these sections, decide where you want to include pauses and which words you want to emphasize by changes in volume and pitch.

3. Watch a videotape of yourself presenting a speech. Pay close attention to your delivery style—your volume, rate, and pitch variations; whether you use vocalized pauses; your eye contact, posture, and gestures; and so on. List the things about your delivery style that currently detract from your message and that you would like to improve. How might you go about improving them?

1. For an excellent overview of the physiology of the voice mechanism and a wide selection of exercises to improve the speaker's voice, see Linda Gates, *Voice for Performance*, New York: Applause Books, 2000.

2. For a humorous treatment of the tendency to slur words, see William Safire, "Slurvian," *New York Times Magazine* (Sept. 17, 2000): 37, 40.

3. Studies have shown that a speaker's attractiveness has an influence on the persuasiveness of the message. Attractiveness can be achieved at least partly through clothing and grooming. See Shelly Chaiken, "Physical Appearance and Social Influence," *Physical Appearance, Stigma, and Social Behavior: The Ontario Symposium*, Vol. 3, ed. C. Peter Herman, Mark P. Zanna, and E. Tory Higgins, Hillsdale, N.J.: Lawrence Erlbaum, 1986, pp. 143–177.

4. For examples of this, see John Bulwer, *Chirologia: Or the Natural Language of the Hand*; and *Chironomia: Or the Art of Manual Rhetoric*, first published 1644, ed. James W. Cleary, Carbondale: Southern Illinois Univ. Press, 1974; and Gilbert Austin, *Chironomia: Or, A Treatise on Rhetorical Delivery*, first published 1806, ed. Mary Margaret Robb and Lester Thonssen, Carbondale: Southern Illinois Univ. Press, 1966.

5. For more discussion of gestures in informal conversation and in speeches, see Peter E. Bull, *Posture and Gesture*, New York: Pergamon Press, 1987, especially Chapter 10: "The Use of Hand Gesture in Political Speeches: Some Case Studies."

6. Researchers Herbert W. Hildebrandt and Walter W. Stevens discovered this rather accidentally when trying to determine whether extemporaneous or manuscript delivery was more effective. See their "Manuscript and Extemporaneous Delivery in Communicating Information," *Communication Monographs* 30 (November 1963): 369–372.

7. It is important to remember that delivery should match the speaker's material, intent, and personality. See Harry W. Bowen, "A Reassessment of Speech Delivery," *Communication Quarterly* 14 (November 1966): 21–24.

Chapter Twelve

Using Visual Aids

In this chapter, we will:

- Identify the main benefits of using visual aids in a speech as well as the potential drawbacks of using them.

- Examine major categories of visual aids and how each might contribute to the effectiveness of the speech.

- Describe materials for making visual aids and address some considerations governing the choice of materials.

- Explain the principles of preparing visual aids and of using them during the speech.

- Consider how computer technology expands the options for preparing and presenting effective visual aids.

In a classroom speech about the benefits and harms of a popular diet plan, Sarah McGonigle used an overhead projector to show cartoons that related to each point she made. Similarly, in a speech about diabetes, Dimitra Apostolopoulos showed her listeners a blood-sugar tester and a syringe, explaining how each is used by a diabetic. And in a speech arguing that the legal drinking age should be lower, Justin Whitney presented a graph to show the relationship between age and drunk-driving accidents. All three speakers enabled their listeners to see as well as hear by using one or more **visual aids** (any materials shown to the audience during the speech). Such materials are "aids" because they help the speaker by adding a visual dimension to the verbal message.

Each of these speakers carefully selected visual aids by keeping the audience and specific purpose in mind. Sarah knew that her audience regarded a diet as a formidable problem, and so she thought that humorous cartoons would serve her purpose of making it seem less imposing (so long as she chose cartoons that did not make fun of obesity or threaten listeners' self-esteem). Dimitra decided that her speech would be clearer if listeners could see the instruments she described. And Justin believed that the information in his speech would be more memorable if the audience saw it in chart form.

Benefits of Using Visual Aids

Not every speech calls for visual aids. Sometimes, the message and its structure are so simple that visual aids aren't needed. Sometimes, a speaker prefers to achieve an effect through voice and personality alone. And sometimes, visual aids may even distract the audience from the message. Nonetheless, visual aids often can be used to good effect. As visual media play a growing role in our culture, knowing how to design and construct images will become just as important as knowing how to plan and develop essays or speeches.

Computer technology has made the preparation of sophisticated visual aids much easier than before. Some have suggested that *every* presentation will be a Web-based presentation or that only rarely will a speaker fail to use visual media. In the future, media literacy will be a required characteristic of the educated person. Right now, it is a strategic resource speakers can use to enhance their effectiveness by combining visual and verbal means of presentation. In some situations, such as a sales presentation or a business proposal, visual aids are already required; audiences expect to see them and will regard the speaker as unprepared without them.

There are three main benefits of using visual aids:

1. Visual aids make the speech more interesting.
2. Visual aids enhance the speaker's credibility.
3. Visual aids improve comprehension and retention.[1]

Interest

Throughout our study, we have seen that a speech is strengthened by variety—in the speaker's voice, gesture, and movement, for example. Similarly, visual aids can enhance listeners' interest by adding variety to your mes-

visual aids

Materials that the speaker shows to the audience during the speech.

sage. When you stop to point to a chart or graph, or to show a slide, you alter your delivery pattern. Moreover, adding visual to aural stimuli is itself a means of making the speech interesting. Because listeners must "switch gears" to look at a poster or a map, they are less likely to fall into the trap of passive listening and more likely to attend to the message. By attracting attention, gaining interest, and possibly generating emotion, visual aids enhance the affective dimension of understanding.

WWW. Using the Internet

Analyze a Speech for Potential Use of Visual Aids

Read a speech delivered by one of the members of the Federal Reserve Board by pointing your browser to **http://www.federalreserve.gov/boarddocs/speeches/2002/**, where you can find speeches delivered by the Chair and by various members of the Board of Governors of the Federal Reserve Board. After reading the speech you have selected, identify what kind of visual aids would enhance the speech. What benefits from using visual aids could be achieved with the visuals you recommend?

Credibility

A speaker who prepares and uses visual aids well often makes a better impression on the audience.[2] Carefully prepared and appropriate visual aids suggest to the audience that you know the subject and think highly enough of them to do extra work. Again, careful audience analysis is the key to knowing how visual aids might enhance your credibility. When Sarah McGonigle used cartoons to illustrate her speech about a diet plan, she knew that these aids were appropriate for an audience that expected to be entertained. But had her audience been nutritionists who anticipated a technical presentation, or people for whom dieting posed serious issues of self-esteem, the cartoons might have backfired and caused listeners to downgrade Sarah as a speaker.

In some cases, the absence of visual aids can undermine a speaker's *ethos*. For example, if you were making a presentation to a board of directors and the norm was for such presentations to include computer-generated slides and video, your failure to use visual aids might suggest that you hadn't done the necessary preparation, didn't have your speech ready ahead of time, or weren't taking the audience seriously.[3]

Comprehension and Retention

A critical benefit of visual aids is that they often make it easier for listeners to understand and remember the speech.[4] Words by their nature are abstract; listeners have to translate them into mental images. But visual aids are concrete. They make it easy for listeners to see what you are talking about and to remember what you said. Listeners may remember a map, a graph, or a picture and associate it with a particular idea in your speech. In this way, visual and aural stimuli work together to affect audience members' cognitive understanding by making ideas clear and easily remembered. They also affect information processing by providing previews and summaries, making it easier for audiences to follow the speech.

For instance, you can effectively supplement a listing of the number of workers enrolled in various types of health care plans by showing a pie chart in which each component is a proportionate slice of the overall pie. You can strengthen a statement such as "The number of workers enrolled in managed-care plans—health maintenance organizations or, as commonly known, HMOs—grew from 52 percent in 1993 to 85 percent in 1997" by using two side-by-side pie charts that show your audience exactly how the proportion of workers enrolled in HMOs has grown over time. Similarly, listeners may not immediately grasp a verbal description of highway directions from Chicago to Detroit; but showing them a simple map is an effective way to strengthen the message.

Even in printed messages—when readers have the luxury of proceeding at their own pace and can go back over the text—complex material is often accompanied by visual aids. In public speaking, when the message cannot be slowed down or replayed, the variety achieved through visual aids is even more important.

To these three benefits of using visual aids we must add one major drawback. Visual aids can be a powerful distraction, drawing attention to themselves rather than to the heart of your speech. If listeners begin to notice how frequently you change slides or that you have misspelled a word on a chart, then they are not paying attention to the main idea of the speech, and they will be far less likely to remember what you said.

Usually, however, when visual aids distract, it is because the speaker did not use them properly. If posters and charts are not large enough for audience members to see or read easily, they may frustrate or bore the audience. But that is not a reason to avoid all use of posters and charts. If slides are out of focus or are changed so quickly that audience members fail to grasp their purpose, they will distract from the message of the speech. But that is not a reason never to use slides. These problems can be avoided. The fault lies not in the decision to use visual aids, but in how they are used.

From this discussion, it should be clear that the preparation and use of visual aids are not casual matters; in fact, they are an integral part of your strategic planning for the speech. The remainder of this chapter will describe different types of visual aids, the materials from which they can be made, and some guidelines for their preparation and use.

Some speakers will give their speeches in "smart" classrooms that are equipped with up-to-date technology; these settings may resemble those of business or professional presentations. Others will speak in rooms equipped only with an overhead projector, if that. Such settings are more like those of neighborhood organizations or simple meeting rooms. This chapter therefore describes a mixture of "low-tech" and "high-tech" visual aids and considers some of the design principles common to both. Based on your understanding of this material, you should be able to adapt your use of visual aids to whatever level of technology you find.

Checklist 12.1 Strategic Planning for Visual Aids

1. **In making decisions about visual aids, ask yourself these questions:**
   - Does the audience expect me to use visual aids, making their absence distracting?
   - Would my speech be clearer if I illustrated important points?
   - Can I retain the audience's interest through visual aids?
   - Can visual aids make it easier for listeners to remember and understand my important points?
   - Can I prevent visual aids from distracting from my message?

Types of Visual Aids

The varieties of visual aids can be grouped conveniently under five headings: charts, graphs, representations, objects or models, and people.

Charts

A **chart** simplifies complex material by arranging it visually according to some obvious principle. The listener is helped not only by being able to see as well as hear the information but also by the way in which the chart organizes the material.

One common type of chart is the *statistical chart* (see Figure 12.1). Because statistics are so abstract, they are often hard to comprehend or remember when heard; displaying them on a chart makes them easier to grasp. But remember that the purpose of a statistical chart is to *simplify* complex information. All too often, statistical charts used in speeches contain too much information, making them hard to read and hard to grasp. The energy that the audience spends trying to decode them is a distraction from the main point of the speech. Generally speaking, a statistical chart should illustrate only one point or support only one conclusion. A series of

chart
A visual arrangement of words or numbers according to some obvious principle.

Child Mortality Rates
(per 1,000 live births)

	1960			2000	
1. Afghanistan	360		1. Angola	260	
2. Angola	345		2. Afghanistan	257	
3. Haiti	253		3. Iraq	133	
4. Bangladesh	248		4. Haiti	123	
5. China	225		5. Bangladesh	82	
6. Iraq	171		6. China	40	
7. Colombia	125		7. Colombia	24	
8. Russia	64		8. Russia	21	
9. United States	30		9. United States	8	
10. Sweden	20		10. Sweden	3	

Figure 12.1 A statistical chart should show important relationships clearly. Here, the figures are contrasted in parallel columns and arranged in order of decreasing rates.

Source: UNICEF, available at http://www.childinfo.org/cmr/revis/dbz.htm.

simple charts is easier to understand than a single complex table that includes all the information.

See Figure 12.2 for an example of a chart that contains too much information for use in a speech. The value of this chart will be further reduced if, as often happens, it is projected onto a screen for only a few seconds. Also, charts should not present information that is *too* precise to grasp. And generally, order-of-magnitude numbers (those that are rounded off) will be better than numbers that are precise but complicated and hard to remember. Rather than showing the U.S. population as 285,183,427, you can just use 285 million.

Another common chart is one that shows the *sequence of steps* in a process. Many speeches give instructions about how to do something, or they describe the evolution of a process. For example, a speech about how to apply for college might cover the steps of (1) determining which criteria are most important—such as size, cost, distance from home, or the presence of special curricular programs; (2) assessing your aptitudes and interests; (3) determining a range of schools that satisfy your criteria and match your interests; (4) obtaining literature about those schools and eliminating some as options; (5) arranging to take whatever standardized tests are necessary; (6) obtaining application materials; and (7) filling out the applica-

Figure 12.2 This is an example of a chart that contains too much information to be useful in a speech.

Top Twenty Religions in the United States

Religion	1990 Est. Adult Pop.	2001 Est. Adult Pop.	% of U.S. Pop., 2000	% Change 1990–2000
Christianity	151,225,000	159,030,000	76.5%	+5%
Nonreligious/Secular	13,116,000	27,539,000	13.2%	+110%
Judaism	3,137,000	2,831,000	1.3%	−10%
Islam	527,000	1,104,000	0.5%	+109%
Buddhism	401,000	1,082,000	0.5%	+170%
Agnostic	1,186,000	991,000	0.5%	−16%
Atheist		902,000	0.4%	
Hinduism	227,000	766,000	0.4%	+237%
Unitarian Universalist	502,000	629,000	0.3%	+25%
Wiccan/Pagan/Druid		307,000	0.1%	
Spiritualist		116,000		
Native American Religion	47,000	103,000		+119%
Baha'i	28,000	84,000		+200%
New Age	20,000	68,000		+240%
Sikhism	13,000	57,000		+338%
Scientology	45,000	55,000		+22%
Humanist	29,000	49,000		+69%
Deity (Deist)	6,000	49,000		+717%
Taoist	23,000	40,000		+74%
Eckankar	18,000	26,000		+44%

Source: Adherents.com, 2001.

tion forms and submitting them online or mailing them. These seven steps might form the subheadings of the speech. A chart listing the seven steps in order would help listeners to remember the steps and to keep track of where you are in the speech. The chart would make clear not only what the steps are but also the appropriate sequence to follow in completing them.

Although the entire sequence of steps in a process might be listed on a single chart, consider whether you could heighten interest in the speech by developing the chart gradually. You could use a *series* of charts, with each one revealing additional new information. For example, in a speech about how the territory of the United States expanded beyond the original thirteen colonies, you might start with a chart listing only the Northwest and Southwest Territories. After discussing those acquisitions, you might then flip to another chart that lists those territories and also adds the Louisiana Purchase as a second stage in the sequence. By using a series of charts, you can control the information so that it evolves as your speech progresses, and listeners will not be distracted by items that you have not yet discussed.

Another common type of chart that emphasizes a sequence of steps is a **decision tree.** In this case, the focus is on the points at which *choices* are made—and the likely consequences of various choices. Suppose that your speech about selecting a college focused on the question "Should I go to a selective private university?" You could present this question as one that requires the answers to a series of other questions. The first question might be "Can I meet the academic standards?" If so, proceed to consider the main question; if not, that issue is moot. But if the answer was "Yes, I can meet the standards," the next question might be "Can I afford a private school?" If so, then write for information about the school. If not, there might be another question, such as "Am I eligible for financial aid?" The decision tree identifies the points at which each choice must be made, and lines on the chart connect each decision with its consequences.

Another way to present a decision tree is as a *flowchart*, which—rather than arranging the sequence as a tree with branches—suggests how each decision "flows." The chart consists of labeled boxes connected by arrows; at key points, one decision flows in one direction, and a different decision leads in a different direction. Figure 12.3 shows a flowchart on the topic of "How to choose whether to apply to a selective private university."

Even when you are not presenting a series of statistics or describing a sequence of events, a chart can be a helpful visual aid. For instance, as you present a verbal list in your speech, you might support it with a *visual list*. Lists fly past an audience rather quickly, and without visual support your point might be lost. A visual list also helps listeners to recognize and follow the structure of your message. For example, in a speech describing different types of home remedies, student speaker Amy Ahlfeld displayed a chart that named each remedy, identified its most probable active ingredients, and listed the ailments it was supposed to cure. The chart helped listeners to organize and remember all this information.

A slight variation of the visual list is a *columnar chart* that conceptually maps the main ideas or key terms by relating them to others. The items in one column of the chart are keyed to corresponding items in another column. An example is shown in Figure 12.4 on page 333, which was prepared by student Maria Rosado at a campus in the southwestern United States, where she was speaking about the prevalence of drugs in the region and

decision tree
A chart showing points in a sequence at which decisions must be made, and the likely consequences of various choices.

flowchart
A chart showing the "flow," or progress, through several steps, with alternative paths showing the outcome of different decisions.

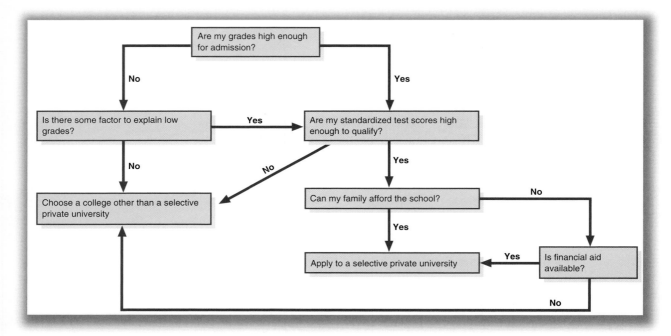

Figure 12.3 A sample flowchart.

their potential harm to teenage users. Because some listeners were Anglo and others were Latino, Maria thought that some would recognize drug names in English and some in Spanish. Knowing little Spanish herself, she prepared a three-column chart that listed the drugs in one column and their English street names in the adjacent column. The third column she left blank. Then she asked the audience to help her fill the blanks by providing the Spanish street names. This "unfinished" visual aid thus helped Maria to make the point that it was important to recognize these common names anywhere in the region. (Figure 12.2 is also a columnar chart, but as you can see by comparing it with Figure 12.4, it contains too much information—and probably too many columns—to be very useful.)

Graphs

A **graph** is a visual display of relationships that shows how change in one thing is related to change in another. The most common types are line graphs, bar graphs, and pie graphs (see Figure 12.5).

A **line graph** charts one variable as a function of another. The values for one variable are shown on the horizontal axis, and those of the other variable are shown on the vertical axis. Any pair of values can thus be represented by a point on the graph. A line connects the various points to show the relationship between the variables.

For example, suppose you wanted to demonstrate that the crime rate increases in hot weather. The two variables might be "temperature" (on the vertical axis) and "average reported crimes per hour per 1,000 population" (on the horizontal axis). At 60 degrees Fahrenheit, you find that there are an average of 25 reported crimes per hour per 1,000 population, so you

graph
A visual display of relationships, showing how change in one thing is related to change in another.

line graph
A graph in which a line connects points, each of which represents a combination of the two items being compared.

would find the point on the chart where a horizontal line from the "60 degrees" mark and a vertical line from the "25 crimes" mark intersect. Suppose that at 80 degrees Fahrenheit, there are an average of 40 reported crimes and at 100 degrees Fahrenheit, there are 65. These points could also be located on the graph. Then a line could be drawn to connect all three points. The line would show clearly that the crime rate goes up as the temperature increases. The relationship between the crime rate and the temperature will be clear and memorable.

Sometimes, however, things are more complicated. The trend will go one way up to a point, but then it will reverse. For example, grades have been shown to motivate improved student performance. Up to a point, a teacher who gives more A's may prompt students to do better work. But if it becomes clear that large numbers of students will receive an *A*, there is *less* incentive to do better work because students know that grades will be high anyway. Line graphs can show complex relationships as well as simple ones.

A **bar graph** is used to show comparisons and contrasts among one or two variables. Unlike a line graph, a bar graph shows units of measurement on only one axis; the other axis identifies the categories to be assessed. Then, for each category, a bar is drawn to the appropriate value. The relative lengths of the bars permit easy comparison.

Figure 12.4 A columnar chart for discussing drug names.

bar graph
A graph in which the length of bars indicates the amount or extent of items being compared.

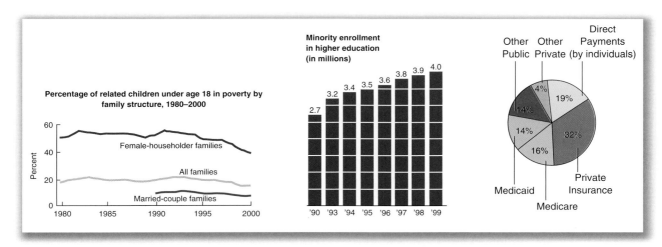

Figure 12.5 Graphs should be kept as simple as possible, with all elements labeled and a minimum number of variables displayed. Left to right: line graph, bar graph, pie graph.

Sources: U.S. Census Bureau March Current Population Survey, www.childstats.gov; American Council on Education, www.washingtonpost.com, the *Washington Post;* U.S. Congress, House Committee on Ways and Means, "1992 Report of The Board of Trustees of the Federal Old-Age and Survivors Insurance and Disability Insurance Trust Funds," 182.

For instance, you might wish to show how gender and race affect the likelihood of completing a college degree. In this graph, the two genders and the various races are the primary variable. The vertical axis could show percentages from 0 to 100. On the horizontal axis are labeled the categories of the variable. One space would be labeled "Men," and another would be labeled "Women." Then bars would be drawn to the appropriate percentages for each gender, making it easy for listeners to compare them. Farther along the horizontal axis, additional spaces might be labeled "White," "Black," "Hispanic," "Asian," and so on, and again bars would show the appropriate values.

You can extend a bar graph to make comparisons using a second variable as well, such as time. For example, the first space could have three bars showing how many men completed college degrees in 1980, in 1990, and in 2000. The spaces for women, whites, blacks, and so on, would show the same information. Visual inspection of the sets of three bars will let the audience see how completion rates vary for each gender/race as well as whether the gap between men and women or between races has widened, narrowed, or stayed about the same over time.

Finally, a **pie graph** is used to show proportions, or percentages, of a whole. (It is called a pie graph because it is usually round and shows the different components as slices of the pie.) If you were speaking about how tax dollars are spent, for example, you might show a pie graph with slices of different sizes representing the proportions of tax money spent on defense, social security, education, welfare programs, interest on the national debt, and so on. Like bar graphs, pie graphs can be used to illustrate two variables. Two pies—one showing the distribution of the budget of the United States and the other showing its distribution in Canada—will make clear that a larger percentage of the federal budget has been required for defense in the United States.[5]

Representations

Representations are visual portrayals of reality. They include textual graphics, diagrams, maps, still photographs or slides, and film or videotape.

A **textual graphic** is a display of words. It is used so that the audience can simultaneously see and hear the words. At the most basic level, a teacher is using a textual graphic when he or she writes an unfamiliar word on the chalkboard. Seeing the word helps students to learn it. In speeches, textual graphics may be used to show a simple outline of the main ideas, to show the central thesis of the speech, or to show the action the speaker wants the audience to take. If you are asking listeners to write to their senator, for example, you could use a textual graphic that shows the senator's address.

A **diagram** is a simple drawing or sketch that represents a more complex object (see Figure 12.6). A diagram is more abstract than a photograph, and because it leaves out many details, you can emphasize the parts of the object that you think are most important. If you were describing how to raise a sail, you might display a diagram of a boat in order to refer to its parts as you proceed. The diagram will not look exactly like a boat, as a photograph would, but it will let listeners know what the principal parts are and how they are used in the process of raising the sail.

pie graph
A graph in the shape of a circle in which the various components of the whole are shown as portions of the circle, like various-sized slices of a pie.

representations
Visual portrayals of reality.

textual graphic
A display of words so that the audience can both see and hear them.

diagram
A simplified drawing or sketch that represents a more complex object.

Maps can be particularly useful visual aids if the speech focuses on directions to, or relationships among, places. For example, a speech about the history of U.S. Route 66 would be aided by a map showing the major points on the famous highway that, in the years before interstates, stretched from Chicago to Los Angeles. But a map almost always needs to be simplified for a speech. Even an enlarged Rand McNally map would not be effective in this case, because it would include so much detail that the audience would not be able to see or focus on Route 66. A much simpler map, showing only the outline of the states and the approximate path of Route 66, would be much more useful (see Fig. 12.7). Nor should the map identify all the points of interest along this famous road; it should show only the points featured in the speech— perhaps three or four. Finally, the map need not be drawn to scale or provide an exact representation, since you are using it primarily to help listeners picture the relationships among the places on Route 66.

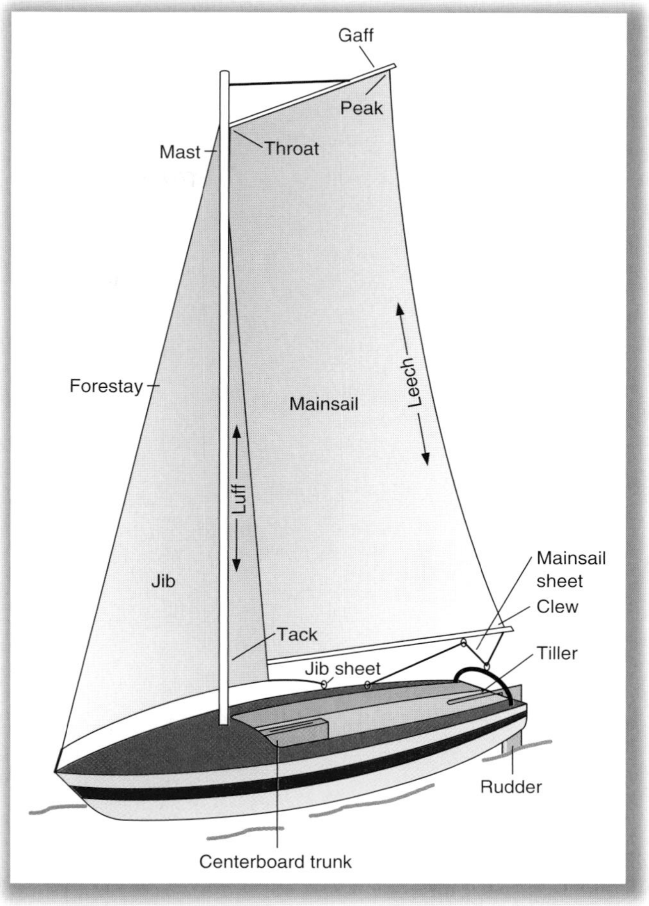

Photographs, too, should be used cautiously as visual aids. Because a photograph portrays reality in all its complexity, it may contain far more information than is important to the speech. What you wish to emphasize may not stand out from the background, and background elements may distract the audience from your intended focus. For example, if you show a photograph of a traffic accident to support your speech about safe driving, your point

Figure 12.6 A diagram for instructional purposes should show only the key features needed for demonstration, as in basic sail instruction.

will be obscured if the audience instead pays attention to the unusual billboards near the scene of the accident.

Some photographs, however, so clearly capture the essence of their subject that they are indeed "worth a thousand words." Examples include such famous photos as the soldiers raising the U.S. flag at Iwo Jima in World War II; President Truman holding up a newspaper headline that had mistakenly announced his defeat in 1948; President Clinton's wagging his finger in early 1998, denying that that he had engaged in a sexual relationship with a White House intern; or the puzzled look on the face of the Florida election official in 2000 who held a punch-card ballot up to the light in order to see whether the chad had been detached. But such photos are rare. Before deciding to illustrate your speech with a photograph, ask yourself (1) whether what you want to show in the photo is clear enough and easy enough to see that it will engage listeners' attention and (2) whether any background elements in the photo will distract the audience from what you want to emphasize.

Film and videotape add the dimension of motion to still photography and raise the possibility of editing to remove distracting scenes (but not to re-

Figure 12.7 Maps should be simplified to display only the key features needed for the presentation—in this case the states and main stopovers on Route 66 from Chicago to Los Angeles.

move distractions in any given shot). These visual aids require special equipment, of course, but videocassette recorders and monitors, in particular, are easy to carry and set up. There is, however, a potential danger in showing moving images. Videos are like television, and people have learned to become relatively passive when they watch. Once you turn on the video, your audience may expect to be entertained and may stop listening actively. To offset this danger, show only short segments of film or tape, and surround them with your oral presentation. Probably the biggest mistake would be to make a short introduction and then just turn the presentation over to videotape. Active listening will decrease markedly.

Objects and Models

Sometimes, the best visual aid is the actual object you are talking about—as when a lawyer holds up key evidence for the jury to see. Chefs on television, for instance, usually explain recipes by using real ingredients, real pots and pans, and real ovens. Similarly, to speak about the different types of seashells found off the coast near your town, you could display examples of shells and point out their unique features. Be aware, though, that objects require you to use your hands more extensively than if you were just pointing to a diagram.[6] You will need to hold things, to manipulate them, and to move them around. All this may solve the problem of what to do with your hands, but you must be careful. Hold the objects firmly and steadily, avoid accidentally knocking them over with sweeping gestures, and be sure to put them away when you are finished with them so that they will not distract the audience.

If it is not feasible to use the actual object, either because it is too large or because it is not portable, you may be able to use a model of the object. For example, a developer who is making a presentation about how a pedestrian mall would improve the downtown area might find it useful to prepare a scale model of the development to refer to during the talk. Similarly, lawyers trying to fix responsibility for an accident might find it useful to refer to a scale model of the accident scene. The one general principle to follow in using a model is that it must be large enough for listeners to see easily. If they have to strain to see the model or you have to apologize because some feature of it is not visible to everyone, it will not be an effective visual aid.

Use good judgment in deciding what to use as models. Occasionally, student speakers, seeking visual aids that add color and interest to the speech, will bring in objects that are illegal or dangerous, such as drugs, guns, or toxic materials. These not only will distract the audience but may startle or frighten them out of proportion to any benefit the speaker might gain. This practice is not only ineffective but ethically dubious.

Finally, animals should not be used as objects or models. Too many problems arise, for example, if you try to use your pet to demonstrate obedience training. The animal will be in a most unfamiliar situation, it may react with fear, and you may lose control. Animals may make noise, get loose, move about, perform bodily functions, or otherwise embarrass you. Even at best, they will distract from your speech by drawing the audience's attention immediately to whatever they are doing rather than to what you are saying.

People

Having just warned against using live models in a speech, it may seem odd that the final category of visual aids is people; it may seem odd, too, to think of yourself or others as visual aids. It almost sounds demeaning. But people presumably are better behaved than animals are, and there are obvious and simple ways in which they can add visual impact to the content of a speech.

Your own body can serve as a visual aid. For example, if your topic is "Power Walking," you can demonstrate the high-intensity movements involved in this type of walking. The demonstration not only will show listeners how to do it but also will help make credible your claim that power walking is vigorous exercise.

Your appearance and grooming can also serve as a visual aid. It obviously makes a difference whether you arrive for a business presentation in a suit or in sweatshirt and jeans. Your clothing either reinforces or undercuts your message that you are seriously interested in obtaining the account. This is not to say that you always have to wear a suit to make a good impression as a speaker. The critical thing is to match your appearance to

Using Visual Aids

The Situation

Your campus organization is underfunded, especially when compared to similar campus organizations. You're getting ready to present your case for more funding to the members of the student government. You've put the final touches on the text of your speech, but now you need to consider using visual aids.

Making Choices

1. What type(s) of visual aids might you use? Why?

2. How should you determine what visual aids would be most appropriate and most useful for this speaking situation?

What If . . .

Your choice of visual aids likely will be affected not only by the type of information available to you but also by the audience to whom you are speaking and your purpose. Decide what type(s) of visual aids you might use and why you would use them for the following situations:

1. You are speaking to a group of ten student government officers instead of the entire student government.

2. You are speaking to all 10,000 students on campus.

3. You are speaking to ten members of the administration.

the situation. If your speech is about lifeguarding, a pair of shorts and a Red Cross T-shirt may be the most effective clothing.

For many people, dress is an important means of asserting cultural identity. Covering your head, wearing non-Western clothing, or dressing in dark colors may be ways to express your heritage and values. At the same time, however, less conventional styles of dress may lead listeners to stereotype you and perhaps to be distracted from your message by your unfamiliar (to them) appearance. Your audience analysis and strategic planning may need to focus on this aspect of the situation. Should you dress to accommodate the expectations of your audience? Or should you "be yourself" and deliberately assert your different cultural identity? The answers to these questions should reflect your analysis of the audience and your specific purpose.

Other people can also serve as visual aids. The obvious example is a speech in which someone helps you demonstrate something. If you plan to use the help of others, it is best to make arrangements with them ahead of time. You will avoid being embarrassed if no one responds when you ask for a volunteer, and you will also be able to coordinate the presentation so that the "volunteer" doesn't seem surprised and you don't seem poorly prepared. Talk candidly with the volunteer about why it is important to perform the task skillfully but quietly, without visible facial responses or other reactions that might upstage you and draw attention away from your speech.

Of all these different types of visual aids, which is the best to use? Charts? Graphs? Representations? Objects and models? People? By now, you know, of course, that there is no "correct" answer to such questions. The decision depends on your topic, on where you are speaking, on the size of the audience, on what the audience is likely to expect, and on how comfortable you are with using visual aids. Any visual aid can be used well or badly. The important thing is to choose it knowingly and with a specific purpose in mind. Once again, critical thinking about your rhetorical situation and strategic planning to achieve your goal will help you make decisions about visual aids.

WWW. Using the Internet

Analyze the Visual Aids Used by Bill Gates

Read the text of one of the speeches delivered by Bill Gates, Chairman of Microsoft, as he gave the keynote address to the Comdex Convention on November 19, 1996. His speech was entitled "The Future of the Personal Computer." You can read the speech at **http://www .microsoft.com/billgates/speeches/comdex96/ keynote.asp.** Next, review the PowerPoint slides that were used to accompany the speech. These are found at **http://www.microsoft.com/billgates/speeches/ comdex96/gates/sld001.asp.** Did the visual aids that Gates used provide interest, enhance credibility, and improve the comprehension and retention of his main points?

Choosing Materials for Visual Aids

Besides your decisions about the types of visual aids to use, you have many options about the materials from which they can be made. Some materials are simple and are available almost everywhere, while others depend on sophisticated equipment and technology. Here, we will examine the chalkboard, flip charts, posterboard, handouts, transparencies, slides, and videotape. A later section of the chapter will provide much more detail about computer-generated visual aids.

Chalkboard

In many speaking situations, using the chalkboard is the easiest way to provide visual aids. Student speakers in classrooms can almost always count on the availability of a chalkboard, and most meeting rooms and presentation settings also include one. Or you might find a variation on the chalkboard—the white board on which you can draw with erasable markers.

Although chalkboards are easily accessible, using them for visual aids presents some problems. For one thing, a chalkboard drawing usually has an amateur quality that may affect the audience's impressions of your speech. Moreover, there is the problem of deciding *when* to draw the visual aid. If you try to draw and talk at the same time, you risk losing eye contact with the audience as well as your concentration. Your vocal qualities will be affected, because your voice will be directed toward the board rather than the audience. But if you stop speaking while you draw, there is an obvious break in the flow of your speech and in the audience's attention. Finally, if you draw the visual aid before beginning to speak, it will remain visible throughout the speech and may distract listeners. (You might avoid this last danger by covering the chalkboard until you are ready to present the visual aid. In some rooms this can be done conveniently by pulling down a screen that is already attached to the chalkboard; but if there is no screen, it may be difficult to cover the visual aid.)

If you do decide to use the chalkboard, make every effort to maintain eye contact with the audience; avoid turning your back on listeners to face the chalkboard. Also make sure that your body does not block anyone's view of the visual aid. Using a ruler, a laser pointer, or some other object to point to it and practicing where to stand and how to move around will help you to remember that the critical relationship is between you and your listeners, not between you and the visual aid.

Flip Charts

A **flip chart** is a writing tablet made of large sheets of paper, usually newsprint, that rests on an easel; you can "flip" each sheet over the binding at the top of the tablet after you have used it. You can create a flip chart by using markers that let you write large enough, wide enough, and dark enough for the audience to see without difficulty.

Flip charts are as easy to make as chalkboard drawings, but they offer two advantages. First, you can develop your visual aids in a sequence. This is especially effective when you want to show the audience a verbal list without including everything at once. For example, you can prepare a series of charts that gradually reveal and elaborate the outline of your speech. The first chart might show only your first main heading. After discussing that idea, you could flip the chart to reveal the next heading; or you could repeat the first heading in one color but also show the new main heading in a contrasting color. As you move through the outline, you can help the audience focus only on the idea that you are discussing at that particular time.

Second, you can easily hide a particular visual or dispose of the flip chart when it is not in use. Instead of erasing or covering up the chalkboard, all you have to do is flip the chart to a blank page. Because you are unlikely to need the chart at the beginning of the speech, you can leave the top sheet blank; simply flip it over when you are ready to discuss your first visual aid.

Posterboard

Anything you can draw on a flip chart can also be prepared on posterboard. Posterboard is as firm as stiff cardboard, making it easier to hold and to handle than a flip chart. If you do not need a lot of visual aids, posterboard may be easier to use.

Where do you put the posterboard? Like other visual aids, it should be concealed when you are not referring to it. You might lay it face down on a table or stand it in the tray of a chalkboard, with the poster facing away from the audience. Or you might attach a blank posterboard to the front of your poster until you are ready to show it. All these methods will prevent listeners from focusing on the poster until you want them to do so. Just be sure that your means of concealment does not make the posterboard hard to reach and uncover when you are ready to use it.

How to display the poster is another consideration. You could hold it, of course; but if it is large and bulky or you need to display it for a long time, holding it will limit your ability to make other appropriate gestures and movements. Another possibility is to place the poster on an easel, much as you would a flip chart. If you prepare several posters, you could stack them on the easel in the order you plan to use them. (Remember to make sure that the easel is available when you begin to speak.) Or you might mount the poster to the wall with thumbtacks or tape (being careful not to damage

flip chart
A writing tablet made of large sheets of paper, usually newsprint, the pages of which can be flipped over after they are used.

the wall, of course). This approach can make it harder to remove the poster during your speech, after you have used it, but the short distraction might be offset by the freedom of movement that you gain when you don't have to worry about holding the poster up.

Handouts

The logical extension of the chalkboard, flip chart, or poster is the **handout**—one or more sheets of paper that you or an assistant literally hand out to audience members to refer to during the speech.

Teachers of public speaking disagree about using handouts. On the positive side, handouts make it easier for a speaker to present complex information, because listeners have their own copy of key terms and definitions or can follow the details of a diagram or the text of a slide. Handouts reduce the need for audience members to take detailed notes, which *may* permit them to concentrate more fully on the substance of the speech. And in some situations—such as a sales presentation—leaving a handout with prospective customers is a highly desirable way to reinforce the message.

But handouts are also a potential source of distraction. The audience may pay more attention to the handout than to what you are saying. This is especially likely to happen if you distribute a handout at the very beginning of the speech but do not refer to it until several minutes have elapsed. Nor is it usually a good idea to distribute handouts in the middle of the speech; that breaks the flow of thought and disturbs listeners who want to concentrate on the speech.

The difficulties with handouts are magnified if you do not have enough copies for everyone. Although some people will share, others are likely to be left out. The worst situation is to pass photographs or a book around the audience while you are speaking. Listeners' attention will lapse in waves as the material reaches them and they focus on it rather than on your speech.

Transparencies

Transparencies are celluloid sheets that are projected onto a screen with the use of an overhead projector. The celluloid sheets are inexpensive, and the projector enlarges the transparency and makes it easily visible to the audience. Finally, since the room does not have to be as dark for an overhead projector as for slides or film, there is less disruption of the speech.

Transparencies are easy to prepare. Using special markers, you can draw charts or diagrams or write key words. (Prepare transparencies only with permanent-ink markers; all your efforts will be wasted if the ink lifts off.) You can prepare text on a word processor, print it on a sheet of paper, and then photocopy it onto a transparency; you can also photocopy charts or graphs. As with flip charts, you can develop and display transparencies in sequence. You can even add to a transparency by drawing on it while it is being shown. And you can stand at the projector and use a pencil or a pen to point to specific objects on the transparency.

handout
One or more sheets of paper given out to audience members before or during the speech; at some point the speaker refers to the handout.

transparencies
Celluloid sheets that are projected onto a screen with the use of an overhead projector.

Visual aids and projection equipment need to be placed properly in the room so that you can refer to the visual aid while also maintaining eye contact with the audience and so that listeners can see you and the visual aid at the same time.

Like any visual aid, however, you have to plan the use of transparencies. First, you will need to stand next to the overhead projector if you want to work with your transparencies as you are speaking. If the size of the print on the transparencies requires you to be a certain distance from the wall, or if the electrical outlet is located inconveniently, you might have to stand behind some members of the audience. You can limit this difficulty by checking the room carefully in advance to determine how large the print should be in order to place the projector where you want it.

Second, you will need to check the projection equipment carefully. To have greater flexibility in positioning it, you might bring a long extension cord with you (but find out whether the cord needs a three-pronged plug; a household extension cord may not be suitable). And it's always a good idea to carry a spare lightbulb for the projector. If the bulb fails, your visual aids will be useless.

Third, realize that the audience will be distracted if the transparencies are too complex, if the print is too small, if you use too many transparencies, or if you change them too rapidly. Above all, be sure to check in advance that the transparencies are in the order you plan to present them. You will break the audience's concentration if you stop either to rearrange the transparencies or to project some of them onto the screen to determine which is which.

For all their benefits, transparencies are effective only with an audience of about 50 or fewer people. With larger audiences, transparencies have to be enlarged so much to fit the screen that they lose their focus and impact.

Slides

Not all forms of visual aids lend themselves to projection by transparencies. Photographs and complex graphs may be easier to project with slides. In addition, if the audience is too large for you to use transparencies effectively, any visual aid on a transparency can be photographed and shown on a slide. But slides are harder to prepare than transparencies, and they are more expensive. You should shoot extra rolls of film so that you can select the slides that most clearly capture the images you want.

Most speakers who use slides arrange them in a **carousel**—a circular tray that fits onto a slide projector. The slides are placed in the desired order for presentation, and the carousel rotates to bring each slide into view. The rate of display can be set to a predetermined number of seconds, or you can change slides by pressing a button. It may not be necessary to stand at the projector while you speak. You can avoid being tied to that space if the projector has a remote control to advance the carousel or if you can find an assistant who will stand at the projector and advance it according to your directions.

As with transparencies, the positioning of the slide projector is critical to the success of the speech. It must be placed so that the slides will be enlarged to the proper size on the screen and so that the path of light from projector to screen is above the heads of the audience. For this reason, you may want to place the screen in a corner at the front of the room rather than directly in the center. As in using an overhead projector, you should check the equipment carefully in advance; find out whether you need and can use an extension cord, and carry a spare lightbulb.

Changes in technology may make slides obsolete. With a digital camera, you can store pictures on a disk, transfer them to a compact disc (CD), and play them on a digital video display (DVD) player. This eliminates the need for film, slides, or a carousel. But the basic principles for the use of the medium remain the same.

Speakers who use slides often overuse them. They have more slides than their speech really requires, and they change them very quickly. This can be extremely distracting, both because audience members really do not have the time to absorb one slide before another is presented and because the constant clicking of the carousel as it advances calls attention to itself.[7]

Videotape

As was noted earlier, videotape makes it possible to present moving images as visual aids. As in using slides, you'll want to tape more material than you

---

WWW. Using the Internet

Find Images for Visual Aids

A speaker can search for relevant images from a variety of resources. The **UMD Locating Visual Images** Web site provides a list of resources and image databases. Point your browser to **http://www.lib.umd.edu/ART/guides/images.html** to access these resources.

Suppose you were giving a speech on the worldwide spread of Acquired Immune Deficiency Syndrome (AIDS). Point your browser to the **Google Image Search** Web page (**http://images.google.com/**) and enter the search term "AIDS map." How could you use one of these images in creating a visual aid for that speech?

Images also can be found at a variety of Internet sites. Go to the **HubbleSite Gallery** Web page (**http://hubblesite.org/gallery/**) for examples of images from space.

---

carousel
A circular tray that holds slides and fits onto a projector; it is usually advanced by remote control.

---

can use, to ensure that you get the most effective images. Because you can show only short segments of videotape, review and edit it carefully before the speech. Remove everything that is not directly relevant to the points you want to make. Today's technology makes it easy to tape with a portable camcorder and then to edit the tape for presentation. In fact, the results are so professional-looking that you'll need to exercise restraint. Your tape must do more than just entertain. Remember that it is a visual aid and that its purpose is to *support* the ideas you articulate.

Preparing Visual Aids

Whatever materials you use in creating visual aids, the most important strategic consideration is that visual aids should be carefully matched to the contents of the speech.

Storyboarding

The process of matching visual aids to points in the speech is called story-boarding. A **storyboard** is a page containing the verbal outline for a single idea in the presentation, along with a sketch of the visual aid that will illustrate that idea. Taken together, the storyboards for a speech provide both a visual and a verbal outline. Storyboarding will force you to:

- Limit yourself to one visual aid per idea.
- Select the types of visual aids that will be most appropriate and most effective.

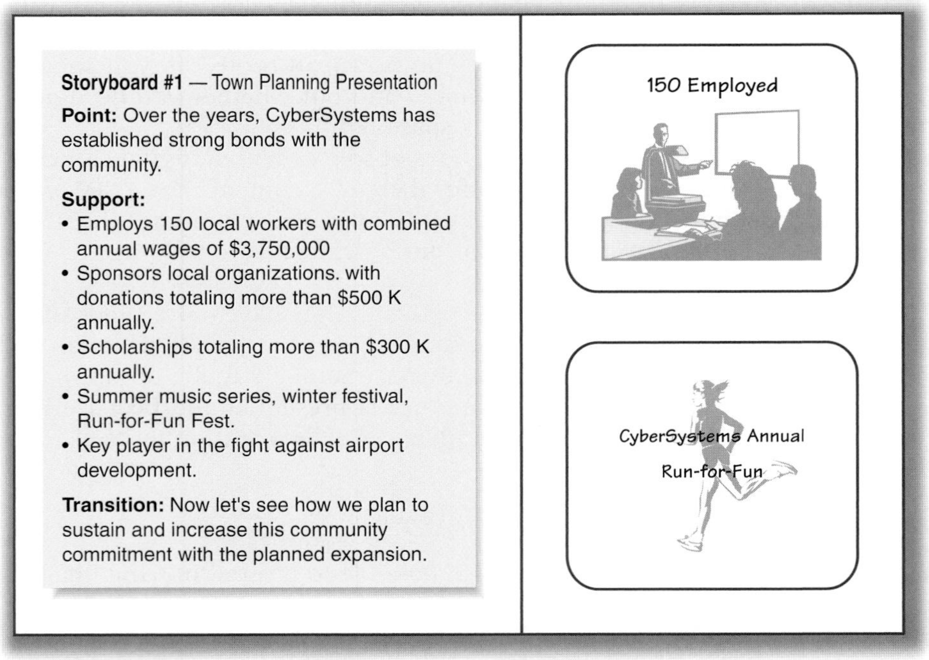

storyboard
A page containing the verbal outline for a single idea, along with a sketch of the visual aid to illustrate that idea.

Figure 12.8 A storyboard for a persuasive presentation.

Storyboard #1 — Town Planning Presentation

Point: Over the years, CyberSystems has established strong bonds with the community.

Support:
- Employs 150 local workers with combined annual wages of $3,750,000
- Sponsors local organizations. with donations totaling more than $500 K annually.
- Scholarships totaling more than $300 K annually.
- Summer music series, winter festival, Run-for-Fun Fest.
- Key player in the fight against airport development.

Transition: Now let's see how we plan to sustain and increase this community commitment with the planned expansion.

150 Employed

CyberSystems Annual Run-for-Fun

When you plan your storyboards, be conservative about the number of visuals to include. Not every idea needs to be illustrated, and you should give the audience enough time to absorb what you show and to listen carefully to your verbal information before you make them shift attention to another image. Figure 12.8 is an example of a storyboard. It is neither an outstanding nor a bad example, but a fairly typical one.

Designing Visual Aids

The following design principles will help you to prepare effective visual aids that support your presentation.

1. *Visual aids should be seen easily by members of the audience.* If people must strain to see, if the visual aid is too small, or if it is too complex, the benefit of using the visual aid is lost. This principle dictates that visual aids be *simple*. Each visual aid should illustrate only one idea in the speech, and each should be as uncluttered as possible.

This principle also requires that you pay attention to the size and proportion of visual aids. For example, the lettering in textual graphics should be at least two or three inches high. You should have a good sense of the distance from the visual aid to the back of the room; stand at that distance from the visual aid as you prepare it, and be certain that you can see and read it easily. Also, you should select the kind of visual aid that is appropriate to the situation. A flip chart or a chalkboard drawing might work perfectly for an audience of 25, but for an audience of 200, you probably need slides or videotape to ensure that everyone can see well.

2. *Visual aids should be easy for the speaker to handle.* Your aids should be portable, not heavy or cumbersome, and they should not restrict your movements or gestures during the speech. In addition, you should be able to set up and remove them quickly, because it is unlikely that the room will be available for any great length of time either before or after your speech. Finally, you should design the visual aids with an eye toward how they will be kept in place during your presentation. Imagine the "choreography" of your speech, and determine whether the aids need to be placed on an easel; if so, be sure that one is available. If you plan to mount your visual aids on the wall or to hand them out to the audience, consider carefully how best to do this and at what point during the speech you will need to use them. If you plan to hold the visual aids, be sure that their size and materials permit you to do so easily.

3. *Visual aids should be aesthetically pleasing without distracting from the speech.* This principle suggests that you determine what the central element of the visual aid is and what elements are in the background. You might use color to heighten the appeal and focus of your aids and to make points clearly. Color is more vivid than black and white and usually will grab the audience's attention. To make your meaning clearer, you might use variations of a single color (shades of green, for example), colors that are close to one another on a color wheel (to suggest similarities), or colors that are usually thought of as opposites (to emphasize distinctions). Aesthetic considerations might also lead you to choose, for example, whether to use a

chart or a graph and whether a bar graph or a pie graph is a more compelling way to illustrate a central idea.

On the other hand, you do not want your speech to be like the movie that is remembered primarily for its special effects. Be careful that elaborate visual aids do not run away with your speech, causing listeners to remember your attractive charts and graphs rather than what you said. Follow two key principles: Restrict your visual aids to those that really are crucial, and keep the design of each visual aid as simple as possible. Although visual aids will help make your ideas clearer, remember that the speech is ultimately about those ideas, not about the visual aids.

Checklist 12.2 Designing Visual Aids

Keep in mind the following principles:

1. **Visual aids should be carefully matched to the contents of the speech.**
2. **Visual aids should be easily seen by members of the audience.**
3. **Visual aids should be easy for the speaker to handle.**
4. **Visual aids should be aesthetically pleasing without distracting from the speech.**

Computer-Generated Visual Aids

Computers make it possible to produce high-quality, sophisticated visual aids and to present them imaginatively during the speech. Computer-generated visual aids have become the norm in many business and professional presentations. Even beginning speakers find many uses for computer technology.

Preparing Visual Aids on the Computer

The most common use of the computer is to generate visual aids that will be printed on slides or transparencies, or, more likely, projected directly from the computer onto a screen. Almost any word-processing program can help you make attractive charts, tables, and textual graphics. Computers also can be used to produce images and representations. With the presentation graphics software products that have been developed in recent years, it is possible for anyone with access to a computer outfitted with the appropriate software to prepare effective graphics. And, with the use of a scanner, you can retrieve photographs, maps, or documents electronically. Some programs also permit you to include video clips or to mix sound with graphics.

WWW. Using the Internet

Use Online Tools to Create a Computer-generated Visual Aid

There are a host of software programs that you can use to develop effective visual aids. To explore some of these, go to the **Allyn & Bacon Public Speaking Web Site** page "Multimedia Tools." Point your browser to **http://www.abacon.com/pubspeak/deliver/webtools.html**.

Beyond providing a wide range of visual aids, an obvious advantage to using the computer is that you can experiment with different sizes and shapes, and you can correct errors easily. You can vary the size and font (type style) of textual graphics and can modify the color, proportions, background, and other elements of an image. In fact, it is tempting to use too much of the computer's capability, leading to visual aids that ignore the principle of simplicity—too many colors, too many fonts, and too much information. The following suggestions should help you to resist this temptation.

1. *Choose a basic design and color scheme for the entire presentation.* You might repeat a word, symbol, style, or font throughout your visual aids, or maintain a consistent color scheme, or use consistent spacing. Any of these will help to create a sense of unity for your presentation.

2. *Select fonts carefully.* Graphic designers usually divide typefaces into four basic classes of fonts: serif, sans serif, script, and ornamental (or decorative). *Serif* fonts, like the one you are reading, have little lines (serifs) at the tops and bottoms of letters, and the letters are usually made up of both thick and thin lines. *Sans serif* fonts do not have the extra lines at the tops and bottoms, and all lines in the letters are usually the same thickness. Of the two, serif fonts are easier to read for longer passages, because the serifs guide the eye from one letter to the next. *Script* fonts imitate handwriting but are far more precise and uniform. They can be very fancy and complicated, which can make them hard to read. Finally, *ornamental*, or *decorative*, fonts are designed not so much for ease in reading as to convey a particular feeling or tone. Figure 12.9 shows examples of each class of font.

Figure 12.9 Typefaces grouped by font type.

Most designers agree that you should use no more than two typefaces on a single visual aid and that they should be from two different font categories. The most common combination is to use a sans serif font for displayed titles or headings and a serif font for text passages. Of course, designers sometimes violate these guidelines to achieve special effects.

3. *Choose an appropriate type size.* Visual aids are of little use if the type is not large enough for everyone in the audience to see. Designers at Microsoft have specified general guidelines for visual aids. They recommend using 44-point type for titles, 32-point type for subtitles or text if there is no subtitle, and 28-point type for the text if there is also a subtitle. (To give a sense of what this means, there are 72 "points" in an inch.) The smallest sizes recommended for visuals other than slides are 36-point type for titles, 24-point for subtitles, and 18-point for text. Slides can be somewhat smaller, since projection enlarges the image. You might use 24-point for titles, 18-point for subtitles, and 14-point for text. Figure 12.10 shows how these sizes look in print. In any case, avoid using capital letters for emphasis except in short titles. Long stretches of all-capital text are hard to read, because our eyes rely on contrasting letter shapes to decode quickly.

4. *Use color to create a mood and sustain attention.* Graphic designers have long known that warm colors (oranges and reds) appear to come forward and have an exciting effect, whereas cool colors (greens and blues) seem to recede and have a more calming effect. When you choose colors, think about how you want your audience to react to your visual aid. Your topic,

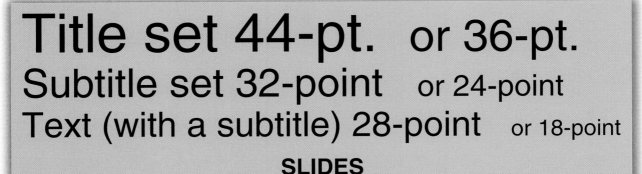

Figure 12.10 Variations of a typeface.

occasion, and purpose should influence this decision. For example, in a business setting, you might use cool colors to convey disappointing news and warm colors to convey good news.

It is also important to choose colors for backgrounds and for text or graphics that contrast with one another but do not conflict. Figure 12.11 provides examples of an effective and an ineffective color combination. Using yellow against a blue background is effective; the colors contrast yet are harmonious. Using purple against a blue background, on the other hand, is not effective; both colors are dark, and so the purple letters do not stand out from the background. Be cautious about combining red and green. Some audience members may have a type of color blindness that makes these two colors indistinguishable. Even for those without color blindness, this combination is not effective because it is difficult to read.

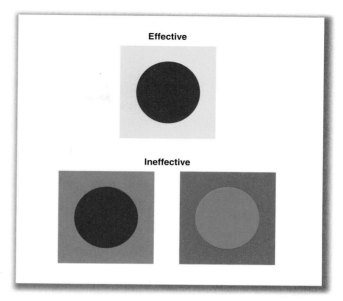

Figure 12.11 Examples of effective and ineffective color combinations.

Multimedia Presentations

It is now possible, with computer programs such as PowerPoint by Microsoft, to incorporate drawings, photographs, video segments, animation, and sound into your visual aids, along with charts, graphs, and text. Such a combination is called a *multimedia presentation*. Presentation software programs such as PowerPoint, Persuasion by Adobe, Corel Presentations, Shockwave, or Freelance Graphics by Lotus can also assist you in making more traditional, professional-quality visual aids, including transparencies, 35mm slides, handouts, or even posters. You can download photographs directly from the Internet (even more easily if you have wireless access), or you can import images that you have entered into your computer by using a scanner. Then you can produce a series of quick images that look like animation, integrating sound clips and even displaying short video clips.

Most of the professional software programs provide a tutorial to help you learn the program easily. They also provide a selection of templates to guide your designs. Using these templates, you can input the text for your graphics in outline form and the program will automatically format it into slides for a presentation. The programs often incorporate design elements discussed in this chapter, such as font size and color coordination, which makes preparing the graphics even easier.

With a multimedia presentation, you have to use the computer to present the visual aids during your speech, and you may wish to do this even if you have created "electronic slides" without multimedia. For a small audience, you can display the finished presentation on the computer monitor, but for most speeches, you will need to project the visual aids onto a larger screen. You can set the computer to advance the visuals automatically at the pace you choose—to match where you expect to be in the speech—or you can advance the visuals manually. You can also use the "build" feature to control the information the audience sees. The presentation will begin with the first major bullet point on your slide and then display progressively more information as you speak about the various points. You can also vary the transitions between slides (how they move on and off the screen), such as making the slides fade in and out or move across, up, or down.

Some of the functions of the computer can be performed using personal data assistants (PDAs). These handheld devices, with names such as Palm Pilot, were originally designed to function as electronic calendars and address books. As technology has advanced, they now are able to do more; some can be used to develop multimedia presentations. Because PDAs are even more portable than laptop computers, they make it even easier to access advanced technology.

Because it is easy to generate visual aids on the computer, it is tempting to make too many of them and to show them throughout the speech. This can distract from your main ideas just as much as can the overuse of charts, slides, or other "low-tech" visual aids. Just as you would not want to show them throughout your speech, you should be equally sparing with the images in a PowerPoint presentation. Keep in mind the fundamental principle: Visual aids are not ends in themselves; their purpose is to support your main ideas.

You always should rehearse the presentation on the equipment that you will actually use when you deliver the speech. Then you can deal in advance with any technical mishaps. Also be sure to bring backup diskettes with you to the speech, in case you run into problems with the files on your computer's hard drive. If you will not be using your own computer, be sure that the computers at the speaking site are compatible with your software.

As a precaution, you should have a backup plan in case the computer program fails to run. For instance, you might use your slides to make a set of transparencies that you could show on an overhead projector in an emergency. Or you could print and duplicate copies of your slides so that you could use them as handouts in case your technology fails. By anticipating technical difficulties, you can use the time right before the presentation to collect your thoughts, knowing that the technical aspects of your visual aids are under control.[8]

Using Visual Aids in the Speech

To plan the effective use of visual aids, you must be sensitive to your audience, your purpose, and the physical circumstances. The composition and culture of the audience will affect your decisions about which visual aids are appropriate, and the size of the audience will affect how large or how complex the visual aids should be. You also need to think about how to use the aids during the speech—and to practice the speech including them.

One of the first decisions is where to place the visual aids. Will they be in the center of the room or to the side? Will they be mounted or free-standing? Will they be visible throughout the speech or concealed except when you refer to them? Make these decisions consciously, not by accident. Then gather whatever materials you need—thumbtacks, tape, extension cord, easel, lightbulb, laptop computer, and so on.

As you practice your speech incorporating the visual aids, keep two important considerations in mind:

1. *Do not obstruct the audience's view of the visual aid.* Position the aid so that, when you stand to speak, listeners will be able to see it as well as to see you. Otherwise, there is no point in preparing the visual aid. For example, if you plan to stand at the center of the room, place the visual aid to the side. If you are using a projection screen, try placing it in one of the front corners of the room rather than in the center.

Consider carefully the details of the room. If your audience is in tiered ("stadium style") seating, you can display your visual aid at your own eye level. But if audience members are seated at the same level (at banquet tables or in an ordinary classroom, for instance), you will need to position the visual aid above your head so that everyone can see it. If you are speaking in a wide room, place the visual aid far enough from the front row that people at the sides can see it; if the room is long and narrow, be sure that the visual aid is large enough that people seated at the back can see it.

Remember, though, that you need to have access to the visual aid. If you plan to point to it, you must stand close enough that your pointer will identify the specific spot you want to highlight. If you plan to turn flip charts, you have to be able to reach them. If you need to be near the overhead projector, that should govern where the projector is placed.

If possible, experiment with the placement of your visual aids in the room where you will speak. If you can arrive early, try out different locations for the visual aids, and find out what works best. If you can't do that because the room is occupied or because you must speak immediately after others, at least think ahead of time about what placement will make the most sense.

If the visual aid is positioned some distance from you and you will need to point to it, select the type of pointer that will work best in the situation. You could consider using your hands, although some find that to be awkward or even impolite. You might use a ruler or a yardstick, or you could buy a retractable pointer that is made for the purpose. Laser pointers throw a beam of light onto the screen, but these must be used with care. They are hard to hold steady, and the audience may think you are nervous if the pointer moves back and forth. With a laser pointer, it is usually best to circle the object you want to highlight rather than focusing directly on it; then turn the light off so it won't be distracting.

2. *Speak to the audience, not to the visual aid.* Many speakers forget this. They face the screen or the chalkboard, pointing to the visual aid, moving their arms around, but with their back to the audience. This is obviously ineffective—first, because it prevents listeners from seeing the visual aid and, second, because the speaker cannot maintain eye contact with the audience. When you turn to the visual aid, do so briefly, to highlight or point out certain features, and then be sure to turn around to face the audience again.

These two considerations suggest the importance of practicing the use of visual aids. Plan where to put them, how and when to refer to them, how to use your hands, and how to put them away. If you practice these steps several times, the visual aids will become a natural part of the speech rather than a distraction.

If you can, simulate the actual conditions in the room where you will speak. Bring your visual aids, and make sure that all needed equipment is in place. Plan where to position yourself and your visual aids. Be prepared with extension cords, spare lightbulbs, and other things you may need. Go through the speech just as you would with the audience present. And if much time lapses between this pre-speech practice and your actual speech, check again that everything is still in working order. Even with the very best preparation, however, equipment sometimes fails during a speech, and you may not be able to use the visual aids as planned. If that happens, be confident that your practice has made you familiar with your visual aids and that you can either improvise some other ones or, if necessary, can even deliver the speech without visual aids.

Strategies for Speaking to Diverse Audiences

Respecting Diversity Through Visual Aids

In preparing visual aids, it is important to make them accessible to all members of the audience. The following strategies recognize that members of diverse audiences may process visual aids differently.

1. Because some members of your audience may be visually impaired, be sure that the visual aids supplement but do not replace verbal content.
2. Remember that some images may convey different meanings in other cultures.
3. Realize that cultures may differ in the processing of different kinds of visual information such as statistics, flow charts, graphs, and the like.

Summary

Although visual aids are not usually required, they can help make your message clear and hold the audience's attention. They permit an appeal to multiple senses, they add variety to the message, they focus the audience's attention, and they make it easier for listeners to remember the speech. If visual aids are not used carefully, however, they may call attention to themselves and distract from your message. The challenge is to reap the benefits of using visual aids while avoiding the pitfalls.

Virtually anything can serve as a visual aid, but it is useful to think in terms of primary categories. Charts can be used to present statistical material, to show the sequence of steps in a process, to reflect patterns of decision or action, and to introduce lists. Graphs show the relationships between variables and are usually depicted as line graphs, bar graphs, or pie graphs. Physical representations can include textual graphics, diagrams, maps, photographs, and film or videotape. Objects and models can be used as visual aids, and the body—whether the speaker's or someone else's—is often a powerful aid to demonstrate actions or processes.

Speakers must decide which materials to use in making visual aids. The main issue is what will be most effective in the given situation. Some possibilities include drawings on the chalkboard, flip charts, posters, handouts, transparencies, slides, and videotape. Each offers certain benefits and has possible drawbacks. Whatever materials are used, the most important consideration is that visual aids should be carefully matched to the contents of the speech. This can be accomplished through storyboarding.

In designing visual aids, key principles include visibility to the audience, ease of handling by the speaker, and aesthetic considerations. To take full advantage of well-prepared visual aids, it is important to practice the speech using the visual aids—if possible, simulating the conditions in the room where you will present the speech.

Computer technology makes it possible to design sophisticated visual aids and to present them from the computer during the speech. You can create text and graphics, making strategic choices about such matters as font, type size, and color. Some computer programs permit you to develop multimedia presentations combining text, clip art, drawings, photographs, video clips, and sound.

Not every speech needs visual aids, but some, such as a sales presentation, virtually require them. In most cases, the decision to use visual aids is a strategic choice that is made to enhance the effectiveness of the speech.

Discussion Questions

1. During the 1992 presidential campaign, candidate Ross Perot was fond of using visual aids to support his messages. Watching a videotape of some of Perot's speeches, what do you make of those visual aids? Did they support or detract from the impact of his speeches? Was the use of visual aids appropriate for the situation? Which visual aid was the most effective? Which was the least effective?

2. Sixty years ago, people listened to the radio for news and entertainment. Today, most young people are raised on the visual medium of television, and on personal computers having sophisticated graphics capabilities. How has the rise of television and the computer altered expectations about visual support in speeches? How in turn do these considerations affect the strategic decisions you make about your speech?

3. What type of visual aid would be most appropriate for the following purposes? Could the speaker get away with not using a visual aid? What would visual aids add to these oral discussions?

   - Describing your trip to Paris
   - Informing your audience about the length of sentences for certain crimes and the length of time that criminals actually serve for those crimes
   - Explaining the technique of crab picking
   - Teaching an audience how to fill out a 1040EZ tax form
   - Teaching the Heimlich maneuver

- Describing the change in expected life spans over the last 500 years
- Getting your audience excited about a new use of the Internet

4. Sometimes visual aids not only increase interest, credibility, and memory but also add to the persuasiveness of a message. Can you think of any examples of visual aids (in speeches, newspapers, advertisements, or the courtroom) that would have an especially powerful persuasive impact?

Activities

1. Take some statistics from one of your speeches, and try to display those statistics in the following forms:

   - As a chart
   - As a line graph
   - As a bar graph
   - As a pie graph

   Which form seems to best communicate the information that you want to get across in your speech? Why?

2. Evaluate each piece of support in your speech to determine whether or not a visual aid will contribute significantly to the message. In making this determination, be sure to consider the many types of visual aids that you might use.

3. Using the visual aids that you have chosen in activity 2, practice your speech in the room where you are going to give it. Note the potential pitfalls (e.g., lack of an easel for the poster, unfocused overhead projector, low volume on a tape player), and be prepared to avoid them in the actual presentation.

Notes

1. For more about these three benefits, see Virginia Johnson, "Picture-Perfect Presentations," *Training and Development Journal* 43 (May 1989): 45–47.
2. William J. Seiler, "The Effects of Visual Materials on Attitudes, Credibility, and Retention," *Speech Monographs* 38 (November 1971): 331–334.
3. Visual aids are often the norm in business speeches. For a good discussion of the minimal standards for visual aids in corporate presentations, see Michael Antonoff, "Presentations that Persuade," *Personal Computing* (July 1990): 60–68.
4. William J. Seiler, "The Conjunctive Influence of Source Credibility and the Use of Visual Materials on Communicative Effectiveness," *Southern Speech Communication Journal* 37 (Winter 1971): 174–185.
5. For more about the mechanics of constructing charts and graphs without the aid of a computer, see Robert Lefferts, *Elements of Graphics: How to Prepare Charts and Graphs for Effective Reports*, New York: Harper & Row, 1981.
6. Lawyers often use objects in their persuasive messages. For a description of one lawyer who was particularly skilled at the use of visual aids, see Edward Palzer, "Visual Materials with a Point," *Today's Speech* 10 (April 1962): 15–16. For additional suggestions regarding the use of visual aids by lawyers, see Ronald Waicukauski, Paul Mark Sandler,

and JoAnne Epps, *The Winning Argument,* Chicago: American Bar Association, 2001, pp. 94–102.

7. More advice about the use of slides in a speech can be found in J. R. Van Pelt, "Lantern Slides and Such," *Quarterly Journal of Speech* 36 (February 1950): 44–50. This is a very early article. As slides become obsolete, its primary value may be as a relic!

8. For further practical advice about the design of computer-generated visual aids, see Dan Cavanaugh, *Preparing Visual Aids for Presentations,* 2d ed., Boston: Allyn & Bacon, 2000. This booklet also includes a step-by-step description of how to prepare visual aids using PowerPoint.

Chapter Thirteen

Informing

In this chapter, we will:

- Refine our understanding of strategic planning as the process of determining how the speech can most effectively achieve its purpose.

- Distinguish between informing and persuading as purposes for a speech while recognizing that they often overlap.

- Consider how the goal of informing dictates clarifications or refinements in the specific purpose and the organizational pattern of the speech.

- Become familiar with various strategies that achieve the goal of educating the audience.

- Examine ways by which you can encourage listeners to remember the knowledge or insight your speech provides.

Now that we have explored audience analysis, research, reasoning, organization, language, and presentation, we are ready to bring these skills together into a complete speech. To do so, we should revisit two related concepts: purpose and strategy. A speech is designed to achieve a purpose, and strategic planning is the process of deciding how your speech can best do that.

In Chapter 4, we examined seven different kinds of purpose:

- Providing new information or sharing a perspective
- Setting the agenda
- Intensifying or weakening a feeling
- Strengthening commitment to a position
- Weakening commitment to a position
- Converting the audience away from one belief and toward another
- Inducing a specific action

Now the question is, which strategies are most appropriate for achieving these purposes?

Planning Your Strategy

Broadly speaking, speech goals are achieved through the strategies of informing, persuading, and entertaining. These are sometimes mistakenly seen as resulting in three fundamentally different kinds of speeches. In fact, though, because successful sharing of information also affects people's attitudes, informing and persuading occur together. Likewise, a successful persuasive speech is also entertaining and enjoyable to listen to, and an entertaining speech usually also conveys new information.

The broad strategies overlap, then, and they do not exclude each other. So if your assignment is to present "an informative speech," this does not mean that you should avoid saying anything entertaining or persuasive. Rather, you should achieve your purpose primarily through strategies of informing.

Defining Your Specific Purpose

But what if the assignment does not specify a purpose? Or what if you are speaking outside the classroom setting? Then you must decide what you want to achieve (for example, to teach people something new, to get them to contribute money to a cause, or to make them laugh). You will need to assess how the audience and the occasion create opportunities or constraints. Finally, based on this analysis, you will define your specific purpose.

For example, suppose that many of your listeners believe that the Internet should be regulated to protect children from indecent material. Your own opinion is exactly the opposite, and you would like to change their minds. But you know (or will learn in the next chapter) that people do not usually make major changes in their beliefs because of a single speech. You also realize that most of your listeners do not really understand exactly what the Internet is. Of course, they have used e-mail and have used the World Wide Web for research, but they don't know the structure of the In-

ternet itself and why that makes regulation difficult. Finally, you will be speaking at an educational conference that is exploring how the
Internet can be used in the home. All these factors lead you not to try to convert your audience
but to seek the more realistic goal of providing
new information about the Internet. You hope
that this new information, in turn, will weaken
the audience's commitment to the view that the
Internet should be regulated, but that is not your
goal for this speech. Rather, you have undertaken
to provide new ideas or a new perspective. To accomplish this goal, you will rely more on strategies to inform than on strategies to persuade.

On the other hand, sometimes an audience
must be persuaded before it can be informed.
Consider another example. During the Cold War
years, most Americans approached foreign policy
issues from the premise that the world was locked in a mortal struggle between freedom and communism. Information about world events was understood within the framework provided by this dominant assumption. For
a speaker even to discuss nationalism in Eastern Europe, it first was necessary to challenge the prevailing view that all of Eastern Europe was a mono-
lith dominated by the Soviet Union. In order to share information
effectively, it first was necessary to change listeners' attitudes.

Informing Your Audience

In this chapter, we are concerned with informing. **Informative strategies**
presume that a principal goal of the speech is to share ideas with the audience. They rely on the metaphor of the speaker as teacher and the speech
as a lesson. The speaker is expected to be clear, accurate, and interesting.
Listeners are asked to be attentive, to understand what is being said, and to
modify their knowledge and belief systems to take this new information and
perspective into account.

In a speech about the microscopic world around us, Kimo Sanderson
made his classmates think about something they had previously ignored:

> There are millions of living creatures in your house right now. They crawl
> through your carpet, reproduce under your bed, and snack in your closet.
> When examined under a microscope, they look like creatures from your worst
> nightmares. They are dust mites, and we live with them every day.

In her speech about the Beat Generation, Elizabeth Wright introduced
her audience to an era that was unfamiliar to them:

> During the late 1940s and early 1950s, the Beat Generation began to explore
> the country in search of something to believe in. People like Jack Kerouac,
> Allen Ginsberg, and Gary Snyder listened to jazz, wrote "stream of conscious-
> ness" poetry, and celebrated freedom. Let's take a closer look at these people
> and their ideas.

Informative strategies do not explicitly ask listeners to believe or do any
particular thing. Rather, they ask that listeners alter their understanding of

informative strategies
Approaches to preparing a
speech in which the overall
goal is to share ideas with an
audience.

a subject. Sometimes this can be done by taking new information into account, such as when one learns that the local community was founded by immigrants 150 years ago. At other times, listeners' understanding is changed because they see the subject in a different light, such as when confusing instructions for filling out a tax form are made clear, or when the speaker explains the counterintuitive fact that the Panama Canal is farther east on the Pacific side than on the Atlantic side (the canal mainly runs north–south).

Of course, learning something new might stimulate listeners to take some action. For example, imagine that you heard a speech about the depletion of the ozone layer, knowing nothing previously about this scientific and ecological issue. The speaker's purpose was to share information about the extent of the thinning of the ozone layer so far, the role of the ozone layer in shielding us from the sun's ultraviolet rays, and projections for the future rate of ozone depletion. The speaker did not actually call on you to do anything; the goal was only to make you aware of a previously neglected issue. But it would not be surprising if, after hearing such a speech, you chose to stop using aerosol spray cans and to urge legislators to ban their use. In the next chapter, we will contrast informative strategies with strategies of persuasion, which seek to influence listeners' beliefs, values, or actions.

Clarifying Your Informative Goal

Two of the speech purposes discussed in Chapter 4 rely primarily on informative strategies: providing new information or perspective and agenda setting. Information is essential if you are to induce listeners to think about something new, to view it from a unique perspective, or to take into account something they had previously ignored. In addition, the purpose of creating positive or negative feeling relies heavily on both informative and persuasive strategies, as well as on entertaining.

Providing New Information or Perspective. Common knowledge about a subject is often quite general. It is widely acknowledged, for example, that many eligible voters in the United States do not vote. But most people have little understanding of what lies behind this statement—whether the percentage of voters has been increasing or decreasing, how participation varies among different groups, factors that tend to increase or limit participation, the relationship between registration and voting, and so on. One informational goal for a speech would be to enrich the audience's common knowledge about voting rates, moving listeners from a broad understanding to a more detailed awareness of the issue.

Sometimes, a speaker's objective is not merely to supply more details but to update and revise the audience's common knowledge. Part of what people generally believe may be mistaken, and social knowledge changes with the times. There is probably no clearer example than what people in the United States "know" about Russia. For most of the period from 1945 to 1990, people "knew" that the Soviet Union (which included Russia) was engaged in a deadly economic and political struggle with the United States. But in the years since 1990, people have come to "know" that this is no longer the case. You probably will not be able to alter your listeners' perspective so dramatically. But if your Internet speech gives listeners information that leads to a new way of thinking about "indecency," you will have accomplished the same purpose.

Agenda Setting. A speaker whose purpose is **agenda setting** wants to create awareness of a subject that listeners did not know about or think about before, thus putting it on the agenda of topics that warrant their concern. Until fairly recently, for example, the majority of Americans simply didn't think about whether there was a pattern to the race or ethnicity of drivers who are stopped by police officers and searched in an effort to reduce crime. Most Americans went about their errands, assuming that if a person was stopped and searched by an officer, that person was suspected of engaging in illegal activity. But many African American drivers who have been pulled over and searched without reasonable cause have protested against "racial profiling," the practice of making traffic or other investigative stops on the basis of a person's race or ethnicity. As a result, the subject now warrants our attention, and increasing numbers of people are becoming aware of the problem. Speakers and writers focused attention on a topic that had been ignored, and at some point it was put on the agenda. The September 11, 2001, terrorist attacks added yet another dimension to the issue, as people who had not thought one way or another about profiling during security screening at airports had to consider how it was being used to combat terrorism.

The AIDS memorial quilt is brought to communities all over the country where audiences flock to see it. Local speakers attempt to bring positive feelings to their audiences about treatment for people with AIDS and new research to find a cure.

Creating Positive or Negative Feeling. It borders on cliché to say that information gives people power. Knowledge and understanding enable people to perform competently and to make intelligent choices. Providing information empowers listeners to feel better about their ability to control their lives. Ellen Benson, for example, did not think that she was good at managing her time. She never seemed to have enough time to get everything done; tasks took much longer than she thought they should, and she often forgot what she needed to do. But then she attended a speech about time management skills, and the speaker's information helped Ellen to understand her problems and gave her some techniques to manage time better. After the speech, she told a friend, "I feel like this speech has given me a new way to take control of my own life." The speech had created a positive feeling.

The ability to make intelligent choices is also a source of power. When you have to make a difficult choice—where to go to college, what to study, whether to return home or to stay on campus for the summer, whether to buy a stereo or to save the money—you will be frustrated if you do not know how to decide which alternative is better. Informative speeches do not tell

agenda setting
Creating awareness about a subject that listeners did not know about or think about before.

the audience which option to choose. But if they lay out the costs and benefits of alternatives, they may help listeners to form criteria for making a decision. By resolving a difficult question, people feel better both about the subject and about themselves.

Providing new information or perspective, agenda setting, and creating a positive or negative feeling are examples of speech goals that rely heavily on informative strategies. Now we will explore some of these strategies. The strategies are not matched uniquely with any one of the three purposes because, as you will see, several of them can be used to achieve more than one purpose.

Checklist 13.1 Speech Purposes and Strategies

1. **Purposes achieved primarily through informative strategies**
   - Providing new information or sharing a perspective
   - Agenda setting
2. **Purposes achieved through a combination of informative and persuasive strategies**
   - Creating positive or negative feeling
3. **Purposes achieved primarily through persuasive strategies**
   - Strengthening commitment to a position
   - Weakening commitment to a position
   - Converting the audience away from one belief and toward another
   - Inducing the audience to perform a specific action

Informative Strategies

For ease of explanation, we shall examine informative strategies one at a time, as though speakers used only one strategy in a given speech. Although that is possible, informative strategies are seldom found in pure form. Most speeches combine a number of strategies to achieve the speaker's purpose and to make it more likely that listeners will remember the information.

Defining

Definition is a strategy to clarify a term or concept that is vague or troublesome. Or definition may be used to introduce a new or unexpected way of viewing the subject, so that the speech can develop the details and implications of this new approach. Definition is unnecessary when a term's meaning is clear-cut; it is used precisely because the term's usage cannot be settled just by consulting a dictionary.

Definition is absolutely required, though, when a concept is not clear at all, as when new technical terminology makes its way into general usage. In the early 1980s, when personal computers came into use, most people suddenly needed to learn a whole new vocabulary: floppy disk, booting up, bytes, download, modem, and so on. A speech entitled "Deciphering the Personal Computer"—which included definitions of such terms—would have been well received. In this case, definition would serve as the means

definition
A strategy to clarify a term or concept that is vague or troublesome, or to introduce a new way of viewing the subject.

to provide new information or perspective. In the example about racial profiling, definition serves as a means of agenda setting, because understanding the meaning of the term helps audiences to think about the problem.

At other times, definition is used to create a positive feeling. Student Sonia Rubenstein, for example, believed that many of the unfortunate racial incidents and cases of "hate speech" on college campuses during the 1990s arose partly because the key concept "affirmative action" was misunderstood. She used the strategy of definition to clarify the concept and to establish a preferred meaning:

> Mention the term *affirmative action,* and some people will tell you that it means special recruiting efforts to attract minorities and women. Others say it means identifying a specific goal for the number of minorities and women to be hired. Still others think it means reserving a specific number of places for minorities and women. And people speak so often of the mechanics of affirmative action that they lose sight of the goal: We all benefit from the perspectives offered by a culturally diverse student body. If we keep track of that goal, then the best way to think of affirmative action is as special efforts to seek out qualified students who will enable us to achieve the goal.

Intelligent discussion is unlikely when the participants have different ideas of what they are talking about. For that reason, Sonia Rubenstein's

WWW. Using the Internet

Identify Informative Strategies of Web Pages on the Discovery Channel Page

Which informative strategies can you find from the links on the Discovery Channel? Point your browser to **http://www.discovery.com/**. Select at least three of the links on the home page to observe how the developers of each page achieved goals of sharing information with you. Which of the following informative strategies did you find?

- Defining
- Reporting
- Describing
- Demonstrating
- Comparing

The goal of a speech of definition is to clarify a difficult concept. The speaker at this Planned Parenthood training session explains exactly what is meant by *domestic violence.*

goals were to identify different possible meanings, to explain the implications of accepting one meaning or another, and to describe a preferred point of view. She made definition the focus of her speech and organized the body like this:

I. Affirmative action has multiple meanings.

    A. It may mean aggressive recruiting.

    B. It may mean numerical goals.

    C. It may mean tie-breaking preferences.

    D. It may mean quotas.

II. Selecting a meaning makes a difference.

    A. It will influence how actively the government takes an interest in the question.

    B. It will clarify whom affirmative action seeks to help.

    C. It will determine whether it is fair to place at a disadvantage people who have not themselves caused previous discrimination.

    D. It will influence how actively committed we should be to the goal.

III. Affirmative action really means aggressive recruiting.

    A. This meaning is consistent with our belief that people should be evaluated as individuals, not as groups.

    B. It is consistent with our belief that decisions should ultimately be made on the basis of merit.

    C. It recognizes the historical underrepresentation of minorities and the fact that qualified minority candidates may not be identified through normal means.

In this example the speaker uses definition to identify and explain a preferred meaning. As we saw in Chapter 10, however, such definitions are not neutral; they shape how we view or think about a subject. In educating listeners about a definition, the speaker is also influencing them to think about the topic in a particular way, and to prefer one definition over another. This illustrates why the purposes of informing and persuading cannot be strictly separated. Although the strategy of definition is intended mainly to be informative, definitions also are persuasive.

Reporting

Reporting is journalism in the oral mode. It answers the question "What happened?" and usually does so in strict chronological order with little overt analysis or interpretation. Select this strategy if your analysis of audience, occasion, and purpose suggests that you need to explain a complex event by identifying each of its components.

If you were giving a speech about the recent trip to India by a group of students to build a house for a low-income family, and your goal was to share what happened, the body of the speech would report the major events of the trip:

reporting
A strategy to relate what happened with little analysis or interpretation.

The Informative Speech

Excerpt from Kyle's Informative Speech on "The Uses of Hemp Products"

Kyle Rogers

First of all, hemp does not equal THC. It's not true. Hemp is a term used to indicate industrial fiber varieties. You can't even grow the two together, according to Franklin Nguyen. He says that hemp plants typically grow ten to twelve feet tall, whereas marijuana plants grow about three feet. If the two were grown together, the hemp plant would obviously overshadow the marijuana plant, which wouldn't allow the latter a sufficient amount of light to live. Darrell T. Ehrensing from Oregon State University says, "Although the plants belong to a single species, the term is used to distinguish industrial fiber varieties from the drug varieties of *Cannabis*."

Let's move on to hemp products, more specifically food. As food, hemp is very nutritious. The seeds are very high in protein, and it tastes pretty good, too. Many people prefer the taste of hemp to soy, and I agree. Hemp seeds are usually processed into cheese or ice cream, or into cooking oils. Believe it or not, most birdseed contains hemp seeds, so even your pets are eating it.

According to the North American Industrial Hemp Council (NAIHC), it can also be made into oils and lubricants for your car, and hemp can be processed into soap, shampoo, and even beer. That's a pretty good deal. In fact, hemp has so many uses that the NAIHC has published a great resource detailing its uses.

Fabrics are a major hemp product. Hemp rope is very strong, and, according to *The American Story*, published in 1998, every boat in the American fleet in 1942 had thirteen thousand feet plus of hemp rope. If it's strong enough for maritime use, it can hold whatever you want to hang from the ceiling.

The fabric that's used to make the shirts and pants is kind of heavy, but also very breathable. Less so than cotton, but it's comfortable, and a much stronger cloth, so the possibility of ripping is lower.

High pressure polymer plastics contain hemp fiber that give them a resilient texture. Nalgene is a very up and coming company that makes water bottles that are virtually indestructible. You can bend them, you can burn them, but you can't break them. They actually use hemp fiber.

Prof. Blivens

Kyle, your speech could use several more sources. The sources you do use need to be explained. *The American Story,* for example, needs to be put into context for the audience. Is it a book or article, and who wrote it? Also the information you give needs to be organized. First, clearly define what hemp is and then begin to tell us what it's used for. While all of your information is good, it seems like it's out of order, which confuses the audience. For example, you start by telling us that it is different from THC. But at that point you haven't explained what hemp is and what THC stands for. The cites from NAIHC are credible, consider having more similar sources. Also, I know of several articles written about this topic that are more recent. Newspapers are generally more current. It seems you know a substantial amount of information about this topic, but remember, for an informative speech you still need sources to support your speech with researched evidence. The speech could be more dynamic if it were organized better. Consider someone who was not familiar with hemp. This speech would have been hard to follow. Instead of giving us cool facts about hemp, organize it into main points. Sections could discuss hemp in industry, food and another section about how it differs from THC would've made the speech stronger. This could offer you a chance to go into further details and explanations. This is a good topic for an informative speech, because many people confuse THC with hemp.

I. Travel to India

    A. Who was part of the group

    B. Arrival at airport

    C. Coping with jet lag

II. Meeting charity organizers

    A. Why the low-income housing is needed

    B. Who will benefit from the housing

    C. Understanding cross-cultural differences

III. Building the house

    A. Where the house is located

    B. What materials were used

    C. How long it took to build

IV. Arrival of the new occupants

    A. What the new occupants thought of the house

    B. What the charity organizers thought of the house

V. Returning to campus

    A. What student participants thought of the experience

    B. How to participate next year

Reporting is primarily a means to provide new information or perspective, but it can also contribute to other goals. Knowing about this trip might lead listeners to think about sponsoring others. Moreover, although the image of reporting is that it is purely factual, usually far more has occurred than can be conveyed in a relatively short speech. Selecting which items to include and which to leave out therefore involves the speaker in making subjective judgments; in turn, these can influence what listeners think about the topic. Even reporting, then, is not a purely informative strategy.

Describing

Many passages in novels use words to try to paint a picture of the scene. When readers can "see" the characters, setting, and action in their minds, they become more actively involved in the novel.

This process of painting a mental picture is **description,** and it can benefit a speech as well as a novel.[1] In a speech about travel to the French Riviera, we are unlikely to hear a set of arguments about why we should go. Rather, the speaker will develop so appealing an image of the Riviera that we will want to go. Similarly, a speech about the San Francisco earthquake of 1906 might use description to convey a sense of what it was like rather than just reporting what happened. In this way, description achieves the purpose of creating positive or negative feeling.

A mental picture becomes vivid through its details. Instead of a general reference to a person, an effective speaker describes specific details—the color of the eyes or hair, whether the person was standing erect or leaning against a post, the expression on the person's face, and so on. But a steady stream of details quickly becomes tedious, so the speaker selects details that evoke a larger picture. The expression on the person's face, for example, might convey a certain attitude. In a speech about the professor who had the greatest influence on her life, student Janet Wickstrom described many such details to her audience:

description

A strategy in which a cumulation of details characterizes, or evokes a mental image of, the subject.

I walked into Professor Alvarez's office and immediately noticed her desk. Or, rather, I noticed that I couldn't *see* her desk. One corner was piled high with new books. The telephone was covered with reminder notes. Students' papers and memos were strewn across the desk. There was yesterday's newspaper opened to the crossword puzzle. A napkin with crumbs from a leftover bagel was on top. Somewhere nearby was a coffee cup. Class notes were piled on top of the computer. A grade book was buried underneath a stack of paper. "What a desk," I thought. Yet I soon would discover that behind that desk was the most organized woman I ever have met.

Description is an especially useful strategy when you believe that listeners will share your appraisal of the details and will regard them as signs or examples of some characteristic that you could not observe or report directly—such as, in this example, the generalization that first appearances can be deceptive. Stated directly, the claim would seem a cliché. But if it is developed indirectly through detailed description, listeners' interest in the details will help them to appreciate the generalization.

Explaining

Beyond simply defining a term or making an idea precise, speakers sometimes want to share with an audience a deeper understanding of events, people, policies, or processes. This is done through explanation, which goes beyond reporting to consider different views of what happened, to ask how or why it happened, or to speculate about what it means or implies.

For example, if you wanted to explain the 1962 Cuban missile crisis to listeners who were not yet born and who don't really understand that event, you would not simply report what took place from October 16 to October 28, 1962. You would discuss such topics as how and why Soviet missiles were placed in Cuba, why Americans regarded them as so threatening, what options for a response were weighed by President Kennedy and his advisers, how the crisis was resolved, and what it meant for U.S.–Soviet relations at the height of the Cold War. If your explanation is successful, listeners not only will know more of the facts but also will grasp the significance of the crisis and will appreciate why the issues it raised have fascinated people for nearly four decades. In this example, you would be both providing new perspectives on the missile crisis and setting an agenda by encouraging listeners to think critically about what they might otherwise have regarded as just a series of facts.

Speeches that explain events or people often begin simply and then build toward greater richness or complexity. In contrast, speeches that explain policies or processes generally proceed in the opposite direction. For most of the years between 1945 and 1990, for example, the chief military policy of the United States toward the Soviet Union was deterrence. A speaker who wants to explain this abstract concept would have to break it down into its components: what weapons were developed and maintained, which diplomatic channels were important, how the United States tried to reassure the Soviet Union that it would not begin a war—while also inducing the belief that, if war started, the United States might use nuclear weapons—and so on. Only by understanding these components well could listeners really know what deterrence was and how it worked.

When explaining a difficult concept, it is important to distinguish between its essential meaning and other meanings that may be associated with it but that are less central. Often this can be done by offering a variety of examples to capture the essential meaning of a concept. For instance, if you told an audience unfamiliar with the concept of "encountering red tape" that filling out a long application form was a good example, they might misunderstand the central idea and think that encountering red tape occurred only when they had to fill out forms, or that every form was an example of red tape. Your explanation would be clearer if you also mentioned having to stand in a long line only to be directed somewhere else when you reached the front, and circulating through voice mail and being disconnected just when you expected to hear a human voice.[2]

Similarly, speeches that explain a process proceed by breaking down complex operations into a simple sequence of steps. Such a speech enables listeners to understand how a complicated process works even if they cannot do it themselves. For example, because public opinion polls are reported so often in the news, you might want to speak about how such polls are conducted. You would explain all the steps in the process: the framing of the questions, identification of the population to be sampled, procedures for obtaining responses from the sample, recording and coding of responses, performing statistical analyses, and interpreting significant results. After hearing your speech, listeners will not be able to design and conduct polls themselves but they will recognize and understand the key steps in the polling process.

Demonstrating

Sometimes, it is not enough to explain a process; it is necessary as well for the audience to see it. Or sometimes, the goal is not just for listeners to understand something; the object is to enable them to do it themselves. In such a case, a speaker may offer a demonstration, describing a seemingly mysterious or complicated procedure as a series of fairly simple steps performed in a particular order. Such a speech that demonstrates how to cook something, how to wallpaper a room, how to prepare a simple tax return, or how to organize a cluttered desk demystifies the topic for listeners, so that they learn to do something that they could not do before. The speech obviously provides new information; in making the subject less mysterious to listeners, it also helps to create a positive feeling.

Demonstration could be the only focus of a speech, or it could be part of a speech that employs other strategies as well. In either case, as you prepare the demonstration, the following considerations are particularly important:

1. Do listeners really need to see the process to understand it? If not, a demonstration may seem superfluous or boring; but if so, a demonstration will be strategically essential.

2. Is the subject precise enough that it can be demonstrated in the time available? Complicated operations, such as rebuilding an automobile engine, can't possibly be covered in a single speech. And even without a time limit, it's unlikely that an audience will attend to, much less remember, a long demonstration about how to rebuild an engine. On the other hand, such topics as how to make an apple pie, how to plan one's study time, and

Sometimes explanation is not enough; the speaker must show listeners how to do something. The speech of demonstration enables listeners to view a process so that they may be able to repeat it themselves.

how to pack a suitcase efficiently lend themselves well to brief demonstrations.

3. Are the steps of the process clear, distinct, and in proper sequence? Listeners will not understand what they are supposed to do if your instructions are vague or incomprehensible or if you demonstrate the steps out of order. Start at the beginning, and go through all the steps leading to the finished product. Do not skip any necessary steps, and do not duplicate steps.

4. Are your actions and your verbal instructions coordinated? Avoid any long gaps in the speech while you are doing something or waiting for something to happen. You will lose both the continuity of the speech and the audience's attention if you must pause and wait for results. This problem often weakens a demonstration of how to cook something.

Demonstration speeches usually benefit from visual aids, which we examined in Chapter 12.

Comparing

The final informative strategy is comparing, which seeks to clarify for listeners the similarities and differences between the items compared. It can be used to make things seem more similar than an audience had imagined. For example, word-processing programs often are thought to be quite different from one another, but a speech comparing features of two leading programs could convince the audience that they are so similar that anyone who knows one can learn the other quickly. Alternatively, a comparison might heighten awareness of differences between things thought to be alike.

If listeners think that all systems of Parliamentary procedure are basically the same, they might learn otherwise by hearing a speech that compares different systems. Or the strategy could accomplish both of these purposes. A speech comparing the curriculum in engineering with that in liberal arts could make listeners aware of both similarities and differences that they had not recognized.

Another use of the strategy of comparing is to decide in what category something should be placed. Deciding whether Social Security is basically an insurance program or basically a welfare program could be helped by a speech exploring its similarities to and differences from each of those concepts.

Finally, comparing can provide listeners with a basis for making a choice. The speaker does not tell them what to do or urge them to accept one perspective over another but instead identifies the options available and compares the benefits and costs.

The public debate about affirmative action in university admissions policies provides a good example. In 2003, the Supreme Court heard arguments in two separate cases from two students who believed that they were denied admission to the University of Michigan as a result of reverse discrimination. In 1978, the Supreme Court had ruled that American universities might consider an applicant's race in making admissions decisions but could not establish quotas for the admission of racial minorities. The 1978 Court decision helped to establish diversity as a social value, but in recent years, opponents have charged that affirmative action is itself racist, admitting unqualified applicants based on their race. Opponents have suggested some alternatives, such as affirmative action focused on economics rather than race, and "affirmative access" that guarantees state university admission to top high-school seniors from any high school in the state. Other opponents have called for race-neutral admissions policies. Supporters of affirmative action believe that it is still necessary to take race into account in order to achieve truly equal educational opportunity. A speech of comparison might have increased public understanding by identifying the problem, describing the proposed options, and determining the strengths and weaknesses of each. The purpose of the speech would not be to urge any particular choice, but to make the alternatives clear so that listeners could apply their own criteria in deciding.

In June of 2003, the Supreme Court ruled that, while the affirmative action program at the University of Michigan Law School was constitutional, the undergraduate admissions program (in which minority applicants automatically were awarded extra points) was too much like a quota, and hence was unconstitutional. The body of a speech comparing the options to modify plans like the Michigan undergraduate plan might be organized this way:

I. Subjective individual review of each applicant is a possible solution.

    A. It offers certain benefits.

    B. It poses certain drawbacks.

II. Race-neutral admissions is a possible solution.

    A. It offers certain benefits.

    B. It poses certain drawbacks.

III. Admissions focused on economic diversity is a possible solution.

   A. It offers certain benefits.

   B. It poses certain drawbacks.

IV. "Affirmative access" guarantees of admission to all top students is a possible solution.

   A. It offers certain benefits.

   B. It poses certain drawbacks.

V. Race-conscious admissions for a limited time period is a possible solution.

   A. It offers certain benefits.

   B. It poses certain drawbacks.

VI. Summary: The choices that we must consider are subjective review of individual applications, race-neutral admissions, admissions focused on economic diversity, "affirmative access," and race-conscious admissions for a limited time period.

WWW. Using the Internet

Evaluate an Informative Speech

Read the speech by Conoco Executive Vice President Jim Nokes and evaluate how he presents complex technical information. Go to **http://www.conoco.com/pa/02nr/nokes_fuel.asp** and evaluate the speech based on:

- The informative purpose of the speech
- The informative strategies used in the speech
- Efforts to encourage retention of information

The principal purpose of this speech was to provide new information for listeners unfamiliar with alternatives to systems like the University of Michigan's affirmative action program for undergraduates. A secondary purpose might well be to create a positive feeling of sympathy for the complex nature of the issue.

Although we have examined the informative strategies as though they were completely separate and distinct, remember that speakers often combine them. A speech may both report what happened and attempt to interpret what it means, or may both explain and compare, or may both define and describe, or may both demonstrate and explain. Always, however, the goal is to share understanding and insight in order to provide new information or perspective, set an agenda, or create a positive or negative feeling.

Encouraging Retention

It might be said that the true test of learning is not how much knowledge or insight one takes in but how much one retains. There are cases in which the speaker seeks only an immediate response. If the purpose of the speech is to convince people to donate to a fund-raising effort, then the immediate response—Did people actually give money?—may be the sole test of success. But with informing, it is different. Speakers want the audience not only to attend to and understand what they said but also to remember it.[3]

Over a century ago, psychologists explained what is called the **forgetting curve.** This concept is applied to public speaking in Figure 13.1, where the horizontal axis represents the amount of time after the speech and the vertical axis shows the percentage of content that is remembered. As you can see from the fast-falling curve, a large portion of the speech is forgotten quickly; the line begins with a sharp negative slope and then levels out later. The forgetting curve applies both to the main points of the speech and to

forgetting curve
A curve that displays the rate at which something learned is forgotten over time.

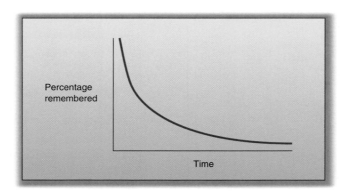

Figure 13.1 The forgetting curve.

the sources of information. Over a short period of time, listeners quickly forget who said what. We might say that the information conveyed in a speech typically has a short half-life. Indeed, this is the biggest constraint on the effectiveness of informative strategies.

Although the forgetting curve typically takes the shape shown in Figure 13.1, the sharp decline does not have to appear at the same place on the graph. It is possible to "shift the curve upward," to increase the likelihood that listeners will remember more content at any given time. In Chapter 3, we examined ways to gain and keep an audience's attention, such as making the speech personally relevant to listeners, making the message stand out, and making it easy to follow. Fortunately, the methods used to increase attention apply to retention as well.

Moreover, in Chapter 2, we learned the importance of active listening, which occurs when the speaker challenges listeners to think, to role-play situations mentally, and to ask and answer questions. Compared with passively receiving information, active listening requires a higher level of participation. And because participation enhances motivation, it should be no surprise that active involvement by listeners (rather than just passive hearing of the speech) increases the chances that they will remember the message.

Retention is also strengthened through **reinforcement,** a response by the speaker that rewards the listener and thereby strengthens the listener's positive attitudes toward the speech. In the public speaking classroom, listeners often reinforce speakers. If audience members nod their heads in agreement whenever a speaker expresses an opinion, the speaker is likely to increase the number of opinion statements.

As a speaker, though, you also can use reinforcement strategically to ensure that the audience remembers the message. As you learned in Chapter 7, if your organizational pattern enables listeners to anticipate what will come next and the subsequent development of your speech confirms their guess, then by confirming their expectation you reward their shrewd judgment.

You can also reinforce audience members by how you refer to them. Saying "we" instead of "you" conveys the message that you identify with listeners and regard them as your equals; you signal that they are in the know and that you respect their thoughtful judgment. Explicit references to them within the speech may have the same effect. A speaker whose transition

reinforcement

A response by a speaker that rewards the listener to strengthen the listener's positive attitude toward the speech.

says, in effect, "Since you've followed this complex topic so far, I'm sure you can see why the next point is valid," is speaking well of the audience and providing reinforcement. This, along with strategies that draw attention and encourage active listening, will shift the forgetting curve and improve the odds of ensuring retention.

Finally, some of the stylistic elements discussed in Chapter 10 also encourage retention. Parallel wording makes it easier to remember ideas, vivid language will keep a description in the listener's mind, and simple sentences enable a listener to follow the message and focus more easily on what is being said. These elements help to make ideas not only more readily understood, but also more likely to be remembered. They are strategic resources that can be used to achieve any informative purpose.

Strategies for Speaking to Diverse Audiences

Respecting Diversity Through Informing

Information is not neutral. How people understand information is affected by their backgrounds and perspectives. These strategies will help you in presenting information to a diverse audience.

1. Consider the range of your audience members' beliefs and experiences when deciding about what they need to be informed.
2. When providing new information or perspective, recognize that anyone's perspective on a topic is influenced by one's culture.
3. Acknowledge that cultures may differ with respect to what topics legitimately can be placed on the agenda.
4. Do not knowingly bias audience members' views. Insofar as possible, present all sides of an issue.

Summary

In this chapter, we have examined how informative strategies achieve several speech purposes: providing new information or perspective, agenda setting, and creating positive feeling by making listeners aware of how to do something or by involving them in making an important choice. Speeches that rely mainly on informative strategies do not seek directly to influence listeners' actions, and yet it would be unfair to say that they have no persuasive effects.

After completing your research, developing an outline, and testing your reasoning, you should review your speech plan in terms of your specific goals. Based on analysis of the audience, occasion, and purpose, you can select appropriate informative strategies. These include defining, reporting, describing, explaining, demonstrating, and comparing. Many speakers combine these strategies.

Because listeners quickly forget much of what was said in a speech, you will want to use strategies that encourage and reinforce retention. Providing information that draws attention, using an organizational structure that enables listeners to anticipate what is coming next, making complimentary references to the audience, and making strategic choices about style are ways to improve retention.

Discussion Questions

1. In the public speeches that you've heard lately, were informative strategies or persuasive strategies dominant? Consider speeches from outside the public speaking classroom, such as:

   - A presidential address.
   - A speech at a protest rally.
   - A lecture in your history class.
   - An oral research report presented by a student in another class.
   - The closing argument in a trial.

   Was any of these speeches completely devoid of persuasive strategies? Were any completely devoid of informative strategies? Can a speaker inform listeners without influencing them in some way? Can a speaker persuade listeners without providing information?

2. Speakers encourage retention by reinforcing listeners, by drawing their attention, and by encouraging them to listen actively. Two strategies for doing these things are (a) to provide a clear organizational pattern and (b) to refer to "we" instead of "you." What other strategies help a speaker to encourage retention in a speech with a primarily informative goal? Discuss the strategies that in your experience were most effective in making you remember the message long after the speech was over.

Activities

1. Watch a news report on television. In what ways is it like a speech to inform? In what ways is it different? Can you take anything from this model to help you create speeches with informative strategies?
2. Describe five strategies that you plan to use in your next speech to increase the audience's retention of information.
3. Create one of the following:
   a. A speech of explanation about the process of developing informative strategies in speeches
   b. A speech of comparison that discusses informative and persuasive strategies
   c. A speech of definition about the concept of "strategic planning" in speech preparation

1. For more about description in speeches, see Gerard A. Hauser, "Empiricism, Description, and New Rhetoric," *Philosophy and Rhetoric* 5 (Winter 1972): 24–44.

2. For a fuller discussion of explanatory discourse, see Katherine E. Rowan, "Informing and Explaining Skills: Theory and Research on Informative Communication," *Handbook of Communication and Social Interaction Skills,* eds. John O. Greene and Brant R. Burleson, Mahwah, N.J.: Erlbaum, 2003, pp. 419–430.

3. For more about retention, see Robert L. Greene, *Human Memory: Paradigms and Paradoxes,* Mahwah, N.J.: Lawrence Erlbaum, 1992.

Chapter Fourteen

Persuading

In this chapter, we will:

- Explore the differences between informative and persuasive strategies for speeches and identify the speech purposes that are achieved through persuasive strategies.

- Describe how determining the target audience and analyzing the audience's motivation and the speaker's purpose can help the speaker plan for persuasion.

- Learn how audiences resist persuasion and what resources help a speaker overcome resistance.

- Identify strategies that speakers can use, both in general and for each specific goal.

- Examine two basic structures for persuasive speeches: the problem–solution structure and the motivated sequence.

Being Catholic, student Molly Keegan was upset and angry to learn about the recent sex scandal in the Catholic Church. She wanted to give a speech to inform her public speaking classmates about the problems in the Church. She decided to focus on the controversial practices of moving priests who had been accused of molesting children to another parish and paying money to victims in order to settle accusations.

As she researched her topic, Molly soon realized that the media were covering only part of the story. Most of her classmates probably knew already about the problems in the Catholic Church. What they most likely did not know was that the percentage of sexual offenses in the Catholic Church was less than the percentage of sexual offenses in other faith traditions and in society at large. Also, Molly discovered that celibacy was not a proven cause of pedophilia. She wanted to call for reforms in seminary education so that it would no longer ignore issues of sexuality and also to persuade her audience to question sensationalistic media headlines.

As Molly discovered, informative goals are sometimes insufficient. They do not require listeners to commit themselves to any belief or action. Sometimes, a speaker may want not only to make listeners think about something but also to influence what they think about it; or may want to move listeners beyond having a belief to taking action; or may want listeners to change their minds, to abandon one belief and accept another. In all these cases, the speaker's goal is to persuade the audience, to prompt listeners to feel, act, or believe in a particular way.

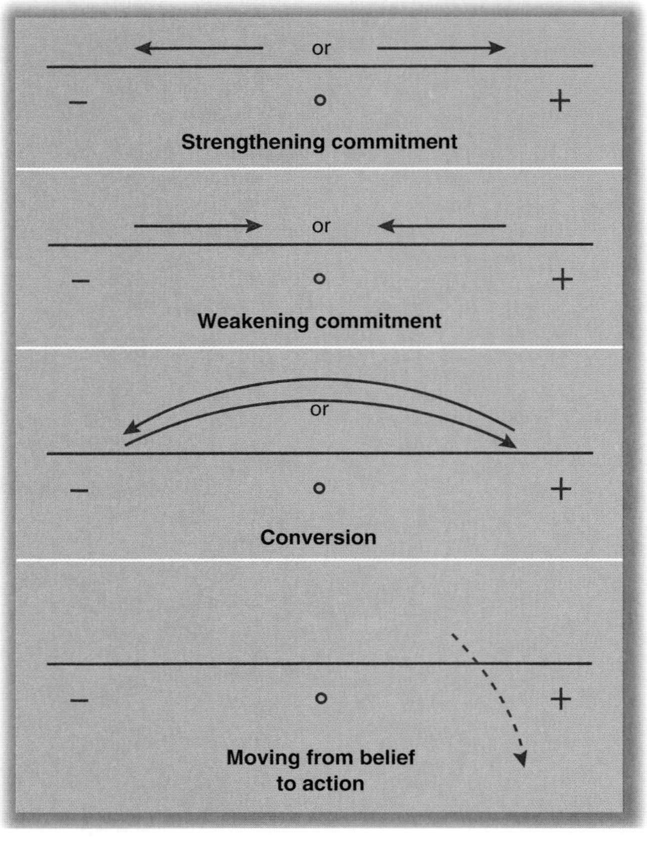

When you ask listeners to make a particular choice about believing or doing something, you are eliminating other possible choices and asking listeners to put their beliefs or values on the line. For this reason, you must be sensitive to your ethical responsibility not to manipulate listeners. A speaker can so "load the deck" that the audience has an illusion of choice even though the speech predetermines what that choice will be. If a speaker moves listeners to action by persuasive but unsound appeals, or withholds crucial information or arguments because they might lead to an unwanted conclusion, or rushes listeners to judgment by pronouncing an issue more urgent than it actually is, then the audience has been manipulated. In Molly's case, she presented her arguments, supported by sound evidence, and let her audience decide whether they were persuaded to agree with her.

Figure 14.1 Directions of persuasion.

Purposes Achieved Through Persuasive Strategies

Chapter 4 introduced seven specific speech purposes, and we saw in Chapter 13 that both agenda setting and providing new information or perspective are achieved mainly through informative strategies. The goals of strengthening commitment, weakening commitment, conversion, and inducing specific action all depend primarily on persuasive strategies.

The term *persuasion* is sometimes misunderstood as referring only to situations in which a speaker *reverses* an audience's beliefs. According to this view, if your roommate is strongly opposed to taking a public speaking course and you talk him or her into taking one, only then have you persuaded your roommate. But this is an overly limited view of persuasion. A person's commitment to a position is not just a matter of yes or no; there is a range, and listeners can become either more committed or less committed to a position. By reasoning with audience members, the speaker seeks to move them from one point to another along a scale reflecting degrees of commitment. As shown in Figure 14.1, the speaker might want to *strengthen commitment* to a belief, moving listeners farther along the scale in the direction toward which they are already headed. Your roommate might be thinking about taking public speaking, and your advocacy leads him or her to feel more strongly that it would be a good idea. In this case, you would be trying to move the listener from a positive position on the scale to an even more positive position. (Or, if your roommate were opposed and you wanted to strengthen his or her opposition, you would be trying to move the listener toward an even more negative position.) Or the speaker might want to *weaken commitment* to a belief, moving listeners closer to the middle of the scale. Your roommate might be strongly opposed to taking public speaking, and your message leads him or her not to rule out the idea completely. The option is "back on the table" even though your roommate is still leaning against it. Or the speaker might even want to try to change listeners' minds, moving them from one side of the scale to the other—a process of *conversion* that seldom results from a single speech. (This is what we mentioned above as the reversal of positions, and it's a mistake to think of it as the only situation in which persuasion occurs.) Finally, the speaker might try to shift the entire scale, aiming to move listeners from a strong belief to approval of a *specific action*. Your roommate has been thinking seriously about taking a public speaking class for some time, but after hearing your remarks, he or she finally goes to next semester's registration and signs up for the course.

As you know from Chapter 13, informing and persuading are not entirely separate goals, and both create positive or negative feelings in the audience. If you want listeners to remember new information, you need to persuade them that the information is important. And to persuade them to take action, you need to be sure that they understand what the action means. Nevertheless, there are differences between informative and persuasive strategies. Both seek to change the audience's perspective, but informative

WWW. Using the Internet

How Persuasive Were the Bradys?

At the 1996 Democratic Party Convention in Chicago, Sarah and Jim Brady spoke to the delegates at the convention and to a national audience on television about gun control.

Point your browser to **http://www.pbs.org/ newshour/convention96/floor_speeches/brady.html.** After reading and/or listening to the speech, analyze how strategies of persuasion were used.

- What seemed to be the specific persuasive goal of the speech?
  To strengthen or weaken convictions?
  To convert opponents?
  To call for an action?
- How well did Sarah and Jim Brady analyze their audience and the situation to adjust to these constraints?
  Did they create identification with the audience?
  Did they call on the audience members to be true to their own beliefs?
  Did they create trust?
  Were they effective in using evidence and reasoning?
  Did they effectively appeal to the audience members' emotions?

strategies do so by enlarging the audience's scope of awareness and concern, whereas persuasive strategies do so by altering the audience's position.

Strengthening Commitment

Speakers often address audiences that already agree with them. Why, then, do listeners need to be persuaded?

Suppose that you believe your school should hire more faculty to teach undergraduate courses, even if that means an increase in tuition. Since most students dislike tuition increases, objections from your classmates could outweigh support for more faculty. A speaker who favors hiring more faculty would know that the agreement of people like you is essential and would want to strengthen your commitment as well as insulate you from the possibility of conversion. The body of this speaker's outline might look like this:

I. A tuition increase would benefit undergraduate education.

    A. It would make it possible to hire more faculty.

    B. It would enable the university to offer more small classes and seminars.

    C. These, in turn, would enrich faculty–student interaction.

II. The risks of a tuition increase are slight.

    A. The size of the increase would be modest.

    B. Financial aid would be increased along with tuition.

    C. After a slight initial decline, applications for admission would increase in response to the strengthened faculty.

You may have been vaguely familiar with these arguments, but you had not considered them carefully. Therefore, the speaker succeeds in *strengthening your commitment* to the belief that the benefits of additional faculty are worth the cost of tuition increases.

Is this really a form of persuasion? Yes, because your attitude about the subject differs after the speech as a direct result of the speech. The speaker has influenced you to believe more strongly about the subject than you did before. Strengthening commitment is a very common approach to persuasion because it takes advantage of people's tendency to seek out and accept messages with which they already agree.

In the next chapter, we will examine ceremonial speaking—speeches of introduction, greeting, tribute, and anniversary celebration, for example. While these speeches serve primarily to mark occasions, they also strengthen listeners' commitment to the community that comes together for the occasion. Just as informative and persuasive speeches cannot be sharply separated, ceremonial speeches employ persuasive strategies as well.

Weakening Commitment

hostile audience
An audience that is strongly committed in opposition to the views of the speaker.

Sometimes a speaker will face a **hostile audience.** This does not mean that audience members are personally unfriendly but that they have strong commitments that are opposed to the speaker's view. During the 2000 presidential campaign, for example, Vice President Al Gore and Senator Joseph

Lieberman told audiences in the entertainment industry that the industry should more carefully regulate the marketing of adult entertainment to children. Their audiences largely believed otherwise, and some in the industry even accused Gore and Lieberman of undermining the First Amendment to the Constitution. In this situation, Gore and Lieberman were trying to weaken the commitment of their industry audience (and, even more, of the larger nationwide audience to whom their speeches were being reported) to the belief that a completely free market should govern the distribution of entertainment programs.

A speaker who tries to weaken the audience's commitment to a position is not asking them to abandon it completely. That is usually too much to hope for, and it may not even be what the speaker wants. Gore and Lieberman, for instance, did not want to advocate censorship of movies and popular music. Rather, the goal is to make listeners less sure of their commitment and at least willing to examine alternative positions. In terms of the scale in Figure 14.1, the goal is to move listeners closer to the middle of the scale, which represents noncommitment. An audience member who, after the speech, said, "I certainly believe in artistic freedom, but we do need to take more care with marketing," would have been persuaded to weaken his or her prior commitment.

Conversion

Far more difficult than strengthening or weakening a commitment is *changing* it. Speakers who attempt **conversion** aim to alter listeners' beliefs, either by convincing them to accept something they had previously rejected or to reject something they had previously accepted. This would involve moving them from one side of the scale in Figure 14.1 all the way to the other side of the scale.

Because people defend themselves against persuasion, no speaker is likely to achieve conversion through a single speech, unless listeners' opinions about the subject are not deeply held in the first place. The most obvious case of conversion is old-time religious revivals in which the emotion of the situation and the magic of the preacher's words cause listeners to feel in a flash the seriousness of their situation and the need for reform. At various times in U.S. history, there has been a wave of religious revivalism. During the mid-1700s and again during the early 1800s, traveling preachers converted thousands who attended nighttime revivals and experienced a flash of insight and inspiration that they described as religious rebirth.

Conversion also occurs at times in the secular realm. During the 1960s, for example, many people completely changed their views about the role of African Americans and women in American life from what they had thought at the beginning of the decade. Many others changed their views about foreign policy and the Cold War as a result of the war in Vietnam. And many changed their views about family lifestyles, dress and grooming, and taste in music as a result of exposure to alternatives. For some people, the terrorist attacks of September 11, 2001, had a similar effect, completely changing their view of U.S. foreign policy, or of the importance of homeland defense compared with the protection of civil liberties.

Even in the classroom, there are occasional cases of conversion. Students who have previously denied that they harbor any racial prejudice might come to see that, at least subconsciously, they do. Or a student who was

conversion
Abandoning one belief or value and replacing it with another.

convinced that the administration's policy on scheduling final examinations was unfair could be led to the opposite position.

Inducing a Specific Action

Finally, there are situations in which modifying belief is not enough. The speaker wants audience members actually to do something as a result of the speech. The most obvious examples are the candidate who is seeking votes, the charitable organization seeking contributions, the advertiser who is trying to sell a product, and the neighborhood organizer who is seeking signatures on a petition. They will not achieve their purpose if listeners simply say they like the message or that they agree with it. Listeners have to take the next step and act on the message.

Moving from belief to action is sometimes difficult. In part, it is a matter of inertia. It is usually easier to say that you agree with a message than it is to exert yourself to do something in response. Beyond that, there is sometimes a discrepancy between people's attitudes and their behavior. They may agree that they ought to modify their eating habits (attitude) without actually altering what they choose to eat (behavior). Or they may say what is socially desirable—what they think others wish to hear—and then act otherwise. This is illustrated by the case of the smoker who is convinced by an antismoking message and yet continues to smoke, or by the person who denies that he or she has any religious or racial prejudice but will not vote for any minority candidate for office. Conversely, listeners might be induced to modify their behavior without changing their underlying attitudes. Thus, a speech decrying racial slurs might persuade listeners to avoid them when speaking with members of other racial groups and yet not change in any way how they feel about race. In such a situation, you will need to decide whether achieving a change only in behavior is sufficient for your purposes or whether you need to alter the underlying attitude as well.

Plan Your Strategy

Throughout our study, we have emphasized speechmaking as strategic planning. Being able to analyze the audience, to size up the situation, and to determine its constraints and opportunities—the basic skills you learned in Chapters 3 and 4—will enable you to make the best use of persuasive strategies.

In Chapter 13, we reviewed the steps in strategic planning. Because persuasive strategies seek an altered commitment from listeners, you need to perform a more detailed audience analysis aimed at identifying your target audience and at assessing that audience's motivation.

Determine Your Target Audience

target audience
Within a larger audience, those individuals whom a speaker especially wants to address, usually people whose response will determine whether the speech succeeds.

If your audience is diverse and you are not seeking unanimity, the first step is to determine as precisely as possible which members are your **target audience.** Although you would be happy if you could persuade everybody,

these are the people you really seek to influence. They may be the key decision makers or their own prestige and credibility might help to influence others. For example, suppose you are speaking at a corporate meeting attended by upper management and by the heads of all departments that might be affected by your presentation—even though any decisions ultimately will be made by only the president and the chair of the board. It would be nice to influence the department heads by your speech, but your real target audience is the president and the board chair. They are the decision makers, and it is they whom you want to persuade.

Assess Your Audience's Motivation

Listeners will be *motivated* to let your speech influence them if they perceive that your appeal is linked to their own motives and needs.

Psychologists have offered many different accounts of the nature of human **motivation.** At the most general level, people seek to attain pleasure and to avoid pain. This motive is the basis for persuasive speeches about everything from the dangers of air pollution to the benefits of good nutrition—as student speaker Michael Masdea demonstrated in urging his audience to stop drinking so much caffeine:

> Caffeine can help us stay up during those frequent student all-nighters. But it can also cause severe headaches, stomachaches, and insomnia. The psychological and behavioral effects of caffeine are frightening. It is a highly addictive drug, and it may be the cause of many problems you are experiencing right now.

Another general account of human motivation was offered by psychologist Abraham Maslow, who theorized that human beings have a *hierarchy of needs;* we first seek to satisfy biological and safety needs, which include food, clothing, shelter, and protection from harm, and then proceed to higher-order needs, such as identity, meaningful relationships, and self-

motivation

The incentive to do something that requires effort, such as considering a persuasive message.

Persuading

The Situation

You are on the board of directors for your local community theatre. The plays that the company produces are popular with people of all ages in the community and serve as an important community activity for both the people involved and the audiences. However, the revenues raised through ticket sales and the small grant from the state council for the arts do not cover the expenses of the productions, and many of the formerly active members have moved out of town. At its last meeting, the theatre board decided it was time to take action. The strategy will be two pronged: to attempt to expand the base of people who take part in the productions or volunteer to work behind the scenes for the theatre, and to solicit contributions from individuals and local businesses. You are appointed to speak for the board to several community organizations.

Making Choices

1. What groups will you choose to approach as your target audience for each of the two prongs of your strategy? Will you concentrate on arts-related groups or include a variety of organizations?

2. What motivations might various audience members have for supporting your organization? How will you use these motivations to your advantage?

3. What resistance do you expect to encounter, and what strategies will you use to overcome it?

4. What basic persuasive speech structure will be most effective for realizing your group's goals?

What If . . .

Your specific speaking goals and how you will structure your speech to achieve these goals will likely be affected by the type of audience. Decide what purpose and motivation you will emphasize in the following situations:

1. You are speaking to the local Chamber of Commerce, whose membership is made up of business managers and small-business owners.

2. You are speaking to a group of retired persons at the local senior center.

3. You are speaking to the theatre club at the local high school.

---

actualization.[1] Maslow argued that a person's higher-order motives become important only after lower-order needs are satisfied. It is useless, for instance, to discuss abstract ideals with someone who doesn't know where his or her next meal is coming from. On the other hand, people who have been able to satisfy their lower-order needs often find that they are not truly fulfilled; then higher-order needs and motives become important. According to this view of motivation, the persuasive speaker's task is to determine approximately where in Maslow's hierarchy listeners are and then both to arouse the appropriate motive and to show how it can be satisfied by the recommended action or belief. Often, of course, different members of an audience will have different kinds of motivation, and the speaker accordingly will include appeals to different levels in the hierarchy.

Student speaker Kevin Krebs appealed to motives on different levels of Maslow's hierarchy in a speech favoring the NCAA policy of enforcing stricter rules about athletes' minimum grade-point averages and test scores. Kevin first appealed to the athletes' basic need to make a living:

How many of you really think you're going to get a job playing professional sports? If you do, the odds are stacked against you. Only a small percentage will actually make a living playing the game. Chances are, when you get out of college, you're going to need the education being forced upon you by the NCAA rules.

Then, for athletes and sports fans alike, Kevin appealed to the higher need to enjoy winning:

The policy at this university is already stricter than the NCAA rules. By accepting these guidelines, some of our competitors with lower standards will be eliminated from the field. Our school will finally get a chance to win a game or two!

Determine Your Purpose

We have been speaking about the *audience's* level of motivation, but the *speaker* also can have different motives for speaking. At the most obvious level, you may want to fulfill an assignment in the class and receive a good grade. You may be motivated by the practical desire to achieve specific results that you think are realistic. Or you may have a passionate commitment to a cause and feel impelled to inspire others.

Your audience analysis and your own motivation, taken together, will help you to determine your general purpose—strengthening commitment, weakening commitment, conversion, or inducing a specific action—and your specific purpose (exactly what it is you want audience members to believe or to do). Unless you know explicitly what you want to achieve, you will have a difficult time making the strategic choices that will develop your speech and you will be less likely to recognize and respect the free choice of your listeners.

Checklist 14.1 Strategic Planning for Persuasion

1. **Ask yourself these questions:**
   - Who is my target audience?
   - What is the audience's motivation?
   - What specifically do I want to achieve?
   - What means of audience resistance might be present?
2. **Decide whether your specific purpose is realistic in light of your answers. If not, modify it. If so, then determine:**
   - Which of the purpose-specific strategies will be most useful.
   - Which general strategies represent resources you can use.
   - How to organize the overall speech.

The Elaboration Likelihood Model

In thinking through your strategic purpose, it may be helpful to know more about how people are persuaded. One answer to that question is offered through the *elaboration likelihood model*. This model reflects the communication process described in Chapter 1, especially the fact that speakers and listeners cooperate jointly to develop meaning and understanding.

Elaboration refers to listeners' tendency to think about information related to the topic of the speech. The likelihood of elaboration varies among people, and for any given person it varies among topics. With relatively high elaboration, a person will be persuaded—if at all—by systematic thinking about the message and the topic. This is the result of critical listening, which was discussed in Chapter 2, and includes careful assessment of the speaker's arguments in light of other things the listener knows. Messages that hold up under such scrutiny will be persuasive.

In contrast, with relatively low elaboration, a person is more likely to be persuaded as a result of "short cuts" that simplify thinking (for example, whether the speaker is attractive or whether the delivery is animated). These are easier bases for decision because they are triggered more by intuitive reactions than by detailed analysis.

Put another way, the more that listeners are likely to elaborate, the more persuasion will depend on the message's arguments, and the less that they are likely to elaborate, the more it will depend on intuitive judgments that suggest simple decision rules. In principle, critical listening is a sounder basis for persuasion, but no one has the time or energy to listen critically to every message on every topic. In fact, listeners will position themselves at points all along the range of elaboration, from high to low, and each listener is likely to use a mix of critical listening and simplifying devices.

For the speaker, it is important to know what factors will make a listener more likely to elaborate, and then to determine whether these factors are present in the particular audience. Helpfully, many of the same factors that influence attention and perception work here as well. If the topic is personally relevant, or if the listeners generally enjoy thinking about things, or have prior knowledge about the topic, or if there are few distractions, they are more likely to elaborate the message.

Of course, the fact that listeners think critically about a message is no guarantee that they will be persuaded by it. That will depend on the outcome of their thought. When elaboration is high, speakers who follow the standards of evidence and reasoning discussed in Chapters 5 and 6 are more likely to be persuasive than those who do not. When elaboration is low, speakers who follow the advice we have offered in Chapters 1, 3, and 11, to establish positive *ethos,* to appear likable, and to seem interesting are more likely to be persuasive than those who do not.

Finally, it's not the case that a person's elaboration likelihood is firmly fixed in advance; it can be affected by the speech itself. A listener who doesn't think that a topic affects him or her personally can come to feel differently during the speech, or a person who thinks he or she knows a lot about the topic already may discover otherwise. If the message can encourage listeners to elaborate, and if it succeeds in persuading them, it is more likely that their attitudes will persist over time and that their attitudes will correspond to their behavior.

What the elaboration likelihood model implies is that persuasion is complex and that there is more than one route to the goal. For the speaker, it suggests the need for careful audience analysis and selection of strategic resources to recognize the multiplicity of ways in which people are persuaded.[2]

Constraints on Effective Persuasive Speaking

As you know very well by now, the strategic plan for a speech requires that you identify the constraints in the situation and that you use your resources to take advantage of opportunities. When you seek to persuade, the constraints are often greater than when you seek to inform or to entertain. Listeners often resist attempts to persuade them. They do so because their identities may be tied closely to their opinions; thus, an appeal to change their opinions might threaten their identities. The nature and strength of such resistance varies significantly among listeners and situations, and it often takes one of the following forms.[3]

- Selective listening
- Selective perception
- Selective influence

These patterns were introduced in Chapter 3. They are described here in slightly different terms in order to highlight the constraints that are especially significant for persuasion.

Selective Listening

As we have seen, audiences typically attend to messages, interpret them, and remember them selectively. But a message that reinforces what the audience already believes does not arouse defensive reactions, perhaps because it is less threatening or because it offers reassurance. For example, if you already support national health insurance, you are more likely to attend to, understand, and remember messages that also support it. But selective listening goes beyond selective exposure—seeking out and paying attention to messages with which you agree. It also includes how you listen to messages. If the focus of a speech is vague or unclear, listeners will "clarify" it by interpreting it in a way that supports what they already believe. Odd as it seems, a speech that decries the cost of health care and demands reform but does not propose a specific solution might be seen by supporters of national health insurance as "really" agreeing with their views. Likewise, those opposed to national health insurance might see the same ambiguous message as "really" against such a policy, even though the speaker never said so.[4]

Because these barriers to persuasion are potentially powerful, it is important to plan strategies that surmount them. One often-used approach is to begin with areas of agreement and gradually move to areas of difference. If your listeners are known to favor national health insurance but you oppose it, you could start by agreeing with them that costs are out of hand, that reform is needed, and that government must play a role. Only then would you make the case that national health insurance is an undesirable solution. The audience will react more favorably to this strategy than if you broadly attack national health insurance without acknowledging the positive aspects of the issue or the intensity of their feelings.

However, when you acknowledge common ground in a persuasive speech, you have to be careful. Selective listening may lead the audience to hear the common ground but to ignore your message. For example, one student speaker thought that she was being considerate of opposing viewpoints when she began a pro-life speech by acknowledging, "A pregnancy at this point in my life would be a disaster." Somehow, half the audience failed to hear her later statements that abortion would make the disaster even worse and that adoption would make it bearable. The speaker did not move clearly enough from common ground to her own thesis; as a result, her confusing speech was made even more confusing by the selective listening of the audience.

Selective Perception

Even if your persuasive message urging listeners to change gets past the filters of selective listening, audiences may selectively perceive and respond to the message in still other ways that result in their not being persuaded.

Denial. Listeners sometimes refuse to accept a message that challenges them to change, no matter how well that message is supported or defended. Wanting to believe otherwise, they simply will not accept the truth of the message; they are in **denial.**

For example, since the mid-1970s, various public figures have maintained that there are limits to what the United States can do in the world. Even when this message has been clearly explained, well supported, and articulately presented, it usually has not been well received. Many Americans—influenced by a two-century tradition that views the United States as a land of unlimited opportunity and promise—simply will not accept that there are limits to what they can achieve.

In a public speaking class, Christy Verneuil learned just how powerful a constraint denial can be. Her persuasive speech urged that gay couples be allowed to serve as adoptive parents. Christy presented study after study proving that children of homosexual parents are as happy and well adjusted as children of heterosexual parents. After the speech, the audience questioned her extensively about those studies. Yet, even though Christy answered every question, her classmates' strong beliefs about this issue kept them from accepting her proposal.

Dismissal. A second way that audiences may selectively perceive an unfavorable message is to dismiss it as not really applying to them. Unlike denial, in which they refuse to accept the *general* truth of the message, in **dismissal** they dispute that the truth applies *specifically* to them.

Dismissal is a common response to unsettling messages about health. A smoker, for example, may hear a speech that describes the harmful effects of nicotine and urges smokers to quit, may conclude that the speech was well reasoned and probably correct in its claims, and yet light a cigarette after the speech because, "It won't happen to me." If you can imagine reasons why your audience might dismiss the message, plan strategies that respond directly to those reasons. You may have to accept, however, that dismissal is sometimes purely self-delusion—and insurmountable.

Belittling the Source. A third way of selectively perceiving a threatening message is to attack the credibility of the source. If your persuasive appeal

---

denial
The refusal to accept the claim in a message no matter how strong its justification is.

dismissal
Disregarding a message (even if it is generally true) because one disputes that it applies to oneself.

relies almost entirely on a single source, you run the risk that listeners might discredit the source and thereby avoid your message.

An example of belittling the source occurred during the early months of 1998, when former White House intern Monica Lewinsky alleged that President Clinton had had an affair with her and then encouraged her to lie about it. Before the release of the independent counsel's report and before the president's admission of wrongdoing, some of Clinton's supporters responded to the allegations by suggesting that Lewinsky was an unstable person whose perceptions were warped by her infatuation with him. Because positive *ethos* is a requirement for persuasion and because there was not yet any solid external evidence of the alleged events, belittling Lewinsky's credibility as a source was an effective way to belittle her accusations as well. Later, some of the president's supporters challenged the motives of the independent counsel, for the same reasons.

WWW. Using the Internet

Resistance to Persuasion

How might audience members be unwilling to be persuaded by AIDS activist Mary Fisher as she testifies before the U.S. House of Representatives Committee on Banking and Financial Services? Point your browser to **http://www.house.gov/banking/3800fis.htm** to read her statement to the committee. Then consider whether some audience members might be likely to dispose of the message by denying it, by believing that it does not apply to them, by belittling the source, by compartmentalizing their beliefs without affecting their values or behavior, or by responding in light of the boomerang effect.

Compartmentalization. If a message challenges what listeners already believe, they may avoid its influence by keeping it separate from their conflicting belief, so that the two ideas do not seem at odds. This defense against persuasion is called **compartmentalization** because it is like putting the conflicting ideas into separate mental boxes. It usually is not a conscious decision by audience members to compartmentalize their beliefs, but the effect is the same as if it were.

People often have different compartments for their general beliefs and their specific beliefs. For example, some people who say they are environmentalists nevertheless buy sport utility vehicles with lower fuel economy and higher air pollution levels than smaller cars.

One approach to influencing people who are sustaining an inconsistent position is simply to make apparent to them that they are defending something in the abstract which they are unwilling to apply in practice. Student Robert Myers, for example, believed that everyone should have the right to speak; yet he was agitated when a campus group scheduled a speaker who claimed that white Americans were responsible for poverty in the Third World and who urged U.S. minority groups to revolt. Robert, like many white students on campus, resented the college giving this speaker a platform.

Classmate Susan Martinson decided to discuss this issue in her next speech. She began by identifying with her listeners, noting that they all shared the value of freedom of speech. She then argued that we diminish this value by applying it only to easy cases and supporting free speech only for those whose messages we approve. The real test, she said, is whether we are secure enough in our own beliefs to extend freedom of speech to "disreputable" speakers whose ideas we hate. By focusing on this criterion for what makes freedom of speech really meaningful, Susan convinced Robert and her classmates to reexamine their opposition to allowing this controversial speaker to speak on campus.

compartmentalization
Keeping two conflicting beliefs separated so that one need not be conscious of the conflict between them.

In exposing listeners' inconsistencies to them, it is important to be gentle and sympathetic. If you are too direct, they naturally could become defensive and even deny that there is any inconsistency. Instead, you want to inspire them to recognize that they have not fully embraced their own ideals.

Selective Influence

In addition to selective listening and perception, which we first encountered in Chapter 3, audiences also may be selective in how they are influenced by the message. Two conditions that can prompt selective influence are a polysemic message and the boomerang effect.

Multiple Meanings: Polysemy. It is a characteristic of many messages that, depending on what a listener emphasizes, they can be understood in more than one way. Such messages are called **polysemic** (pronounced pol-i-SEEM-ic). It is not that audience members actively distort the message but rather that the message interacts with listeners' different prior experiences, beliefs, and expectations in different ways.[5]

For a simple example of how a message can be polysemic, look at the famous speech by Dr. Martin Luther King, Jr., "I Have a Dream," in Appendix B. This speech was delivered at the conclusion of the March on Washington in 1963. As you read the text, ask yourself whether this speech is a call for militancy or for moderation on the part of the African American community. You'll find evidence in the text to support both views. Although the introduction to this speech describes it as a "delicate balancing act," it is not hard to imagine how different listeners could think they were accepting different messages: for one person, the speech might be accepted as a call to action; for another, it might be accepted as a call for caution and patience.

A more recent instance of polysemy can be found in President George W. Bush's address to Congress following the terrorist attacks of 2001 (also in Appendix B). At one point, President Bush stated, "We are in a fight for our principles and our first responsibility is to live by them." Many listeners interpreted this statement as calling for protection of civil liberties and avoidance of racial prejudice. Others, however, viewed it as a call to live by the principles of patriotism and national unity.

In Chapter 10, we discussed condensation symbols. These are symbols, like the American flag, that are highly valued although people value them for different reasons. They condense a wide range of divergent viewpoints in a common expression. By their nature, condensation symbols are polysemic. They are used principally to bring people together around a common symbol or meaning, as Dr. King sought to do with his unifying symbol of the dream. But they also can foster selective acceptance, if people understand the symbol-laden message in different and conflicting ways.

The Boomerang Effect. A final defense of listeners against being influenced is called the **boomerang effect,** because the message turns back on the speaker. This can happen if an appeal is so powerful that it overwhelms the audience. Concluding that nothing they can do will help matters, listeners

polysemic
Capable of being understood in more than one way.

boomerang effect
The opposite effect from that which a speaker intends.

may actually do the opposite of what the speaker has urged, thinking, "What I do won't matter anyway."

Julie Richardson knew that depletion of the ozone layer was a serious environmental and public health issue. In trying to convince listeners of its importance, she explained that much of this protective atmospheric layer has been lost already, resulting in great health risks both for us in the present and also for future generations. Specifically, Julie wanted her audience to stop using products in aerosol spray cans because many of them release fluorocarbons that deplete the ozone layer.

Several classmates reacted as Julie had hoped and were persuaded to stop using aerosol cans. But Jeff Martin had quite a different reaction. Julie's speech convinced him that the problem was so vast in scope that nothing he personally might do could affect it. His occasional use of aerosol cans couldn't possibly make much difference, Jeff reasoned, and if he changed his behavior and stopped using them, that would do hardly anything to improve such a serious situation. Moreover, he thought that the problem was already so far advanced that a change in his behavior wouldn't reverse the damage. Because his actions would be futile in the face of such a massive problem, why bother? Why not continue using the aerosol cans, which he likes and which are easy to use? Julie's speech boomeranged and had the opposite effect from what she desired. Hoping to persuade Jeff to stop using aerosol sprays, she actually convinced him to keep using them.

To avoid the boomerang effect, you must assess carefully just how much to arouse the audience about an issue. Obviously, you want to convey a sense of seriousness or urgency when discussing a significant problem. At the same time, however, your speech should leave listeners optimistic about their ability to contribute to the problem's solution and confident that concerted efforts along the lines recommended in the speech really can make a difference.

Fortunately, these methods by which audiences resist persuasion—selective listening, perception, and acceptance—are not absolute. Speakers can overcome them by making wise use of their resources and opportunities.[6]

Checklist 14.2 Audience Constraints on Persuasion

1. **Selective listening**
2. **Selective perception**
   - Denial of the message
   - Dismissal of the message as not personally applicable
   - Belittling the source
   - Compartmentalization
3. **Selective influence**
   - Multiple meanings (polysemy)
   - Boomerang effect

Strategic Resources for Specific Purposes

In reviewing the constraints facing speakers who wish to persuade, we hinted at some of the ways in which the constraints can be overcome. Now, we want to focus more carefully on the strategic resources available to the speaker. In the last chapter, we discussed a variety of strategies—defining, reporting, describing, explaining, demonstrating, and comparing—that applied across a range of informative goals. With persuasion, it is a bit more complicated. Some of the strategies pertain to a particular purpose, whereas others are more general in their application. This section of the chapter will focus on the former category, and the next section will deal with the latter.

Strengthening Commitment

Here are several common approaches that speakers use to strengthen commitment.

Consciousness Raising. You undoubtedly have beliefs or values that you are barely aware of because you take them for granted. Only when you deliberately focus attention on those values will you acknowledge and reaffirm support for them. For example, people often don't realize how important families and loved ones are until they are separated from them or someone becomes ill.

In the 1970s, the emerging women's movement used the term **consciousness raising** to refer to the process of making people aware of values and commitments that they had taken for granted.[7] Consider the issue of sexual harassment in the workplace. Prior to the movement toward public awareness, many people believed that sexual harassment was wrong, but they were not aware of how this conviction applied to everyday occurrences at work. By bringing such values to the surface and applying them to a specific situation, a speaker can cause listeners to identify with them consciously, thereby strengthening their convictions.

Moving from Education to Commitment. Informative strategies might provide listeners the background that they need to understand an issue. For example, listeners need to be informed of the workings of the Electoral College to recognize that it will not necessarily select as president of the United States the candidate favored by a majority of the voters. Before the election of 2000, many people were not aware of this fact, because the last disparity between popular and electoral vote occurred in 1888. Now, however, it will be easier for listeners to understand how it could happen. A persuasive speech would go further, building on listeners' intellectual awareness of the issue and seeking to convince them that the problem is serious and should be addressed. The speaker's goal might be to convince listeners to support a Constitutional amendment that abolishes the Electoral College or maybe even to lobby for passage of such an amendment.

Increasing the Sense of Urgency. Political campaign managers face the difficult problem of convincing a candidate's supporters that their ongoing support really matters. Tracy Baxter saw the need to fire up supporters when she was managing a political campaign for her neighbor, Martha Scott, who was running for the city council. Martha was well known in the neighborhood for such projects as increasing crime patrols, beautifying parks, and encouraging parents to volunteer at their child's school. She seemed certain to win the election—and that's what troubled Tracy. She was worried that

consciousness raising
Making people aware of values and commitments that they previously took for granted.

Martha's supporters might think their efforts weren't needed and wouldn't bother to contribute to the campaign or even to vote. If enough people felt that way, Martha could lose the election. So Tracy addressed a rally of Martha's supporters, stressing that the race could go either way and that their efforts, money, and votes were essential to victory.

Tracy was worried that a **self-fulfilling prophecy** might derail Martha's campaign. If supporters believed that their efforts weren't needed and thus didn't contribute, the campaign wouldn't have the resources to advertise and mobilize voters; Martha's chance of winning would be reduced. Then, if Martha were defeated, supporters would conclude that they were right not to waste their money and time. To break this circular, self-fulfilling reasoning, Tracy needed to establish a sense of urgency among listeners. She convinced listeners that each person's action would make a real difference in averting defeat and ensuring victory. Her speech carefully balanced how serious the problem was and how easily listeners could be effective in solving it.

In such situations, speakers typically argue that (1) the issue is important, (2) it could be decided either way, (3) it will be decided soon, and (4) the listener's action could tip the scales. Properly crafted, such a message will jolt listeners out of complacency and intensify their commitment to the cause.

Weakening Commitment

There are two general approaches to weakening commitment. You can try to qualify or limit the audience's commitment, or you can try to disprove or dispute the claims that support it. The former approach involves finding a critical distinction; the latter involves refutation.

Finding a Critical Distinction. One way to weaken commitment to a principle is to deflect it by invoking a different principle. Think again about the example of Vice President Gore and Senator Lieberman. Their audience believed strongly that government should not interfere in the artistic process, even if the result was the production of popular music, television, or movies that many people found objectionable. Gore and Lieberman made a distinction between *creating* and *marketing* works of popular culture. They disclaimed any interest in involving government in the process of artistic creation while insisting that improper marketing (promoting adult films to children, for example) was subject to government action if the industry did not regulate itself.[8] In this way, they sought to weaken the audience's commitment to the belief that government has no role to play in popular culture, while at the same time they tried not to challenge the core belief in artistic freedom.

What makes this strategic move possible is that audiences' commitments are complex. They may *seem* simple, but upon inspection they usually can be found to contain multiple perspectives, not all of which work in perfect harmony. For example, a person may believe in the death penalty and also believe that it should be imposed only in cases in which there is absolute certainty of guilt. A speaker might weaken the commitment to capital punishment by using the second belief to argue for mandatory DNA testing of defendants, for provision of highly qualified defense counsel, or even for a

self-fulfilling prophecy
A prediction that comes true because of actions that people take upon hearing the prediction.

moratorium on executions until doubts about the fairness of capital punishment could be resolved. In some cases, the accumulation of these qualifying principles eventually can cause the first principle to collapse. That is what happened in the process that convinced the Supreme Court to declare segregated public schools unconstitutional. The constitutionality of "separate but equal" schools was not challenged directly until a series of cases had established that there was no way that segregated facilities really could be equal.

To employ this means of weakening commitment, you should identify the audience's commitment as precisely as you can and then ask what considerations might limit or qualify the commitment. Mentally explore these possibilities until you find one or more that would compete with the original commitment for the approval of your listeners.

Refutation. If finding a critical distinction serves to *deflect* the audience's commitment, **refutation** is an approach that *challenges* it directly. It tries to disprove or dispute the arguments or appeals made by others. Of course, if you convince listeners not to be persuaded by someone else, you actually have persuaded them yourself.[9]

Before you can refute an argument or appeal, you first need to be sure that you understand what it says. This is where the tests of reasoning that were offered in Chapter 6 are important. Once you have decided that the other person's argument is weak and should be refuted, you can use either or both of the following strategies.

- *Object to the claim itself, and develop a contrary claim.* This form of refutation does not target the internal workings of the argument; instead, it suggests that the conclusion is mistaken and offers an alternative conclusion. For example, on hearing a speaker maintain that abortion should be restricted, you decide to refute the speaker by presenting your own arguments that restrictions should not be established. Your arguments are independent of the other speaker's. You develop them not by analyzing the internal workings of the speaker's argument but through your own careful and independent thought.
- *Object to the speaker's inferences, and thereby refuse to accept the conclusion.* In this case, you analyze the internal workings of the other person's argument, applying the same tests of reasoning (see Chapter 6) that you used in developing your own speech. If the speaker employs hasty generalization, confuses cause with sign, develops a faulty analogy, or commits any other error in reasoning, the conclusion may well be faulty even if supporting evidence is true. You will want to point out these deficiencies in reasoning if your goal is refutation.

Whether you want to refute a particular argument or an entire speech, the basic steps in developing your own message are similar. You must specify what you are refuting, make your refutation convincing, and explain to listeners what the refutation has accomplished. To achieve these goals, the following steps are recommended.

1. *Identify the position to be attacked.* State the position as clearly and as fairly as you can. It is especially important to state the position in a way that

refutation
The attack or defense of a challenged statement or claim.

its supporters would accept. Advocates who fail to do this usually end up speaking past each other rather than truly refuting each other's positions.

For example, if you opposed abortion and began to refute a pro-choice speech by stating, "Pro-choice speakers support the killing of innocent babies," you would not be stating the position fairly. You may regard the fetus as an innocent baby, but pro-choice supporters do not. In fact, that is probably the essential difference between those who support and those who oppose abortion. A fairer statement of the position might be, "Pro-choice supporters don't think the fetus is a human being, but I believe we must assume that it is."

2. *Explain the significance of the position you are attacking.* This often-omitted step lets the audience know why your refutation is important. Most people dislike hearing disagreement for disagreement's sake. If your refutation can be granted and yet do no real damage to the opponent's position, then listeners will probably not take your speech seriously.

Consider the abortion example again, but this time imagine that the speaker is pro-choice and is refuting the statement that protesters stayed ten yards away from the entrance to an abortion clinic, instead insisting that they were within five yards of it. In this case, the refutation is probably not very important; it is hard to imagine why the difference between five and ten yards would matter. But suppose that the speaker were to say, "Pro-life supporters violated a local ordinance by entering the ten-yard radius and blocking the entrance to an abortion clinic," and then went on to explain, "This is important because the law was designed to balance the rights of protesters with the rights of women seeking abortions. If the ten-yard rule is too difficult to maintain, then it should be changed by the City Council, not by protesters." Now the speaker has both identified the argument to be refuted and explained why the refutation matters.

3. *Present and develop the attack.* State your position, and support it with appropriate materials. This step will probably take the most time. The process is basically the same as if you were developing a constructive position of your own. Pay special attention to the tests of evidence (Chapter 5) and reasoning (Chapter 6).

4. *Explain the impact of the refutation.* Having presented and supported your own claim, do not assume that the significance of your achievement is self-evident. Include a sentence or two to explain exactly what your refutation has accomplished. If you are refuting the argument that all students should have parking privileges on campus, and you show that there are not enough parking spaces to go around and that the cost of building additional space is prohibitive, you may believe that you have been very clear about what you've accomplished. But the audience often still needs help. It will not hurt to draw the argument together by saying, "So this proposal is infeasible with the current supply of parking spaces, and creating more spaces is out of the question. Even though the proposal appeals to your desire for parking privileges, therefore, you ought not to be swayed by it." Recognize that listeners will attend to the speech with different degrees of intensity, and provide a clear statement of what your refutation has accomplished.

Checklist 14.3 Steps in Refutation

1. **Decide on the grounds for refutation.**
   - Object to the claim, and develop a contrary claim.
   - Object to the inferences, and thereby refuse to accept the conclusion.
2. **Develop the refutation.**
   - Identify the position to be attacked.
   - Explain the significance of the position you are attacking.
   - Present and develop the attack.
   - Explain the impact of the refutation.

Rebuilding Arguments. Refutation is not solely a process of criticizing arguments; it is also a means of rebuilding an argument that has been attacked. You can rebuild an argument by responding to criticism against it—either by showing that the attack was flawed or by developing independent reasons for the audience to believe the original claim.

If your thesis was "Many people have argued that space limitations make it infeasible to guarantee parking to all students, but I wish to defend the guaranteed-parking proposal against these attacks," your analytical process would be exactly the same as if you were developing the attack. Both attack and defense therefore come under the heading of refutation, and both should be seen as basically alike in analysis and composition.

Conversion

We have observed that conversion is difficult, yet it does take place. People do change their minds, do abandon positions that they have held and replace them with others. How does this happen? Typically, a speaker attempts conversion through the following strategies.

Chip Away at the Edges of Beliefs. Rather than attack beliefs head-on, where they are most strongly defended, work first on the periphery. During the civil rights movement of the 1950s and early 1960s, for example, many resistant Southerners who did not abandon racial prejudice were nonetheless convinced by marches and demonstrations that inhumane treatment of blacks was wrong. That was often the first step toward conversion because it aroused sympathy for the demonstrators and led listeners to examine whether other aspects of the treatment of blacks were also wrong.

One effective way to chip away at the edges of beliefs is to defend a value that initially coexists with the value you want to challenge but that eventually will undermine it. Again, the civil rights movement furnishes an example. Many who believed in racial segregation also revered the Constitution. These two values could coexist as long as the Constitution was not seen as prohibiting segregation; indeed, many opposed integration based on the belief that it violated the Constitution. When laws and court rulings indicated that it was segregation that was unconstitutional, President Lyndon Johnson appealed to many Southerners not so much by discrediting racial prejudice (although he attempted that as well) as by appealing instead to reverence for the Constitution. Suddenly, the two values were in opposition, and one was used to undermine the other.

Identify a Pattern of Anomalies. People change beliefs when their old beliefs no longer explain things adequately. *Anomalies* are puzzling situations that an explanation does not fit. When we first discover them, we tend to dismiss them as freak coincidences or point to them as exceptions to the rule. But if anomalies continue, and especially if they intensify, they eventually call a position into question. Then, the old view may collapse of its own weight and the listener might convert to a new belief.

Such a pattern has been used to explain why many Democrats during the 1980s converted to support Republican Ronald Reagan. Believing in the effectiveness of government programs, they watched through the 1960s and 1970s as those programs grew; yet, in their view, social problems worsened rather than improved. At first, this was just a puzzle for them. But as evidence (and their taxes) continued to mount, they eventually came to believe that government was not a solution to social ills but was itself part of the problem. This, of course, was the position advocated by President Reagan.

Employ Consciousness Raising. Besides being a means of strengthening commitment, consciousness raising can be used when a speaker wants the audience to change. Let's look again at the example of the women's movement. Early advocates of consciousness raising maintained that women had accepted their subordinate role because they had never regarded their role as subordinate. By raising women's consciousness about the dominant/submissive pattern in many of their existing relationships with men, advocates were able not only to sensitize them to their situation but also to evoke an alternative toward which they might strive.

In another example, student speaker Laura Davisson gave a speech to raise listeners' consciousness about their daily acts of discrimination against overweight people:

> You might just laugh at them behind their backs. Perhaps you call them names like "whale" or "pig." Maybe they are the butt of your jokes. Or maybe it's something much more subtle than that. Maybe you just assume that fat people have no self-control, that they eat too much and too often, or that they get no exercise.

By pointing out the existence of listeners' discriminatory feelings and actions, Laura was able to begin altering them. Consciousness raising made listeners sufficiently uncomfortable with their own actions that they could be induced to change.

Seek Incremental Changes. Usually, conversion comes about slowly, in a series of small and gradual steps. Knowing that people typically change their views incrementally rather than radically, keep your goals modest. Don't ask for too much too soon.

Imagine, for example, that your goal is to defend public funding for the arts, even though you know that the audience is hostile to it, considers most contemporary art unnecessary or even perverse, and sees public funding as a waste of tax money. Successful persuasion will probably require several steps, beginning with asking the audience to acknowledge the importance of art both in fostering self-expression and advancing culture; then perhaps moving to the position that one need not like or support all examples of art to believe strongly in the value of the arts; then explaining why it is in the public interest to support art; then defending the overall administration of public funding programs and establishing that errors and mistaken judgments are few; and only then moving to the question of whether the government should reduce funding for the arts. Getting to this point might require several speeches, over a long period of time. But a frontal assault on the audience's values is likely to fail, whereas a gradual, incremental approach has at least a chance of success. People often accept in small doses a belief that they would reject outright if it were presented all at once.

Use Reluctant Testimony. Your statements will be weakened if listeners think that you have something to gain by stating them. If your audience believes that you have a vested interest—whether economic, political, or ideological—in a particular outcome of the speech, listeners will tend to discount what you say. On the other hand, if you make a statement that is at odds with your own interest, that statement is considered to be **reluctant testimony.** Because you are working against your own interests by making this statement, listeners presume that you would not make it unless it were true. Likewise, if you quote sources who are widely known to favor your position, the audience you are seeking to convert may simply dismiss the sources out of hand. On the other hand, using sources who generally support the audience's position but disagree with it in this case will give their words added credibility.

Consider how reluctant testimony has worked in the political world. Only Ronald Reagan, for example—a Cold Warrior who had called the Soviet Union an "evil empire"—could really begin to dismantle the Cold War apparatus and seek arms reduction agreements with the Soviet Union. If someone else had attempted this, it might have seemed like a cave-in to Soviet demands. But President Reagan was trustworthy because people believed that he would not betray conservative interests. Similarly, George W. Bush, although he had opposed the use of U.S. military forces for "nation building," was able to convince many Americans that this was an appropriate, even necessary, use of U.S. troops in Afghanistan, Iraq, and Liberia. And when the actor Charlton Heston, well-known as a political conservative, supported public funding of the National Endowment for the Arts, his words were reluctant testimony that helped convert some conservatives in Congress to support continued funding for the endowment.

Because reluctant testimony generally is more credible than is evidence reflecting the source's self-interest, you should look for it when conducting your research. Reluctant testimony is the opposite of **biased evidence,** which you should try particularly hard to avoid.[10]

Reluctant testimony enhances the credibility of classroom speakers too. Western State University had a tradition of strong social fraternities, a system that had come under fire because several recent initiation rituals clearly had been excessive. A vocal group of faculty members charged that all fraternities were anti-intellectual, and the campus newspaper called them "social clubs for the privileged rich." Two students of public speaking addressed this issue, arguing that major changes were needed if fraternities

reluctant testimony
Statements that are not in the speaker's self-interest.

biased evidence
Statements that are suspect because they are influenced by the self-interest of the source.

were to survive on campus. Ben Peters was an independent who was known to dislike fraternities. Although his speech was well prepared, it had little impact on his classmates; it said exactly what everyone expected Ben to say. But when Charles Thompson, a fraternity president, acknowledged that the system had serious problems, listeners noticed. If a prominent fraternity man criticized the system, his views had to be taken seriously.

Just as the insider was more persuasive in this example, so will a dorm resident who is a smoker be more credible than one who is a nonsmoker in urging a smoke-free dormitory environment. Similarly, a biology student who argues that animal experiments on campus need to be monitored and reduced will be more believable than an English major who makes the same argument. As a speaker, you can enhance your credibility by pointing out when you are offering reluctant testimony.

Inducing a Specific Action

Two strategies will be especially helpful if your goal is to induce a specific action.

Identify the Desired Action Precisely. A speaker who says, "So I urge you to do something about this," is not likely to accomplish much. The action is so general that no one will know what to do. Identify the specific behavior that you want listeners to perform—to stop using the car for trips of fewer than five blocks, to contribute money to a charitable organization, to write legislators in support of a pending bill, and so on.

Make the Action as Easy to Perform as Possible. Audiences are subject to inertia. If a difficult action is requested of them, they are less likely to go to the trouble of performing it. So, for example, if you want your listeners to sign a petition, have a copy of the petition with you. If you want them to write a legislator, provide the specific address (and maybe even hand out stamped self-addressed envelopes). The easier you make it for the audience to do what you ask, the more likely you are to succeed.

Checklist 14.4 Strategies for Specific Purposes

1. **Strengthening commitment**
   - Consciousness raising
   - Moving from education to commitment
   - Increasing the sense of urgency
2. **Weakening commitment**
   - Finding a critical distinction
   - Refutation
3. **Conversion**
   - Identify a pattern of anomalies.
   - Employ consciousness raising.
   - Seek incremental changes.
   - Use reluctant testimony.
4. **Inducing a specific action**
   - Identify the desired action precisely.
   - Make the action as easy to perform as possible.

Generally Available Strategic Resources

In addition to the approaches that are tailored to specific persuasive goals, there are resources available to all persuasive speakers. The earliest theorists of public speaking, during classical times, identified three general means of persuasion: *logos, ethos,* and *pathos. Logos* referred to the speaker's argument; *ethos,* to the speaker's apparent character and credibility; and *pathos,* to appeals to appropriate emotions. In different combinations, these resources are employed whenever speakers try to persuade. Without always using the classical terms, we have discussed many of these resources in earlier chapters, so it is appropriate to review them briefly here.

Select Appropriate Supporting Materials

In Chapter 5, we explored the various forms of supporting material, and in Chapter 7, we considered how to select supporting materials for the speech. Astute selection is particularly important when persuasion is the goal.[11] A startling statistic, for example, might move listeners to take notice of an issue that is far more vast than they might think. For example, student speaker Mitchell Johnson, a Chicago native, talked about the fact that many ballots cast in an election are not counted:

> In 2000, the country focused on uncounted ballots in Florida. But did you know that over 120,000 ballots were discarded as uncountable in Cook County, Illinois, my home? In fact, across the country there were *millions* of punch-card ballots that could not be counted by machine readers.

He then pointed out that this total easily could be larger than the winning margin in a close election. Insisting that every legally cast vote should be counted, Mitchell sought to persuade listeners that all states should replace punch-card voting systems with a more reliable instrument.

A personal narrative also can be a potent form of supporting material, making an abstract problem concrete and showing its effects on the lives of real people. If you discuss how "taxpayer resistance has squeezed the public sector of the economy," the problem may seem distant, removed, and impersonal. Instead, you can make the issue more vivid and immediate by telling listeners, "the local elementary school has been forced to close its library, depriving children of books and the librarian of a job."

Of course, startling statistics and personal narratives are not the only types of supporting material to use in persuasion. *Any* type of supporting material can work well if it is carefully chosen and clearly related to the speaker's purpose.

Use Sound Reasoning

Because in a persuasive speech you are asking the audience to believe or to do something, it is particularly important that you offer good reasons for your claims. Good reasons are those that meet the tests of reasoning we developed in Chapter 6. They will show listeners that you have used inference patterns that generally yield reliable results. People who are confident about your reasoning will be more likely to accept your conclusions and less likely to quibble with your thinking. If listeners think that your reasoning is shoddy, they will be far less likely to conclude that you have made a good case for what you want them to believe or do. And if your case is weak, it is easy for them to disregard your request for their response. You may wish to review the discussion of reasoning in Chapter 6.

Although reasoning is used only in persuasive messages, it is especially important for them. Good reasons increase the likelihood that audience members will adopt the attitudes or behavior that the speaker recommends.[12] Remember that we have focused on reasoning with the audience in mind, not on reasoning as an abstract exercise in formal logic.

Follow Appropriate Organizational Patterns

Not only does being organized itself enhance persuasiveness but also the choice of one organizational pattern over another can make a difference. Review the organizational patterns we developed in Chapter 7. Many speakers find the problem–solution pattern to be particularly effective for persuasion. It makes listeners aware of a problem and then advocates its solution. But other patterns can be effective too, especially cause–effect and comparison–contrast.

A slight variation on the problem–solution pattern is to identify the criteria that a solution would need to satisfy and then to argue that one's proposal best satisfies them. For example, on the subject of diversity in college admissions, a speaker might first establish that a good policy was one that admitted a diverse student body, did not grant preferences based on race or ethnicity, and did not incorporate a quota system. Then, the speaker could suggest that the best way to meet these criteria was to guarantee admission to the top 10 percent of each high school graduating class.

You can inject a number of other helpful patterns into any organizational framework. For instance, narrative sequence lets you tell the story of how the problem developed, topical structure allows you to examine various dimensions of the problem, and biographical structure enables you to focus on key individuals in the evolution of the problem.

Not only are organizational choices important in individual sections of the speech but also organization is an important strategic resource for the speech as a whole. In the next major section of this chapter, "Organizing Persuasive Speeches," we will identify two common organizational plans for a speech in which persuasion is the principal goal.

Establish Positive Ethos

Your *ethos* is a powerful resource in persuasive speeches. If listeners trust you, they will be more inclined to give your ideas a fair hearing. Particularly important among the many factors that engender trust are a speaker's previous record and association with trustworthy sources.

Previous Record. A speaker who has established a record of being trustworthy is likely to be trusted in the specific situation at hand. Federal Reserve Board Chairman Alan Greenspan enjoys positive *ethos* when he speaks about the economy because of his excellent record in managing the economic growth of the 1990s. If in earlier speeches you've convinced the audience that you are careful, faithful to the evidence, and critical in reasoning and don't make claims beyond what the evidence supports, you have created

A speaker who wants to persuade an audience usually must establish positive ethos. James Brady, who was injured in the assassination attempt on President Ronald Reagan, speaks with experience and credibility to promote gun control.

a strong presumption that what you say in this speech will be trustworthy as well.

Association with Trustworthy Sources. Particularly when your topic is something about which you are not yourself an expert, you need to draw on the statements of people who do have expertise in the subject. If your sources themselves have a reputation for trustworthiness, your association with them will suggest that you are trustworthy too. George W. Bush followed this advice during the 2000 presidential campaign. When he spoke about foreign policy, with which he had little previous experience, he often mentioned that he received valuable information from General Colin Powell, former Stanford provost Condoleezza Rice, and former Defense Secretary Richard Cheney, all of whom were quite experienced and were held in high regard, and all of whom he brought into his administration and assigned significant roles.

Encourage Retention Through Reinforcement

We saw in Chapter 13 that the slope of the forgetting curve is steep, particularly when the message involves new, unfamiliar, or uncomfortable ideas (see Figure 13.1). Unless your persuasive goal is very specific and can be achieved through the speech itself, you should think creatively about how to reinforce what you want listeners to believe or to do. Your strategies might range from the simple act of thanking the audience for hearing you out to the extreme of asking listeners to participate actively in encouraging others to accept the view you propose.

Student Margaret Orsinger used an interesting metaphor to reinforce her message that bicyclists and motorcyclists should wear helmets:

> We do more to protect the melons in our grocery stores than we do to protect our own heads! Every time you see a cyclist without a helmet, take a good hard look at these "melon-heads." They are people in need of a good, solid crate around their ears.

There is no magic recipe for reinforcing a persuasive message. In general, though, you are more likely to succeed if you give listeners opportunities to rehearse and remind themselves of your conclusion and how you arrived at it and if you can make acceptance of your position seem to enhance listeners' self-worth.

Achieve Identification

identification
Establishing common bonds between speaker and audience so that the speaker appears to be at one with listeners.

Establishing common bonds between speaker and audience is referred to as **identification.**[13] The more that listeners believe themselves to be basically like the speaker and to share the same values or experiences, the more willing they are to be influenced by what the speaker says. Speakers can develop common bonds explicitly, by stating the features they share with the audience. Or bonds can be developed implicitly, when the speaker relates a personal experience that many listeners also have had. Common bonds can even be developed with no mention at all. For example, the fact that a college student speaks to an audience of college students about concerns of college students is itself a source of common bonds. Not surprisingly, listeners are more likely to be persuaded by a peer than by a more distant figure with whom it is difficult to identify.

Identification with the audience helps to create a good feeling. It is, in a sense, an emotional connection, suggesting that you understand and share the emotions you have aroused in the audience. Your speech can evoke emotions (such as happiness, anger, relief, satisfaction, or fear) that match your own emotions and that you believe are appropriate to your topic. Together with good reasons and good character, good feeling helps you to persuade.

To keep identification from being perceived as pandering to the audience or telling listeners whatever they want to hear, apply the test you learned in Chapter 4: Use appeals that will satisfy not only the specific audience that is immediately present but also the broader audience of unseen critical listeners whom you might imagine as your court of appeal.

Even facing a potentially hostile audience, speakers employ some level of identification. The common bond that leads an audience at least to listen attentively to ideas with which they disagree might be a shared procedural value, such as a belief in fair play or a willingness to hear the speaker out. Or the bond might be a shared value, such as respect for a speaker who has the courage of his or her convictions.

Do not conclude, then, that you can't disagree with your audience. In fact, a speaker who always tailors the message to what listeners believe is suspect. But when you cannot achieve identification with the audience on the basis of your content, do so on the basis of some overarching value.

Checklist 14.5 Generally Applicable Strategies

1. Select appropriate supporting materials.
2. Use sound reasoning.
3. Follow appropriate organizational patterns.
4. Establish positive *ethos*.
5. Encourage retention through reinforcement.
6. Achieve identification.

Organizing Persuasive Speeches

As we have seen, persuasion can be accomplished in any speech. Often, however, the principal purpose of the speech is to persuade. In this section, we will consider briefly two very common patterns for structuring the persuasive speech: the problem–solution pattern and the motivated sequence.

Some writers describe persuasion as though it is a series of steps performed in a specific sequence. For example, social psychologist William J.

McGuire holds that a person's attitudes are changed in a six-step process: receiving a communication, paying attention to it, comprehending it, yielding to it, retaining the new attitude, and performing the desired behavior.[14] Even if these steps are not always separate and do not always come in the same order, McGuire's scheme is useful for understanding what happens when someone is persuaded.

The Problem–Solution Speech

As its name suggests, the problem–solution speech establishes a serious problem and then identifies what should be done about it.[15] Problem–solution speeches can be organized in a variety of ways, but they generally apply to an entire speech the four-stage structure that you learned in Chapter 7:

1. Describe the situation.
2. Evaluate the situation as a problem.
3. Propose a solution.
4. Argue for the solution.

Describe the Situation. This part of the speech is primarily informative. Your goal is to make listeners aware of the magnitude or importance of the problem. For example, in discussing the use of tobacco among teenagers, you might report how many teenagers use cigarettes, smokeless tobacco, and cigars; how teenagers feel about tobacco use; and the relationship between teen smoking and adults' use of tobacco. The outline for this part of the body of your speech might be:

I. Tobacco use among teenagers is significant and high.

   A. Rates of tobacco use among teenagers are high.

   B. Teenagers continue to believe that using tobacco enhances their image.

   C. Most adults who use tobacco began when they were teenagers.

The problem–solution speech requires you first to persuade the audience that there is a serious threat or problem and then to persuade them that your solution is the best approach to the problem. This speaker is arguing that handgun-related deaths are excessive and that limitations must be placed on handgun ownership.

Critique of a Persuasive Speech

Excerpt from John's Persuasive Speech, "Drug Testing in High Schools"

John Hernandez

I'm John Hernandez, and my speech today is about drug testing in extracurricular activities in high schools. To give you a little background about it, according to the Austin *American Statesman*, only ten school districts in Texas have drug tests. They pay up to $18.50 for the drug test. It tests for ten substances, including marijuana, cocaine, and alcohol. To add steroids to the test would be an extra $75. Out of the 1200 schools in Texas, only 196 actually have some sort of drug testing program.

I did a little research on the three main drug tests used in schools. The first one is the immunoassay test, which is the basic urinary test. It costs $20 to $40 and has a low accuracy. Other chemicals can produce false positives. It's similar to the litmus test where a strip changes color when any drug is detected. Another problem is this test can only detect one drug at a time.

The second test is the gas chromatograph, which is a high tech color analysis of chemical structure. It costs anywhere from $80 to $100 per test. It detects masking agents, and it has no chance of false negatives or false positives. It takes a lot longer and requires a highly trained staff in a sophisticated laboratory.

If you use the urinary test, and the results are contested, you have to go back to the gas chromatograph to prove the false or suspected positive. Either way, I'd rather go with the gas chromatograph.

The third test is the hair test, which is $75 per one-and-a-half inch of sample. It gives you a thirty-day feedback of substance abuse. The only problem with this is the high cost and the highly trained staff needed in a sophisticated laboratory.

To get a little insight as far as what people in school districts think, I interviewed Tim James, who is the Athletic Director at Louisa High School. He feels they should drug test the school as a whole and not just focus on athletes, since athletes are not more prone to drug abuse. However, he feels that many legal complications would arise from such a policy, and that there's not enough money to handle any legal problems that arise or even to start a drug-testing program. Another complication he saw is that most tests are not foolproof, and those who want to get by them, can.

Prof. Blivens

John, your opening is well written but doesn't have a stated position on this issue.

After introducing the topic you need to give us your claim. Is drug testing in high schools good or an invasion of privacy? You don't provide the audience with a clear argument. This is a persuasive speech, so we need to be clear on your claims and how you plan to support them. It's great that you told us the types of drug tests and the current status quo. But you bring up several things that could formulate an argument against drug testing; for example, the accuracy rate, privacy issues, and finally the targeting of certain student groups. But you never develop any one of those into a concise argument against testing. Also, why is this topic important? If only 12 school districts in the state of Texas are currently testing students, that number is not significant enough to warrant a speech. Are more schools thinking of initiating this policy? We need clear main points that are developed logically. Starting off by explaining the drug tests was good, but you need two other main points that support your claim. The amount of cited evidence is little to none. Where did the information on the drug tests and the current status of testing in schools come from? Don't forget to cite. Look up the outlining chapter in Zarefsky. Figure out which persuasive format would be better for your speech. Pick one and then go back through and reorganize your speech. Consider the section on supporting materials. What evidence did Zarefsky say was more reliable? Was it interviews? Consider the number of interviews that should be done. Take that into consideration when researching.

Evaluate the Situation as a Problem. The second stage is to convince listeners that the situation you described really does represent a problem—that it is cause for genuine concern. People will endure all sorts of inconveniences without taking action; they become concerned only about what they regard as serious problems.

To establish that a situation is a problem, you need to show that it violates a value that is important to your audience. In the case of teenage tobacco use, for example, you might establish that the use of tobacco products is strongly associated with premature death. In addition, tobacco-related diseases add billions of dollars to the cost of health care. These conditions probably will be accepted as problems in their own right. They also might lead people to question the quality of life not only for tobacco users but also for those who live, work, and play with them. They might also call into question whether it is economically just for society at large to bear the costs of tobacco-related illnesses. Because people care about these values, they are likely to be disturbed by the high rate of tobacco use among teenagers.

Values are rooted in emotions, and so persuasive strategies must be concerned with emotional appeals. In Chapter 6, you learned that an inappropriate appeal to emotions is an error in reasoning. The key word here is *inappropriate*. Although emotional appeals can be misused, there is nothing irrational about responding to an appropriate appeal. When you decide not to go out alone at night because of safety concerns, when you try to mend fences with parents or siblings because family harmony is important, or when you strive to do your best in response to competition, your choices are perfectly reasonable and sensible.

The second part of the speech's body might be outlined like this:

II. High tobacco use among teenagers is a serious problem.

    A. Use of tobacco products is strongly associated with premature death.

    B. Tobacco-related diseases add billions of dollars to the cost of health care.

    C. People question the quality of life for smokers and others.

    D. It undermines economic justice to burden society with the costs of tobacco-related illness.

A speaker cannot create in listeners an emotion that they do not feel. However, the speaker can make audience members aware of their emotions and indicate the importance of those emotions. When you evoke fear, pride, anxiety, or any other emotion, you also create a need to satisfy that emotion. Some emotions, such as fear and anxiety, can become highly disturbing if they are left unrelieved. Your power as a speaker lies in the ability not only to arouse the emotion but also to satisfy it by providing a positive course of action. We have seen that arousing too much fear can cause a boomerang effect. But if you arouse an appropriate level of fear in the audience and you then offer the means to relieve the fear—by talking to a school counselor, by taking advantage of over-the-counter aids to stop smoking, or by joining a community organization that works to reduce teenagers' use of tobacco products—the speech is likely to be persuasive.

Propose a Solution. Your solution might be simple (a single option) or complex (a range of options). You might identify it at once, or you might first rule out alternatives. But your solution should be detailed enough to address the problem as you have described it. If you have presented three separate dimensions of the problem, for instance, each should be addressed by your solution.

In the example of teenagers' use of tobacco, few listeners would feel that a statement such as "We have to have faith and hope that things will turn out for the best" is an appropriate solution. You are more likely to be persuasive if a section of the body of your speech details the solution, such as:

III. A successful solution to the problem has several components.

    A. It includes efforts to eliminate the root causes of teenage tobacco use.

    B. It includes more effective enforcement of laws regarding the purchase of tobacco.

    C. It includes creating more persuasive appeals to tobacco companies.

Argue for the Solution. The final step in the problem–solution speech is to convince listeners that your solution really works—that it resolves the problem, is feasible, and produces benefits that outweigh its costs. Speakers too often neglect this final step, as though the value of the solution were self-evident. But if that were so, the solution would probably have been tried already!

Instead of taking the value of your solution for granted, give listeners reasons to believe that your solution is the best option. In the tobacco example, this final section of the body of your speech might be organized in the following way:

IV. The comprehensive solution I have proposed is the best way to deal with the use of tobacco among teenagers.

    A. It will stop tobacco use at the source when possible.

    B. It will deter the sale of tobacco products to teenagers.

    C. It will improve the quality of life for both smokers and nonsmokers.

From this example, you can see that the basic problem–solution organizational pattern adapts easily to persuasive speeches. Although each step of the structure includes informative elements, the principal purpose of the speech is to affect the audience's beliefs, attitudes, values, or actions.

The Motivated Sequence

A sequential scheme for achieving persuasion in a speech was developed many years ago by Alan H. Monroe.[16] His **motivated sequence** is similar to the problem–solution speech, but instead of being organized with reference to the specific subject—health care or crime, for instance—it is organized in terms of the audience's motivation. The sequence has five steps and includes the introduction and conclusion of the speech as well as the body:

motivated sequence
A persuasive message that is organized in terms of steps in the audience's motivation rather than in terms of the specific subject.

I. Attention step	Introduction
II. Need step	
III. Satisfaction step	Body
IV. Visualization step	
V. Action step	Conclusion

The *attention step,* as its name suggests, is intended to engage listeners' attention. It serves as the introduction to the speech and includes such appropriate devices as visual narratives, engaging anecdotes, and startling statistics.

The *need step* is intended to convince the audience that something is amiss. The goal is to arouse listeners to believe that an important value is being lost, an opportunity is being wasted, or an objective is not being met. This belief will motivate them to take corrective action if they know what to do.

The *satisfaction step* provides listeners with the means to fulfill the motivation that the need step aroused. People seldom respond to broad and abstract generalizations, however, and so slogans such as "Stimulate the economy" or "Affirmative action: mend it but don't end it" are unlikely to satisfy listeners. To avoid this problem, the speaker goes on to explain how the solution will work and how it will affect listeners personally.

The *visualization step* gives the audience a mental picture of the solution. Instead of saying, "Stimulate the economy," the speaker shows what the solution will mean: "Putting an extra $1,000 saved from taxes into the hands of the average family will make it easier for them to buy the things they need. Increased demand for those products will create millions of new jobs, so that even more people will be better off."

The final step in the motivated sequence is the *action step,* in which the speaker asks the audience to do specific things to bring about the solution that they have visualized: change your personal behavior, sign a petition, patronize some stores but not others, write to senators and representatives, make a donation, and so on. The action step resembles the final plea that is one of the traditional functions of the conclusion of a speech.

An outline based on a persuasive speech by student Sarah Crist on the problems of the commercialization of America's classrooms could be organized into the motivated sequence as follows:

I. Attention Step

    A. Description of fondness for Coke products, but school sells only Pepsi because of an exclusive contract.

    B. Statistics showing percent of school day spent watching commercial "information" video programs.

    C. Statistics documenting the profits of commercialized education companies.

    D. Translation of these statistics into the probability that a younger relative is being treated as a consumer, not a student, by their school.

II. Need Step

    A. Commercialized education promotes consumerism, not education.

    B. Commercialized education exploits schools' financial problems.

    C. Commercialized education benefits advertisers, not students.

    D. Commercialized education promotes unhealthy food and beverage options.

III. Satisfaction Step

    A. End contracts with commercialized education companies such as Channel One.

    B. Vote to pass school levies to alleviate financial problems.

    C. Lobby lawmakers to pass laws prohibiting exploitation of students as consumers.

    D. Provide healthy food and beverage alternatives at school.

IV. Visualization Step

    A. Students will not be held captive to advertisers.

    B. Students will spend more class time learning, not consuming.

    C. Students will eat healthier and live healthier.

V. Action Step

    A. Write a letter to school board officials urging them to end contracts with commercialized education companies.

    B. Support your school by voting in favor of school levies.

    C. Participate in school fundraisers as an alternative to commercialized funding.

The criticisms that were raised against McGuire's theory of persuasion also apply to the motivated sequence. First, these steps are not always completely separate. It's possible, for example, that visualizing a solution is what alters the perception of a need. Second, not all listeners experience the steps in precisely the same order. Someone might be attracted to the satisfaction step, for example, without having grasped the full dimensions of the need. But even if the motivated sequence is not a universal account of human motivation, it still can provide a clear, coherent, and compelling way to organize speeches when the goal is persuasion.

Summary

Persuasive strategies aim not only to provide information but also to affect audience members' attitudes and behavior. They ask for a greater degree of commitment from listeners than informative strategies do, although no speaker can manipulate an unwilling audience.

The purposes of strengthening commitment, weakening commitment, conversion, and inducing a specific action are usually achieved through strategies of persuasion. It is important for speakers to know clearly the purpose they wish to achieve. They also need to understand that listeners must be motivated, must comprehend and agree with the message, and must incorporate the message into their overall system of beliefs and attitudes. They must determine the target audience that they are trying to influence, which may not be identical to the sum of people who hear the message.

The elaboration likelihood model explains how people are persuaded. Elaboration is the listener's tendency to think about the message and topic. When elaboration is high, persuasion is more likely to result from systematic analysis of the speaker's arguments; when it is low, it is likely to result from more intuitive judgments about the speaker. When elaboration is at moderate levels, listeners are likely to use a mix of these bases for judgment.

Listeners are often resistant to persuasion and may selectively listen to, perceive, and be influenced by the message. Among their means of resistance are regarding an ambiguous message as "really" supporting their own position, denying the message, dismissing it as inapplicable to them, belittling the source, compartmentalizing the message in their minds so that it affects beliefs without affecting values or behavior, understanding it to mean different things from what the speaker intended, or actually doing the opposite of what the speaker recommends, through a boomerang effect.

To attain results, speakers draw on their ability to analyze the audience and the situation, on their own credibility, and on the effective use of evidence, reasoning, and emotional appeals. Some strategies are specific to a particular purpose and others are applicable generally. A speaker may seek to strengthen commitment by moving from education to commitment, from subconscious to conscious values, or from belief to action. To weaken commitment, the speaker might try to qualify commitment by drawing a critical distinction, or the speaker might engage in refutation. Conversion can be achieved by chipping away at the edges of beliefs, drawing on a pattern of anomalies, using consciousness raising, seeking incremental changes, and employing reluctant testimony. Inducing a specific action will be facilitated by stating clearly just what is to be done and by making the action easy for listeners to perform.

In addition to these specific strategies, persuasive speakers have several generally applicable resources. They try to achieve identification by establishing common bonds with the audience. They may call upon listeners to be true to their own beliefs. They try to give listeners a sense of trust that they then can draw upon to support their message, which should reflect an appropriate organizational plan and include appropriate supporting materials. Finally, speakers should provide opportunities for listeners not only to say that they agree but also to perform some action.

One common type of speech based on persuasive strategies is the problem–solution speech, which (1) describes a situation, (2) evaluates it as a problem, (3) proposes a solution, and (4) argues for the solution. The problem–solution speech may achieve one or more of the specific purposes that persuasive strategies advance.

The motivated sequence offers another way to organize persuasive appeals. Similar to the problem–solution speech, it is organized for the purpose of arousing and then satisfying the audience's motivation. Including the introduction and conclusion, the message has five key parts: the attention step, need step, satisfaction step, visualization step, and action step.

Discussion Questions

1. What are the most urgent issues of controversy in the public forum of your classroom? List issues that most interest your community and your generation. Which of those topics would be good for a persuasive speech that:

   • Strengthens commitment?
   • Weakens commitment?
   • Converts opponents?
   • Calls for a specific action?

2. When a speaker has strong beliefs about a controversial issue, how can that speaker achieve identification with an opponent without compromising his or her own beliefs? What common bonds might be established between the opposing sides on the following controversial topics?

- Abortion
- The death penalty
- Affirmative action

How could a speaker use those common bonds as an aid to persuasion?
3. In what ways do persuasive strategies differ for the various speech purposes? As a class, create a chart that describes what you think would be likely differences in organization, choice of supporting material, and style for the following persuasive goals.

Organization   Supporting Material   Style

Strengthening commitment
Weakening commitment
Conversion
Inducing a specific action

Activities

1. Identify a topic and develop a thesis statement for each of the persuasive goals in the chart above. In a sentence or two, explain why you think each of these would be a good topic and thesis statement for a speech aimed at your target audience.
2. Choose one of your thesis statements from activity 1, and develop a persuasive speech. In a short essay, explain how you intend to motivate your audience. To which values do you plan to appeal?
3. From an opponent's perspective, examine the issue that you have chosen for your persuasive speech. Honestly try to step into the shoes of someone who disagrees with and might refute you.
   a. Which argument is most important for your opponent?
   b. What concerns would your opponent have if your position is argued successfully?
   c. How will your opponent view the supporting material that you plan to use in your speech?
4. Watch a debate. It can be a campaign debate, an academic debate, or a debate between two friends. In a short essay, answer the following questions about each speaker:
   a. Did the speaker fairly identify the opponent's position?
   b. Did the speaker refute the claims or the inferences being made by the other side?
   c. Did the speaker explain the significance of the position being attacked?
   d. Did the speaker explain the impact of the refutation?
   e. Who do you think won the debate, and why?

1. A. H. Maslow, "A Dynamic Theory of Personality," *Psychological Review* 50 (July 1943): 370–396.

2. For a more complete review of the elaboration likelihood model and research supporting it, see Daniel J. O'Keefe, *Persuasion: Theory and Research*, 2d ed. Thousand Oaks, Cal.: Sage, 2002, pp. 137–167.

3. A review of the psychological literature about persuasion further explains the resistances discussed in this chapter. See Chester A. Insko, *Theories of Attitude Change*, New York: Appleton-Century-Crofts, 1967.

4. The tendency to make ambiguous messages seem closer to one's own position than they actually are is one of the major conclusions of social judgment theory. For more on social judgment theory, see Carolyn W. Sherif, Muzafer Sherif, and Roger E. Nebergall, *Attitudes and Attitude Change: The Social Judgment-Involvement Approach*, Philadelphia: W. B. Saunders, 1965.

5. For an excellent overview of the concept of polysemy as it applies to the analysis of speeches, see Leah Ceccarelli, "Polysemy: Multiple Meanings in Rhetorical Criticism," *Quarterly Journal of Speech* 84 (November 1998): 395–415.

6. For more discussion of persuasive strategies, see Herbert W. Simons, *Persuasion: Understanding, Practice, and Analysis*, Reading, Mass.: Addison-Wesley, 1976.

7. Consciousness raising often occurred in group discussions but could also be the result of a more formal speech. See Anita Shreve, *Women Together, Women Alone: The Legacy of the Consciousness-Raising Movement*, New York: Viking Press, 1989.

8. The technical term for this kind of distinction drawing is *dissociation*. For a thorough treatment of the concept, see Chaim Perelman and L. Olbrechts-Tyteca, *The New Rhetoric*, translated by John Wilkinson and Purcell Weaver, Notre Dame, Ind.: Univ. of Notre Dame Press, 1969, pp. 411–459.

9. Research has shown that messages which provide both arguments for a position and refutation of the opposition are more persuasive than messages that simply present arguments for a position. Mike Allen, Jerold Hale, Paul Mongeau, et al., "Testing a Model of Message Sidedness: Three Replications," *Communication Monographs* 57 (December 1990): 275–291.

10. A recent study questions whether reluctant testimony is more persuasive than neutral testimony. See William L. Benoit and Kimberly A. Kennedy, "On Reluctant Testimony," *Communication Quarterly* 47 (Fall 1999): 376–387. Both reluctant testimony and neutral testimony, however, are clearly more persuasive than biased testimony.

11. See John C. Reinard, "The Empirical Study of the Persuasive Effects of Evidence: The Status after Fifty Years of Research," *Human Communication Research* 15 (Fall 1988): 3–59.

12. The relationship between good reasons and attitudes or behavior is established by the theory of reasoned action. For a discussion of this theory, see O'Keefe, *Persuasion: Theory and Research*, pp. 101–113.

13. See Kenneth Burke, *A Rhetoric of Motives*, New York: Prentice-Hall, 1950. For a discussion of Burke's theory of identification, see Dennis G. Day, "Persuasion and the Concept of Identification," *Quarterly Journal of Speech* 46 (October 1960): 270–273.

14. William J. McGuire, "Personality and Attitude Change: An Information-Processing Approach." In A. G. Greenwald, T. C. Brock, and T. M. Ostrom, ed., *Psychological Foundations of Attitudes*, Orlando: Atlantic Press, 1968, pp. 171–196.

15. A message that first arouses a need and then attempts to satisfy that need is more persuasive than a message organized in the reverse order. See Arthur R. Cohen, "Need for Cognition and Order of Communication as Determinants of Opinion Change," *The Order of Presentation in Persuasion*, New Haven, Conn.: Yale Univ. Press, 1966, pp. 79–97.

16. Alan H. Monroe, *Principles and Types of Speech*, Glenview, Ill.: Scott Foresman, 1935. The book has multiple editions with various authors. In the most recent edition, the lead author is Bruce E. Gronbeck.

Chapter Fifteen

Occasions for Public Speaking

In this chapter, we will:

- Explore how the nature of the speaking occasion and the purpose influence the speech.

- Understand what expectations are raised for a speech by the concept of decorum, or "fittingness to the occasion."

- Identify the differences between deliberative and ceremonial speaking occasions.

- Examine various specific kinds of deliberative and ceremonial speaking.

In preparing classroom speeches, you probably have been careful to follow specific instructions. If the assignment was to demonstrate a process, you made certain that your speech did that. If you were supposed to include three different types of supporting material, you probably paid extra attention to that aspect of preparation. And if the speech could not be longer than eight minutes, you most likely worked carefully with your outlines to be sure that you could cover the topic in that time.

Fitting Your Speech to the Occasion

Although the requirements of an assignment may sometimes seem arbitrary, they help you to focus on your goals for a speech, and they make the point that all speeches—whether inside or outside the classroom—are given in specific situations. Strategies of informing and persuading are selected and combined so that you and your listeners will have the greatest chance of achieving your goals in a particular situation. (Although we have not focused specifically on them, the same is true of strategies of entertaining.) Now that you have mastered the general tools for constructing and presenting effective speeches, you are ready to explore some of these specific situations in which they take place.

What's needed in one situation is different from what's needed in another. Just as an hour-long lecture is out of place when an eight-minute speech is expected, so is self-congratulation inappropriate in a speech to accept an award. On the other hand, just as including a variety of supporting material makes a persuasive speech effective, so does well-intentioned humor play an enhancing role in a "roast."

Influence of the Occasion

So far, we have examined the *speech,* the *speaker,* and the *audience,* as well as the relationships among them. It is time to consider the final dimension of any rhetorical situation—the *occasion.* The concept of the occasion was introduced briefly in Chapter 4 when we explored the components of a rhetorical situation. Now it is time to consider more carefully how the occasion influences the development of a speech. Then we can examine types of speeches that are appropriate to different occasions.

We begin with three premises: (1) speeches are presented for specific occasions, (2) occasions create constraints, and (3) constraints are not absolute.

Speeches Are Presented for Specific Occasions. At its best, literature is meaningful regardless of the circumstances in which it is written or read. Speeches, however, achieve their power by responding effectively to a particular occasion.

Even an occasion that is as formal and well-defined as a president's State of the Union address can be influenced by specific circumstances. President Reagan's, for example, responded to special circumstances that the nation faced in 1986. His State of the Union address was to be his first televised speech since the astronauts died in the *Challenger* explosion, so he changed the address into a tribute that reflected the occasion. Had he ignored the circumstances and delivered his original State of the Union address, that response would have been far less appropriate. Similarly, in 1998, President Clinton believed that the occasion called for statesmanship, and he delivered his State of the Union address without commenting on allegations that he was involved in a personal scandal. Although the two presidents had the same "assignment," their responses were quite different. Yet both were appropriate to the occasion.

Some speeches—such as Lincoln's Gettysburg Address and Martin Luther King, Jr.'s "I Have a Dream"—resonate with great force and power long after delivery, largely because they both responded to the specific occasion and also made that response more universal.

Occasions Create Constraints. Certain expectations arise on any occasion. If you attend a commencement speech, for instance, you expect that it will do certain things and not others. Undoubtedly, it will pose some challenge for the graduates; most likely, it will not criticize their parents and families. At a funeral or memorial service, you expect speakers to talk about the noble character of the deceased and to recall significant events in the person's life; you do not expect anyone to urge the audience to see an important new movie.

Constraints Are Not Absolute. Satisfying the expectations of a particular occasion still leaves the speaker much room for making creative and strategic choices. Not only are there many different ways to meet expectations but also a speech might go beyond them. In the process, it could change listeners' understanding of a situation.

Consider the example of the commencement speech again. Once it has posed a challenge to the graduates, it might proceed to discuss an important issue of public policy. Secretary of State George Marshall used the 1947 Harvard commencement address to announce what became known as the Marshall Plan to rebuild Europe after World War II. When First Lady Barbara Bush spoke at commencement at Wellesley College in 1990, she used the occasion to focus on lifestyle choices of women. United Nations Secretary General Kofi Annan used the 1997 Massachusetts Institute of Technology commencement address to urge Americans to support the United Nations and to spread tolerance and compassion globally. And speakers in 2002 and 2003, after noting that the graduates' lives were affected by the September 11, 2001, terrorist attacks, often proceeded to predict how their experience and the country's future would be different because of this tragedy.

In each of these examples, the speech not only responded to but also altered the situation. It met the audience's expectations for what they should hear, and yet it transformed those expectations. Each speaker presented a commencement address but also announced or proposed policies or placed significant public issues on the nation's agenda.

Moreover, experienced speakers sometimes choose deliberately to violate the audience's expectations. For example, in a series of speeches thanking teachers and parents, one speaker might choose to be humorous to set the speech apart from the others and to entertain the audience. Deliberately violating the expectations of the occasion can sometimes be an effective strategy. But beginning speakers are wise to understand and fit a speech to the expectations of the occasion before seeking to subvert them.

In any situation, speakers both respond to and actively shape the rhetorical situation. That is why any occasion for public speaking requires not that you follow a prescribed formula but that you make strategic choices while also recognizing the constraints imposed by the occasion.[1]

The Concept of Decorum

Centuries ago, theorists of public speaking developed the concept of **decorum** to identify "fittingness to the occasion."[2] Decorum implies more than common courtesy. A *decorous* speech is one that conforms to the expectations of a particular occasion. As we've just seen, these expectations differ from one occasion to another, but the following variables are important.

Formality. Some occasions are highly formal, such as the inauguration of a president or the keynote address at a conference. These may call for a carefully worded speech delivered from manuscript. Other occasions are informal and call for a conversational delivery, use of familiar maxims, and plain language. Although neither approach is right or wrong in the abstract, either one can be successful or disastrous in the context of a specific situation.

Length. Some occasions call for lengthy remarks; others demand brevity. If your campus organization spends thousands of dollars to present a distinguished guest speaker who talks for only two minutes about the topic and then asks, "Any questions?" the audience will feel cheated. On the other hand, a nomination speech should not go on for more than a few minutes because the speaker would eclipse the nominee.

For most occasions, brevity is preferred. Speeches that are too long challenge the audience's attention, undercut the import of the occasion, and may even expose the speaker to ridicule.

Intensity. If you are speaking at a dinner to honor a retiring faculty member, how lavish should your praise be? If you are extravagant, the honoree may be embarrassed, and the audience may not take you seriously. But if your remarks are perfunctory, listeners may think that you don't really know or care about the person.

Determining just how intense to make your remarks is a particularly difficult challenge. As you gain experience in speaking, however, you should develop an almost-intuitive sense of what an occasion calls for.

Supporting Material. In a speech of introduction, you may decide to highlight an incident from the person's early life to characterize him or her for the audience. As supporting material, that anecdote should truly represent the person. Other occasions call for different types of supporting materials. Formal arguments might be appropriate in congressional testimony, narratives in a speech of tribute, and examples in a pep talk.

Identification. Most speakers try to evoke a sense of common bonds among listeners and between the audience and themselves. Sometimes, the bonding is explicit, as in a speech that commemorates an important occasion and seeks to draw attention to the community. At other times, the bonding is implicit, as when the chair of a meeting summarizes a discussion. To be decorous, a speech also matches expectations about identification.

decorum
Fittingness or appropriateness to the occasion.

Considering the factors that we have just reviewed, the most general standard for decorum is the answer to the question "Does the speech capture the thoughts and emotions appropriate to the occasion?" Every aspect of the speech—selection of materials, arrangement, language, and delivery—should help to express the sentiments which, if they thought about it, listeners would agree were the things that ought to be said on the occasion. This doesn't mean that audience members would necessarily agree with everything the speaker said, but rather that they would agree that the speaker, given his or her standpoint and purpose, selected the right topics and presented them in the right way.

Identifying Your Purpose

Some theorists believe that the only purpose of speeches for special occasions is to entertain, but this position is misleading. First, entertaining is sometimes not the goal at all. An oral report or a small-group deliberation is likely to focus on presenting information or on reaching a decision, not on entertaining. Second, speeches that are entertaining often serve other purposes as well. They have a deeper underlying message. Just as we saw that no speeches are purely informative or persuasive, the same is true for entertaining. Even accomplished comedians often use humor in order to make an important point, believing that they can be more effective if they do so gently and disarmingly. The goal is not to be funny as an end in itself, but to use humor in order to achieve a strategic purpose. In fact, speeches that have no purpose other than entertaining for its own sake will often appear to listeners as silly or shallow.

Recall once again the seven speech purposes we identified in Chapter 4. Speeches on special occasions often serve to strengthen commitment. For example, an anniversary commemoration allows audiences to reexperience their common past, strengthening listeners' commitment to a person, group, or organization. Special-occasion speeches also create positive or negative feeling. A speech to present an award, for example, may describe the awardee and narrate his or her life in order that listeners may feel good about the person and the values for which he or she stands. Other occasions, such as group presentations, may have the goal of inducing a specific action. In short, while strengthening commitment and creating a positive or negative feeling are common purposes of special-occasion speeches, these speeches can be used to achieve any of the purposes described in Chapter 4.

When giving a speech to mark an occasion, therefore, you need to know just what your purpose is and then to make strategic choices so that the speech will be designed to achieve it. Don't just follow a standard formula or pattern that you think covers speeches of a particular kind. Guided by knowledge of your purpose, you are more likely to prepare speeches that hold together well and accomplish your goal.

Deliberative Speaking

In ancient Greece, the earliest theorists of public speaking distinguished among three types of occasions: forensic, deliberative, and ceremonial (also called epideictic).[3] **Forensic speaking** occurs in a court of law and is concerned with establishing justice. Because this type of speaking is highly

forensic speaking
Speaking in a court of law; concerned with establishing justice.

specialized and is largely the province of lawyers, judges, and legal panels, we will not examine forensic speaking here. But both deliberative and ceremonial speaking warrant our close attention. Also, many occasions, including pep talks, political campaigns, commencement speeches, and inaugural addresses, call for combinations of deliberative and ceremonial speaking. We shall examine some of these situations as well.

The Nature of Deliberative Speaking

Just as the law court is the model setting for forensic discourse, the legislature is the model for deliberative speaking. Actually, though, it occurs in any formal or informal decision-making group. **Deliberative speaking** aims to answer the question "What shall we do?" Its focus is on action, and it occurs when two conditions arise:

1. The answer to "What shall we do?" is not self-evident. Matters are uncertain, perhaps because they deal with the future, because they involve questions of value, or because the information needed for certainty is simply not available.
2. A decision is required. Action cannot be deferred until everything is known and the outcome is self-evident. Either that may never occur, or, if it does, it will happen too late.

Many of the examples discussed throughout this book involve deliberative speaking occasions. For instance, suppose you were addressing the topic "How to solve America's health care crisis." The topic itself is oriented to action and implies that you might choose among potential actions or at least review your solution options. Not everything about the topic can be known. Even if you know how the current health care system works, you obviously will not know the results of untried alternatives. Yet a decision must be made because health costs represent a large and growing share of national expenditures and new programs would increase federal spending significantly. Needing to make a decision under uncertain conditions, listeners turn to you for help in answering the question, "What should we do?"

It should be apparent from this description that deliberative speaking uses the strategies of informing and persuading, which we examined in Chapters 13 and 14. By providing needed information or by giving good reasons to favor one choice over another, a deliberative speech helps the audience to determine what should be done. Following are some of the most common occasions that call for deliberative speaking. Although several of these occasions call for presentations in informal settings that we do not always commonly associate with public speaking (dialogues and group meetings, for instance), they are in fact important speaking situations, so we need to understand them.

deliberative speaking
Speaking in a decision-making assembly; concerned with matters of expediency; addresses the question "What shall we do?"

Checklist 15.1 Deliberative Speaking Occasions

1. **Oral reports and presentations**
2. **Group presentations**
   - Group reports
- Speaking in small groups
- Chairing a meeting
3. **Responding to questions**

Oral Reports and Presentations

Staff members in businesses and government agencies often have to brief their supervisors about important issues and situations. Such a briefing is simply an oral report in which the staff member identifies the topic or issue and gives background information to help the supervisor reach a decision. Similarly, when you describe a problem facing the company or explain to coworkers how to perform a task, you are presenting an oral report.

You probably have made oral reports in some of your classes in school. Although your purpose might not have been to help someone make a decision about what to do, such reports are much like the oral briefings expected in business and government settings. In preparing an oral report, the organizational pattern that you select is particularly important because you want to present the material in an order that is appropriate and easy to understand. If you are describing a process, for example, you want to be sure to list its specific steps in the right order. If you are proposing a solution, you want to be sure that the problem is explained first. Then, after establishing a clear organizational structure, you want to use effective transitions and signposting to help listeners to follow the speech. For example, you can hold their attention with vivid or unfamiliar details, and, by including concise summaries, you can tie together the main points.

Laura Winston was the project manager responsible for developing new information systems for her company. She and her staff were experts in handling the technical aspects of databases, networking, and data security, but these systems also were used by managers who did not understand them well. So when Laura was asked to describe a new system at a meeting of company executives, she wisely began with a clear forecast of her speech:

> The company will soon develop a new information system. Let me describe its key features, explain the major differences from the old system, and show you how it will benefit us all. I know that change is sometimes difficult, but once we get used to this new system, I think we'll find it to be a big improvement. So please follow along, and be sure to ask questions if there's something you don't understand.

Laura might have met the expectations for a briefing even without this careful preview. But by including it, she altered the occasion to make it also a time for reassuring her listeners in the face of uncertainty.

Laura's presentation was primarily informative, but sometimes a speech's goal is to be persuasive: not just to present information but to urge decision makers to select your proposal over others. Persuasive presentations are common in the sales environment, where they emphasize how the benefits of your proposal are most in line with the decision makers' values.

For example, if you know that a corporation's decision makers will select the advertising campaign that most appeals to the values of youthfulness and creativity, you will make primary reference to those values in presenting and defending your proposal. If you know that the city council will select the parking plan that makes parking easiest in the downtown area, you will point out that your proposal creates the greatest number of spaces at the lowest cost. And knowing that your professors represent diverse interests, you may want to defend a proposed research paper by pointing out that it will contribute to several different schools of thought. In cases like these, the principles of audience analysis and persuasion that we examined in earlier chapters will be of great help.

Jon Hobbs applied these principles when he was president of New Images, a student group that made films and videos. Appearing at a meeting of the Student Activities Funding Board, which was responsible for allocating all student activity fees, he made a convincing presentation. He emphasized the large number of students involved in New Images, the artistic merit of the group's previous work, the fact that the group had won production awards that brought prestige to the college, and the group's track record in attracting outside donors and staying under budget. These themes matched the values of the funding board, whose members were interested in benefiting large numbers of students, bringing favorable recognition and publicity to the college, and stretching its resources as much as possible. Although several other student organizations left the budget meeting unsatisfied, Jon's effective presentation resulted in full funding for New Images.

Group Presentations

Group Reports. It is quite common for people to join groups that investigate an issue, propose solutions, and then present the results of their work to others. Group reports are often presented orally, as the starting point for discussion by a larger public audience. For example, a citizens' panel might be asked to propose ways to improve public education in the community. When the group presents its findings for public discussion, one member might talk about curriculum, another might talk about extracurricular programs, another might discuss cultural diversity, another might stress the significance of parental involvement, and yet another might address matters of school finance.

An example of a group report on campus is one that focused on how fraternities and sororities were making the transition to alcohol-free rush as required by their national organizations. The report's purpose was to inform fraternity and sorority members of their responsibilities and options under the new plan. One panelist outlined the new regulations, a second talked about alcohol-free events being organized by her sorority, and a third discussed the values that would lead students to affiliate with fraternities and sororities in the absence of alcohol.

When a group report is presented in this fashion, the occasion is called a **symposium.** As in the example of the citizens' panel, the organizational structure of a symposium is usually topical. All participants in a symposium should understand how the issue has been divided into topics and what will be discussed under each topic heading. That will make them less likely either to repeat each other's points or to omit some important dimension of the issue. Each participant should present only a limited number of main points, being careful that these relate to his or her portion of the larger discussion.

Speaking in Small Groups. Although this discussion has emphasized formal occasions, people are far more likely to engage in deliberative speaking when they participate in small groups. The task of the group is to reach a decision or to propose a solution to a particular problem, and participants advocate specific suggestions in a collaborative effort to find the best solution.

symposium

A group presentation in which a subject is organized topically and each speaker addresses a limited portion of the subject.

In the previous example about an alcohol-free rush, the symposium was preceded by group meetings in the individual fraternities and sororities. Members discussed whether they should challenge, ignore, or observe the new regulations. They talked about the benefits and drawbacks of alcohol-free events. And they reflected on whether or not alcohol played any role in their own decisions to join a fraternity or sorority. Some argued that the houses would be at a real disadvantage without alcohol, while others said that they would be better off if their parties were "dry." As the groups worked through these issues, members made short speeches advancing ideas and arguments for their point of view. Although their remarks were brief and quite informal, the students made use of the strategies of informing and persuading that we have considered in this book.

By participating in a group, members gain access to the thinking of many other people about the question at hand. They can draw on more information in reaching a decision, and those who participate in problem solving tend to have a better understanding of the issues and to be more committed to the group's solution. On the other hand, a member who has a particularly strong personality may dominate the discussion and influence others to go along unthinkingly. And people sometimes propose more extreme solutions within a group setting because they do not feel personally responsible for the outcome. Be especially alert in a group, and avoid these dangers, sometimes labeled **groupthink.** Make sure that in advocating a position you do not close the door to other possibilities, that you listen as carefully to other people's ideas as you want them to listen to yours, and that you do not urge the group to adopt any course of action that you would not adopt personally. The idea is to take advantage of the assets that a group offers while minimizing the risks.[4]

Chairing a Meeting. Deliberative decisions are often made during a meeting, whether small and informal or large and public. Unless the occasion is very informal or spontaneous, someone will act as the **chair,** or presiding officer, of the meeting. This person may be appointed or elected or may simply assume the role by performing its functions. Some of the chair's functions are themselves deliberative in nature, particularly stating the issues, summarizing what group members have said, and identifying the issues to be decided.

Chairing a meeting is an important skill in its own right. **Parliamentary procedure** is a set of rules for a public meeting to ensure that the majority will reach the most effective decision while protecting the rights of the minority. It involves **motions,** or statements, that propose what the group should do. But even in informal meetings, the chair has such responsibilities as:[5]

1. Ensuring that the physical space is set up appropriately—that there are enough seats, that they are arranged in the best pattern for the meeting (circle, theatre style, and so on), that lighting is adequate, that noise is controlled, and that the temperature is comfortable.
2. Previewing what will be discussed or decided—the equivalent of preparing an agenda for formal meetings.
3. Stating the issues precisely.
4. Summarizing major points that emerge in discussion and indicating how they are related.
5. Stating clearly what has been decided.

groupthink
The tendency for groups to approve more extreme solutions than would an individual because no one is personally responsible for the group's decision.

chair
The presiding officer of a meeting.

parliamentary procedure
Rules for the conduct of public meetings.

motion
A statement proposing what an assembly should do.

Not all questions are straightforward. Listen to your audience's questions and remember that your answers give evidence of your *ethos*. Here, the Dalai Lama carefully listens and responds to university students.

People chair meetings far more often than you might think. You may emerge as the leader of an informal study group that is deciding on the best way to prepare for an examination. You may function as the leader of a current-events discussion group. Or you may be elected or appointed to a leadership position in student government. Experienced public speakers are often selected to chair meetings because their skills of analysis and argument are of great value in these situations as well as at a podium.

Responding to Questions

One situation that calls for deliberative speaking does not seem like a prepared speech at all. After you speak, listeners may ask questions. Or, in an informal situation such as a campaign rally, they may interrupt your speech to ask questions. Sometimes, as in a press conference, the entire point of speaking is to respond to questions.

Answering questions can be a way to share information. After a speech, you may be asked to explain an idea in greater detail or to develop an interesting point further. Sometimes, a questioner will confront you with an alternative or even an opposing view of your topic, and you will have the opportunity to defend your position.

Sometimes, questions may not be so straightforward. Skeptics or critics may try to discredit your speech under the guise of asking a question. The classic example is the **loaded question,** one that presupposes an adverse value judgment. The comedian who asks, "Have you stopped beating your wife?" has loaded the question because it can't be answered satisfactorily if taken at face value. Instead, one must identify the shaky premise on which it is based—in this case, that the husband was ever beating his wife in the first place.

Another trick question is one that poses a **false dilemma** by identifying two unacceptable options and assuming that they are the only alternatives. Ellen Williams faced such a question after a speech urging her classmates to spend their vacations in the United States rather than abroad. She had pointed out the many natural wonders and historical sites that many Americans have never seen, and she had argued that domestic tourism could strengthen the U.S. economy and improve the balance of payments. After the speech, she was immediately confronted by another student who asked, "Well, Ellen, if you don't support foreign travel, are you saying that we should all be ignorant of the rest of the world?" Obviously, these are not the only alternatives available, and a speaker should identify the false dilemma rather than being trapped by attempting to answer such a question.

If a listener asks multiple questions or a complex question that requires multiple answers, it is usually wise to divide the question and respond to its parts separately. Doing so will keep your organizational structure clear and

loaded question
A question that presupposes a value judgment adverse to the speaker.

false dilemma
Identifying two unacceptable options and assuming that they are the only alternatives.

make it easy for listeners to follow you. Sometimes, humor or even obvious evasion can deflect an inappropriate question without antagonizing the audience. One lecturer, after speaking about changes in political campaigns over the years, was asked, "Did you vote for Bush or Gore in 2000?" Believing that his personal political choices were irrelevant to the discussion but not wanting to offend the questioner, he answered, "Yes." Chuckles from audience members signaled their recognition that the speaker had answered the literal question but chose not to provide the information the questioner sought. Because the speaker smiled and obviously was in good humor, listeners interpreted his response to mean that the question was inappropriate rather than that the lecturer was evasive.

Although no speaker can anticipate every possible question, it's a good idea in preparing a speech to think about what listeners may ask. Try particularly to imagine questions that will challenge your position, and be ready to answer those. People who hold press conferences often prepare in advance by asking others to act as hostile questioners; then, they rehearse the answers they plan to give. Thinking about possible questions will allow you to plan your answers mentally and to select among different ways of responding.

During the question-and-answer session itself, remember that you are both answering questions and giving listeners more evidence of your *ethos*. If you become defensive, they may decide that you are not really confident about what you said in the speech. If you become aggressive or hostile, they may conclude that you are not being fair to your questioner. If you take advantage of a vague or unclear question, you may seem to be playing a game rather than being genuinely committed to your topic. As a general rule, use question-and-answer periods to enhance your image as being fair, genuinely interested in your subject, and committed to the goals of sharing information and making intelligent decisions.

Ceremonial Speaking

The third type of speaking occasion identified by ancient theorists was called **epideictic** (ep-uh-DIKE-tik), but **ceremonial** is a more contemporary term. Epideictic speeches are delivered at ceremonial occasions. Speeches of tribute at a retirement dinner, speeches introducing a distinguished guest, speeches upon receiving an award, and speeches commemorating a significant event are all examples of ceremonial speaking.

Although ceremonial speeches have informative and persuasive elements, their basic purpose is different from deliberative speeches. Instead of sharing information and guiding decisions, ceremonial speeches strengthen the bonds between speaker and listeners and among listeners themselves, building a sense of community. Epideictic speakers often use humor to entertain listeners and to make them more aware of their common bonds. To achieve that sense of community, they usually create a sense of **presence** for particular ideas and values. They bring to the forefront of consciousness some value or belief that a group holds but may not have thought much about, which makes people aware that they share important values and beliefs. Although deliberative speeches also may emphasize values, they do so to guide an audience in decision making. Ceremonial speeches tend to focus on values to draw people closer together.

epideictic
Ceremonial.

ceremonial speaking
Speaking at ceremonial occasions; it reaffirms a community's common bonds and values, strengthening ties between individuals and the group.

presence
Conscious awareness, salience.

Reexperiencing a Common Past

By recalling events or stories that are important to the group, the speaker enables the audience to relive its history vicariously. If the group faced or overcame a major obstacle, references to that obstacle strengthen a sense that the group has been tested and has met an important challenge. That common experience sustains the group's identity.

Invoking Common Values. By explicitly reminding listeners of the principles or values they share, the speaker knits them together as a community. President Ronald Reagan frequently used this technique in speeches that identified positive values with Americans, reminding listeners that they shared these values. His successors often continued this practice in their State of the Union addresses by singling out individuals who represented these socially desirable values.

Reinterpreting Events. It is often said that events do not speak; they must be spoken for. By giving meaning to events, the speaker may interpret them within a frame of reference that draws the group together. If, for example, the group's membership has declined over the past year, is that a life-threatening crisis or a challenge to be met creatively? If the group has a history of rallying in the face of challenges, the speaker will want to interpret the event as a challenge. That interpretation will bring the event within the group's shared values and frame of reference.

Emphasizing People. In any community, some individuals play an especially important symbolic role. They may be the founders, or those who sustained the community in a time of trouble, or those who have been its leaders. Images of these heroic figures themselves become shared by the community. To suggest that the heroes would approve or disapprove of something or to imply that their memory is being carried forward or violated is to keep them alive, to draw upon their unifying power, and to add emotional force to the issue being discussed. For example, a civil rights group might invoke the memory of Martin Luther King, Jr.; a service organization might call forth a feeling of patriotism through reference to Revolutionary War heroes; and a football team might be asked to "win this one for the Gipper."

Guidelines for Ceremonial Speaking

The strength of a ceremonial speech does not depend primarily on its informative or persuasive dimensions, as a deliberative speech might, but on the speaker's ability to craft words and images that capture the occasion. The speaker's ability to articulate the audience's unexpressed feelings is called **resonance,** because the speaker's words echo listeners' feelings. This, of course, also enables the speaker to better identify with the audience.

The speaker chooses a mix of stories, images, and arguments to use in responding to the occasion and enjoys great flexibility in the selection of specific purposes. But the tone must be appropriate for the occasion; the speech should build to an emotional climax; its length has to be controlled carefully; and humor must contribute to, rather than weaken, the presentation. Do not leave these elements and other key decisions to chance.

Because a ceremonial speech helps to define the occasion it marks, the

resonance
Articulating the unexpressed feelings of listeners, who then conclude that the speaker's message rings true with them.

audience usually has high expectations. Although successful ceremonial speeches seem natural, even effortless, they are actually difficult to prepare. The great variety of ceremonial occasions makes it impossible to explore them all, but the following sections describe some of the most common.

Ceremonial Speaking Occasions

Many of the most typical occasions for ceremonial speaking can be grouped under three broad headings: speeches of greeting, speeches of tribute, and speeches marking awards.

Speeches of Greeting

Introductions. Early in this course, you may have delivered a speech of introduction, either of yourself or of another student. This is a common type of ceremonial speech. When a group invites a speaker to address it, a member of the group usually introduces the speaker. The goals of such a speech of introduction are to make the speaker feel welcome, to give listeners relevant information about the speaker, and to contribute to the speaker's *ethos*.

Weddings are a common occasion for public speaking. Toasts to the bride and groom often involve celebrating the joining of two individuals and wishing them a lifetime of happiness together.

These general purposes suggest guidelines for the speech of introduction. It should be selective, since a lengthy list of all the speaker's achievements may embarrass the speaker and bore the audience. Mention only significant accomplishments that are directly related to the occasion, carefully avoiding any incidents or information that might digress from the point. Also avoid lavish praise, which either might be embarrassing or might raise the audience's expectations to an unattainable level. Listeners who are told, "Our special guest is simply the most captivating speaker you will ever hear," are likely to be disappointed, which can only undercut the speaker's efforts.

A speech of introduction should not be read, because a manuscript suggests that the introducer doesn't really know the speaker very well. If you are to introduce a speaker whom you don't know well, learn about him or her in advance. In particular, be absolutely certain that you use and correctly pronounce the speaker's preferred name. Finally, never anticipate or try to summarize what the speaker will say; besides stealing attention from the speaker, you might be mistaken. Few things weaken the introducer's *ethos* more than being corrected immediately by the speaker.

Here is how student Jonathan Cherry introduced a guest speaker on campus:

> Welcome, and thank you for coming tonight. Our guest has been called socially conscious, family-oriented, and a business wizard. She has served on planning commissions under the last three mayors of our city and has been responsible for innovations in housing, human relations, and education. Her many years of practical experience, combined with her undergraduate degree in sociology and her master's degree from Eastern State in urban planning, make her especially qualified to discuss "The Future of the City." Please join me in welcoming to our campus Laura Westerfield.

Speeches of Welcome. A visiting individual or group is often greeted on arrival with a speech of welcome. This aims not only to introduce the guest to the host but also to make the guest feel comfortable and at ease. Your tone should be upbeat and optimistic. You should explicitly express greetings to the guest, identify some common bond or interest between you and the guest (such as "We look forward to learning more about each other"), and honor the guest by saying how pleased you are by the visit.

Speeches of Tribute

Testimonials. One of the most common ceremonial speeches is the **testimonial,** a speech to honor someone. Testimonials are presented on many occasions, such as a significant wedding anniversary, a transition to new responsibilities, an outstanding achievement, retirement from a career or profession, and, of course, death.

The honoree's accomplishments are the organizing principle for a testimonial speech. You should discuss achievements that are significant in their own right as well as representative of the person's general character. To keep listeners interested, mention specific incidents and describe them vividly. If possible, select at least some incidents that might not be known to the audience. Be cautious about focusing on incidents or situations in which you played a part, since the point of the testimonial is to focus on

testimonial
A speech honoring a person.

the honoree rather than on you. And although your goal is to praise the person, you again should be careful not to exaggerate. Doing so could embarrass the honoree, cause listeners to doubt your sincerity, or suggest that you are so enthralled by the person that you cannot exercise independent judgment.

Eulogies. A **eulogy** is a special form of testimonial speech that is concerned with praising the dead. Eulogies are often delivered at funerals or memorial services or on special occasions such as the birthday of the deceased. Eulogies typically celebrate the essential character of the person, so the organizing principle is the person's virtues rather than accomplishments. Cite specific examples that illustrate the virtues. A caring individual, for example, might have donated much time and money to various charity organizations. Someone who was "ahead of her time" might have recognized a cultural trend before it became popular.

A eulogy is positive in tone, magnifying the person's strengths and minimizing weaknesses. Still, if it praises too lavishly, it may become maudlin or sound insincere. The goal is to help listeners recall the honoree's personality and character. As in a testimonial, in a eulogy you should limit personal references so that the focus remains on the honoree.

Earlier in this chapter, we briefly mentioned President Ronald Reagan's eulogy for the astronauts killed in the 1986 explosion of the space shuttle *Challenger*. (You will find this speech in Appendix B.) President Reagan spoke again five days later at a memorial service in Houston. His remarks on that occasion illustrate many of the characteristic features of a eulogy:

> We come together today to mourn the loss of seven brave Americans, to share the grief that we all feel and, perhaps in that sharing, to find the strength to bear our sorrow and the courage to look for the seeds of hope. . . .
>
> Their truest testimony will not be in the words we speak but in the way they lived their lives and in the way they lost their lives—with dedication, honor, and an unquenchable desire to explore this mysterious and beautiful universe.
>
> The best we can do to remember our seven astronauts—our *Challenger* Seven—remember them as they lived, bringing life and love and joy to those who knew them and pride to a nation.[6]

This excerpt combines praise for the dead with advice for the living, the two most common components of a eulogy.

President Clinton likewise delivered a public eulogy for the victims of the Oklahoma City bombing in 1995. Another notable eulogy was delivered in the summer of 1999, when the private plane piloted by John F. Kennedy, Jr., crashed into the Atlantic Ocean, killing him, his wife, and his sister-in-law. His uncle, Senator Edward M. Kennedy, delivered the eulogy. And, of course, there were many eulogies for the firefighters and rescue workers who died while trying to save the victims of the September 11, 2001, terrorist attacks, just as there were many eulogies for the victims themselves.

Toasts. A **toast** is a miniature version of the testimonial speech. It is usually delivered in the presence of the honoree and often concludes by raising a glass to salute the person.

eulogy
A special form of the testimonial speech, honoring someone who has died.

toast
A brief testimonial speech, usually delivered in the presence of the person honored and accompanied by raising a glass in the person's honor.

Many people who give toasts—at wedding receptions, at dinners honoring someone, or at the beginning of a new career or position—perform awkwardly. They are unsure of what to say, their remarks are often trite, and they don't do justice to the honoree. Such problems often result from failing to plan the toast in advance.

One useful way to think of the toast is as a variation of the one-point speech discussed in Chapter 1. It should celebrate one key characteristic of the honoree; supporting materials should include one or two incidents which illustrate that characteristic, talent, or virtue. A toast at a wedding reception, for example, might emphasize the devotion of the newlyweds by referring to an eight-year engagement that spanned three different states and two time zones. After stating the key characteristic and providing the examples, the person giving the toast should recognize the honoree, wish for continued strength and success, and conclude.

Here is a simple example of a toast:

> When offered a job that paid more money, Bob Howlett turned it down because he was loyal to this company and he didn't want to move. When an employee made a mistake, he took the responsibility for it himself. When offered a higher position that would require him to work longer hours, he said that his family came first. Ladies and gentlemen, please join me in honoring Bob Howlett, a man who always has his priorities straight.

Roasts. A slightly different variation on the speech of tribute is the **roast,** which both honors and pokes fun at a person. When you roast someone, your deft handling of the humor is essential to the success of the roast. Yet, the humor can backfire. Humor is used to put listeners at ease and also to demystify the honoree, suggesting that he or she is "just one of us." But it should never embarrass the person, nor should it distract from the fact that you and the audience are engaged in a tribute.

Like other forms of the speech of tribute, a roast should focus on only one or two key themes or incidents in the honoree's life. Select incidents that poke fun in a good-natured way and yet also have an underlying positive message. For example, the person you are roasting may have done something that seemed unusual or silly at the time, yet revealed a positive character trait. Avoid humor that could be misunderstood as prejudice. Although the roast may begin humorously, it should always end by pointing to the honoree's strengths. Like the toast, the roast should be relatively brief.

Speeches Marking Awards

Presentation Speeches. Suppose that an organization to which you belong sponsors an award for a student who has done an outstanding job of community or volunteer service. The award is presented at a dinner at the end of the year, and your job is to present the award. Rather than just calling out the winner's name and handing over the certificate or trophy, which might suggest either that you don't care much about the award or that you think the wrong person won it, on most occasions the presentation of an award calls for a speech.

The **presentation speech** typically has two basic elements, and there are choices to make about each. First, it establishes the importance of the

roast
A speech of tribute that both honors and pokes fun at a person.

presentation speech
A speech marking the issuance of an award.

Abraham Lincoln's second inaugural address, delivered in 1865, is one of the most eloquent. He used the ceremonial occasion to look beyond the end of the Civil War and to call for a peace "with malice toward none."

award itself. You might say something about the values it represents—in this case, community or volunteer service. If the award is named after someone, you might say a word or two about that person, to pay continuing tribute and to remind the audience of how he or she is connected to the award. Or you might emphasize the award's importance by stating how it relates to other awards that the organization presents—perhaps it is the oldest award, the most prestigious award, or the most competitive award.

Second, the presentation speech establishes the winner's fitness to receive the award by sharing with the audience the actions or achievements that render the person particularly qualified. Often, this step can be linked directly to the preceding part of the speech. For example, if you have shown that scholastic achievement and participation in extracurricular activities are the qualities honored by the award, you then could describe the winner's accomplishments in these respects. This step of the speech symbolically links the winner with the award, establishing that the winner is a fitting recipient.

Besides these two basic elements, presentation speeches may include other components. It may be appropriate to explain the selection process for choosing the recipient. If the choice reflects the subjective judgment of a committee, for instance, you might want to discuss some of the criteria the committee used. If a large number of applicants or nominees were considered for the award, you might describe how they were screened down to the finalists. There is no need to describe the selection process if the criteria for the award are purely mechanical, such as an award to the student with the highest grade-point average.

If the finalists who did not win the award are known to the audience, it may be appropriate to praise them as well. You might indicate that anyone in this strong group could have received the award, that the choice of the selection committee was especially difficult, or that the judges wished they could have made multiple awards. Make such statements only if they are true, of course; insincerity can seldom be concealed. But if the competition for the award really was keen, it takes nothing away from the winner to suggest that other candidates were also highly qualified. If anything, winning may magnify the recipient's achievement.

If your speech concludes with the physical presentation of the award, manage your gestures carefully to avoid any awkwardness. Present the award with your left hand into the recipient's left hand so that you can use your right hands to shake.

Acceptance Speeches. The recipient of an award is usually expected to "say a few words." An honoree who just says, "Thanks," and sits down quickly may seem not to value the award or the audience very much. Such a brief acknowledgment is successful only when the recipient is genuinely overcome with emotion and cannot put his or her feelings into words.

Like the presentation speech, the **speech of acceptance** has certain basic elements. First, you should express gratitude for the honor that the award represents. Be modest; it is always more appealing to say that you are surprised by the award than to say that you know you deserve it. Thank those who presented the award for the honor they have shown you. If it is appropriate, praise the runners-up, or indicate that you are accepting the award on behalf of all the candidates. (This courtesy may be especially diplomatic if the selection process was close or if the runners-up are good friends or are highly regarded by the audience.)

Second, when appropriate, thank those who helped make it possible for you to receive the award. Few people are solely responsible for their own achievements; most have been helped along the way by parents, teachers, friends, and colleagues. Worthy recipients usually seek to share the honor with those whose influence has led to their success. Yet this seemingly simple step has potential dangers. Mentioning a very long list of people not only might bore the audience but also might imply that no single person made a significant contribution to your success. And if you are too specific in identifying helpful people, you may omit someone unintentionally. Sometimes references to people in categories, such as "my parents, my teachers, and my coworkers," may be the safest approach, unless the influence of certain individuals truly was exceptional.

Third, you should indicate your understanding of the values that the award represents. This step not only makes clear that you understand why you are being honored but, more important, also makes the point that you

---

speech of acceptance
A speech presented when one receives an award or a nomination for office.

appreciate and pay tribute to those same values in accepting the award. This statement gives the award symbolic significance that transcends you personally.

Probably the most prestigious award of all is the Nobel Prize, given annually in several different fields for distinctive achievement. Accepting the 1986 Nobel Prize for Peace, Elie Wiesel began by speaking about the significance of the award:

> It is with a profound sense of humility that I accept the honor you have chosen to bestow upon me. I know. Your choice transcends me. This both frightens and pleases me.
>
> It frightens me because I wonder: Do I have the right to represent the multitudes who have perished? Do I have the right to accept this great honor on their behalf? I do not. That would be presumptuous. No one may speak for the dead, no one may interpret their mutilated dreams and visions.
>
> It pleases me because I may say that this honor belongs to all the survivors and their children, and through us, to the Jewish people with whose destiny I have always identified.

Wiesel chose to put his selection for the Nobel Prize in the broader context of the survivors of the Holocaust. Taking a different approach, Toni Morrison, recipient of the 1993 Nobel Prize for Literature, spoke about the social significance of language and literature, for which she had been honored. Referring to a hypothetical woman writer, she said:

> She is convinced that when language dies, out of carelessness, disuse, and absence of esteem, indifference or killed by fiat, not only she herself, but all users and makers are accountable for its demise. In her country children have bitten their tongues off and use bullets instead to iterate the voice of speechlessness, of disabled and disabling language, of language adults have abandoned altogether as a device for grappling with meaning, providing guidance, or expressing love. But she knows tongue-suicide is not only the choice of children. It is common among the infantile heads of state and power merchants whose evacuated language leaves them with no access to what is left of their human instincts, for they speak only to those who obey, or in order to force obedience.

The complete text of Morrison's speech is included in Appendix B.

Like most ceremonial speeches, a speech of acceptance should be brief. Audiences want to hear a few words of thanks, not a long speech. Indeed, an overly long acceptance speech may suggest that you are using the receipt of the award as a launching pad for a presentation of your own. Usually, a few minutes will be quite enough for an acceptance speech. Then, quit while you are ahead, and return to your seat.

Checklist 15.2 Ceremonial Speaking Occasions

1. **Speeches of greeting**
   - Introductions
   - Speeches of welcome
2. **Speeches of tribute**
   - Testimonials
   - Eulogies
   - Toasts
   - Roasts
3. **Speeches marking awards**
   - Presentation speeches
   - Acceptance speeches

Speeches Combining Deliberative and Ceremonial Goals

We categorize speeches to help recognize differences among them. Some speeches clearly fit into the deliberative category (such as proposal presentations and oral reports); others clearly fit into the ceremonial category (such as introductions and roasts); and some speeches share the basic characteristics of both categories. This should not be surprising. A single speech may well attempt both to guide decision making and to celebrate values in a community. In fact, on certain occasions, the two goals are expected to come together, and the speech should be designed to achieve both deliberative and ceremonial purposes.

Speeches Posing Challenges

Pep Talks. A **pep talk** is virtually any speech that is intended to motivate and inspire, ranging from a seminar presentation for sales executives to a coach's locker-room address to professional athletes. This speech has two basic purposes: (1) to heighten a sense of community, so that listeners believe that they are "all in this together" and are working for one another, and (2) to increase motivation, so that listeners will put forth extra effort willingly.

To inspire enthusiasm, you need to be enthusiastic yourself. In a pep talk, your emotional tone, intensity, and body language will communicate at least as much as your words do. You should remind listeners of shared goals, both to strengthen commitment to the goals and to move listeners beyond belief to action. To help unify the audience, you may remind everyone of past successes. Recalling a shared experience in narrative form will bind the group together. Reference to past successes will suggest that future successes also are possible and are called for, to honor the successes of the past. Sometimes a pep talk will remind the audience of their shared sacrifices, suggesting that their efforts will be justified if success is forthcoming. Finally, the speech should end on a strong positive note. Indicate that success is possible in the task at hand, and directly exhort every listener to perform as well as possible, not only for personal gain but for the achievement of the group's goals.

pep talk
A speech that is intended to motivate a group and inspire enthusiasm for a task.

after-dinner speech
A speech presented following a ceremonial meal, usually humorous in tone but with a serious message.

After-Dinner Speeches. A second example of a speaking occasion that challenges the audience is the **after-dinner speech,** so named because it typically follows a banquet or other meal, which could be anything from a continental breakfast to a state dinner. This type of speech is deceptively simple. On the surface, it has no serious content but aims primarily to entertain. Like the roast, however, it is delivered with serious intent and ultimately does challenge listeners. It is a speech of celebration that also contains a serious message.

The theme of the after-dinner speech should be easy to state and easy for listeners to grasp. The speech's development should be light-hearted and humorous. Again, though, be careful in how you use humor. It cannot be forced; your stories or anecdotes must be genuinely funny. Your use of humor cannot involve religious, racial, gender, or ethnic jokes. Although all were commonplace in the past, today they are offensive to most audiences and will reflect negatively on you as a speaker. And humor should not become an end in itself, or the point of the speech will be lost. As a general rule, the safest humor is that which seemingly comes at one's own expense. Poking fun at yourself may cause listeners to see their own situations in a more lighthearted vein.[7]

WWW. Using the Internet

Assess Ceremonial Speaking for Commemorating the Fourth of July

Go to the **Fourth of July Database** for discussion of Fourth of July orations and other symbolic means of celebrating the holiday. Point your browser to **http://gurukul.american.edu/heintze/fourth.htm**. Choose from some of the examples of Fourth of July addresses that are included in the database in order to make your assessment.

- How does the celebration of the Fourth of July represent a ceremonial occasion?
- How did speakers use the strategies for ceremonial speaking?
- How did the addresses made by speakers satisfy the requirements of decorum?
- How did speakers create common bonds among people by invoking particular ideas, beliefs, or values?
- How did speakers recall past events and celebrate symbolic heroes?

Commencement Speeches

Few speaking occasions are more common—or more the object of satire and ridicule—than are graduation ceremonies. Although a formal speech is not essential, custom is strong enough that the absence of a commencement speaker is noted, usually negatively. Much energy goes into identifying just the right speaker, for the *ethos* of the speaker is somehow thought to transfer to the graduates. Yet most commencement speeches are eminently forgettable. Only a few—such as the speeches by George Marshall, Kofi Annan, and Barbara Bush, all mentioned earlier in the chapter—outlive the occasion.

The obvious purpose of the commencement speech is to challenge the graduates, urging them to go out into "the real world" and dedicate themselves to a task that is larger than they. Yet the speech cannot be that simple. First, although it is directed primarily to the graduating students, it somehow must acknowledge the presence of others, particularly the parents and families of the graduates, who may be of different generations and who have had different experiences; for them, the same basic message may not be appropriate.

Second, although the speech is intended mainly for this specific occasion, it also needs to suggest a broader scope without sounding "canned." Presumably, the commencement speaker at Eastern State University would not give a dramatically different speech at Western State; and yet something must be said to the graduates of Eastern that distinguishes them from their counterparts at Western.

In 1997, as noted earlier, United Nations Secretary General Kofi Annan spoke at the Massachusetts Institute of Technology commencement about the importance of the United Nations and America's role in a globalized future. His remarks were significant because they offered advice and encouragement to the graduates while challenging all Americans to think of their role in the world in a different way:

> On the plane of international affairs, the outbursts of unreason in this century surpass in horror and human tragedy any the world has seen in the entire modern era. From Flanders' fields to the Holocaust and the aggressions that produced World War II; from the killing fields of Cambodia and Rwanda to ethnic cleansing in Bosnia; from the twenty-five million refugees who roam the world today to untold millions, many of them children, who die the slow death of starvation or are maimed for life by land-mines—our century, even this generation, has much to answer for. . . .
>
> All of you in the Class of 1997, wherever you go from here and whatever you do in the future, will participate in a world that is becoming increasingly globalized. . . . As you enter this new world, I call upon you to remember this: as powerful and as progressive a bond that market rationality constitutes, it is not a sufficient basis for human solidarity. It must be coupled with an ethic of caring for those whom the market disadvantages, an ethic of responsibility for the collective goods that the market under-produces, an ethic of tolerance for those whom the market pits as your adversary.

The complete text of Annan's speech is included in Appendix B.

Some commencement exercises include a student speaker. If you perform this role, you will face additional challenges. You will appear presumptuous if you seem to have more experience or expertise than your classmates. You want to issue a challenge, and yet you do not want to talk down to an audience of your peers. Student speakers are most successful when they do not try to issue a challenge themselves but rather discover and articulate one that is already "out there"; it also helps to speak frequently in the first person rather than the second person, referring to challenges facing "us" rather than "you" and indicating what "we," not "you," must do to meet those challenges.

Strategies for Speaking to Diverse Audiences

Respecting Diversity Through Occasions for Public Speaking

In some situations, speakers may be tempted to say things that unintentionally demean listeners, such as by using inappropriate humor or falsely assuming that listeners share their values. These strategies will help you to avoid these pitfalls and to recognize audience diversity on the occasions when you speak.

1. Consider the particular constraints and opportunities in your speaking occasion.
2. Avoid "group-think" in group presentations. Listen carefully to others' ideas.
3. Answer questions directly and with respect for the questioner.
4. In a ceremonial speech, invoke common values and experiences that unite audience members.
5. Avoid inappropriate or demeaning humor in a roast or after-dinner speech.

Just as the speaker, the speech, and the audience are important components of a rhetorical situation, so too is the occasion. Any occasion creates expectations that the speaker may want to observe or to modify, but in any case will need to understand. *Decorum,* or fittingness to the occasion, influences a speaker's decisions about the appropriate degree of formality, length, and intensity of a speech; about the representativeness and types of supporting materials to use; and how explicitly to identify with the audience. A decorous speech is one that gives voice to the heretofore unexpressed sentiments of the audience.

Speaking occasions can be classified in various ways. The ancients distinguished among forensic, deliberative, and epideictic (ceremonial) speaking. Forensic speaking, conducted in courts of law, today is the work of professionally trained advocates, but all public speakers engage in deliberative and ceremonial speaking.

Deliberative speaking aims to answer the question "What shall we do?" Its focus is on action, which involves sharing information to resolve matters that are uncertain but require decisions. It takes place in a wide range of settings and includes oral reports and presentations, group meetings and presentations of various kinds, and responding to questions.

Ceremonial speaking aims to emphasize common bonds among people and to give a greater sense of presence to particular ideas, beliefs, or values. These goals are achieved by recalling a common past, invoking shared values, interpreting past events within a frame of reference that ties them to the community, and paying tribute to a group's symbolic heroes. Ceremonial speaking is both argumentative and emotional in nature. It is seemingly simple yet requires difficult judgments and careful preparation. Many occasions for ceremonial speaking can be grouped into three broad categories—speeches of greeting, speeches of tribute, and speeches marking awards. Opportunities for ceremonial speaking arise often.

Some occasions call for speeches that serve both deliberative and ceremonial functions, often posing challenges to the audience. In particular, we examined pep talks, after-dinner speeches, and commencement speeches.

1. What occasions have you experienced on which speeches were given? What were your expectations as an audience member? Did the speaker meet or neglect your expectations? Discuss your impressions with both deliberative and ceremonial speeches, including their appropriateness for the occasions at which they were presented.

2. In what ways might the strategic design of a speech differ for ceremonial and deliberative occasions? Identify the general goals of these two types of speaking, and discuss the various strategies that a speaker

might use to achieve them. As part of your analysis, create a chart that identifies potential differences in the speaker's arrangement of ideas, choice of supporting materials, and stylistic decisions.

3. When you discussed questions 1 and 2, how did the group dynamic of your class work? Did one person dominate the discussion? Did group-think become a problem? Did anyone provide testimony to guide decision making? Was an individual who offered a claim asked to respond to questions? Were there any debates? Discuss and evaluate the public speaking that occurs in the group discussions of your class.

Activities

1. Attend a ceremony at which at least one speech will be given. In a short essay, critique a speech that you heard at that ceremony. Was the speech decorous? In what ways was it designed to fit the constraints of the occasion?

2. Observe a group discussion, taking care not to engage in that discussion yourself. Write an essay describing what you learned from that experience. Considering the size of the group, the function of the meeting, and the particular dynamics of the group, comment on some of these speech goals:

   - Drawing up a group report
   - Speaking in small groups
   - Chairing a meeting
   - Responding to questions

3. Think about the expectations raised by the following real or imagined occasions, and prepare a decorous speech for one of them:
   a. A roast of your public speaking teacher
   b. An acceptance speech for an award that you hope to win someday
   c. A pep talk to your favorite sports team
   d. A eulogy for a friend, family member, or public figure

Notes

1. Two articles together capture this balance between constraint and creativity. Lloyd F. Bitzer, "The Rhetorical Situation," *Philosophy and Rhetoric* 1 (Winter 1968): 1–14, focuses on the need to respond to a rhetorical situation. Richard E. Vatz, "The Myth of the Rhetorical Situation," *Philosophy and Rhetoric* 6 (Summer 1973): 154–161, emphasizes that choices made by speakers actually shape the rhetorical situation.

2. Cicero emphasized the concept of decorum and made much of it. See Marcus Tullius Cicero, *Orator*, translated by H. M. Hubbel, Cambridge, Mass: Harvard Univ. Press, 1939, 70–74.

3. For example, see Aristotle, *The Rhetoric*, translated by W. Rhys Roberts, New York: The Modern Library, 1954, Book I, Chapter 3.

4. For more about speaking in small groups, see John K. Brilhart, *Effective Group Discussion*, Fifth Edition, Dubuque, Ia.: Wm. C. Brown, 1986.

5. For more about parliamentary procedure, see Henry Martyn Robert, *Robert's Rules of Order,* Newly Revised, Glenview, Ill.: Scott Foresman, 1981.

6. The way in which Reagan's eulogy was designed to respond to the occasion is discussed in more detail in Steven M. Mister, "Reagan's *Challenger* Tribute: Combining Generic Constraints and Situational Demands," *Central States Speech Journal* 37 (Fall 1986): 158–165.

7. For more about the use of humor in speeches, see Charles R. Gruner, "Advice to the Beginning Speaker on Using Humor—What the Research Tells Us," *Communication Education* 34 (April 1985): 142–147.

Beyond the Classroom: Speaking in the Public Forum

In this appendix, we will:

- Explore what the public forum is and how your study of public speaking prepares you to participate effectively in it.

- Describe a variety of speaking situations that are likely to arise as you move from the classroom to the public forum.

Your public speaking skills are applicable beyond the classroom, of course. You will use them in addressing your neighborhood civic club, church group, or PTA. You'll use them when making presentations in your business or professional life. And you'll use them when a public issue matters to you and you decide to speak out about it.

A course in public speaking prepares you to express yourself and perhaps to influence others in each of these settings. Diverse as the settings are, they all embody a public forum; that is, they meet the conditions under which skilled speakers can conduct meaningful public discussion of important issues.

The Public Forum

The word **public** in "public speaking" is important in at least two respects. First, it designates speaking that is open and accessible by others. A person who speaks publicly is inviting others to listen carefully and to think about and appraise the message. The speaker's goal is that of informed choice, not forced compliance, on the part of the audience.

Second, speaking is public when it affects people beyond the immediate audience. If you urge classmates to lobby for higher student activity fees, your remarks will have consequences for people who are not even present to hear you. If you explain how to examine the terms of a lease before signing it, listeners can follow your directions in ways that will affect others as well.

From the speaker's point of view, giving a speech means entering into the **public forum.** Centuries ago, the forum was a physical place where citizens gathered to discuss issues affecting them. Today, the public forum is not an actual place to which we go; instead, it is an imagined "space" that exists wherever people have the freedom to exchange ideas. The public forum is created whenever the following conditions are met:

1. *Some problem affects people collectively* as well as individually.
2. *Cooperative action is needed* to address the problem. Speakers and listeners participate in deciding what to do.
3. *The decision requires subjective judgment.* What should be done is not obvious; there is more than one possible solution, and there is no way for anyone to gather all the information that conceivably might bear on the decision.
4. Nevertheless, *a decision is required.* People stand at a fork in the road, and a choice cannot be avoided.

Just as the public forum exists in many places, so do many subjects call for communication in the public forum. The subject of health care is an example. Consider how it reflects each of the four conditions for a public forum:

1. For many years, health care was seen as a private matter. People either did or did not obtain insurance, did or did not seek preventive care, did or did not receive treatment, and were healthy or ill—all as a series of individual choices and actions that were not seen as affecting others. Gradually, however, people realized that health care is *not just an individual matter.* Many people are unable to obtain insurance on their own. If someone be-

public
Open to or accessible by others; affects others.

public forum
A space (imagined, rather than physical) in which citizens gather to discuss issues affecting them; discussion characterized by certain assumptions about the need for cooperative action and subjective judgment to resolve a problem.

comes seriously ill and goes without treatment, he or she may become a real burden to family members. And the cost of providing health care limits economic growth and hurts everyone.

2. When people came to see health care as more than a private matter, *speakers and listeners together began to discuss* how to provide and pay for it. Audiences heard descriptions of how various plans would work. They identified and evaluated speakers' claims, arguments, and evidence. They considered a variety of proposals, accepting some ideas and rejecting others. Speakers analyzed their audiences' beliefs and values and tried to adapt their ideas to what listeners regarded as most important.

3. *No one person can just impose a solution.* No one can be certain which proposal is best, and no one can ever get all the information that might help in making that decision. So there is a process of give-and-take as speakers and listeners consider alternative ideas and proposals, trying their best to decide which are the most sensible or compelling.

4. *And yet a decision has to be made,* because doing nothing will make the problems of health care worse—for individuals as well as for society as a whole.

Over time, the participants in the public forum come to an understanding about which approach should be tried. The understanding that they reach is always tentative and always subject to revision if better ideas emerge into the forum. Indeed, because no final answer has been found, the subject of health care returns to the public forum every few years.

National health insurance, for example, was proposed as long ago as the 1940s, and this proposal has been reintroduced on several occasions since. During the 1960s, public discussion focused on medical care for the elderly, and that subject is back in the public forum in the early 2000s. Proposals for large-scale reform of the health care system in the early 1990s were unsuccessful, but the result was a focus in the 2000s on individual issues such as children's health insurance, regulating health maintenance organizations, and providing coverage for the cost of prescription drugs for the elderly. The topic of health care is typical of many subjects in the public forum. The specifics of the discussion change over time, decisions are subject to change as a result of new information or perspective, and the issue is not settled with finality.

Public Speaking and Democracy

You may not have thought about it this way, but as you become skilled in public speaking, you become a more effective participant in the public forum. You are able to analyze important issues of public concern, to articulate your ideas and to relate them to others, to listen carefully and critically to other points of view, to weigh and evaluate arguments and evidence, and to bring your best judgment to issues that have no easy or automatic

---

WWW. Using the Internet

The Public Forum on the Internet

Examine some of the ways that Internet users participate in a Web-based public forum by visiting some of the following Web sites:

Monitor Talk at the *Christian Science Monitor*	http://www.csmonitor.com/monitortalk/index.html
Live Online at the *Washington Post*	http://washingtonpost.com/wp-srv/liveonline/
Post and Ripost at *Atlantic Unbound*	http://www.theatlantic.com/pr/
Town Hall	http://www.townhall.com/
Forum One	http://forumone.com/

---

answer. As you exercise these skills, you strengthen the ties that unite participants in the public forum into a community or society. This is a benefit above and beyond the gains in personal self-esteem and performance on the job that come with competence in communication.

Traditionally, the public forum has been associated with large political questions. These questions may present themselves quite close to home, however. A zoning controversy in the community will bring citizens forward to speak for and against proposed changes. The allocation of student activity fees on campus requires collective decisions that are subjective, and speakers come out to defend the activities they represent. A proposed change in residence hall regulations will lead those who will be affected by it to voice their opinions and to deliberate publicly.

Moreover, the boundary between public and private is always shifting, and any subject might easily find its way into the public forum. Styles in popular music, for example, become more than just private or individual choices in response to claims that the noise level is harmful to health or that the content leads children to violence. Personal choices of deodorants or clothing are no longer just private matters when they are are alleged to cause destruction of the ozone layer or exploitation of Third World labor markets. And speculating in the stock market becomes a public matter when one's investment choices affect so many others. Whatever subject you discuss—whether or not it is usually regarded as political—you are entering into the public forum.

Discussion of public issues is best advanced when the public forum is active and vibrant. Unfortunately, there are many signs that today's public forum is not healthy. Increasing numbers of people claim to have little interest in public affairs. Even in informal conversation, according to recent research, many people are reluctant to talk about public issues.[1] Many are put off by the complexity and difficulty of understanding important issues. Others are satisfied with sources of information that oversimplify issues and turn them into slogans. Large numbers of people see no point in participating in the public forum because they think they are powerless to effect any public change. Others generally perceive public figures to be deceptive or dishonest. Still others say that they are interested only in themselves.

These are warning signals for a free society. If the public forum is allowed to weaken, critical public decisions will be made unilaterally, whether by experts or by rulers, so those who are affected by the decisions really won't have any part in making them. Without a well-cultivated public forum, as we noted in Chapter 1, the two alternatives are autocratic rule and anarchy.

At the same time, many who disdain traditional politics are involved actively in their own communities on issues that affect the general good. It may be that the public forum, rather than weakening, is becoming more localized and that many new forums are emerging. If so, what it means to be a citizen is changing but not necessarily eroding.[2] This would be an encouraging development but one that would require that many more people be able to participate actively.

Nationwide, colleges and universities are stressing "civic engagement" and are developing programs that will help students to become more competent citizens who will become involved with public issues. Fortunately, studying public speaking equips you to better participate in the public forum by enabling you to understand issues and evaluate claims. The processes of discovering, assessing, arranging, and presenting ideas will be valuable as you read and think about public issues, discuss them with others, and speak out when the issue and the occasion move you. You'll be able to make decisions even about matters that do not directly affect you. And when an issue does affect you, your involvement and participation will count.

Occasions for Speaking in Public

In Chapter 15, we examined a number of occasions for public speaking in which student speakers are likely to find themselves outside the classroom, such as making an oral report or presentation, chairing a meeting, or giving a speech of greeting or tribute. Here are additional speaking occasions you are likely to encounter as you move into the larger public forum. Even if you do not speak on all these occasions, you will listen to others who do. Your understanding of public speaking will enable you to listen critically, making you a more effective citizen when the time comes to express your preferences or to record your vote.

Community Service and Involvement

As you become active in your community, there will be many occasions for you to speak in the public forum. You may represent your point of view in speeches to service clubs, neighborhood groups, the Chamber of Commerce, or the PTA. In the process, you will help to make people aware of the public dimensions of issues they might not have recognized previously. You will both inform and persuade, pursuing goals that range from agenda setting to inducing a specific action.

For some years, there had been a disparity in the academic achievement of students of different races in the Central City public schools. For some, this had been accepted as a "fact of life," and for others, each student's achievement was an individual and private matter. But George Rivers and Linda Sanchez decided to draw people's attention to this situation. They thought it had larger consequences for the school district. Property values would decline if the school district had a reputation for poor performance by students of different races. Even more important, this differential was not encouraging for the future of race relations in Central City, which was becoming increasingly multiethnic and multicultural. George had children in the Central City schools; Linda did not. But they both insisted that the issue affected the entire community, and their speeches to neighborhood associations, church groups, and PTAs caused the school district to acknowledge the issue and recognize it as a priority.

George and Linda's situation is like many that you will face. They did not regard themselves as "politicians" in any way. Their major concerns were personal—their families and their careers. But they became aware of an issue that affected the general welfare of the community and about which they felt strongly. That issue prompted them to speak in public, and doing so brought them into the public forum.

Community service and involvement is the way in which you are most likely to be an active participant in the public forum. What is more, if the issue engages you and you become strongly committed, you are likely to find that becoming involved by speaking out is personally meaningful and rewarding.

Public Hearings and Debates

Sometimes, you may wish to speak out by providing testimony at public hearings or participating in debates.

Providing Testimony. A development firm is proposing to build a major shopping center in your neighborhood. The plan offers great potential economic benefits to the town, but it's likely to increase neighborhood traffic and will create a commercial presence in a residential area. The development firm seeks a zoning variance to build the center even though it will not comply fully with regulations. The zoning board holds a public hearing at which interested citizens can testify.

Individuals who testify in public hearings present deliberative speeches; their goal is to persuade those conducting the hearings to their point of view. Because many people testify at a hearing, each statement must be brief. An analysis of the decision makers helps a speaker to determine which points to emphasize and how best to be persuasive in the situation.

Janet Carpenter and Richard Brinkley were both well informed about the proposed shopping center. They both knew that the city would welcome the additional tax revenue from the center, especially since citizens had recently voted against higher taxes. But they were also aware that the shopping center might damage the residential character of the neighborhood. They both testified before the zoning board that would have to approve the project. Janet favored the development and began by saying:

> This shopping center will revive the sagging economy of our town. That's worth a lot. It will strengthen the value of our homes and make money available for schools and parks without our tax rates having to go up. Now, I know that the residential character of this area is important, but tough zoning regulations will still protect that, even after the shopping center is built.

Richard opposed the project. In his testimony, he argued:

> We must be careful to avoid being lured too strongly by money. Sure, we all recognize the need to bring more money into the town, and let's find better ways to do that. But this shopping center will change the quality of our lives forever. That's a far more harmful effect, even though it can't be measured in dollars.

Both Janet and Richard focused on a small number of arguments and made each as clear and concise as possible. Those are excellent goals to strive for if you are called upon to provide testimony.

Debates. Sometimes, an organization will sponsor a debate about a controversial issue. You may be invited to advocate one side of the issue while someone else supports the other side. Debaters not only present speeches they have thought about in advance but also respond to the statements of their opponents. The purpose of a debate is to enable the audience, by hearing the opposing positions at the same time, to understand the issues better and to decide which side they wish to support.

Some debates are highly structured, with rules prescribing the number of speeches and the time limits. Other debates are loosely structured; one advocate presents a speech, the opponent responds, and then the speakers alternate their responses until everyone feels that the issue has been exhausted. Debates employ all the techniques of informative and persuasive speaking, with special emphasis on testing reasoning. Participants not only develop their own arguments but also refute opposing arguments.

In election campaigns, candidates appear in debates to enable voters to decide whom to support. In legislative bodies discussing a proposal, members engage in debates both to make a record for their constituents and to clarify issues to influence their undecided colleagues' votes. In local communities, civic organizations hold debates so that people will be informed about important issues and can decide what they believe. Although it may be some time before you participate in debates that will affect your community, school or campus organizations may give you practice in debating issues ranging from the nation's foreign policy to the allocation of student funds for campus activities.

Anniversary Celebrations

The most common example of an **anniversary celebration** is the Fourth of July oration, a patriotic speech delivered annually on the anniversary of American independence. Anniversaries of major historical events are often celebrated with speeches. For example, in 1994, President Clinton delivered an address to mark the fiftieth anniversary of the D-Day landing during World War II, just as President Reagan had done on the fortieth anniversary in 1984. Referring to D-Day, Clinton said:

> My fellow Americans, we have gathered to remember those who stormed this beach for freedom who never came home. We pay tribute to what a whole generation of heroes won here. But let us also recall what was lost here. We must never forget that thousands of people gave everything they were, or what they might have become, so that freedom might live.

Anniversary celebrations share common features. First, the speaker typically refers to the event being commemorated, perhaps recounting it as a narrative and perhaps emphasizing a few key points. This reminds listeners of their historical roots in the event. Second, the speaker may abstract certain virtues or special characteristics from the event. The Fourth of July orator may highlight the selflessness and farsightedness of the nation's founders, much as President Clinton noted the courage and dedication of those who landed at Normandy on D-Day. These virtues are discussed to remind listeners why the event is celebrated and to show that the event has significance beyond its historical details. Third, the speaker relates these features to listeners' lives, perhaps challenging the audience to adhere to

anniversary celebration
A speech of remembrance delivered on the anniversary of an important event.

the standards evidenced in the event, to behave as nobly today as their predecessors did in the event commemorated, or to keep the memory of the event alive as it recedes into history. Through these steps, the anniversary celebration combines tribute to the past with a challenge for the future.

Speeches Marking Candidacy and Election

Important moments in the process of selecting candidates for public office are marked by speeches. These include nominating, acceptance, and inaugural speeches. Although the most obvious place for these speeches is in national politics, you may find that they also are used in the public forum in which you participate, whether on campus, in your community, or in organizations to which you belong.

Nominating Speeches. Every four years in the United States, each major political party holds a national convention to nominate its candidates for president and vice president. Especially when there is a contest for these offices, the **nominating speech** becomes a centerpiece of the convention. Each candidate is nominated by a delegate who makes a speech on his or her behalf, concluding by formally placing the person's name in nomination. Candidates select their nominating speakers with care, and delegates who are chosen for this task consider it a great honor and prepare their speeches with equal care. A similar process occurs in any organization that proposes candidates for office and then deliberates and votes on them. Nominating speeches are made in student government, in housing units, and in civic and religious organizations of all kinds.

While a nominating speech has deliberative goals, it also has a ceremonial aspect that makes it somewhat different from other campaign speeches. Although the speech attempts to guide and persuade people in choosing a leader, it is usually presented at a formal celebration and is meant to draw an audience together in support of common values.

A nominating speech has three basic goals. The first is to *make the importance of the office clear.* A speaker usually does this by alluding to the responsibilities of the office, describing the issues that the victorious candidate will have to confront or explaining the traits and attitudes that a successful office holder must demonstrate. This part of the speech both magnifies the significance of the office and makes it clear that the nominating speaker understands what is involved.

The second goal should be apparent: *to show the fitness of the candidate for the office.* If certain traits and attitudes are important, then the candidate should be shown to have them. The goal is to link the candidate with the office so that listeners can imagine that outcome and will consider it natural. For example, if previous experience is important, you might emphasize the candidate's record in other positions. If the candidate shares your beliefs about important issues and how to handle them, it will be helpful to note that you have similar priorities.

To demonstrate your candidate's fitness for the office, you may find it desirable to say something about other candidates. Here, you need to be careful. Several recent national elections have been marked by negative campaigns that emphasized the opponents' weaknesses rather than the candidate's strengths, and voters have begun to resist this approach. In any case, negative campaigning is almost always inappropriate in a nominating

nominating speech
A speech in which a person is named for an office or honor.

speech. Appeals that compare your candidate with others will be more effective if they are generic and emphasize the candidate's positive features without attacking specific opponents. Your own conviction and enthusiasm will convey a strong positive message about your candidate; attacks on others may suggest that you lack confidence about your choice and see your candidate simply as the least of evils.

The third goal of the nominating speech is *to formally place the candidate's name in nomination.* Speakers sometimes save this formality for the end of the speech, to build to a dramatic climax. At national political conventions, for instance, nominating speeches often avoid mentioning the candidate's name because it might set off a demonstration by the audience that would compete for attention with the speaker's intended message. Even when everyone already knows which candidate you will nominate, saving the formal step of the nomination for the very end focuses listeners on why you think your candidate is best suited for the job.

Acceptance of Candidacy. Sometimes, the nominating process selects the person who will actually occupy the office. In that case, election to office is similar to receiving an award, and the winner might make the sort of speech described in Chapter 15. But when the nominating process determines only who will run for office in an upcoming election, then the acceptance speech needs to be slightly different.

First, of course, the candidate should formally accept the nomination, pledging his or her best efforts in the subsequent campaign and, if elected, in office. It is appropriate to acknowledge the supporters who made it possible to gain the nomination. Particularly if the contest for the nomination was hard fought, the winning candidate should appeal to the losers for support in the race ahead and should express appreciation for their campaign and principles. If it is at all possible, incorporation of elements from the losers' positions into one's own campaign will help to draw the community together.

The acceptance speech should also acknowledge the magnitude of the tasks ahead: winning office and carrying out its duties. It takes a careful combination of modesty and self-confidence to emphasize how difficult and important the position is and yet to pledge to perform capably if elected. Finally, the acceptance speech often concludes with a direct appeal for help from the audience. In accepting the Democratic presidential nomination in 1960, for example, John F. Kennedy asked listeners, "Give me your help, and your hand, and your heart, and your vote."

Acceptance speeches by presidential candidates in the United States have taken on new significance in recent years. Not since 1980 has there been any doubt by the time of the national conventions who the nominees will be. Rather than focus on the formalities of accepting the nomination, there-

---

WWW. Using the Internet

Research the Progression of a Presidential Campaign

Presidential campaigns include a range of types of speeches from an initial announcement of candidacy through the inauguration of a new presidency. Explore some of the following Web links to find representative types of discourse:

USA Today Speech Index	**http://www.usatoday.com/news/conv/speechindex.htm**
National Public Radio Online	**http://www.npr.org/news/national/election2000/index.html**
Project VoteSmart	**http://www.vote-smart.org/speeches/index.phtml?checking=/**
Issues 2000	**http://www.issues2000.org/**
Inaugural Addresses of the Presidents of the United States	**http://www.bartleby.com/124/index.html**
Library of Congress American Memory on Presidential Inaugurations	**http://memory.loc.gov/ammem/pihtml/pihome.html**

---

fore, this speech has become a means for the introduction of the candidate to a national audience and the launching of the general election campaign. For many people, the acceptance speeches are the first occasions when they pay attention to the political contest. Consequently, these speeches have dealt less with rallying the committed and more with swaying the undecided. They have become occasions for citizens to use the critical listening skills we explored in Chapter 2.

A slight variation on the acceptance speech occurs when there is no election campaign but the person nominated must still be approved by others. In 1993, when President Clinton nominated Judge Ruth Bader Ginsburg for a seat on the U.S. Supreme Court, her remarks revealed the typical features of an acceptance speech, as these brief excerpts indicate:

> Mr. President, I am grateful beyond measure for the confidence you have placed in me, and I will strive with all that I have to live up to your expectations in making this appointment. . . .

> The announcement the president just made is significant, I believe, because it contributes to the end of the days when women, at least half the talent pool in our society, appear in high places only as one-at-a-time performers. . . .

> I am indebted to so many for this extraordinary chance and challenge: to a revived women's movement in the 1970s that opened doors for people like me, to the civil rights movement of the 1960s from which the women's movement drew inspiration, to my teaching colleagues at Rutgers and Columbia and for thirteen years my D.C. Circuit colleagues who shaped and heightened my appreciation of the value of collegiality.

Justice Ginsburg expresses her appreciation for the nomination, notes the significance of the office, places her selection in a broader context, and acknowledges the help of those who have enabled her to reach this important milestone.

Inaugural Addresses. If the acceptance speech marks only the acceptance of candidacy rather than the assumption of office, the latter event is also often celebrated with a speech. Every four years, at the beginning of a term, the president of the United States delivers an **inaugural address.** Presidents of other organizations—whether colleges or universities, business or civic clubs, or professional organizations—may also be called upon to deliver an inaugural address. The inaugural may actually define the assumption of office, but sometimes, as with a university president, there is an interval of time between the official's taking over the office and delivering the inaugural address.

An inaugural address includes several basic elements. First, the leader formally accepts the responsibilities of the office, stating that he or she understands the duties and will make every effort to fulfill them. Second, the new leader explicitly seeks to unify the audience. This is especially important if the campaign for office has been divisive; in effect, the new leader says that the campaign is over and reaches out for the help and support of everyone in the audience. After the bitter and close election of 1800, Thomas Jefferson introduced this aspect to the presidential inaugural address when he proclaimed:

> Let us then, fellow citizens, unite with one heart and one mind. Let us restore to social intercourse that harmony and affection without which liberty and

inaugural address
A speech delivered when assuming an office to which one has been elected.

even life itself are dreary things. . . . But every difference of opinion is not a difference of principle. We have called by different names brethren of the same principle. We are all Republicans, we are all Federalists.

President Jefferson's goal was to urge members of the two political parties of his day to overcome their differences and to unite for the common good. Most subsequent U.S. presidents have expressed similar sentiments in their inaugural address.

Third, the newly installed leader typically outlines the general goals to be pursued during his or her time in office. The inaugural address usually does not spell out specific proposals but rather identifies general themes or goals. For example, in 2001, President George W. Bush emphasized the themes of civility, courage, compassion, and character, and asked his listeners to be citizens, rather than spectators or subjects.

Finally, the inaugural address often puts the new leader's service into a larger context. He or she may speak of perpetuating the ideals of the organization or of fulfilling a dream held since childhood. Presidents of the United States have often concluded their inaugurals with a plea for divine assistance, which not only suggests humility but also places the presidency in the larger context of carrying out God's will.

Inaugural speeches in other contexts, though less lofty, are also significant. As you assume leadership of a campus organization, a brief speech thanking members for their support, stating your objectives, and appealing for help as you go forward, will mark the occasion in an appropriate way.

Keynote Speeches. Meetings of business, academic, professional, or political organizations often feature a speaker near the beginning of the program to set the tone of the event. You may find yourself inviting a keynote speaker for a meeting that you organize, or you may be asked to deliver a keynote speech yourself.

Coming near the beginning of a meeting, the **keynote speech** has two special purposes. First, it *draws together and defines the diverse members of the audience as a community.* The individual delegates at a state convention of a civic organization, for example, have come from cities and towns that have diverse issues and concerns. The fact that the delegates all belong to the same organization may not seem important to them individually. But when they assemble at the convention, the keynote speech helps to focus their attention and energy on what they share.

Second, the keynote speech helps to *set the meeting's thematic agenda.* This refers not to the listing of specific items of business but to the larger matters of topics, themes, or issues that will dominate the meeting. Sometimes a meeting has a designated theme, for example, "achieving unity through diversity," and the keynote speaker is asked to address that theme. What the speaker says will help listeners to think about the meeting's theme and to refer to it in their deliberations. On other occasions, the meeting itself may have no theme; the keynote speaker, if successful, will help to determine what listeners will be thinking and talking about for the rest of the meeting.

The keynote speech is a platform enabling you to identify what you deem important and to urge others to think about it as well. It also serves to rally or inspire listeners, presenting them with a challenge and the motivation to meet it. Although a keynote speaker has considerable latitude, some cautions are appropriate. Remember that the purpose of the keynote is to open,

keynote speech
A speech presented near the beginning of a meeting to guide its thematic agenda and to help set its tone.

multivocal
Capable of being heard in different ways by different listeners, all of whom find the term or concept positive.

not close, discussion. A successful keynote address poses issues or questions for delegates to ponder; it does not offer dogmatic proclamations. Stating your own views too strongly, unless you know that the audience holds the same views, can hurt the keynote speech. Recognize that the audience is likely to be diverse, at least on some dimensions. Design the keynote so that it seems to speak to everyone without excluding significant segments of the audience. This means that the speech has to be somewhat **multivocal,** including terms and phrases that individual listeners can interpret in light of their own experiences and concerns. A reference to "the American dream," for example, will mean different things to different listeners, and yet it can be a positive symbol for everyone. This is an example of a *polysemic* message, which we described in Chapter 14, because there are different layers or dimensions of meaning that will appeal to different people. Polysemic messages are multivocal, and vice versa.

Summary

Public speaking skills are applied not only in the classroom, but also in a wide variety of situations that have the characteristics of the public forum. In these situations an issue confronts people collectively as well as individually, cooperative action is needed to address the issue, it is impossible to know with certainty the best course to take, and yet a decision is required. Examples of such situations include community service and involvement, public hearings and debates, ceremonial speeches, and speeches marking candidacy and election. Your understanding of public speaking will help you both to speak effectively in situations like these and to listen more carefully to others.

Notes

1. An example of recent research demonstrating that people often tend to avoid the discussion of public issues is Nina Eliasoph, *Avoiding Politics: How Americans Produce Apathy in Everyday Life,* New York: Cambridge Univ. Press, 1998.
2. For an excellent analysis of how the concept of citizenship has changed over time along with changing norms about public communication, see Michael Schudson, *The Good Citizen,* New York: Free Press, 1998.

Speeches for Analysis and Discussion

Botox

Priya Mydur

Priya Mydur is a student at Texas Tech University. You have followed her work throughout this book. In this speech, presented in class in 2003, she seeks to explain Botox treatments and to describe their effects. The speech relies primarily on informative strategies. Consider how Priya applies the strategies discussed in Chapter 13. What features of the speech enable it to hold your interest? What changes, if any, would you suggest? How well is the speech adapted to a student audience? How might it be modified for a different audience?

If a salesman told you that a single drug could cure headaches, obesity, sore muscles, and even body odor for the extremely low price of $300, would you believe him? Most likely not. But many doctors and scientists say there is such a drug that does all this and so much more. And believe it or not, it's Botox, the wonder drug.

Now, most people are just learning what Botox is. For those of you who have never heard of it, trust me, you'll want to learn more. It's gaining fame for its methods in reducing the signs of wrinkles, but little do people know that it relieves numerous muscle problems, making life just a little easier for those with a limited range of movement.

The name Botox is derived from the poison botulinum toxin. Botulinum toxin causes botulism, a food poisoning that causes paralysis that can sometimes be fatal. The toxin attaches itself to nerve endings so that neurotransmitters can't be released to trigger muscle contractions. Therefore, botulinum toxin blocks the signals that would tell your muscles to contract. If the poison attacks the muscles in your chest, the respiratory muscles would be impacted, thus breathing could be prevented. This is usually the case of how most people die from botulism.

Telling you all this, I'm sure you're wondering why anybody would want to have such a deadly poison injected into them. According to *Newsweek*, Botox is so diluted that any such reaction is impossible to occur, but it still has the same effects of interrupting the transmission of nerve impulses to the injected muscles.

Botox, as I stated, is most widely used for the minimizing of the appearance of wrinkles in between the eyebrows and around the eyes, which are known as crow's feet. When Botox is injected into this region, the muscles there will not be able to move, thus it cannot wrinkle. And it only affects the injected area. If it's used correctly, it can dissolve laugh lines, furrows, and crow's feet, all by paralyzing the muscle.

Botox applications last for about three to five months, and after that the wrinkles slowly appear again. But at the affordable cost of $300 to $400, many people return to have the quick ten-minute procedure done. According to the journal *Young Investigators*, nearly 1.6 million treatments took place in 2001, a 2356 percent increase since 1997.

Surprisingly, Botox does not have very drastic side effects. The discomfort during the procedure is quite minimal, and there is no recovery time needed. In fact, most people get it done during their lunch hour and return to work immediately. The worst that could happen if your authorized doctor, and I stress authorized doctor, slips, is that you would lose the ability to move that part of your face, like raise your eyebrows all the way for a short period of time.

Slip-ups are pretty rare, because a few tiny injections are inserted into the muscle or the skin, as reported by the Botox Web site and *How Stuff Works*. Other side effects are headaches, neck pain, and soreness at the injection site.

Botox is not only used to diminish wrinkles anymore. From *Popular Science*, as many as one in five hundred babies are born with club foot, a condition where their feet are turned inwards. Before the introduction of Botox, babies had to undergo tendon-lengthening surgery so that their feet could be comfortably turned to the proper position.

Dr. Christina Alvarez of the Children's Hospital in Vancouver now does simple procedures where she inserts Botox into babies' calves, repositions the feet, and then stabilizes them with casts. Since Botox weakens the muscles, it is also used for treating disorders that stem from involuntary muscle spasms or clenching such as writer's cramps.

Some doctors injected Botox into the gastric muscles to make obese patients empty more slowly. The patients felt full for longer and ate less. Botox also helps people with hyperhidrosis, a condition of excessive sweating. By paralyzing the sweat glands, the injection prevents them from overproducing sweat.

Donna Goldamer of Sioux Falls receives Botox injections in her neck because she has dystonia, a condition where she has a tension in her neck, causing her head to have an abnormal rotation towards the right, and shake chaotically. After her first dosage of Botox, she was convinced it was well worth it. Right after the procedure, the patient experienced an immediate feeling of relaxation, and since her dystonia is considered a medical condition, her insurance pays for a large portion of the medication.

In addition to muscle treatments, it can also bring relief to migraine and headache sufferers. Plastic surgeon Dr. William Binder used Botox in his patients for wrinkles, and many of them returned saying not only had their wrinkles disappeared, but so had their headaches. Though Botox has not yet been approved by the FDA for the treatment of headaches, many neurologists have been using it for a number of years.

Though many miracles are performed daily using the injection, there are downfalls that current and prospective patients of Botox should know about. First of all, it's not permanent. Patients must go back periodically to receive follow-up treatments in order to maintain their achieved look. Not all people are capable of affording the treatment. Though in some cases, insurance provides coverage. But most Botox patients receive it for cosmetic reasons, which is not covered by insurance.

Not everybody is a candidate for Botox. Botox treatments work wonderfully for wrinkles that are caused by muscle weakness. If the patient has wrinkles caused by loss of elasticity in the skin due to aging, sun exposure, or smoking, they should look to other treatments such as collagen.

Perhaps Botox may be a wonder drug. It may not cure AIDS and other ailing conditions, but it can help people have a freer range of movement by helping to relax their muscles. Botox works so well that pretty soon some people may give up searching for the fountain of youth, but simply go out on their lunch breaks and get Botox injections instead.

Social Insecurity

Josh Gregersen

Josh Gregersen is a student at Northwestern University. He presented this speech in his Public Speaking class in 2003. It follows a pattern of comparison similar to that developed in Chapter 13. Decide whether the speech reflects mainly informative or mainly persuasive strategies, or if you can tell the difference. Josh has chosen a controversial public issue, so consider how, by speaking out, he has involved himself in the public forum as described in Appendix A. Finally, this speech illustrates the use of reasoning and the inclusion of many kinds of supporting materials. How effectively does this speech meet the standards developed in Chapters 5 and 6?

We've all probably paid them, Social Security payments, that is. A little over six percent of what we gross is taken out as a payment toward the social security of others. We know that some day we will be supported in the same way, and that gives us assurance that it is okay to pay.

But when we listen to the government now, what do they say about our investment in our security? In a 2003 annual report, the Senate Finance Committee gave us an answer. We, as young people, are not socially secure, because by the year 2018 Social Security will begin running on deficit. By the year 2042, social security will be bankrupt, as the trust fund that backs it runs out of money.

Though many of us will be approaching sixty, we will not get our fair share of what we have contributed over our forty years in the workforce. According to Eric Ernst of the *Sarasota-Herald Tribune* in an article printed just two days ago, when the Social Security Act was signed in 1935, there were forty-five workers to every one beneficiary. Now the ratio is four workers to every one beneficiary. Forty years from now, it will be two to one. This is a result of an increase in life expectancy combined with a proportional decrease of workers to support these older people.

In response to this reality, George W. Bush has outlined a plan that would allow some of our Social Security to be privatized, to be put under our control until we reach the minimum age at which we can begin to withdraw. Privatization of Social Security could help to remedy this problem with its benefits, but could also prove inferior to the current system because of its drawbacks. We'll look at both sides of the issue to see whether privatization is, or is not, the best course of action in response to this dilemma.

Privatization gives three main benefits to the individual that you should understand. It gives individuals control over risk, control over money, and control over their financial future. Let's go through them one at a time. Privatization gives us control over the amount of risk we can handle. The plan allows people to put a percentage of their Social Security funds into a private account where they can invest in stocks, as opposed to investing in government bonds, which is how the money is currently invested. The S&P 500 Index returned an average of 8.44 percent from 1950 to 2003 based on historical data. This is considerably higher than the 5.38 percent return you would get if you bought a thirty-year treasury bond this morning, which is what the government would buy. With higher risks, generally there are higher returns, so in picking stocks, the individuals can decide how aggressive or conservative he or she wants to be.

We've seen how control over risk helps individuals, now let's look at what having control over your money—that YOU earned—could do for you. In a survey conducted by the Cato Institute, the most common factor in support of privatization of Social Security funds is the control of money, as 39 percent listed that as the biggest benefit of privatization. Under the privatization plan, we as individuals would have the say as to how much or how little of our money would be invested in stocks. We also are able to pick which stocks we want to invest in, or we could leave it up to a mutual fund manager. It is our choice, it is our money. This lets us invest at whatever level we feel comfortable with, whatever we can handle. It also gives investment capital to companies whose stock we buy, giving them the opportunity to grow, further strengthening the economy.

We have control over risk, control over our money, and thirdly, we have control over our financial future. Privatization would provide us with the tools to shape our own financial future instead of praying that the Social Security trust fund doesn't go bankrupt. Aside from giving us insurance over the bankruptcy of the Social Security system, privatization would give us control over our financial future in that we would be guarded from decreases in benefits that would likely come if bankruptcy were an immediate issue, as it may be forty years from now. By being able to invest some of your Social Security, you could counter a depreciation in benefits by investing in a private account, where the government couldn't touch it.

These worries about the future trouble everyone, but another side of the issue says that privatization is not the way to go. As we examine the negative aspects of privatization, I will show you three reasons why privatization is not the best course of action to take concerning this issue. The plan costs too much money, it has too much risk, and it has too much influence. First, the plan costs too much money. Implementing this plan would create a shortage of funds in the short term, as some of the money intended for people who are currently receiving money would be allocated to private accounts. This money would need to be borrowed in order to pay those to whom it is guaranteed. The plan also costs too much money in that it takes away from some of the flexibility of the government. The government often uses surpluses in the Social Security account to cover shortages in other areas of the government. The government would then have to pay a higher interest rate on money that it needs because it would need to borrow it from a bank. This would increase the national debt and discourage economic growth.

Privatizing Social Security not only costs too much money, it is also too risky. For someone looking to receive payments just after a market crash, the results can be devastating. People who were hoping to retire today who were invested in the NASDAQ index have seen their accounts lose over two-thirds of their value since January 2001. Privatization takes the security out of Social Security. More than 42 percent of American families had no other retirement plan in 2001 other than Social Security, according to a February 27, 2003, *Christian Science Monitor* article. What can the government do to help these people if they don't have a safety net to protect them? The government will have used its last resources, so families will need to take on the burden of aging parents, a situation few children look forward to. The plan would also put financially uneducated people in charge of some of their own retirement. Without training in evaluating their own level of acceptable risk, these people may be playing the lottery with their future.

I've shown you how this plan costs too much money, how it is too risky, and now I want to show you that it gives the market too much influence over politics. Thomas Frank wrote in the January 2002 issue of *Harper's* magazine that "With our Social Security money entrusted to Wall Street, its priorities will become the nation's priorities; its demands for deregulation, de-unionization, low wages, and generous "stimulus" packages whenever the Dow looks a little weak will be recast as the demands of little old ladies in Beardstown and blue-collar workers in Providence." Wall Street will gain political power, as what is good for Wall Street will be what is best for the people. As rules regarding business law become more lax, as Wall Street would like it, another Enron awaits, but this time, far more people may be affected.

We've found that privatizing Social Security can offer more control of risks, money, and the future to individuals, but we have also found that the plan can be too costly, too risky, and too influential. I hope that you now can look at the issue in an educated way, and that you can now make a judgment for yourself as to whether or not privatization is the best way to fix the problems of the Social Security system. The next time you look at your paycheck, pay attention to the amount that is deducted for Social Security. Remember what you heard in your college speech class: that Social Security is no longer safe, and that it might not be there when you need it, whether it gets privatized or not.

Making the Grade

Nicole Tremel

This speech utilizes the problem–solution structure described in Chapter 14. Nicole Tremel, a student at the University of Northern Iowa, wanted to persuade her listeners that grade inflation is a serious problem and that the solutions she proposed should be adopted. Consider the difficulties she faces in addressing a student audience on this topic. Is she suggesting that her listeners might not have achieved as much academically as they think? What might lead a student audience to favor making their work harder through higher standards and more rigorous grading? Examine Nicole's choices of organization, supporting material, reasoning, and language to see how well they meet the requirements of the situation. This speech was presented in Lexington, Kentucky, in 1999.

The letter *D* is in serious danger. So is the *C–*. And the *F* is almost nonexistent. From the *Arizona Daily Star* of September 6–10, 1998, explanations are given that the chime of the bell curve has not been heard in a long time at the state's three universities. At the University of Arizona, Arizona State University, and Northern Arizona University, 70 percent of all grades awarded to undergraduates were *A*s or *B*s. But how is it possible that these students can be so uniformly excellent, so perfect that nearly all of them do grade-A work?

College grades are much higher today than in the 1960s. Is it due to better academic programs, more intense studying, or due to a phenomenon affecting schools and universities nationwide called grade inflation? The latter is the answer, according to *College Teaching* from Summer 1997; due to grade inflation, grade point averages have risen 15 to 20 percent in the past 30 years. Trends in achievement and GPA support the idea that 15 percent of today's present college graduates would not have earned a diploma by mid-60s standards. This inflation of grades has numerous problems that affect nearly everyone. Students are getting higher grades from less work, professors are able to be tenured because of students' evaluations, and employers are struggling to decipher who is really qualified when all applicants are equipped with college degrees with high GPAs. To better understand the problem of grade inflation, we will first explore the extent of grade inflation; second, the harms of grade inflation; and finally, seek solutions to end the practice of grade inflation.

How bad is grade inflation? *Newsweek*, March 3, 1997, details the rapid increase of grades at some of the nation's finest universities down to it affecting community college and high schools. National research done by the President of the Teachers College at Columbia University, Arthur Levine, found that students averaging *A*– or better rose from 7 percent in 1969 to 26 percent in 1993. Students receiving a *C* have dramatically fallen from 25 percent to 9 percent. At Stanford University, in 1996, 93 percent of the grades were *A*s or *B*s. Brown University's *Registrar's Report* showed that in 1995–96, 40 percent of the letter grades earned were *A*s, where in 1985–86 only 31 percent were rewarded an *A*, a direct indication of grade inflation. The *Indiana Daily Student* of March 27, 1998, also discusses how Indiana University has been plagued by grade inflation. The average grade is a *C* according to all universal transcripts, but at Indiana University, the average grade is a *B*. With scores and transcripts like this, it is nearly impossible to distinguish the fair students from the outstanding scholars. The *Associated Press* of February 13, 1998, explains that today at Princeton, it is getting very crowded at the head of the class. Eighty-three percent of all Princeton students are receiving grades between *B*– and *A*+, compared to just 69 percent in 1977. The problem isn't just at the Ivy League schools but at universities throughout the nation. This increase is causing concern and causing the reexamination of grading because of this escalation of GPAs.

Grade inflation does not result in numerous deaths or physically harmful situations, but it has serious harms that are very real. The key harms are the lack of fundamental knowledge, students don't gain an accurate view of evaluation in the real world, and a consumer mentality.

One of the most dangerous harms is that students today are less educated than their predecessors. Today's students, as it is argued in the *Detroit News* of April 26, 1998, are not required to master as much material as they once were. If students are receiving better grades and have not mastered the material they later will be using, the education has not had a lasting value. This can hinder any student, but consider the ramifications of a pilot, surgeon, or teacher. Their high grades are nice looking, but if any one of these professionals fails to master the skills, millions will be affected by their lack of knowledge, be it the people on the plane, on the operating table, and the ones in the classroom. Grade inflation results in students' lackadaisical attitude toward improving performance.

National Public Radio shares in the worries of grade inflation with an interview with James Twitchell, an English Professor at the University of

Florida. He emphasizes that standardized test scores are dropping, but students are somehow getting higher grades. He believes that the University of Florida will be graduating grade-based "geniuses" who perform no better than average.

Grade inflation gives students higher grades, a universal symbol of academic achievement. But there is no grade inflation in the real world, according to South Carolina University's Web page of October 1997. Henry Price, a veteran professor and administrator of the College of Journalism and Mass Communication states, "The *F* you get in the real world stands for fired." We in higher education are not preparing our students by handing out undeserved high grades. Once the degree is earned and the real world faces these students, it creates problems for graduate schools and employers. An Associated Press report of February 13, 1998, emphasizes the struggles of deciphering excellence and ordinary, because all students have relatively the same grade point average.

In the previously cited *College Teaching*, it describes why grade inflation is affecting colleges and universities. It is because these institutions adopt a student-as-consumer model, that knowledge is a product to be sold, students exchange money for a diploma. This consumer model undermines education's value as it places too much emphasis on student satisfaction. The satisfied consumers evaluate their professors positively and professors reciprocate kindness with inflated or higher grades than they deserve. This creates a problem because teachers concentrate on making class fun and entertaining while trying to raise the self-esteem of the students. This encourages passive learning and students do not know the operation of the world, because it allows students to buy degrees rather than work for them. In these colleges, the value of persistent work, responsibility, and resilience are discouraged.

With these dangerous harms in mind, let's examine how this grade inflation can be solved. Some potential solutions to this problem include transcript make-overs, faculty development, and getting rid of the GPA and replacing it with the AI, Achievement Index.

College Teaching of Summer 1997 gave several ideas of solving the inflation of grades. They believe that using the overall class grade on the transcript will better show the students' "true" ability. One variation is to print the student's grade in the class, but also list the median grade for the class and the number of students in the class. A different option would be to use a grading system where the class grade has two parts. The first number would be my grade in the class and the second would be the overall grade for the class. It would look like this: Nicole Tremel 3.0/2.7. It would show that I received a *B*, while the overall grade in my class was a 2.7. This lets graduate, medical, and law schools know my exact ability in conjunction to my peers.

Faculty development is another vital solution. Today, faculty is discouraged from raising higher standards for students. Faculty members fear reinstating higher standards because the use of student evaluations affects the process of promotion to tenure. If a professor demands students to work really hard, their evaluations will generally be negative, and lessen the professor's chance of becoming a tenured faculty member.

The other solution that looks successful is given by *Newsweek* of March 3, 1997. It suggests that colleges discontinue the use of the GPA and use a new system called AI, or Achievement Index. Vater Johnson, a statistics professor at Duke, is responsible for the AI's creation. The procedure for grading would have professors grade students in the usual way, but the results would be fed through a computer to adjust for levels of difficulty. This index relies on an algorithm that measures the student against other students, not against the 4.0 ideal. This method rewards the students who can excel in a variety of classes, those with the highest AI scores would be the most well-rounded. If you receive an *A* in an art history class when the average grade is a *B*–, then your AI rises. If you get a *C*+ in Biology when the average grade is a *B*, then your AI falls. When institutions like the state universities in Arizona give out such a high percentage of *A*s and *B*s, two particular things can happen. The top-notch work in the class receives the same grade as the average and even below-average students. This eventually leads to top students expecting high grades for mediocre work. This pummels into a vicious cycle where work expectations go downward with grades spiraling upward. This increase does nothing for students but harm them.

Grade inflation has affected my education in many ways. At my university, the average GPA has risen significantly, from 2.72 in 1985 to 2.98 in 1998.

There is a danger with our current grading system, according to the aforementioned *College Teaching*. Grades are supposed to be the primary indicator of education achievement. If today's grades do not reflect actual achievement, it is crucial that we do something different to record achievement. From today's focus on the causes of grade inflation, to dangerous harms, and the potential relief of this problem, we can see just what needs to be done to give the proper letter grade. Many universities and colleges are having such trouble figuring out who are excellent students and who are the mediocre ones. This problem needs to be addressed by administrators, faculty, and the students. Students need to know success comes from hard work; it is not revealed in the beautiful 4.0 on one's transcript. Daniel Pedersen seems to wrap it up best in *Newsweek*, March 3, 1997: "When *A* stands for average, do grades mean anything at all?"

Address to the National Women's Rights Convention, 1855

Lucy Stone

The movement for women's rights had its beginnings in the United States in the early nineteenth century. For many women, even being able to speak in public required overcoming obstacles, especially a particular interpretation of the Bible that held that women should remain quiet. Women who became involved in the antislavery movement came to believe that their position in society was, in some respects, not too different from that of the slaves. With their sensitivities thus heightened, leaders of the women's rights movement held conventions during the 1850s all across the nation.

Lucy Stone spoke at one of these meetings. She was educated at Oberlin College, where she studied rhetoric and became the first woman from Massachusetts to earn a college degree. She was a popular lecturer on both abolitionism and women's rights. In this speech, she is responding to another speaker at the 1855 Cincinnati women's rights convention who had claimed that the movement was nothing more than a few disappointed women. Rather than denying the charge, she turns the image of the "disappointed woman" to her advantage. How does she do it? How well?

Although not ignoring ideology or principles, Stone tries to emphasize the practical aspect of the women's rights issue by talking about the economic and legal harms suffered by women. In doing so, how is Stone able to avoid trivializing the larger issues? How do her appeals compare with those of the contemporary women's movement? Are the same appeals used by speakers from other traditionally marginalized groups as they seek inclusion in the public forum?

The last speaker alluded to this movement as being that of a few disappointed women. From the first years to which my memory stretches, I have been a disappointed woman. When, with my brothers, I reached forth after the sources of knowledge, I was reproved with "It isn't fit for you; it doesn't belong to women." Then there was but one college in the world where women were admitted, and that was in Brazil. I would have found my way there, but by the time I was prepared to go, one was opened in the young State of Ohio—the first in the United States where women and negroes could enjoy opportunities with white men. I was disappointed when I came to seek a profession worthy an immortal being—every employment was closed to me, except those of the teacher, the seamstress, and the housekeeper. In education, in marriage, in religion, in everything, disappointment is the lot of woman. It shall be the business of my life to deepen this disappointment in every woman's heart until she bows down to it no longer. I wish that women, instead of being walking show-cases, instead of begging of their fathers and brothers the latest and gayest new bonnet, would ask of them their rights.

The question of Woman's Rights is a practical one. The notion has prevailed that it was only an ephemeral idea: that it was but women claiming the right to smoke cigars in the streets, and to frequent barrooms. Others have supposed it a question of comparative intellect; others still, of sphere. Too much has already been said and written about woman's sphere. Trace all the doctrines to their source and they will be found to have no basis except in the usages and prejudices of the age. This is seen in the fact that what is tolerated in woman in one country is not tolerated in another. In this country women may hold prayer-meetings, etc., but in Mohammedan countries it is written upon their mosques, "Women and dogs, and other impure animals, are not permitted to enter." Wendell Phillips says, "The best and greatest thing one is capable of doing, that is his sphere." I have confidence in the Father to believe that when He gives us the capacity to do anything He does not make a blunder. Leave women, then, to find their sphere. And do not tell us before we are born even, that our province is to cook dinners, darn stockings, and sew on buttons. We are told woman has all the rights she wants; and even women, I am ashamed to say, tell us so. They mistake the politeness of men for rights—seats while men stand in this hall to-night, and their adulations; but these are mere courtesies. We want rights. The flour-merchant, the house-builder, and the postman charge us no less on account of our sex; but when we endeavor to earn money to pay all these, then, indeed, we find the difference. Man, if he have energy, may hew out for himself a path where no mortal has ever trod, held back by nothing but what is in himself; the world is all before him, there to choose; and we are glad for you, brothers, men, that it is so. But the same society that drives forth the young man keeps woman at home—a dependent—working little cats on worsted, and little dogs on punctured paper; but if she goes heartily and bravely to give herself to some worthy purpose, she is out of her sphere and she loses caste. Women working in tailor-shops are paid one-third as much as men. Some one in Philadelphia has stated that women make fine shirts for twelve and a half cents apiece; that no woman can make more than nine a week, and the sum thus earned, after deducting rent, fuel, etc., leaves her just three and a half cents a day for bread. Is it a wonder that women are driven to prostitution? Female teachers in New York are paid fifty dollars a year, and for every such situation there are five hundred applicants. I know not what you believe of God, but I believe He gave yearnings and longings to be filled, and that He did not mean all our time should be devoted to feeding and clothing the body. The present condition of woman causes a horrible perversion of the marriage relation. It is asked of a lady, "Has she married well?" "Oh, yes, her husband is rich." Woman must marry for a home, and you men are the sufferers by this; for a woman who loathes you may marry you because you have the means to get money which she can not have. But when woman can enter the lists with you and make money for herself, she will marry you only for deep and earnest affection.

I am detaining you too long, many of you standing, that I ought to apologize, but women have been wronged so long that I may wrong you a little. [*Applause*]. A woman undertook in Lowell to sell shoes to ladies. Men laughed at her, but in six years she has run them out, and has a monopoly of the trade. Sarah Tyndale, whose husband was an importer of china, and died bankrupt, continued his business, paid off his debts, and has made a fortune and built the largest china warehouse in the world. [*Mrs. Mott here corrected Lucy. Mrs. Tyndale has not the largest china warehouse, but the largest assortment of china in the world.*] Mrs. Tyndale, herself, drew the plan of her warehouse, and it is the best plan ever drawn. A laborer to whom the architect showed it, said: "Don't she know e'en as much as some men?" I have seen a woman at manual labor turning out chair-legs in a cabinet-shop with a dress short enough not to drag in the shavings. I wish other women would imitate her in this. It made her hands harder and broader, it is true, but I think a hand with a dollar and a quarter a day in it, better than one with a crossed ninepence. The men in the shop didn't use tobacco, nor swear—they can't do those things where there are women, and we owe it to our brothers to go wherever they work to keep them decent. The widening of woman's sphere is to improve her lot. Let us do it, and if the world scoff, let it scoff—if it sneer, let it sneer—but we will go on emulating the example of the sisters Grimke and Abby Kelly. When they first lectured against slavery they were not listened to as respectfully as you listen to us. So the first female physician meets many difficulties, but to the next the path will be made easy.

Lucretia Mott has been a preacher for years; her right to do so is not questioned among Friends. But when Antionette Brown felt that she was commanded to preach, and to arrest the progress of thousands that were on the road to hell; why, when she applied for ordination they acted as though they had rather the whole world should go to hell, than that Antionette Brown should be allowed to tell them how to keep out of it. She is now ordained over a parish in the State of New York, but when she meets on the Temperance platform the Rev. John Chambers, or your own Gen. Carey [*APPLAUSE*] they greet her with hisses. Theodore Parker said: "The acorn that the school-boy carries in his pocket and the squirrel stows in his cheek, has in it the possibility of an oak, able to withstand, for ages, the cold winter and the driving blast." I have seen the acorn men and women, but never the perfect oak; all are but abortions. The young mother, when first the newborn babe nestles in her bosom, and a heretofore unknown love springs up in her heart, finds herself unprepared for this new relation in life, and she sends forth the child scarred and dwarfed by her own weakness and imbecility, as no stream can rise higher than its fountain.

Second Inaugural Address, 1865

Abraham Lincoln

By the time Lincoln took the presidential oath of office a second time, the outcome of the Civil War was certain. The disagreement was not about who would win the war but about the nature of the postwar Union. Lincoln needed to articulate how he planned to bring the nation back together, knowing that his approach would be highly controversial. To provide context for his reconstruction plan, he needed to explain or to account for the war. His Second Inaugural Address is devoted to this task. He both reaffirms that the war was about preservation of the Union and acknowledges that slavery was the underlying cause.

Lincoln's explanation fuses secular and sacred. He sees the war as divine punishment for human sins. By implication, changing attitudes about slavery was necessary to atone for sin, and only when that was done would "the scourge of war" pass away. It recalls values drawn from the past, puts forward the broad political principles of reconstruction, and acknowledges Executive limitations by placing the ultimate outcome in the hands of God.

Six weeks after delivering this speech, Abraham Lincoln lay dead, the first president to fall victim to assassination. In retrospect, the Second Inaugural Address takes on added significance as a kind of valedictory or farewell address, although it surely was not constructed with these purposes in mind.[1]

Fellow Countrymen: At this second appearing to take the oath of the Presidential office there is less occasion for an extended address than there was at the first. Then a statement somewhat in detail of a course to be pursued seemed fitting and proper. Now, at the expiration of four years, during which public declarations have been constantly called forth on every point and phase of the great contest which still absorbs the attention and engrosses the energies of the nation, little that is new could be presented. The progress of our arms, upon which all else chiefly depends, is as well known to the public as to myself, and it is, I trust, reasonably satisfactory and encouraging to all. With high hope for the future, no prediction in regard to it is ventured.

On the occasion corresponding to this four years ago all thoughts were anxiously directed to an impending civil war. All dreaded it, all sought to avert it. While the inaugural address was being delivered from this place, devoted altogether to *saving* the Union without war, insurgent agents were in the city seeking to *destroy* it without war—seeking to dissolve the Union and divide effects by negotiation. Both parties deprecated war, but one of them would make war rather than let the nation survive, and the other would *accept* war rather than let it perish, and the war came.

One-eighth of the whole population were colored slaves, not distributed generally over the Union, but localized in the southern part of it. These slaves constituted a peculiar and powerful interest. All knew that this interest was somehow the cause of the war. To strengthen, perpetuate, and extend this interest was the object for which the insurgents would rend the Union even by war, while the Government claimed no right to do more than to restrict the territorial enlargement of it. Neither party expected for the war the magnitude or the duration which it has already attained. Neither anticipated that the *cause* of the conflict might cease with or even before the conflict itself should cease. Each looked for an easier triumph, and a result less fundamental and astounding. Both read the same Bible and pray to the same God, and each invokes His aid against the other. It may seem strange that any men should dare to ask a just God's assistance in wringing their bread from the sweat of other men's faces, but let us judge not, that we be not judged. The prayers of both could not be answered. That of neither has been answered fully. The Almighty has His own purposes. "Woe unto the world because of offenses; for it must needs be that offenses come, but woe to that man by whom the offense cometh." If we shall suppose that American slavery is one of those offenses which, in the providence of God, must needs come, but which having continued through His appointed time, He now wills to remove, and that He gives to both North and South this terrible war as the woe due to those by whom the offense came, shall we discern therein any departure from those divine attributes which the believers in a living God always ascribe to Him? Fondly do we hope, fervently do we pray, that this mighty scourge of war may speedily pass away. Yet, if God wills that it continue until all the wealth piled by the bondsman's two hundred and fifty years of unrequited toil shall be sunk, and until every drop of blood drawn with the lash shall be paid by another drawn with the sword, as was said three thousand years ago, so still it must be said, "the judgments of the Lord are true and righteous altogether."

With malice toward none, with charity for all, with firmness in the right as God gives us to see the right, let us strive on to finish the work we are in, to bind up the nation's wounds, to care for him who shall have borne the battle and for his widow and his orphan, to do all which may achieve and cherish a just and lasting peace among ourselves and with all nations.

First Inaugural Address, 1933

Franklin D. Roosevelt

Like Lincoln's Second Inaugural, this speech was delivered in a time of national crisis. By 1932, after the stock market crash and the ensuing Depression, industrial production had been cut by half and more than 13 million people were unemployed. Many were without homes; more were without hope. The situation actually worsened during 1932 after a brief recovery during the summer. Five thousand banks failed; 9 million savings accounts were lost; unemployment rose to 15 million.

Where Roosevelt stood on most issues was not clear, and he had the reputation of being a vacillating politician who would temper his principles to the requirements of the situation. During the campaign, he sounded inconsistent themes, and his advisers were divided about what he should do. Many people said the country had reached the end of an era, and some even predicted revolution.

Nearly 100,000 people gathered for the inaugural ceremonies at the Capitol, and millions listened on their radio sets. The new president's first task was to restore confidence, and he spoke to that need early in the speech. He promised action, called for sacrifice, promised to seek whatever powers he would need, and asked for the help of God. The president had promised to take charge, and from that moment the restoration of national confidence began.[2]

I am certain that my fellow Americans expect that on my induction into the Presidency I will address them with a candor and a decision which the present situation of our Nation impels. This is preeminently the time to speak the truth, the whole truth, frankly and boldly. Nor need we shrink from honestly facing conditions in our country today. This great Nation will endure as it has endured, will revive and will prosper. So, first of all, let me assert my firm belief that the only thing we have to fear is fear itself—nameless, unreasoning, unjustified terror which paralyzes needed efforts to convert retreat into advance. In every dark hour of our national life a leadership of frankness and vigor has met with that understanding and support of the people themselves which is essential to victory. I am convinced that you will again give that support to leadership in these critical days.

In such a spirit on my part and on yours we face our common difficulties. They concern, thank God, only material things. Values have shrunken to fantastic levels; taxes have risen; our ability to pay has fallen; government of all kinds is faced by serious curtailment of income; the means of exchange are frozen in the currents of trade; the withered leaves of industrial enterprise lie on every side; farmers find no markets for their produce; the savings of many years in thousands of families are gone.

More important, a host of unemployed citizens face the grim problem of existence, and an equally great number toil with little return. Only a foolish optimist can deny the dark realities of the moment.

Yet our distress comes from no failure of substance. We are stricken by no plague of locusts. Compared with the perils which our forefathers conquered because they believed and were not afraid, we have still much to be thankful for. Nature still offers her bounty and human efforts have multiplied it. Plenty is at our doorstep, but a generous use of it languishes in the very sight of the supply. Primarily this is because the rulers of the exchange of mankind's goods have failed, through their own stubbornness and their own incompetence, have admitted their failure, and abdicated. Practices of the unscrupulous money changers stand indicted in the court of public opinion, rejected by the hearts and minds of men.

True, they have tried, but their efforts have been cast in the pattern of all outworn tradition. Faced by failure of credit they have proposed only the lending of more money. Stripped of the lure of profit by which to induce our people to follow their false leadership, they have resorted to exhortations, pleading tearfully for restored confidence. They know only the rules of a generation of self-seekers. They have no vision, and when there is no vision the people perish.

The money changers have fled from their high seats in the temple of our civilization. We may now restore that temple to the ancient truths. The measure of the restoration lies in the extent to which we apply social values more noble than mere monetary profit.

Happiness lies not in the mere possession of money; it lies in the joy of achievement, in the thrill of creative effort. The joy and moral stimulation of work no longer must be forgotten in the head chase of evanescent profits. These dark days will be worth all they cost us if they teach us that our true destiny is not to be ministered unto but to minister to ourselves and to our fellow men.

Recognition of the falsity of material wealth as the standard of success goes hand in hand with the abandonment of the false belief that public office and high political position are to be valued only by the standards of pride of place and personal profit; and there must be an end to a conduct in banking and in business which too often has given to a sacred trust the likeness of callous and selfish wrongdoing. Small wonder that confidence languishes, for it thrives only on honesty, on honor, on the sacredness of obligations, on faithful protection, on unselfish performance; without them it can not live.

Restoration calls, however, not for changes in ethics alone. This Nation asks for action, and action now.

Our greatest primary task is to put people to work. This is no unsolvable problem if we face it wisely and courageously. It can be accomplished in part by direct recruiting by the Government itself, treating the task as we would treat the emergency of a war, but at the same time, through this employment, accomplishing greatly needed projects to stimulate and reorganize the use of our natural resources.

Hand in hand with this we must frankly recognize the overbalance of population in our industrial centers and, by engaging on a national scale in a redistribution, endeavor to provide a better use of the land for those best fitted for the land. The task can be helped by definite efforts to raise the values of agricultural products and with this the power to purchase the output of our cities. It can be helped by preventing realistically the tragedy of the growing loss through foreclosure of our small homes and our farms. It can be helped by insistence that the Federal, State, and local governments act forthwith on the demand that their cost be drastically reduced. It can be helped by the unifying of relief activities which today are often scattered, uneconomical, and unequal. It can be helped by national planning for and supervision of all forms of transportation and of communications and other utilities which have a definitely public character. There are many ways in which it can be helped, but it can never be helped merely by talking about it. We must act and act quickly.

Finally, in our progress toward a resumption of work we require two safeguards against a return of the evils of the old order; there must be a strict supervision of all banking and credits and investments; there must be an end to speculation with other people's money, and there must be provision for an adequate but sound currency.

There are the lines of attack. I shall presently urge upon a new Congress in special session detailed measures for their fulfillment, and I shall seek the immediate assistance of the several States.

Through this program of action we address ourselves to putting our own national house in order and making income balance outgo. Our international trade relations, though vastly important, are in point of time and necessity secondary to the establishment of a sound national economy. I favor as a practical policy the putting of first things first. I shall spare no effort to restore world trade by international economic readjustment, but the emergency at home can not wait on that accomplishment.

The basic thought that guides these specific means of national recovery is not narrowly nationalistic. It is the insistence, as a first consideration, upon the interdependence of the various elements in all parts of the United States—a recognition of the old and permanently important manifestation of the American spirit of the pioneer. It is the way to recovery. It is the immediate way. It is the strongest assurance that the recovery will endure.

In the field of world policy I would dedicate this Nation to the policy of the good neighbor—the neighbor who resolutely respects himself and, because he does so, respects the rights of others—the neighbor who respects his obligations and respects the sanctity of his agreements in and with a world of neighbors.

If I read the temper of our people correctly, we now realize as we have never realized before our interdependence on each other; that we can not merely take but we must give as well; that if we are to go forward, we must move as a trained and loyal army willing to sacrifice for the good of a common discipline, because without such discipline no progress is made, no leadership becomes effective. We are, I know, ready and willing to submit our lives and property to such discipline, because it makes possible a leadership which aims at a larger good. This I propose to offer, pledging that the larger purposes will bind upon us all as a sacred obligation with a unity of duty hitherto evoked only in time of armed strife.

With this pledge taken, I assume unhesitatingly the leadership of this great army of our people dedicated to a disciplined attack upon our common problems.

Action in this image and to this end is feasible under the form of government which we have inherited from our ancestors. Our Constitution is so simple and practical that it is possible always to meet extraordinary needs by changes in emphasis and arrangement without loss of essential form. That is why our constitutional system has proved itself the most superbly enduring political mechanism the modern world has produced. It has met every stress of vast expansion of territory, of foreign wars, of bitter internal strife, of world relations.

It is to be hoped that the normal balance of executive and legislative authority may be wholly adequate to meet the unprecedented task before us. But it may be that an unprecedented demand and need for undelayed action may call for temporary departure from that normal balance of public procedure.

I am prepared under my constitutional duty to recommend the measures that a stricken nation in the midst of a stricken world may require. These measures, or such other measures as the Congress may build out of its experience and wisdom, I shall seek, within my constitutional authority, to bring to speedy adoption.

But in the event that the Congress shall fail to take one of these two courses, and in the event that the national emergency is still critical, I shall not evade the clear course of duty that will then confront me. I shall ask the Congress for the one remaining instrument to meet the crisis—broad Executive power to wage a war against the emergency, as great as the power that would be given to me if we were in fact invaded by a foreign foe.

For the trust reposed in me I will return the courage and the devotion that befit the time. I can do no less.

We face the arduous days that lie before us in the warm courage of the national unity; with the clear consciousness of seeking old and precious moral values; with the clean satisfaction that comes from the stern performance of duty by old and young alike. We aim at the assurance of a rounded and permanent national life.

We do not distrust the future of essential democracy. The people of the United States have not failed. In their need they have registered a mandate that they want direct, vigorous action. They have asked for discipline and direction under leadership. They have made me the present instrument of their wishes. In the spirit of the gift I take it.

In this dedication of a Nation we humbly ask the blessing of God. May He protect each and every one of us. May He guide me in the days to come.

I Have a Dream, 1963

Martin Luther King, Jr.

After months of organization and planning, civil rights leaders held a "March on Washington for Jobs and Freedom" on August 28, 1963. A civil rights bill seemed stalled in Congress, and leaders hoped the march would spur legislative action. Two hundred thousand people, black and white, massed in peaceful protest in front of the Lincoln Memorial, where they heard a series of speakers. Each speaker had to decide whether to appeal to the conscience of white Americans, regarding them as potential allies, or to regard them as the adversary who should be blamed for the problems in race relations.

The last speaker of the day, the Reverend Dr. Martin Luther King, Jr., delivered a speech that has become one of the most famous of the twentieth century. You undoubtedly have studied it in other classes or perhaps watched it on film on Martin Luther King Day. Although the speech is usually studied as an embodiment of Dr. King's ideals, look at it also as a public speech reflect-

ing strategic choices in response to the opportunities and constraints of the situation. King walked a tightrope between militancy and moderation, stressing the urgency of the moment but avoiding attacks on whites and repudiating violence. He stressed the ideals to be achieved but rooted them in "the American dream" so that they would not seem new or radical. And he merged political oratory with the preaching style of the Southern black church.

How did King accomplish these objectives? What role was played by the metaphor of "cashing a check" or of "the American dream"? How did King's use of his voice contribute to his effect? What did King accomplish through parallel structure and repetition? It is clear that the speech was effective, at least for a time, in unifying the various elements of the civil rights movement. In 1999, a national poll identified "I Have a Dream" as the best speech given by an American during the twentieth century. What factors in the speech help us to understand why it is considered a masterpiece of public speaking?[3]

I am happy to join with you today in what will go down in history as the greatest demonstration for freedom in the history of our nation.

Five score years ago, a great American, in whose symbolic shadow we stand today, signed the Emancipation Proclamation. This momentous decree came as a great beacon light of hope to millions of Negro slaves, who had been seared in the flames of withering injustice. It came as a joyous daybreak to end the long night of their captivity.

But one hundred years later, the Negro still is not free. One hundred years later, the life of the Negro is still sadly crippled by the manacles of segregation and the chains of discrimination. One hundred years later, the Negro lives on a lonely island of poverty in the midst of a vast ocean of material prosperity. One hundred years later, the Negro is still languished in the corners of American society and finds himself an exile in his own land.

And so we've come here today to dramatize a shameful condition. In a sense we've come to our nation's Capitol to cash a check. When the architects of our republic wrote the magnificent words of the Constitution and the Declaration of Independence, they were signing a promissory note to which every American was to fall heir. This note was a promise that all men—yes, black men as well as white men—would be guaranteed the unalienable rights of life, liberty, and the pursuit of happiness.

It is obvious today that America has defaulted on this promissory note insofar as her citizens of color are concerned. Instead of honoring this sacred obligation, America has given the Negro people a bad check—a check which has come back marked "insufficient funds."

But we refuse to believe that the bank of justice is bankrupt. We refuse to believe that there are insufficient funds in the great vaults of opportunity of this nation. And so we've come to cash this check—a check that will give us upon demand the riches of freedom and the security of justice.

We have also come to this hallowed spot to remind America of the fierce urgency of now. This is no time to engage in the luxury of cooling off or to take the tranquilizing drug of gradualism. Now is the time to make real the promises of democracy. Now is the time to rise from the dark and desolate valley of segregation to the sunlit path of racial justice. Now is the time to lift our nation from the quicksands of racial injustice to the solid rock of brotherhood. Now is the time to make justice a reality for all of God's children.

It would be fatal for the nation to overlook the urgency of the moment. This sweltering summer of the Negro's legitimate discontent will not pass until there is an invigorating autumn of freedom and equality. Nineteen sixty-three is not an end, but a beginning. Those who hope that the Negro needed to blow off steam and will now be content will have a rude awakening if the nation returns to business as usual. There will be neither rest nor tranquility in America until the Negro is granted his citizenship rights. The whirlwinds of revolt will continue to shake the foundations of our nation until the bright day of justice emerges.

But there is something that I must say to my people, who stand on the warm threshold which leads into the palace of justice. In the process of gaining our rightful place, we must not be guilty of wrongful deeds. Let us not seek to justify our thirst for freedom by drinking from the cup of bitterness and hatred.

We must forever conduct our struggle on the high plane of dignity and discipline. We must not allow our creative protest to degenerate into physical violence. Again and again we must rise to the majestic heights of meeting physical force with soul force.

The marvelous new militancy which has engulfed the Negro community must not lead us to a distrust of all white people. For many of our white brothers, as evidenced by their presence here today, have come to realize that their destiny is tied up with our destiny. They have come to realize that their freedom is inextricably bound to our freedom. We cannot walk alone.

As we walk, we must make the pledge that we shall always march ahead. We cannot turn back. There are those who are asking the devotees of civil rights, "When will you be satisfied?" We can never be satisfied as long as a Negro is the victim of the unspeakable horrors of police brutality. We can never be satisfied as long as our bodies, heavy with the fatigue of travel, cannot gain lodging in the motels of the highways and the hotels of the cities. We cannot be satisfied as long as a Negro in Mississippi cannot vote and a Negro in New York believes he has nothing for which to vote. No, no, we are not satisfied, and we will not be satisfied until justice rolls down like waters, and righteousness like a mighty stream.

I am not unmindful that some of you have come here out of great trials and tribulations. Some of you have come fresh from narrow jail cells. Some of you have come from areas where your quest for freedom left you battered by the storms of persecution and staggered by the winds of police brutality. You have been the veterans of creative suffering. Continue to work with the faith that unearned suffering is redemptive.

Go back to Mississippi, go back to Alabama, go back to South Carolina, go back to Georgia, go back to Louisiana, go back to the slums and ghettos of our Northern cities, knowing that somehow this situation can and will be changed. Let us not wallow in the valley of despair.

I say to you today, my friends, so even though we face the difficulties of today and tomorrow, I still have a dream. It is a dream deeply rooted in the American dream.

I have a dream that one day this nation will rise up and live out the true meaning of its creed, "We hold these truths to be self-evident, that all men are created equal."

I have a dream that one day on the red hills of Georgia the sons of former slaves and the sons of former slaveowners will be able to sit down together at the table of brotherhood.

I have a dream that one day even the state of Mississippi, a state sweltering with the heat of injustice, sweltering with the heat of oppression, will be transformed into an oasis of freedom and justice.

I have a dream that my four little children will one day live in a nation where they will not be judged by the color of their skin but by the content of their character. I have a dream today.

I have a dream that one day, down in Alabama, with its vicious racists, with its governor having his lips dripping with the words of interposition and nullification, one day right there in Alabama little black boys and black girls will be able to join hands with the little white boys and white girls as sisters and brothers. I have a dream today.

I have a dream that one day every valley shall be exalted, every hill and mountain shall be made low, the rough places will be made plain and the crooked places will be made straight, and the glory of the Lord shall be revealed, and all flesh shall see it together.

This is our hope. This is the faith that I go back to the South with. With this faith we will be able to hew out of the mountain of despair a stone of hope. With this faith we will be able to transform the jangling discords of our nation into a beautiful symphony of brotherhood. With this faith we will be able to work together, to pray together, to struggle together, to go to jail together, to stand up for freedom together, knowing that we will be free one day.

This will be the day—this will be the day when all of God's children will be able to sing with new meaning, "My country 'tis of thee, sweet land of liberty, of thee I sing. Land where my fathers died, land of the pilgrim's pride, from every mountainside, let freedom ring." And if America is to be a great nation, this must become true.

So let freedom ring from the prodigious hilltops of New Hampshire. Let freedom ring from the mighty mountains of New York. Let freedom ring from the heightening Alleghenies of Pennsylvania!

Let freedom ring from the snowcapped Rockies of Colorado! Let freedom ring from the curvaceous slopes of California!

But not only that. Let freedom ring from Stone Mountain of Georgia!

Let freedom ring from Lookout Mountain of Tennessee!

Let freedom ring from every hill and molehill of Mississippi. From every mountainside, let freedom ring.

And when this happens, when we allow freedom to ring—when we let it ring from every village and every hamlet, from every state and every city—we will be able to speed up that day when all of God's children, black men and white men, Jews and Gentiles, Protestants and Catholics, will be able to join hands and sing in the words of the old Negro spiritual, "Free at last! Free at last! Thank God Almighty, we are free at last!"

Eulogy for the *Challenger* Astronauts, 1986

Ronald Reagan

Giving meaning to tragic events is one key function of the eulogy. It honors the memory of the dead by finding a message for the living. Eulogies typically stress the virtues of the deceased to guide the beliefs and actions of listeners. Most eulogies are of interest to only a small number of people. When the tragedy is public, the eulogy takes on added significance.

Such a highly public tragedy occurred on the morning of January 28, 1986, when the space shuttle Challenger exploded barely a minute after liftoff, killing all seven astronauts aboard. Schoolchildren and families across the country especially watched the launch because one of the astronauts was a teacher, Christa McAuliffe, the first civilian to travel in space. The explosion of the spacecraft was seen by millions of people on live television. These factors probably made the tragedy seem more immediate and "real" than the explosion of the Columbia as it reentered the earth's atmosphere in early 2003. Certainly for those old enough to remember, the Columbia disaster brought back to mind the tragic end of the Challenger.

President Ronald Reagan had been scheduled to give a State of the Union address, but he postponed it and eulogized the Challenger *astronauts instead. Concerned that the tragedy might cause listeners to doubt the value of the space program, he chose instead to emphasize the pioneer virtues of the astronauts and to regard their death as an unfortunate but necessary price for progress. Did Reagan select an appropriate meaning to give to this tragedy? How did his choices in the speech work to accomplish his effect? Were better choices available? Was Reagan the most appropriate spokesperson on this occasion? Why or why not?*

Ladies and gentlemen, I'd planned to speak to you tonight to report on the state of the Union, but the events of earlier today have led me to change those plans. Today is a day of mourning and remembering. Nancy and I are pained to the core by the tragedy of the shuttle *Challenger*. We know we share this pain with all of the people of our country. This is truly a national loss.

Nineteen years ago, almost to the day, we lost three astronauts in a terrible accident on the ground. But we've never lost an astronaut in flight; we've never had a tragedy like this. And perhaps we've forgotten the courage it took for the crew of the shuttle. But they, the *Challenger* Seven, were aware of the dangers, but overcame them and did their jobs brilliantly. We mourn seven heroes: Michael Smith, Dick Scobee, Judith Resnik, Ronald McNair, Ellison Onizuka, Gregory Jarvis, and Christa McAuliffe. We mourn their loss as a nation together.

For the families of the seven, we cannot bear, as you do, the full impact of this tragedy. But we feel the loss, and we're thinking about you so very much. Your loved ones were daring and brave, and they had that special grace, that special spirit that says, "Give me a challenge, and I'll meet it with joy." They had a hunger to explore the universe and discover its truths. They wished to serve, and they did. They served all of us. We've grown used to wonders in this century. It's hard to dazzle us. But for twenty-five years the United States space program has been doing just that. We've grown used to the idea of space, and perhaps we forget that we've only just begun. We're still pioneers. They, the members of the *Challenger* crew, were pioneers.

And I want to say something to the schoolchildren of America who were watching the live coverage of the shuttle's take-off. I know it is hard to understand, but sometimes painful things like this happen. It's all part of the process of exploration and discovery. It's all part of taking a chance and expanding man's horizons. The future doesn't belong to the fainthearted; it belongs to the brave. The *Challenger* crew was pulling us into the future, and we'll continue to follow them.

I've always had great faith in and respect for our space program, and what happened today does nothing to diminish it. We don't hide our space program. We don't keep secrets and cover things up. We do it all up front and in public. That's the way freedom is, and we wouldn't change it for a minute. We'll continue our quest in space. There will be more shuttle flights and more shuttle crews and, yes, more volunteers, more civilians, more teachers in space. Nothing ends here; our hopes and our journeys continue. I want to add that I wish I could talk to every man and woman who works for NASA or who worked on this mission and tell them: "Your dedication and professionalism have moved and impressed us for decades. And we know of your anguish. We share it."

There's a coincidence today. On this day 390 years ago, the great explorer Sir Francis Drake died aboard ship off the coast of Panama. In his lifetime the great frontiers were the oceans, and an historian later said, "He lived by the sea, died on it, and was buried in it." Well, today we can say of the *Challenger* crew: Their dedication was, like Drake's, complete.

The crew of the space shuttle *Challenger* honored us by the manner in which they lived their lives. We will never forget them, nor the last time we saw them, this morning, as they prepared for their journey and waved goodbye and "slipped the surly bonds of earth" to "touch the face of God."

Nobel Prize Lecture, 1993

Toni Morrison

This speech was delivered by Toni Morrison after she won the Nobel Prize for literature. She made much briefer remarks to accept the award, and then delivered a formal lecture. Morrison both describes and illustrates the power of storytelling. An extended example serves to develop her thesis that narrative is a means of knowledge as well as entertainment.

After introducing the story on a literal level, Morrison then treats it metaphorically. A bird stands for language; an old woman, for writers. At this level, Morrison is able to explain the writer's responsibility to keep language alive in the face of threats to its "nuanced, complex" character. As she points out, attending to language does not serve to displace experience but rather to imbue it with meaning. How well do you think she establishes her claim?

Successful speeches often blend forms—in this case narrative and exposition. Morrison does not simply talk about storytelling; she tells stories. The variety in her approach and her supporting materials add interest and power to the speech. Also, although the speech is not about any specific policy or proposal, it does address an issue of significant concern that is appropriately discussed in the public forum.

Members of the Swedish Academy, Ladies and Gentlemen:

Narrative has never been merely entertainment for me. It is, I believe, one of the principal ways in which we absorb knowledge. I hope you will understand, then, why I begin these remarks with the opening phrase of what must be the oldest sentence in the world, and the earliest one we remember from childhood: "Once upon a time . . ."

"Once upon a time there was an old woman. Blind but wise." Or was it an old man? A guru, perhaps. Or a *griot* soothing restless children. I have heard this story, or one exactly like it, in the lore of several cultures.

"Once upon a time there was an old woman. Blind. Wise."

In the version I know the woman is the daughter of slaves, black, American, and lives alone in a small house outside of town. Her reputation for wisdom is without peer and without question. Among her people she is both the law and its transgression. The honor she is paid and the awe in which she is held reach beyond her neighborhood to places far away; to the city where the intelligence of rural prophets is the source of much amusement.

One day the woman is visited by some young people who seem to be bent on disproving her clairvoyance and showing her up for the fraud they believe she is. Their plan is simple: they enter her house and ask the one question the answer to which rides solely on her difference from them, a difference they regard as a profound disability: her blindness. They stand before her, and one of them says,

"Old woman, I hold in my hand a bird. Tell me whether it is living or dead."

She does not answer, and the question is repeated. "Is the bird I am holding living or dead?"

Still she does not answer. She is blind and cannot see her visitors, let alone what is in their hands. She does not know their color, gender, or homeland. She only knows their motive.

The old woman's silence is so long, the young people have trouble holding their laughter.

Finally she speaks, and her voice is soft but stern. "I don't know," she says. "I don't know whether the bird you are holding is dead or alive, but what I do know is that it is in your hands. It is in your hands."

Her answer can be taken to mean: if it is dead, you have either found it that way or you have killed it. If it is alive, you can still kill it. Whether it is to stay alive is your decision. Whatever the case, it is your responsibility.

For parading their power and her helplessness, the young visitors are reprimanded, told they are responsible not only for the act of mockery but also for the small bundle of life sacrificed to achieve its aims. The blind women shifts attention away from assertions of power to the instrument through which that power is exercised.

Speculation on what (other than its own frail body) that bird in the hand might signify has always been attractive to me, but especially so now, thinking as I have been about the work I do that has brought me to this company. So I choose to read the bird as language and the woman as a practiced writer.

She is worried about how the language she dreams in, given to her at birth, is handled, put into service, even withheld from her for certain nefarious purposes. Being a writer, she thinks of language partly as a system, partly as a living thing over which one has control, but mostly as agency—as an act with consequences. So the question the children put to her, "Is it living or dead?," is not unreal, because she thinks of language as susceptible to death, erasure, certainly imperiled and salvageable only by an effort of the will. She believes that if the bird in the hands of her visitors is dead, the custodians are responsible for the corpse. For her a dead language is not only one no longer spoken or written, it is unyielding language content to admire its own paralysis. Like statist language, censored and censoring. Ruthless in its policing duties, it has no desire or purpose other than to maintain the free range of its own narcotic narcissism, its own exclusivity and dominance. However moribund, it is not without effect, for it actively thwarts the intellect, stalls conscience, suppresses human potential. Unreceptive to interrogation, it cannot form or tolerate new ideas, shape other thoughts, tell another story, fill baffling silences. Official language smitheried to sanction ignorance and preserve privilege is a suit of armor, polished to shocking glitter, a husk from which the knight departed long ago. Yet there it is; dumb, predatory, sentimental. Exciting reverence in schoolchildren, providing shelter for despots, summoning false memories of stability, harmony among the public.

She is convinced that when language dies, out of carelessness, disuse, indifference, and absence of esteem, or killed by fiat, not only she herself but all users and makers are accountable for its demise. In her country children have bitten their tongues off and use bullets instead to iterate the void of speechlessness, of disabled and disabling language, of language adults have abandoned altogether as a device for grappling with meaning, providing guidance, or expressing love. But she knows tongue-suicide is not only the choice of children. It is common among the infantile heads of state and power merchants whose evacuated language leaves them with no access to what is left of their human instincts, for they speak only to those who obey, or in order to force obedience.

The systematic looting of language can be recognized by the tendency of its users to forgo its nuanced, complex, midwifery properties, replacing them with menace and subjugation. Oppressive language does more than represent violence; it is violence; does more than represent the limits of knowledge; it limits knowledge. Whether it is obscuring state language or the faux language of mindless media; whether it is the proud but calcified language of the academy or the commodity-driven language of science; whether it is the maligned language of law-without-ethics, or language designed for the estrangement of minorities, hiding its racist plunder in its literary cheek—it must be rejected, altered, and exposed. It is the language that drinks blood, laps vulnerabilities, tucks its fascist boots under crinolines of respectability and patriotism as it moves relentlessly toward the bottom line and the bottomed-out mind. Sexist language, racist language, theistic language—all are typical of the policing languages of mastery, and cannot, do not, permit new knowledge or encourage the mutual exchange of ideas.

The old woman is keenly aware that no intellectual mercenary or insatiable dictator, no paid-for politician or demagogue, no counterfeit journalist would be persuaded by her thoughts. There is and will be rousing language to keep citizens armed and arming; slaughtered and slaughtering in the malls, courthouses, post offices, playgrounds, bedrooms, and boulevards; stirring, memorializing language to mask the pity and waste of needless death. There will be more diplomatic language to countenance rape, torture, assassination. There is and will be more seductive, mutant language designed to throttle women, to pack their throats like pâté-producing geese with their own unsayable, transgressive words; there will be more of the language of surveillance disguised as research; of politics and history calculated to render the suffering of millions mute; language glamorized to thrill the dissatisfied and bereft into assaulting their neighbors; arrogant pseudo-empirical language crafted to lock creative people into cages of inferiority and hopelessness.

Underneath the eloquence, the glamour, the scholarly associations, however stirring or seductive, the heart of such language is languishing, or perhaps not beating at all—if the bird is already dead.

She has thought about what could have been the intellectual history of any discipline if it had not insisted upon, or been forced into, the waste of time and life that rationalizations for and representations of dominance required—lethal discourses of exclusion blocking access to cognition for both the excluder and the excluded.

The conventional wisdom of the Tower of Babel story is that the collapse was a misfortune. That it was the distraction or the weight of many languages that precipitated the tower's failed architecture. That one monolithic language would have expedited the building, and heaven would have been reached. Whose heaven, she wonders? And what kind? Perhaps the achievement of Paradise was premature, a little hasty if no one could take the time to understand other languages, other views, other narratives. Had they, the heaven they imagined might have been found at their feet. Complicated, demanding, yes, but a view of heaven as life; not heaven as post-life.

She would not want to leave her young visitors with the impression that language should be forced to stay alive merely to be. The vitality of language lies in its ability to limn the actual, imagined, and possible lives of its speakers, readers, writers. Although its poise is sometimes in displacing experience, it is not a substitute for it. It arcs toward the place where meaning may lie. When a president of the United States thought about the graveyard his country had become, and said, "The world will little note nor long remember what we say here. But it will never forget what they did here," his simple words were exhilarating in their life-sustaining properties because they refused to encapsulate the reality of 600,000 dead men in a cataclysmic race war. Refusing to monumentalize, disdaining the "final word," the precise "summing up," acknowledging their "poor power to add or detract," his words signal deference to the uncapturability of the life it mourns. It is the deference that moves her, that recognition that language can never live up to life once and for all. Nor should it. Language can never "pin down" slavery, genocide, war. Nor should it yearn for the arrogance to be able to do so. Its force, its felicity, is in its reach toward the ineffable.

Be it grand or slender, burrowing, blasting or refusing to sanctify; whether it laughs out loud or is a cry without an alphabet, the choice word or the chosen silence, unmolested language surges toward knowledge, not its destruction. But who does not know of literature banned because it is interrogative; discredited because it is critical; erased because alternate? And how many are outraged by the thought of a self-ravaged tongue?

Word-work is sublime, she thinks, because it is generative; it makes meaning that secures our difference, our human difference—the way in which we are like no other life.

We die. That may be the meaning of life. But we *do* language. That may be the measure of our lives.

"Once upon a time . . ." Visitors ask an old woman a question. Who are they, these children? What did they make of that encounter? What did they hear in those final words: "The bird is in your hands"? A sentence that gestures toward possibility, or one that drops a latch? Perhaps what the children heard was, "It is not my problem. I am old, female, black, blind. What wisdom I have now is in knowing I cannot help you. The future of language is yours."

They stand there. Suppose nothing was in their hands. Suppose the visit was only a ruse, a trick to get to be spoken to, taken seriously as they have not been before. A chance to interrupt, to violate the adult world, its miasma of discourse about them. Urgent questions are at stake, including the one they have asked: "Is the bird we hold living or dead?" Perhaps the question meant: "Could someone tell us what is life? What is death?" No trick at all; no silliness. A straightforward question worthy of the attention of a wise one. An old one. And if the old and wise who have lived life and faced death cannot describe either, who can?

But she does not; she keeps her secret, her good opinion of herself, her gnomic pronouncements, her art without commitment. She keeps her distance, enforces it and retreats into the singularity of isolation, in sophisticated, privileged space.

Nothing, no word follows her declaration of transfer. That silence is deep, deeper than the meaning available in the words she has spoken. It shivers, this silence, and the children, annoyed, fill it with language invented on the spot.

"Is there no speech," they ask her, "no words you can give us that help us break through your dossier of failures? through the education you have just given us that is no education at all because we are paying close attention to what you have done as well as to what you have said? to the barrier you have erected between generosity and wisdom?

"We have no bird in our hands, living or dead. We have only you and our important question. Is the nothing in our hands something you could not bear to contemplate, to even guess? Don't you remember being young, when language was magic without meaning? When what you could say, could not mean? When the invisible was what imagination strove to see? When questions and demands for answers burned so brightly you trembled with fury at not knowing?

"Do we have to begin consciousness with a battle heroes and heroines like you have already fought and lost, leaving us with nothing in our hands except what you have imagined is there? Your answer is artful, but its artfulness embarrasses us and ought to embarrass you. Your answer is indecent in its self-congratulation. A made-for-television script that makes no sense if there is nothing in our hands.

"Why didn't you reach out, touch us with your soft fingers, delay the sound bite, the lesson, until you knew who we were? Did you so despise our trick, our modus operandi, that you could not see that we were baffled about how to get your attention? We are young. Unripe. We have heard all our short lives that we have to be responsible. What could that possibly mean in the catastrophe this world has become; where, as a poet said, "nothing needs to be exposed since it is already barefaced"? Our inheritance is an affront. You want us to have your old, blank eyes and see only cruelty and mediocrity. Do you think we are stupid enough to perjure ourselves again and again with the fiction of nationhood? How dare you talk to us of duty when we stand waist deep in the toxin of your past?

"You trivialize us and trivialize the bird that is not in our hands. Is there no context for our lives? No song, no literature, no poem full of vitamins, no history connected to experience that you can pass along to help us start strong? You are an adult. The old one, the wise one. Stop thinking about saving your face. Think of our lives and tell us your particularized world. Make up a story. Narrative is radical, creating us at the very moment it is being created. We will not blame you if your reach exceeds your grasp; if love so ignites your words that they go down in flames and nothing is left but their scald. Or if, with the reticence of a surgeon's hands, your words suture only the places where blood might flow. We know you can never do it properly—once and for all. Passion is never enough; neither is skill. But try. For our sake and yours forget your name in the street; tell us what the world has been to you in the dark places and in the light. Don't tell us what to believe, what to fear. Show us belief's wide skirt and the stitch that unravels fear's caul. You, old woman, blessed with blindness, can speak the language that tells us what only language can: how to see without pictures. Language alone protects us from the scariness of things with no names. Language alone is meditation.

"Tell us what it is to be a woman so that we may know what it is to be a man. What moves at the margin. What it is to have no home in this place. To be set adrift from the one you knew. What it is to live at the edge of towns that cannot bear your company.

"Tell us about ships turned away from shorelines at Easter, placenta in a field. Tell us about a wagonload of slaves, how they sang so softly their breath was indistinguishable from the falling snow. How they knew from the hunch of the nearest shoulder that the next stop would be their last. How, with hands prayered in their sex, they thought of heat, then sun. Lifting their faces as though it was there for the taking. Turning as though there for the taking. They stop at an inn. The driver and his mate go in with the lamp, leaving them humming in the dark. The horse's void steams into the snow beneath its hooves and the hiss and melt are the envy of the freezing slaves.

"The inn door opens: a girl and a boy step away from its light. They climb into the wagon bed. The boy will have a gun in three years, but now he carries a lamp and a jug of warm cider. They pass it from mouth to mouth. The girl offers bread, pieces of meat, and something more: a glance into the eyes of the one she serves. One helping for each man, two for each woman. And a look. They look back. The next stop will be their last. But not this one. This one is warmed."

It's quiet again when the children finish speaking, until the woman breaks into the silence.

"Finally," she says. "I trust you now. I trust you with the bird that is not in your hands because you have truly caught it. Look. How lovely it is, this thing we have done—together."

_____

© The Nobel Foundation 1993.

Inaugural Address, 1994

Nelson Mandela

The inaugural addresses of Abraham Lincoln and Franklin D. Roosevelt were delivered in a very different context from that faced by Nelson Mandela as the first post-apartheid president of South Africa. Some had predicted that the end of the racial caste system would be marked by violent revolution, but South Africa has made a peaceful, yet dramatic, transition to majority rule.

As you read the speech, notice how Mandela tries both to identify with his audience and to unify the audience by regarding its members as a single community. How does Mandela use symbolic references to the land in order to evoke other values of unity and solidarity? How does the favorable reference to his predecessor, F. W. de Klerk (who had accepted a position in Mandela's government), serve the same purpose?

In Appendix A, we discussed the typical features of an inaugural address within the culture of the United States. To what degree does Mandela's address exhibit these same features? How is it different from a speech that might be delivered in the United States?

Your Majesties, Your Highnesses, Distinguished Guests, Comrades and Friends:

Today, all of us do, by our presence here, and by our celebrations in other parts of our country and the world, confer glory and hope to newborn liberty.

Out of the experience of an extraordinary human disaster that lasted too long, must be born a society of which all humanity will be proud.

Our daily deeds as ordinary South Africans must produce an actual South African reality that will reinforce humanity's belief in justice, strengthen its confidence in the nobility of the human soul, and sustain all our hopes for a glorious life for all.

All this we owe both to ourselves and to the peoples of the world who are so well represented here today.

To my compatriots, I have no hesitation in saying that each one of us is as intimately attached to the soil of this beautiful country as are the famous jacaranda trees of Pretoria and the mimosa trees of the bushveld.

Each time one of us touches the soil of this land, we feel a sense of personal renewal. The national mood changes as the seasons change.

We are moved by a sense of joy and exhilaration when the grass turns green and the flowers bloom.

That spiritual and physical oneness we all share with this common homeland explains the depth of the pain we all carried in our hearts as we saw our country tear itself apart in a terrible conflict, and as we saw it spurned, outlawed, and isolated by the peoples of the world, precisely because it has become the universal base of the pernicious ideology and practice of racism and racial oppression.

We, the people of South Africa, feel fulfilled that humanity has taken us back into its bosom, that we, who were outlaws not so long ago, have today been given the rare privilege to be host to the nations of the world on our own soil.

We thank all our distinguished international guests for having come to take possession with the people of our country of what is, after all, a common victory for justice, for peace, for human dignity.

We trust that you will continue to stand by us as we tackle the challenges of building peace, prosperity, non-sexism, non-racialism, and democracy.

We deeply appreciate the role that the masses of our people and their political mass democratic, religious, women, youth, business, traditional and other leaders have played to bring about this conclusion. Not least among them is my Second Deputy President, the Honorable F. W. de Klerk.

We would also like to pay tribute to our security forces, in all their ranks, for the distinguished role they have played in securing our first democratic elections and the transition to democracy, from blood-thirsty forces which still refuse to see the light.

The time for the healing of the wounds has come.

The moment to bridge the chasms that divide us has come.

The time to build is upon us.

We have, at last, achieved our political emancipation. We pledge ourselves to liberate all our people from the continuing bondage of poverty, deprivation, suffering, gender, and other discrimination.

We succeeded to take our last steps to freedom in conditions of relative peace. We commit ourselves to the construction of a complete, just and lasting peace.

We have triumphed in the effort to implant hope in the breasts of the millions of our people. We enter into a covenant that we shall build the society in which all South Africans, both black and white, will be able to walk tall, without any fear in their hearts, assured of their inalienable right to human dignity—a rainbow nation at peace with itself and the world.

As a token of its commitment to the renewal of our country, the new Interim Government of National Unity will, as a matter of urgency, address the issue of amnesty for various categories of our people who are currently serving terms of imprisonment.

We dedicate this day to all the heroes and heroines in this country and the rest of the world who sacrificed in many ways and surrendered their lives so that we could be free.

Their dreams have become reality. Freedom is their reward.

We are both humbled and elevated by the honor and privilege that you, the people of South Africa, have bestowed on us, as the first President of a united, democratic, non-racial, and non-sexist South Africa, to lead our country out of the valley of darkness.

We understand it still that there is no easy road to freedom.

We know it well that none of us acting alone can achieve success.

We must therefore act together as a united people, for national reconciliation, for nation building, for the birth of a new world.

Let there be justice for all.

Let there be peace for all.

Let there be work, bread, water, and salt for all.

Let each know that for each the body, the mind and the soul have been freed to fulfill themselves.

Never, never and never again shall it be that this beautiful land will again experience the oppression of one by another and suffer the indignity of being the skunk of the world.

Let freedom reign.

The sun shall never set on so glorious a human achievement!

God bless Africa!

Thank you.

Commencement Address at the Massachusetts Institute of Technology, 1997

Kofi A. Annan

We saw in Chapter 15 that commencement exercises are an example of special occasions for public speaking. This address was delivered by the Secretary General of the United Nations. Notice how the speech is directed specifically to the graduates and yet also explores broader public issues. What are Annan's strategies for identifying with his audience? How does he make his larger message relevant to the immediate audience, so that the speech will have a unity of purpose? Is the commencement address an appropriate occasion at which to urge support for the United Nations? Why or why not?

This speech also illustrates how the speaker tries to shift the audience's focus from a primarily national to a primarily international perspective. One way in which to respect cultural diversity is to place issues in a broader context, so that listeners recognize that theirs is not the only way to imagine and think about a topic. How effective is Secretary General Annan in offering a new perspective? Would a U.S. speaker be more or less effective at achieving this goal with a U.S. audience? Why?

Thank you, Dr. Gray, for your most gracious welcome. I am honored and pleased to have been asked to speak to you on this grand occasion and in these familiar surroundings. The Boston area boasts of several excellent institutions of higher learning. But there is only one MIT.

Mr. President, Trustees, ladies and gentlemen: Let us congratulate the best, the brightest, the most dedicated, the most thoughtful, and the most likely to succeed MIT class ever—the class of 1997!

But, graduates, you know better than anyone that you did not do it alone. Accordingly, please join me in a big round of applause for those who have stood by you throughout the years and who are with you today, in person or in spirit, your loving parents and dear friends. Let's give them a hand.

Now you are free. Free of the pressure of exams. Free to begin the next stage of your life. And free to pay back your student loans. I wish you well.

I once sat where you sit today. Sharing these joyous moments with you today in Killian Court takes me back more than a quarter century to my own studies at MIT. As a Sloan Fellow, I learned management skills that I draw on still today in refashioning the United Nations for the new century that is upon us. But I learned an even more important lesson.

At the outset, there was competition—rather intense competition—among my cohorts. Each was equally determined to shine and to demonstrate his leadership abilities. I say "his," because there were no women among us; I am certainly glad that has changed.

Walking along the Charles River one day, in the middle of my first term, I reflected on my predicament. How could I survive, let alone thrive, in this group of over-achievers? And the answer came to me most emphatically: NOT by playing it according to their rules. "Follow your own inner compass," I said to myself, "listen to your own drummer." To live is to choose. But to choose well, you must know who you are, what you stand for, where you want to go, and why you want to get there. My anxieties slowly began to dissolve.

What I took away from MIT, as a result, was not only the analytical tools but also the intellectual confidence to help me locate my bearings in new situations, to view any challenge as a potential opportunity for renewal and growth, and to be comfortable in seeking the help of colleagues, but not fearing, in the end, to do things my way.

When the world thinks of MIT alumni and alumnae who have gone on to assume positions of visibility in their respective fields, as so many have, it correctly imagines Nobel laureates in physics, chemistry, and economics, or business tycoons, or engineers improving our daily lives in countless ways. But a Secretary General of the United Nations? That's hardly the first answer anyone would blurt out on a TV quiz show!

And yet, it is not as much of a stretch as it may seem at first. For the ethos of science and engineering shares deep and profound similarities with the twentieth century project of international organization. Science and international organization alike are constructs of reason, engaged in a permanent struggle against the forces of unreason. Science and international organization alike are experimental; both learn by trial and error and strive to be self-correcting. Lastly, science and international organization alike speak a universal language and seek universal truths. Allow me to expand briefly on each of these features of the project of international organization.

I begin with the struggle between reason and unreason. When the history of the twentieth century is written, this struggle will figure very prominently in it. On the plane of international affairs, the outbursts of unreason in this century surpass in horror and human tragedy any the world has seen in the entire modern era. From Flanders' fields to the Holocaust and the aggressions that produced World War II; from the killing fields of Cambodia and Rwanda to ethnic cleansing in Bosnia; from the twenty-five million refugees who roam the world today to untold millions, many of them children, who die the slow death of starvation or are maimed for life by landmines—our century, even this generation, has much to answer for.

But we have also managed to build up the international edifice of reason. By deliberate institutional means, we have better positioned humankind to cope with pressing global problems. Measures to enhance peace and security rank among these accomplishments. As the twentieth century draws to a close, we can take pride in numerous advances in, for example, the area of arms control and disarmament. Perhaps the bedrock is the Nuclear Non-Proliferation Treaty, in force for nearly three decades now. Negotiated through the United Nations and monitored by one of its Agencies, the N.P.T. has more adherents than any arms control treaty in history. In September 1996, the United Nations General Assembly approved the Comprehensive Nuclear Test Ban Treaty, which has since been signed by more than 140 countries, including all five nuclear-weapons States.

In April of this year, we witnessed the entry into force of the Chemical Weapons Convention. It helps to ensure that these vile weapons never again will be the scourge of any battlefield, the silent but certain doom of any civilian population.

Finally, states that are party to the Biological Weapons Convention are seeking ways to reinforce its authority through a verification mechanism.

Much remains to be done, especially in reducing the vast and rapidly growing flow of conventional weapons; ridding the world of the viciousness of land-mines, whose primary targets are the innocents of any conflict; strengthening the methods of preventive diplomacy; and inventing the next generation of peacekeeping operations. But only a decade ago the achievements I have enumerated seemed unimaginable. Now they are real.

Similar accomplishments are transforming other aspects of international life. Few are more noble than safeguarding and enhancing human rights. Few yield more practical benefits than deepening and expanding multilateral rules for international economic relations. Few are more rewarding than helping the world's children to achieve healthy and productive lives. Few are more critical than preserving the human environment even as we achieve greater economic opportunity for all. And so, as this century draws to a close, we are justified in concluding that international organization has helped tilt the balance toward the domain within which the power of reason prevails.

A second attribute that the project of international organization shares with science is the experimental method. Indeed, international organization is an experiment. It is an experiment in human cooperation on a planetary scale. Those of us who serve in international organizations must never forget the fact that they are not an end in themselves. They are a means to empower both governments and people to realize goals through collaboration that would otherwise elude them. International organizations, therefore, must be closely attuned to their environment, quickly correct their mistakes, build cumulatively on their achievements, and constantly generate new modalities as previous ways of doing things become outdated.

I am very pleased, therefore, to report to you today that we at the United Nations are amidst the most thoroughgoing institutional reforms ever attempted there. I would go a step further and express my conviction that when our reform plans are announced next month, they will compare favorably with any such reforms yet undertaken by any public sector, anywhere.

We seek a United Nations that will view change as a friend, not change for its own sake but change that permits us to do more good by doing it better. We seek a United Nations that is leaner, more focused, more flexible, and more responsive to changing global needs. We seek a United Nations that is organized around its core competencies vis-à-vis other international organizations and an ever-more robust global civil society. We seek a United Nations that serves more effectively not only its Member States but also the people of the world whose hopes we embody.

In short, we at the United Nations are working hard to firm up the grounds on which the project of international organization rests. And we are doing so by recognizing its experimental nature and embracing the imperative of inventiveness that it implies.

A third similarity between the ethos of science and the project of international organization is this: we do what we do in the realm of international organization because we strive, in our own fashion, to give expression to universal truths. What might these be in so contested an arena as international affairs? I believe that they include the truths of human dignity and fundamental equality, whereby a child born in the smallest village of the poorest land is valued as much as one born on Beacon Hill. I believe they include a yearning for peace, the awareness that we are but stewards of this extraordinary only one earth, the understanding that even though the world is divided by many particularisms we are united as a human community.

This noble cause requires your help. All of you in the Class of 1997, wherever you go from here and whatever you do in the future, will participate in a world that is becoming increasingly globalized. You will interact, directly or indirectly, with others just like you across the far reaches of the world. They will represent colleagues, competitors, customers. As you enter this new world, I call upon you to remember this: as powerful and as progressive a bond that market rationality constitutes, it is not a sufficient basis for human solidarity. It must be coupled with an ethic of caring for those whom the market disadvantages, an ethic of responsibility for the collective goods that the market under produces, an ethic of tolerance for those whom the market pits as your adversary.

The United Nations has no peer in this regard. It is the unparalleled nerve center of the global village, exploring and negotiating emerging issues, setting priorities, and creating norms of conduct. Since the 1970s, the United Nations has been at the forefront of instituting concern with the human environment, world population, world hunger, the extension of fundamental human rights to encompass the status of women and of children, as well as sustainable development in its many facets. We have done so through a series of global conferences that have brought together governments and non-governmental organizations from every corner of the world.

By means of this novel form of multilateral diplomacy, the universal truths of which I spoke slowly but steadily are making themselves heard. Slowly but steadily they are stretching the "we" in "we the peoples of the United Nations," as the opening words of our Charter put it—not at the expense of you or me, of this or that country, but in fulfillment of that which we share in common.

Moreover, most of you here today are citizens of this great and bountiful United States of America. For you I have a special plea. Your country, the world's most powerful, even now is debating its future role in the new world community, and the place of the United Nations within that overall foreign policy vision.

I call upon you to work tirelessly to anchor the United States firmly to the course of internationalism, to its historic mission as an agent of progressive change and to a world order that reflects your country's commitment to the rule of law, equal opportunity, and the irreducible rights of all individuals. The need is pressing; the moment is now. Let us continue the productive partnership between the United States and the United Nations and go forward together with a positive, can-do attitude to win the peace and prosperity that beckons.

Thank you, Mr. President, honored guests—and most of all, my fellow alumni and alumnae. Yes, I can call you that now. Good luck!

Speech at Yad Vashem Holocaust Memorial, 2000

Pope John Paul II

As the year 2000 dawned, many religious people found deep significance in the coming of a new millennium. They expressed hope for spiritual renewal and for drawing the world's diverse peoples closer together. For the Catholic Church in particular, under the leadership of Pope John Paul II, the Holy Year of 2000 was the occasion for frank acknowledgment of the sinfulness of religious persecution in which many Christians had engaged over the years. A highlight of the year was the Pope's trip to the Holy Land, the sacred space of Judaism, Christianity, and Islam.

This speech was delivered in Jerusalem at Yad Vashem, the Israeli national Holocaust memorial. Even for those who are not religious, the speech is an astute response to a very delicate rhetorical situation. The place called for reverence and remembering. The occasion and the speaker made it necessary to acknowledge that many perpetrators of evil claimed to be Christians. And yet, since the teaching of the Church is considered by believers to be perfect, the Pope had to distinguish between the actions of alleged Christians and the doctrines of Christianity.

It conveys no disrespect that we examine religious discourse as strategic public speaking. Throughout this book, we have examined speakers' choices that use their opportunities in the face of constraints. What choices does the Pope's speech reflect? How skillfully did he analyze his audience and rhetorical situation? What, if any, alternatives were available to him?

The words of the ancient Psalm rise from our hearts: "I have become like a broken vessel. I hear the whispering of many—terror on every side! as they scheme together against me, as they plot to take my life. But I trust in you. O Lord, I say, 'You are my God.' "

In this place of memories, the mind and heart and soul feel an extreme need for silence. Silence in which to remember. Silence in which to try to make sense of the memories which come flooding back. Silence because there are no words strong enough to deplore the terrible tragedy of the Shoah. My own personal memories are of all that happened when the Nazis occupied Poland during the war. I remember my Jewish friends and neighbors, some of whom perished, while others survived.

I have come to Yad Vashem to pay homage to the millions of Jewish people who, stripped of everything, especially of their human dignity, were murdered in the Holocaust. More than half a century has passed, but the memories remain.

Here, as at Auschwitz and many other places in Europe, we are overcome by the echo of the heart-rending laments of so many. Men, women, children cry out to us from the depths of the horror that they knew. How can we fail to heed their cry? No one can forget or ignore what happened. No one can diminish its scale. We wish to remember. But we wish to remember for a purpose, namely to ensure that never again will evil prevail as it did for the millions of innocent victims of Nazism.

How could man have such utter contempt for man? Because we had reached the point of contempt for God. Only a Godless ideology could plan and carry out the extermination of a whole people.

The honour given to the "just gentiles" by the State of Israel at Yad Vashem for having acted heroically to save Jews, sometimes to the point of giving their own lives, is a recognition that not even in the darkest hour is every light extinguished. That is why the Psalms, and the entire Bible, though well aware of the human capacity for evil, also proclaim that evil will not have the last word. Out of the depths of pain and sorrow, the believer's heart cries out: "I trust in you, O Lord: I say You are my God" (Psalms 31:14). Jews and Christians share an immense spiritual patrimony, flowing from God's self-revelation. Our religious teachings and our spiritual experience demand that we overcome evil with good. We remember, but not with any desire for vengeance or an incentive to hatred. For us, to remember is to pray for peace and justice, and to commit ourselves to their cause. Only a world at peace, with justice for all, can avoid repeating the mistakes and terrible crimes of the past.

As Bishop of Rome and successor of the Apostle Peter, I assure the Jewish people that the Catholic Church, motivated by the Gospel law of truth and love and by no political considerations, is deeply saddened by the hatred, acts of persecution, and displays of anti-Semitism directed against the Jews by Christians at any time and in any place. The Church rejects racism in any form as a denial of the image of the Creator inherent in every human being.

In this place of solemn remembrance, I fervently pray that our sorrow for the tragedy which the Jewish people suffered in the twentieth century will lead to a new relationship between Christians and Jews. Let us build a new future in which there will be no more anti-Jewish feeling among Christians or anti-Christian feeling among Jews, but rather the mutual respect required of those who adore the one Creator and Lord, and look to Abraham as our common father in faith.

The world must heed the warning that comes to us from the victims of the Holocaust and from the testimony of the survivors. Here at Yad Vashem the memory lives on, and burns itself into our souls. It makes us cry out:

"I hear the whispering of many—terror on every side! But I trust in you, O Lord; I say, 'You are my God'" (Psalms 31:15).

Address to a Joint Session of Congress and the American People, 2001

George W. Bush

The terrorist attacks of September 11, 2001, shocked and angered Americans. People wondered what the attacks meant, who ordered them, and how the United States would respond. In times of national crisis and trauma, people look to the President for meaning, reassurance, and action. Nine days after the attacks, President George W. Bush addressed a joint session of Congress and a nationwide television audience to explain the policy of his administration.

Notice how the president characterizes the attacks as "war" yet distinguishes these incidents from earlier wars. Notice, too, how he calls upon the American people to respond. Does anything strike you as unusual about what he asks of the people? Finally, notice how the speech is organized as answers to a series of questions the American people are said to be asking. Does this organizational pattern help the president to achieve his purpose?

In Chapter 15, we considered speeches that combine deliberative and ceremonial strategies. How does this speech do so? What enables it both to articulate and defend a policy and also to celebrate national unity and to mobilize support for the war?

Public approval of the President's performance rose markedly after the terrorist attacks, from just over 50 percent to almost 90 percent. How, if at all, does this speech help to explain the marked increase in President Bush's public support?[4]

Mr. Speaker, Mr. President Pro Tempore, members of Congress, and fellow Americans:

In the normal course of events, Presidents come to this chamber to report on the state of the Union. Tonight, no such report is needed. It has already been delivered by the American people.

We have seen it in the courage of passengers, who rushed terrorists to save others on the ground—passengers like an exceptional man named Todd Beamer. And would you please help me to welcome his wife, Lisa Beamer, here tonight.

We have seen the state of our Union in the endurance of rescuers, working past exhaustion. We have seen the unfurling of flags, the lighting of candles, the giving of blood, the saying of prayers—in English, Hebrew, and Arabic. We have seen the decency of a loving and giving people who have made the grief of strangers their own.

My fellow citizens, for the last nine days, the entire world has seen for itself the state of our Union—and it is strong.

I thank the Congress for its leadership at such an important time. All of America was touched on the evening of the tragedy to see Republicans and Democrats joined together on the steps of this Capitol, singing "God Bless America." And you did more than sing; you acted, by delivering $40 billion to rebuild our communities and meet the needs of our military.

Speaker Hastert, Minority Leader Gephardt, Majority Leader Daschle, and Senator Lott, I thank you for your friendship, for your leadership, and for your service to our country.

And on behalf of the American people, I thank the world for its outpouring of support. America will never forget the sounds of our National Anthem playing at Buckingham Palace, on the streets of Paris, and at Berlin's Brandenburg Gate.

We will not forget South Korean children gathering to pray outside our embassy in Seoul, or the prayers of sympathy offered at a mosque in Cairo. We will not forget moments of silence and days of mourning in Australia and Africa and Latin America.

Nor will we forget the citizens of 80 other nations who died with our own: dozens of Pakistanis; more than 130 Israelis; more than 250 citizens of India; men and women from El Salvador, Iran, Mexico, and Japan; and hundreds of British citizens. America has no truer friend than Great Britain. Once again, we are joined together in a great cause—so honored the British Prime Minister has crossed an ocean to show his unity of purpose with America. Thank you for coming, friend.

On September the 11th, enemies of freedom committed an act of war against our country. Americans have known wars—but for the past 136 years, they have been wars on foreign soil, except for one Sunday in 1941. Americans have known the casualties of war—but not at the center of a great city on a peaceful morning. Americans have known surprise attacks—but never before on thousands of civilians. All of this was brought upon us in a single day—and night fell on a different world, a world where freedom itself is under attack.

Americans have many questions tonight. Americans are asking: Who attacked our country? The evidence we have gathered all points to a collection of loosely affiliated terrorist organizations known as al Qaeda. They are the same murderers indicted for bombing American embassies in Tanzania and Kenya and responsible for bombing the USS Cole.

Al Qaeda is to terror what the mafia is to crime. But its goal is not making money; its goal is remaking the world—and imposing its radical beliefs on people everywhere.

The terrorists practice a fringe form of Islamic extremism that has been rejected by Muslim scholars and the vast majority of Muslim clerics—a fringe movement that perverts the peaceful teachings of Islam. The terrorists' directive commands them to kill Christians and Jews, to kill all Americans, and make no distinction among military and civilians, including women and children.

This group and its leader—a person named Osama bin Laden—are linked to many other organizations in different countries, including the Egyptian Islamic Jihad and the Islamic Movement of Uzbekistan. There are thousands of these terrorists in more than 60 countries. They are recruited from their own nations and neighborhoods and brought to camps in places like Afghanistan, where they are trained in the tactics of terror. They are sent back to their homes or sent to hide in countries around the world to plot evil and destruction.

The leadership of al Qaeda has great influence in Afghanistan and supports the Taliban regime in controlling most of that country. In Afghanistan, we see al Qaeda's vision for the world.

Afghanistan's people have been brutalized—many are starving and many have fled. Women are not allowed to attend school. You can be jailed for owning a television. Religion can be practiced only as their leaders dictate. A man can be jailed in Afghanistan if his beard is not long enough.

The United States respects the people of Afghanistan—after all, we are currently its largest source of humanitarian aid—but we condemn the Taliban regime. It is not only repressing its own people, it is threatening people everywhere by sponsoring and sheltering and supplying terrorists. By aiding and abetting murder, the Taliban regime is committing murder.

And tonight, the United States of America makes the following demands on the Taliban: Deliver to United States authorities all the leaders of al Qaeda who hide in your land. Release all foreign nationals, including American citizens, you have unjustly imprisoned. Protect foreign journalists, diplomats, and aid workers in your country. Close immediately and permanently every terrorist training camp in Afghanistan, and hand over every terrorist, and every person in their support structure, to appropriate authorities. Give the United States full access to terrorist training camps, so we can make sure they are no longer operating.

These demands are not open to negotiation or discussion. The Taliban must act, and act immediately. They will hand over the terrorists, or they will share in their fate.

I also want to speak tonight directly to Muslims throughout the world. We respect your faith. It's practiced freely by many millions of Americans, and by millions more in countries that America counts as friends. Its teachings are good and peaceful, and those who commit evil in the name of Allah blaspheme the name of Allah. The terrorists are traitors to their own faith, trying, in effect, to hijack Islam itself. The enemy of America is not our many Muslim friends; it is not our many Arab friends. Our enemy is a radical network of terrorists, and every government that supports them.

Our war on terror begins with al Qaeda, but it does not end there. It will not end until every terrorist group of global reach has been found, stopped and defeated.

Americans are asking, why do they hate us? They hate what we see right here in this chamber—a democratically elected government. Their leaders are self-appointed. They hate our freedoms—our freedom of religion, our freedom of speech, our freedom to vote and assemble and disagree with each other.

They want to overthrow existing governments in many Muslim countries, such as Egypt, Saudi Arabia, and Jordan. They want to drive Israel out of the Middle East. They want to drive Christians and Jews out of vast regions of Asia and Africa.

These terrorists kill not merely to end lives, but to disrupt and end a way of life. With every atrocity, they hope that America grows fearful, retreating from the world and forsaking our friends. They stand against us, because we stand in their way.

We are not deceived by their pretenses to piety. We have seen their kind before. They are the heirs of all the murderous ideologies of the 20th century. By sacrificing human life to serve their radical visions—by abandoning every value except the will to power—they follow in the path of fascism, and Nazism, and totalitarianism. And they will follow that path all the way, to where it ends: in history's unmarked grave of discarded lies.

Americans are asking: How will we fight and win this war? We will direct every resource at our command—every means of diplomacy, every tool of intelligence, every instrument of law enforcement, every financial influence, and every necessary weapon of war—to the disruption and to the defeat of the global terror network.

This war will not be like the war against Iraq a decade ago, with a decisive liberation of territory and a swift conclusion. It will not look like the air war above Kosovo two years ago, where no ground troops were used and not a single American was lost in combat.

Our response involves far more than instant retaliation and isolated strikes. Americans should not expect one battle, but a lengthy campaign, unlike any other we have ever seen. It may include dramatic strikes, visible on TV, and covert operations, secret even in success. We will starve terrorists of funding, turn them one against another, drive them from place to place, until there is no refuge or no rest. And we will pursue nations that provide aid or safe haven to terrorism.

Every nation, in every region, now has a decision to make. Either you are with us, or you are with the terrorists. From this day forward, any nation that continues to harbor or support terrorism will be regarded by the United States as a hostile regime.

Our nation has been put on notice: We are not immune from attack. We will take defensive measures against terrorism to protect Americans. Today, dozens of federal departments and agencies, as well as state and local governments, have responsibilities affecting homeland security. These efforts must be coordinated at the highest level. So tonight I announce the creation of a Cabinet-level position reporting directly to me—the Office of Homeland Security.

And tonight I also announce a distinguished American to lead this effort, to strengthen American security: a military veteran, an effective governor, a true patriot, a trusted friend—Pennsylvania's Tom Ridge. He will lead, oversee and coordinate a comprehensive national strategy to safeguard our country against terrorism, and respond to any attacks that may come. These measures are essential. But the only way to defeat terrorism as a threat to our way of life is to stop it, eliminate it, and destroy it where it grows.

Many will be involved in this effort, from FBI agents to intelligence operatives to the reservists we have called to active duty. All deserve our thanks, and all have our prayers. And tonight, a few miles from the damaged Pentagon, I have a message for our military: Be ready. I've called the Armed Forces to alert, and there is a reason. The hour is coming when America will act, and you will make us proud.

This is not, however, just America's fight. And what is at stake is not just America's freedom. This is the world's fight. This is civilization's fight. This is the fight of all who believe in progress and pluralism, tolerance and freedom.

We ask every nation to join us. We will ask, and we will need, the help of police forces, intelligence services, and banking systems around the world. The United States is grateful that many nations and many international organizations have already responded—with sympathy and with support. Nations from Latin America, to Asia, to Africa, to Europe, to the Islamic world. Perhaps the NATO Charter reflects best the attitude of the world: An attack on one is an attack on all.

The civilized world is rallying to America's side. They understand that if this terror goes unpunished, their own cities, their own citizens may be next. Terror, unanswered, can not only bring down buildings, it can threaten the stability of legitimate governments. And you know what—we're not going to allow it.

Americans are asking: What is expected of us? I ask you to live your lives, and hug your children. I know many citizens have fears tonight, and I ask you to be calm and resolute, even in the face of a continuing threat.

I ask you to uphold the values of America, and remember why so many have come here. We are in a fight for our principles, and our first responsibility is to live by them. No one should be singled out for unfair treatment or unkind words because of their ethnic background or religious faith.

I ask you to continue to support the victims of this tragedy with your contributions. Those who want to give can go to a central source of information, libertyunites.org, to find the names of groups providing direct help in New York, Pennsylvania, and Virginia.

The thousands of FBI agents who are now at work in this investigation may need your cooperation, and I ask you to give it.

I ask for your patience, with the delays and inconveniences that may accompany tighter security; and for your patience in what will be a long struggle.

I ask your continued participation and confidence in the American economy. Terrorists attacked a symbol of American prosperity. They did not touch its source. America is successful because of the hard work, and creativity, and enterprise of our people. These were the true strengths of our economy before September 11th, and they are our strengths today.

And, finally, please continue praying for the victims of terror and their families, for those in uniform, and for our great country. Prayer has comforted us in sorrow, and will help strengthen us for the journey ahead.

Tonight I thank my fellow Americans for what you have already done and for what you will do. And ladies and gentlemen of the Congress, I thank you, their representatives, for what you have already done and for what we will do together.

Tonight, we face new and sudden national challenges. We will come together to improve air safety, to dramatically expand the number of air marshals on domestic flights, and take new measures to prevent hijacking. We will come together to promote stability and keep our airlines flying, with direct assistance during this emergency.

We will come together to give law enforcement the additional tools it needs to track down terror here at home. We will come together to strengthen our intelligence capabilities to know the plans of terrorists before they act, and find them before they strike.

We will come together to take active steps that strengthen America's economy, and put our people back to work.

Tonight we welcome two leaders who embody the extraordinary spirit of all New Yorkers: Governor George Pataki and Mayor Rudolph Giuliani. As a symbol of America's resolve, my administration will work with Congress, and these two leaders, to show the world that we will rebuild New York City.

After all that has just passed—all the lives taken, and all the possibilities and hopes that died with them—it is natural to wonder if America's future is one of fear. Some speak of an age of terror. I know there are struggles ahead, and dangers to face. But this country will define our times, not be defined by them. As long as the United States of America is determined and strong, this will not be an age of terror; this will be an age of liberty, here and across the world.

Great harm has been done to us. We have suffered great loss. And in our grief and anger we have found our mission and our moment. Freedom and fear are at war. The advance of human freedom—the great achievement of our time, and the great hope of every time—now depends on us. Our nation—this generation—will lift a dark threat of violence from our people and our future. We will rally the world to this cause by our efforts, by our courage. We will not tire, we will not falter, and we will not fail.

It is my hope that in the months and years ahead, life will return almost to normal. We'll go back to our lives and routines, and that is good. Even grief recedes with time and grace. But our resolve must not pass. Each of us will remember what happened that day, and to whom it happened. We'll remember the moment the news came—where we were and what we were doing. Some will remember an image of a fire, or a story of rescue. Some will carry memories of a face and a voice gone forever.

And I will carry this: It is the police shield of a man named George Howard, who died at the World Trade Center trying to save others. It was given to me by his mom, Arlene, as a proud memorial to her son. This is my reminder of lives that ended, and a task that does not end. I will not forget this wound to our country or those who inflicted it. I will not yield; I will not rest; I will not relent in waging this struggle for freedom and security for the American people.

The course of this conflict is not known, yet its outcome is certain. Freedom and fear, justice and cruelty, have always been at war, and we know that God is not neutral between them.

Fellow citizens, we'll meet violence with patient justice—assured of the rightness of our cause, and confident of the victories to come. In all that lies before us, may God grant us wisdom, and may He watch over the United States of America.

Thank you.

Notes

1. For a thorough analysis of this speech, see Ronald C. White, *Lincoln's Greatest Speech*, New York: Simon and Schuster, 2002.
2. A detailed analysis of the development of Roosevelt's First Inaugural can be found in Davis W. Houck, *FDR and Fear Itself*, College Station, Tex.: Texas A&M Univ. Press, 2002.
3. Despite the prominence of this speech, it has received little systematic analysis. An exception is Carolyn Calloway-Thomas and John Louis Lucaites, *Martin Luther King, Jr., and the Sermonic Power of Public Discourse*, Tuscaloosa: Univ. of Alabama Press, 1993.
4. A recent analysis of this speech, and of the significance of rhetorical choices in combating terrorism is David Zarefsky, "George W. Bush Discovers Rhetoric: September 20, 2001 and the U.S. Response to Terrorism," in Michael J. Hyde, ed., *The Ethos of Rhetoric*, Columbia, S.C.: Univ. of South Carolina Press, 2004.

Index

Examples (*continued*)
  length of, 167
  tests for effectiveness of, 167–168
  using, 125–126
Exigence, defined, 11
Experiments, 128
Expert testimony, 179–180
Explanation
  causal inference as, 176
  as informative strategy, 367–368
Extemporaneous speech, 22, 94, 318
Eye contact, 25, 314
  with large audience, 315
  when using notes, 315

Facial expression
  eye contact, 314, 315
Fact books, 135
Facts
  defined, 6, 51
  finding aids for, 102–103
Factual testimony, 129
Fallacy, 185
  analyzing, 186
  defined, 167
  types of, 168
False dilemma, 424
Familiarity, advantages of, 203–204
Feedback, 7
  listening and, 41
  nonverbal, 7
  and quality, 28
  videotape as, 28–29
  regarding volume, 303–304
Feeling, creating, 107, 361–362
Fields, defined, 85
Figurative analogy, 170
Filing, of information, 151
Films, as visual aids, 335–336
Finding aids, 102–103
  online, 103
Fisher, Mary, 389
Flip charts, 340
Flowchart, 331, 332
Focus groups, 82
Follow-up questions, 132
Forensic speech, 98, 419–420
Forgetting curve, 371–372
Formal occasions, 418
Fourth of July, as speech setting, 435, 447
Fugitive materials, 140

Gates, Bill, 339
General public, defined, 84
General purpose statement, 113
Generally held beliefs, 124
Gerson, Michael, 96
Gestures, importance of, 313–314
Ginsburg, Ruth Bader, 450
Goals
  and causal inferences, 176
  of speech, 12–13, 15
Google, 142, 143
Gore, Al, 86, 176, 287, 290, 380, 381, 393

Government sources
  indexes of, 138–139
  online, 138
Grade inflation sample speech, 458–461
Grand style, 292
Graphs, 332–334
Greenspan, Alan, 401–402
Greeting, speeches of, 427–428
Group reports, 422
Groupthink, 423

Handouts, 341
Hearing, 40
Heston, Charlton, 398
Hitler, Adolf, 59, 159
Horowitz, David, 75
Hostile audience, 380–381
Humor, in speech introduction, 231–232
Hypotheticals, 125
  examples using, 166–167

Identification
  with audience, 11, 97, 225–226, 402–403
  defined, 10
  in persuasion, 402–403
Ignoring the question, 186
Implementation step, 314
Impromptu presentation, 316
Inaugural addresses, 450–451
  Lincoln's second, 464–465
  Mandela's, 480–482
  Franklin Roosevelt's first, 466–469
Inducing an action, 109
  facilitating the action, 399
  identifying the action, 399
  strategies for, 379, 382, 399
Inference, 160
  from analogy, 169–172
  causal, 174–179
  from example, 165–168
  from narrative, 183–185
  from signs, 172–174
  from testimony, 179–183
  tests of, 185–187
Inflection, 310
Informative speech and strategies, 26, 359–360
  comparison as, 369–371
  definition as, 362–364
  demonstration as, 368–369
  description as, 366–367
  diversity and, 373
  example of, 365
  explanation as, 367–368
  goal of, 360–362
  reporting as, 364–366
  sample of, 454–455
Institutional regularity, 173
Interests
  of audience, 70–71
  of speaker, 99–100, 101–102
Internal preview, 242–243, 244
Internal summary, 243
Internet
  citing sources from, 139, 152, 260

evaluation of sources on, 19
as information resource, 17, 20
interplay on, 7
searching for information on, 141–143
types of information on, 140
See also World Wide Web
Interviews
  documentation of, 132–133
  format of, 131–132
  guidelines for, 133
  question types in, 132
  subject of, 131
Introduction
  of self to audience, 20
  of speaker to audience, 21, 427–428
Introduction of speech, 15–16
  defined, 222
  developing wording of, 23
  example of, 224–225, 240
  importance of, 25
  outline of, 257–258
  purposes of, 222–224
  strategies for preparing, 232–234
  types of, 225–232
Invention, defined, 94
Inversion of word order, 289
Irony, 286
Issue
  defined, 115
  identifying, 115–117

Jackson, Jesse, 292, 307
Jargon, 284
Jefferson, Thomas, 450–451
John Paul II, speech at Yad Hashem Holocaust memorial, 486–487
Johnson, Lyndon, 231–232
Jordan, Barbara, 76
Journalistic questions, 198
Jumping to conclusions, 43–44, 45–46
  avoiding, 85

Kennedy, Edward M., 429
Kennedy, John F., 74, 77, 231, 273, 289, 311, 367, 449
Kennedy, John F., Jr., 429
Keynote speeches, 451–452
King, Martin Luther, 226, 238, 294, 307, 390
  I Have a Dream speech text, 469–472

Lay testimony, 180
Librarian's Index to the Internet, 17
Library
  books in, 133–134
  catalog of, 135, 136
  online resources, 134
  references in, 134–136
Lieberman, Joseph, 77, 380–381, 393
Lincoln, Abraham, 57–58, 86, 184, 231, 238–239, 273, 431
  second Inaugural address of, 464–465
Line graphs, 332